Psychology of Personality:

Readings in Theory   Third Edition

William S. Sahakian, Editor
Suffolk University

Houghton Mifflin Company / Boston
Dallas   Geneva, Ill.   Hopewell, N.J.
Palo Alto   London

William S. Sahakian, Advisory Editor

ACKNOWLEDGMENTS

The editor wishes to credit the original publishers of the selections in this reader and to express his gratitude to them, to the authors, and to the many other individuals and institutions who hold the copyrights, for their generosity and cooperation in making the source materials available to him.

Reprinted from *An Autobiographical Study* by Sigmund Freud, authorized translation by James Strachey. By permission of W. W. Norton & Company, Inc., New York, and The Hogarth Press Ltd., London. Copyright 1952 by W. W. Norton & Company, Inc. Copyright 1935 by W. W. Norton & Company, Inc., under the title *Autobiography*. Copyright renewed © 1963 by James Strachey.

Reprinted from *Certain Neurotic Mechanisms in Jealousy, Paranoia and Homosexuality* by Sigmund Freud, translated by Joan Riviere. From *The Collected Papers of Sigmund Freud*, edited by Ernest Jones, Basic Books, New York, 1959. By permission of Basic Books, Inc., New York, and The Hogarth Press Ltd., London.

Reprinted from *The Ego and the Id* by Sigmund Freud, newly translated from the German and edited by James Strachey. By permission of W. W. Norton & Company, Inc., New York, and The Hogarth Press Ltd., London. Copyright © 1960 by James Strachey.

Reprinted from *A General Introduction to Psycho-Analysis* by Sigmund Freud. By permission of Liveright, Publishers, New York, and George Allen & Unwin, London. Copyright renewed © 1963 by Joan Riviere.

Reprinted from *Inhibitions, Symptoms and Anxiety* by Sigmund Freud. Originally published by *The Psychoanalytic Quarterly*, volume V, 1936. By permission of *The Psychoanalytic Quarterly*, New York, and The Hogarth Press Ltd., London.

ACKNOWLEDGMENTS

Reprinted from *Instincts and Their Vicissitudes* by Sigmund Freud, translated by James Strachey, from *The Collected Papers of Sigmund Freud*, edited by Ernest Jones, Basic Books, New York, 1959. By permission of Basic Books, Inc., New York, and The Hogarth Press Ltd., London.

Reprinted from *Neurosis and Psychosis* by Sigmund Freud, translated by Joan Riviere, from *The Collected Papers of Sigmund Freud*, edited by Ernest Jones, Basic Books, New York, 1959. By permission of Basic Books, Inc., New York, and The Hogarth Press Ltd., London.

Reprinted from *New Introductory Lectures on Psycho-Analysis* by Sigmund Freud, translated by W. J. H. Sprott. By permission of W. W. Norton & Company, Inc., New York, and The Hogarth Press Ltd., London. Copyright 1933 by Sigmund Freud. Copyright renewed © 1961 by W. J. H. Sprott.

Reprinted from *An Outline of Psychoanalysis* by Sigmund Freud, authorized translation by James Strachey. By permission of W. W. Norton & Company, Inc., New York, and The Hogarth Press Ltd., London. Copyright 1949 by W. W. Norton & Company, Inc. Copyright © 1969 by The Institute of Psychoanalysis and Alix Strachey.

Reprinted from *The Psychopathology of Everyday Life* by Sigmund Freud, translated by Alan Tyson and edited by James Strachey. By permission of The Macmillan Company, New York, and Ernest Benn Limited, London. Copyright © 1960 by The Macmillan Company.

Reprinted from *Studies in Hysteria* by Josef Breuer and Sigmund Freud, translated and edited by James Strachey. 1957. By permission of Basic Books, Inc., New York, and The Hogarth Press Ltd., London.

Reprinted from *Two Encyclopaedia Articles* by Sigmund Freud, translated by James Strachey, from *The Collected Papers of Sigmund Freud*, edited by Ernest Jones, Basic Books, New York, 1959. By permission of Basic Books, Inc., New York, and the Hogarth Press Ltd., London.

Reprinted from *Aion: Researches into the Phenomenology of the Self*, volume IX, part 2, in *The Collected Works of Carl G. Jung*. By permission of Bollingen Foundation, New York.

Reprinted from *Archetypes and the Collective Unconscious*, volume IX, part 1, in *The Collected Works of Carl G. Jung*. By permission of Bollingen Foundation, New York.

Reprinted from *Contributions to Analytical Psychology* by Carl G. Jung. By permission of Bollingen Foundation, New York, and Routledge & Kegan Paul Ltd., London.

Reprinted from *Freud and Psychoanalysis*, volume IV in *The Collected Works of Carl G. Jung*. By permission of Bollingen Foundation, New York, and Routledge & Kegan Paul Ltd., London.

Reprinted from *Psychological Types*, by C. G. Jung (Pantheon Books, a Division of Random House, Inc.). By permission of Random House, Inc., New York, and Routledge & Kegan Paul Ltd., London.

Reprinted from *The Practice and Theory of Individual Psychology* by Alfred Adler. By permission of Humanities Press Inc., New York, and Routledge & Kegan Paul Ltd., London.

Reprinted from *The Science of Living* by Alfred Adler. By permission of **Dr.** Kurt A. Adler and George Allen & Unwin Ltd., London.

From *Escape from Freedom* by Erich Fromm. Copyright 1941 by Erich Fromm. Reprinted by permission of Holt, Rinehart and Winston, Inc., New York, Routledge & Kegan Paul Ltd., London, and the author.

From *The Sane Society* by Erich Fromm. Copyright © 1955 by Erich Fromm. Reprinted by permission of Holt, Rinehart and Winston, Inc., New York, Routledge & Kegan Paul Ltd., London, and the author.

Reprinted from *Our Inner Conflicts* by Karen Horney, M.D. By permission of W. W. Norton & Company, Inc., New York, and Routledge & Kegan Paul Ltd., London. Copyright 1945 by W. W. Norton & Company, Inc., Copyright renewed 1972 by Renate Mintz, Marianne Von Eckardt, and Briggitte Horney Swarzenski.

Reprinted from *Self-Analysis* by Karen Horney, M.D. By permission of W. W. Norton & Company, Inc., New York, and Routledge & Kegan Paul Ltd., London. Copyright 1942 by W. W. Norton & Company, Inc. Copyright renewed 1969 by Marianne von Eckardt, Renate Mintz, and Brigitte Swarzenski.

Reprinted from *The Interpersonal Theory of Psychiatry* by Harry Stack Sullivan, M.D. By permission of W. W. Norton & Company, Inc., New York, and Tavistock Publications, London. Copyright 1953 by The William Alanson White Psychiatric Foundation.

Excerpted from "Outline of Analysis" in *Psychoanalysis and Daseinanalysis* by Medard Boss, translated by Ludwig B. Lefebre. Copyright © 1963 by Basic Books, Inc., Publishers, New York.

Excerpted from *Being-in-the-World* by Ludwig Binswanger, translated by Jacob Needleman. Copyright © 1963 by Basic Books, Inc., Publishers, New York.

Excerpted from *Existence: A New Dimension in Psychiatry and Psychology*, edited by Rollo May, Ernest Angel and Henri F. Ellenberger. Copyright © 1958 by Basic Books, Inc., Publishers, New York.

Reprinted from "The Concept of Man in Logotherapy" by Viktor E. Frankl, in *Journal of Existentialism*, VI (1965). By permission of the publisher and the author.

Reprinted from "Determinism and Humanism" by Viktor E. Frankl, in *Humanitas, Journal of the Institute of Man*, VII (1971). By permission of the publisher and the author.

Reprinted from "Dynamics, Existence and Values" by Viktor E. Frankl, in *Journal of Existential Psychiatry*, II (1961). By permission of the publisher and the author.

Reprinted from "Existential Dynamics and Neurotic Escapism" by Viktor E. Frankl, in *Journal of Existential Psychiatry*, IV (1963). By permission of the publisher and the author.

Reprinted from "Logotherapy and the Challenge of Suffering" by Viktor E. Frankl, in *Review of Existential Psychology and Psychiatry*, I (1961). By permission of the publisher and the author.

ACKNOWLEDGMENTS

Reprinted from "The Spiritual Dimension in Existential Analysis and Logo-therapy" by Viktor E. Frankl, in *Journal of Individual Psychology*, XV (1959). By permission of the publisher and the author.

Reprinted from "What Is Meant by Meaning" by Viktor E. Frankl, in *Journal of Existentialism*, VII (1966). By permission of the publisher and the author.

Reprinted from Carl Rogers, *Client-Centered Therapy*, excerpts from pages 483-524. Copyright 1951 by Houghton Mifflin Company. By permission of the publisher and the author.

Reprinted from "A Theory of Therapy, Personality, and Interpersonal Relationships as Developed in the Client-Centered Framework" by Carl R. Rogers. From *Psychology: A Study of a Science*, volume III, edited by Sigmund Koch. Copyright 1959 by McGraw-Hill. Used with the permission of McGraw-Hill Book Company.

Reprinted from *The Psychology of Personal Constructs* by George A. Kelly. By permission of W. W. Norton & Company, Inc., New York. Copyright © 1955.

From *Explorations in Personality*, edited by Henry A. Murray. Copyright 1938 by Oxford University Press, Inc. Reprinted by permission of the publisher and the author.

Reprinted from "Defining the 'Field at a Given Time'" by Kurt Lewin, in *Psychological Review*, L (1943). By permission of the American Psychological Association.

Reprinted from Kurt Lewin. "Forces Behind Food Habits and Methods of Change" in *Bulletin of the National Research Council*, 108. Washington, D. C., 1943, pp. 35-36. By permission of the National Research Council.

Reprinted from *Principles of Topological Psychology* by Kurt Lewin. Copyright 1936 by McGraw-Hill Book Company. Used by permission.

Reprinted by permission of the publishers and the author from Kurt Goldstein, *Human Nature in the Light of Psychopathology*. Cambridge, Mass.: Harvard University Press. Copyright 1940 by the President and Fellows of Harvard College.

From "Dynamics of Personality Organization. I" by Abraham H. Maslow, in *Psychological Review*, L (1943). Reprinted by permission of the American Psychological Association and the author.

From "The Instinctoid Nature of Basic Needs" by Abraham H. Maslow, in *Journal of Personality*, XXII (1954). Reprinted by permission of the *Journal of Personality* and the author.

From pp. 27-31, 136-145, 345-352, *Motivation and Personality* by A. H. Maslow. Copyright 1954 by Harper & Brothers. Reprinted with the permission of Harper & Row, Publishers, and the author.

From *Religions, Values, and Peak-Experiences* by Abraham H. Maslow, published by The Ohio State University Press. Copyright © 1964 by Kappa Delta Pi, an Honor Society in Education. Reprinted by permission of Kappa Delta Pi and the author.

From *Personality: A Biosocial Approach to Origins and Structure* by Gardner Murphy. Copyright 1947 by Harper & Brothers. Reprinted with the permission of the publisher and the author.

From *The Varieties of Temperament* by W. H. Sheldon. Copyright 1942 by Harper & Brothers. Reprinted with the permission of the publisher and the author.

Reprinted from Gordon W. Allport, *Pattern and Growth in Personality*. Copyright 1937, © 1961, Holt, Rinehart and Winston, Inc. By permission of the publisher and the author.

Reprinted from Gordon W. Allport, *Personality: A Psychological Interpretation*. Copyright 1937, Holt, Rinehart and Winston, Inc. By permission of the publisher and the author.

Reprinted from *An Introduction to Personality Study* by Raymond B. Cattell, published by Hutchinson University Library, London. By permission of the publisher and the author.

Reprinted from *Personality: A Systematic Theoretical and Factual Study* by Raymond B. Cattell, published by McGraw-Hill Book Company. By permission of the author.

Reprinted from "The Principles of Experimental Design and Analysis in Relation to Theory Building" and "Psychological Theory and Scientific Method," by Raymond B. Cattell, in *Handbook of Multivariate Experimental Psychology*, edited by Raymond B. Cattell. Copyright © 1966 by Rand McNally and Company, Chicago. By permission of the publisher.

Reprinted from "Criterion Analysis—An Application of the Hypothetico-Deductive Method to Factor Analysis" by H. J. Eysenck, in *Psychological Review*, LVII (1957). By permission of the American Psychological Association and the author.

Reprinted from *Dimensions of Personality* by H. J. Eysenck. By permission of Routledge & Kegan Paul Ltd., London, and the author.

Reprinted from *The Scientific Study of Personality* by H. J. Eysenck. By permission of Routledge & Kegan Paul Ltd., London, and the author.

Reprinted from *The Structure of Human Personality*, 3rd. ed., by H. J. Eysenck. Copyright 1970 by Methuen & Company, Ltd., London. By permission of the publisher.

From *The Behavior of Organisms*, by B. F. Skinner. Copyright © 1966 (Paper edition). By permission of the publisher, Prentice-Hall, Inc.

Excerpted from *Beyond Freedom and Dignity*, by B. F. Skinner. Copyright © 1971. By permission of Alfred A. Knopf, Inc.

From the book *B. F. Skinner: The Man and His Ideas* by Richard I. Evans. Copyright © 1969 by Richard I. Evans. Published by E. P. Dutton & Co., Inc. in a paperback edition and used with their permission.

From *Contingencies of Reinforcement*, by B. F. Skinner. Copyright © 1969 (Paper edition copyright © 1972). By permission of the publisher, Prentice-Hall, Inc.

Reprinted with permission of The Macmillan Company from *Science and Human Behavior* by B. F. Skinner. Copyright © 1953 by The Macmillan Company.

Reprinted from *Personality and Psychotherapy* by John Dollard and Neal E. Miller. Copyright 1950 by McGraw-Hill Book Company. Used by permission of the publisher and the authors.

ACKNOWLEDGMENTS

From *Principles of Behavior Modification* by Albert Bandura. Copyright ©
1969 by Holt, Rinehart and Winston, Inc. Reprinted by permission of Holt,
Rinehart and Winston, Inc.

Reprinted from Albert Bandura, editor, *Psychological Modeling: Conflicting
Theories* (Chicago: Aldine-Atherton, Inc., 1971); copyright © 1971 by Aldine-
Atherton, Inc. Reprinted by permission of the author and Aldine-Atherton, Inc.

From *Social Learning and Personality Development* by Albert Bandura and
Richard H. Walters. Copyright © 1963 by Holt, Rinehart and Winston, Inc.
Reprinted by permission of Holt, Rinehart and Winston, Inc.

From *Social Learning Theory* by Albert Bandura, published by General Learning Press. Copyright © 1971 General Learning Corporation. Reprinted by
permission.

From *Applications of a Social Learning Theory of Personality* by Julian B.
Rotter, June E. Chance and E. Jerry Phares. Copyright © 1972 by Holt, Rine-
hart and Winston, Inc. Reprinted by permission of Holt, Rinehart and Winston,
Inc.

Dedicated to
Those valuable factors
in the development of my personality:
My wife, Mabel Marie
My sons, Jim and Rick
My daughters, Barbara and Paula

Preface to the First Edition

The psychology of personality is unlike other areas of psychology in which a single textbook is sufficient to cover an entire field. Here one cannot lecture on *the* psychology of personality; rather he must discuss *psychologies* of personality. Consequently, a book which presents the leading theories of personality held by those psychologists who pioneered the field and have successfully emerged with definite contributions is the only adequate approach to the subject.

Since the psychology of personality is a relatively young field, the student must investigate a wide variety of points of view if he is to be adequately equipped to construct his own theory or at least view the problem with discernment and discrimination. Toward this end the readings collected here will serve by presenting the germane and salient portions of the finest works in personality theory which are at present available to the psychological community.

With the exception of the chapter on Freud, who wrote his autobiography (excerpts of which are included here), each chapter is prefaced with a synopsis of the psychologist's predominant attitude in personality theory, plus a note concerning his background, education, and published writings. It is hoped that the introductory material will not only prove of interest to the reader, but also direct him in his reading of the masters by furnishing him with points of orientation, and make it easier for him to perceive the central concepts in their theories of personality.

Where feasible, the particular terminology of each psychologist has been used in the section titles, and his line of procedural development has been employed. Occasionally, however, in order to make the material more coherent or to bring out more clearly the structure of a particular system, it has seemed advisable to depart from this basic plan. Ellipses marks are used to indicate brief omissions; asterisks are inserted, however not only to indicate the deletion of intervening material of considerable length, but also to denote the absence of material which would prove interesting and enlightening should the reader care to pursue the matter further.

The individuals whose writings are included here were not arbitrarily selected; rather, each was chosen for specific reasons: because he established a school of personality theory or has been the foremost authority in the development of such a school, because his theories have had an important influence on other psychologists in the field, and because his contributions have been of value in the continuing development of the field.

The editor wishes to thank those persons who assisted in the various phases of the production of this book, particularly Dr. Mabel Sahakian of Northeastern University for proofreading the original manuscript, and James William Sahakian for his part in typing.

WILLIAM S. SAHAKIAN

Beacon Hill,
Boston, Massachusetts

Preface to the Second Edition

Since the compilation of the first edition of this work, no momentous change has occurred in the theories of any of the individuals treated. In those cases where these theorists have published, their writings have for the most part been reiterations of their original positions. If such is the case, why, then, publish a second edition? There are two major reasons. The first is to update in a few cases where it is vital to give a complete account of a theorist's position. This updating has been accomplished in two ways: (*a*) by bringing the original material of the theorists up to date, and (*b*) by updating the introductory material, especially the bibliographies.

The second major purpose for publishing a second edition is to add influential personality theories of men who were not treated before. These additions include the operant reinforcement theory of personality developed by B. F. Skinner, the modeling theory of personality espoused by Albert Bandura, the social learning theory of personality expounded by Julian Rotter, an existential theory of personality represented by Ludwig Binswanger, Medard Boss, and Rollo May, and the logotherapeutic approach to personality sired by Viktor E. Frankl. In order to make these additions and still maintain the usefulness of this book as a text, three theorists, who failed to command growing interest in the psychological community with respect to personality theory, were regrettably deleted from the present edition.

Finally, to facilitate the approach to personality theory by grouping kindred approaches together, some of the chapters have been rearranged. This rearrangement should provide, especially to initiates of personality, a perspective that would otherwise be laborious and time-consuming to acquire.

WILLIAM S. SAHAKIAN

Beacon Hill,
Boston, Massachusetts

Preface to the Third Edition

The third edition is more than an updating of earlier editions; it
is an enlargement and rearrangement of earlier ones. The major
addition has been the presentation of the personality system of
George A. Kelly, who contributed a personal construct theory to
psychology. In keeping with the current trend in psychological
circles, a new part has also been added to the third edition entitled
"Cognitive Approaches to Personality." Cognitivism in psychology
has gained considerable momentum in the decade of the 1970s, so
much so that an entire volume has been dedicated to cognitive personality theory. Moreover, the opening of the decade even saw the
publication of a journal of *Cognitive Psychology*, which well ar-
ticulates the sign of the times.

WILLIAM S. SAHAKIAN

Beacon Hill,
Boston, Massachusetts

Contents

Part 1   The Dynamic Approach: The Freudian And Neopsychoanalytic Tradition

Psychoanalytic Theory of Personality. Autobiography. Topography of the Mind (Conscious, Preconscious, Unconscious). The Structure of Personality (Id, Ego, Superego). Neurosis and Psychosis. The Ego's Mechanisms of Defence. The Ego's Three Varieties of Anxiety (Objective, Neurotic, and Moral). Libido Theory (Instincts and Their Sublimation). Stages of Personality (Libidinal) Development. Dreams as Wish Fulfillments. Psychopathology of Everyday Life (Freudian Slips). Traumas: Their Abreaction and Catharsis.

Personality Theory from the Standpoint of Analytical Psychology. Analytical Psychology Versus Psychoanalysis. The Collective Unconscious. The Ego. The Shadow. The

Contents

Constructs. Constructs Classified According to the Nature of Their Control over Their Elements. General Diagnostic Constructs. Constructs Relating to Transition. Constructive Alternativism. Man-the-Scientist. Roles and Role-Playing.

All books on the psychology of personality are at the same time books on the philosophy of the person. It could not be otherwise.

Gordon W. Allport

The Dynamic Approach:
The Freudian and
Neopsychoanalytic Tradition

CHAPTER 1

SIGMUND FREUD

PSYCHOANALYTIC THEORY
OF PERSONALITY

AUTOBIOGRAPHY[1]

I was born on May 6th, 1856, at Freiberg in Moravia, a small town in what is now Czechoslovakia. My parents were Jews, and I have remained a Jew myself. . . . When I was a child of four I came to Vienna, and I went through the whole of my education there. At the "Gymnasium" (Grammar School) I was at the top of my class for seven years; I enjoyed special privileges there, and had scarcely ever to be examined in class. Although we lived in very limited circumstances, my father insisted that, in my choice of a profession, I should follow my own inclinations alone. Neither at that time, or indeed in my later life, did I feel any particular predilection for the career of a doctor.

*   *   *   *   *

When, in 1873, I first joined the University, I experienced some appreciable disappointments. Above all, I found that I was expected to feel myself inferior and an alien because I was a Jew. I refused absolutely to do the first of these things.

*   *   *   *   *

At length, in Ernst Brücke's physiological laboratory, I found rest and full satisfaction. . . . I worked at this Institute, with short interruptions, from 1876 to 1882, and it was generally thought that I was marked out to fill the next post of Assistant that might fall vacant there. The various branches of medicine proper, apart from psychiatry, had no attraction for me. I was

[1]*An Autobiographical Study*, trans. James Strachey (New York: Norton, 1952), from pp. 13-139.

decidedly negligent in pursuing my medical studies, and it was not until 1881 that I took my somewhat belated degree as a Doctor of Medicine.

The turning point came in 1882, when my teacher, for whom I felt the highest possible esteem, corrected my father's generous improvidence by strongly advising me, in view of my bad financial position, to abandon my theoretical career. I followed his advice, left the physiological laboratory and entered the General Hospital as an *Aspirant* (Clinical Assistant). I was soon afterwards promoted to being a *Sekundararzt* (Junior or House Physician), and worked in various departments of the hospital, among others for more than six months under Meynert, by whose work and personality I had been greatly struck while I was still a student.

* * * * *

In the distance shone the great name of Charcot; so I formed a plan of first obtaining an appointment as University Lecturer (*Dozent*) on Nervous Diseases in Vienna and of then going to Paris to continue my studies. . . . In the spring of 1885 I was appointed Lecturer (*Dozent*) in Neuropathology on the ground of my histological and clinical publications. Soon afterwards, as the result of a warm testimonial from Brücke, I was awarded a Travelling Bursary of considerable value ($250.00). In the autumn of the same year I made the journey to Paris. I became a student at the Salpetrière. . . . Before leaving Paris I discussed with the great man (Charcot) a plan for a comparative study of hysterical and organic paralyses.

* * * * *

I will now return to the year 1886, the time of my settling down in Vienna as a specialist in nervous diseases. The duty devolved upon me of giving a report before the "Gesellschaft der Aerzte" [Society of Medicine] upon what I had seen and learnt with Charcot. But I met with a bad reception.

* * * * *

While I was still working in Brücke's laboratory I had made the acquaintance of Dr. Josef Breuer, who was one of the most respected family physicians in Vienna. . . . Breuer had told me about a case of hysteria which, between 1880 and 1882, he had treated in a peculiar manner which had allowed him to penetrate deeply into the causation and significance of hysterical symptoms. This was at a time, therefore, when Janet's works still belonged to the future. . . . In 1893 we issued a preliminary communication, "On the Psychical Mechanism of Hysterical Phenomena," and in 1895 there followed our book, *Studies on Hysteria*.

* * * * *

For more than ten years after my separation from Breuer I had no followers. I was completely isolated. In Vienna I was shunned; abroad no notice was taken of me. My *Interpretation of Dreams,* published in 1900, was scarcely reviewed in the technical journals.

*   *   *   *   *

In 1909 G. Stanley Hall invited Jung and me to America to go to Clark University, Worcester, Mass., of which he was President, and spend a week giving lectures (in German) at the celebration of that body's foundation. . . . In Europe during the years 1911-1913 two secessionist movements from psycho-analysis took place, led by men who previously played a considerable part in the young science, Alfred Adler and C. G. Jung. Both movements seemed most threatening and quickly obtained a large following. . . . The history of psycho-analysis falls from my point of view into two phases: In the first of these I stood alone and had to do all the work myself: this was from 1895-6 until 1906 or 1907. In the second phase, lasting from then until the present time, the contributions of my pupils and collaborators have been growing more and more in importance, so that to-day, when a grave illness warns me of the approaching end, I can think with a quiet mind of the cessations of my own labours. . . . And here I may be allowed to break off these autobiographical notes. The public has no claim to learn any more of my personal affairs. . . .[2]

TOPOGRAPHY OF THE MIND
(CONSCIOUS, PRECONSCIOUS, UNCONSCIOUS)[3]

The state in which the ideas existed before being made conscious is called by us *repression,* and we assert that the force which instituted the repression and maintains it is perceived as *resistance* during the work of analysis. Thus we obtain our concept of the unconscious from the theory of repression. The repressed is the prototype of the unconscious for us. We see however, that we have two kinds of unconscious—the one which is latent but capable of becoming conscious, and the one which is repressed and which is not, in itself and without more ado, capable of becoming conscious. The piece of insight into psychical dynamics cannot fail to affect terminology and description. The latent, which is unconscious only descriptively, not in the dynamic sense, we call *preconscious;* we restrict the term *unconscious* to the dynamically unconscious repressed; so that now we have three terms, conscious (*Cs.*) preconscious (*Pcs.*), and unconscious (*Ucs.*), whose sense is no longer purely descriptive. The *Pcs.* is presumably a great deal closer to the *Cs.* than is the *Ucs.,* and since we have called the *Ucs.* psychical we shall with even less hesitation call the latent *Pcs.* psychical. But why do we not rather, instead of this, remain in agreement with the philosophers

[2]The illness of which Freud speaks, cancer of the jaw, culminated in his death at London, Sept. 23, 1939.

[3]*The Ego and the Id,* trans. James Strachey (New York: Norton, 1961), from pp. 4-10.

and, in a consistent way, distinguish the *Pcs.* as well as the *Ucs.* from the conscious psychical? The philosophers would then propose that the *Pcs.* and the *Ucs.* should be described as two species or stages of the "psychoid," and harmony would be established. But endless difficulties in exposition would follow; and the one important fact, that these two kinds of "psychoid" coincide in almost every other respect with what is admittedly psychical, would be forced into the background in the interests of a prejudice dating from a period in which these psychoids, or the most important part of them, were still unknown.

We can now play about comfortably with our three terms, *Cs., Pcs.,* and *Ucs.,* so long as we do not forget that in the descriptive sense there are two kinds of unconscious, but in the dynamic sense only one.

* * * * *

For our conception of the unconscious, however, the consequences of our discovery are even more important. Dynamic considerations caused us to make our first correction; our insight into the structure of the mind leads to the second. We recognize that the *Ucs.* does not coincide with the repressed; it is still true that all that is repressed is *Ucs.,* but not all that is *Ucs.* is repressed. A part of the ego, too—and Heaven knows how important a part—may be *Ucs.,* and undoubtedly is *Ucs.* And this *Ucs.* belonging to the ego is not latent like the *Pcs.;* for if it were, it would not be activated without becoming *Cs.,* and the process of making it conscious would not encounter such great difficulties. When we find ourselves thus confronted by the necessity of postulating a third *Ucs.,* which is not repressed, we must admit that the characteristic of being unconscious begins to lose significance for us. It becomes a quality which can have many meanings, a quality which we are unable to make, as we should have hoped to do, the basis of far-reaching and inevitable conclusions. Nevertheless we must beware of ignoring this characteristic, for the property of being conscious or not is in the last resort our one beacon-light in the darkness of depth-psychology.

* * * * *

All perceptions which are received from without (sense-perceptions) and from within—what we call sensations and feelings—are *Cs.* from the start. But what about those internal processes which we may—roughly and inexactly—sum up under the name of thought processes? They represent displacements of mental energy which are effected somewhere in the interior of the apparatus as this energy proceeds on its way toward action. Do they advance to the surface, which causes consciousness to be generated? Or does consciousness make its way to them? This is clearly one of the difficulties that arise when one begins to take the spatial or "topographical" idea of mental life seriously. Both of these possibilities are equally unimaginable; there must be a third alternative.

I have already, in another place, suggested that the real difference between an *Ucs.* and a *Pcs.* idea (thought) consists in this: that the former is carried out on some material which remains unknown, whereas the latter (the *Pcs.*) is in addition brought into connection with word-presentations. This is the first attempt to indicate distinguishing marks for the two systems, the *Pcs.* and the *Ucs.*, other than their relation to consciousness. The question, "How does a thing become conscious?" would thus be more advantageously stated: "How does a thing become preconscious?" And the answer would be: "Through becoming connected with the word-presentations corresponding to it."

These word-presentations are residues of memories; they were at one time perceptions, and like all mnemonic residues they can become conscious again. . . . It dawns upon us like a new discovery that only something which has once been a *Cs.* perception can become conscious, and that anything arising from within (apart from feelings) that seeks to become conscious must try to transform itself into external perceptions: this becomes possible by means of memory-traces.

THE STRUCTURE OF PERSONALITY (ID, EGO, SUPEREGO)[4]

We have arrived at our knowledge of this psychical apparatus by studying the individual development of human beings. To the oldest of these mental provinces or agencies we give the name of *id.* It contains everything that is inherited, that is present at birth, that is fixed in the constitution—above all, therefore, the instincts, which originate in the somatic organization and which find their first mental expression in the id in forms unknown to us.

Under the influence of the real external world which surrounds us, one portion of the id has undergone a special development. From what was originally a cortical layer, provided with organs for receiving stimuli and with apparatus for protection against excessive stimulation, a special organization has arisen which henceforth acts as an intermediary between the id and the external world. This region of our mental life has been given the name of *ego.*

The principal characteristics of the ego are these. In consequence of the relation which was already established between sensory perception and muscular action, the ego is in control of voluntary movement. It has the task of self-preservation. As regards *external* events, it performs that task by becoming aware of the stimuli from without, by storing up experiences of them (in the memory), by avoiding excessive stimuli (through flight), by dealing with moderate stimuli (through adaptation) and, finally, by learning to bring about appropriate modifications in the external world

[4]*An Outline of Psychoanalysis*, trans. James Strachey (New York: Norton, 1949), from pp. 14-123.

to its own advantage (through activity). As regards *internal* events, in relation to the id, it performs that task by gaining control over the demands of the instincts, by deciding whether they shall be allowed to obtain satisfaction, by postponing that satisfaction to times and circumstances favorable in the external world or by suppressing their excitations completely. Its activities are governed by consideration of the tensions produced by stimuli present within it or introduced into it. The raising of these tensions is in general felt as *unpleasure* and their lowering as *pleasure.* It is probable, however, that what is felt as pleasure or unpleasure is not the *absolute* degree of the tensions but something in the rhythm of their changes. The ego pursues pleasure and seeks to avoid unpleasure. An increase in unpleasure which is expected and foreseen is met by a *signal of anxiety;* the occasion of this increase, whether it threatens from without or within, is called a *danger.* From time to time the ego gives up its connection with the external world and withdraws into the state of sleep, in which its organization undergoes far-reaching changes. It may be inferred from the state of sleep that that organization consists in a particular distribution of mental energy.

The long period of childhood, during which the growing human being lives in dependence upon his parents, leaves behind it a precipitate, which forms within his ego a special agency in which this parental influence is prolonged. It has received the name of *superego.* Insofar as the superego is differentiated from the ego or opposed to it, it constitutes a third force which the ego must take into account.

Thus, an action by the ego is as it should be if it satisfies simultaneously the demand of the id, of the superego and of reality, that is to say if it is able to reconcile their demands with one another. The details of the relationship between the ego and the superego become completely intelligible if they are carried back to the child's attitude toward his parents. The parents' influence naturally includes not merely the personalities of the parents themselves but also the racial, national, and family traditions handed on through them as well as the demands of the immediate social *milieu* which they represent. In the same way, an individual's superego in the course of his development takes over contributions from late successors and substitutes of his parents, such as teachers, admired figures in public life, or high social ideals. It will be seen that, in spite of their fundamental difference, the id and the superego have one thing in common: they both represent the influences of the past (the id the influence of heredity, the superego essentially the influence of what is taken over from other people), whereas the ego is principally determined by the individual's own experience, that is to say by accidental and current events.

*   *   *   *   *

Id

The core of our being, then, is formed by the obscure *id,* which has no direct relations with the external world and is accessible even to our own knowledge only through the medium of another agency of the mind. Within this id the organic *instincts* operate, which are themselves composed of fusions of two primal forces (Eros and destructiveness) in varying proportions and are differentiated from one another by their relation to organs or systems of organs. The one and only endeavor of these instincts is toward satisfaction, which it is hoped to obtain from certain modifications in the organs by the help of objects in the external world. But an immediate and regardless satisfaction of instinct, such as the id demands, would often enough lead to perilous conflicts with the external world and to extinction. The id knows no precautions to ensure survival and no anxiety; or it would perhaps be more correct to say that, though it can produce the sensory elements of anxiety, it cannot make use of them. The processes which are possible in and between the assumed mental elements in the id (the *primary process*) differ largely from those which are familiar to us by conscious perception in our intellectual and emotional life; nor are they subject to the critical restrictions of logic, which repudiates some of these processes as invalid and seeks to undo them.

The id, which is cut off from the external world, has its own world of perception. It detects with extraordinary clarity certain changes in its interior, especially oscillations in the tension of its instinctual needs, especially oscillations which become conscious as feelings in the pleasure-unpleasure series. It is, to be sure, hard to say by what means and with the help of what sensory terminal organs these perceptions come about. But it remains certain that self-perceptions—coenesthetic feelings and feelings of pleasure-unpleasure—govern events in the id with despotic force. The id obeys the inexorable pleasure principle. But not the id alone. It seems as though the activity of the other agencies of the mind is able only to modify the pleasure principle but not to nullify it; and it remains a question of the greatest theoretical importance, and one that has not yet been answered, when and how it is ever possible for the pleasure principle to be overcome. The consideration that the pleasure principle requires a reduction, or perhaps ultimately the extinction, of the tension of the instinctual needs (that is, a state of *Nirvana*) leads to problems that are still unexamined in the relations between the pleasure principle and the two primal forces, Eros and the death instinct.

Ego

The other agency of the mind, which we appear to know the best and in which we recognize ourselves the most easily—what is known as the *ego*—was developed out of the cortical layer of the id, which, being adapted for the reception and exclusion of stimuli, is in direct contact with the external world. Starting from conscious perception, it has brought under its influence ever larger regions and ever deeper layers of the id; and, in the persistence with which it maintains its dependence upon the external world, it bears the incredible stamp of its origin (as it might be "Made in Germany"). Its psychological function consists in raising the processes in the id to a higher dynamic level (perhaps by transforming freely mobile into bound energy, such as corresponds to the preconscious condition); its constructive function consists in interposing, between the demand made by an instinct and the action that satisfies it, an intellective activity which, after considering the present state of things and weighing up earlier experiences, endeavors by means of experimental actions to calculate the consequences of the proposed line of conduct. In this way the ego comes to a decision whether the attempt to obtain satisfaction is to be carried out or postponed or whether it may not be necessary for the demand of the instinct to be altogether suppressed as being dangerous. (Here we have the *reality principle*.) Just as the id is directed exclusively to obtaining pleasure, so the ego is governed by considerations of safety. The ego has set itself the task of self-preservation, which the id appears to neglect. It makes use of sensations of anxiety as a signal to give a warning of dangers threatening its integrity. Since memory-traces can become conscious just as much as perceptions, especially through their association with verbal residues, the possibility arises of a confusion which would lead to a mistaking of reality. The ego guards itself by establishing a function for *reality-testing*, which can be allowed to fall into abeyance in dreams on account of the conditions governing the state of sleep. In its efforts to preserve itself in an environment of overwhelming mechanical forces, the ego is threatened with dangers that come in the first instance from external reality, but not from there alone. Its own id is a source of similar dangers and that for two different reasons. In the first place, an excessive strength of instinct can damage the ego in the same way as an excessive "stimulus" from the external world. It is true that such an excess cannot destroy it; but it *can* destroy its characteristic dynamic organization, it can turn the ego back into a portion of the id. In the second place, experience may have taught the ego that the satisfaction of some instinctual demand that is not in itself unbearable would involve dangers in the external world, so that an instinctual demand of that kind itself becomes a danger. Thus the ego is fighting on two fronts: it has to defend its existence both against the external world that threatens it with annihilation and against an internal world that makes excessive demands. It adopts the same methods of protection against both, but its defense against the internal foe is particularly inadequate. As a result of having been originally identical with this enemy and of having since lived with it upon the most intimate terms, the ego has the greatest difficulty in escaping from the internal dangers. They persist as threats, even if they can be temporarily held in check.

* * * * *

Superego

A portion of the external world has, at least partially, been given up as an object and instead, by means of identification, taken into the ego—that is, has become an integral part of the internal world. This new mental agency continues to carry on the functions which have hitherto been performed by the corresponding people in the external world: it observes the ego, gives it orders, corrects it and threatens it with punishments, exactly like parents whose place it has taken. We call this agency the *superego* and are aware of it, in its judicial functions, as our *conscience.* It is a remarkable thing that the superego often develops a severity for which no example has been provided by the real parents, and further that it calls the ego to task not only on account of its deeds but just as much on account of its thoughts and unexecuted intentions, of which it seems to have knowledge. We are reminded that the hero of the Oedipus legend too felt guilty for his actions and punished himself, although the compulsion of the oracle should have made him innocent in our judgment and in his own. The superego is in fact the heir to the Oedipus complex and only arises after that complex has been disposed of. For that reason its excessive severity does not follow a real prototype but corresponds to the strength which is used in fending off the temptation of the Oedipus complex.

*   *   *   *   *

So long as the ego works in complete agreement with the superego, it is not easy to distinguish between their manifestations; but tensions and estrangements between them become very plainly visible. The torments caused by the reproaches of conscience correspond precisely to a child's dread of losing his parents' love, a dread which has been replaced in him by the moral agency. On the other hand, if the ego has successfully resisted a temptation to do something that would be objectionable to the superego, it feels its self-respect raised and its pride increased, as though it had made some precious acquisition. In this way the superego continues to act the role of an external world toward the ego, although it has become part of the internal world. During the whole of man's later life it represents the influence of childhood, of the care and education given to him by his parents, of his dependence on them—of the childhood which is so greatly prolonged in human beings by a common family life. And in all of this time what is operating is not only the personal qualities of these parents but also everything that produced a determining effect upon them themselves, the tastes and standards of the social class in which they live and the characteristics and traditions of the race from which they spring. Those who have a liking for generalizations and sharp distinctions may say that the external world, in which the individual finds himself exposed after being detached from his parents, represents the power of the present; that his id, with its inherited trends, represents the organic past; and that the superego, which comes to join them later, represents more than anything the cultural past, an after-experience of which, as it were, the child has to pass through during the few years of his early life.

*   *   *   *   *

Neurosis and Psychosis[5]

The essay referred to [*The Ego and the Id*] describes the various al-legiances the ego owes, its mediate position between the outer world and the *id*, and its struggles to serve all its masters at one and the same time. Now it so happened that a train of thought suggested elsewhere, which had to do with the causes giving rise to the psychoses and with prevention of them, furnished me with a simple formula concerning what is perhaps the most important genetic difference between neurosis and psychosis: *Neurosis is the result of a conflict between the ego and its id, whereas psychosis is the analogous outcome of a similar disturbance in the relation between the ego and its environment (outer world).*

* * * * *

All our analyses go to show that the transference neuroses originate from the ego's refusing to accept a powerful instinctual impulse existing in its *id* and denying it motor discharge, or disputing the object toward which it is aimed. The ego then defends itself against the impulse by the mechanism of repression; the repressed impulse struggles against this fate, and finds ways which the ego cannot control to create for itself substitutive gratifica-tion (a symptom), which is forced upon the ego in the form of a compro-mise; the ego finds its unity menaced and injured by this interloper, pur-sues against the symptom the struggle it had formerly maintained against the original impulse, and all this together produces the clinical picture of a neurosis. It is no matter that in undertaking the repression the ego is at bot-tom following the dictates of its super-ego, which dictates originated in in-fluences of the same kind from the real environment that subsequently found representation in the super-ego. The fact remains that the ego takes sides with these powers that be, that their demands are stronger in it than the claims of instinct from the *id*, and that the force which sets repression to work against that part of the *id* and fortifies it by the anti-cathexis of re-sistance is the ego. In the service of its super-ego and of reality the ego has come into conflict with its *id*, and this state of affairs is found in all the trans-ference neuroses.

It is just as easy, on the other hand, from what we already know of the mechanism of the psychoses, to quote examples from them pointing to a disturbance in the relation between the ego and its environment. In Mey-nert's amentia, the acute hallucinatory confusion which is perhaps the most extreme and striking form of psychosis, the outer world is either not per-ceived in the very least or else any perception of it remains absolutely with-out effect. Normally, indeed, the outer world commands the ego in two ways:

[5]*Neurosis and Psychosis*, trans. Joan Riviere, in vol. II, THE COLLECTED PAPERS OF SIGMUND FREUD, ed. Ernest Jones (New York: Basic Books, 1959), from pp. 250-54.

first, by current perceptions which it is constantly able to engender afresh, and secondly, by the store of memories of former perceptions which, as its "inner world," has become the possession and a constituent part of the ego. Now in amentia not only is acceptance denied to fresh perceptions, but the importance (cathexis) of the inner world—that inner world which formerly reflected the outer world as an image of it—is withdrawn too; the ego creates for itself in a lordly manner a new outer and inner world; and there is no doubt about two facts, that this new world is constructed after the pattern of the impulses in the *id*, and that the motive of this collapse of the ego's relation with the outer world is a <u>severe frustration</u> by reality of a wish, a frustration which seemed too unendurable to be borne. The close affinity of this psychosis with normal dreams is unmistakable. A pre-condition of dreaming, however, is a state of sleep, and complete abandonment of perceptive capacity and of the outer world is one of the features of sleep.

*   *   *   *   *

There always remains as a common feature in the <u>aetiology</u> both of the psychoneuroses and the psychoses the factor of frustration—the lack of fulfilment of one of those eternal uncontrollable childhood's wishes that are so deeply rooted in our composition, phylogenetically fore-ordained as it is. In the last resort this frustration is always an outer one; in the individual case it may proceed from that internal institution (in the super-ego) which has taken over the part played by the demands of reality. Now the pathogenic effect depends on whether, in the tension of such a conflict, the ego remains true in its allegiance to the outer world and endeavours to subjugate the *id*, or whether it allows itself to be overwhelmed by the *id* and thus torn away from reality. In this apparently simple situation, however, a complication is introduced by the existence of the super-ego, which, in some connection not yet clear to us, combines in itself influences from the *id* as well as from the outer world, and is to some extent an ideal prototype of that state towards which all the ego's endeavours are bending, a reconciliation of its manifold allegiances. The attitude of the super-ego should be taken into account, as has not hitherto been done, in all forms of mental disorder. For the moment, however, we can postulate that there must be diseases founded on a conflict between ego and super-ego. Analysis gives us the right to infer that melancholia is the model of this group, and then we should put in a claim for the name of "narcissistic psychoneuroses" for these disorders. It does not fit in badly with our impressions if we find reasons for distinguishing conditions such as melancholia from the other psychoses. We then observe, however, that we were able to complete our simple genetic formula without abandoning it. A transference neurosis corresponds to a conflict between ego and *id*, a narcissistic neurosis to that between ego and super-ego, and a psychosis to that between ego and outer world. To be sure, we can hardly say at a glance whether this really represents new knowledge or is merely an addition to our list of formulas; but I think that after all its capacity for application must give us courage to keep in mind this dissection of the mental apparatus that I have proposed, namely, into ego, super-ego and *id*.

The proposition that neuroses and psychoses originate in the ego's conflicts with the various powers ruling it, that is, that they correspond with a failure in the function of the ego, which after all is straining to reconcile all these different claims with one another, requires supplementing in a further point. One would like to know in what circumstances and by what means the ego succeeds in surviving such conflicts, which are undoubtedly always present, without falling ill. Now this is a new field for research in which the most various factors will certainly demand consideration. Two of them, however, can be indicated at once. The outcome of such situations will assuredly depend upon economic conditions, upon the relative strength of the forces striving with one another. And further, it is always possible for the ego to avoid a rupture in any of its relations by deforming itself, submitting to forfeit something of its unity, or in the long run even to being gashed and rent. Thus the illogicalities, eccentricities and follies of mankind would fall into a category similar to their sexual perversions, for by accepting them they spare themselves repressions.

In conclusion there remains to be considered the question what that mechanism analogous to repression may be by which the ego severs itself from the outer world. This is not to be answered, in my opinion, without fresh investigations, but, like repression, the content of this mechanism must include a withdrawal of the cathexes emanating from the ego.

THE EGO'S MECHANISMS OF DEFENCE

Resistance and Repression[6]

When we undertake to cure a patient of his symptoms he opposes against us a vigorous and tenacious *resistance* throughout the entire course of the treatment. . . . The resistance shown by patients is highly varied and exceedingly subtle, often hard to recognize and protean in the manifold forms it takes; the analyst needs to be continually suspicious and on his guard against it. . . . We require the patient to put himself into a condition of calm self-observation, without trying to think of anything, and then to communicate everything which he becomes inwardly aware of, feelings, thoughts, remembrances, in the order in which they arise in his mind. We expressly warn him against giving way to any kind of motive which would cause him to select from or to exclude any of the ideas (associations), whether because they are too "disagreeable," or too "indiscreet" to be mentioned, or too "unimportant" or "irrelevant" or "nonsensical" to be worth saying. . . . We know from the technique of dream-interpretation that it is precisely

[6]*A General Introduction to Psycho-Analysis*, trans. Joan Riviere (New York: Liveright, 1935), from pp. 253-62.

those associations against which innumerable doubts and objections are raised that invariably contain the material leading to the discovery of the unconscious.

* * * * *

Whenever we are on the point of bringing to his consciousness some piece of unconscious material which is particularly painful to him, then he is critical in the extreme; even though he may have previously understood and accepted a great deal, yet now all these gains seem to be obliterated; in his struggles to oppose at all costs he can behave just as though he were mentally deficient, a form of "emotional stupidity."

In what way can we now account for this fact observed, that the patient struggles so energetically against the relief of his symptoms and the restoration of his mental processes to normal functioning? We say that we have come upon the traces of powerful forces at work here opposing any change in the condition; they must be the same forces that originally induced the condition. In the formation of symptoms some process must have been gone through, which our experience in dispersing them makes us able to reconstruct. . . . It follows from the existence of a symptom that some mental process has not been carried through to an end in a normal manner so that it could become conscious; the symptom is a substitute for that which has not come through. Now we know where to place the forces which we suspect to be at work. A vehement effort must have been exercised to prevent the mental process in question from penetrating into consciousness and as a result it has remained unconscious; being unconscious it had the power to construct a symptom. The same vehement effort is again at work during analytic treatment, opposing the attempt to bring the unconscious into consciousness. This we perceive in the form of resistances. The pathogenic process which is demonstrated by the resistances we call REPRESSION.

It will now be necessary to make our conception of this process of *repression* more precise. . . . Let us take as a model an impulse, a mental process seeking to convert itself into action: we know that it can suffer rejection, by virtue of what we call "repudiation" or "condemnation"; whereupon the energy at its disposal is withdrawn, it becomes powerless, but it can continue to exist as a memory. The whole process of decision on the point takes place with the full cognizance of the ego. It is very different when we imagine the same impulse subject to *repression*: it would then retain its energy and no memory of it would be left behind; the process of repression, too, would be accomplished without the cognizance of the ego.

* * * * *

The unconscious system may be compared to a large ante-room, in which the various mental excitations are crowding upon one another, like individual beings. Adjoining this is a second, smaller apartment, a sort of reception-room, in which consciousness resides. But on the threshold between the two there stands a personage with the office of door-keeper, who examines the various mental excitations, censors them, and denies them admittance to the reception-room when he disapproves of them. You will see at once that it does not make much difference whether the door-keeper turns any one impulse back at the threshold, or drives it out again once it has entered the reception-room; that is merely a matter of the degree of his vigilance and promptness in recognition. Now this metaphor may be employed to widen our terminology. The excitations in the unconscious, in the antechamber, are not visible to consciousness, which is of course in the other room, so to begin with they remain unconscious. When they have pressed forward to the threshold and been turned back by the door-keeper, they are *"incapable of becoming conscious"*; we call them then *repressed*. But even those excitations which are allowed over the threshold do not necessarily become conscious; they can only become so if they succeed in attracting the eye of consciousness. This second chamber therefore may be suitably called *the preconscious system*. In this way the process of becoming conscious retains its purely descriptive sense. Being repressed, when applied to any single impulse, means being unable to pass out of the unconscious system because of the door-keeper's refusal of admittance into the preconscious. The door-keeper is what we have learnt to know as resistance in our attempts in analytic treatment to loosen the repressions. . . . I should like to assure you that these crude hypotheses, the two chambers, the door-keeper on the threshold between the two, and consciousness as a spectator at the end of the second room, must indicate an extensive approximation to the actual reality. I should like to hear you admit that our designations, unconscious, preconscious, and conscious, are less prejudicial and more easily defensible than some others which have been suggested or have come into use, e.g. subconscious, inter-conscious, co-conscious, etc.

*   *   *   *   *

The door-keeper between the unconscious and the preconscious is nothing else than the *censorship* to which we found the form of the manifest dream subjected. The residue of the day's experiences which we found to be the stimuli exciting the dream, was preconscious material which at night during sleep had been influenced by unconscious and repressed wishes and excitations; and had thus by association with them been able to form the latent dream, by means of their energy. Under the dominion of the unconscious system this material had been elaborated (worked over)—by condensation and displacement—in a way which in normal mental life, i.e., in the preconscious system, is unknown or admissible very rarely. This difference in their manner of functioning is what distinguishes the two systems for us; the relationship to consciousness, which is a permanent feature of the preconscious, indicates to which of the systems any given process belongs. Neither is dreaming a pathological phenomenon; every healthy person may dream while asleep. Every inference concerning the constitution of both dreams and neurotic symptoms has an irrefutable claim to be regarded as applying also to normal mental life.

This is as much as we will say about repression. . . . Moreover, it is but a necessary preliminary condition, a prerequisite, of symptom-formation. We know that the symptom is a substitute for some other process which was held back by repression.

Fixation and Regression[7]

Let me simply say that we consider it possible that single portions of every separate sexual impulse may remain in an early stage of development, although at the same time other portions of it may have reached their final goal. You will see from this that we conceive each such impulse as a current continuously flowing from the beginning of life and that we have divided its flow to some extent artificially into separate successive forward movements. Your impression that these conceptions require further elucidation is correct, but the attempt would lead us too far afield. We will, however, decide at this point to call this *arrest* in a component impulse at an early stage a FIXATION (of the impulse).

The second danger in a development by stages such as this we call RE-GRESSION; it also happens that those portions which have proceeded further may easily revert in a backward direction to these earlier stages. The impulse will find occasion to *regress* in this way when the exercise of its function in a later and more developed form meets with powerful external obstacles, which thus prevent it from attaining the goal of satisfaction. It is a short step to assume that fixation and regression are not independent of each other; the stronger the fixations in the path of development the more easily will the function yield before the external obstacles, by regressing on to those fixations; that is, the less capable of resistance against the external difficulties in its path will the developed function be. If you think of a migrating people who have left large numbers at the stopping-places on their way, you will see that the foremost will naturally fall back upon these positions when they are defeated or when they meet with an enemy too strong for them. And again, the more of their number they leave behind in their progress, the sooner will they be in danger of defeat.

*　　*　　*　　*　　*

After what you have heard about the development of the libido you may anticipate two kinds of regression; a return to the first objects invested with libido, which we know to be incestuous in character, and a return of the whole sexual organization to earlier stages. . . . I think, however, that I had better warn you now above all not to confound *Regression* with *Repression* and that I must assist you to clear your minds about the relation between the two processes. *Repression*, as you will remember, is the process by which

[7]*Ibid.*, from pp. 298-301.

a mental act capable of becoming conscious (that is, one which belongs to the preconscious system) is made unconscious and forced back into the unconscious system. And we also call it *repression* when the unconscious mental act is not permitted to enter the adjacent preconscious system at all, but is turned back upon the threshold by the censorship. There is therefore no connection with sexuality in the concept *repression;* please mark this very carefully. It denotes a purely psychological process; and would be even better described as *topographical,* by which we mean that it has to do with the spatial relationships we assume within the mind, or, if we again abandon these crude aids to the formulation of theory, with the structure of the mental apparatus out of separate psychical systems.

The comparisons just now instituted showed us that hitherto we have not been using the word *regression* in its general sense but in a quite specific one. If you give it its general sense, that of a reversion from a higher to a lower stage of development in general, then repression also ranges itself under regression; for repression can also be described as reversion to an earlier and lower stage in the development of a mental act. Only, in repression this retrogressive direction is not a point of any moment to us; for we also call it repression in a dynamic sense when a mental process is arrested before it leaves the lower stage of the unconscious. Repression is thus a topographic-dynamic conception, while regression is a purely descriptive one. But what we have hitherto called *regression* and considered in its relation to fixation signified exclusively the return of *the libido* to its former halting-places in development, that is, something which is essentially quite different from repression and quite independent of it. Nor can we call repression of the libido a purely psychical process; neither do we know where to localize it in the mental apparatus; for though it may exert the most powerful influence upon mental life, the organic factor in it is nevertheless the most prominent.

*   *   *   *   *

Frustration and Sublimation[8]

People fall ill of a neurosis when the possibility of satisfaction for the libido is removed from them—they fall ill in consequence of a "frustration," as I called it, therefore—and that their symptoms are actually substitutes for the missing satisfaction. This of course does not mean that every frustration in regard to libidinal satisfaction makes everyone who meets with it neurotic, but merely that in all cases of neurosis investigated the factor of frustration was demonstrable.

*   *   *   *   *

Now in order to consider this proposition further we do not know whether to begin upon the nature of the frustration or the particular character of the

8*Ibid.,* from pp. 301-3.

person affected by it. The frustration is very rarely a comprehensive and absolute one; in order to have a pathogenic effect it would probably have to strike at the only form of satisfaction which that person desires, the only form of which he is capable. In general, there are very many ways by which it is possible to endure lack of libidinal satisfaction without falling ill. Above all we know of people who are able to take such abstinence upon themselves without injury; they are then not happy, they suffer from unsatisfied longing, but they do not become ill. We therefore have to conclude that the sexual impulse-excitations are exceptionally "plastic," if I may use the word. One of them can step in in place of another; if satisfaction of one is denied in reality, satisfaction of another can offer full recompense. They are related to one another like a network of communicating canals filled with fluid, and this in spite of their subordination to the genital primacy, a condition which is not at all easily reduced to an image. Further, the component-instincts of sexuality, as well as the united sexual impulse which comprises them, show a great capacity to change their object, to exchange it for another—i.e., for one more easily attainable; this capacity for displacement and readiness to accept surrogates must produce a powerful counter-effect to the effect of a frustration. One amongst these processes serving as protection against illness arising from want has reached a particular significance in the development of culture. It consists in the abandonment, on the part of the sexual impulse, of an aim previously found either in the gratification of a component-impulse or in the gratification incidental to reproduction, and the adoption of a new aim—which new aim, though genetically related to the first, can no longer be regarded as sexual, but must be called social in character. We call this process SUBLIMATION, by which we subscribe to the general standard which estimates social aims above sexual (ultimately selfish) aims. Incidentally, sublimation is merely a special case of the connections existing between sexual impulses and other, asexual ones.

* * * * *

Your impression now will be that we have reduced want of satisfaction to a factor of negligible proportions by the recognition of so many means of enduring it. But no; this is not so: it retains its pathogenic power. The means of dealing with it are not always sufficient. The measure of unsatisfied libido that the average human being can take upon himself is limited. The plasticity and free mobility of the libido is not by any means retained to the full in any of us; and sublimation can never discharge more than a certain proportion of libido, apart from the fact that many people possess the capacity for sublimation only in a slight degree. The most important of these limitations is clearly that referring to the mobility of the libido, since it confines the individual to the attaining of aims and objects which are very few in number. Just remember that incomplete development of the libido leaves behind it very extensive (and sometimes numerous) libido-fixations upon earlier phases of organizations and types of object-choice, mostly incapable of satisfaction in reality; you will then recognize fixation of libido as the second powerful factor working together with frustration in the causation of illness. We may condense this schematically and say that libido-fixation represents the internal, predisposing factor, while frustration represents the external, accidental factor, in the aetiology of the neuroses.

* * * * *

Undoing and Isolation[9]

Obsessional neurosis presents such a vast multiplicity of phenomena that no efforts have yet succeeded in making a coherent synthesis of all its variations. . . . The overacute conflict between id and superego which has dominated the illness from the very beginning may assume such extensive proportions that the ego, unable to carry out its office of mediator, can undertake nothing which is not drawn into the sphere of that conflict.

In the course of these struggles we come across two activities of the ego which form symptoms and which deserve special attention because they are obviously surrogates of repression and therefore well calculated to illustrate its purpose and technique. The fact that such auxiliary and substitute techniques emerge may argue that true repression has met with difficulties in its functioning. If one considers how much more the ego is the scene of action of symptom-formation in obsessional neurosis than it is in hysteria and with what tenacity the ego clings to its relations to reality and to consciousness, employing all its intellectual faculties to that end—and indeed how the very process of thinking becomes hypercathected and eroticized—then one may perhaps come to a better understanding of these variations of repression.

The two techniques I refer to are *undoing what has been done* and *isolating.* The first of these has a wide range of application and goes back very far. It is, as it were, negative magic, and endeavours, by means of motor symbolism, to "blow away" not merely the *consequences* of some event (or experience or impression) but the event itself. I choose the term "blow away" advisedly, so as to remind the reader of the part played by this technique not only in neuroses but in magical acts, popular customs and religious ceremonies as well. In obsessional neurosis the technique of undoing what has been done is first met with in the "diphasic" symptoms, in which one action is cancelled out by a second, so that it is as though neither action had taken place, whereas, in reality, both have. This aim of undoing is the second underlying motive of obsessional ceremonials, the first being to take precautions in order to prevent the occurrence of reoccurrence of some particular event. The difference between the two is easily seen: the precautionary measures are rational, while trying to get rid of something by "making it not to have happened" is irrational and in the nature of magic. It is of

[9]"Inhibitions, Symptoms and Anxiety," trans. James Strachey, in vol. XX, THE STANDARD EDITION OF THE COMPLETE PSYCHOLOGICAL WORKS OF SIGMUND FREUD, ed. James Strachey (London: Hogarth, 1952), from pp. 118-22.

course to be suspected that the latter is the earlier motive of the two and proceeds from the animistic attitude toward the environment. This endeavour to undo shades off into normal behaviour in the case in which a person decides to regard an event as not having happened. But whereas he will take no direct steps against the event, and will simply pay no further attention to it or its consequences, the neurotic person will try to make the past itself non-existent. He will try to repress it by motor means. The same purpose may perhaps account for the obsession for *repeating* which is so frequently met with in this neurosis and the carrying out of which serves a number of contradictory intentions at once. When anything has not happened in the desired way it is undone by being repeated in a different way; and thereupon all the motives that exist for lingering over such repetitions come into play as well. As the neurosis proceeds, we often find that the endeavour to undo a traumatic experience is a motive of first-rate importance in the formation of symptoms. We thus unexpectedly discover a new, motor technique of defence, or (as we may say in this case with less inaccuracy) of repression.

The second of these techniques which we are setting out to describe for the first time, that of isolation, is peculiar to obsessional neurosis. It, too, takes place in the motor sphere. When something unpleasant has happened to the subject or when he himself has done something which has a significance for his neurosis, he interpolates an interval during which nothing further must happen—during which he must perceive nothing and do nothing. This behaviour, which seems strange at first sight, is soon seen to have a relation to repression. We know that in hysteria it is possible to cause a traumatic experience to be overtaken by amnesia. In obsessional neurosis this can often not be achieved: the experience is not forgotten, but, instead, it is deprived of its affect, and its associative connections are suppressed or interrupted so that it remains as though isolated and is not reproduced in the ordinary processes of thought. The effect of this isolation is the same as the effect of repression with amnesia. This technique, then, is reproduced in the isolations of obsessional neurosis; and it is at the same time given motor reinforcement for magical purposes. The elements that are held apart in this way are precisely those which belong together associatively. The motor isolation is meant to ensure an interruption of the connection in thought. The normal phenomenon of concentration provides a pretext for this kind of neurotic procedure: what seems to us important in the way of an impression or a piece of work must not be interfered with by the simultaneous claims of any other mental processes or activities. But even a normal person uses concentration to keep away not only what is irrelevant or unimportant, but, above all, what is unsuitable because it is contradictory. He is most disturbed by those elements which once belonged together but which have been torn apart in the course of his development—as, for instance, by manifestations of the ambivalence of his father-complex in his relation to God, or by impulses attached to his excretory organs in his emotions of love. Thus, in the normal course of things, the ego has a great deal of isolating work to do in its function of directing the current of thought. And, as we know, we are obliged, in carrying out our analytic technique, to train it to relinquish that function for the time being, eminently justified as it usually is.

We have all found by experience that it is especially difficult for an obsessional neurotic to carry out the fundamental rule of psychoanalysis. His ego is more watchful and makes sharper isolations, probably because of the high degree of tension due to conflict that exists between his super-ego and his id. While he is engaged in thinking, his ego has to keep off too much— the intrusion of unconscious phantasies and the manifestation of ambivalent trends. It must not relax, but is constantly prepared for a struggle. It fortifies this compulsion to concentrate and to isolate by the help of the magical acts of isolation which, in the form of symptoms, grow to be so noticeable and to have so much practical importance for the patient, but which are, of course, useless in themselves and are in the nature of ceremonials.

* * * * *

Since obsessional neurosis begins by persecuting erotic touching and then, after regression has taken place, goes on to persecute touching in the guise of aggressiveness, it follows that nothing is so strongly proscribed in that illness as touching nor so well suited to become the central point of a system of prohibitions. But isolating is removing the possibility of contact; it is a method of withdrawing a thing from being touched in any way. And when a neurotic isolates an impression or an activity by interpolating an interval, he is letting it be understood symbolically that he will not allow his thoughts about that impression or activity to come into associative contact with other thoughts.

Identification[10]

I cannot tell you as much as I could wish about the change from the parental function to the super-ego. . . . You will have to be satisfied with the following indications. The basis of the process is what we call an identification, that is to say, that one ego becomes like another, one which results in the first ego behaving itself in certain respects in the same way as the second; it imitates it, and as it were takes it into itself. This identification has been not inappropriately compared with the oral cannibalistic incorporation of another person. Identification is a very important kind of relationship with another person, probably the most primitive, and is not to be confused with object-choice. One can express the difference between them this way: when a boy identifies himself with his father, he wants to *be like* his father; when he makes him the object of his choice, he wants to *have* him, to possess him; in the first case his ego is altered on the model of his father, in

[10]*New Introductory Lectures on Psycho-Analysis*, trans. W. J. H. Sprott (New York: Norton, 1933), from pp. 90-92.

the second case that is not necessary. Identification and object-choice are broadly speaking independent of each other; but one can identify oneself with a person, and alter one's ego accordingly, and take the same person as one's sexual object. It is said that this influencing of the ego by the sexual object takes place very often with women, and is characteristic of femininity. . . . It can be as easily observed in children as in adults, in normal as in sick persons. If one has lost a love-object or has had to give it up, one often compensates oneself by identifying oneself with it; one sets it up again inside one's ego, so that in this case object-choice regresses, as it were, to identification.

*   *   *   *   *

Another thing that we must not forget is that the child values its parents differently at different periods of its life. At the time at which the Oedipus complex makes way for the super-ego, they seem to be splendid figures, but later on they lose a good deal of their prestige. Identifications take place with these later editions of the parents as well, and regularly provide important contributions to the formation of character; but these only affect the ego, they have no influence on the super-ego, which has been determined by the earliest parental imagos.

*   *   *   *   *

Projection[11]

The three layers or grades of jealousy may be described as (1) *competitive* or normal, (2) *projected*, and (3) *delusional* jealousy.

There is not much to be said from the analytic point of view about normal jealousy. . . . The jealousy of the second layer, *projected* jealousy, is derived in both men and women either from their own actual unfaithfulness in real life or from impulses toward it which have succumbed to repression. It is a matter of everyday experience that fidelity, especially that degree of it required in marriage, is only maintained in the face of continual temptations. Anyone who denies these temptations in himself will nevertheless feel their pressure so strongly that he will be glad enough to make use of an unconscious mechanism to alleviate his situation. He can obtain this alleviation —and, indeed, acquittal by his conscience—if he projects his own impulses to faithlessness on to the partner to whom he owes faith. This strong motive can then make use of the perceptual material which betrays unconscious impulses of the same kind in the partner, and the subject can justify himself with the reflection that the other is probably not much better than he is himself.[a]

*   *   *   *   *

---

[11]*Certain Neurotic Mechanisms in Jealousy, Paranoia and Homosexuality*, trans. Joan Riviere, in vol. II, COLLECTED PAPERS, *op. cit.*, from pp. 232-34.

[a]"I called my love false love; but what said he then?

"If I court more women, you'll couch with more men."   (*Othello*, IV, 3)

The jealousy that arises from such a projection has, it is true, an almost delusional character; it is, however, amenable to the analytic work of exposing the unconscious phantasies of the subject's own infidelity.

* * * * *

THE EGO'S THREE VARIETIES OF ANXIETY (OBJECTIVE, NEUROTIC, AND MORAL)[12]

Anxiety is an affective condition—that is to say, a combination of certain feelings of the pleasure-pain series with their corresponding efferent innervations, and a perception of them—but we asserted that anxiety is probably also the trace of a certain important event, taken over by inheritance, and therefore comparable to the ontogenetically acquired hysterical attack. . . . The first anxiety of all would thus have been a toxic one. We then started[13] from the distinction between objective anxiety and neurotic anxiety, the former being what seems to us an intelligible reaction to danger—that is, to anticipated injury from without—and the latter altogether puzzling and, as it were, purposeless. In our analysis of objective anxiety we explained it as a condition of increased sensory attention and motor tension, which we called "*anxiety-preparedness.*" Out of this the anxiety-reaction arises. The anxiety-reaction may run one of two courses. Either the *anxiety-development,* the repetition of the old traumatic experience, is restricted to a signal, in which case the rest of the reaction can adapt itself to the new situation of danger, whether by flight or defence; or the old experience gets the upper hand, and the whole reaction exhausts itself in anxiety-development, in which case the affective state is paralysing and unadapted to the present situation.

We then turned our attention to neurotic anxiety, and pointed out that it could be observed in three forms. Firstly, we have free-floating, general apprehensiveness, ready to attach itself for the time being to any new possibility that may arise in the form of what we call expectant dread, as happens, for instance, in the typical anxiety-neurosis. Secondly, we find it firmly attached to certain ideas, in what are known as *phobias,* in which we can still recognize a connection with external danger, but cannot help regarding the anxiety felt toward it as enormously exaggerated. Thirdly and finally, we have anxiety as it occurs in hysteria and in other severe neuroses; this anxiety either accompanies symptoms or manifests itself independently, whether as an attack or as a condition which persists for some time, but always without having any visible justification in an external danger. We then ask ourselves two questions: "What are people afraid of when they have neurotic anxiety?" and "How can one bring this kind of anxiety into line with objective anxiety felt toward an external danger?"

[12]*New Introductory Lectures, op. cit.,* from pp. 113-24.
[13]Throughout this section, Freud is recapitulating former lectures.

... The most frequent cause of anxiety-neurosis is undischarged excitation. A libidinal excitation is aroused, but is not satisfied or used; in the place of this libido which has been diverted from its use, anxiety makes its appearance. This view found some support in certain almost universal phobias of small children. Many of these phobias are altogether enigmatic, but others, such as the fear of being left alone and the fear of unfamiliar people, can be definitely explained. Being left alone or seeing strange faces stirs up the child's longing for the familiar presence of its mother; it cannot control this libidinal excitation; it cannot keep it in a state of suspension, but turns it into anxiety. This anxiety in children, therefore, is not objective anxiety, but must be classed among the neurotic anxieties. Children's phobias, and the anxious expectation in anxiety-neurosis, serve as two examples of one way in which neurotic anxiety comes about; *i.e.* through direct transformation of libido.

*　　*　　*　　*　　*

For it is to the process of repression that we attribute the appearance of anxiety in hysteria and other neuroses. We now believe that it is possible to give a fuller description of this process ... if we separate the history of the idea that has to be repressed from that of the libido which is attached to it. It is the idea that undergoes repression and may be distorted so as to become unrecognizable; its associated affect is always turned into anxiety, regardless of its nature, whether, that is to say, it is aggression or love. Now it makes no essential difference on what grounds a given quantity of libido has become unusable, whether on account of the infantile weakness of the ego, as in the case of children's phobias, or on account of somatic processes in sexual life, as in the case of anxiety neuroses, or no account of repression, as in the case of hysteria. The two mechanisms which give rise to neurotic anxiety are therefore essentially the same.

While we were engaged in these investigations, we noticed a very important connection between anxiety-development and symptom-formation. It was that the two are interchangeable. The agoraphobiac, for example, begins his illness with an attack of anxiety in the street. This is repeated every time he walks along the street again. He now develops a symptom—a street phobia—which can also be described as an inhibition or a functional restriction of the ego, and thus he preserves himself from anxiety attacks. One can observe the reverse process if one interferes with the formation of symptoms, as is possible, for instance, in the case of obsessive acts. If one prevents a patient from carrying out his washing ceremonial, he is thrown into an intolerable state of anxiety, against which his symptom has obviously protected him. And, indeed, it seems as though anxiety-development is the earlier and symptom-formation the later of the two, as though the symptom were created in order to prevent the outbreak of a state of anxiety. And it is in keeping with this that the first neuroses of childhood are phobias—conditions, that is to say, in which one sees quite clearly how what began as anxiety-development is later replaced by symptom-formation: one gets an impression that this circumstance affords the best starting-point from which to approach an understanding of neurotic anxiety. At the same time we succeeded in discovering the answer to the question of what it is that one fears in neurotic anxiety, and thus restoring the connection between neurotic anxiety and objective anxiety. What one fears is obviously one's own libido. The difference between this and objective anxiety lies in two points—that the danger is an internal instead of an external one, and that it is not consciously recognized.

In the case of phobias one can see clearly how this internal danger is transformed into an external one; how, that is to say, neurotic anxiety turns into apparent objective anxiety. Let us simplify a state of affairs which is often very complicated, and suppose that the agoraphobiac is always afraid of his impulses in connection with temptations aroused in him by meeting people in the street. In his phobia he makes a displacement and is now afraid of an external situation. What he gains thereby is obvious; it is that he feels he can protect himself better in that way. One can rescue oneself from an external danger by flight, whereas to attempt to fly from an internal danger is a difficult undertaking.

. . . I expressed the opinion that, though these various results of our investigations did not actually contradict one another, they were nevertheless not entirely consistent. As an affective condition, anxiety is the reproduction of an old danger-threatening event; anxiety serves the purposes of self-preservation as being a signal of the presence of a new danger; it arises from libido that has become unusable for some reason or other, including the process of repression; it is replaced by symptom-formation, and thus, as it were, psychically bound; in all of this one feels that something is missing which would combine these fragments into a unity.

. . . The division of the mental personality into a super-ego, ego and id . . . has forced us to take up a new position with regard to the problem of anxiety. In assuming that the ego is the only seat of anxiety, we have taken up a new and secure position, from which many facts take on a new aspect. And when you come to think of it, it is difficult to see what sense there could be in speaking of an "anxiety of the id," or how we could ascribe a capacity for feeling anxiety to the super-ego. On the contrary, we have found a satisfactory confirmation of our theory in the fact that the three main varieties of anxiety—objective anxiety, neurotic anxiety and moral anxiety —can so easily be related to the three directions in which the ego is dependent, on the external world, on the id and on the super-ego. Our new position, too, has brought to the fore the function of anxiety as a signal indicating the presence of a danger-situation, a function with which we were already not unfamiliar. The question of the stuff out of which anxiety is made loses interest for us, and the relations between objective anxiety and neurotic anxiety are clarified and simplified in a surprising way. And, besides this, it is to be noticed that we now understand the apparently complicated cases of anxiety-formation better than we do those which seem to be simple.

We have recently investigated the manner in which anxiety comes about in certain phobias, which we class with anxiety-hysteria. . . . I cannot tell you all the individual steps of an investigation of this kind; let it suffice to say that, to our astonishment, the result was the reverse of what we had expected. It is not the repression that creates the anxiety, but the anxiety is there first and creates the repression!

*   *   *   *   *

We have discovered two new facts: first, that anxiety causes repression, and not the other way round as we used to think, and secondly, that frightening *instinctual* situations can in the last resort be traced back to *external* situations of danger. Our next question will be: How can we picture the process of repression carried out under the influence of anxiety? I think this is what happens: the ego becomes aware that the satisfaction of some nascent instinctual demand would evoke one among the well-remembered danger-situations. This instinctual cathexis must, therefore, somehow or other be suppressed, removed, made powerless. We know that the ego succeeds in this task if it is strong, and if it has assimilated the impulse in question into its organization.

THE LIBIDO THEORY
(INSTINCTS AND THEIR SUBLIMATION)

The Libido

Libido[14] is a term used in the theory of instincts for describing the dynamic manifestations of sexuality. . . .

The[15] power of the id expresses the true purpose of the individual organism's life. This consists in the satisfaction of its innate needs. No such purpose as that of keeping itself alive or of protecting itself from dangers by means of anxiety can be attributed to the id. That is the business of the ego, which is also concerned with discovering the most favorable and least perilous method of obtaining satisfaction, taking the external world into account. The superego may bring fresh needs to the fore, but its chief function remains the *limitation* of satisfactions.

The forces which we assume to exist behind the tensions caused by the needs of the id are called *instincts*. They represent the somatic demands upon mental life. Though they are the ultimate cause of all activity, they are by nature conservative; the state, whatever it may be, which a living thing has

---

[14]"Two Encyclopaedia Articles," trans. James Strachey, in vol. V, COLLECTED PAPERS, *op. cit.*, from p. 131.

[15]*An Outline of Psychoanalysis, op. cit.*, from pp. 19-22.

reached, gives rise to a tendency to re-establish that state so soon as it has been abandoned. It is possible to distinguish an indeterminate number of instincts and in common practice this is in fact done. For us, however, the important question arises whether we may not be able to derive all of these various instincts from a few fundamental ones. We have found that instincts can change their aim (by displacement) and also that they can replace one another—the energy of one instinct passing over to another. This latter process is still insufficiently understood. After long doubts and vacillations we have decided to assume the existence of only two basic instincts, *Eros* and *the destructive instinct*. (The contrast between the instincts of self-preservation and of the preservation of the species, as well as the contrast between ego-love and object-love, fall within the bounds of Eros.) The aim of the first of these basic instincts is to establish ever greater unities and to preserve them thus—in short, to bind together; the aim of the second, on the contrary, is to undo connections and so to destroy things. We may suppose that the final aim of the destructive instinct is to reduce living things to an inorganic state. For this reason we also call it the *death instinct*. If we suppose that living things appeared later than inanimate ones and arose out of them, then the death instinct agrees with the formula that we have stated, to the effect that instincts tend toward a return to an earlier state. We are unable to apply the formula to Eros (the love instinct). That would be to imply that living substance had once been a unity but had subsequently been torn apart and was now tending toward re-union.

In biological functions the two basic instincts work against each other or combine with each other. Thus, the act of eating is a destruction of the object with the final aim of incorporating it, and the sexual act is an act of aggression having as its purpose the most intimate union. This interaction of the two basic instincts with and against each other gives rise to the whole variegation of the phenomena of life. The analogy of our two basic instincts extends from the region of animate things to the pair of opposing forces—attraction and repulsion—which rule in the inorganic world.

Modifications in the proportions of the fusion between the instincts have the most noticeable results. A surplus of sexual aggressiveness will change a lover into a sexual murderer, while a sharp diminution in the aggressive factor will lead to shyness or impotence.

There can be no question of restricting one or the other of the basic instincts to a single region of the mind. They are necessarily present everywhere. We may picture an initial state of things by supposing that the whole available energy of Eros, to which we shall henceforward give the name of *libido,* is present in the as yet undifferentiated ego-id and serves to neutralize the destructive impulses which are simultaneously present. (There is no term analogous to "libido" for describing the energy of the destructive instinct.) It becomes relatively easy for us to follow the later vicissitudes of the libido; but this is more difficult with the destructive instinct.

*   *   *   *   *

Sexual Instincts and Ego Instincts

The[16] first sphere to be studied by psycho-analysis comprised what is known as the transference neuroses (hysteria and obsessional neuroses). It was found that their symptoms came about by sexual instinctive impulses being rejected (repressed) by the subject's personality (his ego) and then finding expression by circuitous paths through the unconscious. These facts could be met by drawing a contrast between the sexual instincts and ego instincts (*instincts of self-preservation*), which was in line with the popular saying that hunger and love are what make the world go round; libido was the manifestation of the force of love in the same sense as was hunger of the self-preservation instinct. The nature of the ego instincts remained for the time being undefined and, like all the other characteristics of the ego, inaccessible to analysis. There was no means of deciding whether, and if so what, qualitative differences were to be assumed to exist between the two classes of instincts.

*　　*　　*　　*　　*

Sublimation

What is described as the sexual instinct turns out to be of a highly composite nature and is liable to disintegrate once more into its component instincts. Each component instinct is unalterably characterized by its *source*, that is, by the region or zone of the body from which its excitation is derived. Each has furthermore as distinguishable features an *object* and an *aim*. The aim is always discharge accompanied by satisfaction, but it is capable of being changed from activity to passivity. The object is less closely attached to the instinct than was at first supposed; it is easily exchanged for another one, and, moreover, an instinct which had an external object can be turned round upon the subject's own self. The separate instincts can either remain independent of one another or—in what is still an inexplicable manner—can be combined and merged into one another to perform work in common. They are also able to replace one another and to transfer their libidinal cathexis to one another, so that the satisfaction of one instinct can take the place of the satisfaction of others. The most important vicissitude which an instinct can undergo seems to be *sublimation*. Here both object and aim are changed, so that what was originally a sexual instinct finds satisfaction in some achievement which is no longer sexual but has a higher social or ethical valuation. These different features do not as yet combine to form an integral picture.

Narcissism

It was found that the pathogenic process in dementia praecox is the withdrawal of the libido from objects and its introduction into the ego, while

16"Two Encyclopaedia Articles," *op. cit.*, from pp. 131-33.

the clamorous symptoms of the disease arise from the vain struggles of the libido to find a pathway back to objects. It thus turned out to be possible for object-libido to change into cathexis of the ego and *vice versa*. Further reflection showed that this process must be presumed to occur on the largest scale and that the ego is to be regarded as a great reservoir of libido from which libido is sent out *to* objects and which is always ready to absorb libido flowing back *from* objects. Thus the instincts of self-preservation were also of a libidinal nature: they were sexual instincts which, instead of external objects, had taken the subject's own ego as an object. Clinical experience had made us familiar with people who behaved in a striking fashion as though they were in love with themselves and this perversion had been given the name of narcissism. The libido of the self-preservative instincts was now described as narcissistic libido and it was recognized that a high degree of this self-love constituted the primary normal state of things. The earlier formula laid down for the transference neuroses consequently required to be modified, though not corrected. It was better, instead of speaking of a conflict between sexual instincts and ego instincts, to speak of a conflict between object-libido and ego-libido, or, object-cathexes and the ego.

*   *   *   *   *

The Two Classes of Instincts: Eros and Thanatos

I[17] have lately developed a view of the instincts. . . . According to this view we have to distinguish two classes of instincts, one of which, the sexual instincts or Eros, is by far the more conspicuous and accessible to study. It comprises not merely the uninhibited sexual instinct proper and the instinctual impulses of an aim-inhibited or sublimated nature derived from it, but also the self-preservative instinct, which must be assigned to the ego and which at the beginning of our analytic work we had good reason for contrasting with the sexual object-instincts. The second class of instincts was not so easy to point to: in the end we came to recognize sadism as its representative. On the basis of theoretical considerations, supported by biology, we put forward the hypothesis of a death instinct, the task of which is to lead organic life back into the inanimate state; on the other hand, we supposed that Eros, by bringing about a more and more far-reaching combination of the particles into which living substance is dispersed, aims at complicating life and at the same time, of course, at preserving it. Acting in this way, both the instincts would be conservative in the strictest sense of the word, since both would be endeavoring to re-establish a state of things that was disturbed by the emergence of life. The emergence of life would thus be the cause of the continuance of life and also at the same time of the striving toward death; and life itself would be a conflict and compromise between these two trends. The problem of the origin of life would remain a cosmo-

17*The Ego and the Id, op. cit.,* from pp. 30-35.

logical one; and the problem of the goal and purpose of life would be answered dualistically.

* * * * *

The Bipolarity or Ambivalency of Emotions

For the opposition between the two classes of instincts we may put the polarity of love and hate. There is no difficulty in finding a representative of Eros; but we must be grateful that we can find a representative of the elusive death instinct in the instinct of destruction, to which hate points the way. Now, clinical observation shows not only that love is with unexpected regularity accompanied by hate (ambivalence), and not only that in human relationships hate is frequently a forerunner of love, but also that in a number of circumstances hate changes into love and love into hate. If this change is more than a mere succession in time—if, that is, one of them actually turns into the other—then clearly the ground is cut away from under a distinction so fundamental as that between erotic instincts and death instincts, one which presupposes physiological processes running in opposite directions.

. . . We know of several instances in the psychology of the neuroses in which it is more plausible to suppose that a transformation does take place. In persecutory paranoia the patient fends off an excessively strong homosexual attachment to some particular person in a special way; and as a result this person whom he loved most becomes a persecutor, against whom the patient directs an often dangerous aggressiveness. Here we have the right to interpolate a previous phase which has transformed the love into hate.

* * * * *

It will be noticed, however, that by introducing this other mechanism of changing love into hate, we have tacitly made another assumption which deserves to be stated explicitly. We have reckoned as though there existed in the mind—whether in the ego or in the id—a displaceable energy, which, neutral in itself, can be added to a qualitatively differentiated erotic or destructive impulse, and augment its total cathexis. . . . I am putting forward a hypothesis; I have no proof to offer. It seems a plausible view that this displaceable and neutral energy, which is no doubt active both in the ego and in the id, proceeds from the narcissistic store of libido—that it is desexualized Eros. (The erotic instincts appear to be altogether more plastic, more readily diverted and displaced than the destructive instincts.) . . . If this displaceable energy is desexualized libido, it may also be described as *sublimated* energy; for it would still retain the main purpose of Eros—that of uniting and binding —insofar as it helps towards establishing the unity, or tendency to unity, which is particularly characteristic of the ego. If thought-processes in the wider sense are to be included among these displacements, then the activity of thinking is also supplied from the sublimation of erotic motive forces.

Here we arrive again at the possibility which has already been discussed that sublimation may take place regularly through the mediation of the ego.

The Nature of Instincts

This[18] view would enable us to characterize instincts as tendencies in living substance towards restoring an earlier state of things: that is to say, they would be historically determined and of a conservative nature and, as it were, the expression of an inertia or elasticity present in what is organic. Both classes of instincts, Eros as well as the death instinct, would, on this view, have been in operation and working against each other from the first origin of life.

* * * * *

We[19] are now in a position to discuss certain terms which are used in reference to the concept of an instinct—for example, its "pressure," "aim," its "object" and its "source."

By the pressure (*Drang*) of an instinct we understand its motor factor, the amount of force or the measure of the demand for work which it represents. The characteristic of exercising pressure is common to all instincts; it is in fact their very essence. Every instinct is a piece of activity; if we speak loosely of passive instincts, we can only mean instincts whose *aim* is passive.

The aim (*Ziel*) of an instinct is in every instance satisfaction, which can only be obtained by removing the state of stimulation at the source of the instinct. But although the ultimate aim of each instinct remains unchangeable, there may yet be different paths leading to the same ultimate aim; so that an instinct may be found to have various nearer or intermediate aims, which are combined or interchanged with one another. Experience permits us also to speak of instincts which are "inhibited in their aim," in the case of processes which are allowed to make some advance towards instinctual satisfaction but are then inhibited and deflected. We may suppose that even processes of this kind involve a partial satisfaction.

The object (*Objekt*) of an instinct is the thing in regard to which or through which the instinct is able to achieve its aim. It is what is most variable about an instinct and is not originally connected with it, but becomes assigned to it only in consequence of being peculiarly fitted to make satisfaction possible. The object is not necessarily something extraneous: it may equally well be a part of the subject's own body. It may be changed any number of times in the course of the vicissitudes which the instinct undergoes during its existence; and highly important parts are played by this displacement of instinct. It may happen that the same object serves for the satisfaction of several instincts simultaneously, a phenomenon which Adler called a "confluence" of instincts. A particularly close attachment of the instinct

---

[18]"Two Encyclopaedia Articles," *op. cit.*, p. 135.

[19]"Instincts and Their Vicissitudes," trans. James Strachey, in vol. XIV (1957), STANDARD EDITION, *op. cit.*, from pp. 122-23.

to its object is distinguished by the term "fixation." This frequently occurs at very early periods of the development of an instinct and puts an end to its mobility through its intense opposition to detachment.

By the source (*Quelle*) of an instinct is meant the somatic process which occurs in an organ or part of the body and whose stimulus is represented in mental life by an instinct. We do not know whether this process is invariably of a chemical nature or whether it may also correspond to the release of other, e.g. mechanical, forces. The study of the sources of instincts lies outside the scope of psychology. Although instincts are wholly determined by their origin in a somatic source, in mental life we know them only by their aims. An exact knowledge of the sources of an instinct is not invariably necessary for purposes of psychological investigation; sometimes its source may be inferred from its aim.

* * * * *

STAGES OF PERSONALITY (LIBIDINAL) DEVELOPMENT

From[20] the third year onwards there is no longer any doubt about the sexual life in the child; at this period the genital organs begin to show signs of excitation; there is a perhaps regular period of infantile masturbation, that is, of gratification in the genital organs. The mental and social sides of sexual life need no longer be overlooked: choice of object, distinguishing of particular persons with affection, even decision in favor of one sex or the other, and jealousy, were conclusively established independently by impartial observation before the time of psychoanalysis; they may be confirmed by any observer who will use his eyes. You will object that you never doubted the early awakening of affection but only that this affection was of "sexual" quality. Children between the ages of three and eight have certainly learnt to conceal this element in it; but nevertheless if you will look attentively you will collect enough evidence of the "sensual" nature of this affection, and whatever still escapes your notice will be amply and readily supplied by analytic investigation. The sexual aims of this period of life are in closest connection with the sexual curiosity arising at the same time. . . . The perverse character of some of these aims is a natural result of the immature constitution of the child who has not yet discovered the aim of the act of intercourse.

* * * * *

We[21] find ourselves on firmer ground when we turn to the question of how the instinctual life serves the sexual function. Here we have obtained decisive

[20]*A General Introduction, op. cit.,* from p. 286.
[21]*New Introductory Lectures, op. cit.,* from pp. 134-36.

information; but you are already familiar with it. We do not, that is to say, believe that there is a single sexual instinct, which is from the first the vehicle of the impulse towards the aim of the sexual function, that is, the union of the two sex cells. On the contrary, we see a large number of component instincts, arising from various regions of the body, which strive for satisfaction more or less independently of one another, and find this satisfaction in something that may be called "*organ-pleasure*." The genitals are the latest of these *erotogenic zones;* and their organ-pleasure must certainly be called "sexual." Not all of these pleasure-seeking impulses are incorporated in the final organization of the sexual function. Many of them are put aside as useless, by means of repression or in some other way. . . . You have heard that in this long-drawn-out course of development several phases of provisional organization are to be recognized, and that aberrations and maldevelopments of the sexual function are to be explained by reference to its history. The first of these *pregenital* phases is called the *oral* phase, because, in accordance with the fact that the infant is nourished through the mouth, the erotogenic zone of the mouth dominates what we may call the sexual activity of this period of life. At a second stage the *sadistic* and *anal* impulses come to the fore, obviously in connection with the cutting of the teeth, the strengthening of the musculature, and the control of the sphincters. We have learnt a great many interesting details about this remarkable stage of development in particular. Third comes the *phallic* phase, in which for both sexes the penis (and what corresponds to it in the girl) achieves an importance which can no longer be overlooked. We have reserved the name of *genital* phase for the final sexual organization, established after puberty, in which the female genitals receive for the first time the recognition which the male genitals have long since obtained.

* * * * *

From[22] about the sixth or eighth year onwards a standstill or retrogression is observed in the sexual development, which in those cases reaching a high cultural standard deserves to be called a *latency period*. This latency period, however, may be absent; nor does it necessarily entail an interruption of sexual activities and sexual interests over the whole field. Most of the mental experiences and excitations occurring before the latency period then succumb to the infantile amnesia . . . which veils our earliest childhood from us and estranges us from it.

* * * * *

The Oedipus Complex

From the third year onwards the sexual life of children shows much in common with that of adults; it is differentiated from the latter . . . by the absence of a stable organization under the primacy of the genital organs, by

[22]*A General Introduction, op. cit.,* from pp. 286-96.

inevitable traits of a preverse order, and of course, also by far less intensity in the whole impulse. But those phases of the sexual development, or as we will call it, of the *libido-development,* which are of greatest interest theoretically lie before this period. This development is gone through so rapidly that direct observation alone would perhaps never have succeeded in determining its fleeting forms.

*   *   *   *   *

We will follow up another aspect of this development—namely, the relation of the sexual component-impulses to an object. . . . Certain of the component-impulses of the sexual instinct have an object from the very beginning and hold fast to it: such are the impulses to mastery (sadism), to gazing (skotophilia) and curiosity. . . . Thus the first object of the oral component of the sexual instinct is the mother's breast which satisfies the infant's need for nutrition. In the act of sucking for its own sake the erotic component, also gratified in sucking for nutrition, makes itself independent, gives up the object in an external person, and replaces it by a part of the child's own person. The oral impulse becomes *auto-erotic,* as the anal and other erotogenic impulses are from the beginning. Further development has, to put it as concisely as possible, two aims: first, to renounce auto-erotism, to give up again the object found in the child's own body in exchange again for an external one; and secondly, to combine the various objects of the separate impulses and replace them by one single one. This naturally can only be done if the single object is again itself complete, with a body like that of the subject; nor can it be accomplished without some part of the auto-erotic impulse-excitations being abandoned or useless.

The processes by which an object is found are rather involved, and have not so far received comprehensive exposition. For our purposes it may be emphasized that, when the process has reached a certain point in the years of childhood before the latency period, the object adopted proves almost identical with the first object of the oral pleasure impulse, adopted by reason of the child's dependent relationship to it; it is, namely, the mother, although not the mother's breast. We call the mother the first *love*-object. We speak of "love" when we lay the accent upon the mental side of the sexual impulses and disregard, or wish to forget for a moment, the demands of the fundamental physical or "sensual" side of the impulses. At about the same time when the mother becomes the love-object, the mental operation of repression has already begun in the child and has withdrawn from him the knowledge of some part of his sexual aims. Now with this choice of the mother as love-object is connected all that which, under the name of *"the Oedipus complex,"* has become of such great importance in the psycho-analytic explanation of the neuroses, and which has had a perhaps equally important share in causing the opposition against psycho-analysis.

*   *   *   *   *

Now you will be impatiently waiting to hear what this terrible Oedipus complex comprises. The name tells you: you all know the Greek myth of King Oedipus, whose destiny it was to slay his father and to wed his mother, who did all in his power to avoid the fate prophesied by the oracle, and who in self-punishment blinded himself when he discovered that in ignorance he had committed both these crimes. . . . And psychological truth is contained in this; even though a man has repressed his evil desires into his Unconscious and would then gladly say to himself that he is no longer answerable for them, he is yet compelled to feel his responsibility in the form of a sense of guilt for which he can discern no foundation. There is no possible doubt that one of the most important sources of the sense of guilt which so often torments neurotic people is to be found in the Oedipus complex. More than this: in 1913, under the title of *Totem and Tabu*, I published a study of the earliest form of religion and morality in which I expressed a suspicion that perhaps the sense of guilt of mankind as a whole, which is the ultimate source of religion and morality, was acquired in the beginnings of history through the Oedipus complex.

*　　*　　*　　*　　*

When the little boy shows the most open sexual curiosity about his mother, wants to sleep with her at night, insists on being in the room while she is dressing, or even attempts physical acts of seduction, as the mother so often observes and laughingly relates, the erotic nature of this attachment to her is established without a doubt. . . . It is easy to see that the little man wants his mother all to himself, finds his father in the way, and shows his dissatisfaction when the latter takes upon himself to caress her, and shows his satisfaction when the father goes away or is absent. He often expresses his feelings directly in words and promises his mother to marry her.

*　　*　　*　　*　　*

From the time of puberty onward the human individual must devote himself to the great task of *freeing himself from the parents;* and only after this detachment is accomplished can he cease to be a child and so become a member of the social community. For a son, the task consists in releasing his libidinal desires from his mother, in order to employ them in the quest of an external love-object in reality; and in reconciling himself with his father if he has remained antagonistic to him, or in freeing himself from his domination if, in the reaction to the infantile revolt, he has lapsed into subservience to him. These tasks are laid down for every man; it is noteworthy how seldom they are carried through ideally, that is, how seldom they are solved in a manner psychologically as well as socially satisfactory. In neurotics, however, this detachment from the parents is not accomplished at all; the son remains all his life in subjection to his father, and incapable of transferring his libido to a new sexual object. In the reversed relationship the daughter's fate may be the same. In this sense the Oedipus complex is justifiably regarded as the kernel of the neuroses.

DREAMS AS WISH FULFILMENTS[23]

We hoped to find a path to an understanding of the problems presented by dreams in the fact that certain very transparent phantasy-formations are called "day-dreams." Now these day-dreams are literally wish-fulfilments, fulfilments of ambitious or erotic wishes, which we recognize as such; they are, however, carried out in thought, and, however vividly imagined, they never take the form of hallucinatory experiences. Here, therefore, the less certain of the two main characteristics of the dream is retained, whereas the other, to which the condition of sleep is essential and which cannot be realized in waking life, is entirely lacking. So in language we find a hint that a wish-fulfilment is a main characteristic of dreams. And further, if the experience we have in dreams is only another form of imaginative representation, a form which becomes possible under the peculiar conditions of the sleeping state—"a nocturnal day-dream," as we might call it—we understand at once how it is that the process of dream-formation can abrogate the stimulus operating at night and can bring gratification; for day-dreaming also is a mode of activity closely linked up with gratification, which is in fact the only reason why people practise it.

* * * * *

Now see how much information we have gained, and that with hardly any trouble, from our study of children's dreams! We have learnt that the function of dreams is to protect sleep; that they arise out of two conflicting tendencies, of which the one, the desire for sleep, remains constant, whilst the other endeavours to satisfy some mental stimulus; that dreams are proved to be mental acts, rich in meaning; that they have two main characteristics, i.e., they are wish-fulfilments and hallucinatory experiences.

* * * * *

There is another class of dreams at least in which no distortion is present and which, like children's dreams, we easily recognize to be wish-fulfilments. These are dreams which are occasioned all through life by imperative physical needs—hunger, thirst, sexual desire—and are wish-fulfilments in the sense of being reactions to internal somatic stimuli.

* * * * *

Dreams are the means of removing, by hallucinatory satisfaction, mental stimuli that disturb sleep. . . . Every time that we fully understand a dream

[23]*Ibid.*, from pp. 117-37.

it proves to be a wish-fulfilment; and this coincidence cannot be accidental or unimportant. Dreams of another type are assumed by us to be distorted substitutes for an unknown content, which first of all has to be traced; we have various grounds for this assumption, amongst others the analogy to our conception of errors. Our next task is to investigate and understand this *dream-distortion.*

It is dream-distortion which makes dreams seem strange and incomprehensible. There are several things we want to know about it: first, whence it comes (its dynamics), secondly, what it does, and finally, how it does it. Further, we can say that distortion is the production of the *dream-work.*

*   *   *   *   *

We actually use the term DREAM-CENSORSHIP, and ascribe part of the distortion to its agency. Wherever there are gaps in the manifest dream we know that the censorship is responsible; and indeed we should go further and recognize that wherever, amongst other more clearly defined elements, one appears which is fainter, more indefinite or more dubious in recollection, it is evidence of the work of the censorship. . . . Omission, modification, regrouping of material—these then are the modes of the dream-censorship's activity and the means employed in distortion. The censorship itself is the originator, or one of the originators, of distortion, the subject of our present enquiry. Modification and alteration in arrangement are commonly included under the term "displacement."

*   *   *   *   *

We have found out that the distortion in dreams which hinders our understanding of them is due to the activities of a censorship, directed against the unacceptable, unconscious wish-impulses. . . . We call a constant relation . . . between a dream-element and its translation a *symbolic* one, and the dream-element itself a *symbol* of the unconscious dream-thought. . . . The number of things which are represented symbolically in dreams is not great. The human body as a whole, parents, children, brothers and sisters, birth, death, nakedness—and one thing more. The only typical, that is to say, regularly occurring, representation of the human form as a whole is that of a *house.* . . . When walls are quite smooth, the house means a man; when there are ledges and balconies which can be caught hold of, a woman. Parents appear in dreams as *emperor* and *empress, king* and *queen* or other exalted personages; in this respect the dream attitude is highly dutiful. Children and brothers and sisters are less tenderly treated, being symbolized by *little animals* or *vermin.* Birth is almost invariably represented by some reference to *water:* either we are falling into water or clambering out of it, saving someone from it or being saved by them, i.e. the relation between mother and child is symbolized. For dying we have setting out upon a *journey* or *travelling* by train, while the state of death is indicated by various obscure and, as it were, timid allusions; *clothes* and *uniforms* stand for nakedness.

You see that here the dividing line between the symbolic and the allusive kinds of representation tends to disappear.

PSYCHOPATHOLOGY OF EVERYDAY LIFE (FREUDIAN SLIPS)[24]

We shall now begin, not with postulates, but with an investigation. For this purpose we shall select certain phenomena which are very frequent, very familiar and much overlooked, and which have nothing to do with illness, since they may be observed in every healthy person. I refer to errors that everyone commits: as when anyone wishes to say a certain thing but uses the wrong word ("slip of the tongue"); or when the same sort of mistake is made in writing ("slip of the pen"), in which case one may or may not notice it; or when anyone reads in print or writing something other than what is actually before his ("misreading"); or when anyone mis-hears what is said to him, naturally when there is no question of disease of the auditory sense-organ. Another series of such phenomena are those based on forgetting something temporarily, though not permanently; as, for instance, when anyone cannot think of a name which he knows quite well and is always able to recognize whenever he sees it; or when anyone forgets to carry out some intention, which he afterwards remembers, and had therefore forgotten only for a certain time. This element of transitoriness is lacking in a third class, of which mislaying things so that they cannot be found is an example. This is a kind of forgetfulness which we regard differently from the usual kind; one is amazed or annoyed at it, instead of finding it comprehensible. Allied to this are certain *mistakes,* in which the temporary element is again noticeable, as when one believes something for a time which both before and afterwards one knows to be untrue, and a number of similar manifestations which we know under various names.

*   *   *   *   *

The commonest and also the most noticeable form of slip of the tongue ... is that of saying the exact opposite of what one meant to say. These cases are quite outside the effect of any relations between sounds or confusion due to similarity, and in default one may therefore turn to the fact that opposites have a strong conceptual connection with one another and are psychologically very closely associated. There are well-known examples of this sort. For instance, the President of our Parliament once opened the session with the words, "Gentlemen, I declare a quorum present and herewith declare the session *closed.*" ...

As an instance of an interchange (in the position of words) someone might say "The Milo of Venus" instead of "The Venus of Milo." The well-known

[24]*Ibid.,* from pp. 25-67.

slip of the hotel-boy who, knocking at the bishop's door, nervously replied to the question "Who is it?" "The Lord, my boy!" is another example of such an interchange in the position of words. . . . And when a member of the House of Commons referred to another as the "honourable member for Central *Hell*," instead of "Hull," it was a case of perseveration; as also when a soldier said to a friend "I wish there were a thousand of our men *mortified* on that hill, Bill," instead of "fortified." In the one case the *ell* sound has perseverated from the previous words "member for Central," and in the other the *m* sound in "*m*en" has perseverated to form "mortified."

* * * * *

We encounter a principle which will later on reveal itself to be of quite prodigious importance in the causation of neurotic symptoms: namely, the aversion on the part of memory against recalling anything connected with painful feelings that would revive the pain if it were recalled. In this tendency towards *avoidance of pain* from recollection or other mental processes, this flight of the mind from that which is unpleasant, we may perceive the ultimate purpose at work behind not merely the forgetting of names, but also many other errors, omissions, and mistakes. The forgetting of names seems, however, to be especially facilitated psycho-physiologically, and therefore does occur on occasions where the intervention of an unpleasantness-motive cannot be established. When anyone has a tendency to forget names, it can be confirmed by analytic investigation that names escape, not merely because he does not like them or because they remind him of something disagreeable, but also because the particular name belongs to some other chain of associations of a more intimate nature.

* * * * *

Bungled[25] actions can, of course, also serve a whole number of other obscure purposes. Here is a first example. It is very rare for me to break anything. I am not particularly dexterous but a result of the anatomical integrity of my nerve-muscle apparatus is that there are clearly no grounds for my making clumsy movements of this kind, with their unwelcome consequences. I cannot therefore recall any object in my house that I have ever broken. Shortage of space in my study has often forced me to handle a number of pottery and stone antiquities (of which I have a small collection) in the most uncomfortable positions, so that onlookers have expressed anxiety that I should knock something down and break it. That however has never happened. Why then did I once dash the marble cover of my plain inkpot to the ground so that it broke?

My inkstand is made out of a flat piece of Untersberg marble which is hollowed out to receive the glass inkpot; and the inkpot has a cover with a knob made of the same stone. Behind this inkstand there is a ring of bronze

[25]*The Psychopathology of Everyday Life*, trans. Alan Tyson, ed. James Strachey, in vol. VI (1960), STANDARD EDITION, *op. cit.*, from pp. 167-68, 178-79.

statuettes and terra cotta figures. I sat down at the desk to write, and then moved the hand that was holding the pen-holder forward in a remarkably clumsy way, sweeping on to the floor the inkpot cover which was lying on the desk at the time.

The explanation was not hard to find. Some hours before, my sister had been in the room to inspect some new acquisitions. She admired them very much, and then remarked: "Your writing table looks really attractive now; only the inkstand doesn't match. You must get a nicer one." I went out with my sister and did not return for some hours. But when I did I carried out, so it seems, the execution of the condemned inkstand. Did I perhaps conclude from my sister's remark that she intended to make me a present of a nicer inkstand on the next festive occasion, and did I smash the unlovely old one so as to force her to carry out the intention she had hinted at? If that is so, my sweeping movement was only apparently clumsy; in reality it was exceedingly adroit and well-directed, and understood how to avoid damaging any of the more precious objects that stood around.

* * * * *

It is well known that in the severer cases of psychoneurosis instances of self-injury are occasionally found as symptoms and that in such cases suicide can never be ruled out as a possible outcome of the psychical conflict. I have now learnt and can prove from convincing examples that many apparently accidental injuries that happen to such patients are really instances of self-injury. What happens is that an impulse to self-punishment, which is constantly on the watch and which normally finds expression in self-reproach or contributes to the formation of a symptom, takes ingenious advantage of an external situation that chance happens to offer, or lends assistance to that situation until the desired injurious effect is brought about. Such occurrences are by no means uncommon in cases even of moderate severity, and they betray the part which the unconscious intention plays by a number of special features—e.g. by the striking composure that the patients retain in what is supposed to be an accident.

TRAUMAS: THEIR ABREACTION AND CATHARSIS[26]

Observations . . . seem to us to establish an analogy between the pathogenesis of common hysteria and that of traumatic neuroses, and to justify an extension of the concept of traumatic hysteria. In traumatic neuroses the operative cause of the illness is not the trifling physical injury but the affect of fright—the psychical trauma. In an analogous manner, our investigations reveal, for many, if not for most, hysterical symptoms, precipitating causes which can only be described as psychical traumas. Any experience

[26]Josef Breuer and Sigmund Freud, *Studies on Hysteria*, trans. James Strachey, in vol. II (1955), STANDARD EDITION, *op. cit.*, from pp. 5-17.

which calls up distressing affects—such as those of fright, anxiety, shame or physical pain—may operate as a trauma of this kind; and whether it in fact does so depends naturally enough on the susceptibility of the person affected (as well as on another condition which will be mentioned later). In the case of common hysteria it not infrequently happens that, instead of a single, major trauma, we find a number of partial traumas forming a *group* of provoking causes. These have only been able to exercise a traumatic effect by summation and they belong together in so far as they are in part components of a single story of suffering. There are other cases in which an apparently trivial circumstance combines with the actually operative event or occurs at a time of peculiar susceptibility to stimulation and in this way attains the dignity of a trauma which it would not otherwise have possessed but which thenceforward persists.

But the causal relation between the determining psychical trauma and the hysterical phenomenon is not of a kind implying that the trauma merely acts like an *agent provocateur* in releasing the symptom, which thereafter leads an independent existence. We must presume rather that the physical trauma —or more precisely the memory of the trauma—acts like a foreign body which long after its entry must continue to be regarded as an agent that is still at work; and we find the evidence for this in a highly remarkable phenomenon which at the same time lends an important *practical* interest to our findings.

For we found, to our great surprise at first, that *each individual hysterical symptom immediately and permanently disappeared when we had succeeded in bringing clearly to light the memory of the event by which it was provoked and in arousing its accompanying affect, and when the patient had described that event in the greatest possible detail and had put the affect into words.* Recollection without affect almost invariably produces no result. The psychical process which originally took place must be repeated as vividly as possible; it must be brought back to its *status nascendi* and then given verbal utterance. Where what we are dealing with are phenomena involving stimuli (spasms, neuralgias and hallucinations) these re-appear once again with the fullest intensity and then vanish for ever. Failures of function, such as paralyses and anaesthesias, vanish in the same way, though, of course, without the temporary intensification being discernible.

It is plausible to suppose that it is a question here of unconscious suggestion: the patient expects to be relieved of his sufferings by this procedure, and it is this expectation, and not the verbal utterance, which is the operative factor. This, however, is not so. The first case of this kind that came under observation dates back to the year 1881, that is to say the "presuggestion" era. A highly complicated case of hysteria was analysed in this way, and the symptoms, which sprang from separate causes, were separately removed. This observation was made possible by spontaneous auto-hypnoses on the part of the patient, and came as a great surprise to the observer.

We may reverse the dictum "*cessante causa cessat effectus*" ["when the cause ceases the effect ceases"] and conclude from these observations that the determining process continues to operate in some way or other for years —not indirectly, through a chain of intermediate causal links, but as a *directly* releasing cause—just as a psychical pain that is remembered in waking consciousness still provokes a lachrymal secretion long after the event. *Hysterics suffer mainly from reminiscences.*

At first sight it seems extraordinary that events experienced so long ago should continue to operate so intensely—that their recollection should not be liable to the wearing away process to which, after all, we see all our memories succumb. The following considerations may perhaps make this a little more intelligible.

The fading of a memory or the losing of its affect depends on various factors. The most important of these is *whether there has been an energetic reaction to the event that provokes an affect.* By "reaction" we here understand the whole class of voluntary and involuntary reflexes—from tears to acts of revenge—in which, as experience shows us, the affects are discharged. If this reaction takes place to a sufficient amount a large part of the affect disappears as a result. Linguistic usage bears witness to this fact of daily observation by such phrases as "to cry oneself out" ["*sich ausweinen*"], and to "blow off steam" ["*sich austoben*," literally "to rage oneself out"]. If the reaction is suppressed, the affect remains attached to the memory. An injury that has been repaid, even if only in words, is recollected quite differently from one that has had to be accepted. Language recognizes this distinction, too, in its mental and physical consequences; it very characteristically describes an injury that has been suffered in silence as "a mortification" ["*Kränkung*," lit. "making ill"].—The injured person's reaction to the trauma only exercises a completely "cathartic" effect if it is an *adequate* reaction—as, for instance, revenge. But language serves as a substitute for action; by its help, an affect can be "abreacted" almost as effectively. In other cases speaking is itself the adequate reflex, when, for instance, it is a lamentation or giving utterance to a tormenting secret, e.g. a confession. If there is no such reaction, whether in deeds or words, or in the mildest cases in tears, any recollection of the event retains its affective tone to begin with.

"Abreaction," however, is not the only method of dealing with the situation that is open to a normal person who has experienced a psychical trauma. A memory of such a trauma, even if it has not been abreacted, enters the great complex of associations, it comes alongside other experiences, which may contradict it, and is subjected to rectification by other ideas. After an accident, for instance, the memory of the danger and the (mitigated) repetition of the fright becomes associated with the memory of what happened afterwards—rescue and the consciousness of present safety. Again, a person's memory of a humiliation is corrected by his putting the facts right, by considering his own worth, etc. In this way a normal person is able to bring about the disappearance of the accompanying affect through the process of association.

To this we must add the general effacement of impressions, the fading of memories which we name "forgetting" and which wears away those ideas in particular that are no longer affectively operative.

Our observations have shown, on the other hand, that the memories which have become the determinants of hysterical phenomena persist for a long time with astonishing freshness and with the whole of their affective colouring. We must, however, mention another remarkable fact, which we shall later be able to turn to account, namely, that these memories, unlike other memories of their past lives, are not at the patients' disposal. On the contrary, *these experiences are completely absent from the patients' memory when they are in a normal psychical state, or are only present in a highly summary form.* Not until they have been questioned under hypnosis do these memories emerge with the undiminished vividness of a recent event.

Thus, for six whole months, one of our patients reproduced under hypnosis with hallucinatory vividness everything that had excited her on the same day of the previous year (during an attack of acute hysteria). A diary kept by her mother without her knowledge proved the completeness of the reproduction. Another patient, partly under hypnosis and partly during spontaneous attacks, re-lived with hallucinatory clarity all the events of a hysterical psychosis which she had passed through ten years earlier and which she had for the most part forgotten till the moment at which it re-emerged. Moreover, certain memories of aetiological importance which dated back from fifteen to twenty-five years were found to be astonishingly intact and to possess remarkable sensory force, and when they returned they acted with all the affective strength of new experiences.

This can only be explained on the view that these memories constitute an exception in their relation to all the wearing-away processes which we have discussed above. *It appears, that is to say, that these memories correspond to traumas that have not been sufficiently abreacted;* and if we enter more closely into the reasons which have prevented this, we find at least two sets of conditions under which the reaction to the trauma fails to occur.

In the first group are those cases in which the patients have not reacted to a psychical trauma because the nature of the trauma excluded a reaction, as in the case of the apparently irreparable loss of a loved person or because social circumstances made a reaction impossible or because it was a question of things which the patient wished to forget, and therefore intentionally repressed from his conscious thought and inhibited and suppressed. It is precisely distressing things of this kind that, under hypnosis, we find are the basis of hysterical phenomena (e.g. hysterical deliria in saints and nuns, continent women and well-brought-up children).

The second group of conditions are determined, not by the content of the memories but by the psychical states in which the patient received the experiences in question. For we find, under hypnosis, among the causes of hysterical symptoms ideas which are not in themselves significant, but whose persistence is due to the fact that they originated during the prevalence of severely paralyzing affects, such as fright, or during positively abnormal psychical states, such as the semi-hypnotic twilight state of day-dreaming, auto-hypnoses, and so on. In such cases it is the nature of the states which makes a reaction to the event impossible.

Both kinds of conditions may, of course, be simultaneously present, and this, in fact, often occurs. It is so when a trauma which is operative in itself takes place while a severely paralyzing affect prevails or during a modified state of consciousness. But it also seems to be true that in many people a psychical trauma *produces* one of these abnormal states, which, in turn, makes reaction impossible.

Both of these groups of conditions, however, have in common the fact that the psychical traumas which have not been disposed of by reaction cannot be disposed of either by being worked over by means of association. In the first group the patient is determined to forget the distressing experiences and accordingly excludes them so far as possible from association; while in the second group the associative working-over fails to occur because there is no extensive associative connection between the normal state of consciousness and the pathological ones in which the ideas made their appearance. We shall have occasion immediately to enter further into this matter.

It may therefore be said that the ideas which have become pathological have persisted with such freshness and affective strength because they have been denied the normal wearing-away processes by means of abreaction and reproduction in states of uninhibited association.

We have stated the conditions which, as our experience shows, are responsible for the development of hysterical phenomena from psychical traumas. In so doing, we have already been obliged to speak of abnormal states of consciousness in which these pathogenic ideas arise, and to emphasize the fact that the recollection of the operative psychical trauma is not to be found in the patient's normal memory but in his memory when he is hypnotized. The longer we have been occupied with these phenomena the more we have become convinced that *the splitting of consciousness which is so striking in the well-known classical cases under the form of "double conscience" is present to a rudimentary degree in every hysteria, and that a tendency to such a dissociation, and with it the emergence of abnormal states of consciousness (which we shall bring together under the term "hypnoid") is the basic phenomenon of this neurosis.* In these views we concur with Binet and the two Janets, though we have had no experience of the remarkable findings they have made on anaesthetic patients.

We should like to balance the familiar thesis that hypnosis is an artificial hysteria by another—the basis and *sine qua non* of hysteria is the existence of hypnoid states. These hypnoid states share with one another and with hypnosis, however much they may differ in other respects, one common feature: the ideas which emerge in them are very intense but are cut off from associative communication with the rest of the content of consciousness. Associations may take place between these hypnoid states, and their ideational content can in this way reach a more or less high degree of psychical organization. Moreover, the nature of these states and the extent to which they are cut off from the remaining conscious processes must be supposed to vary just as happens in hypnosis, which ranges from a light drowsiness to somnambulism, from complete recollection to total amnesia.

If hypnoid states of this kind are already present before the onset of the manifest illness, they provide the soil in which the affect plants the pathogenic memory with its consequent somatic phenomena. This corresponds to *dispositional* hysteria. We have found, however, that a severe trauma (such as occurs in a traumatic neurosis) or a laborious suppression (as of a sexual affect, for instance) can bring about a splitting-off of groups of ideas even in people who are in other respects unaffected; and this would be the mechanism of *psychically acquired* hysteria. Between the extremes of these two forms we must assume the existence of a series of cases within which the liability to dissociation in the subject and the affective magnitude of the trauma vary inversely.

We have nothing new to say on the question of the origin of these dispositional hypnoid states. They often, it would seem, grow out of the daydreams which are so common even in healthy people and to which needlework and similar occupations render women especially prone. Why it is that the "pathological associations" brought about in these states are so stable and why they have so much more influence on somatic processes than ideas are usually found to do—these questions coincide with the general problem of the effectiveness of hypnotic suggestions. Our observations contribute nothing fresh on this subject. But they throw a light on the contradiction between the dictum "hysteria is a psychosis" and the fact that among hysterics may be found people of the clearest intellect, strongest will, greatest character and highest critical power. This characterization holds good of their waking thoughts; but in their hypnoid states they are insane, as we all are in dreams. Whereas, however, our dream-psychoses have no effect upon our waking state, the products of hypnoid states intrude into waking life in the form of hysterical symptoms.

*   *   *   *   *

It will now be understood how it is that the psychotherapeutic procedure which we have described in these pages has a curative effect. *It brings to an end the operative force of the idea which was not abreacted in the first instance, by allowing its strangulated affect to find a way out through speech; and it subjects it to associative correction by introducing it into normal consciousness (under light hypnosis) or by removing it through the physician's suggestion, as is done in somnabulism accompanied by amnesia.*

In our opinion the therapeutic advantages of this procedure are considerable. It is of course that we do not cure hysteria in so far as it is a matter of disposition. We can do nothing against the recurrence of hypnoid states. Moreover, during the productive stage of an acute hysteria our procedure cannot prevent the phenomena which have been so laboriously removed from being at once replaced by fresh ones. But once this acute stage is past, any residues which may be left in the form of chronic symptoms or attacks are often removed, and permanently so, by our method, because it is a radical one; in this respect it seems to us far superior in its efficacy to removal through direct suggestion, as it is practised to-day by psychotherapists.

If by uncovering the psychical mechanism of hysterical phenomena we have taken a step forward along the path first traced so successfully by Charcot with his explanation and artificial imitation of hysterotraumatic paralyses, we cannot conceal from ourselves that this has brought us nearer to an understanding only of the *mechanism* of hysterical symptoms and not of the internal causes of hysteria. We have done no more than touch upon the aetiology of hysteria and in fact have been able to throw light only on its acquired forms—on the bearing of accidental factors on the neurosis.

CHAPTER 2

CARL G. JUNG

PERSONALITY THEORY FROM THE STANDPOINT OF ANALYTICAL PSYCHOLOGY

Carl G. Jung, the first president of the Psychoanalytical Society, severed relations with the Freudian camp in 1912 by establishing his own school of psychological thought which he named ANALYTICAL PSYCHOLOGY. Several psychological concepts distinguish the thinking of his school from Freudian psychoanalysis: the belief in a *collective unconscious* as well as a personal unconscious, *i.e.*, a universal or unconscious mind which is shared by all members of the human race; the belief in two basic personality types, extraverts and introverts; the belief in archetypes, complexes, and symbols; the belief that man is telically as well as causally motivated; the belief that man has noble or divine impulses as well as animal impulses; the repudiation of the Freudian belief in pansexualism; and the belief in the soul of man.

Jung, who was born in Switzerland in 1875 and died in 1961, spent most of his life in the country of his birth. The son of a minister, he trained as a medical doctor at the University of Basel and entered personality theory from the field of psychiatry, where he had specialized in the treatment of schizophrenia. He studied six months with the noted Janet and was Bleuler's assistant at the mental hospital at Burghölzli in Zurich. Jung's wife, Emma Rauschenbach, also a Swiss, was an analyst in her own right.

During World War I Jung served in the Swiss army as a medical officer in charge of British prisoners of war. In 1933 he became head of the General Medical Society for Psychotherapy, and he was co-editor of its journal from 1936 to 1940, when he resigned from both posts. From 1933 to 1941 he was Professor of Psychology at Zurich, and in 1944 Professor of Medical Psychology at Basel.

Jung's work profited from his monumental background of cultural learning. His researches took him the world over: in 1921 he made a trip to North Africa to observe the habits and psychology of the natives; and in 1924-1925 he made a similar trip to Arizona and New Mexico to study the behavior and thinking of the Pueblo Indians. In 1932 he was the recipient of the Literary Prize of the city of Zurich, and in 1937 he delivered the Terry Lectures at Yale University. His achievements have been recognized by academic communities from America to India, and he holds honorary degrees from Harvard University, Oxford University, the University of Calcutta, the University of Geneva, Banaras Hindu University, and the University of Allahabad, Indian. When Oxford University conferred upon him the honorary D.Sc., he became the first psychologist to receive such an honor in England.

Jung is remembered as a genial man, brown-eyed, white-haired, and ruddy-complexioned, tall and fine-looking, with an equally impressive personality. By way of recreation he enjoyed walking in the nearby Swiss mountains, stonecarving, and swimming in the Lake of Zurich. Upon the lintel over the door of his home in Küsnacht there hung a sign which read, *Vocatus at ave non vocatus deus aderit* (called or not called, God is present), a most appropriate motto for the religious man that Jung was.

The English-speaking world has been provided with *The Collected Works of Carl G. Jung*, published by the Bollingen Foundation, under the editorship of Herbert Read, Michael Fordham, and Gerhard Adler, and translated by R. F. C. Hull.

ANALYTICAL PSYCHOLOGY VERSUS PSYCHOANALYSIS[1]

As is well known, the merit of discovering the new analytical method of general psychology belongs to Professor Freud of Vienna. His original views have had to undergo many important modifications, some of them

---

[1]"Prefaces to 'Collected Papers on Analytical Psychology,'" in *Freud and Psychoanalysis*, vol. IV of COLLECTED WORKS, ed. Herbert Read *et al.*, trans. R. F. C. Hull (Bollingen Series XX; New York: Pantheon, 1961), from pp. 290-97.

owing to the work done at Zurich, in spite of the fact that he himself is far from agreeing with the standpoint of this school.

*   *   *   *   *

The Viennese School adopts an exclusively sexualistic standpoint while that of the Zurich School is symbolistic. The Viennese School interprets the psychological symbol semiotically, as a sign or token of certain primitive psychosexual processes. Its method is analytical and causal. The Zurich School recognizes the scientific possibility of such a conception but denies its exclusive validity, for it does not interpret the psychological symbol semiotically only but also symbolistically, that is, it attributes a positive value to the symbol.

The value of the symbol does not depend merely on historical causes; its chief importance lies in the fact that it has a meaning for the actual present and for the future, in their psychological aspects. For the Zurich School the symbol is not merely a sign of something repressed and concealed, but is at the same time an attempt to comprehend and to point the way to the further psychological development of the individual. Thus we add a prospective meaning to the retrospective value of the symbol.

The method of the Zurich School, therefore, is not only analytical and causal but synthetic and prospective, in recognition of the fact that the human mind is characterized by *fines* (aims) as well as by *causae*. This deserves particular emphasis, because there are two types of psychology, the one following the principle of hedonism, the other the power principle. The philosophical counterpart of the former type is scientific materialism and of the latter the philosophy of Nietzsche. The principle of the Freudian theory is hedonism, while the theory of Adler (one of Freud's earliest personal pupils) is founded on the power principle.

The Zurich School, recognizing the existence of these two types (also remarked by the late Professor William James), considers that the views of Freud and Adler are one-sided and valid only within the limits of their corresponding type. Both principles exist in every individual though not in equal proportions.

Thus, it is obvious that every psychological symbol has two aspects and should be interpreted in accordance with both principles. Freud and Adler interpret in the analytical and causal way, reducing to the infantile and primitive. Thus with Freud the conception of the "aim" is the fulfillment of the wish, while with Adler it is the usurpation of power. In their practical analytical work both authors take the standpoint which brings to light only infantile and grossly egoistic aims.

The Zurich School is convinced that within the limits of a diseased mental attitude the psychology is such as Freud and Adler describe. It is, indeed, just on account of such an impossible and childish psychology that the individual is in a state of inner dissociation and hence neurotic. The Zurich School, therefore, in agreement with them so far, also reduces the psychological symbol (the phantasy-products of the patient) to his fundamental infantile hedonism or infantile desire for power. Freud and Adler content themselves with the result of mere reduction, which accords with their scientific biologism and naturalism.

But here a very important question arises. Can man obey the fundamental and primitive impulses of his nature without gravely injuring himself or his fellow beings? He cannot assert either his sexual desire or his desire for power unlimitedly in the face of limits which are very restrictive. The Zurich School has in view the end-result of analysis, and it regards the fundamental thoughts and impulses of the unconscious as symbols, indicative of a definite line of future development. We must admit, however, that there is *no scientific justification* for such a procedure, because our present-day science is based wholly on causality. But causality is only one principle, and psychology cannot be exhausted by causal methods only, because the mind lives by aims as well. Besides this controversial philosophical argument we have another of much greater value in favour of our hypothesis, namely that of *vital necessity*. It is impossible to live according to the promptings of infantile hedonism or according to a childish desire for power. If these are to be given a place they must be taken symbolically. Out of the symbolic applications of infantile trends there evolves an attitude which may be termed philosophic or religious, and these terms characterize sufficiently well the lines of the individual's further development. The individual is not just a fixed and unchangeable complex of psychological facts; he is also an extremely variable entity. By an exclusive reduction to causes the primitive trends of a personality are reinforced; this is helpful only when these primitive tendencies are balanced by a recognition of their symbolic values. Analysis and reduction lead to causal truth; this by itself does not help us to live but only induces resignation and hopelessness. On the other hand, the recognition of the intrinsic value of a symbol leads to constructive truth and helps us to live; it inspires hopefulness and furthers the possibility of future development.

The functional importance of the symbol is clearly shown in the history of civilization. For thousands of years the religious symbol proved a most efficacious device in the moral education of mankind. Only a prejudiced mind could deny such an obvious fact. Concrete values cannot take the place of the symbol; only new and more effective symbols can be substituted for those that are antiquated and outworn and have lost their efficacy through the progress of intellectual analysis and understanding. The further development of the individual can be brought about only by means of symbols which represent something far in advance of himself and whose intellectual meanings cannot yet be grasped entirely. The individual unconscious produces such symbols, and they are of the greatest possible value in the moral development of the personality.

Man almost invariably has philosophic and religious views concerning the meaning of the world and of his own life. There are some who are proud to have none. But these are exceptions outside the common path of mankind; they lack an important function which has proved itself to be indispensible to the human psyche.

In such cases we find in the unconscious, instead of modern symbolism, an antiquated, archaic view of the world and of life. If a necessary psychological function is not represented in the sphere of consciousness it exists in the unconscious in the form of an archaic or embryonic prototype.

* * * * *

It cannot be disputed that, psychologically speaking, we are living and working day by day according to the principle of directed aim or purpose as well as that of causality. A psychological theory must necessarily adapt itself to this fact. What is plainly directed towards a goal cannot be given an exclusively causalistic explanation, otherwise we should be led to the conclusion expressed in Moleschott's famous dictum: "Man ist was er isst" (Man *is* what he eats). We must always bear in mind that *causality is a point of view. . . . Finality is also a point of view,* and it is empirically justified by the existence of series of events in which the causal connection is indeed evident *but the meaning of which only becomes intelligible in terms of end-products (final effects).* Ordinary life furnishes the best instances of this. The causal explanation must be mechanistic if we are not to postulate a metaphysical entity as first cause. For instance, if we adopt Freud's sexual theory and assign primary importance psychologically to the function of the genital glands, the brain is seen as an appendage of the genital glands. If we approach the Viennese concept of sexuality, with all its vague omnipotence, in a strictly scientific manner and reduce it to its physiological basis, we shall arrive at the first cause, according to which psychic life is for the most important part, tension and relaxation of the genital glands. If we assume for the moment that this mechanistic explanation is "true," it would be the sort of truth which is exceptionally tiresome and rigidly limited in scope. A similar statement would be that the genital glands cannot function without adequate *nourishment,* the inference being that sexuality is a subsidiary function of nutrition. The truth of this forms an important chapter in the biology of the lower forms of life.

But if we wish to work in a really psychological way we shall want to know the *meaning* of psychological phenomena. After learning what kinds of steel the various parts of a locomotive are made of, and what iron-works and mines they come from, we do not really know anything about the locomotive's *function,* that is to say its *meaning.* But "function" as conceived by modern science is by no means exclusively a causal concept; it is especially a final or "teleological" one. For it is impossible to consider the psyche from the causal standpoint only; we are obliged to consider it also from the final point of view.

* * * * *

As a matter of fact, modern physics has necessarily been converted from the idea of pure mechanism to the finalistic concept of the conservation of energy, because the mechanistic explanation recognizes only reversible processes whereas the actual truth is that the processes of nature are irreversible. This fact led to the concept of an energy that tends towards relief of tension and hence towards a definite final state.

Obviously, I consider both these points of view necessary, the causal as well as the final, but would at the same time stress that since Kant's time we have come to realize that the two viewpoints are not antagonistic if they are regarded as regulative principles of thought and not as constituent principles of the process of nature itself.

THE COLLECTIVE UNCONSCIOUS

The Personal and Collective Unconscious

A[2] more or less superficial layer of the unconscious is undoubtedly personal. I call it the *personal unconscious.* But this personal unconscious rests upon a deeper layer, which does not derive from personal experience and is not a personal acquisition but is inborn. This deeper layer I call the *collective unconscious.* I have chosen the term "collective" because this part of the unconscious is not individual but universal; in contrast to the personal psyche, it has contents and modes of behaviour that are more or less the same everywhere and in all individuals. It is, in other words, identical in all men and thus constitutes a common psychic substrate of a supra-personal nature which is present in every one of us.

Psychic existence can be recognized only by the presence of contents that are *capable of consciousness.* We can therefore speak of an unconscious only in so far as we are able to demonstrate its contents. The contents of the personal unconscious are chiefly the *feeling-toned complexes,* as they are called; they constitute the personal and private side of psychic life. The contents of the collective unconscious, on the other hand, are known as *archetypes.*

*   *   *   *   *

The[3] collective unconscious is a part of the psyche which can be negatively distinguished from a personal unconscious by the fact that it does not, like the latter, owe its existence to personal experience and consequently is not a personal acquisition. While the personal unconscious is made up essentially of contents which have at one time been conscious but which have disappeared from consciousness through having been forgotten or re-

---

[2]"Archetypes of the Collective Unconscious," in *Archetypes and the Collective Unconscious* (1959), vol. IX, pt. 1 of COLLECTED WORKS, *op. cit.,* from pp. 3-4.

[3]"The Concept of the Collective Unconscious," in *Archetypes and the Collective Unconscious, ibid.,* from pp. 42ff.

pressed, the contents of the collective unconscious have never been in consciousness, and therefore have never been individually acquired, but owe their existence exclusively to heredity. Whereas the personal unconscious consists of the most part of *complexes,* the content of the collective unconscious is made up essentially of *archetypes.*

The concept of the archetype, which is an indispensable part of the idea of the collective unconscious, indicates the existence of definite forms in the psyche which seem to be present always and everywhere. Mythological research calls them "motifs"; in the psychology of primitives they correspond to Lévy-Bruhl's concept of "représentations collectives," and in the field of comparative religion they have been defined by Hubert and Mauss as "categories of the imagination." Adolf Bastian long ago called them "elementary" or "primordial thoughts." From these references it should be clear enough that my idea of archetype—literally a pre-existent form—does not stand alone but is something that is recognized and named in other fields of knowledge.

My thesis, then, is as follows: In addition to our immediate consciousness, which is of a thoroughly personal nature and which we believe to be the only empirical psyche (even if we tack on the personal unconscious as an appendix), there exists a second psychic system of a collective, universal, and impersonal nature which is identical in all individuals. The collective unconscious does not develop individually but is inherited. It consists of pre-existent forms, the archetypes, which can only become conscious secondarily and which give definite form to certain psychic contents.

Instincts and the Collective Unconscious

Medical psychology, growing as it did out of professional practice, insists on the *personal* nature of the psyche. By this I mean the views of Freud and Adler. It is a *psychology of the person,* and its aetiological or causal factors are regarded almost wholly as personal in nature. Nonetheless, even this psychology is based on certain general biological factors, for instance on the sexual instinct or on the urge for self-assertion, which are by no means merely personal peculiarities. It is forced to do this because it lays claim to being an explanatory science. Neither of these views would deny the existence of *a priori* instincts common to man and animals alike, or that they have a significant influence on personal psychology. Yet instincts are impersonal, universally distributed, hereditary factors of a dynamic or motivating character, which very often fail so completely to reach consciousness that modern psychotherapy is faced with the task of helping the patient to become conscious of them. Moreover, the instincts are not vague and indefinite by nature, but are specifically formed motive forces which, long before there is any conscousness, and in spite of any degree of consciousness later on, pursue their inherent goals. Consequently they form very close analogies to the archetypes, so close, in fact, that there is good reason for supposing that the archetypes are the unconscious images of the instincts themselves, in other words, that they are *patterns of instinctual behaviour.*

THE EGO[4]

Investigations of the psychology of the unconscious confronted me with facts which required the formulation of new concepts. One of these concepts is the *self.* The entity so denoted is not meant to take the place of the one that has always been known as the *ego,* but includes it in a supraordinate concept. We understand the ego as the complex factor to which all conscious contents are related. It forms, as it were, the centre of the field of consciousness; and, in so far as this comprises the empirical personality, the ego is the subject of all personal acts of consciousness. The relation of a psychic content to the ego forms the criterion of its consciousness, for no content can be conscious unless it is represented to a subject.

With this definition we have described and delimited the *scope* of the subject. Theoretically, no limits can be set to the field of consciousness, since it is capable of indefinite extension. Empirically, however, it always finds its limit when it comes up against the *unknown.* This consists of everything we do not know, which, therefore, is not related to the ego as the centre of the field of consciousness. The unknown falls into two groups of objects: those which are outside and can be experienced by the senses, and those which are inside and are experienced immediately. The first group comprises the unknown in the outer world; the second the unknown in the inner world. We call this latter territory the *unconscious.*

The ego, as a specific content of consciousness, is not a simple or elementary factor but a complex one which, as such, cannot be described exhaustively. Experience shows that it rests on two seemingly different bases: the *somatic* and the *psychic.* The somatic basis is inferred from the totality of endosomatic perceptions, which for their part are already of a psychic nature and are associated with the ego, and are therefore conscious. They are produced by endosomatic stimuli, only some of which cross the threshold of consciousness. A considerable proportion of these stimuli occur unconsciously, that is, subliminally.

*   *   *   *   *

The somatic basis of the ego consists, then, of conscious and unconscious factors. The same is true of the psychic basis: on the one hand the ego rests on the *total field of consciousness,* and on the other, on the *sum total of unconscious contents.* These fall into three groups: first, temporarily subliminal contents that can be reproduced voluntarily (memory); second, unconscious contents that cannot be reproduced voluntarily; third, contents that

4"The Ego," in *Aion: Researches into the Phenomenology of the Self* (1959), vol. IX, pt. 2 of COLLECTED WORKS, *op. cit.,* from pp. 3-6.

are not capable of becoming conscious at all. Group two can be inferred from the spontaneous irruption of subliminal contents into consciousness. Group three is hypothetical; it is a logical inference from the facts underlying group two. This contains contents which have *not yet* irrupted into consciousness, or which never will.

When I said that the ego "rests" on the total field of consciousness I do not mean that it *consists* of this. Were that so, it would be indistinguishable from the field of consciousness as a whole. The ego is only the latter's point of reference, grounded on and limited by the somatic factor described above.

Although its bases are in themselves relatively unknown and unconscious, the ego is a conscious factor par excellence. It is even acquired, empirically speaking, during the individual's lifetime. It seems to arise in the first place from the collision between the somatic factor and the environment, and, once established as a subject, it goes on developing from further collisions with the outer world and the inner.

Despite the unlimited extent of its bases, the ego is never more and never less than consciousness as a whole. As a conscious factor the ego could, theoretically at least, be described completely. But this would never amount to more than a picture of the *conscious personality*; all those features which are unknown or unconscious to the subject would be missing. A total picture would have to include these. But a total description of the personality is, even in theory, absolutely impossible, because the unconscious portion of it cannot be grasped cognitively. This unconscious portion, as experience has abundantly shown, is by no means unimportant. On the contrary, the most decisive qualities in a person are often unconscious and can be perceived only by others, or have to be laboriously discovered with outside help.

Clearly, then, the personality as a total phenomenon does not coincide with the ego, that is, with the conscious personality, but forms an entity that has to be distinguished from the ego. Naturally the need to do this is incumbent only on a psychology that reckons with the fact of the unconscious, but for such a psychology the distinction is of paramount importance. Even for jurisprudence it should be of some importance whether certain psychic facts are conscious or not—for instance, in adjudging the question of responsibility.

I have suggested calling the total personality which, though present, cannot be fully known, the self. The ego is, by definition, subordinate to the self and is related to it like a part to the whole. . . . Since it is the point of reference for the field of consciousness, the ego is the subject of all successful attempts at adaptation so far as these are achieved by the will. The ego therefore has a significant part to play in the psychic economy. Its position there is so important that there are good grounds for the prejudice that the ego is the centre of the personality, and that the field of consciousness is the psyche *per se*.

THE SHADOW[5]

Whereas the contents of the personal unconscious are acquired during the individual's lifetime, the contents of the collective unconscious are invariably archetypes that were present from the beginning. Their relation to the instincts has been discussed elsewhere. The archetypes most clearly characterized from the empirical point of view are those which have the most frequent and the most disturbing influence on the ego. These are the *shadow,* the *anima,* and the *animus.* The most accessible of these, and the easiest to experience, is the shadow, for its nature can in large measure be inferred from the contents of the personal unconscious. The only exceptions to this rule are those rather rare cases where the positive qualities of the personality are repressed, and the ego in consequence plays an essentially negative or unfavorable role.

The shadow is a moral problem that challenges the whole ego-personality, for no one can become conscious of the shadow without considerable moral effort. To become conscious of it involves recognizing the dark aspects of the personality as present and real. This act is the essential condition for any kind of self-knowledge, and it therefore, as a rule, meets with considerable resistance. Indeed, self-knowledge as a psychotherapeutic measure frequently requires much painstaking work extending over a long period.

Closer examination of the dark characteristics—that is, the inferiorities constituting the shadow—reveals that they have an *emotional* nature, a kind of autonomy, and accordingly an obsessive or, better, possessive quality. Emotion, incidentally, is not an activity of the individual but something that happens to him. Affects occur usually where adaptation is weakest, and at the same time they reveal the reason for its weakness, namely a certain degree of inferiority and the existence of a lower level of personality. On this lower level with its uncontrolled or scarcely controlled emotions one behaves more or less like a primitive, who is not only the passive victim of his affects but also singularly incapable of moral judgment.

Although, with insight and good will, the shadow can to some extent be assimilated into the conscious personality, experience shows that there are certain features which offer the most obstinate resistance to moral control and prove almost impossible to influence. These resistances are usually bound up with *projections,* which are not recognized as such, and their recognition is a moral achievement beyond the ordinary. While some traits peculiar to the shadow can be recognized without too much difficulty as one's own personal qualities, in this case both insight and good will are unavailing because the cause of the emotion appears to lie, beyond all possibility of doubt, in the *other person.* No matter how obvious it may be to the neutral observer that it is a matter of projections, there is little hope that the subject will perceive this himself. He must be convinced that he

[5]"The Shadow," in *Aion, ibid.,* from pp. 8-10.

throws a very long shadow before he is willing to withdraw his emotionally-toned projections from their object.

Let us suppose that a certain individual shows no inclination whatever to recognize his projections. The projection-making factor then has a free hand and can realize its object—if it has one—or bring about some other situation characteristic of its power. As we know, it is not the conscious subject but the unconscious which does the projecting. Hence one meets with projections, one does not make them. The effect of projection is to isolate the subject from his environment, since instead of a real relation to it there is now only an illusory one. Projections change the world into the replica of one's own unknown face. In the last analysis, therefore, they lead to an autoerotic or autistic condition in which one dreams a world whose reality remains forever unattainable. The resultant *sentiment d'incomplétude* and the still worse feeling of sterility are in their turn explained by projection as the malevolence of the environment, and by means of this vicious circle the isolation is intensified. The more projections are thrust in between the subject and the environment, the harder it is for the ego to see through its illusions.

* * * * *

It is often tragic to see how blatantly a man bungles his own life and the lives of others yet remains totally incapable of seeing how much the whole tragedy originates in himself, and how he continually feeds it and keeps it going. Not *consciously*, of course—for consciously he is engaged in bewailing and cursing a faithless world that recedes further and further into the distance. Rather, it is an unconscious factor which spins the illusions that veil his world. And what is being spun is a cocoon, which in the end will completely envelop him.

One might assume that projections like these, which are so very difficult if not impossible to dissolve, would belong to the realm of the shadow —that is, to the negative side of the personality. This assumption becomes untenable after a certain point, because the symbols that then appear no longer refer to the same but to the opposite sex, in a man's case to a woman and vice versa. The source of projections is no longer the shadow—which is always of the same sex as the subject—but a contrasexual figure. Here we meet the animus of a woman and the anima of a man, two corresponding archetypes whose autonomy and unconsciousness explain the stubbornness of their projections. Through the shadow is a motif as well known to mythology as anima and animus, it represents first and foremost the personal unconscious, and its content can therefore be made conscious without too much difficulty. In this it differs from anima and animus, for whereas the shadow can be seen through and recognized fairly easily, the anima and animus are much further away from consciousness and in normal circumstances are seldom if ever realized. With a little self-criticism one can see through the shadow—so far as its nature is personal. But when it appears as an archetype, one encounters the same difficulties as with anima and animus. In other words, it is quite within the bounds of possibility for a man to recognize the relative evil of his nature, but it is a rare and shattering experience for him to gaze into the face of absolute evil.

THE ANIMA AND ANIMUS[6]

What, then, is this projection-making factor? The East calls it the "Spinning Woman"[a]—Maya, who creates illusion by her dancing. . . . In the case of the son, the projection-making factor is identical with the mother-imago, and this is consequently taken to be the real mother. The projection can only be dissolved when the son sees that in the realm of his psyche there is an image not only of the mother but of the daughter, the sister, the beloved, the heavenly goddess, and the chthonic Baubo. Every mother and every beloved is forced to become the carrier and embodiment of this omnipresent and ageless image, which corresponds to the deepest reality in a man. It belongs to him, this perilous image of Woman; she stands for the loyalty which in the interests of life he must sometimes forgo; she is the much needed compensation for the risks, struggles, sacrifices that all end in disappointment; she is the solace for all the bitterness of life. . . . This image is "My Lady Soul," as Spitteler called her. I have suggested instead the term "anima," as indicating something specific, for which the expression "soul" is too general and too vague. The empirical reality summed up under the concept of the anima forms an extremely dramatic content of the unconscious.

*   *   *   *   *

The projection-making factor is the anima, or rather the unconscious as represented by the anima. Whenever she appears, in dreams, visions, and fantasies, she takes on personified form, thus demonstrating that the factor she embodies possesses all the outstanding characteristics of a feminine being. She is not an invention of the conscious, but a spontaneous product of the unconscious. Nor is she a substitute figure for the mother. On the contrary, there is every likelihood that the numinous qualities which make the mother-imago so dangerously powerful derive from the collective archetype of the anima, which is carnated anew in every male child.

Since the anima is an archetype that is found in men, it is reasonable to suppose that an equivalent archetype must be present in women; for just as the man is compensated by a feminine element, so woman is compensated by a masculine one. . . . Just as the mother seems to be the first carrier of the projection-making factor for the son, so is the father for the

---

[6]"The Syzygy: Anima and Animus," in *Aion, ibid.*, from pp. 11ff.
[a]I have defined the anima as a personification of the unconscious.

daughter. Practical experience of these relationships is made up of many individual cases presenting all kinds of variations on the same basic theme.

* * * * *

Woman is compensated by a masculine element and therefore her unconscious has, so to speak, a masculine imprint. This results in a considerable psychological difference between men and women, and accordingly I have called the projection-making factor in women the animus, which means mind or spirit. The animus corresponds to the paternal Logos just as the anima corresponds to the maternal Eros. But I do not wish or intend to give these two intuitive concepts too specific a definition. I use Eros and Logos merely as conceptual aids to describe the fact that woman's consciousness is characterized more by the cognition associated with Logos. In men, Eros, the function of relationship, is usually less developed than Logos. In women, on the other hand, Eros is an expression of their true nature, while their Logos is often only a regrettable accident. It gives rise to misunderstandings and annoying interpretations in the family circle and among friends. This is because it consists of *opinions* instead of reflections, and by opinions I mean *a priori* assumptions that lay claim to absolute truth. Such assumptions, as everyone knows, can be extremely irritating. As the animus is partial to argument, he can best be seen at work in disputes where both parties know they are right. Men can argue in a very womanish way, too, when they are anima-possessed and have thus been transformed into the animus of their own anima. With them the question becomes one of personal vanity and touchiness (as if they were females); with women it is a question of power, whether of truth or justice or some other "ism"—for the dressmaker and hairdresser have already taken care of their vanity. The "Father" (i.e., the sum of conventional opinions) always plays a great role in female argumentation. No matter how friendly and obliging a woman's Eros may be, no logic on earth can shake her if she is ridden by the animus.

* * * * *

When animus and anima meet, the animus draws his sword of power and the anima ejects her poison of illusion and seduction. The outcome need not always be negative, since the two are equally likely to fall in love (a special instance of love at first sight). The language of love is of astonishing uniformity, using the well-worn formulas with the utmost devotion and fidelity, so that once again the two partners find themselves in a banal collective situation. Yet they live in the illusion that they are related to one another in a most individual way.

In both its positive and its negative aspects the anima/animus relationship is always full of "animosity," i.e., it is emotional, and hence collective. . . . Whereas the cloud of "animosity" surrounding the man is composed chiefly of sentimentality and resentment, in woman it expresses itself in the form of opinionated views, interpretations, insinuations, and misconstructions, which all have the purpose (sometimes attained) of severing the relations between two human beings. The woman, like the man, becomes wrapped in a veil of illusions by her demon-familiar, and, as the daughter who alone understands her father, she is translated to the land of sheep, where she is put to graze by the shepherd of her soul, the animus.

Like the anima, the animus too has a positive aspect. Through the figure of the father he expresses not only conventional opinion but—equally— what we call "spirit," philosophical or religious ideas in particular, or rather the attitude resulting from them. Thus the animus of the psychopomp, a mediator between the conscious and the unconscious and a personification of the latter.

$$* \quad * \quad * \quad * \quad *$$

Recapitulating, I should like to emphasize that the integration of the shadow, or the realization of the personal unconscious, marks the first stage in the analytic process, and that without it a recognition of anima and animus is impossible. The shadow can be realized only through a relation to the opposite sex, because only in such a relation do their projections become operative. The recognition of anima or animus gives rise, in a man, to a trias, one third of which is transcendent: the masculine subject, the opposing feminine subject, and the transcendent anima. With a woman the situation is reversed.

ARCHETYPES
(CONTENTS OF THE COLLECTIVE UNCONSCIOUS)[7]

The term "archetype" occurs as early as Philo Judaeus, with reference to the *Imago Dei* (God-image) in man. It can also be found in Irenaeus, who says: "The creator of the world did not fashion these things directly from himself but copied them from archetypes outside himself." In the *Corpus Hermeticum*, God is called *to archetupon phos* (archetypal light). . . . "Archetype" is an explanatory paraphrase of the Platonic *eidos*. For our purposes, this term is apposite and helpful, because it tells us that so far as the collective unconscious contents are concerned we are dealing with archaic or—I would say—primordial types, that is, with universal images that have existed since the remotest times. The term "représentations collectives," used by Lévy-Bruhl to denote the symbolic figures in the primitive view of the world, could easily be applied to unconscious contents as well, since it means practically the same thing. Primitive tribal lore is concerned with archetypes that have been modified in a special way. They are no longer contents of the unconscious, but have already been changed

[7]"The Archetypes and the Collective Unconscious," in *Aion, op. cit.,* from pp. 4-5.

into conscious formulae taught according to tradition, generally in the form of esoteric teaching. This last is a typical means of expression for the transmission of collective contents originally derived from the unconscious.

Another well-known expression of the archetypes is myth and fairytale. But here too we are dealing with forms that have received a specific stamp and have been handed down through long periods of time. The term "archetype" thus applies only indirectly to the "représentations collectives," since it designates only those psychic contents which have not yet been submitted to conscious elaboration and are therefore an immediate datum of psychic experience. In this sense there is considerable difference between the archetype and the historical formula that has evolved. Especially on the higher levels of esoteric teaching the archetypes appear in a form that reveals quite unmistakably the critical and evaluating influence of conscious elaboration. Their immediate manifestation, as we encounter it in dreams and visions, is much more individual, less understandable, and more naive than myths, for example. The archetype is essentially an unconscious content that is altered by becoming conscious and by being perceived, and it takes its colour from the individual consciousness in which it happens to appear.

* * * * *

Primordial Images[8]

The image is a concentrated *expression of the total psychic situation,* not merely, nor even pre-eminently, of unconscious contents pure and simple. It undoubtedly does express the contents of the unconscious, though not the whole of its contents in general, but merely those momentarily constellated. This constellation is the product of the specific activity of the unconscious on the one hand, and of the momentary conscious situation on the other: this always stimulates the activity of associated subliminal material at the same time as it also inhibits the irrelevant. Accordingly the image is equally an expression of the unconscious as of the conscious situation of the moment.

* * * * *

I term the image *primordial* when it possesses an archaic character. I speak of its archaic character when the image is in striking unison with familiar mythological motives. In this case it expresses material primarily derived from the collective unconscious, while, at the same time, it indicates that the momentary conscious situation is influenced not so much from the side of the personal as from the collective.

A *personal* image has neither archaic character nor collective significance, but expresses contents of the personal unconscious and a personally conditioned, conscious situation.

[8]*Psychological Types* (London: Routledge & Kegan Paul, 1923), from pp. 555ff.

The primordial image (elsewhere termed the "archetype") is always collective, *i.e.* it is at least common to entire nations or epochs. In all probability the most important mythological motives are common to all times and races; I have, in fact, demonstrated a whole series of motives from Grecian mythology in the dreams and phantasies of thoroughbred negroes suffering from mental disorders.

The primordial image is a mnemic deposit, an *imprint* ("engramm"— Semon), which has arisen through a condensation of innumerable, similar processes. It is primarily a precipitate or deposit, and therefore a typical basic form of a certain ever-recurring psychic experience. As a mythological motive, therefore, it is a constantly affective and continually recurring expression which is either awakened, or appropriately formulated, by certain psychic experiences. The primordial image, then, is the psychic expression of an anatomically and physiologically determined disposition. If one supports the view that a definite anatomical structure is the product of environmental conditions upon living matter, the primordial image in its constant and universal distribution corresponds with an equally universal and continuous external influence, which must, therefore, have the character of a natural law.

The Self[9]

We shall now turn to the question of whether the increase in self-knowledge resulting from the withdrawal of impersonal projections—in other words, the integration of the contents of the collective unconscious —exerts a specific influence on the ego-personality. To the extent that the integrated contents are *parts of the self,* we can expect this influence to be considerable. Their assimilation augments not only the area of the field of consciousness but also the importance of the ego, especially when, as usually happens, the ego lacks any critical approach to the unconscious. In that case it is easily overpowered and becomes identical with the contents that have been assimilated. In this way, for instance, a masculine consciousness comes under the influence of the anima and can even be possessed by her.

I have discussed the wider affects of the integration of unconscious contents elsewhere and can therefore omit going into details here. I should only like to mention that the more numerous and the more significant the unconscious contents which are assimilated to the ego, the closer the approximation of the ego to the self, even though this approximation must be a never-ending process. This inevitability produces an inflation of the ego, unless a critical line of demarcation is drawn between it and the unconscious figures. But this act of discrimination yields practical results only if

[9]"The Self," in *Aion, op. cit.,* from pp. 23-24.

it succeeds in fixing reasonable boundaries to the ego and in granting the figures of the unconscious—the self, anima, animus, and shadow—relative autonomy and reality (of a psychic nature). To psychologize this reality out of existence is ineffectual, or else merely increases the inflation of the ego. One cannot dispose of facts by declaring them unreal. The projection-making factor, for instance, has undeniable reality. Anyone who insists on denying it becomes identical with it, which is not only dubious in itself but a positive danger to the well-being of the individual.

* * * * *

It must be reckoned a psychic catastrophe when the *ego is assimilated by the self.* The image of wholeness then remains in the unconscious, so that on the one hand it shares the archaic nature of the unconscious and on the other finds itself in the psychically relative space-time continuum that is characteristic of the unconscious as such. Both these qualities are numinous and hence have an unlimited determining effect on ego-consciousness, which is differentiated, i.e., separated, from the unconscious and moreover exists in an absolute space and an absolute time. It is a vital necessity that this should be so. If, therefore, the ego falls for any length of time under the control of an unconscious factor, its adaptation is disturbed and the way opened for all sorts of possible accidents.

* * * * *

Comparison of Self and Ego[10]

By ego, I understand a complex of representations which constitutes the centrum of my field of consciousness and appears to possess a very high degree of continuity and identity. Hence I also speak of an *ego-complex.*

• The ego-complex is as much a content as it is a condition of consciousness, since a psychic element is conscious to me just in so far as it is related to my ego-complex. But, inasmuch as the ego is only the centrum of my field of consciousness, it is not identical with the totality of my psyche, being merely a complex among other complexes. Hence I discriminate between the ego and the Self, since the ego is only the subject of my consciousness, while the Self is the subject of my totality: hence it also includes the unconscious psyche. In this sense the Self would be an (ideal) factor which embraces and includes the ego. In unconscious phantasy the Self often appears as a super-ordinated or ideal personality, as Faust in relation to Goethe and Zarathustra to Nietzsche. In the effort of idealization the archaic features of the Self are represented as practically severed from the "higher" Self, as in the figure of Mephisto with Goethe or in that of Epimetheus with Spitteler. In the Christian psychology the severance is ex-

---

[10]*Psychological Types, op. cit.,* from p. 540.

treme in the figures of Christ and the devil or Anti-christ; while with Nietzsche Zarathustra discovers his shadow in the "ugliest man."

THE PSYCHE, SOUL, AND ANIMA[11]

I have found sufficient cause, in my investigations into the structure of the unconscious, to make a conceptual distinction between the *soul* and the *psyche*. By the psyche I understand the totality of all the psychic processes, both conscious as well as unconscious; whereas by *soul* I understand a definitely demarcated function-complex that is best characterized as a "personality."

*   *   *   *   *

We have only to observe a man rather closely under varying circumstances, to discover that a transition from one milieu to another brings about a striking alteration in his personality, whereby a sharply-outlined and distinctly changed character emerges. The proverbial expression "angel abroad, and devil at home" is a formulation of the phenomenon of character-splitting derived from everyday experience. A definite milieu demands a definite attitude. Corresponding with the duration or frequency with which such a milieu-attitude is demanded, the more or less habitual it becomes. Great numbers of men of the educated classes are obliged to move in two, for the most part totally different, milieux—viz. in the family and domestic circle and in the world of affairs. These two totally different environments demand two totally different attitudes, which, in proportion to the degree of identification of the ego with the monetary attitude, produce a duplication of character. In accordance with social conditions and necessities, the social character is orientated, on the one hand by the expectations or obligations of the social milieu, and on the other by the social aims and efforts of the subject. The domestic character is, as a rule, more the product of the subject's laissez-aller indolence and emotional demands; whence it frequently happens that men who in public life are extremely energetic, bold, obstinate, wilful, and inconsiderate appear good-natured, mild, accommodating, even weak, when at home within the sphere of domesticity. Which, then, is the true character, the real personality?

*   *   *   *   *

This brief consideration will show that, even in the normal individual, character-splitting is by no means an impossibility. We are, therefore, perfectly justified in treating the question of dissociation of personality also as a problem of normal psychology. According to my view then—to pursue the discussion—the above question should be met with a frank avowal that such a man has no real character at all, i.e. he is not *individual* but *collective*, i.e.

[11]*Ibid.*, from pp. 588-97.

he corresponds with general circumstance and expectations. Were he an individual, he would have but one and the same character with every variation of attitude. It would not be identical with the momentary attitude, neither could it nor would it prevent his individuality from finding expression in one state just as clearly as in another. He is an individual, of course, like every being; but an unconscious one. Through his more or less complete identification with the attitude of the moment, he at least deceives others, and also often himself, as to his real character. He puts on a _mask,_ which he knows corresponds with his conscious intentions, while it also meets with the requirements and opinions of his environment, so that first one motive then the other is in the ascendant. The mask, viz. the ad hoc adopted attitude, I have called the *persona,* which was the designation given to the mask worn by actors of antiquity. A man who is identified with this mask I would call "personal" (as opposed to "individual").

Both the attitudes of the case considered above are collective personalities, which may be simply summed up under the name "persona" or "personae." I have already suggested that the real individuality is different from both. Thus, the persona is a function-complex which has come into existence for reasons of adptation or necessary convenience, but by no means is it identical with the individuality. The function-complex of the persona is exclusively concerned with the relation to the object.

*   *   *   *   *

Those cases in which the inner psychic processes appear to be entirely overlooked are lacking a typical inner attitude just as little as those who constantly overlook the outer object and the reality of facts lack a typical outer attitude. The persona of these latter, by no means infrequent, cases has the character of unrelatedness, or at times even a blind inconsiderateness, which frequently yields only to the harshest blows of fate. Not seldom, it is just those individuals whose persona is characterized by a rigid inconsiderateness and absence of relations who possess an attitude to the unconscious processes which suggests a character of extreme susceptibility. As they are inflexible and inaccessible outwardly, so are they weak, flaccid, and determinable in relation to their inner processes. In such cases, therefore, the inner attitude corresponds with an inner personality diametrically opposed and different from the outer. I know a man, for instance, who without pity blindly destroyed the happiness of those nearest to him, and yet he would interrupt his journeys when travelling on important business just to enjoy the beauty of a forest scene glimpsed from the carriage window. . . . With the same justification as daily experience furnishes us for speaking of an outer personality are we also justified in assuming the existence of an inner personality. The inner personality is the manner of one's behaviour towards the inner psychic processes; it is the inner attitude, the character, that is turned towards the unconscious. I term the outer attitude, or the outer character, the *persona,* the inner attitude I term the *anima,* or *soul.*

In the same degree as an attitude is habitual, is it a more or less firmly welded function-complex, with which the ego may be more or less identified. This is practically expressed in language: of a man who has an habitual attitude towards certain situations, we are accustomed to say: He is quite *another man* when doing this or that. This is a practical demonstration of the independence of the function-complex of an habitual attitude; it is as though another personality had taken possession of the individual, as "though another spirit had entered into him." The same autonomy as is so often granted to the outer attitude is also claimed by the soul or inner attitude. One of the most difficult of all educational achievements is the task of changing the outer attitude, or persona. But to change the soul is just as difficult, since its structure tends to be just as firmly welded as is that of the persona. Just as the persona is an entity, which often appears to constitute the whole character of a man, even accompanying him practically without change throughout his entire life, so the soul is also a definitely circumscribed entity, with a character which may prove unalterably firm and independent. Hence, it frequently offers itself to characterization and description.

As regards the character of the soul, my experience confirms the validity of the general principle that it maintains, on the whole, a *complementary* relation to the outer character. Experience teaches us that the soul is wont to contain all those general human qualities the conscious attitude lacks. The tyrant tormented by bad dreams, gloomy forebodings, and inner fears, is a typical figure. Outwardly inconsiderate, harsh and unapproachable, he is inwardly susceptible to every shadow, and subject to every fancy, as though he were the least independent, and the most impressionable, of men. Thus his soul contains those general human qualities of suggestibility and weakness which are wholly lacking in his outer attitude, or persona. Where the persona is intellectual, the soul is quite certainly sentimental. That the complementary character of the soul is also concerned with the sex-character is a fact which can no longer seriously be doubted. A very feminine woman has a masculine soul, and a very manly man a feminine soul. This opposition is based upon the fact that a man, for instance, is not in all things wholly masculine, but has also certain feminine traits. The more manly his outer attitude, the more will his womanly traits be effaced; these then appear in the soul. This circumstance explains why it is that the very manly men are most subject to characteristic weaknesses; their attitude to the unconscious has a womanly weakness and impressionability. And, vice versa, it is often just the most womanly women who, in respect of certain inner things, have an extreme intractableness, obstinacy, and wilfulness; which qualities are found in such intensity only in the outer attitude of men. These are manly traits, whose exclusion from the womanly outer attitude makes them qualities of the soul. If, therefore, we speak of the *anima* of a man, we must logically speak of the *animus* of a woman, if we are to give the soul of a woman its right name. Whereas logic and objective reality commonly prevail in the outer attitude of man, or are at least regarded as an ideal, in the case of woman it is feeling. But in the soul the relations are reversed: inwardly it is the man who feels, and the woman who reflects. Hence man's liability to total despair, while the woman can always find comfort and hope; hence man is more liable to put an end to himself than woman. However prone a woman may be to fall a victim to social circumstances, as in prostitution for instance, a man is equally delivered over to impulses from the unconscious in the form of alcoholism and other vices.

As regards the general human characters, the character of the soul may be deduced from that of the persona. Everything which should normally be in the outer attitude, but is decidedly wanting there, will invariably be found in the inner attitude. This is a basic rule, which my experience has borne out again and again. But, as regards individual qualities, nothing can be deduced about them in this way. We can be certain that, when a man is identical with his persona, the individual qualities are associated with the soul. It is this association which gives rise to the symbol, so often appearing in dreams, of the soul's pregnancy; this symbol has its source in the primordial image of the hero-birth. The child that is to be born signifies the individuality, which, though existing, is not yet conscious. Hence in the same way as the persona, which expresses one's adaptation to the milieu, is as a rule strongly influenced and shaped by the milieu, so the soul is just as profoundly moulded by the unconscious and its qualities. Just as the persona, almost necessarily, takes on primitive traits in a primitive milieu, so the soul assumes the archaic characters of the unconscious as well as its prospective, symbolic character. Whence arise the "pregnant" and "creative" qualities of the inner attitude. Identity with the persona automatically conditions an unconscious identity with the soul, because, when the subject or ego is not differentiated from the persona, it can have no conscious relation to the processes of the unconscious. Hence it *is* these processes: it is identical with them. The man who is unconditionally his outer role therewith delivers himself over unquestionably to the inner processes, i.e. he will even frustrate his outer role by absolute inner necessity, reducing it *ad absurdum*. A steady holding to the individual line is thereby excluded, and his life runs its course in inevitable opposition. Moreover, in such a case the soul is always projected into a corresponding, real object, with which a relation of almost absolute dependence exists. Every reaction proceeding from this object has an immediate, inwardly arresting effect upon the subject. Tragic ties are frequently found in this way (Soul-image).

*   *   *   *   *

The soul-image is a definite image among those produced by the unconscious. Just as the persona, or outer attitude, is represented in dreams by the images of certain persons who possess the outstanding qualities of the persona in especially marked form, so the soul, the inner attitude of the unconscious, is similarly represented by definite persons whose particular qualities correspond with those of the soul. Such an image is called a "soul-image." Occasionally these images are quite unknown or mythological figures. With men the soul, i.e. the anima, is usually figured by the unconscious in the person of a woman; with women it is a man. In every case where the individuality is unconscious, and therefore associated with the soul, the soul-image has the character of the same sex.

Two Psychological Types

Extraversion[12]

Extraversion means an outward-turning of the libido. With this concept I denote a manifest relatedness of subject to object in the sense of a positive movement of subjective interest towards the object. Everyone in the state of extraversion thinks, feels, and acts in relation to the object, and moreover in a direct and clearly observable fashion, so that no doubt can exist about his positive dependence upon the object. In a sense, therefore, extraversion is an outgoing transference of interest from the subject to the object. If it is an intellectual extraversion, the subject thinks himself into the object; if a feeling extraversion, then the subject feels himself into the object. The state of extraversion means a strong, if not exclusive, determination by the object. One should speak of an *active* extraversion when deliberately willed, and of a *passive* extraversion when the object compels it, i.e. attracts the interest of the subject of its own accord, even against the latter's intention. Should the state of extraversion become habitual, the *extraverted type* appears.

Introversion[13]

Introversion means a turning inwards of the libido whereby a negative relation of subject to object is expressed. Interest does not move towards the object, but recedes towards the subject. Everyone whose attitude is introverted thinks, feels, and acts in a way that clearly demonstrates that the subject is the chief factor of motivation while the object at most receives only a secondary value. Introversion may possess either a more intellectual or more emotional character, just as it can be characterized by either intuition or sensation. Introversion is *active*, when the subject *wills* a certain seclusion in face of the object; it is *passive* when the subject is unable to restore again to the object the libido which is streaming back from it. When introversion is habitual, one speaks of an *introverted type*.

The Four Functions[14]

By psychological function I understand a certain form of psychic activity that remains theoretically the same under varying circumstances. From the

[12]*Ibid.*, from pp. 542-43.
[13]*Ibid.*, from p. 567.
[14]*Ibid.*, from p. 547.

energic standpoint a function is a phenomenal form of libido which theoretically remains constant, in much the same way as physical force can be
considered as the form or momentary manifestation of physical energy. I
distinguish four basic functions in all, two rational and two irrational—viz.
thinking and *feeling, sensation* and *intuition.*

* * * * *

I differentiate these functions from one another, because they are neither
mutually relatable nor mutually reducible. The principle of thinking, for
instance, is absolutely different from the principle of feeling, and so forth.
I make a capital distinction between this concept of function and phantasy-
activity, or reverie, because, to my mind, phantasying is a peculiar form of
activity which can manifest itself in all the four functions.

In my view, both will and attention are entirely secondary psychic
phenomena.

Thinking[15]

Thinking is that psychological function which, in accordance with its own
laws, brings given presentations into conceptual connection. It is an apper-
ceptive activity and, as such, must be differentiated into *active* and *passive*
thought-activity. Active thinking is an act of will, passive thinking an occurrence. In the former case, I submit representation to a deliberate act of judgment; in the latter case, conceptual connections establish themselves, and
judgments are formed which may even contradict my aim—they may lack all
harmony with my conscious objective, hence also, for me, any feeling of
direction, although by an act of active apperception I may subsequently
come to a recognition of their directedness. Active thinking would correspond, therefore, with my idea of directed thinking. Passive thinking was
inadequately characterized in my previous work as "phantasying." To-day
I would term it *intuitive* thinking. . . .

The faculty of directed thinking, I term *intellect:* the faculty of passive, or
undirected, thinking, I term *intellectual* intuition. Furthermore, I describe
directed thinking or intellect as the *rational* function, since it arranges the
representations under concepts in accordance with the presuppositions of my
conscious rational norm. Undirected thinking, or intellectual intuition, on
the contrary is, in my view, an *irrational* function, since it criticizes and
arranges the representations according to norms that are unconscious to me
and consequently not appreciated as reasonable. . . . Thinking that is regulated by feeling, I do not regard as intuitive thinking, but as thought dependent upon feeling; it does not follow its own logical principle, but is subordinated to the principle of feeling. In such thinking the laws of logic are only
ostensibly present; in reality they are suspended in favour of the aims of
feeling.

[15]*Ibid.*, from pp. 611-12.

Feeling[16]

I am unable to support the psychological school that regards feeling as a secondary phenomenon dependent upon "presentations" or sensations, ... I regard it as an independent function sui generis.

Feeling is primarily a process that takes place between the ego and a given content, a process, moreover, that imparts to the content a definite *value* in the sense of acceptance or rejection ("like" or "dislike"); but it can also appear, as it were, isolated in the form of "mood," quite apart from the momentary contents of consciousness or momentary sensations. . . . The mood, whether it be regarded as a general or only a partial feeling, signifies a valuation; not, however, a valuation of one definite, individual, conscious content, but of the whole conscious situation at the moment, and, once again, with special reference to the question of acceptance or rejection.

Feeling, therefore, is an entirely *subjective* process, which may be in every respect independent of external stimuli, although chiming in with every sensation. Even an "indifferent" sensation possesses a "feeling tone," namely, that of indifference, which again expresses a certain valuation. Hence feeling is also a kind of *judging*, differing, however, from an intellectual judgment, in that it does not aim at establishing an intellectual connection but is solely concerned with the setting up of a subjective criterion of acceptance or rejection. The valuation by feeling extends to *every* content of consciousness, of whatever kind it may be. When the intensity of feeling is increased an *affect* results, which is a state of feeling accompanied by appreciable bodily innervations. Feeling is distinguished from affect by the fact that it gives rise to no perceptible physical innervations, i.e. just as much or as little as the ordinary thinking process.

* * * * *

The nature of a feeling-valuation may be accompanied with intellectual apperception as an *apperception of value*. An *active* and a *passive* feeling-apperception can be distinguished. The passive feeling-act is characterized by the fact that a content excites or attracts the feeling; it compels a feeling-participation on the part of the subject. The active feeling-act, on the contrary, confers value from the subject—it is a deliberate evaluation of contents in accordance with feeling and not in accordance with intellectual intention. Hence active feeling is a *directed* function, an act of will, as for instance loving as opposed to being in love. This latter state would be *undirected*, passive feeling, as, indeed, the ordinary colloquial term suggests, since it describes the former as activity and the latter as a condition. Undirected feeling is *feeling-intuition*. Thus, in the stricter sense, only the active, directed feeling should be termed *rational:* the passive is definitely *irrational*, since it establishes values without voluntary participation, occasionally even against the subject's intention.

[16]*Ibid.*, from pp. 543-47.

When the total attitude of the individual is orientated by the function of feeling, we speak of a feeling-type.

Sensation[17]

Sensation, or sensing, is that psychological function which transmits a physical stimulus to perception. It is, therefore, identical with perception. Sensation must be strictly distinguished from feeling, since the latter is an entirely different process, although it may, for instance, be associated with sensation as "feeling-tone." Sensation is related not only to the outer stimuli, but also to the inner, i.e. to changes in the internal organs.

Primarily, therefore, sensation is *sense-perception,* i.e. perception transmitted *via* the sense organs and "bodily senses" (kinaesthetic, vaso-motor sensation, etc.). On the one hand, it is an element of presentation, since it transmits to the presenting function the perceived image of the outer object; on the other hand, it is an element of feeling, because through the perception of bodily changes it lends the character of affect to feeling. Because sensation transmits physical changes to consciousness, it also represents the physiological impulse. But it is not identical with it, since it is merely a perceptive function.

* * * * *

Insofar as sensation is an elementary phenomenon, it is something absolutely given, something that, in contrast to thinking and feeling, is not subject to the laws of reason. I therefore term it an *irrational* function, although reason contrives to assimilate a great number of sensations into rational associations.

A man whose whole attitude is orientated by the principle of sensation belongs to the sensation type.

Intuition[18]

It is that psychological function which transmits perceptions *in an unconscious way.* Everything, whether outer or inner objects or their associations, can be the object of this perception. Intuition has this peculiar quality: it is neither sensation, nor feeling, nor intellectual conclusion, although it may appear in any of these forms. Through intuition any one content is presented as a complete whole, without our being able to explain or discover in what way this content has been arrived at. Intuition is a kind of instinctive apprehension, irrespective of the nature of its contents. Like sensation it is an *irrational* perceptive function. Its contents, like those of sensation, have the character of being given, in contrast to the "derived" or "deduced" character of feeling and thinking contents. Intuitive cognition, therefore, possesses an intrinsic character of certainty and conviction which enabled Spinoza to uphold the "scientia intuitiva" as the highest form of cognition. (Similarly Bergson). Intuition has this quality in common with sensation,

[17]*Ibid.,* from pp. 585-88.
[18]*Ibid.,* from pp. 567-69.

whose physical foundation is the ground and origin of its certitude. In the same way, the certainty of intuition depends upon a definite psychic matter of fact, of whose origin and state of readiness, however, the subject was quite unconscious.

*   *   *   *   *

Intuition maintains a compensatory function to sensation, and, like sensation, it is the maternal soil from which thinking and feeling are developed in the form of rational functions. Intuition is an irrational function, notwithstanding the fact that many intuitions may subsequently be split up into their component elements, whereby their origin and appearance can also be made to harmonize with the laws of reason. Everyone whose general attitude is orientated by the principle of intuition, i.e. perception by way of the unconscious, belongs to the *intuitive type.*

According to the manner in which intuition is employed, whether directed within in the service of cognition and inner perception or without in the service of action and accomplishment, the introverted and extraverted intuitive types can be differentiated.

PSYCHIC ENERGY (LIBIDO) [19]

The theory of libido which I have advanced has met with many misunderstandings and, in some quarters, complete repudiation; it may therefore not be amiss if I again take up the fundamental concepts of this theory.

It is a generally recognized truth that physical events can be looked at in two ways, that is, from the mechanistic and from the energic standpoint. The mechanistic view is purely causal; from this standpoint an event is conceived as the result of a cause, in the sense that immutable substances change their relationships to one another according to fixed laws.

The energic view-point on the other hand is in essence final; the event is traced from effect to cause on the assumption that energy forms the essential basis of changes in phenomena, that it maintains itself as a constant throughout these changes, and finally leads to an entrophy, a condition of general equilibrium. The flow of energy has a definite direction (goal), in that it follows the fall of potential in a way that cannot be reversed. The idea of energy is not that of a substance moved in space; it is a concept abstracted from relations of movement. The concept, therefore, is not founded on substances themselves, but on their relations; while the moving substance itself is the basis of the mechanistic theory.

*   *   *   *   *

I am in hearty agreement with von Grot—one of the first to propose the concept of psychic energy—when he says: "The idea of psychic energy is

[19]"On Psychical Energy," in *Contributions to Analytical Psychology*, trans. H. G. and Cary F. Baines (London: Routledge & Kegan Paul, 1928), from pp. 1-32.

as much justified in science as is that of physical energy, and psychic energy equally with physical energy has quantitative measurements and a variety of forms."

The Subjective System of Values

The applicability of the energic standpoint to psychology rests, then, exclusively upon the question as to whether a quantitative evaluation of psychic energy is possible. This question is to be met with unconditional affirmation, because our minds possess what is in fact an exceedingly well-developed evaluating system, namely, the *system of psychological values*. Values are indices of amounts of energy. Here it is to be noted that in the collective moral and aesthetic values we have at our disposal an objective system that is not merely one of values but also of measure. This system of measure is certainly not immediately available for our purposes, for it is a generally established scale of values which takes account, in an indirect way only, of subjective, that is, individual psychological conditions.

* * * * *

We can weigh our subjective valuations one against the other and determine their *relative* strength. The measure of them is certainly relative to the value of other contents, and therefore not absolute and objective, but it is sufficient for our purpose, inasmuch as different intensities of value within similar qualities can be recognized with confidence, while equal values under the same conditions plainly maintain themselves in equilibrium. . . . In subjective evaluation feeling and insight are of immediate assistance, because feeling is a function that has been developing through an inconceivably long period of time, and has become most firmly differentiated.

The Objective Measure of Quantity

In the study of the phenomena of association I have shown that there are certain groupings of psychic elements about emotionally-toned contents, which have been called complexes. The emotionally-toned content, the complex, consists of a nuclear element and a great number of secondarily constellated associations. The nucleus is made up of two components, first, a condition determined by experience, an event in other words, that is causally related to the environment, and, secondly, a condition innate in the individual character, that is, determined by disposition.

The nuclear element is characterized by the so-called feeling tone, or the emphasis given through affect. This stress, expressed in terms of energy, is a value quantity. Insofar as the nuclear element is conscious, the quantity can be subjectively estimated, at least relatively. But if, as frequently happens, the nuclear element is unconscious, or at least unconscious in its psychological significance, then the subjective evaluation is impossible, and one must substitute the indirect method of arriving at the value. This indirect method rests in principle on the following facts: the nuclear element creates a complex automatically in so far as it is affectively toned, that is, possessed of energic value. I have shown this in detail in the second and third chapters of my *Psychology of Dementia Praecox.* The nuclear element has a constellating power corresponding to its energic value. From this power there follows a specific constellation of the psychic contents; and thus is developed the complex, which is a constellation of psychic contents dynamically conditioned by the energic value. The resulting constellation, however, is not a simple irradiation of the stimulus, but a selection of stimulated psychic contents, conditioned by the quality of the nuclear element—a selection which naturally cannot be explained on an energic basis, because the energic explanation is quantitative and not qualitative. For a qualitative explanation we must have recourse to the causal viewpoint. The statement, then, upon which the objective estimation of psychological value-intensities is founded, runs as follows: the constellating power of the nuclear element corresponds to its value intensity, which in turn represents its energy.

But what means have we of estimating in its energic value the constellating power that can enrich a complex with associations? We can estimate this amount of energy in various ways:—

(1) from the relative number of constellations effected by the nuclear element;

(2) from the relative frequency and intensity of the so-called disturbance- or complex-indices;

(3) from the intensity of accompanying affect-phenomena.

1. The data required to determine the relative number of constellations effected by the nuclear element may be obtained in part through direct observation, and in part by means of analytical deductions. The rule of our estimate is: the more frequently we come upon constellations that are conditioned by one and the same complex, the greater must be the psychological value that we assign to this complex.

2. By the disturbance- or complex-indices we must not understand merely the indicators that appear in the association experiments. These are really nothing but complex-effects, the form of which is determined by the special situation of the experiment. . . .

3. For the determination of the intensity of affective phenomena we have objective methods which, though not measuring the amount of the affect, still permit an estimation. Experimental psychology has given us a string of such methods. Apart from time measurements, which determine the inhibition in the association-process rather than the actual affect, we have in particular the following means:—

(a) the pulse curve.

(b) the respiration curve.

(c) the psycho-galvanic phenomenon.

The easily recognizable changes in these curves permit estimates to be made concerning the intensity of the disturbing cause. It is possible, as experience has sufficiently shown, to induce affect-phenomena in the person experimented upon by means of intentional psychological stimuli, which one knows to be especially stressed with affect for the particular individual in his relation to the experimenter.

The Conservation of Energy

If we undertake to view the psychical life-processes from the energic standpoint, we must not be content with mere theory, but must take up the task of testing its applicability to empirical material. An energic viewpoint is superfluous if its main principle, that of the conservation of energy, proves inapplicable. We must follow here the recommendation of Busse, and distinguish between the principle of equivalence and that of constancy. The equivalence principle states that "for every energy spent or consumed in bringing about a condition, a similar quantity of the same or other forms of energy shall appear elsewhere"; the constancy principle is to the effect that "the sum total of energy remains constant, and is neither susceptible of increase, nor of decrease." The constancy principle is therefore a logically necessary but generalized inference from the equivalence principle; it has no practical significance, since our experience is based only on relative systems. Thus, for our task, the equivalence principle is the only one of immediate concern.

Entropy

The principle of equivalence is one practically important postulate in the theory of energy; the other necessary complementary position is the principle of entropy. Transformations of energy are possible only as a result of differences in intensity. According to the statement of Carnot, heat can be transformed into work only by passing from a warmer to a colder body, but mechanical work is continually being transformed into heat, which on account of its diminished intensity cannot be retransformed into work again. In this way a closed energic system gradually reduces its differences in intensity to an even temperature, whereby any further change is prohibited. This is the so-called death in "trepidity."

The principle of entropy is known in experience only as a principle of partial processes which make up a relatively closed system. The psyche can be regarded as such a relatively closed system, in which the transpositions of energy also lead to an equilization of differences. According to Boltzmann's formulation, this levelling process corresponds to a transition from an improbable to a probable condition, but with an increasing limitation of the possibilities of further change. We see this process, for example, in the development of a lasting and relatively unchanging attitude. After violent oscillations at the beginning the contradictions balance each other, and gradually a new attitude develops, the final stability of which is the greater in proportion to the magnitude of the initial differences. The greater the tension between the pairs of opposites, the greater the energy, the stronger will be its constellating, attracting power. This greater attracting power represents a wider range of constellated psychical material, and the further this range extends, the less chance there is of later disturbances that might arise from differences with the material not previously constellated. For this reason an attitude that has been formed out of a far-reaching process of equalization is an especially lasting one. Daily psychological experience offers proof of this statement. Most intense conflicts, if overcome, leave behind a sense of security and rest, or a brokenness, that it is scarcely possible to disturb again, or to cure, as the case may be. . . . Since our experience is confined to relatively closed systems,[b] we are never in the position to observe an absolute psychological entropy; but the more complete the isolation of the psychological system is, the more clearly is the phenomenon of entropy manifested. We can see this particularly well in those mental disturbances which are characterized by an extreme seclusion from the environment. The so-called "dulling of affect" of dementia praecox, of schizophrenia, is to be understood as a phenomenon of entropy. The same also applies to those so-called degenerative phenomena which develop into psychological attitudes that permanently exclude all connexions with the world around. Similarly, such voluntary directed processes as directed thought or feeling can be viewed as relatively closed psychological systems. These functions are based on the principle of the exclusion of the inappropriate, or unsuitable, which could bring about a deviation from the chosen way. The elements that "belong" are protected from outside, disturbing influences. Thus after some time they reach their "probable" condition, which manifests its firmness, for example, in a "lasting" conviction, or in a "deeply ingrained" view-point, etc. How firmly rooted such things are can be tested by anyone who attempts to dissolve such a structure, for example, to uproot a prejudice, or change a habit of thought. In the history of peoples such changes have cost rivers of blood. But insofar as an absolute closing off is impossible (pathological cases excepted) the energic process goes on as development, though, because of "loss by friction," with lessening intensity and decreased potential.

This way of looking at things has long been familiar. Everybody speaks of the "storms of youth" which yield to the "tranquility of age." We speak too of a "strengthened opinion" after "battling with doubts," of a "relief from inner tension," etc. This is the arbitrary energic standpoint shared by everyone. This standpoint remains valueless to the scientific psychologist as long as he feels no need of estimating psychological values. For physiological psychology the problem does not come into question at all.

Energism and Dynamism

The psychological concept of energy is not a pure concept, but also a concrete and applied concept, that appears in the form of sexual, vital, mental, moral "energy"; in other words it appears in the form of instinct,

---

[b]A system is absolutely closed when energy from without can no longer be fed into it. Only in such a case can entrophy occur.

the undeniably dynamic nature of which justifies us in a conceptual parallelism with physical forces. . . .

I have advocated calling the energy-concept used in analytical psychology by the name "libido." The choice of the word may not be ideal in some ways, yet it seems to me that this concept merits the name libido as a matter of historical justice. . . . Since Freud confines himself exclusively to sexuality and its manifold ramifications in the mind, the sexual definition of energy as a specific instinctive force is quite sufficient for his purpose. In a general psychological theory, however, it is impossible to use sexuality, that is, one specific instinct, as an explanatory concept, since psychical energy-transformation is not merely a matter of sexual dynamics. Sexual dynamics is only a special case in a general theory of mind. When so regarded its existence is not denied, but merely given its proper place.

Since the applied theory of energy immediately becomes hypostasized on perceptual grounds into the forces of the mind (instincts, affects, and other dynamic processes), the perceived manifestation of psychic energy is in my opinion excellently characterized by the word "libido"; inasmuch as similar perceptions have always made use of like terms, as, for example, Schopenhauer's "will," the *horme* of Aristotle, the *eros* of the elements, or the *élan vital* of Bergson. From these concepts I have taken only the graphic or perceptual character of my term, not the definition of the concept.

*   *   *   *   *

With the word "libido" I do not connect, as I said, a sexual definition, yet it must not therefore be inferred that I exclude a sexual dynamism, more than any other dynamism, as, for example, that of the hunger instinct. In my book, *The Psychology of the Unconscious*, I called attention to my notion of a general life instinct, termed libido, which replaces the concept "psychic energy" that I used in the *Psychology of Dementia Praecox*.

THE INDIVIDUATION PROCESS[20]

I use the term "individuation" to denote the process by which a person becomes a psychological "in-dividual," that is, a separate, indivisible unity or "whole." It is generally assumed that consciousness is the whole of the psychological individual. But knowledge of the phenomena that can only be explained on the hypothesis of unconscious psychic processes makes it doubtful whether the ego and its contents are in fact identical with the

[20]"Conscious, Unconscious, and Individuation," in *Archetypes and the Collective Unconscious, op. cit.*, from pp. 275-89.

"whole." If unconscious processes exist at all, they must surely belong to the totality of the individual, even though they are not components of the conscious ego. If they were part of the ego they would necessarily be conscious, because everything that is directly related to the ego is conscious. Consciousness can even be equated with the relation between the ego and the psychic contents. But unconscious phenomena are so little related to the ego that most people do not hesitate to deny their existence outright. Nevertheless, they manifest themselves in an individual's behaviour. An attentive observer can detect them without difficulty, while the observed person remains quite unaware of the fact that he is betraying his most secret thoughts or even things he has never thought consciously. It is, however, a great prejudice to suppose that something we have never thought consciously does not exist in the psyche. There is plenty of evidence to show that consciousness is very far from covering the psyche in its totality. Many things occur semiconsciously, and a great many more remain entirely unconscious. Thorough investigation of the phenomena of dual and multiple personalities, for instance, has brought to light a mass of material with observations to prove this point.

* * * * *

Consciousness grows out of an unconscious psyche which is older than it, and which goes on functioning together with it or even in spite of it. Although there are numerous cases of conscious contents becoming unconscious again (through being repressed, for instance), the unconscious as a whole is far from being a mere remnant of consciousness. Or are the psychic functions of animals remnants of consciousness?

As I have said, there is little hope of finding in the unconscious an order equivalent to that of the ego. It certainly does not look as if we were likely to discover an unconscious ego-personality. . . . Just as a human mother can only produce a human child, whose deepest nature lay hidden during its potential existence within her, so we are practically compelled to believe that the unconscious cannot be an entirely chaotic accumulation of instincts and images. There must be something to hold it together and give expression to the whole. Its centre cannot possibly be the ego, since the ego was born out of it into consciousness and turns its back on the unconscious, seeking to shut it out as much as possible. Or can it be that the unconscious loses its centre with the birth of the ego? In that case we would expect the ego to be far superior to the unconscious in influence and importance. The unconscious would then follow meekly in the footsteps of the conscious and that would be just what we wish.

Unfortunately, the facts show the exact opposite: consciousness succumbs all too easily to unconscious influences, and these are often truer and wiser than our conscious thinking. Also, it frequently happens that unconscious motives overrule our conscious decisions. . . . Another example is intuition, which is chiefly dependent on unconscious processes of a very complex nature. Because of this peculiarity, I have defined intuition as "perception via the unconscious."

Normally the unconscious collaborates with the conscious without friction or disturbance, so that one is not even aware of its existence. But when an individual or a social group deviates too far from their instinctual foundations, they then experience the full impact of unconscious forces.

* * * * *

Consciousness needs a centre, an ego to which something is conscious. We know of no other kind of consciousness, nor can we imagine a consciousness without an ego. There can be no consciousness when there is no one to say: "*I* am conscious." . . . It was never possible for me to discover in the unconscious anything like a personality comparable with the ego. But although a "second ego" cannot be discovered (except in the rare case of dual personality), the manifestations of the unconscious do at least show *traces of personalities. . . . Personality need not imply consciousness. It can just as easily be dormant or dreaming.*

The general aspect of unconscious manifestations is in the main chaotic and irrational, despite certain symptoms of intelligence and purposiveness. The unconscious produces dreams, visions, fantasies, emotions, grotesque ideas, and so forth. This is exactly what we would expect a dreaming personality to do. It seems to be a personality that was never awake and was never conscious of the life it had lived and of its own continuity. The only question is whether the hypothesis of a dormant and hidden personality is possible or not.

* * * * *

I am convinced that such evidence exists. Unfortunately, the material to prove this belongs to the subtleties of psychological analysis. . . . I shall begin with a brief statement: in the unconscious of every man there is hidden a feminine personality, and in that of every woman a masculine personality.

It is a well-known fact that sex is determined by a majority of male or female genes, as the case may be. But the minority of genes belonging to the other sex does not simply disappear. A man therefore has in him a feminine side, an unconscious feminine figure—a fact of which he is generally quite unaware. I may take it as known that I have called this figure the "anima," and its counterpart in a woman the "animus." . . .

Another, no less important and clearly defined figure is the "shadow." Like the anima, it appears either in projection on suitable persons, or personified as such in dreams. The shadow coincides with the "personal" unconscious (which corresponds to Freud's conception of the unconscious). . . . The shadow personifies everything that the subject refuses to acknowledge about himself and yet is always thrusting itself upon him directly or indirectly—for instance, inferior traits of character and other incompatible tendencies.

The fact that the unconscious spontaneously personifies certain affectively toned contents in dreams is the reason why I have taken over these personifications in my terminology and formulated them as names.

Besides these figures there are still a few others, less frequent and less striking, which have likewise undergone poetic as well as mythological formulation. I would mention, for instance, the figure of the hero and of the wise old man, to name only two of the best known. All these figures irrupt autonomously into consciousness as soon as it gets into a pathological state.

* * * * *

The unconscious psyche is not only immensely old, it is also capable of growing into an equally remote future. It moulds the human species and is just as much a part of it as the human body, which, though ephemeral in the individual, is collectively of immense age.

The anima and animus live in a world quite different from the world outside—in a world where the pulse of time beats infinitely slowly, where the birth and death of individuals count for little. No wonder their nature is strange, so strange that their irruption into consciousness often amounts to a psychosis. They undoubtedly belong to the material that comes to light in schizophrenia.

What I have said about the collective unconscious may give you a more or less adequate idea of what I mean by this term. If we now turn back to the problem of individuation, we shall see ourselves faced with a rather extraordinary task: the psyche consists of two incongruous halves which together should form a whole. One is inclined to think that ego-consciousness is capable of assimilating the unconscious, at least one hopes that such a solution is possible. But unfortunately the unconscious really is unconscious; in other words, it is unknown. And how can you assimilate something unknown? Even if you can form a fairly complete picture of the anima and animus, this does not mean that you have plumbed the depths of the unconscious. One hopes to control the unconscious, but the past masters in the art of self-control, the yogis, attain perfection in *samādhi*, a state of ecstasy, which so far as we know is equivalent to a state of unconsciousness. It makes no difference whether they call our unconscious a "universal consciousness"; the fact remains that in their case the unconscious has swallowed up ego-consciousness. They do not realize that a "universal consciousness" is a contradiction in terms, since exclusion, selection, and discrimination are the root and essence of everything that lays claim to the name "consciousness." "Universal consciousness" is logically identical with unconsciousness.

* * * * *

We believe in ego-consciousness and in what we call reality. . . . Our European ego-consciousness is therefore inclined to swallow up the unconscious, and if this should not prove feasible we try to suppress it. But if we understand anything of the unconscious, we know that it cannot be swallowed. We also know that it is dangerous to suppress it, because the unconscious is life and this life turns against us if suppressed, as happens in neurosis.

Conscious and unconscious do not make a whole when one of them is suppressed and injured by the other. If they must contend, let it at least be a fair fight with equal rights on both sides. Both are aspects of life. Consciousness should defend its reason and protect itself, and the chaotic life of the unconscious should be given the chance of having its way too— as much of it as we can stand. This means open conflict and open collaboration at once. That, evidently, is the way human life should be. It is the old game of hammer and anvil: between them the patient iron is forged into an indestructible whole, an "individual."

This, roughly, is what I mean by the individuation process. As the name shows, it is a process or course of development arising out of the conflict between the two fundamental psychic facts. . . . How the harmonizing of conscious and unconscious data is to be undertaken cannot be indicated in the form of a recipe. It is an irrational life-process which expresses itself in definite symbols. It may be the task of the analyst to stand by this process with all the help he can give. In this case, knowledge of the symbols is indispensable, for it is in them that the union of conscious and unconscious contents is consummated. Out of this union emerge new situations and new conscious attitudes. I have therefore called the union of opposites the "transcendent function." This rounding out of the personality into a whole may well be the goal of any psychotherapy that claims to be more than a mere cure of symptoms.

CHAPTER 3

ALFRED ADLER

INDIVIDUAL PSYCHOLOGY
AS A PERSONALITY THEORY

When Alfred Adler, one of Freud's first disciples, was requested to withdraw from the Vienna Psychoanalytic Society, he founded his own school of INDIVIDUAL PSYCHOLOGY to which he attracted approximately 25 per cent of the members (roughly three dozen in number) of the Freudian society. The main tenets and central interests of Adler's psychology are (1) the inferiority complex, (2) compensation (for inferiority), (3) the striving for superiority, (4) style of life, (5) social interest, (6) fictional finalism, (7) the superiority complex, (8) the creative self, (9) the neurotic constitution, (10) organic inferiority, and (11) old remembrances.

These basic concepts in Adler's system of psychology are not disconnected ideas, but the mutually related elements of an integrated whole. Personality problems in the individual stem from an inferiority complex, which arises because of organ inferiority or his style of life (philosophical attitude or outlook on life), and for which he compensates in a variety of ways, one of which is the superiority complex. The neurotic constitution or any other personality phase springs from the creative self which produces a style of life. One's very old, i.e., earliest, memories are indicators of a given style of life. Particularly in the neurotic constitution, fictional finalism plays an important role, but every person pursues unreal ideals which function as stabilizers for his personality. The normal person shares the characteristics of the neurotic, from whom he differs principally in degree. A social interest, that is, the desire to become socialized and to free oneself from self-centeredness (narcissism), is indicative of a stable personality and a definitive sign of wholesome mental health.

Adler was born in 1870 in Vienna and died in 1937. He too entered the field of psychology through psychiatry. A charter member of the Vienna Psychoanalytic Society, he became its president and one of its foremost original thinkers, second only to Freud (Jung belonged to the international group). Encouraged by Freud, Adler engaged in those original investigations in psychoanalysis which led to his gradual but unmistakable departure from Freudian thought and to his resignation, in 1911, from the society of which he was then president. His own school of psychology he termed "individual" because it stresses the uniqueness with which each individual person develops his own style of life. In 1935 Adler's school began to publish its own organ, *International Journal of Individual Psychology*. Following World War I, Adler became interested in the psychology of children and instituted child guidance clinics in Vienna.

Among his many writings, now available in English translations, are *The Neurotic Constitution* (1917), *A Study of Organ Inferiority and Its Psychical Compensation* (1917), *The Practice and Theory of Individual Psychology* (1927), *Understanding Human Nature* (1927), *Problems of Neurosis* (1929), *The Science of Living* (1929), *The Pattern of Life* (1930), *What Life Should Mean to You* (1931), and *Social Interest: A Challenge to Mankind* (1938).

INDIVIDUAL PSYCHOLOGY[1]

Individual Psychology tries to see individual lives as a whole and regards each single reaction, each movement and impulse as an articulated part of an individual attitude towards life. Such a science is of necessity oriented in a practical sense, for with the aid of knowledge we can correct and alter our attitudes. Individual Psychology is thus *prophetic* in a double sense: not only does it predict what will happen, but, like the prophet Jonah, it predicts what *will* happen in order that it should *not* happen.

The science of Individual Psychology developed out of the effort to understand that mysterious creative power of life—that power which expresses itself in the desire to develop, to strive and to achieve—and even to compensate for defeats in one direction by striving for success in another.

[1] *The Science of Living* (London: George Allen & Unwin, 1929), from ch. 1.

This power is *teleological*—it expresses itself in the striving after a goal, and in this striving every bodily and psychic movement is made to co-operate. It is thus absurd to study bodily movements and mental conditions abstractly without relation to an individual whole. It is absurd, for instance, that in criminal psychology we should pay so much more attention to the crime than to the criminal. It is the criminal, not the crime that counts, and no matter how much we contemplate the criminal act we shall never understand its criminality unless we see it as an episode in the life of a particular individual. The same outward act may be criminal in one case and not criminal in another. The important thing is to understand the individual context—the goal of an individual's life which marks the line of direction for all of his acts and movements. This goal enables us to understand the hidden meaning behind the various separate acts—we see them as parts of a whole. Vice versa when we study the parts—provided we study them as parts of a whole—we get a better sense of the whole.

LEADING PRINCIPLES OF INDIVIDUAL PSYCHOLOGY[2]

I. Every neurosis can be understood as an attempt to free oneself from a feeling of inferiority in order to gain a feeling of superiority.

II. The path of a neurosis does not lead in the direction of social functioning, nor does it aim at solving given life-problems but finds an outlet for itself in the small family circle, thus achieving the isolation of the patient.

III. The larger unit of the social unit is either completely or very extensively pushed aside by a mechanism consisting of hypersensitiveness and intolerance. Only a small group is left over for the manoeuvres aiming at the various types of superiority to expend themselves upon. At the same time protection and the withdrawal from the demands of the community and the decisions of life are made possible.

IV. Thus estranged from reality, the neurotic man lives a life of imagination and phantasy and employs a number of devices for enabling him to side-step the demands of reality and for reaching out toward an ideal situation which would free him from any service for the community and absolve him from responsibility.

V. These exemptions and the privileges of illness and suffering give him a substitute for his original hazardous goal of superiority.

VI. Thus the neurosis and the psyche represent an attempt to free oneself from all the constraints of the community by establishing a counter-compulsion. This latter is so constituted that it effectively faces the peculiar nature of the surroundings and their demands. Both of these con-

[2]*The Practice and Theory of Individual Psychology*, trans. P. Radin (rev. ed.; London: Routledge & Kegan Paul, 1929), from ch. 3.

vincing inferences can be drawn from the manner in which this counter-compulsion manifests itself and from the neuroses selected.

VII. The counter-compulsion takes on the nature of a revolt, gathers its material either from favourable affective experiences or from observations. It permits thoughts and affects to become preoccupied either with the above-mentioned stirrings or with unimportant details, as long as they at least serve the purpose of directing the eye and the attention of the patient away from his life-problems. In this manner, depending upon the needs of the situation, he prepares anxiety- and compulsion-situations, sleeplessness, swooning, perversions, hallucinations, slightly pathological affects, neurasthenic and hypochondriacal complexes and psychotic pictures of his actual condition, all of which are to serve him as excuses.

VIII. Even logic falls under the domination of the counter-compulsion. As in psychosis this process may go as far as the actual nullification of logic.

IX. Logic, the will to live, love, human sympathy, co-operation and language, all arise out of the needs of human communal life. Against the latter are directed all the plans of the neurotic individual striving for isolation and lusting for power.

X. To cure a neurosis and a psychosis it is necessary to change completely the whole up-bringing of the patient and turn him definitely and unconditionally back upon human society.

XI. All the volition and all the strivings of the neurotic are dictated by his prestige-seeking policy, which is continually looking for excuses which will enable him to leave the problems of life unsolved. He consequently automatically turns against allowing any community-feeling to develop.

XII. If therefore we may regard the demand for a complete and unified understanding of man and for a comprehension of his (undivided) individuality as justified—a view to which we are forced both by the nature of reason and the individual-psychological knowledge of the urge toward and integration of the personality—then the method of *comparison*, the main tool of our method, enables us to arrive at some conception of the power-lines along which an individual strives to attain superiority.

The Development of Personality[3]

In the light of Individual Psychology the problem of inheritance . . . decreases in importance. It is not what one has inherited that is important, but what one does with his inheritance in the early years—that is to say, the prototype that is built up in the childhood environment. Heredity is of course responsible for inherited organic defects, but our problem there is simply to relieve the particular difficulty and place the child in a favorable situation.

[3]*The Science of Living*, from *op. cit.*

As a matter of fact we have even a great advantage here, inasmuch as when we see the defect we know how to act accordingly. Ofttimes a healthy child without any inherited defects may fare worse through malnutrition or through any of the many errors in upbringing.

In the case of children born with imperfect organs it is the psychological situation which is all-important. Because these children are placed in a more difficult situation they show marked indications of an exaggerated feeling of inferiority. At the time the prototype is being formed they are already more interested in themselves than in others, and they tend to continue that way later on in life. Organic inferiority is not the only cause of mistakes in the prototype: other situations may also cause the same mistakes—the situations of pampered and hated children, for instance. . . . These children grow up handicapped and . . . they constantly fear attacks inasmuch as they have grown up in an environment in which they never learned indepedence.

It is necessary to understand the social interest from the very outset since it is the most important part of our education, of our treatment and of our cure. Only such persons as are courageous, self-confident and at home in the world can benefit both by the difficulties and by the advantages of life. They are never afraid. They know that there are difficulties, but they also know that they can overcome them. They are prepared for all the problems of life, which are invariably social problems. From a human standpoint it is necessary to be prepared for social behavior. The three types of children we have mentioned develop a prototype with a lesser degree of social interest. They have not the mental attitude which is conducive to the accomplishment of what is necessary in life or to the solution of its difficulties. Feeling defeated, the prototype has a mistaken attitude towards the problems of life and tends to develop the personality on the useless side of life. On the other hand our task in treating patients is to develop behavior on the useful side and to establish in general a useful attitude towards life and society.

Lack of social interest is equivalent to being oriented towards the useless side of life. The individuals who lack social interest are those who make up the groups of problem children, criminals, insane persons, and drunkards. Our problem in their case is to find a means to influence them to go back to the useful side of life and to make them interested in others. In this way it may be said that our so-called Individual Psychology is actually a social psychology.

* * * * *

THE INFERIORITY COMPLEX[4]

We must always look at the whole social context of the facts we study. We must look at the social environment in order to understand the particular

[4]*Ibid.,* from ch. 2.

"goal of superiority" an individual chooses. We must look at the social situation, too, in order to understand a particular maladjustment. Thus many persons are maladjusted because they find it impossible to make normal contact with others by means of language. The stammerer is a case in point. If we examine the stammerer we shall see that since the beginning of his life he was never socially well adjusted. He did not join in activities, and he did not want friends or comrades. His language development needed association with others, but he did not want to associate. Therefore his stammering continued. There are really two tendencies in stammerers—one to associate with others, and another that makes them seek isolation for themselves.

Later in life, among adult persons not living a social life, we find that they cannot speak in public and have a tendency to stage fright. This is because they regard their audiences as enemies. They have a feeling of inferiority when confronted by a seemingly hostile and dominating audience. The fact is that only when a person trusts himself and his audience can he speak well, and only then will he not have stage fright.

The feeling of inferiority and the problem of social training are thus intimately connected. Just as the feeling of inferiority arises from a social maladjustment, so social training is the basic method by which we can all overcome our feelings of inferiority.

*　*　*　*　*

While the feeling of inferiority and the striving for superiority are universal, it would be a mistake to regard this fact as indicating that all men are equal. Inferiority and superiority are the general conditions which govern the behavior of men, but besides these conditions there are differences in bodily strength, in health, and in environment. For that reason different mistakes are made by individuals in the same given conditions. If we examine children we shall see that there is no one absolutely fixed and right manner for them to respond. They respond in their own individual ways. They strive towards a better style of life, but they all strive in their own way, making their own mistakes and their own type of approximations to success.

*　*　*　*　.*

Children strive, make mistakes, and develop in various ways according to the prototypes they formed in the first four or five years of life. The goal of each is different. One child may want to be a painter, while another may wish himself out of this world where he is a misfit. We may know how he can overcome his imperfection, but he does not know it, and too often the facts are not explained to him in the right way.

*　*　*　*　*

A given defect does not always lead to the same result. There is no necessary cause and effect relation between a physical imperfection and a bad style of life. For the physical imperfection we can often give good treatment in the form of right nutrition and thereby partly obviate the physical situation. But it is not the physical defect which causes the bad results: it is the patient's attitude which is responsible. That is why for the individual psychologist mere physical defects or exclusive physical causality does not exist, but only mistaken attitudes towards physical situations. Also that is why the individual psychologist seeks to foster a striving against the feeling of inferiority during the development of the prototype.

* * * * *

Whenever we see persons constantly in motion, with strong tempers and passions, we can always conclude that they are persons with a great feeling of inferiority. A person who knows he can overcome his difficulties will not be impatient. On the other hand he may not always accomplish what is necessary. Arrogant, impertinent, fighting children also indicate a great feeling of inferiority. It is our task in their case to look for the reasons—for the difficulties they have—in order to prescribe treatment. We should never criticise or *punish* mistakes in the style of life of the prototype.

We can recognize these prototype traits among children in very peculiar ways—in their unusual interests, in their scheming and striving to surpass others, and in building toward the goal of superiority. There is a type that does not trust himself in movement and expression. He prefers to exclude others as far as possible. He prefers not to go where he is confronted with new situations but to stay in a little circle in which he feels sure. In school, in life, in society, in marriage he does the same. He is always hoping to accomplish much in his little place in order to arrive at a goal of superiority. We find this trait among many human beings. They all forget that to accomplish results, one must be prepared to meet all situations. Everything must be faced. If one eliminates certain situations and certain persons, one has only private intelligence to justify oneself, and this is not enough. One needs all the renovating winds of social contact and common sense.

* * * * *

The key to the entire social process is to be found in the fact that persons are always striving to find a situation in which they excel. Thus children who have a great feeling of inferiority want to exclude stronger children and play with weaker children whom they can rule and domineer. This is an abnormal and pathological expression of the feeling of inferiority, for it is important to realize that it is not the sense of inferiority which matters but the degree and character of it.

The abnormal feeling of inferiority has acquired the name of "inferiority complex." But complex is not the correct word for this feeling of inferiority that permeates the whole personality. It is more than a complex, it is almost a disease whose ravages vary under different circumstances. Thus we sometimes do not notice the feeling of inferiority when a person is on his job because he feels sure of his work. On the other hand he may not be sure of himself in society or in his relations with the opposite sex, and in this way we are able to discover his true psychological situation.

We notice mistakes in a greater degree in a tense or difficult situation. It is in the difficult or new situation that the prototype appears rightly, and in fact the difficult situation is nearly always the new one. That is why . . . the expression of the degree of social interest appears in a new social situation.

*　　*　　*　　*　　*

The psychologist, if he looks closely can often see contradictions in men. Such contradictions may be considered as a sign of a feeling of inferiority. But we must also observe the movements of a person who constitutes our problem on hand. Thus, his approach, his way of meeting people, may be poor, and we must observe if he comes toward persons with a hesitating step and bodily attitude. This hesitation will often be expressed in other situations of life. There are many persons who take one step forward and one backward—a sign of a great feeling of inferiority.

Our whole task is to train such persons away from their hesitating attitude. The proper treatment for such persons is to encourage them—never to discourage them. We must make them understand that they are capable of facing difficulties and solving the problems of life. This is the only way to build self-confidence, and this is the only way the feeling of inferiority should be treated.

*　　*　　*　　*　　*

STRIVING FOR SUPERIORITY[5]

Now we have to turn to the inverse topic, the superiority complex. . . . The two complexes are naturally related. We should not be astonished if in the cases where we see an inferiority complex we find a superiority complex more or less hidden. On the other hand, if we inquire into a superiority complex and study its continuity, we can always find a more or less hidden inferiority complex.

We must bear in mind of course that the word complex as attached to inferiority and superiority merely represents an exaggerated condition of the sense of inferiority and the striving for superiority. If we look at things this way it takes away the apparent paradox of two contradictory tendencies, the inferiority complex and the superiority complex, existing in the same individual. For it is obvious that as normal sentiments the striving for superiority and the feeling of inferiority are naturally complementary. We should not strive to be superior and to succeed if we did not feel a certain lack in our present condition. Now inasmuch as the so-called complexes de-

[5]*Ibid.*, from ch. 3.

velop out of the natural sentiments, there is no more contradiction in them than in the sentiments.

The striving for superiority never ceases. It constitutes in fact the mind, the psyche of the individual. As we have said, life is the attainment of a goal or form, and it is the striving for superiority which sets the attainment of form into motion. It is like a stream which drags along all the material it can find. If we look at lazy children and see their lack of activity, their lack of interest in anything, we should say that they do not seem to be moving. But nonetheless we find in them a desire to be superior.

* * * * *

We see children who start stealing suffering from the feeling of superiority. They believe they are deceiving others; that others do not know they are stealing. Thus they are richer with little effort. This same feeling is very pronounced among criminals who have the idea that they are superior heroes. . . . If a murderer thinks himself a hero, it is a private idea. He is lacking in courage since he wants to arrange matters so that he escapes the solution of the problems of life. Criminality is thus the result of a superiority complex and not the expression of fundamental and original viciousness.

* * * * *

Melancholy and insane persons are always the center of attention in the family. In them we see the power wielded by the inferiority complex. They complain that they feel weak and are losing weight, etc., but nonetheless they are the strongest of all. They dominate healthy persons. This fact should not surprise us, for in our culture weakness can be quite strong and powerful. (In fact if we were to ask ourselves who is the strongest person in our culture, the logical answer would be, the baby. The baby rules and cannot be dominated.)

Let us study the connection between the superiority complex and inferiority. Let us take for example a problem child with a superiority complex—a child that is impertinent, arrogant and pugnacious. We shall find that he always wants to appear greater than he really is. We all know how children with temper tantrums want to control others by getting a sudden attack. Why are they so impatient? Because they are not sure they are strong enough to attain their goal. They feel inferior. We will always discover in fighting, aggressive children an inferiority complex and a desire to overcome it. It is as if they were trying to lift themselves on their toes by this easy method of success, pride and superiority.

* * * * *

If a person is a show-off it is only because he feels inferior, because he does not feel strong enough to compete with others on the useful side of life. That is why he stays on the useless side. He is not in harmony with society. He is not socially adjusted, and he does not know how to solve the social problems of life. And so we always find a struggle between him and his parents and teachers during his childhood.

* * * * *

Now we will find among these other children that they all have an inferiority complex and are striving toward a superiority complex. So long as they are interested not only in themselves but in others, they will solve their problems of life satisfactorily. But if their inferiority complex is clearly marked, they find themselves living, as it were, in an enemy country—always looking out for their own interests rather than for those of others, and thus not having the right amount of communal sense. They approach the social question of life with a feeling that is not conducive to their solution. And so, seeking relief, they go over to the useless side of life. We know that this is not really relief, but it seems like relief not to solve questions but to be supported by others. They are like beggars, who are being supported by others and who feel comfortable neurotically exploiting their weakness.

It seems to be a trait of human nature that when individuals—both children and adults—feel weak, they cease to be interested socially but strive for superiority. They want to solve the problems of life in such a way as to obtain personal superiority without any admixture of social interest. As long as a person strives for superiority and tempers it with social interest, he is on the useful side of life and can accomplish good. But if he lacks social interest, he is not really prepared for the solution of the problems of life. . . . A superiority complex may sometimes be hidden, not recognized as present, yet existing in fact as a compensation for the inferiority complex.

* * * * *

The superiority complex and inferiority complex agree on one point, namely, that they are always on the useless side. We can never find an arrogant, impertinent child, one with a superiority complex, on the useful side of life.

* * * * *

Our civilization does not regard pampered children with favor. Sometimes the father realizes this and wants to end this state of affairs. Sometimes the school comes into the situation. The position of such a child is always in danger and for this reason the pampered child feels inferior. We do not notice this feeling of inferiority among pampered children so long as they are in a favorable situation, but the moment an unfavorable situation arises we see these children either breaking down and becoming depressed or developing a superiority complex.

* * * * *

Individual Psychology was trying to find out the importance of positions in sleep indicating a person's feeling of superiority or inferiority. One can see that such information might prove useful. Some persons lie in bed in a curved line like a hedgehog, covering their heads with the covers. This expresses an inferiority complex. Can we believe such a person to be courageous? Or if we see a person stretched out straight, can we believe him weak or bent in life? Both in a literal and metaphorical way he will appear great, as he does in sleep. It has been observed that persons who sleep on their stomachs are stubborn and pugnacious.

*   *   *   *   *

There is the case of a boy of fifteen who entered an asylum for the insane because of his hallucinations. . . . We are able to understand what happened in the case of this boy. In the beginning he had an inferiority complex because he was undersized and hence derided by the guests in the restaurant. But he was constantly striving for superiority. He wanted to be a teacher. But because he was blocked in attaining this occupation, he found another goal of superiority by making a detour to the useless side of life. He became superior in sleep and dreams.

Thus we see that the goal of superiority may be on the useless or useful side of life. If a person is benevolent, for instance, it may mean either of two things—it may mean that he is socially adjusted and wants to help, or else it may mean simply that he wants to boast. The psychologist meets with many whose main goal is to boast. There is the case of a boy who was not very accomplished in school; in fact he was so bad that he became a truant and stole things, but he was always boastful. He did these things because of his inferiority complex. He wanted to accomplish results in some line—be it only the line of cheap vanity. . . . In all his behavior his great striving was to appear greater than others—and greater than he really was.

A similar tendency may be remarked in the behavior of criminals—the tendency to claim easy success, which we have already discussed in another connection. The New York newspapers some time ago reported how a burglar broke into the home of some schoolteachers and had a discussion with them. The burglar told the women they did not know how much trouble there was in ordinary honest occupations. It was much easier to be a burglar than to work. This man had escaped to the useless side of life. But by taking this road he had developed a certain superiority complex. He felt stronger than the women, particularly since he was armed·and they were not. But did he realize that he was a coward? We know he is because we see him as a person who had escaped his inferiority complex by going over to the useless side of life. He thought himself to be a hero, however, and not a coward.

Some types turn to suicide and desire in this way to throw off the whole world with its difficulties. They seem not to care for life and so feel superior, although they are really cowards. We see that a superiority complex is a second phase. It is a compensation for the inferiority complex. We must always try to find the organic connection—the connection which may seem to be a contradiction but which is quite in the course of human nature, as we have already shown. Once this connection is found we are in a position to treat both the inferiority and superiority complexes.

We should not conclude the general subject of inferiority and superiority complexes without saying a few words as to the relation of these complexes to normal persons. Everyone, as we have said, has a feeling of inferiority. But the feeling of inferiority is not a disease, it is rather a stimulant to healthy normal striving and development. It becomes a pathological condition only when the sense of inadequacy overwhelms the individual, and so far from stimulating him to useful activity, makes him depressed and incapable of development. Now the superiority complex is one of the ways which a person with an inferiority complex may use as a method of escape from difficulties. He assumes that he is superior when he is not, and this false success compensates him for the state of inferiority which he cannot bear. The normal person does not have a superiority complex, he does not even have a sense of superiority. He has the striving to be superior in the sense that we all have ambition to be successful, but so long as this striving is expressed in work it does not lead to false valuations, which is at the root of mental disease.

STYLE OF LIFE[6]

If we look at a pine tree growing in the valley we will notice that it grows differently from one on top of a mountain. It is the same kind of a tree, a pine, but there are two distinct styles of life. Its style on top of the mountain is different from its style when growing in the valley. The style of life of a tree is the individuality of a tree expressing itself and moulding itself in an environment. We recognize a style when we see it against a background of an environment different from what we expect, for then we realize that every tree has a life pattern and is not merely a mechanical reaction to the environment.

It is much the same way with human beings. We see the style of life under certain conditions of environment and it is our task to analyze its exact relation to the existing circumstances, inasmuch as mind changes with alteration of the environment. As long as a person is in a favorable situation we cannot see his style of life clearly. In new situations, however, where he is confronted with difficulties, the style of life appears clearly and distinctly. A trained psychologist could perhaps understand a style of life of a human being even in a favorable situation, but it becomes apparent to everybody when the human subject is put into unfavorable or difficult situations.

*   *   *   *   *

[6]*Ibid.*, from ch. 4.

The style of life is a unity because it has grown out of the difficulties of early life and out of the striving for a goal. But we are not so much interested in the past as in the future. And in order to understand a person's future we must understand his style of life. Even if we understand instincts, stimuli, drive, etc., we cannot predict what must happen. Some psychologists indeed try to reach conclusions by noting certain instincts, impressions or traumas, but on closer examination it will be found that all these elements presuppose a consistent style of life. Thus whatever stimulates, stimulates only to *save* and *fix* a style of life.

*　　*　　*　　*　　*

We have seen how human beings with weak organs, because they face difficulties and feel insecure, suffer from a feeling or complex of inferiority. But as human beings cannot endure this for long, the inferiority feeling stimulates them, as we have seen, to movement and action. This results in a person having a goal. Now Individual Psychology has long called the consistent movement toward this goal a plan of life. But because this name has sometimes led to mistakes among students, it is now called a style of life.

Because an individual has a style of life, it is possible to predict his future sometimes just on the basis of talking to him and having him answer questions. It is like looking at the fifth act of a drama, where all the mysteries are solved. We can make predictions in this way because we know the phases, the difficulties and the questions of life. Thus from experience and knowledge of a few facts we can tell what will happen to children who always separate themselves from others, who are looking for support, who are pampered and who hesitate in approaching situations. What happens in the case of a person whose goal it is to be supported by others? Hesitating, he stops or escapes the solution of the questions of life. We know he can hesitate, stop, or escape, because we have seen the same things happen a thousand times. We know that he does not want to proceed alone but wants to be pampered. He wants to stay far away from the great problems of life, and he occupies himself with useless things rather than struggle with the useful ones. He lacks social interests, and as a result he may develop into a problem child, a neurotic, a criminal, or a suicide—that final escape. All these things are now better understood than formerly.

We realize, for instance, that in looking for the style of life of a human being we may use the normal style of life as a basis for measurement. We use the socially adjusted human being as a standard, and we can measure the variations from the normal.

*　　*　　*　　*　　*

And now let us take up the reasons for this style of life. Individual Psychology undertakes to analyze the causes for a style of life. This man established his style of life during the first four or five years. At that time some tragedy happened which moulded and formed him, and so we have to look for the tragedy. . . . We must mention the fact that he was a first child. . . . In many cases we need only ask a patient, Are you the first, second, or third child? Then we have all we need. We can also use an entirely different method: we can ask for old remembrances. . . . This method is worthwhile because these remembrances or first pictures are a part of the building up of the early style of life which we have called the prototype. One comes upon an actual part of the prototype when a person tells of his early re-membrances. Looking back, everybody remembers certain important things, and indeed what is fixed in memory is always important. There are schools of psychology which act on the opposite assumption. They believe that what a person has forgotten is the most important point, but there is really no great difference between the two ideas. Perhaps a person can tell us his conscious remembrances, but he does not know what they mean. He does not know their connection with his actions. Hence the result is the same, whether we emphasize the hidden or forgotten significance of conscious memories or the importance of forgotten memories.

Little descriptions of old remembrances are highly illuminating. Thus a man might tell you that when he was small, his mother took him and his younger brother to market. That is enough. We can then discover his style of life. He pictures himself and a younger brother. Therefore we see it must have been important to him to have had a younger brother. Lead him further and you may find a situation similar to a certain one in which a man recalled that it began to rain that day. His mother took him in her arms, but when she saw the younger brother she put him down to carry the little one. Thus we can picture his style of life. He always has the ex-pectation that another person will be preferred. And so we can understand why he cannot speak in society for he is always looking around to see if another will not be preferred. The same is true with friendship. He is al-ways thinking that another is more preferred by his friend, and as a result he can never have a true friend. He is constantly suspicious, looking out for little things that disturb friendship.

* * * * *

Let us look at another specific case—the case of a man afflicted with melancholia. This is a very common illness, but it can be cured. Such per-sons are distinguishable very early in life. In fact we notice many children who in their approach to a new situation show signs of suffering from melancholia. This melancholy man of whom we are speaking had about ten attacks, and these always occurred when he took a new position. As long as he was in his old position he was nearly normal. But he did not want to go out into society and he wanted to rule others. Consequently he had no friends and at fifty he had not married.

Let us look at his childhood in order to study his style of life. He had been very sensitive and quarrelsome, always ruling his older brothers and sisters by emphasizing his pains and weaknesses. When playing on a couch one day, he pushed them all off. When his aunt reproached him for this, he said, "Now my whole life is ruined because you have blamed me!" And at that time he was only four or five years old.

Such was his style of life—always trying to rule others, always complaining of his weakness and of how he suffered. This trait led in his later life to melancholy, which in itself is simply an expression of weakness. . . . Frequently such a person has been pampered and is so no longer, and this influences his style of life.

Human beings in their reactions to situations are much like the different species of animals. A hare reacts differently to the same situation from a wolf or a tiger. So it is with human individuals. The experiment was once made of taking three different types of boys to a lion's cage in order to see how they would behave on seeing this terrible animal for the first time. The first boy turned and said, "Let's go home." The second boy said, "How nice!" He wanted to appear courageous but he was trembling when he said it. He was a coward. The third boy said, "May I spit at him?" Here then we see three different reactions, three different ways of experiencing the same situation. We see also that for the most part human beings have a tendency to be afraid.

This timidity, when expressed in a social situation, is one of the most frequent causes of maladjustment. . . . We must make all children independent, and this can be done only if we get them to understand the mistakes in their style of life.

OLD REMEMBRANCES[7]

Having analyzed the significance of an individual's style of life, we turn now to the topic of old remembrances, which are perhaps the most important means for getting at a style of life. By looking back through childhood memories we are able to uncover the prototype—the core of the style of life—better than by any other method.

If we want to find out the style of life of a person—child or adult—we should, after we have heard a little about his complaints, ask him for old remembrances and then compare them with the other facts he has given. For the most part the style of life never changes. There is always the same person with the same personality, the same unity. A style of life, as we have shown, is built up through the striving for a particular goal of superiority, and so we must expect every word, act and feeling to be an organic part of the whole "action line." Now at some points this "action line" is more clearly expressed. This happens particularly in old remembrances.

We should not, however, distinguish too sharply between old and new

[7]*Ibid.*, from ch. 5.

remembrances, for in new remembrances also the action line is involved. It is easier and more illuminating to find the action line in the beginning, for then we discover the theme and are able to understand how the style of life of a person does not really change. In the style of life formed at the age of four or five we find the connection between remembrances of the past and actions of the present. And so after many observations of this kind we can hold fast to the theory that in these old remembrances we can always find a real part of the patient's prototype.

(6) When a patient looks back into his past we can be sure that anything his memory will turn up will be of emotional interest to him, and thus we find a clue to his personality. It is not to be denied that the forgotten experiences are also important for the style of life and for the prototype, but many times it is more difficult to find out the forgotten remembrances, or, as they are called, the unconscious remembrances. Both conscious and unconscious remembrances have the common quality of running towards the same goal of superiority. They are both a part of the complete prototype. It is well, therefore, to find both the conscious and unconscious remembrances if possible. Both conscious and unconscious remembrances are in the end about equally important, and the individual himself generally understands neither. It is for the outsider to understand and interpret both of them.

*　　*　　*　　*　　*

As we have explained in the last chapter it is convenient for certain purposes to classify individuals into types. Now old remembrances go according to types and reveal what is to be expected of the behavior of a particular type. For instance, let us take the case of a person who remembers that he saw a marvelous Christmas tree, filled with lights, presents and holiday cakes. What is the most interesting thing in this story? *That he saw.* Why does he tell us that he has seen? Because he is always interested in visual things. He has struggled against some difficulties in sight, and, having been trained, has always been interested and attentive to seeing. Perhaps this is not the most important element of his style of life, but it is an interesting and important part. It indicates that if we are to give him an occupation it should be one in which he will use his eyes.

*　　*　　*　　*　　*

One of the most significant types of old remembrances is the memory of a death during the period of childhood. When children see a person die suddenly and abruptly, the effect on their minds is very marked. Sometimes such children become morbid. Sometimes, without becoming morbid, they devote their whole lives to the problem of death and are always occupied in struggling against illness and death in some form. We may find many of these children interested in medicine later in life, and they may become physicians or chemists. Such a goal of course is on the useful side of life. They not only struggle against death but help others to do so. Sometimes, however, the prototype develops a very egotistical point of view. A child who was very much affected by the death of an older sister was asked what he wanted to be. The answer expected was that he would be a physician; instead he replied: "A grave-digger." He was asked why he wanted to follow this occupation, and he answered, "Because I want to be the one to bury the others and not the one buried." The goal, we see, is on the useless side of life, for the boy is interested only in himself.

*   *   *   *   *

If we can obtain such old remembrances we can predict, as we have said, what will happen later in the life of our patients. However, it must be remembered that old remembrances are not reasons, they are hints. They are signs of what happened and how development took place. They indicate the movement toward a goal and what obstacles had to be overcome. They show how a person becomes more interested in one side of life than another. We see that he may have what we call a trauma, along the lines of sex, for instance; that is, he may be more interested in such matters than in others.

*   *   *   *   *

CHILDHOOD EXPERIENCES AND PROBLEM CHILDREN[8]

We have gathered from previous discussions that the style of life of a child in a family is fixed after it is four or five years old and cannot directly be changed. This indicates the way in which the modern school has to go. It must not criticise or punish, but try to mould, educate and develop the social interest of children. The modern school cannot work on the principle of suppression and censorship, but rather on the idea of trying to understand and solve the personal problems of the child.

*   *   *   *   *

Normal children, if there be such, do not concern us. We would not touch them. If we see children who are fully developed and socially adjusted, the best thing is not to suppress them. They should go their own way because such children can be depended upon to look for a goal on the useful side in order to develop the sense of superiority. Their superiority feeling, precisely because it is on the useful side, is not a superiority complex.

On the other hand both the feeling of superiority and the feeling of inferiority exist on the useless side among problem children, neurotics, criminals, etc. Such persons express a superiority complex as a compen-

8*Ibid.*, from ch. 8.

sation for their inferiority complex. The feeling of inferiority, as we have shown, exists in every human being, but this feeling becomes a complex only when it discourages him to the point of stimulating training on the useless side of life.

All these problems of inferiority and superiority have their root in family life during the period before the child enters school. It is during this period that he has built up his style of life, which in contrast with the adult style of life we have designated as a prototype. This prototype is the unripe fruit, and like an unripe fruit, if there is some trouble with it, if there is a worm, the more it develops and ripens the larger the worm grows.

As we have seen, the worm or difficulty develops from problems over imperfect organs. It is the difficulty with imperfect organs that is the usual root of the feeling of inferiority, and here again we must remember that it is not the organic inferiority that causes the problem but the social maladjustments which it brings in its wake. It is this that provides the educational opportunity. Train a person to adjust himself socially and the organic inferiorities, so far from being liabilities, may become assets. For as we have seen, an organic inferiority may be the origin of a very striking interest, developed through training, which may rule the individual's whole life, and provided this interest runs in a useful channel, it may mean a great deal to the individual.

* * * * *

Besides the children with imperfect organs, a problem is presented by the great number of pampered children who come to school. Now the way schools are organized, it is physically impossible for a single child always to remain the center of attention. It may indeed happen occasionally that a teacher is so kind and soft-hearted that she plays favorites, but as the child moves from grade to grade it falls out of its position of favor. Later in life it is even worse, for it is not considered proper in our civilization for one person always to be the center of attention, without doing anything to merit it.

All such problem children have certain defined characteristics. They are not well fitted for the problems of life; they are very ambitious, and want to rule personally, not in behalf of society. In addition they are always quarrelsome and at enmity with others. They are usually cowards, since they lack interest in all the problems of life. A pampered childhood has not prepared them for life's problems.

Other characteristics which we discover among such children is that they are cautious and continually hesitating. They postpone the solution of the problems that life presents to them. Or else they come to a stop altogether before problems, going off on distractions and never finishing anything.

* * * * *

Both the pampered-child and the organ-inferiority type of children always want to "exclude" the difficulties of life because of their great feeling of inferiority which robs them of strength to cope with them. However, we may control the difficulties at school, and thus gradually put them in a position to solve problems. The school thus becomes a place where we really educate, and not merely give instruction.

Besides these two types, we have to consider the hated child. The hated child is usually ugly, mistaken, crippled, and in no way prepared for social life. He has, perhaps, the greatest difficulty of all three types upon entering school.

* * * * *

Besides these specifically problem children, there are also the children who are believed to be prodigies—the exceptionally bright children. Sometimes because they are ahead in some subjects it is easy for them to appear brilliant in others. They are sensitive, ambitious, and not usually very well liked by their comrades. Children immediately seem to feel whether one of their number is socially adjusted or not. Such prodigies are admired but not beloved.

We can understand how many of these prodigies pass through school satisfactorily. But when they enter social life they have no adequate plan of life. When they approach the three great problems of life—society, occupation, and love and marriage—their difficulties come out. What happened in their prototype years becomes apparent, and we see the effect of their not being well adjusted in the family.

* * * * *

The solution that Individual Psychology offers for the problems of prodigies is the same as that for other problem children. The individual psychologist says, "Everybody can accomplish everything." This is a democratic maxim which takes the edge off prodigies, who are always burdened with expectations, are always pushed forward and become too much interested in their own persons. Persons who adopt this maxim can have very brilliant children, and these children do not have to become conceited or too ambitious. They understand that what they have accomplished was the result of training and good fortune. . . . But, other children, who are less favorably influenced and not as well trained and educated, may also accomplish good things if their teacher can make them understand the method.

* * * * *

SOCIAL INTEREST[9]

The goal of Individual Psychology is *social* adjustment. This may seem a paradox, but if it is a paradox, it is so only verbally. The fact is that it is

[9]*Ibid.*, from chs. 9-11.

only when we pay attention to the concrete psychological life of the individual do we come to realize how all-important is the social element. The individual becomes an individual only in a social context. Other systems of psychology make a distinction between what they call individual psychology and social psychology, but for us there is no such distinction. Our discussions hitherto have attempted to analyze the individual style of life, but the analysis has always been with a social point of view and for a social application.

*   *   *   *   *

We have seen that social maladjustments are caused by the social consequences of the sense of inferiority and the striving for superiority. The terms inferiority complex and superiority complex already express the result after a maladjustment has taken place. These complexes are not in the germplasm, they are not in the blood-stream: they simply happen in the course of the interaction of the individual and his social environment. Why don't they happen to all individuals? All individuals have a sense of inferiority and a striving for success and superiority which makes up the very life of the psyche. The reason all individuals do not have complexes is that their sense of inferiority and superiority is harnessed by a psychological mechanism into socially useful channels. The springs of this mechanism are social interest, courage, and social mindedness, or the logic of common sense.

*   *   *   *   *

As long as the feeling of inferiority is not too great, we know that a child will always strive to be worth while and on the useful side of life. Such a child, in order to gain his end, is interested in others. Social feeling and social adjustment are the right and normal compensations, and in a sense it is almost impossible to find anybody—child or adult—in whom the striving for superiority has not resulted in such development. We can never find anyone who could say truly, "I am not interested in others." He may act this way—he may act as if he were not interested in the world— but he cannot justify himself. Rather does he claim to be interested in others, in order to hide his lack of social adjustment. This is mute testimony to the universality of the social feeling.

Nonetheless maladjustments do take place. We can study their genesis by considering marginal cases—cases where an inferiority complex exists but is not openly expressed on account of a favorable environment. The complex is then hidden, or at least a tendency to hide it is shown. Thus if a person is not confronted with a difficulty, he may look wholly satisfied. But if we look closely we shall see how he really expresses—if not in words or opinions, at least in attitudes—the fact that he feels inferior. This is an inferiority complex and is the result of an exaggerated feeling of inferiority. People who are suffering from such a complex are always looking for relief from the burdens which they have imposed upon themselves through their self-centeredness.

It is rather interesting to observe how some persons hide their inferiority complex, while others confess, "I am suffering from an inferiority complex." The confessors are always elated at their confession. They feel greater than others because they have confessed while others cannot. They say to themselves, "I am honest. I do not lie about the cause of my suffering." But at the very moment that they confess their inferiority complex, they hint at some difficulties in their lives or other circumstances which are responsible for their situation. They may speak of their parents or family, of not being well educated, or of some accident, curtailment, suppression, or other things.

Often the inferiority complex may be hidden by a superiority complex, which serves as a compensation. Such persons are arrogant, impertinent, conceited and snobbish. They lay more weight on appearances than on actions.

*   *   *   *   *

An inferiority complex may also be indicated by such characteristics as slyness, cautiousness, pedantry, the exclusion of the greater problems of life, and the search for a narrow field of action which is limited by many principles and rules. It is also a sign of an inferiority complex if a person always leans on a stick. Such a person does not trust himself, and we will find that he develops queer interests. He is always occupied with little things, such as collecting newspapers or advertisements. They waste their time this way and always excuse themselves. They train too much on the useless side, and this training when long continued leads to a compulsion neurosis.

An inferiority complex is usually hidden in all problem children no matter what type of problem the children present on the surface. Thus to be lazy is in reality to exclude the important tasks of life and is a sign of a complex. To steal is to take advantage of the insecurity or absence of another; to lie is not to have the courage to tell the truth. All these manifestations in children have an inferiority complex as their core.

*   *   *   *   *

In all these cases where complexes develop, the failure to function in social and useful channels is due to a lack of courage on the part of the individual. It is this lack of courage which prevents him from following the social course. Side by side with the lack of courage are the intellectual accompaniments of a failure to understand the necessity and utility of the social course.

All this is most clearly illustrated in the behavior of criminals—who are really cases of inferiority complexes par excellence. Criminals are cowardly and stupid; their cowardice and social stupidity go together as two parts of the same tendency.

Drinking may be analyzed on similar lines. The drunkard seeks relief from his problems, and is cowardly enough to be satisfied with the relief that comes from the useless side of life.

The ideology and intellectual outlook of such persons differentiate themselves sharply from the social common sense which accompanies the courageous attitudes of normal persons. Criminals, for instance, always make excuses or accuse others. They mention unprofitable conditions of labor. They speak of the cruelty of society in not supporting them. Or they say the stomach commands and cannot be ruled. When sentenced, they always find such excuses as that of the child-murderer Hickman, who said, "It was done by a command from above." Another murderer, upon being sentenced, said, "What is the use of such a boy as I have killed? There are a million other boys. . . ."

Social interest is a slow growth. Only those persons who are really trained in the direction of social interest from their first childhood and who are always striving on the useful side of life will actually have social feeling. For this reason it is not particularly difficult to recognize whether a person is really well prepared for life with the other sex or not.

* * * * *

Marriage and Sex[10]

An understanding of the nature of social interest shows us that the problems of love and marriage can be solved satisfactorily only on the basis of entire equality. This fundamental give-and-take is the important thing; whether one partner esteems the other is not very significant. . . . It is only when there is a proper foundation of equality that love will take the right course and make marriage a success.

If either the man or the woman wishes to be a conqueror after marriage, the results are likely to be fatal. Looking forward to marriage with such a view in mind is not the right preparation, and the events after marriage are likely to prove it. It is not possible to be a conqueror in a situation in which there is no place for a conqueror. The marriage situation calls for an interest in the other person and an ability to put oneself in the other's place.

* * * * *

We can see how all the indications manifested in childhood are emphasized and increased when a person faces the problem of love. We can imagine how a person suffering from an inferiority complex will behave in sexual matters. Perhaps because he feels weak and inferior he will express the feeling by always wanting to be supported by other persons. Often such

[10]Ibid., from chs. 11-12.

a type has an ideal which is motherly in character. Or sometimes, by way of compensation for his inferiority, he may take the opposite direction in love and become arrogant, impudent and aggressive.

* * * * *

If we look closely we see that the mate that many a person seeks is really a victim. Such persons do not understand that the sex relationship cannot be exploited for such an end. For if one person seeks to be a conqueror, the other will want to be a conqueror also. As a result life in common becomes impossible. The idea of satisfying one's complexes illuminates certain peculiarities in the choice of a partner which are otherwise difficult to understand. It tells us why some persons choose weak, sick, or old persons: they choose them because they believe things will be easier for them. Sometimes they look for a married person: here it is a case of never wanting to reach a solution of a problem. Sometimes we find people falling in love with two men or two women at the same time, because . . . "two girls are less than one." . . .

Spoiled children show up in marriage true to type. They want to be pampered by their marital partners.

* * * * *

We can understand what happens when a person feels himself misunderstood and his activity curtailed. He feels and wants to escape. Such feelings are especially bad in marriage, particularly if a sense of extreme hopelessness arises. When this happens revenge begins to creep in. One person wants to disturb the life of the other person. The most common way to do this is to be unfaithful. Infidelity is always a revenge. True, persons who are unfaithful always justify themselves by speaking of love and sentiments, but we know the value of feelings and sentiments. Feelings always agree with the goal of superiority, and should not be regarded as arguments.

* * * * *

Questions of love and marriage can be solved only by socially adjusted persons. The mistakes in the majority of cases are due to lack of social interest, and these mistakes can be obviated only if the persons change. Marriage is a task for two persons. Now it is a fact that we are educated either for tasks that can be performed by one person alone or else by twenty persons—never for a task for two persons. But despite our lack of education the marriage task can be handled properly if the two persons recognize the mistakes in their character and approach things in a spirit of equality.

It is almost needless to add that the highest form of marriage is monogamy. There are many persons who claim on pseudoscientific grounds that polygamy is better adapted to the nature of human beings. This conclusion cannot be accepted, and the reason it cannot be accepted is that in our culture love and marriage are social tasks. We do not marry for our private good only, but indirectly for the social good. In the last analysis marriage is for the sake of the race.

*   *   *   *   *

Many doctors and psychologists believe that the development of sexuality is the basis for the development of the whole mind and psyche, as well as for all the physical movements. In the view of the present writer this is not true, inasmuch as the whole form and development of sexuality is dependent upon the personality—the style of life and the prototype.

Thus, for example, if we know that a child expresses his sexuality in a certain way, or that another child suppresses it, we may guess what will happen to both of them in their adult life. If we know that the child always wants to be the center of attention and to conquer, then he will also develop his sexuality so as to conquer and be the center of attention.

Many persons believe that they are superior and dominant when they express their sex instinct polygamously. They therefore have sex relations with many, and it is easy to see that they deliberately overstress their sexual desires and attitudes for psychological reasons. They think that thereby they will be conquerors. This is an illusion, of course, but it serves as a compensation for an inferiority complex.

It is the inferiority complex which is the core of sexual abnormalities. A person who suffers from an inferiority complex is always looking for the easiest way out. Sometimes he finds this easiest way by excluding most of life and exaggerating his sexual life.

*   *   *   *   *

A certain Frenchman has remarked that man is the only animal that eats when he is not hungry, drinks when he is not thirsty and has sex relations at all times. The over-indulgence of the sex instinct is really quite on a par with the over-indulgence of other appetites. Now when any appetite is over-indulged and any interest is overdeveloped, the harmony of life is interfered with. Psychological annals are full of cases of persons who develop interests or appetites to the point where they become a compulsion with them. The cases of misers who overstress the importance of money are familiar to the common man. But there are also the cases of persons who think cleanliness all important. They put washing ahead of all other activities and at times they wash the whole day and half the night. Then there are persons who insist on the paramount importance of eating. They eat all day long, are interested only in eatables, and talk about nothing but eating.

The cases of sexual excess are precisely similar. They lead to an unbalancing of the entire harmony of activity. Inevitably they drag the whole style of life to the useless side.

In the proper training of the sex instinct the sexual drives should be harnessed to a useful goal in which the whole of our activities are expressed. If the goal is properly chosen neither sexuality nor any other expression of life will be overstressed.

On the other hand while all appetites and interests have to be controlled and harmonized, there is danger in complete suppression. Just as in the matter of food, when a person diets to the extreme, his mind and body suffer, so, too, in the matter of sex complete abstinence is undesirable.

What this statement implies is that in a normal style of life sex will find its proper expression. It does not mean that we can overcome neuroses, which are the marks of an unbalanced style of life, merely by sex expression. The belief, so much propagated, that a suppressed libido is the cause of a neurosis is untrue. Rather it is the other way around: Neurotic persons do not find their proper sex expression.

One meets persons who have been advised to give more free expression to their sex instincts and who have followed that advice, only to make their condition worse. The reason things work out that way is that such persons fail to harness their sexual life with a socially useful goal, which alone can change their neurotic condition. The expressions of sex instinct by itself does not cure the neurosis, for the neurosis is a disease in the style of life, if we may use the term, and it can be cured only by ministering to the style of life.

For the individual psychologist all this is so clear that he does not hesitate to fall back on happy marriage as the only satisfactory solution for sex troubles. A neurotic does not look with favor on such a solution, because a neurotic is always a coward and not well prepared for social life. Similarly all persons who overstress sexuality, talk of polygamy, and companionate or trial marriage are trying to escape the social solution of the sex problem. They have no patience for solving the problem of social adjustment on the basis of mutual interest between husband and wife and dream of escape through some new formula. The most difficult road, however, is sometimes the most direct.

STRIVING FOR SUPERIORITY AND FICTIONAL FINALISM[11]

Let me observe that if I know the goal of a person I know in a general way what will happen. I am in a position to bring into their proper order each of the successive movements made, to view them in their connections, to correct them and to make, where necessary, the required adaptations for my approximate psychological knowledge of these associations. If I am acquainted only with the causes, know only the reflexes, the reaction-times,

[11]*The Practice and Theory of Individual Psychology, op. cit.,* from ch. 1.

the ability to repeat and such facts, I am aware of nothing that actually takes place in the soul of the man.

* * * * *

If we look at the matter more closely, we shall find the following law holding in the development of all psychic happenings: *we cannot think, feel, will, or act without perception of some goal.* For all the causalities in the world would not suffice to conquer the chaos of the future nor obviate the planlessness to which we would be bound to fall a victim. All activity would persist in the stage of uncontrolled gropings; the economy visible in our psychic life unattained; we should be unintegrated and in every aspect of our physiognomy, in every personal touch, similar to organisms of the rank of the amoeba.

No one will deny that by assuming an objective for our psychic life we accommodate ourselves better to reality. This can be easily demonstrated. For its truth in individual examples, where phenomena are torn from their proper connections, no doubt exists. Only watch, from this point of view, the attempts at walking made by a small child or a woman recovering from a confinement. Naturally he who approaches this whole matter without any theory is likely to find its deeper significance escape him. Yet it is a fact that before the first step has been taken the objective of a person's movement has already been determined.

In the same way it can be demonstrated that all psychic activities are given direction by means of a previously determined goal. All the temporary and partially visible objectives, after the short period of psychic development of childhood, are under the domination of an imagined terminal goal, of a final point and conceived of as definitely fixed. In other words the psychic life of man is made to fit into the fifth act like a character drawn by a good dramatist.

The conclusion thus to be drawn from the unbiased study of any personality viewed from the standpoint of individual-psychology leads us to the following important proposition: *every psychic phenomenon, if it is to give us any understanding of a person, can only be grasped and understood if regarded as a preparation for some goal.* To what extent this conception promotes our psychological understanding, is clearly apparent as soon as we become aware of the *multiplicity of meaning of those psychical processes that have been torn from their proper context.*

* * * * *

Our science demands a markedly individualizing procedure and is consequently not much given to generalizations. For general guidance I would like to propound the following rule: *as soon as the goal of a psychic movement or its life-plan has been recognized, then we are to assume that all the movements of its constituent parts will coincide with both the goal and the life-plan.*

This formulation, with some minor provisos, is to be maintained in the widest sense. It retains its value even if inverted: *the properly understood part-movements must when combined, give the picture of an integrated life-plan and final goal.* Consequently we insist that, without worrying about the *tendencies, milieu and experiences,* all psychical powers are under the control of a directive idea and all expressions of emotion, feeling, thinking, willing, acting, dreaming as well as psychopathological phenomena, are permeated by one unified life-plan. Let me, by a slight suggestion, prove and yet soften down these heretical propositions: more important than tendencies, objective experience and milieu is *the subjective evaluation,* an evaluation which stands furthermore in a certain, often strange, relation to realities. Out of this evaluation however, which generally results in the development of a permanent mood *of the nature of a feeling of inferiority* there arises, depending upon the unconscious technique of our thought-apparatus, an imagined goal, an attempt at a planned final compensation and a life-plan.

* * * * *

Let me emphasize the fact that the dynamics of psychic life that I am about to describe hold equally for healthy and diseased. What distinguishes the nervous from the healthy individual is the stronger safeguarding tendency with which the former's life-plan is filled. With regard to the "positing of a goal" and the life-plan adjusted to it there are no fundamental differences.

I shall consequently speak of a general goal of man. A thorough-going study has taught us that we can best understand the manifold and diverse movements of the psyche as soon as our *most general presupposition,* that the psyche has as its objective the *goal of superiority,* is recognized. . . . Whether a person desires to be an artist, and first in his profession, or a tyrant in his home, to hold converse with God or humiliate other people: whether he regards his suffering as the most important thing in the world to which everyone must show obeisance, whether he is chasing after unattainable ideals or old deities, overstepping all limits and norms, at every part of his way he is guided and spurred on by his longing for superiority, the thought of his godlikeness, the belief in his special magical power.

* * * * *

This goal of complete superiority, with its strange appearance at times, does not come from the world of reality. Inherently we must place it under "fictions" and "imaginations." Of these Vaihinger (*The Philosophy of "As If"*) rightly says that their importance lies in the fact that whereas in themselves without meaning, they nevertheless possess in practice the greatest importance. For our case this coincides to such an extent that we may say *that this fiction of a goal of superiority so ridiculous from the viewpoint of reality, has become the principal conditioning factor of our life as hith-*

erto known. It is this that teaches us to differentiate, gives us poise and security, moulds and guides our deeds and activities and forces our spirit to look ahead and to perfect itself. There is of course an obverse side, for *this goal introduces into our life a hostile and fighting tendency,* robs us of the simplicity of our feelings and is always the cause for an estrangement from reality since it puts near to our hearts the idea of attempting to over-power reality. Whoever takes this goal of godlikeness seriously or literally, will soon be compelled to flee from real life and compromise, by seeking a life within life; if fortunate in art, but more generally in pietism, neurosis or crime.

* * * * *

If purposely sought it is rarely obtained. However, every bodily or mental attitude indicates clearly its origin in a striving for power and carries within itself the ideal of a kind of perfection and infallibility. In those cases that lie on the confines of neurosis there is always to be discovered a reinforced pitting of oneself against the environment, against the dead or heroes of the past.

A test of the correctness of our interpretation can be easily made. If everyone possesses within himself an ideal of superiority, such as we find to an exaggerated degree among the nervous, then we ought to encounter phenomena whose purpose is the oppression, the minimizing and under-valuation of others. Traits of character such as intolerance, dogmatism, envy, pleasure at the misfortune of others, conceit, boastfulness, mistrust, avarice,—in short all those attitudes that are the substitutes for a struggle, force their way through to a far greater extent, in fact, than self-preservation demands.

Similarly, either simultaneously or interchangingly, depending upon the zeal and the self-confidence with which the final goal is sought, we see emerg-ing indications of pride, emulation, courage, the attitudes of saving, bestow-ing and directing. . . . Finally we must remember that these hostile traits, particularly in the case of the nervous, are often so concealed that their pos-sessor is justifiably astonished and irritated when attention is drawn to them.

* * * * *

The whole weight of the personal striving for power and superiority passes, at a very early age in the case of the child, into the form and the content of its striving, its thought being able to absorb for the time being only so much as the eternal, real and physiologically rooted *community-feeling* permits. Out of the latter are developed tenderness, love of neighbour, friendship and love, the desire for power unfolding itself in a veiled manner and seeking secretly to push its way along the path of group consciousness.

* * * * *

I shall now proceed to explain briefly how the goal of godlikeness transforms the relation of the individual to his environment into hostility and how the struggle drives an individual towards a goal either along a direct path such as aggressiveness or along byways suggested by precaution. If we trace the history of this aggressive attitude back to childhood we always come upon the outstanding fact that *throughout the whole period of development, the child possesses a feeling of inferiority in its relation both to parents and the world at large.* Because of the immaturity of his organs, his uncertainty and lack of independence, because of his need for dependence upon stronger natures and his frequent and painful feeling of subordination to others, a sensation of inadequacy develops that betrays itself throughout life. This feeling of inferiority is the cause of his continual restlessness as a child, his craving for action, his playing of roles, the pitting of his strength against that of others, his anticipatory pictures of the future and his physical as well as mental preparations. The whole potential educability of the child depends upon this feeling of insufficiency. In this way the future becomes transformed into the land that will bring him compensations. His conflict-attitude is again reflected in his feeling of inferiority; and only conflict does he regard as a compensation which will do away permanently with his present inadequate condition and will enable him to picture himself as elevated above others. Thus the child arrives at the positing of a goal, an imagined goal of superiority, whereby his poverty is transformed into wealth, his subordination into domination, his suffering into happiness and pleasure, his ignorance into omniscience and his incapacity into artistic creation. The longer and more definitely the child feels his insecurity, the more he suffers either from physical or marked mental weakness, the more he is aware of life's neglect, the higher will this goal be placed and the more faithfully will it be adhered to. He who wishes to recognize the nature of this goal, should watch a child at play, at optionally selected occupations or when phantasying about his future profession. The apparent change in these phenomena is purely external for in every new goal the child imagines a predetermined triumph. A variant of this weaving of plans, one frequently found among weakly aggressive children, among girls and sickly individuals, might be mentioned here. This consists of so misusing their frailties that they compel others to become subordinate to them. They will later on pursue the same method until their life-plan and life-falsehood have been clearly unmasked.

The attentive observer will find the nature of the *compensatory dynamics* presenting a quite extraordinary aspect as soon as he permits the sexual role to be relegated to one of minor importance and realizes that it is the former that is impelling the individual toward superhuman goals. In our present civilization both the girl and the youth will feel themselves forced to extraordinary exertions and manoeuvres. A large number of these are admittedly of a distinctive progressive nature. To preserve this progressive nature but to ferret out those by-paths that lead us astray and cause illness, to make these harmless, that is our object and one that takes us far beyond the limits of medical art. It is to this aspect of our subject that society, child-education and folk-education may look for germs of a far-reaching kind. *For the aim of this point-of-view is to gain a reinforced sense of reality, the development of a feeling of responsibility and a substitution for latent hatred of a feeling of mutual goodwill, all of which can be gained only by the conscious evolution of a feeling for the commonweal and the conscious destruction of the will-to-power.*

*   *   *   *   *

CONCLUSION[12]

It is time to conclude the results of our survey. The method of Individual Psychology—we have no hesitation in confessing it—begins and ends with the problem of inferiority.

Inferiority, as we have seen, is the basis for human striving and success. On the other hand the sense of inferiority is the basis for all our problems of psychological maladjustment. When the individual does not find a proper concrete goal of superiority, an inferiority complex results. The inferiority complex leads to a desire for escape and this desire for escape is expressed in a superiority complex, which is nothing more than a goal on the useless and vain side of life offering the satisfaction of false success.

This is the dynamic mechanism of psychological life. More concretely, we know that the mistakes in the functioning of the psyche are more harmful at certain times than at others. We know that the style of life is crystallized in tendencies formed in childhood—in the prototype that develops at the age of four or five. And this being so, the whole burden of the guidance of our psychological life rests on proper childhood guidance.

As regards childhood guidance we have shown that the principal aim should be the cultivation of proper social interests in terms of which useful and healthy goals can be crystallized. It is only by training children to fit in with the social scheme that the universal sense of inferiority is harnessed properly and is prevented from engendering either an inferiority or superiority complex.

Social adjustment is the obverse face of the problem of inferiority. It is because the individual man is inferior and weak that we find human beings living in society. Social interest and social cooperation are therefore the salvation of the individual.

[12]*The Science of Living, op. cit.,* from ch. 13.

CHAPTER 4

ERICH FROMM

HUMANISTIC PSYCHOANALYSIS
AS A PERSONALITY THEORY

Erich Fromm labels his school of thought HUMANISTIC PSYCHO-ANALYSIS. As the title implies, Fromm's psychology is, essentially, his attempt to humanize, and to apply to man as a member of society, the fundamental Freudian concepts. The basic thesis of one of Fromm's earliest books, *Escape from Freedom,* is that man, if he fails to accept and endure freedom, will then degenerate so that he is tempted to submit to an authoritarian ideology such as fascism. Fromm, who was the first to advocate a sociological school of psychoanalysis, applies psychoanalytic concepts to man as a social being in a social setting; humanistic psychology is, therefore, concerned with the individual as a member of society, to which he adjusts and contributes only insofar as he has sublimated his Freudian instincts. Unlike Freud, Fromm believes that man is not completely evil, since he possesses many positive attributes, such as the human ability to love, which, if "productively" expressed, issues in the enhancement of his own interests and those of society; it is love which enables man to be sane.

For Fromm, one of the consequences of the medieval society was the creation in man of a feeling of isolation, and it is this isolation from which modern man seeks to escape. However, if his escape is not accomplished through psychologically desirable channels, such as *humanistic communitarian socialism,* then it will lead not to freedom, but to a fascist ideology, *i.e.*, an escape effected by blind devotion to a leader and/or a robotlike submission to an all-powerful state whose aggressive and sadistic program is levelled against minority groups.

Born in Germany in 1900, Fromm studied in Heidelberg, Frankfurt, Munich, and Berlin, receiving his Ph.D. from the University of Heidelberg and studying psychoanalysis at the Berlin Psychoanalytic Institute. He practiced professionally in Berlin and Heidelberg before coming to teach at the Chicago Psychoanalytic Institute in 1933. He is now in private practice in New York.

Among his works are *Escape from Freedom* (1941), *Man for Himself* (1947), "The Oedipus Complex and the Oedipus Myth," in *The Family: Its Function and Destiny* (ed. by Ruth N. Anshen, 1948), *Psychoanalysis and Religion* (1950), *The Forgotten Language* (1951), *The Sane Society* (1955), *The Art of Loving* (1956), *Sigmund Freud's Mission* (1959), *Zen Buddhism and Psychoanalysis* (1960), *Marx's Concept of Man* (1961), *May Man Prevail* (1961), *Beyond the Chains of Illusion* (1962), *The Dogma of Christ and Other Essays* (1963), *The Heart of Man* (1964), *The Revolution of Hope* (1968), and "Values, Psychology, and Human Existence" in *Human Dynamics in Psychology and Education* (ed. by D. E. Hamachek, 1968).

Human Needs[1]

Man's life is determined by the inescapable alternative between regression and progression, between return to animal existence and arrival at human existence. Any attempt to return is painful, it inevitably leads to suffering and mental sickness, to death either physiologically or mentally (insanity). Every step forward is frightening and painful too, until a certain point has been reached where fear and doubt have only minor proportions. Aside from the physiologically nourished cravings (hunger, thirst, sex), all essential human cravings are determined by this polarity. Man has to solve a problem, he can never rest in the given situation of a passive adaptation to nature. Even the more complete satisfaction of all his instinctive passions and needs are not those rooted in his body, but those rooted in the very peculiarity of his existence.

There lies also the key to humanistic psychoanalysis. Freud, searching

[1]*The Sane Society* (New York: Holt, Rinehart and Winston, 1955), from pp. 27-43, 60-65.

for the basic force which motivates human passions and desires believed he had found it in the libido. But powerful as the sexual drive and all its derivations are, they are by no means the most powerful forces within man and their frustration is not the cause of mental disturbance. The most powerful forces motivating man's behavior stem from the condition of his existence, the "human situation."

Man cannot live statically because his inner contradictions drive him to seek for an equilibrium, for a new harmony instead of the lost animal harmony with nature. After he has satisfied his animal needs, he is driven by his human needs. While his body tells him what to eat and what to avoid —his conscience ought to tell him which needs to cultivate and satisfy, and which needs to let wither and starve out. But hunger and appetite are functions of the body with which man is born—conscience, while potentially present, requires the guidance of men and principles which develop only during the growth of culture.

All passions and strivings of man are attempts to find an answer to his existence or, as we may also say, they are an attempt to avoid insanity. (It may be said in passing that the real problem of mental life is not why some people become insane, but rather why most avoid insanity.) Both the mentally healthy and the neurotic are driven by the need to find an answer, the only difference being that one answer corresponds more to the total needs of man, and hence is more conducive to the unfolding of his powers and to his happiness than the other. All cultures provide for a patterned system in which certain solutions are predominant, hence certain strivings and satisfactions. Whether we deal with primitive religions, with theistic or nontheistic religions, they are all attempts to give an answer to man's existential problem. The finest, as well as the most barbaric cultures have the same function—the difference is only whether the answer given is better or worse. The deviate from the cultural pattern is just as much in search of an answer as his more well-adjusted brother. His answer may be better or worse than the one given by his culture—it is always another answer to the same fundamental question raised by human existence. In this sense all cultures are religious and every neurosis is a private form of religion, provided we mean by religion an attempt to answer the problem of human existence. Indeed, the tremendous energy in the forces producing mental illness, as well as those behind art and religion could never be understood as an outcome of frustrated or sublimated physiological needs; they are attempts to solve the problem of being born human. All men are idealists and cannot help being idealists, provided we mean by idealism the striving for the satisfaction of needs which are specifically human and transcend the physiological needs of the organism.

*   *   *   *   *

What are these needs and passions stemming from the existence of man?

RELATEDNESS VERSUS NARCISSISM

Man is torn away from the primary union with nature, which characterizes animal existence. Having at the same time reason and imagination, he is aware of his aloneness and separateness; of his powerlessness and ignorance; of the accidentalness of his birth and of his death. He could not face this state of being for a second if he could not find new ties with his fellow man which replace the old ones, regulated by instincts. Even if all his physiological needs were satisfied, he would experience his state of aloneness and individuation as a prison from which he had to break out in order to retain his sanity. In fact, the insane person is the one who has completely failed to establish any kind of union, and is imprisoned, even if he is not behind barred windows. The necessity to unite with other human beings, to be related to them, is an imperative need on the fulfillment of which man's sanity depends. This need is behind all phenomena which constitute the whole gamut of intimate human relations, of all passions which are called love in the broadest sense of the word.

There are several ways in which this union can be sought and achieved. Man can attempt to become one with the world by *submission* to a person, to a group, to an institution, to God. In this way he transcends the separateness of his individual existence by becoming part of somebody or something bigger than himself, and experiences his identity in connection with the power to which he has submitted. Another possibility of overcoming separateness lies in the opposite direction: man can try to unite himself with the world by having *power* over it, by making others a part of himself, and thus transcending his individual existence by domination.

*   *   *   *   *

There is only one passion which satisfies man's need to unite himself with the world, and to acquire at the same time a sense of integrity and individuality, and this is *love*. *Love is union* with somebody, or something, outside oneself, *under the condition of retaining the separateness and integrity of one's own self.* It is an experience of sharing, of communion, which permits the full unfolding of one's own inner activity. The experience of love does away with the necessity of illusions. There is no need to inflate the image of the other person, or of myself, since the reality of active sharing and loving permits me to transcend my individualized existence, and at the same time to experience myself as the bearer of the active powers which constitute the act of loving. What matters is the particular quality of loving, not the object. Love is the experience of human solidarity with our fellow creatures, it is in the erotic love of man and woman, in the love of the mother for the child, and also in the love for oneself, as a human being; it is in the mystical experience of union. In the act of loving, I am one with All, and yet I am myself, a unique, separate, limited, mortal being. Indeed out of the very polarity between separateness and union, love is born and reborn.

Love is one aspect of what I have called the productive orientation: the active and creative relatedness of man to his fellow man, to himself and nature. In the realm of *thought*, this productive orientation is expressed in the proper grasp of the world by reason. In the realm of *action*, the productive orientation is expressed in productive work, the prototype of which is art and craftsmanship. In the realm of *feeling*, the productive orientation is expressed in love, which is the experience of union with another person, with all men, and with nature, under the condition of retaining one's sense of integrity and independence. . . . Love, paradoxically, makes me more independent because it makes me stronger and happier—yet it makes me one with the loved person to the extent that individuality seems to be extinguished for the moment. In loving I experience "I am you," you—the loved person, you—the stranger, you—everything alive. In the experience of love lies the only answer to being human, lies sanity.

Productive love always implies a syndrome of attitudes; that of *care*, *responsibility*, *respect* and *knowledge*. If I love, I care—that is, I am actively concerned with the other person's growth and happiness; I am not a spectator. I am responsible, that is, I respond to his needs, to those he can express and more so to those he cannot or does not express.

*   *   *   *   *

TRANSCENDENCE—
CREATIVENESS VERSUS DESTRUCTIVENESS

Another aspect of the human situation, closely connected with the need for relatedness, is man's situation as a *creature*, and his need to transcend this very state of the passive creature. . . . Being endowed with reason and imagination, he cannot be content with the passive role of the creature, with the role of dice cast out of a cup. He is driven by the urge to transcend the role of the creature, the accidentalness and passivity of his existence, by becoming a "creator."

Man can create life. This is the miraculous quality which he indeed shares with all living things, but with the difference that he alone is aware of being created and of being a creator. . . . In the act of creation man transcends himself as a creature, raises himself beyond the passivity and accidentalness of his existence into the realm of purposefulness and freedom. In man's need for transcendence lies one of the roots for love, as well as for art, religion and material production.

To create presupposes activity and care. It presupposes love for that which one creates. How then does man solve the problem of transcending himself, if he is not capable of creating, if he cannot love? *There is another answer to this need for transcendence: if I cannot create life, I can destroy it. To destroy life makes me also transcend it.* Indeed, that man can destroy life is just as miraculous a feat as that he can create it, for life is *the* miracle, the inexplicable.

*　　*　　*　　*　　*

✱ Destructiveness is a secondary potentiality, rooted in the very existence of man, and having the same intensity and power as any passion can have. But—and this is the essential point of my argument—it is only the *alternative to creativeness*. Creation and destruction, love and hate, are not two instincts which exist independently. They are both answers to the same need for transcendence, and the will to destroy must rise when the will to create cannot be satisfied. However, the satisfaction of the need to create leads to happiness; destructiveness to suffering, most of all, for the destroyer himself.

ROOTEDNESS—BROTHERLINESS VERSUS INCEST

Man's birth as man means the beginning of his emergence from his natural home, the beginning of the severance of his natural ties. Yet, this very severance is frightening; if man loses his natural roots, where is he and who is he? He would stand alone, without a home; without roots; he could not bear the isolation and helplessness of this position. He would become insane. He can dispense with the *natural* roots only insofar as he finds new *human* roots and only after he has found them can he feel at home again in this world. Is it surprising, then, to find a deep craving in man not to sever the natural ties, to fight against being torn away from nature, from mother, blood and soil?

*　　*　　*　　*　　*

Every adult is in need of help, of warmth, of protection, in many ways differing and yet in many ways similar to the needs of the child. Is it surprising to find in the average adult a deep longing for the security and rootedness which the relationship to his mother once gave him? Is it not to be expected that he cannot give up this intense longing unless he finds other ways of being rooted?

The problem of incest, however, is not restricted to fixation to the mother. The tie to her is only the most elementary form of all natural ties of blood which give man a sense of rootedness and belonging. The ties of blood are extended to those who are blood relatives, whatever the system is according to which such relationships are established. The *family* and the *clan*, and later on the state, nation or church, assume the same function which the individual mother had originally for the child. The individual leans on them, feels rooted in them, has his sense of identity as a part of them, and not as an individual apart from them.

*　　*　　*　　*　　*

The theory of the Oedipus complex is at the same time the acknowledgement *and* denial of the crucial phenomenon: man's longing for mother's love. In giving the incestuous striving paramount significance, the importance of the tie with mother is recognized; by explaining it as sexual the emotional—and true—meaning of the tie is denied.

Whenever fixation to the mother is also sexual—and this undoubtedly happens—it is because the affective fixation is so strong that it also influences the sexual desire, but not because the sexual desire is at the root of the fixation. On the contrary, sexual desire as such is notoriously fickle with regard to its objects, and generally sexual desire is precisely the force which helps the adolescent in his *separation* from mother, and not the one which binds him to her.

*   *   *   *   *

That Freud himself distorted his great discovery may have been due to an unsolved problem in the relationship to his own mother, but it was certainly largely influenced by the strictly patriarchal attitude which was so characteristic of Freud's time, and which he shared so completely.

*   *   *   *   *

SENSE OF IDENTITY— INDIVIDUALITY VERSUS HERD CONFORMITY

Man may be defined as the animal that can say "I," that can be aware of himself as a separate entity. The animal being within nature, and not transcending it, has no awareness of himself, has no need for a sense of identity. Man, being torn away from nature, being endowed with reason and imagination, needs to form a concept of himself, needs to say and to feel: "I am I." Because he is not *lived*, but *lives*, because he has lost the original unity with nature, has to make decisions, is aware of himself and of his neighbor as different persons, he must be able to sense himself as the subject of his actions. As with the need for relatedness, rootedness, and transcendence, this need for a sense of identity is so vital and imperative that man could not remain sane if he did not find some way of satisfying it. Man's sense of identity develops in the process of emerging from the "primary bonds" which tie him to mother and nature. The infant, still feeling one with mother, cannot yet say "I," nor has he any need for it. Only after he has conceived of the outer world as being separate and different from himself does he come to the awareness of himself as a distinct being, and one of the last words he learns to use is "I," in reference to himself.

*   *   *   *   *

Inasmuch as I am not different, inasmuch as I am like the others, and recognized by them as "a regular fellow," I can sense myself as "I." I am—"as you desire me"—as Pirandello put it in the title of one of his plays. Instead of the pre-individualistic clan identity, a new herd identity develops, in which the sense of identity rests on the sense of an unquestionable belonging to the crowd. That this uniformity and conformity are often not recognized as such, and are covered by the illusion of individuality, does not alter the facts.

* * * * *

The need to feel a sense of identity stems from the very condition of human existence, and it is the source of the most intense strivings. Since I cannot remain sane without the sense of "I," I am driven to do almost anything to acquire this sense. Behind the intense passion for status and conformity is this very need, and it is sometimes even stronger than the need for physical survival. What could be more obvious than the fact that people are willing to risk their lives, to give up their love, to surrender their freedom, to sacrifice their own thoughts, for the sake of being one of the herd, of conforming, and thus of acquiring a sense of identity, even though it is an illusory one.

The Need For a Frame of Orientation And Devotion— Reason Versus Irrationality

The fact that man has reason and imagination leads not only to the necessity for having a sense of his own identity, but also for orienting himself in the world intellectually. . . . Man finds himself surrounded by many puzzling phenomena and, having reason, he has to make sense of them, has to put them in some context which he can understand and which permits him to deal with them in his thoughts. The further his reason develops, the more adequate becomes his system of orientation, that is, the more it approximates reality. But even if man's frame of orientation is utterly illusory, it satisfies his need for some picture which is meaningful to him. Whether he believes in the power of a totem animal, in a rain god, or in the superiority and destiny of his race, his need for some frame of orientation is satisfied. Quite obviously, the picture of the world which he has depends on the development of his reason and of his knowledge. Although biologically the brain capacity of the human race has remained the same for thousands of generations, it takes a long evolutionary process to arrive at *objectivity*, that is, to acquire the faculty to see the world, nature, other persons and oneself as they are, and not distorted by desires and fears. The more man develops this objectivity, the more he is in touch with reality, the more he matures, the better can he create a human world in which he is at home. Reason is man's faculty for *grasping* the world by thought, in contradiction to intelligence, which is man's ability to *manipulate* the world with the help of thought. Reason is man's instrument for arriving at the truth, intelligence is man's instrument for manipulating the world more successfully; the former is essentially human, the latter belongs to the animal part of man.

intelligence – animalistic part?
Reason – human

*   *   *   *   *

The need for a frame of orientation exists on two levels; the first and the more fundamental need is to have *some* frame of orientation, regardless of whether it is true or false. Unless man has such a subjectively satisfactory frame of orientation, he cannot live sanely. On the second level the need is to be in touch with reality by reason, to grasp the world objectively. But the necessity to develop his reason is not as immediate as that to develop some frame of orientation, since what is at stake for man in the latter case is his happiness and serenity, and not his sanity. This becomes very clear if we study the function of *rationalization.* However unreasonable or immoral an action may be, man has an insuperable urge to rationalize it, that is, to prove to himself and to others that his action is determined by reason, common sense, or at least conventional morality. He has little difficulty in acting irrationally, but it is almost impossible for him not to give his action the appearance of reasonable motivation.

ESCAPE FROM FREEDOM[2]

The physiologically conditioned needs are not the only imperative part of man's nature. There is another part just as compelling, one which is not rooted in bodily processes but in the very essence of the human mode and practice of life: the need to be related to the world outside oneself, the need to avoid aloneness. To feel completely alone and isolated leads to mental disintegration just as physical starvation leads to death. This relatedness to others is not identical with physical contact. An individual may be alone in a physical sense for many years and yet he may be related to ideas, values, or at least social patterns that give him a feeling of communion and "belonging." On the other hand, he may live among people and yet be overcome with an utter feeling of isolation, the outcome of which, if it transcends a certain limit, is the state of insanity which schizophrenic disturbances represent. This lack of relatedness to values, symbols, patterns, we may call moral aloneness and state that moral aloneness is as intolerable as the physical aloneness, or rather that physical aloneness becomes unbearable if it implies also moral aloneness. The spiritual relatedness to the world can assume many forms; the monk in his cell who believes in God

[2]*Escape from Freedom* (New York: Holt, Rinehart and Winston, 1941), from pp. 19-37.

and the political prisoner kept in isolation who feels one with his fellow fighters are not alone morally. Neither is the English gentleman who wears his dinner jacket in the most exotic surroundings nor the petty bourgeois who, though being deeply isolated from his fellow men, feels one with his nation or its symbols. The kind of relatedness to the world may be noble or trivial, but even being related to the basest kind of pattern is immensely preferable to being alone. Religion and nationalism, as well as any custom and any belief however absurd and degrading, if it only connects the individual with others, are refuges from what man most dreads: isolation.

* * * * *

Any attempt to answer the question why the fear of isolation is so powerful in man would lead us far away from the main road we are following in this book. However, in order not to give the reader the impression that the need to feel one with others has some mysterious quality, I should like to indicate in what direction I think the answer lies.

One important element is the fact that men cannot live without some sort of co-operation with others. In any conceivable kind of culture man needs to co-operate with others if he wants to survive, whether for the purpose of defending himself against enemies or dangers of nature, or in order that he may be able to work and produce. Even Robinson Crusoe was accompanied by his man Friday; without him he would probably not only have become insane but would actually have died. Each person experiences this need for the help of others very drastically as a child. On account of the factual inability of the human child to take care of itself with regard to all-important functions, communication with others is a matter of life and death for the child. The possibility of being left alone is necessarily the most serious threat to the child's whole existence.

There is another element, however, which makes the need to "belong" so compelling: the fact of subjective self-consciousness, of the faculty of thinking by which man is aware of himself as an individual entity, different from nature and other people. Although the degree of this awareness varies, as will be pointed out in the next chapter, its existence confronts man with a problem which is essentially human: by being aware of himself as distinct from nature and other people, by being aware—even very dimly—of death, sickness, aging, he necessarily feels his insignificance and smallness in comparison with the universe and all others who are not "he." Unless he belonged somewhere, unless his life had some meaning and direction, he would feel like a particle of dust and be overcome by his individual insignificance. He would not be able to relate himself to any system which would give meaning and direction to his life, he would be filled with doubt, and this doubt eventually would paralyze his ability to act—that is, to live.

Before we proceed, it may be helpful to sum up what has been pointed out with regard to our general approach to the problems of social psychology. Human nature is neither a biologically fixed and innate sum total of drives nor is it a lifeless shadow of cultural patterns to which it adapts itself smoothly; it is the product of human evolution, but it also has certain inherent mechanisms and laws. There are certain factors in man's nature which are fixed and unchangeable: the necessity to satisfy the physiologically conditioned drives and the necessity to avoid isolation and moral aloneness. We have seen that the individual has to accept the mode of life rooted in the system of production and distribution peculiar for any given society. In the process of dynamic adaptation to culture, a number of powerful drives develop which motivate the actions and feelings of the individual. The individual may or may not be conscious of these drives, but in any case they are forceful and demand satisfaction once they have developed. They become powerful forces which in their turn become effective in molding the social process.

*   *   *   *   *

The discussion will always be centered around the main theme of this book: that man, the more he gains freedom in the sense of emerging from the original oneness with man and nature and the more he becomes an "individual," has no choice but to unite himself with the world in the spontaneity of love and productive work or else to seek a kind of security by such ties with the world as destroy his freedom and the integrity of his individual self.

*   *   *   *   *

To the degree to which the individual, figuratively speaking, has not yet completely severed the umbilical cord which fastens him to the outside world, he lacks freedom; but these ties give him security and a feeling of belonging and of being rooted somewhere. I wish to call these ties that exist before the process of individuation has resulted in the complete emergence of an individual "primary ties." They are organic in the sense that they are part of normal human development; they imply a lack of individuality, but they also give security and orientation to the individual. They are the ties that connect the child with its mother, the member of the primitive community with his clan and nature, or the medieval man with the Church and his social caste. Once the stage of complete individuation is reached and the individual is free from these primary ties, he is confronted with a new task: to orientate and root himself in the world and to find security in other ways than those which were characteristic of his preindividualistic existence. Freedom then has a different meaning from the one it had before this stage of evolution is reached.

*   *   *   *   *

The more the child grows and to the extent to which primary ties are cut off, the more it develops a quest for freedom and independence. But the fate of this quest can only be fully understood if we realize the dialectic quality in this process of growing individuation.

This process has two aspects: one is that the child grows stronger physically, emotionally, and mentally. In each of these spheres intensity and activity grow. At the same time, these spheres become more and more integrated. An organized structure guided by the individual's will and reason develops. If we call this organized and integrated whole of the personality the self, we can also say that the *one side of the growing process of individuation is the growth of self-strength.* The limits of the growth of individuation and the self are set, partly by individual conditions, but essentially by social conditions. For although the differences between individuals in this respect appear to be great, every society is characterized by a certain level of individuation beyond which the normal individual cannot go.

The other aspect of the process of individuation is *growing aloneness.* The primary ties offer security and basic unity with the world outside of oneself. To the extent to which the child emerges from that world it becomes aware of being alone, of being an entity separate from all others. This separation from a world, which in comparison with one's own individual existence is overwhelmingly strong and powerful, and often threatening and dangerous, creates a feeling of powerlessness and anxiety. As long as one was an integral part of that world, unaware of the possibilities and responsibilities of individual action, one did not need to be afraid of it. When one has become an individual, one stands alone and faces the world in all its perilous overpowering aspects.

Impulses arise to give up one's individuality, to overcome the feeling of aloneness and powerlessness by completely submerging oneself in the world outside.

*   *   *   *   *

Phylogenetically, too, the history of man can be characterized as a process of growing individuation and growing freedom. Man emerges from the prehuman stage by the first steps in the direction of becoming free from coercive instincts. If we understand by instinct a specific action pattern which is determined by inherited neurological structures, a clear-cut trend can be observed in the animal kingdom. The lower an animal is in the scale of development, the more are its adaptation to nature and all its activities controlled by instinctive and reflex action mechanisms. The famous social organizations of some insects are created entirely by instincts. On the other hand, the higher an animal is in the scale of development, the more flexibility of action pattern and the less completeness of structural adjustment do we find at birth. This development reaches its peak with man. He is the most hopeless of all animals at birth. His adaptation to nature is based essentially on the process of learning, not on instinctual determination.

*   *   *   *   *

Human existence begins when the lack of fixation of action by instincts exceeds a certain point; when the adaptation to nature loses its coercive character; when the way to act is no longer fixed by hereditarily given mechanisms. In other words, *human existence and freedom are from the beginning inseparable.* Freedom is here used not in its positive sense of "freedom to" but in its negative sense of "freedom from," namely freedom from instinctual determination of his actions.

Freedom in the sense just discussed is an ambiguous gift. Man is born without the equipment for appropriate action which the animal possesses; he is dependent on his parents for a longer time than any animal, and his reactions to his surroundings are less quick and less effective than the automatically regulated instinctive actions are. He goes through all the dangers and fears which this lack of instinctive equipment implies. Yet this very helplessness of man is the basis from which human development springs; *man's biological weakness is the condition of human culture.*

* * * * *

Instead of a predetermined instinctive action, man has to weigh possible courses of action in his mind; he starts to think. He changes his role toward nature from that of purely passive adaptation to an active one: he produces. He invents tools and, while thus mastering nature, he separates from it more and more. He becomes dimly aware of himself—or rather of his group—as not being identical with nature. It dawns upon him that his is a tragic fate: to be part of nature, and yet to transcend it. He becomes aware of death as his ultimate fate even if he tries to deny it in manifold phantasies.

* * * * *

Man has become separate from nature, he has taken the first step toward becoming human by becoming an "individual." He has committed the first act of freedom. The myth [the Biblical myth of man's expulsion from paradise] emphasizes the suffering resulting from this act. To transcend nature, to be alienated from nature and from another human being, finds man naked, ashamed. He is alone and free, yet powerless and afraid. The newly won freedom appears as a curse; he is free *from* the sweet bondage of paradise, but he is not free *to* govern himself, to realize his individuality.

"Freedom from" is not identical with positive freedom, with "freedom to." This emergence of man from nature is a long-drawn-out process; to a large extent he remains tied to the world from which he emerged; he remains part of nature—the soil he lives on, the sun and moon and stars, the trees and flowers, the animals, and the group of people with whom he is connected by the ties of blood. Primitive religions bear testimony to man's feeling of oneness with nature. Animate and inanimate nature are part of his human world or, as one may also put it, he is still part of the natural world.

These primary ties block his full human development; they stand in the way of the development of his reason and his critical capacities; they let him recognize himself and others only through the medium of his, or their, participation in a clan, a social or religious community, and not as human beings; in other words, they block his development as a free, self-determining, productive individual. But although this is one aspect, there is another one. This identity with nature, clan, religion, gives the individual security. He belongs to, he is rooted in, a structuralized whole in which he has an unquestionable place. He suffers from hunger or suppression, but he does not suffer from the worst of all pains—complete aloneness and doubt.

We see the process of growing human freedom has the same dialectic character that we have noticed in the process of individual growth. On the one hand it is a process of growing strength and integration, mastery of nature, growing power of human reason, and growing solidarity with other human beings. But on the other hand this growing individuation means growing isolation, insecurity, and thereby growing doubt concerning one's own role in the universe, the meaning of one's life, and with all that a growing feeling of one's own powerlessness and insignificance as an individual.

If the process of the development of mankind had been harmonious, if it had followed a certain plan, then both sides of the development—the growing strength and the growing individuation—would have been exactly balanced. As it is, the history of mankind is one of conflict and strife. Each step in the direction of growing individuation threatened people with new insecurities. Primary bonds once severed cannot be mended; once paradise is lost, man cannot return to it. There is only one possible, productive solution for the relationship of individualized man with the world: his active solidarity with all men and his spontaneous activity, love and work, which unite him again with the world, not by primary ties but as a free and independent individual.

However, if the economic, social and political conditions on which the whole process of human individuation depends, do not offer a basis for the realization of individuality in the sense just mentioned, while at the same time people have lost those ties which gave them security, this lag makes freedom an unbearable burden. It then becomes identical with doubt, with a kind of life which lacks meaning and direction. Powerful tendencies arise to escape from this kind of freedom into submission or some kind of relationship to man and the world which promises relief from uncertainty, even if it deprives the individual of his freedom.

European and American history since the end of the Middle Ages is the history of the full emergence of the individual. It is a process which started in Italy, in the Renaissance, and which only now seems to have come to a climax. It took over four hundred years to break down the medieval world and to free people from the most apparent restraints. But while in many respects the individual has grown, has developed mentally and emotionally, and participates in cultural achievements in a degree unheard of before, the lag between "freedom from" and "freedom to" has grown too. The result of this disproportion between freedom *from* any tie and the lack of possibilities for the positive realization of freedom and individuality has led, in Europe, to a panicky flight from freedom into new ties or at least into complete indifference.

HUMANISTIC COMMUNITARIAN SOCIALISM[3]

In the nineteenth century the problem was that *God is dead*; in the twentieth century the problem is that *man is dead*. In the nineteenth century inhumanity meant cruelty; in the twentieth century it means schizoid self-alienation. The danger of the past was that men became slaves. The danger of the future is that men may become robots. True enough, robots do not rebel. But given man's nature, robots cannot live and remain sane, they become "Golems," they will destroy their world and themselves because they cannot stand any longer the boredom of a meaningless life.

Our dangers are war and robotism. What is the alternative? To get out of the rut in which we are moving, and to take the next step in the birth and self-realization of humanity. The first condition is the abolishment of the war threat hanging over all of us now and paralyzing faith and initiative. We must take the responsibility for the life of all men, and develop on an international scale what all great countries have developed internally, a relative sharing of wealth and a new and more just division of economic resources. This must lead eventually to forms of international economic co-operation and planning, to forms of world government and to complete disarmament. We must retain the industrial method. But we must decentralize work and state so as to give it *human proportions,* and permit centralization only to an optimal point which is necessary because of the requirements of industry. In the economic sphere we need co-management of all who work in an enterprise, to permit their active and responsible participation. The new forms for such participation can be found. In the political sphere, return to the town meetings, by creating thousands of small face-to-face groups, which are well informed, which discuss, and whose decisions are integrated in a new "lower house." A cultural renaissance must combine work education for the young, adult education and a new system of popular art and secular ritual throughout the whole nation. Our only alternative to the danger of robotism is humanistic communitarianism.

*   *   *   *   *

Building such a society means taking the next step; it means the end of "humanoid" history, the phase in which man had not become fully human. It does not mean the "end of days," the "completion," the state of perfect

[3]*The Sane Society, op. cit.,* from pp. 360-63.

harmony in which no conflicts or problems confront men. On the contrary, it is man's fate that his existence is beset by contradictions, which he has to solve without ever solving them. When he has overcome the primitive state of human sacrifice, be it in the ritualistic form of the Aztecs or in the secular form of war, when he has been able to regulate his relationship with nature reasonably instead of blindly, when things have truly become his servants rather than his idols, he will be confronted with the truly human conflicts and problems; he will have to be adventuresome, courageous, imaginative, capable of suffering and of joy, but his powers will be in the service of life, and not in the service of death. The new phase of human history, if it comes to pass, will be a new beginning, not an end.

Man today is confronted with the most fundamental choice; not that between Capitalism or Communism, but that between *robotism* (of both the capitalist and the communist variety), or Humanistic Communitarian Socialism. Most facts seem to indicate that he is choosing robotism, and that means, in the long run, insanity and destruction. But all these facts are not strong enough to destroy faith in man's reason, good will and sanity. As long as we can think of other alternatives, we are not lost; as long as we can consult together and plan together, we can hope. But, indeed, the shadows are lengthening; the voices of insanity are becoming louder. We are in reach of achieving a state of humanity which corresponds to the vision of our great teachers; yet we are in danger of the destruction of all civilization, or of robotization. A small tribe was told thousands of years ago: "I put before you life and death, blessing and curse—and you chose life." This is our choice too.

CHAPTER 5

KAREN HORNEY

NEO-FREUDIANISM:
THE SOCIOLOGICAL SCHOOL

Karen Horney's theory of personality modifies and builds upon the psychoanalytic orthodoxy of Freud. Recognizing the originality of her contribution to psychological theory and its dependence on the work of Freud, she wrote: "I believe that deference for Freud's gigantic achievements should show itself in building on the foundation he has laid and in this way we can help to fulfill the possibilities which psychoanalysis has for the future."[1]

As an adherent of the SOCIOLOGICAL SCHOOL of psychoanalysis, Horney maintained that personality characteristics, including neurotic ones, "are generated not only by incidental individual experiences, but also by the specific cultural conditions under which we live."[2] This school, whose chief members are Fromm, Horney, Sullivan, and perhaps Adler, contends that the culture in which the individual is reared is primarily responsible for the development of his personality and his resultant adjustment or maladjustment.

Unlike Freud, Dr. Horney believed that "man can change and go on changing as long as he lives";[3] consequently, there is always hope for psychological salvation. She has detected a fundamental character structure which she believes to be common to all neurotics.

[1]*The Neurotic Personality of Our Time* (New York: Norton, 1937), from p. ix.
[2]*Ibid.*, from p. viii.
[3]*Our Inner Conflicts* (New York: Norton, 1945), from p. 19.

Essentially, the neurotic suffers from a basic and dynamic conflict arising from contradictory trends which may be summed up as the attitudes of (1) "moving towards people," (2) "moving against people," and (3) "moving away from people." The neurotic's own desperate, but inadequate, attempts to resolve his conflict (through a denial of the conflicting attitudes and rigid self-control) succeed only in compounding the conflict. Nevertheless, a real resolution of the conflict, effected not by absurdly simple means, but by changes in the personality of the neurotic individual, becomes possible. The personality development of the neurotic individual, particularly in childhood, is similar to that of the average, normal individual; unfortunately, the neurotic's early experiences of rejection, insecurity, contempt, intolerance, disrespect, neglect, were suffered in aggravated form.

Dr. Horney was born in Germany in 1885 and died in New York City in 1952. During her career in psychoanalysis she was lecturer at the Berlin Psychoanalytic Institute, Associate Director of the Chicago Institute for Psychoanalysis, lecturer at The New School for Social Research, and Dean of the American Institute for Psychoanalysis.

Among her published works are *The Neurotic Personality of Our Time* (1937), *New Ways in Psychoanalysis* (1939), *Self Analysis* (1942), *Our Inner Conflicts* (1945), *Neurosis and Human Growth* (1950), *Are You Considering Psychoanalysis?* (1962), *Feminine Psychology* (1967), and "The Technique of Psychoanalytic Therapy" in *American Journal of Psychoanalysis* (1968).

THE NEUROTIC PERSONALITY[4]

Whatever the starting point and however tortuous the road, we must finally arrive at a disturbance of personality as the source of psychic illness. The same can be said of this as of almost any other psychological discovery. Poets and philosophers of all times have known that it is never the serene, well-balanced person who falls victim to psychic disorders, but the one torn by inner conflicts. In modern terms, every neurosis, no matter what the symptomatic picture, is a character neurosis. Hence our endeavor in theory must be directed toward a better understanding of the neurotic character structure.

Actually, Freud's great pioneering work increasingly converged on this concept—though his genetic approach did not allow him to arrive at its

[4]*Ibid.*, from pp. 11-19.

explicit formulation. But others who have continued and developed Freud's work—notably Franz Alexander, Otto Rank, Wilhelm Reich, and Harald Schultz-Hencke—have defined it more clearly. None of them, however, is agreed as to the precise nature and dynamics of this character structure.

My own starting point was a different one. Freud's postulations in regard to feminine psychology set me thinking about the role of cultural factors. Their influence on our ideas of what constitutes masculinity or femininity was obvious, and it became just as obvious to me that Freud had arrived at certain erroneous conclusions because he failed to take them into account. My interest in this subject grew over the course of fifteen years. It was furthered in part by association with Erich Fromm who, through his profound knowledge of both sociology and psychoanalysis, made me more aware of the significance of social factors over and above their circumscribed application to feminine psychology. And my impressions were confirmed when I came to the United States in 1932. I saw then that the attitudes and the neuroses of persons in this country differed in many ways from those I had observed in European countries, and that only the difference in civilizations could account for this. My conclusions finally found their expression in *The Neurotic Personality of Our Time*. The main contention here was that neuroses are brought about by cultural factors—which more specifically meant that neuroses are generated by disturbances in human relationships.

In the years before I wrote *The Neurotic Personality* I pursued another line of research that followed logically from the earlier hypothesis. It revolved around the question as to what the driving forces are in neurosis. Freud had been the first to point out that these were compulsive drives. He regarded these drives as instinctual in nature, aimed at satisfaction and intolerant of frustration. Consequently he believed that they were not confined to neuroses *per se* but operated in all human beings. If, however, neuroses were an outgrowth of disturbed human relationships, this postulation could not possibly be valid. The concepts I arrived at on this score were, briefly, these. Compulsive drives are specifically neurotic; they are born of feelings of isolation, helplessness, fear and hostility, and represent ways of coping with the world despite these feelings; they aim primarily not at satisfaction but at safety; their compulsive character is due to the anxiety lurking behind them. Two of these drives—neurotic cravings for affection and power—stood out at first in clear relief and were presented in detail in *the Neurotic Personality*.

Though retaining what I considered the fundamentals of Freud's teachings, I realized by that time that my search for a better understanding had led me in directions that were at variance with Freud. If so many factors that Freud regarded as instinctual were culturally determined, if so much that Freud considered libidinal was a neurotic need for affection, provoked by anxiety and aimed at feeling safe with others, then the libido theory was no longer tenable. Childhood experiences remained important, but the influence they exerted on our lives appeared in a new light. Other theoretical differences inevitably followed. Hence it became necessary to formulate in my own mind where I stood in reference to Freud. The result of this clarification was *New Ways in Psychoanalysis*.

In the meantime my search for the driving forces in neurosis continued. I called the compulsive drives neurotic trends and described ten of them in my next book. By then I, too, had arrived at the point of recognizing that the neurotic character structure was of central significance. I regarded it at that time as a kind of macrocosm formed by many microcosms interacting upon one another. In the nucleus of each microcosm was a neurotic trend. This theory of neurosis had a practical application. If psychoanalysis did not primarily involve relating our present difficulties to our past experiences but depended rather upon understanding the interplay of forces in our existing personality, then recognizing and changing ourselves with little or even no expert help was entirely feasible. In the face of a widespread need for psychotherapy and a scarcity of available aid, self-analysis seemed to offer the hope of filling a vital need. Since the major part of the book dealt with the possibilities, limitations, and ways of analyzing ourselves, I called it *Self-Analysis*.

I was, however, not entirely satisfied with my presentation of individual trends. The trends themselves were accurately described; but I was haunted by the feeling that in a simple enumeration they appeared in a too isolated fashion. I could see that a neurotic need for affection, compulsive modesty, and the need for a "partner" belonged together. What I failed to see was that together they represented a basic attitude toward others and the self, and a particular philosophy of life. These trends are the nuclei of what I have now drawn together as a "moving toward people." I saw, too, that a compulsive craving for power and prestige and neurotic ambition had something in common. They constitute roughly the factors involved in what I shall call "moving against people." But the need for admiration and the perfectionist drives, though they had all the earmarks of neurotic trends and influenced the neurotic's reaction with others, seemed primarily to concern his relation with himself. Also, the need for exploitation seemed to be less basic than either the need for affection or for power; it appeared less comprehensive than these, as if it were not a separate entity but had been taken out of some larger whole.

My questionings have since proved justified. In the years following, my focus of interest shifted to the role of conflicts in neurosis. I had said in *The Neurotic Personality* that a neurosis came about through the collision of divergent neurotic trends. In *Self-Analysis* I had said that neurotic trends not only reinforced each other but also created conflicts. Nevertheless conflicts had remained a side issue. Freud had been increasingly aware of the significance of inner conflicts; he saw them, however, as a battle between repressed and repressing forces. The conflicts I began to see

were of a different kind. They operated between contradictory sets of neurotic trends, and though they originally concerned contradictory attitudes
towards others, in time they encompassed contradictory attitudes toward
the self, contradictory qualities and contradictory sets of values.

A crescendo of observation opened my eyes to the significance of such
conflicts. What first struck me most forcibly was the blindness of patients
toward obvious contradictions within themselves. When I pointed these
out they became elusive and seemed to lose interest. After repeated experiences of this kind I realized that the elusiveness expressed a profound aversion to tackling these contradictions. Finally, panic reactions in response
to a sudden recognition of a conflict showed me I was working with dy-
namite. Patients had good reason to shy away from these conflicts: they
dreaded their power to tear them to pieces.

Then I began to recognize the amazing amount of energy and intelligence that was invested in more or less desperate efforts to "solve" the
conflicts or, more precisely, to deny their existence and create an artificial
harmony. I saw the four major attempts at solution in about the order in
which they are presented in this book. The initial attempt was to eclipse
part of the conflict and raise its opposite to predominance. The second was
to "move away from" people. The function of the neurotic detachment now
appeared in a new light. Detachment was part of the basic conflict—that is,
one of the original conflicting attitudes towards others; but it also represented an attempt at solution, since maintaining an emotional distance between the self and others set the conflict out of operation. The third attempt
was very different in kind. Instead of moving away from others, the neurotic moved away from himself. His whole actual self became somewhat
unreal to him and he created in its place an idealized image of himself in
which the conflicting parts were so transfigured that they no longer appeared as conflicts but as various aspects of a rich personality. This concept helped to clarify many neurotic problems which hitherto were beyond
the reach of our understanding and hence of our therapy. It also put two
of the neurotic trends which had previously resisted integration into their
proper setting. The need for perfection now appeared as an endeavor to
measure up to this idealized image; the craving for admiration could be
seen as the patient's need to have outside affirmation that he really was his
idealized image. And the farther the image was removed from reality the
more insatiable this latter need would logically be. Of all the attempts at
solution the idealized image is probably the most important by reason of
its far-reaching effect on the whole personality. But in turn it generates a
new inner rift, and hence calls for further patchwork. The fourth attempt
at solution seeks primarily to do away with this rift, though it helps as
well to spirit away all other conflicts. Through what I call externalization,
inner processes are experienced as going on outside the self. If the idealized
image means taking a step away from the actual self, externalization repre-

sents a still more radical divorce. It again creates new conflicts, or rather greatly augments the original conflict—that between the self and the outside world.

I have called these four major attempts at solution, partly because they seem to operate regularly in all neuroses—though in varying degree— and partly because they bring about incisive changes in the personality. But they are by no means the only ones. Others of less general significance include such strategies as arbitrary rightness, whose main function is to quell all inner doubts; rigid self-control, which holds together a torn individual by sheer will power; and cynicism, which, in disparaging all values, eliminates conflicts in regard to ideals.

Meanwhile the consequences of all these unresolved conflicts were gradually becoming clearer to me. I saw the manifold fears that were generated, the waste of energy, the inevitable impairment of moral integrity, the deep hopelessness that resulted from feeling inextricably entangled.

It was only after I had grasped the significance of neurotic hopelessness that the meaning of sadistic trends finally came into view. These, I now understand, represented an attempt at restitution through vicarious living, entered upon by a person who despaired of ever being himself. And the all-consuming passion which can so often be observed in sadistic pursuits grew out of such a person's insatiable need for vindictive triumph. It became clear to me then that the need for destructive exploitation was in fact no separate neurotic trend but only a never-failing expression of that more comprehensive whole which for lack of a better term we call sadism.

Thus a theory of neurosis evolved, whose dynamic center is a basic conflict between the attitudes of "moving toward," "moving against," and "moving away from" people. Because of his fear of being split apart on the one hand and the necessity to function as a unity on the other, the neurotic makes desperate attempts at solution. While he can succeed this way in creating a kind of artificial equilibrium, new conflicts are constantly generated and further remedies are continually required to blot them out. Every step in this struggle for unity makes the neurotic more hostile, more helpless, more fearful, more alienated from himself and others, with the result that the difficulties responsible for the conflicts become more acute and their real resolution less and less attainable. He finally becomes hopeless and may try to find a kind of restitution in sadistic pursuits, which in turn have the effect of increasing his hopelessness and creating new conflicts.

This, then, is a fairly dismal picture of neurotic development and its resulting character structure. Why do I nonetheless call my theory a constructive one? In the first place it does away with the unrealistic optimism that maintains we can "cure" neuroses by absurdly simple means. But it involves no equally unrealistic pessimism. I call it constructive because it allows us for the first time to tackle and resolve neurotic hopelessness. I call it constructive most of all because in spite of its recognition of the severity of neurotic entanglements, it permits not only a tempering of the underlying conflicts but their actual resolution, and so enables us to work toward a real integration of personality. Neurotic conflicts cannot be resolved by rational decision. The neurotic's attempts at solution are not only futile but harmful. But these conflicts *can* be resolved by changing the conditions within the personality that brought them into being. Every piece of analytical work well done changes these conditions in that it makes a person less helpless, less fearful, less hostile, and less alienated from himself and others.

Freud's pessimism as regards neuroses and their treatment arose from the depths of his disbelief in human goodness and human growth. Man, he postulated, is doomed to suffer or to destroy. The instincts which drive him can only be controlled, or at best "sublimated." My own belief is that man has the capacity as well as the desire to develop his potentialities and become a decent human being, and that these deteriorate if his relationship to others and hence to himself is, and continues to be, disturbed. I believe that man can change and go on changing as long as he lives. And this belief has grown with deeper understanding.

THE TEN NEUROTIC NEEDS[5]

Neurotic trends may be classified in various ways. Those entailing strivings for closeness with others might be contrasted with those aiming at aloofness and distance. Those impelling toward one or another kind of dependency might be bundled together in contrast with those stressing independence. Trends toward expansiveness stand against those working toward a constriction of life. Trends toward an accentuation of personal peculiarities could be contrasted with those aiming at adaptation or at an eradication of the individual self, those toward self-aggrandizement with those that entail self-belittling. But to carry through such classifications would not make the picture clearer, because the categories are overlapping. I shall therefore merely enumerate those trends which at the present time stand out as describable entities.

*   *   *   *   *

1. The neurotic need for affection and approval:
Indiscriminate need to please others and to be liked and approved of by others;
Automatic living up to the expectations of others;
Center of gravity in others and not in self, with their wishes and opinions the only thing that counts;
Dread of self-assertion;
Dread of hostility on the part of others or of hostile feelings within self.

[5]*Self-Analysis* (New York: Norton, 1942), from pp. 54-63.

2. The neurotic need for a "partner" who will take over one's life:
Center of gravity entirely in the "partner," who is to fulfill all expectations of life and take responsibility for good and evil, his successful manipulation becoming the predominant task;
Overvaluation of "love" because "love" is supposed to solve all problems;
Dread of desertion;
Dread of being alone.

3. The neurotic need to restrict one's life within narrow borders:
Necessity to be undemanding and contented with little, and to restrict ambitions and wishes for material things;
Necessity to remain inconspicuous and to take second place;
Belittling of existing faculties and potentialities, with modesty the supreme value;
Urge to save rather than to spend;
Dread of making any demands;
Dread of having or asserting expansive wishes.

* * * * *

4. The neurotic need for power:
Domination over others craved for its own sake;
Devotion to a cause, duty, responsibility, though playing some part, not the driving force;
Essential disrespect for others, their individuality, their dignity, their feelings, the only concern being their subordination;
Great differences as to degree of destructive elements involved;
Indiscriminate adoration of strength and contempt for weakness;
Dread of uncontrollable situations;
Dread of helplessness.

4a. The neurotic need to control self and others through reason and foresight:
Belief in the omnipotence of intelligence and reason;
Denial of the power of emotional forces and contempt for them;
Extreme value placed on foresight and prediction;
Feelings of superiority over others related to the faculty of foresight;
Contempt for anything within self that lags behind the image of intellectual superiority;
Dread of recognizing objective limitations of the power of reason;
Dread of "stupidity" and bad judgment.

4b. The neurotic need to believe in the omnipotence of will:
Feeling of fortitude gained from the belief in the magic power of will (like possession of a wishing ring);
Reaction and desolation to any frustration of wishes;
Tendency to relinquish or restrict wishes and to withdraw interest because of a dread of "failure";
Dread of recognizing any limitations of sheer will.

5. The neurotic need to exploit others and by hook or crook get the better of them:
Others evaluated primarily according to whether or not they can be exploited or made use of;
Various foci of exploitation—money (bargaining amounts to a passion), ideas, sexuality, feelings;
Pride in exploitative skill;
Dread of being exploited and thus of being "stupid."

6. The neurotic need for social recognition or prestige:
All things—inanimate objects, money, persons, one's own qualities, activities, and feelings—evaluated only according to their prestige value;
Self-evaluation entirely dependent on nature of public acceptance;
Differences as to use of traditional or rebellious ways of inciting envy or admiration;
Dread of losing caste ("humiliation"), whether through external circumstances or through factors from within.

7. The neurotic need for personal admiration:
Inflated image of self (narcissism);
Need to be admired not for what one possesses or presents in the public eye but for the imagined self;
Self-evaluation dependent on living up to this image and on admiration of it by others;
Dread of losing admiration ("humiliation").

8. The neurotic ambition for personal achievement:
Need to surpass others not through what one presents or is but through one's activities;
Self-evaluation dependent on being the very best—lover, sportsman, writer, worker—particularly in one's own mind, recognition by others vital too, however, and its absence resented;
Admixture of destructive tendencies (toward the defeat of others) never lacking but varying in intensity;
Relentless driving of self to greater achievements, though with pervasive anxiety;
Dread of failure ("humiliation").

* * * * *

9. The neurotic need for self-sufficiency and independence:
Necessity never to need anybody, or to yield to any influence, or to be tied down to anything, any closeness involving the danger of enslavement;
Distance and separateness the only source of security;
Dread of needing others, of ties, of closeness, of love.

10. The neurotic need for perfection and unassailability:
Relentless driving for perfection;
Ruminations and self-recriminations regarding possible flaws;
Feelings of superiority over others because of being perfect;

Dread of finding flaws within self or of making mistakes;
Dread of criticism or reproaches.

A striking consideration in reviewing these trends is that none of the strivings and attitudes they imply is in itself "abnormal" or devoid of human value. Most of us want and appreciate affection, self-control, modesty, consideration of others. To expect fulfillment of one's life from another person is regarded, at least for a woman, as "normal" or even virtuous. Among the strivings are some that we would not hesitate to estimate highly. Self-sufficiency, independence, and guidance through reason are generally regarded as valuable goals.

MOVING TOWARD, AGAINST, AND AWAY FROM PEOPLE[6]

Moving Toward People

It is impossible to present the basic conflict by simply showing it in operation in a number of individuals. Because of its disruptive power the neurotic builds a defensive structure around it which serves not only to blot it from view but so deeply imbeds it that it cannot be isolated in pure form. The result is that what appears on the surface is more the various attempts at solution than the conflict itself.

*　　*　　*　　*　　*

To understand all that is involved in the basic conflict we must start by studying each of the opposing elements separately. We can do this with some success if we observe the types of individuals in whom one or the other element has become predominant, and for whom it represents the more acceptable self. For the sake of simplicity I shall classify such types as the compliant, the aggressive, and the detached personality. We shall focus in each case on the person's more acceptable attitude, leaving out in so far as possible the conflicts it conceals. In each of these types we shall find that the basic attitude toward others has created, or at least fostered, the growth of certain needs, qualities, sensitivities, inhibitions, anxieties, and, last but not least, a particular set of values.

*　　*　　*　　*　　*

Group I, the compliant type, manifests all the traits that go with "moving toward" people. He shows a marked need for affection and approval and an especial need for a "partner"—that is, a friend, lover, husband or wife "who is to fulfill all expectations of life and take responsibility for good and evil, his successful manipulation becoming the predominant task" [*Self-*

---

[6]*Our Inner Conflicts, op. cit.*, from pp. 48-51, 53-55, 63-67, 73-77, 79-81.

Analysis]. These needs have the characteristics common to all neurotic trends; that is, they are compulsive, indiscriminate, and generate anxiety or despondence when frustrated. They operate almost independently of the intrinsic worth of the "others" in question, as well as of the person's real feeling toward them. However these needs may vary in their expression, they all center around a desire for human intimacy, a desire for "belonging." Because of the indiscriminate nature of his needs, the compliant type will be prone to overrate his congeniality and the interests he has in common with those around him and disregard the separating factors. . . . In sum this type needs to be liked, wanted, desired, loved; to feel accepted, welcomed, approved of, appreciated; to be needed, to be of importance to others, especially to one particular person; to be helped, protected, taken care of, guided.

*   *   *   *   *

This type has certain characteristic attitudes toward himself. One is the pervasive feeling that he is weak and helpless—a "poor little me" feeling. When left to his own resources he feels lost, like a boat loosed from its moorings, or like Cinderella bereft of her fairy godmother. This helplessness is in part real; certainly the feeling that under no circumstances would one possibly fight or compete does promote actual weakness. Besides, he frankly admits his helplessness to himself and others. It may be dramatically emphasized in dreams as well. He often resorts to it as a means of appeal or defense: "You must love me, protect me, forgive me, not desert me, *because* I am so weak and helpless."

A second characteristic grows out of his tendency to subordinate himself. He takes it for granted that everyone is superior to him, that they are more attractive, more intelligent, better educated, more worth while than he. There is a factual basis for this feeling in that his lack of assertiveness and firmness does impair his capacities; but even in fields where he is unquestionably able his feeling of inferiority leads him to credit the other fellow—regardless of his merit—with greater competence than his own. In the presence of aggressive or arrogant persons his sense of his own worthiness shrinks still more. However, even when alone his tendency is to undervalue not only his qualities, talents, and abilities but his material possessions as well.

A third typical feature is a part of his general dependence upon others. This is his unconscious tendency to rate himself by what others think of him. His self-esteem rises and falls with their approval or disapproval, the affection or lack of it. Hence any rejection is actually catastrophic for him. . . . In other words any criticism, rejection, or desertion is a terrifying danger, and he may make the most abject effort to win back the regard of the person who has thus threatened him.

*   *   *   *   *

These, then, are the elements involved in a neurotic "moving toward" people. It must be apparent now how inadequate it would be to describe them by any *one* term like submissive or dependent, for a whole way of thinking, feeling, acting—a whole way of life—is implicit in them.

*   *   *   *   *

Moving Against People

In discussing the second aspect of the basic conflict—the tendency to "move against" people—we shall proceed as before, examining here the type in whom aggressive trends predominate.

Just as the compliant type clings to the belief that people are "nice," and is continually baffled by evidence to the contrary, so the aggressive type takes it for granted that everyone is hostile, and refuses to admit that they are not. To him life is a struggle of all against all, and the devil take the hindmost. Such exceptions as he allows are made reluctantly and with reservation. His attitude is sometimes quite apparent, but more often it is covered over with a veneer of suave politeness, fairmindedness and good fellowship. This "front" can represent a Machiavellian concession to expediency. As a rule, however, it is a composite of pretenses, genuine feelings, and neurotic needs. A desire to make others believe he is a good fellow may be combined with a certain amount of actual benevolence as long as there is no question in anybody's mind that he himself is in command. There may be elements of a neurotic need for affection and approval, put to the service of aggressive goals. No such "front" is necessary to the compliant type because his values coincide anyway with approved-of social or Christian virtues.

To appreciate the fact that the needs of the aggressive type are just as compulsive as those of the compliant, we must realize that they are as much prompted by basic anxiety as his. This must be emphasized, because the component of fear, so evident in the latter, is never admitted or displayed by the type we are now considering. In him everything is geared toward being, becoming, or at least appearing tough.

His needs stem fundamentally from his feeling that the world is an arena where, in the Darwinian sense, only the fittest survive and the strong annihilate the weak. What contributes most to survival depends largely on the civilization in which the person lives; but in any case, a callous pursuit of self-interest is the paramount law. Hence his primary need becomes one of control over others. Variations in the means of control are infinite.

*   *   *   *   *

Concomitantly he needs to excel, to achieve success, prestige, or recognition in any form. Strivings in this direction are partly oriented toward power inasmuch as success and prestige lend power in a competitive society. But they also make for a subjective feeling of strength through outside affirmation, outside acclaim, and the fact of supremacy. Here as in the compliant type the center of gravity lies outside the person himself; only the kind of affirmation wanted from others differs. Factually one is as futile as the other. When people wonder why success has failed to make them feel any less insecure, they only show their psychological ignorance, but the fact that they do so indicates the extent to which success and prestige are commonly regarded as yardsticks.

A strong need to exploit others, to outsmart them, to make them of use to himself, is part of the picture. Any situation or relationship is looked at from the standpoint of "What can I get out of it?"—whether it has to do with money, prestige, contact, or ideas. The person is consciously or semiconsciously convinced that everyone acts this way, and so what counts is to do it more efficiently than the rest. The qualities he develops are almost diametrically opposed to those of the compliant type. He becomes hard and tough, or gives that appearance. He regards all feelings, his own as well as others', as "sloppy sentimentality." Love, for him, plays a negligible role. Not that he is never "in love" or never has an affair or marries, but what is of prime concern is to have a mate who is eminently desirable, one through whose attractiveness, social prestige, or wealth he can enhance his own position. He sees no reason to be considerate to others.

*　　*　　*　　*　　*

While the compliant type tends to appease, the aggressive type does everything he can to be a good fighter. He is alert and keen in an argument and will go out of his way to launch one for the sake of proving his right. He may be at his best when his back is to the wall and there is no alternative but to fight. In contrast to the compliant type who is afraid to win a game, he is a bad loser and undeniably wants victory. He is just as ready to accuse others as the former is to take blame on himself. In neither case does the consideration of guilt play a role. The compliant type when he pleads guilty is by no means convinced that he is so, but is driven to appease. The aggressive type similarly is not convinced that the other fellow is wrong; he just assumes he is right because he needs this ground of subjective certainty in much the same way as an army needs a safe point from which to launch an attack. To admit error when it is not absolutely necessary seems to him an unforgivable display of weakness, if not arrant foolishness.

It is consistent with his attitude of having to fight against a malevolent world that he should develop a keen sense of realism—of its kind. He will never be so "naïve" as to overlook in others any manifestation of ambition, greed, ignorance, or anything else that might obstruct his goals. Since in a competitive civilization attributes like these are much more common than real decency, he feels justified in regarding himself as only realistic. Actually, of course, he is just as one-sided as the compliant type. Another facet of his realism is his emphasis on planning and foresight.

Like any good strategist, in every situation he is careful to appraise his own chances, the forces of his adversaries, and the possible pitfalls.

*　　*　　*　　*　　*

Moving Away from People

The third face of the basic conflict is the need for detachment, for "moving away from" people. Before examining it in the type for whom it has become the predominant trend, we must understand what is meant by neurotic detachment. Certainly it is not the mere fact of wanting occasional solitude. Everyone who takes himself and life seriously wants to be alone at times. Our civilization has so engulfed us in the externals of living that we have little understanding of this need, but its possibilities for personal fulfillment have been stressed by philosophies and religions of all times. A desire for meaningful solitude is by no means neurotic; on the contrary most neurotics shrink from their own inner depths, and an incapacity for constructive solitude is itself a sign of neurosis. Only if there is intolerable strain in associating with people and solitude becomes primarily a means of avoiding it is the wish to be alone an indication of neurotic detachment.

Certain of the highly detached person's peculiarities are so characteristic of him that psychiatrists are inclined to think of them as belonging exclusively to the detached type. The most obvious of these is a general estrangement from people. In him this strikes our attention because he particularly emphasizes it, but actually his estrangement is no greater than that of other neurotics. In the case of the two types we have discussed, for instance, it would be impossible to make a general statement as to which was the more estranged. We can only say that this characteristic is covered over in the compliant type, that he is surprised and frightened when he discovers it, because his passionate need for closeness makes him so eager to believe that no gap between himself and others exists. After all, estrangement from people is only an indication that human relationships are disturbed. But this is the case in all neuroses. The extent of estrangement depends more on the severity of the disturbance than on the particular form the neurosis takes.

Another characteristic that is often regarded as peculiar to detachment is estrangement from the self, that is, a numbness to emotional experience, an uncertainty as to what one is, what one loves, hates, desires, hopes, fears, resents, believes. Such self-estrangement is again common to all neuroses. Every person, to the extent that he is neurotic, is like an airplane directed by remote control and so bound to lose touch with himself. . . . Others, again, can have a comparatively rich emotional life. Since such variations exist, we cannot regard self-estrangement, either, as exclusive to detachment. What all detached persons have in common is something quite different. It is their capacity to look at themselves with a kind of objective interest, as one would look at a work of art. Perhaps the best way to describe it would be to say that they have the same "onlooker" attitude toward themselves that they have toward life in general. They may often, therefore, be excellent observers of the processes going on within them. An outstanding example of this is the uncanny understanding of dream symbols they frequently display.

What is crucial is their inner need to put emotional distance between themselves and others. More accurately, it is their conscious and unconscious determination not to get emotionally involved with others in any way, whether in love, fight, co-operation, or competition. They draw around themselves a kind of magic circle which no one may penetrate. And this is why, superficially, they may "get along" with people. The compulsive character of need shows up in their reaction of anxiety when the world intrudes on them.

All the needs and qualities they acquire are directed toward this major need of not getting involved. Among the most striking is the need for *self-sufficiency*. Its most positive expression is resourcefulness. The aggressive type also tends to be resourceful—but the spirit is different; for him it is a prerequisite for fighting one's way in a hostile world and for wanting to defeat others in the fray. In the detached type the spirit is like Robinson Crusoe's: he has to be resourceful in order to live. It is the only way he can compensate for his isolation.

*   *   *   *   *

Another pronounced need is his need for privacy. He is like a person in a hotel room who rarely removes the "Do-Not-Disturb" sign from his door. Even books may be regarded as intruders, as something from outside. Any question put to him about his personal life may shock him; he tends to shroud himself in a veil of secrecy. . . .

Self-sufficiency and privacy both serve his most outstanding need, the need for utter independence. He himself considers his independence a thing of positive value. And it undoubtedly has a value of sorts. For no matter what his deficiencies, the detached person is certainly no conforming automaton. His refusal blindly to concur, together with his aloofness from competitive struggle, does give him a certain integrity.

*   *   *   *   *

The need to feel superior, although common to all neuroses, must be stressed here because of its intrinsic association with detachment. The expressions "ivory tower" and "splendid isolation" are evidence that even in common parlance, detachment and superiority are almost linked. Probably nobody can stand isolation without either *being* particularly strong and resourceful or *feeling* uniquely significant. This is corroborated by clinical experience. . . . The need for superiority in the case of the detached person has certain specific features. Abhorring competitive struggle, he does not want to excel realistically through consistent effort. He feels rather that the treasures within him should be recognized without any effort on his part; his hidden greatness should be felt without his having to make a move. . . . Another way his sense of superiority expresses itself is in his feeling of his own uniqueness. This is a direct outgrowth of his wanting to feel separate and distinct from others.

* * * * *

The emotional life of the detached person does not follow as strict a pattern as that of the other types described. Individual variations are greater in his case chiefly because in contradistinction to the other two, whose predominant trends are directed toward positive goals—affection, intimacy, love in the one; survival, domination, success in the other— his goals are negative: he wants *not* to be involved, *not* to need anybody, *not* to allow others to intrude on or influence him. Hence the emotional picture would be dependent on the particular desires that have developed or been allowed to stay alive within this negative framework, and only a limited number of tendencies intrinsic to detachment as such can be formulated. . . . The all-important function of neurotic detachment, then, is to keep major conflicts out of operation.

CHAPTER 6

HARRY STACK SULLIVAN

THE INTERPERSONAL THEORY

The INTERPERSONAL THEORY OF PSYCHIATRY, as Harry Stack Sullivan designated his theory, defines personality as *"the relatively
enduring pattern of recurrent interpersonal situations which characterize a human life.* The term, *pattern,* in this statement is to be
taken to mean *the envelope of all insignificant differences. Significant* differences in to-be-recurrent interpersonal relations occur, at
times, when personality changes."[1] Implicit in this definition is the
concept that psychiatry is closely related to or identifiable with social psychology. Sullivan stated it explicitly when he wrote: Psychiatry as it is—the preoccupation of extant psychiatric specialists
—is not science nor art but confusion. In defining it as the study
of interpersonal relations, I sought to segregate from everything
else a disciplinary field in which operational methods could be
applied with great practical benefits. This made psychiatry the
probable locus of another evolving discipline, one of the social
sciences, namely, *social psychology*."[2] Therefore, Sullivan believed that the culture to which an individual belongs plays an
essential role in his personality development. Like Fromm and
Karen Horney, Sullivan was an adherent of the cultural school
of psychology.

Sullivan was born in Norwich, New York, on February 21, 1892,

[1]Harry Stack Sullivan, *Conceptions of Modern Psychiatry* (New York: Norton,
1947), from p. xi.
[2]*Ibid.,* from p. x.

and died in Paris, January 16, 1949. He received his M.D. from the Chicago College of Medicine and Surgery in 1917, and entered the medical profession as a medical officer in World War I. Later he specialized in the practice of psychiatry where his work with schizophrenics stimulated his interest in theoretical psychology. His writings are permeated, as someone put it, with "the odor of the clinic." From 1923 to 1930 he was at the University of Maryland Medical School as Associate Professor of Psychiatry; during 1932-1933 he lectured at Yale University, and in 1939 he was appointed Professor and Chairman of the Department of Psychiatry at Georgetown University Medical School. In 1948 he became co-editor of both *Psychiatry: Journal for the Study of Interpersonal Processes* and the *Journal of Biology and Pathology*.

Among his chief works, most of them posthumous publications, are *Conceptions of Modern Psychiatry* (1947), "Tensions Interpersonal and International: A Psychiatrist's View," in *Tensions That Cause War* (ed. by H. Cantril, 1950), *The Interpersonal Theory of Psychiatry* (1953), *The Psychiatric Interview* (1954), *Schizophrenia as a Human Process* (1962), *The Fusion of Psychiatry and Social Science* (1964), and *Personal Psychopathology* (1972).

POSTULATES[3]

Three Principles Borrowed from Biology

I want at this point to mention three principles which are a part of my logical philosophy or theory and are woven into my system of thought. These three principles, which I have borrowed from the biology of Seba Eldridge, are the principle of communal existence, the principle of functional activity, and the principle of organization. It is by dealing with applications of these principles that all basic phenomenology of life can, at the biological level, be thrown into meaningful reference. The principle of communal existence refers to the fact that the living cannot live when separated from what may be described as their necessary environment. While this is not as vividly apparent at some of the higher levels of life as it is at the lowest, because storage capacities somewhat disguise the utter dependence on interchange in the higher organisms, the fact is that the living maintain constant exchange through their bordering membranes with certain elements in the physicochemical universe around them; and the interruption of this exchange is tantamount to death of the organism. Thus

[3]*The Interpersonal Theory of Psychiatry* (New York: Norton, 1953), from pp. 31-43.

by the principle of communal existence I mean that all organisms live in continuous, communal existence with their necessary environment.

*　　*　　*　　*　　*

From a consideration of these three principles, it is possible to think of man as distinguished from plants and animals by the fact that human life—in a very real and not only a purely literary or imaginary sense—requires interchange with an environment which includes culture. When I say that man is distinguished very conspicuously from other members of the biological universe by requiring interchange with a universe of culture, this means, in actual fact, since culture is an abstraction pertaining to people, that man requires interpersonal relationships, or interchange with others. While there are apparent exceptions, which I shall later mention, it is a rare person who can cut himself off from mediate and immediate relations with others for long spaces of time without undergoing a deterioration in personality. In other words, being thus cut off is perhaps not as fatal as for an animal to be cut off from all sources of oxygen; but the lethal aspect of it is nonetheless well within the realm of correct referential speech, and is not merely a figure of speech or an allegory.

The One-Genus Postulate

I now want to present what I used to call the one-genus hypothesis, or postulate. This hypothesis I word as follows: We shall assume that *everyone is much more simply human than otherwise,* and that anomalous interpersonal situations, insofar as they do not arise from differences in language or custom, are a function of differences in relative maturity of the persons concerned. In other words, the differences between any two instances of human personality—from the lowest-grade imbecile to the highest-grade genius—are much less striking than the differences between the least-gifted human being and a member of the nearest other biological genus. Man—however undistinguished biologically—as long as he is entitled to the term, human personality, will be very much more like every other instance of human personality than he is like anything else in the world. As I have tried to hint before, it is to some extent on this basis that I have become occupied with the science, not of individual differences, but of human identities, or parallels, one might say. In other words, I try to study the degrees and patterns of things which I assume to be ubiquitously human.

Heuristic Stages in Development

I would like at this point to set up a heuristic classification of personality development which is very convenient for the organization of thought. These heuristic stages are: infancy, childhood, the juvenile era, preadolescence, early adolescence, late adolescence, and adulthood or maturity.

Infancy extends from a few minutes after birth to the appearance of articulate speech, however uncommunicative or meaningless. *Childhood* extends from the appearance of the ability to utter articulate sounds of or pertaining to' speech, to the appearance of the need for playmates—that is, companions, cooperative beings of approximately one's own status in all sorts of respects. This ushers in the *juvenile era*, which extends through most of the grammar-school years to the eruption, due to maturation, of a need for an intimate relation with another person of comparable status. This, in turn, ushers in the era that we call *preadolescence*, an exceedingly important but chronologically rather brief period that ordinarily ends with the eruption of genital sexuality and puberty, but psychologically or psychiatrically ends with the movement of strong interest from a person of one's own sex to a person of the other sex. These phenomena mark the beginning of *adolescence*, which in this culture (it varies, however, from culture to culture) continues until one has patterned some type of performance which satisfies one's lust, one's genital drives. Such patterning ushers in *late adolescence*, which in turn continues as an era of personality until any partially developed aspects of personality fall into their proper relationship to their time partition; and one is able, at *adulthood*, to establish relationships of love for some other person, in which relationship the other person is as significant, or nearly as significant, as one's self. This really highly developed intimacy with another is not the principal business of life, but is, perhaps, the principal source of the satisfactions of life; and one goes on developing in depth of interest or scope of interest, or in both depth and scope, from that time until unhappy retrogressive changes in the organism lead to old age.

Euphoria and Tension

In our thinking we need, besides biological or human postulates, certain concepts that are borrowed from other fields of human activity, including a few from the field of mathematics. The one I particularly want to mention at this time is the idea of limits, and the notion of the absolute. I use absolute constructs every now and then in thinking about interpersonal relations. That is, I attempt to define something I know does not exist by extrapolation from extreme instances of something that does exist. These ideal constructs or polar constructs are useful for clear discussion of phenomena which fall more or less near one of these polar absolutes.

The two absolutes that I want to present at the moment are absolute *euphoria* and absolute *tension*. Absolute euphoria can be defined as a state of utter well-being. The nearest approach to anything like it that there is any reason for believing one can observe might occur when a very young infant is in a state of deep sleep. Absolute tension might be defined as the maximum possible deviation from absolute euphoria. The nearest approach to absolute tension that one observes is the rather uncommon, and always relatively transient, state of terror.

Now, it is a peculiarity of life that the level of euphoria and the level of tension are in reciprocal relation; that is, the level of euphoria varies inversely with the level of tension. And now I am going to make—partly, I suppose, for my own amusement—a frank and wholehearted reference to mathematics. This reciprocal relation may be expressed by saying that y is a function of x, and the relationship is $y = 1/x$.

Those of you who remember the conversion of the mathematical formula $y = 1/x$ into numerical representation will perhaps recall that y has a boundless limit when x equals zero and that, however much the value of x is increased, y never reaches zero. That is, the limits—zero for the one and infinity for the other—are never actually observed. This is just another way of saying that absolute euphoria and absolute tension are constructs which are useful in thought but which do not occur in nature. These absolutes are approached at times, but almost all of living is perhaps rather near the middle of the trail; that is, there is some tension, and to that extent the level of euphoria is not as high as it could be.

While euphoria need not trouble us very much, tensions are a very important part of our thinking. On this matter of tensions, I should like to include here an excerpt from an article of mine:[a]

> In any discussion about personality considered as an entity, we must use the term *experience*. Whatever else may be said about experience, it is in final analysis experience of *tensions* and experience of *energy transformations*. I use these two terms in exactly the same sense as I would in talking about physics; there is no need to add adjectives such as "mental"—however "mental" experience itself may be conceived to be. . . .

$$\text{EXPERIENCE is of} \begin{cases} \text{tensions} \\ \text{energy transformations} \end{cases}$$

$$\text{occurs in three modes} \begin{cases} \text{prototaxic} \\ \text{parataxic} \\ \text{syntaxic} \end{cases}$$

$$\text{TENSIONS are those of} \begin{cases} \text{needs} \begin{cases} \text{general} \\ \text{zonal} \end{cases} \\ \text{anxiety} \end{cases}$$

$$\text{ENERGY TRANSFORMATIONS are} \begin{cases} \text{overt} \\ \text{covert} \end{cases}$$

Returning now to my account of the development of the human animal in becoming a person, I have suggested that euphoria may be equated to a total equilibrium of the organism, which we know never exists, but which is approached in those time intervals or instants when tension is at its minimum. In the very young infant these intervals occur when the breathing cycle has started on its lifelong course; when there is no deficiency of body temperature, of water supply, and of food supply (in the stomach usu-

[a] *Culture and Personality*, ed. by S. Stansfeld Sargent and Marian Smith (New York: The Viking Fund, Inc., 1947).

ally) ; and when no noxious events are impinging on the so-called periphery of what will later be called awareness.

The Tension of Needs

The tensions that episodically or recurrently lower the level of the infant's euphoria and effect the biologic disequilibrium of his being are *needs* primarily appertaining to his communal existence with the physico-chemical universe. . . . The relaxations of these episodic or recurrent tensions which disturb the equilibrium of the infant's being are, of course, equilibrations with specific respect to the source of disequilibrium, whether it be lack of oxygen, lack of sugar, lack of water, or lack of adequate body temperature. And the relaxation of the tensions called out by lacks of this kind I call *satisfaction* of the specific need which was concerned.

I will mention at this time—and the immediate relevance of this will gradually appear—that satisfaction can be defined by noting the biological disequilibrium which action, that is, energy transformations, of the infant have served to remedy. In other words, a need, while it is in a broad biological sense disequilibrium, acquires its meaning from the action or energy transformations which result in its satisfaction.

* * * * *

The alteration of need and satisfaction gives rise to experience or, if you will, *is* experience—needless to say, in a prototaxic mode. The need —that is, the felt discomfort of the disequilibrium, the specific tensional reduction in euphoria—begins to be differentiated in terms of the direction toward its relief, which amounts to increasingly clear foresight of relief by appropriate action. . . . Thus beginning with the first activities of the infant, the first transformations of energy that are associated with the diminution of need and its ultimate extinction for the time being, the personality develops what is later clearly identifiable as the foresight function.

* * * * *

Concerning the relationship of the very young human and the necessary environment, it becomes possible to draw out a general principle which I used to call a theorem. This principle or theorem is designed to be an especially compact and meaningful way of expressing one of the basic derivatives from this approach.

My theorem is this: *The observed activity of the infant arising from the tension of needs induces tension in the mothering one, which tension is experienced as tenderness and as an impulsion to activities toward the relief of the infant's needs.* In other words, however manifest the increasing tension of needs in an infant may be—and we will study a very important manifestation of that tension in the energy transformations of the cry—the observation of these tensions or of the activity which manifests their presence calls out, in the mothering one, a certain tension, which may be described as that of tenderness, which is a potentiality for or an impulsion to activities suited to—or more or less suited to—the relief of the infant's needs. This, in its way, is a definition of tenderness—a very important conception, very different indeed from the miscellaneous and, in general, meaningless term "love," which confuses so many issues in our current day and age.

The manifest activity by the mothering one toward the relief of the infant's needs will presently be experienced by the infant as the undergoing of tender behavior; and these needs, the relaxation of which require cooperation of another, thereon take on the character of a general *need for tenderness*.

To sum up: The tension called out in the mothering one by the manifest needs of the infant we call *tenderness,* and a generic group of tensions in the infant, the relief of which requires cooperation by the person who acts in the mothering role, can be called *need for tenderness.* As I have said, I regard the first needs that fall into the genus of the need for tenderness as needs arising in the necessary communal existence of the infant and the physicochemical universe.

The Tension of Anxiety

But now I pass to another broadly important statement, where there is much less chance for confusion over whether things are interpersonal or impersonal. This again I call a theorem: *The tension of anxiety, when present in the mothering one, induces anxiety in the infant.* The rationale of this induction—that is, *how* anxiety in the mother induces anxiety in the infant—is thoroughly obscure. This gap, this failure of our grasp on reality, has given rise to some beautifully plausible and perhaps correct explanations of how anxiety of the mother causes anxiety in the infant; I bridge the gap simply by referring to it as a manifestation of an indefinite—that is, not yet defined—interpersonal process to which I apply the term *empathy.* . . . But whether the doctrine of empathy is accepted or not, the fact remains that the tension of anxiety when present in the mothering one induces anxiety in the infant; that theorem can be proved, I believe.

*   *   *   *   *

The tension called anxiety primarily appertains to the infant's, as also to the mother's communal existence with a *personal* environment, in utter contradistinction to the physicochemical environment. For reasons presently to appear, I distinguish this tension from the sundry tensions already called needs by saying that the relaxation of the tension of anxiety, the re-equilibration of being in this specific respect, is the experience, not of satisfaction, but of interpersonal *security.*

*   *   *   *   *

There is in the infant no capacity for action toward the relief of anxiety. While needs, as already suggested, begin to be, as it were, recognized or experimentally represented in terms of the first of the infant's actions associated with their relief, the relief of anxiety has none of that aspect. No action of the infant is consistently and frequently associated with the relief of anxiety; and therefore the need for security, or freedom from anxiety, is highly significantly distinguished from all other needs from its very first hypothetical appearance.

* * * * *

Now my point is that anxiety, in contradistinction to these other tensions, has nothing specific about it; it does not gradually get itself related to hypothetical but reasonably probable contractions in the stomach, or dryness of the throat, or what have you. It does not have any specific characteristics of that kind, and consequently there is no basis in the experience of early anxiety for any differentiation, or clarification, of action appropriate to the avoidance or relief of anxiety. Therefore, I say that the infant has no capacity for action toward the relief of anxiety.

* * * * *

THE STRUCTURE OF PERSONALITY

Dynamisms[4]

Living organisms are often multicellular organizations, and the sundry kinds of living cells which in a sense compose the organism are themselves usefully conceived as dynamisms, or as subdynamisms, one might call them, which are dynamically regulated in their living in accordance with the living of the organism as a whole. Malignancies, the sarcomatous and the carcinomatous evils which befall some organisms, may be regarded as instances of the escape from such dynamic regulation of some cells of the organism which, because they have escaped this regulation, become capable of destructively independent living. . . . This total dynamism of the organism cannot, however, be separated from its necessary environmental milieu without ceasing to be a living organism.

* * * * *

In general, we can say that the ultimate entities usefully abstracted in the study of the morphology, or organization, of living organisms is this living dynamism, the cell. Similarly, the ultimate entity, the smallest useful abstraction, which can be employed in the study of the functional activity of the living organism is the *dynamism* itself, *the relatively enduring pattern of energy transformations which recurrently characterize the*

[4]*Ibid.*, from pp. 102-9.

organism in its duration as a living organism. That is perhaps the most general statement that I can make about the conception of dynamism. . . . The dynamisms of interest to the psychiatrist are the relatively enduring patterns of energy transformation which recurrently characterize the interpersonal relations—the functional interplay of persons and personifications, personal signs, personal abstractions, and personal attributions—which make up the distinctively human sort of being.

The Definition of Pattern.   I spoke, just now, of *relatively enduring patterns,* and since this term will be repeated time and again in this presentation, it may be well at this point to say a few words about the word *pattern* itself. I shall give you a definition of patterns for which I believe I am the sole authority, a situation which always awakens very great suspicion on my part. *A pattern is the envelope of insignificant particular differences.* Taxonomy, the science of classification, which is particularly important in the biological field, deals chiefly with patterns.

* * * * *

I trust that you see that there is something, at least, in my defining a pattern as the envelope—the limit in a tridimensional or multidimensional sense—of insignificant particular differences. As long as the congeries of particular differences is insignificant, then whatever is being discussed fits the pattern, which pattern, you might say, gives it its meaning, its authenticity, or its identity.

Dynamisms in Psychiatry.   Organisms begin by reproduction; grow; mature; resist, or repair the damage caused by, some of the noxious influences which they encounter; reproduce themselves; and, in the higher manifestations of life at least, degenerate and come to an end in death. The patterns of energy transformation which characterize their life span are only *relatively* enduring. These patterns appear, in the higher forms of life at least, by maturation; they are changed variously by growth and by favorable or unfavorable influences; and perhaps in no two recurrent manifestations are they identical in all discoverable particulars. The dynamisms which interest us are relatively enduring patterns which manifest, in some cases at least, postnatal origin by maturation, and in all cases change by experience in the occurrence of which they are a significant factor. To put this very crudely, we might say that dynamisms grow or degenerate as a result of their recurrent manifestations, but that is really a pretty mystical idea. We can be more sure of what we are talking about when we say that dynamisms are modified by experience, which has in a significant sense been brought about by their manifestation.

The thing I particularly want to emphasize about dynamisms at this point is that their manifestation in the living of the organism is, in the sense that we originally used the term, *experience* of the organism. And in a sense which will later become a little clearer, this experience of the organism is particularly related to the manifestation of the particular dynamism at work and is striking, although the change in the dynamism is insignificant from the standpoint of a pattern. It will presently appear that while these changes are insignificant so far as the pattern is conceived, they can be very significant so far as living is concerned. I reiterate this notion of a pattern to emphasize the idea that a conception such as pattern can remain valid, even though, in the long stretch of duration, the objectively observable manifestations may be quite different.

*   *   *   *   *

The dynamisms of particular interest to psychiatry are of two genera: those conceptualized with primary reference to the sundry recurring tensions which manifest themselves as integrating, disjunctive, and isolating tendencies; and, on the other hand, those conceptualized with primary reference to the energy transformations characteristic of particular zones of interaction. Dynamisms of the first kind will be exemplified in our subsequent consideration, for example, of *fear;* of the anti-anxiety system which is called the *self-system*—the system involved in the maintenance of felt interpersonal security; and of *lust*, which is my particular term for certain tensions of or pertaining to the genitals, and which has an excellent historical background. Dynamisms of the second kind will be exemplified in the discussion of, for example, the *oral dynamism.* Any observable behavior may be said to manifest concomitant activity of dynamisms of both sorts, as does the phasic change in awareness concerned in sleep.

*   *   *   *   *

I have brought forward for your consideration two grand divisions, two genera, of dynamisms that are useful conceptions. One conceives the dynamism with primary reference to the tensions which recurrently disturb the euphoria of the living creature and manifest themselves in interpersonal relations as integrating, disjunctive, or isolative tendencies of a particular sort. The second concept of the dynamism, which is equally important, is on the basis of primary reference to the energy-transformation characteristics of particular zones of interaction.

*   *   *   *   *

The Concept of Personality.[5] *Personality is the relatively enduring pattern of recurrent interpersonal situations which characterize a human life.*

Personifications[6]

The infant's personification of the good mother is the prehended pattern of her participation in recurrent nursing situations and integrations of other needful sorts which have been resolved by satisfaction. She—the

[5] *Ibid.*, from pp. 110-11.
[6] *Ibid.*, from pp. 111-13.

infant's personification of the good mother—symbolizes forthcoming satisfaction of the sundry needs—that is, she symbolizes in turn the integration, maintenance, and resolution of situations that include her, through appropriate and adequate activity on the infant's part.

In what I have just said, I have introduced the idea of *personification,* which derives its importance from the fundamental importance of the interpersonal situation in understanding the phenomena with which psychiatry deals. Here, in discussing the personification of the good mother, which is formed in the early days of infancy, we start out on the long course of attempting to understand personifications and their dynamic role.

* * * * *

Now this personification is not the "real" mother—a particular living being considered as an entity. It is an elaborate organization of the infant's experience. The mother's personification of the infant is not the infant, but a growing organization of experience "in" the mother, which includes many factors only remotely pertaining to dealing with this particular "real" infant. It is important to understand that the infant's personification of the mother is composed of, or made up from, or organized from, or elaborated out of, what has occurred in the infant's relation to what you might call the "real" mother in satisfaction-giving integrations with her. And the mother's personification of the infant—which was sometimes rather rudimentary in the days when it was thought that the soul joined the infant at the age of seven months or so, before which I presume the infant could be called *it* instead of *he* or *she*—is not the infant and is not merely an abstract of the events that the mother has encountered when integrated with the infant; it includes also much that is only remotely related to dealing with this particular baby. . . . The mother's personification of the infant includes experience when the infant is anxious as well as when he is not. It includes experience when the infant is sleeping as well as when he is awake. It includes the observation of growth changes in the infant, and perhaps richly formulated expectation of changes yet to come. That which the personified infant signifies to or symbolizes "in" the mother is clearly more than forthcoming satisfaction of the need to give tenderness, or to participate in the integration, maintenance, and resolution of situations integrated by the infant's immediate needs.

* * * * *

Stereotypes.[7] In the juvenile era, one of the additions to acquaintance with social reality which is almost always encountered is the growth of patterns of others' alleged personalities, which, in a great many cases, amount to actual stereotypes. It is apparent that a great many of us make practical use of stereotypes when we say, "He acts like a farmer." This does

[7]*Ibid.,* from pp. 236-38, 300-3.

not mean that we have made a great many observations of farmers and have segregated from all these observations a nuclear group of durable and important traits which are found only in farmers; more probably we are really referring to a stereotype, which may be completely empty of any validifiable meaning. In the juvenile era, the growth of stereotypes which will later disfigure one's ability, or interfere with one's ability, to make careful discriminations about others goes to really lamentable lengths in some instances. These are persons never encountered in reality, or—perhaps next most troublesome—stereotypes of large groups of humanity on the basis of a solitary instance or a very few instances.

* * * * *

Stereotyping can be a source of a very real trouble in later life, especially if one is going into a field of work like psychiatry, where the extremely important thing to do is to observe participantly what goes on with another person. If you have a number of implicit assumptions that have not been questioned by you for twenty or twenty-five years about the alleged resemblance of the person before you to some stereotype that you have in your mind, you may find yourself greatly handicapped, for these stereotypes are often viciously incomplete and meaninglessly erroneous.

* * * * *

Sometimes there are stereotypes about teachers which are all too easy to accept because of previous unpleasantness with authority figures. Quite often there are stereotypes of juveniles' relations to teachers; and if one is actually teacher's pet, or simply for some reason the teacher is especially interested in one, one has to act under the aegis of the juvenile stereotype of the teacher's pet, and cannot therefore derive any simple profit from what would otherwise be a fortunate accident.

* * * * *

People have come to hold views of themselves which are so far from valid formulations that these views are eternally catching them in situations in which the incongruity and inappropriateness are about to become evident, whereupon the person suffers the interference of anxiety. . . . In addition to inadequate and inappropriate personifications of the self, there are, attendant upon that, and in congruity with it, inadequate and inappropriate personifications of others. Such inadequacy and inappropriateness of secondary personifications—secondary because to most people they seem less important than a person's personification of himself—may apply broadly to everyone, or specifically to stereotypes of certain alleged people. A person cannot personify others with any particular refinement except in terms of his own personification of himself. If you regard yourself as generous, then you tend to assume that others will be generous; but since you have a good deal of experience not in keeping with that, you personify many people as ungenerous, *not* generous. Now that doesn't give you any particularly good formulation of what they are; they are just different and opposite from you in one of your better aspects. Thus, to a remarkable degree this limitation in the personification of others is based on inappropriate and inadequate personification of oneself. Particularly troublesome are the inadequate and inappropriate personifications by what I have referred to as stereotypes, which again reflect the limitations in the personification of the self. We often encounter the most accessible part of such things as prejudices, intolerances, fears, hatreds, aversions, and revulsions that pertain to alleged classes of people. . . .

Stereotypes reflect inadequate and inappropriate elements in one's own self-system; thus all the special stereotypes are either poor imitations of ingredients in the personified self, or—even more inadequate in terms of providing a guide in life—they are *not* elements from the personification of the self.

*   *   *   *   *

Supervisory Patterns.[8] Stereotyping, to a striking extent, also characterizes the evolution of the juvenile's own self-system, insofar as the personifications of the self are concerned. An almost inevitable outcome of the most fortunate kind of juvenile experience is the appearance of what I call *supervisory patterns* in the already very complex system of processes and personifications that make up the self-system. These supervisory patterns amount in certain instances to subpersonalities—that is, they are "really" imaginary people who are always with one.

Perhaps I can make my point by mentioning . . . supervisory patterns that everyone knows most intimately from very long experience. When you have to teach, lecture in public, as I am doing, or do any talking in which it's quite important that the other fellow learns something from you, or thinks that you're wonderful, even if obscure, you have as a supervisory pattern a personality whom I might call your *hearer*. . . . My supervisory pattern is such that I often adjust my remarks fairly well to the needs of, let us say, fifty per cent of my audience. Some people's hearers seem to have been more singularly uninformed about other people than mine, and these hearers let pass, as adequate and proper, expressions which communicate to very few indeed of those that hear them. But in any event, it is as if there were two people—one who actually utters statements, and another who attempts to see that what is uttered is fairly well adjusted to its alleged purpose.

The Self-System[9]

Good-Me, Bad-Me, and Not-Me. Now here I have set up three aspects of interpersonal cooperation which are necessary for the infant's survival,

[8]*Ibid.*, from pp. 238-39.
[9]*Ibid.*, from pp. 161-70.

and which dictate learning. That is, these aspects of interpersonal cooperation require acculturation or socialization of the infant. Infants are customarily exposed to all of these before the era of infancy is finished. From
experience of these three sorts—with rewards, with the anxiety gradient, and
with practically obliterative sudden severe anxiety—there comes an initial
personification of three phases of what presently will be *me,* that which is
invariably connected with the sentience of *my body*—and you will remember
that *my body* as an organization of experience has come to be distinguished
from anything else by its self-sentient character. These beginning personifications of three different kinds, which have in common elements of the prehended body, are organized in about mid-infancy—I can't say exactly when.
I have already spoken of the infant's very early double personification of
the actual mothering one as the good mother and the bad mother. Now, at
this time, the beginning personifications of *me* are *good-me, bad-me,* and
not-me. So far as I can see, in practically every instance of being trained
for life, in this or another culture, it is rather inevitable that there shall be
this tripartite cleavage in personifications, which have as their central tie—
the thing that binds them ultimately into one, that always keeps them in
very close relation—their relatedness to the growing conception of "my
body."

Good-me is the beginning personification which organizes experience
in which satisfactions have been enhanced by rewarding increments of
tenderness, which come to the infant because the mothering one is pleased
with the way things are going; therefore, and to that extent, she is free,
and moves toward expressing tender appreciation of the infant. Good-me,
as it ultimately develops, is the ordinary topic of discussion about "I."

Bad-me, on the other hand, is the beginning personification which organizes experience in which increasing degrees of anxiety are associated with
behavior involving the mothering one in its more-or-less clearly prehended
interpersonal setting. That is to say, bad-me is based on this increasing
gradient of anxiety and that, in turn, is dependent, at this stage of life, on
the observation, if misinterpretation, of the infant's behavior by someone
who can induce anxiety. The frequent coincidence of certain behavior on
the part of the infant with increasing tenseness and increasingly evident
forbidding on the part of the mother is the source of the type of experience
which is organized as a rudimentary personification to which we may apply
the term bad-me.

*   *   *   *   *

The personification of the not-me is most conspicuously encountered by
most of us in an occasional dream while we are asleep; but it is very
emphatically encountered by people who are having a severe schizophrenic
episode, in aspects that are to them most spectacularly real. As a matter
of fact, it is always manifest—not every minute, but every day, in every life
—in certain peculiar absences of phenomena where there should be phe-

nomena; and in a good many people—I know not what proportion—it is very striking in its indirect manifestations (dissociated behavior), in which people do and say things of which they do not and could not have knowledge, things which may be quite meaningful to other people but are unknown to them. The special circumstances which we encounter in grave mental disorders may be, so far as you know, outside your experience; but they were not once upon a time. It is from the evidence of these special circumstances . . . that I choose to set up this third beginning personification which is tangled up with the growing acquaintance of "my body," the personification of *not-me*. This is a very gradually evolving personification of an always relatively primitive character—that is, organized in unusually simple signs in the parataxic mode of experience, and made up of poorly grasped aspects of living which will presently be regarded as "dreadful," and which will still later be differentiated into incidents which are attended by awe, horror, loathing, or dread. This rudimentary personification of not-me evolves very gradually, since it comes from the experience of intense anxiety—a very poor method of education. Such a complex and relatively inefficient method of getting acquainted with reality would naturally lead to relatively slow evolution of an organization of experiences; furthermore, these experiences are largely truncated, so that what they are really about is not clearly known.

* * * * *

The Dynamism of the Self-System. From the essential desirability of being good-me, and from the increasing ability to be warned by slight increases of anxiety—that is, slight diminutions in euphoria—in situations involving the increasingly significant other person, there comes into being the start of an exceedingly important, as it were, secondary dynamism, which is purely the product of interpersonal experience arising from anxiety encountered in the pursuit of the satisfaction of general zonal needs. This secondary dynamism I call the *self-system*. As a dynamism it is secondary in that it does not have any particular zones of interaction, any particular physiological apparatus, behind it; but it literally uses all zones of interaction and all physiological apparatus which is integrative and meaningful from the interpersonal standpoint. And we ordinarily find its ramifications spreading throughout interpersonal relations in every area where there is any chance that anxiety may be encountered.

The essential desirability of being good-me is just another way of commenting on the essential undesirability of being anxious. Since the beginning personification of good-me is based on experience in which satisfactions are enhanced by tenderness, then naturally there is an essential desirability of living good-me. . . . The self-system thus is an organization of educative experience called into being by the necessity to avoid or to minimize incidents of anxiety. The functional activity of the self-system —I am speaking of it from the general standpoint of a dynamism—is primarily directed to avoiding and minimizing this disjunctive tension of anxiety, and thus indirectly to protecting the infant from this evil eventuality in connection with the pursuit of satisfactions—the relief of general or zonal tensions.

Thus we may expect, at least until well along in life, that the components of the self-system will exist and manifest functional activity in relation to every general need that a person has, and to every zonal need that the excess supply of energy to the various zones of interaction gives rise to. How conspicuous the "sector" of the self-system connected with any particular general need or zonal need will be, or how frequent its manifestations, is purely a function of the past experience of the person concerned.

* * * * *

I have said that the self-system comes into being because the pursuit of general and zonal needs for satisfaction is increasingly interfered with by the good offices of the mothering one in attempting to train the young. And so the self-system, far from being anything like a function of or an identity with the mothering one, is an organization of experience for avoiding increasing degrees of anxiety which are connected with the educative process.

* * * * *

When I talk about the self-system, I want it clearly understood that I am talking about a *dynamism* which comes to be erroneously important in understanding interpersonal relations. This dynamism is an explanatory conception; it is not a thing, a region, or what not, such as superegos, egos, ids, and so on. Among the things this conception explains is something that can be described as a quasi-entity, the personification of the self. The personification of the self is what you are talking about when you talk about yourself as "I," and what you are often, if not invariably referring to when you talk about "me" and "my." But I would like to make it forever clear that *the relation of personifications to that which is personified is always complex and sometimes multiple;* and that *personifications are not adequate descriptions of that which is personified.*

* * * * *

The origin of the self-system can be said to rest on the irrational character of culture or, more specifically, society. . . . If the cultural prescriptions which characterize any particular society were better adapted to human life, the notions that have grown up about incorporating or introjecting a punitive, critical person would not have arisen. . . . But even at that, I believe that a human being without a self-system is beyond imagination. . . . But do not overlook the fact that the self-system comes into being because of, and can be said to have as its goal, the securing of necessary satisfaction without incurring much anxiety.

The self-system is a product of educative experience, part of which is of the character of reward, and a very important part of which has the graded anxiety element that we have spoken of. But quite early in life, anxiety is also a very conspicuous aspect of the self-dynamism *function*. This is another way of saying that experience functions in both recall and foresight. Since troublesome experience, organized in the self-system, has been experience connected with increasing grades of anxiety, it is not astounding that this element of recall, functioning on a broad scale, makes the intervention of the self-dynamism in living tantamount to the warning, or foresight, of anxiety. And warning of anxiety means noticeable anxiety, really a warning that anxiety will get worse.

Cognitive Processes[10]

What we have in our minds begins in experience, and experience for the purpose of this theory is held to occur in three modes which I shall set up, one of which is usually, but by no means certainly, restricted to human beings. These modes are: the *prototaxic,* the *parataxic,* and the *syntaxic.* I shall offer the thesis that these modes are primarily matters of "inner" elaboration of events. The mode which is easiest to discuss is relatively uncommon—experience in the syntaxic mode; the one about which something can be known, but which is somewhat harder to discuss, is experience in the parataxic mode; and the one which is ordinarily incapable of any formulation, and therefore of any discussion, is experience of the prototaxic or primitive mode. The difference in these modes lies in the extent and the character of the elaboration that one's contact with events has undergone.

The prototaxic mode, which seems to be the rough basis of memory, is the crudest—shall I say—the simplest, the earliest, and possibly the most abundant mode of experience. Sentience, in the experimental sense, presumably relates to much of what I mean by the prototaxic mode. The prototaxic, at least in the very early months of life, may be regarded as the discrete series of momentary states of the sensitive organism, with special reference to the zones of interaction with the environment.

*　　*　　*　　*　　*

SUBLIMATION[11]

When I am talking about sublimation I am not discussing exactly what Freud had in mind when he set up the terms; my thinking about sublimation makes it a very much more inclusive process than a study of classical psychoanalysis might suggest. The manifestations of what I shall continue to call sublimation, for want of a better term, appear in late infancy, be-

[10]*Ibid.,* from pp. 28-29.
[11]*Ibid.,* from pp. 193-96.

come conspicuous in childhood, and become very conspicuous indeed in the succeeding period. Since this is the label of a very important manifestation of changes in behavior and referential pattern, let me make a somewhat precise statement about it:

Sublimation is the unwitting substitution, for a behavior pattern which encounters anxiety or collides with the self-system, of a socially more acceptable activity pattern which satisfies part of the motivational system that caused trouble. In more fortunate circumstances, symbol processes occurring in sleep take care of the rest of the unsatisfied need.

To use the term sublimation in the sense that I use it, one must keep track of the fact that it occurs exterior to the field of conscious content; the reason for that is intricate but nonetheless important, and will perhaps be made clear. . . . What happens in the kind of sublimation that I am now trying to describe is that a need collides with anxiety at the behest of the social censor or acculturating person; a notable example of this—although, of course, no example is perfect—is the very young child who wants to put his thumb in his mouth but his thumb is soiled with, say, feces. If we find that this very young child, when his fingers are soiled in this particular way, always or very frequently picks out a particular toy and sucks it, then we may actually feel with reasonable certainty that there has been a "substitution" of the experience of sucking this toy, in place of the experience of putting this particular type of soiled thumb in the mouth.

*   *   *   *   *

This sublimation, or peculiar substitution of goal may be, and in fact is, in a notable proportion of all instances, almost completely satisfying, so that there is very little leftover, unsatisfied need. . . . In the adult who leads a fairly busy life, the great time for covert operations of that kind is during sleep; although it doesn't have to be, it very commonly is. . . . The point is that the excess of need which is not satisfied by the sublimation is discharged by covert or overt symbolic performances which do not collide particularly with social censure—that is, which are not particularly associated with anxiety. Needless to say, there are some patterns of behavior and covert process in the pursuit of satisfactions that can scarcely be subjected to this process. When we discuss adolescence, we will discover that this is true of lust, at least, in my view. Certain zonal needs which form part of the lust pattern may be sublimated, but if one depends on such processes for handling the whole thing, trouble is right around the corner, if not already present.

A great deal of what is called learning is made up of the refinement of behavior, and the change of covert referential processes, which are accomplished by this relatively simple process of sublimation—by combining activity in partial satisfaction of a need with other patterns of action—perhaps purely in the pursuit of security, perhaps partly in the pursuit of other satisfactions—so that anxiety is successfully avoided. . . . So it is that a very important part of education for living in an essentially irrational culture is found in this type of refinement of behavior and covert process which occurs exterior to awareness, but which has the pattern of giving up immediate, direct, and complete satisfaction of a need, and of utilizing instead some partially satisfying, socially approved pattern, discharging any excess need in sleep or in some other way.

PART TWO

Existential and Phenomenological Approaches to Personality

CHAPTER 7

MEDARD BOSS
LUDWIG BINSWANGER
ROLLO MAY

EXISTENTIAL THEORY OF PERSONALITY

The term *existentialism*, though coined in this century by Jean
Wahl, the French philosopher, finds its origin in the word "existence" as employed by the Danish philosopher Soren Kierkegaard
(1813-1855). Kierkegaard was little known to American philosophers and psychologists until the late thirties and forties, when
his works appeared in translation. But the existentialism that infil-
trated psychology was Heideggerian, though it was in the Kierke-
gaardian tradition. The book that fired the thoughts of psychologists
and psychiatrists was Heidegger's classic *Being and Time*, which
did not appear in English until 1962 though it was originally published in 1927. It was especially the Heideggerian concept of the
human being (or, preferably, being human) that appealed to psychologists, i.e., man as a being-in-the-world, a hyphenated term
because man and his phenomenological world are inseparable, for
man is an in-the-world-being and must be understood from this
phenomenological orientation.

Man as a being-in-the-world was termed *Dasein* (being-there) and
was identified by Heidegger as concern or sorrowful concern, existence, as a being-toward-death, and as moods. Man's essence is
his existence with countless possibilities available to him whereby
he may choose different personalities (kinds of being) for himself.
Heidegger's primary interest was being human and the temporality
of dasein (human existence). The fact that dasein is mine and that
existence has priority over essence characterize dasein. By the latter

is meant that man as existing is primary, not the nonexistential human or universal qualities studied as the principles of psychology, but man as an existing individual. The facticity of dasein is that he understands his own being with awareness, he is a self-conscious existent who is flung into the world as a fact. As such, he exists and *has* to be. As a self-conscious fact within the world, he is subject to fear or dread (anxiety). His nature or structure is care or sorrowful concern, and he is disclosed in anxiety (dread), an entity that can neither be particularized nor objectified, hence is a *nothingness* in which the existent individual finds himself suspended. Without dasein there is no being, no reality. Man's finitude, his consciousness of death, strikes him with a mood of anxiety, impending nothingness. Anxiety is without a corresponding object in the outer world; it lacks intentionality. Thus, man is a being-toward-death; he lives a life that is death oriented. Awareness of death, one's finite existence, makes a difference as to the choices one will make in life. Conscience, too, plays an important role, for man is a *being-guilty*, and in his existential guilt, man never escapes guilt feelings. Whatever choices are made leaves others unresolved to plague man with guilt. All time (past and future) is existentially real, and man is a being-for-the-future, oriented by the future, but the past is never completely gone because it is active in the sense that it holds future possibilities with things that bear repetition. Man's *resoluteness* girds him to face anxiety as he moves through time toward the acheivement of authentic existence. In attaining authentic existence, dasein (man) is a being-a-whole, a fully integrated and whole man. With the Heideggerian psychology and philosophy in mind, grasping the thought of the existential psychologists will prove less arduous.

Both Medard Boss and Ludwig Binswanger were reared in the tradition of Swiss psychiatry. Born in Kreuzlingen on April 13, 1881, Binswanger, the senior of the two by over a score of years, was trained at Lausanne, Heidelberg, and Zurich universities in the early years of the present century. For a brief period of a year, he was a medical assistant at Burghölzli (Zurich), and a second year was invested under the guidance of Eugen Bleuler at the Psychiatric University Clinic in Jena. His long tenure as Medical Superintendent at the Sanatorium Bellevue in Kreuzlingen began in 1910. This leading force in existential psychiatry died in 1966.

Of the many books of Binswanger, only a few have been translated into English; the first full-length book devoted to his writings is *Being-in-the-World*, which appeared in translation in 1963. In 1958, however, some of his writings were translated as part of a volume edited by May, Angel, and Ellenberger, titled *Existence: A New Dimension in Psychiatry and Psychology*. His articles are also appearing in English, among them "Existential Analysis, Psychiatry, Schizophrenia" in *Journal of Existential Psychiatry*, 1960, and a chapter in *Progress in Psychotherapy*, ed. by F. Fromm-Reichman and J. L. Moreno in 1956.

Born on October 4, 1903, in St. Gallen, Switzerland, Medard Boss spent virtually all of his life in Zurich, was educated at its university, and later became Professor of Psychotherapy at the University of Zurich's medical school. One-time president of the International Society for Medical Psychotherapy, Boss has only relatively recently become known to American psychologists. This close friend of Heidegger had his first book in English published by Dagobert D. Runes, the philosopher-head of Philosophical Library, Inc., and roommate of Heidegger when the two were students together. The book, *The Analysis of Dreams*, appeared in English in 1958, and was followed in 1963 by his exposition of existential psychology (including existential personality theory), *Psychoanalysis and Daseinsanalysis*. A half-year sojourn to India in 1956 resulted in *A Psychiatrist Discovers India*, which though written in 1958 was not translated until 1965.

The third existentialist psychologist, Rollo May, is the leading American champion of existentialist personality theory. May, a practicing psychotherapist in New York, was born on April 21, 1909, in Ada, Ohio. After receiving his baccalaureate from Oberlin College in 1930, he turned to theological school, obtaining a B.D. in 1938 before pursuing a Ph.D. at Columbia, which was granted in 1949. In the mid-thirties, May served as counselor to male students at Michigan State College and the mid-forties found him at a similar task at the College of the City of New York. While in private practice as a psychoanalyst, he served on faculties at a number of institutions, including the William Alanson White Institute of Psychiatry, Psychology, and Psychoanalysis (from 1948 to 1955 and again from 1958 to the present); New School for Social Research (1955 to 1960), New York University (1960 to the present), the summer of 1964 at Harvard University, Princeton University (1966 to 1967), and recently at Yale University.

May's works include *The Art of Counseling* (1939), the presentation of counseling as an art and psychotherapy oriented from personality theories espoused by Freud, Jung, Rank, and Kunkel; *The Meaning of Anxiety* (1950), a treatment of anxiety as the central problem of psychotherapy and a review of various theories of anxiety; *Man's Search for Himself* (1953), the search for self-realization, selfhood, and integration; *Psychology and the Human Dilemma* (1967), a collection of essays and papers written during the mid-sixties, and *Love and Will* (1967). He also edited *Existential Psychology* (rev. ed., 1969), six chapters on existential psychology contributed by May, Rogers, Allport, Maslow, and Feifel, and coedited the earlier mentioned *Existence*.

Existential psychology, a humanistic orientation to personality theory, is one of the youngest approaches in psychology. Its life in America is virtually in its embryonic stage.

ANALYSIS OF DASEIN (HUMAN PERSONALITY)[1]

Basic Nature of Man's Being-in-the-World

Man's primordial being-in-the-world is not an abstraction but always a concrete occurrence. His being-in-the-world occurs and fulfills itself only in and as the manifold particular modes of human behavior and of man's different ways of relating toward things and fellow beings. This kind of being presupposes a unique openness of man's existence. It has to be an openness into which the particular beings which man encounters can disclose themselves as the beings they are, with all the context of their meaningful references. How else could man relate to things in the sensible and efficient way he actually is capable of if his relationships toward them were not primarily of the nature of illuminating, of disclosing and understanding the meaning of what he encounters, whether this disclosure of the things of his world occurs as seeing or hearing them, smelling or tasting them, feeling them, thinking or dreaming of them, or as handling them unreflectingly?

* * * * *

This primary awareness of Being-ness is—as the fundamental feature of man's existence—*not* an attribute or a property which man has, but that man *is* this primary awareness of Being-ness, that he is in the world essentially and primarily as such. Man, then, is a light which luminates[a] whatever particular being comes into the realm of its rays. It is of his essence to disclose things and living beings in their meaning and content. This characterization of man's existence should not be mistaken and dismissed as an imaginative or poetic paraphrase without relevance for the

---

[1]Medard Boss, *Psychoanalysis and Daseinsanalysis* (New York: Basic Books, 1963), from pp. 34, 37-38, 40, 42-43, 45-48.

[a]Translator's Note: My translation is intended to differentiate the quality of "shining forth" from that of "giving light to," i.e., from *illuminate*.

investigations of psychologists and psychiatrists who want to deal only with real or so-called empirical facts. To speak here of a luminating light is by no means a far-fetched intellectual or conceptual abstraction either. It is, on the contrary, a very sober and direct description of the most concrete condition of man. For how would any perception, understanding, and elucidation of the meaning of a single thing or living being, any appearing and shining forth of this or that particular matter, be possible at all without an open realm of light, a realm that lends itself to letting shine forth whatever particular being may come into its elucidating openness? No wonder that a synonym of "understanding," "perceiving," and "becoming aware"—the word "elucidate"—has its very root in *lux*, or "light." No thing, no psychic apparatus or system of any kind, possesses the least ability to perceive itself, another thing, or, at least of all, a human being as what it actually is. Nor has any thing ever had the ability to disclose the context of reference of any of these. Only because man—in contrast to the things he deals with—is essentially an understanding, seeing, and luminating being is he capable of going both physically and spiritually blind. To speak of a blind thing—of a blind rock, for instance—does not make sense.

The Existentialia

The fundamental characteristics of (human) *Dasein*, such as being-in-the world, primary comprehending, and luminating, are, in the language of analysis of *Dasein*, "existentialia." They are to be sharply distinguished from the characteristics of particular beings *other* than *Dasein*, for which Heidegger reserves the term "categories." It is possible—and this has occurred—to misunderstand the *existentialia* in the sense of an *a priori* structure of *Dasein* existing in a supersensual realm of its own. All factual, ontic characteristics of existing human beings would then have to be understood as *a posteriori* realizations of such structures. Heidegger's concern happens to be to overcome this very type of metaphysics. He emphasizes continually that one must not picture the essential condition of *Dasein* (as he has shown it) as something which exists in itself, forms a background, and is of the nature of a design (in the sense of Platonic "Ideas"), a design which has to be deduced, by logical procedures, from observable human phenomena which always fall short of the design itself. On the contrary, the *existentialia* always characterize the immediate "essence" of factually observable, concrete behavior of human beings. *Existentialia*, being nothing other than the very meaning and essence of directly observable human behavior, cannot very well be assumed also to exist in some other way, detached from human existence. Most certainly they do not float in some metaphysical realm of their own.

Spatiality of Man's World

We have stated before that Heidegger uses the term *Dasein* in its literal sense: *Dasein* (literally "there-being") is the being of the "there." What is meant by this "there"? It may be best to consider first what the "there" of *Dasein* is *not*. It must not be understood to refer to a specific spot in space. Nor does it refer to the place where my body happens to be. The position of my body does not determine my "there" in space. Actually, an "I" without primary relations to space, an "I" which is not already "there" with the disclosed things from the beginning, an "I" which first has to enter a body and must transport it somewhere in order to be "there" eventually—such an "I" does not exist. The position of a body is, on the contrary, the essential consequence of man's existential spatiality. If we attribute spatiality to *Dasein,* then such "being in space" obviously must be understood on the basis of the mode of being of the particular being which is man. "Spatiality of *Dasein*"—*Dasein* being essentially *not* extant —cannot mean that *Dasein* occurs at some place in the world-case. Nor can it mean that *Dasein* is at hand [*zuhanden*] at a certain place, for both being extant and being at hand are modes of being of objects. Man by no means exists primarily in the segment of space his body happens to fill, limited by its epidermis. To say that *Dasein* is present at the place in space where the body is, is to reveal an ontologically inadequate conception of the particular being which is *Dasein.* Nor does the difference between the spatiality of an extended thing and the spatiality of *Dasein* lie in the peculiarity that *Dasein knows* of space. Taking up space is not only *not* identical with the ability to imagine space, but the former presupposes the latter. It is also inadequate to interpret the spatiality of *Dasein* as an imperfection, due to the fatal bond between spirit and body. *Dasein* is, rather, essentially spatial *because* it is "spiritual." No extended body-thing is spiritual, and for this reason it cannot be spatial in the way *Dasein* is spatial.

Temporality of Man's World

The original spatiality of *Dasein* is closely related to man's original temporality. Indeed, spatiality can be fully understood only on the basis of temporality. For "being" always means being "present" within the "there," within the luminous realm of Being-ness which is man's existence. Presence is derived from *praeesse. Praeesse* implies both "emergence" and "sojourn," and both of these imply "lasting." Something can last only on the basis of "time." For this reason, Western philosophical thought has ever since its beginnings implicitly related the deepest essence of Being-ness, including the essence of human being, to temporality. By the same token, Heidegger's title for his main work—*Being and Time*—underscores the fact that he is asking the fundamental ontological question concerning the meaning of "Being-ness as such."

Man as a being is present [*ein Anwesender*] and he lasts [*ein Während-der*], he is a temporal being. This does not mean that the particular temporality of *Dasein* can be deduced from what is commonly called "time," i.e., from the velocity of the moving stars, from other natural occurrences, or from the turning of the hands of a clock. Far from it. Man's original temporality is as little an item existing by itself and outside of man as his original spatiality. Original time is no external framework consisting of an endless sequence of "nows," on which man eventually can hang up and put into proper order his experiences and the events of his life. Man's temporality *is* not but *is emerging* [*zeitigt sich*], as the unfolding and coming forth of his existence. Man's original temporality always refers to his disclosing and taking care of something. Such original temporality is dated at all times by his meaningful interactions with, his relating to, that which he encounters. Every "now" is primarily a "now as the door bangs," a "now as the book is missing," or a "now when this or that has to be done." The same holds true for every "then." Originally a "then" is a "then when I met my friend, some time in the past" or a "then when I shall go to the university again." Every "now" and every "then" refers to a man's caring for something, and it lasts as long as this caring-for lasts. There is, for example, a "now during the interval in the theater" or the "then while we were having breakfast." Man carries out his existence in such caring for what is disclosed to him. He lasts from his past through his present into his future in letting things come forth and shine into the luminating realm of his existence, in caring for them in one way or the other. Existing in such a way, he is consuming *his* time. Because man's original temporality thus consists "only" in such an occurrence, i.e., *as* the consumption or the carrying out of his existential potentialities, he can know short and long hours, depending on whether his existence is intensely fulfilled at a given phase of its unfolding or is not. Also based on this original, existential temporality are questions such as the one addressed to a friend whom one is reluctant to see depart: "Can't you stay for another cigarette?" The insight into this original temporality of human being (as well as the insight into original spatiality) is of paramount importance for the understanding of otherwise unintelligible "time"-(and space-) phenomena in many dreams, in experiences of schizophrenic patients and drug addicts, and so forth.

Dasein grants itself its original *spatiality* in its relations to the phenomena which show themselves in the *light* of its essence. In such *opening-up of space, Dasein* unfolds its existence, *"consumes" its time,* i.e., it emerges. Without man's existence, unfolding its own temporality and spatiality, there would not be a lighted realm, a "there" into which particular beings can come forth, can appear, and actually come into their own being. There can be no appearance—no "phenomenon" (from *phainesthai:* to appear)—without a light.

Man's Fundamental Engagement

Comprehension of the *existentialia* and of the spatiality and temporality of man's world helps us achieve some of the basic Daseinsanalytic insights into the nature of man's being-in-the-world. Yet these insights constitute only the very beginning of an understanding of man's existence.

Analysis of *Dasein* regards man's unique way of being-in-the-world solely as the necessary presupposition and precondition for a really human existence. Man seems so constituted not just for his own amusement. Man's existence seems claimed by Being-ness as the necessary clearing into which all that has to be may come forth and within which it may shine forth. For everything that can come forth needs a realm into which it can do so. Man is well equipped to be this realm. His task seemingly is to be both "servant and shepherd of Being-ness." This means that man must responsibly take over all his possibilities for world-disclosing relationships, so that whatever may show itself in the light of these relationships can come forth into its being to the best possible extent. In other words, man is to accept all his life-possibilities, he is to appropriate and assemble them to a free, authentic own self no longer caught in the narrowed-down mentality of an anonymous, inauthentic "everybody." Man's freedom consists in becoming ready for accepting and letting be all that is, to let it shine forth in the world-openness *as* which he exists.

How else could it be possible that man is reminded of this task by his conscience, whenever he does not fulfill it? This call of conscience, these feelings of guilt, will not give him any peace until he has borne out all his possibilities in caring for the things and fellow men of his world. As long as man lives he is essentially and inevitably in debt [*Schuld*][b] in this regard. For he is always and necessarily in arrears, as far as carrying out his world-disclosing possibilities of living are concerned. He is in arrears in two ways. First, finite man can exist only in one of the world-relations of which he is constituted at any given time, and all other possibilities of caring for something remain unfulfilled at that moment. Second, man's whole future waits for him. Until the moment of his death, new possibilities for world-disclosure approach him from his future—possibilities which must be taken over, whose fulfillment he still owes. All actual, concrete feelings of guilt and pangs of conscience are grounded in this existential "being-in-debt" [*Schuldigsein*] toward his whole existence, lasting all through life, no matter how grotesquely they sometimes appear, and how far from their source they may have been driven in various neurotic conditions.

MAN AS DASEIN, FACTICITY, AND CARE[2]

Man as a creature of nature is revealed in the thrownness of the Dasein, its "that-it-is," its *facticity*. "Has the Dasein, as such, ever freely decided and will it ever be able to decide as to whether it wants to come into 'ex-

---

[b]Translator's Note: *Schuld* means both "debt" and "guilt." This dual meaning should be kept in mind.

[2]Ludwig Binswanger, *Being-in-the-World*, Jacob Needleman, trans. (New York, Basic Books, 1963), from pp. 212-14.

istence' or not?" The Dasein, although it exists essentially for its own sake (*umwillen seiner*), has nevertheless not itself laid the ground of its *being*. And also, as a creature "come into existence," it is and remains, *thrown*, determined, i.e., enclosed, possessed, and compelled by beings in general. Consequently it is not "completely free" in its world-design either. The "powerlessness" of the Dasein here shows itself in that certain of its possibilities of being-in-the-world are *withdrawn* because of commitment to and by beings, because of its facticity. But it is also just this withdrawal that lends the Dasein its *power*: for it is this that first brings *before* the Dasein the "real," graspable possibilities of world-design.

Transcendence is thus not only a striding or swinging of the Dasein toward the world, but is, at the same time, withdrawal, limitation—and only *in* this limiting does transcendence gain power "over the world." All this, however, is but a "transcendental document" of the Dasein's *finitude*. The thrownness of the Dasein, its facticity, is the transcendental horizon of all that scientific systematic psychiatry delimits as reality under the name of organism, body (and heredity, climate, milieu, etc.), and also for all that which is delimited, investigated, and researched as psychic *determinateness*: namely, as mood and ill humor, as craziness, compulsive or insane "possessedness," as addiction, instinctuality, as confusion, phantasy determination, as, in general, unconsciousness. Now, whereas the science of psychiatry not only observes and establishes connections *between* these two spheres, but also erects the theoretical bridge of the psychophysical—*Daseinsanalyse*, on the other hand, shows that it is the scientific dichotomization of man's ontological wholeness that gives rise to this postulate in the first place. It shows that this dichotomization results from projecting the whole of human being upon the screen of that which is merely objectively present [*vorhanden*]. It also indicates the general world-design of science as stemming from one and the same Dasein, from, namely, the Dasein's ontological potentiality of scientific being-in-the-world. Here, too, it is true to say that what lends the world-design its (limited) scientific power is obtained only through its powerlessness to understand the being of human existence [Dasein] as a whole.

It is to Heidegger's great credit that he summed up the being of the Dasein under the all too easily misunderstood title of Care (= caring for), and to have phenomenologically explored its basic structures and make-up. Thrownness in the sense of the facticity of the Dasein's answerability to its that-it-is, is only *one* component ("existential") of this structure, the others, as we know, being existence (project) and fallenness. Thus what in psychiatry is irreversibly separated into discrete realities of fields of study, namely, the finite human Dasein, is presented here in its basic structural unity. (It cannot be emphasized too often that this presentation signifies something quite different from the approach to man under the aegis of one particular *idea*, such as the idea of the will to power, libido, or any idea involving man as, in general, a creature of nature, or even, indeed, the idea

of man as a child of God, as *homo aeternus*, etc.) But where there is structure there can be no dissociation of one structural member from the structural whole. Each, rather, remains implicated in the others, and a change
in one structural element involves a change in the others. The Dasein can
thus never get "behind" its thrownness and can only project those possibilities into which it is thrown. Only, therefore, as surrendered to its *that*,
as thrown, does the Dasein *exist* within the ground of its power-to-be.
The self of existence, although it has to lay its own ground, can therefore
never have power over this ground. As a being, it has to be "as it is and
can be." Its being is a projection of its own power-to-be, and to this extent
it is always already in *advance*[c] of itself. This being in advance of itself
also concerns the whole of the Dasein's structure. Corresponding to all that
we know of its thrownness (as already-being-in-the-world), the being-in-
advance-of itself of the Dasein, its futurity, is through and through implicated with its past. Out of both these temporal "ecstasies" the authentic
present temporalizes itself. This is what [has been referred to elsewhere]
as the "way" of *Sein und Zeit*: the attempt to understand the basic structure of the Dasein *via* the unitariness of temporality and its ecstasies.

EXISTENTIAL ANALYSIS, TRANSCENDENCE, WORLD-DESIGN AND BEING-BEYOND-THE-WORLD[3]

Existential analysis does not propose an ontological thesis about an
essential condition determining existence, but makes *ontic statements*—
that is, statements of factual findings about actually appearing forms and
configurations of existence. In this sense, existential analysis is an empirical science, with its own method and particular ideal of exactness,
namely with the method and the ideal of exactness of the *phenomenological* empirical sciences.

Today we can no longer evade recognition of the fact that there are
two types of empirical scientific knowledge. One is the *discursive inductive*
knowledge in the sense of describing, explaining, and controlling "natural
events," whereas the second is the *phenomenological empirical* knowledge
in the sense of a methodical, critical exploitation or interpretation of phenomenal contents. It is the old disagreement between Goethe and Newton
which today—far from disturbing us—has changed by virtue of our deep-
ened insight into the nature of experience from an "either/or" into an
"as well as." The same phenomenological empirical knowledge is used re-

[c]Regarding the extent to which the various psychotic forms of manic depression and
schizophrenia are rooted in various modes of this being-in-advance-of-itself of the Dasein
(be it from the aspect of attunement [*Gestimmtheit*] or "Extravagant" ideal-formation),
see my studies *Ober Ideenflucht* and *Schizophrenie*.

[3]Ludwig Binswanger, "The Existential Analysis School of Thought," in Rollo May,
Ernest Angel, and Henri F. Ellenberger, eds., *Existence: A New Dimension in Psychiatry and Psychology* (New York: Basic Books, 1958), from pp. 192-95, 200-1.

gardless of whether we deal with the interpretation of the aesthetic content of an artistic style-period, with the literary content of a poem or a drama, or with the self-and-world content of a Rorschach response or of a psychotic form of existence. In phenomenological experience, the discursive taking apart of natural objects into characteristics or qualities and their inductive elaboration into types, concepts, judgments, conclusions, and theories is replaced by giving expression to the content of what is purely phenomenally given and therefore is not part of "nature as such" in any way. But the phenomenal content can find expression and, in being expressed, can unfold itself only if we approach and question it by the phenomenological method—or else we shall receive not a scientifically founded and verifiable answer but just an accidental *aperçu*. In this, as in every science, everything depends upon the method of approach and inquiry—*i.e.*, on the ways and means of the phenomenological method of experience.

Over the last few decades the concept of phenomenology has changed in some respects. Today, we must strictly differentiate between Husserl's pure or eidetic phenomenology as a transcendental discipline, and the phenomenological interpretation of human forms of existence as an empirical discipline. But understanding the latter is not possible without knowledge of the former.

In this we should be guided, to mention only one factor, by abstinence from what Flaubert calls *la rage de vouloir conclure,* that is, by overcoming our passionate need to draw conclusions, to form an opinion, or to pass judgment—a task which in the light of our one-sided natural-scientific intellectual training cannot be considered an easy one. In short, instead of reflecting on something we should let the something speak for itself or, to quote Flaubert again, "express the thing as it is." However, the "as it is" contains one more fundamental ontological and phenomenological problem; for we finite human beings can acquire information on the "how" of a thing only according to the "world-design" which guides our understanding of things. Therefore, I have to return once more to Heidegger's thesis of existence as "being-in-the-world."

The ontological thesis that the basic constitution or structure of existence is being-in-the-world is not a philosophical *aperçu* but rather represents an extremely consistent development and extension of fundamental philosophical theories, namely of Kant's theory about the conditions of the possibility of experience (in the natural-scientific sense) on the one hand, and of Husserl's theory of transcendental phenomenology on the other. I shall not elaborate on these connections and developments. What I want to emphasize here is only the identification of being-in-the-world and transcendence; for it is through this that we can understand what "being-in-the-world" and "world" signify in their anthropological application. The German word for transcendence or transcending is *Ueberstieg* (climbing over or above, mounting). An *Ueberstieg* requires, first, that toward which the

Ueberstieg is directed and, secondly, that which is *ueberstiegen* or transcended; the first, then, toward which the transcendence occurs, we call "world," whereas the second, which is transcended, is the being itself *(das Seiende selbst)* and especially that in the form of which a human existence itself "exists." In other words, not only "world" constitutes itself in the act of transcending—be it as a mere dawn of world or as objectifying knowledge—but the self also does so.

Why do I have to mention these seemingly complicated matters?

Only because through the concept of being-in-the-world as transcendence has the fatal defect of all psychology been overcome and the road cleared for anthropology, the fatal defect being the theory of a dichotomy of world into subject and object. On the basis of that theory, human existence has been reduced to a mere subject, to a worldless rump subject in which all sorts of happenings, events, functions occur, which has all sorts of traits and performs all sorts of acts, without anybody, however, being able to say (notwithstanding theoretical constructs) how the subject can ever meet an "object" and can communicate and arrive at an understanding with other subjects. In contrast, being-in-the-world implies always being in the world with beings such as I, with coexistents. Heidegger, in his concept of being-in-the-world as transcendence, has not only returned to a point prior to the subject-object dichotomy of knowledge and eliminated the gap between self and world, but has also elucidated the structure of subjectivity as transcendence. Thus he has opened a new horizon of understanding for, and given a new impulse to, the scientific exploration of human existence and its specific modes of being. The split of Being into subject (man, person) and object (thing, environment) is now replaced by the unity of existence and "world," secured by transcendence.[d]

Transcending, therefore, implies far more, and something much more original, than knowing, even more than "intentionality" in Husserl's sense, since "world" becomes accessible to us first and foremost already through our "key" *(Stimmung)*. If for a moment we remember the definition of being-in-the-world as transcendence and view from this point our psychiatric analysis of existence, we realize that by investigating the structure of being-in-the-world we can also approach and explore psychoses; and realize furthermore that we have to understand them as specific modes of

[d]Where we speak of "world" in terms of existential analysis, there world always means that toward which the existence has climbed and according to which it has designed itself: or, in other words, the manner and mode in which that which is *(Seiende)* becomes accessible to the existence. However, we use the expression "world" not only in its transcendental but also in its "objective" sense, as, *e.g.*, when we speak of the "dull resistance of the world," of the "temptations of the world," "retiring from the world," etc., whereby we have primarily the world of our fellow men in mind. Similarly, we speak of a person's environment and of his "own world" as of particular regions of that which exists in the objective world, and not as of transcendental world designs. This is terminologically troublesome, but not open to change any more. Hence, where the meaning is not self-evident, we have to place "world" always in quotation marks, or use the term "world design."

transcending. In this context we do not say: mental illnesses are diseases of the brain (which, of course, they remain from a medical-clinical viewpoint). But we say: In the mental diseases we face modifications of the fundamental or essential structure and of the structural links of being-in-the-world as transcendence. It is one of the tasks of psychiatry to investigate and establish these variations in a scientifically exact way.

As can be seen from all our analyses published so far, spatialization and temporalization of existence play an important part in existential analysis. I shall confine myself here to the still more central problem of time. What makes this problem so central is the fact that transcendence is rooted in the very nature of time, in its unfolding into future, "having been" *(Gewesenheit)*, and present. This will help to explain why, in our anthropological analyses of psychotic forms of being-human, we are not satisfied with our investigation unless we gain at least some insight into the respective variations of the structure of our patients' time. . . .

In those forms of being-in-the-world which are generally called "psychotic" we have so far found two types of modifications of "world"-formation, one characterized by "leaping" (ordered flight of ideas) and by a "whirl" (disorderly flight of ideas), and the other characterized by a shrinking and simultaneous narrowing of existence along with its turning into swamp and earth *(Verweltlichung)*. We may describe the latter also in the following terms: the freedom of letting "world" occur is replaced by the unfreedom of being overwhelmed by a certain "world-design." In the case of Ellen West, for instance, the freedom of forming an "ethereal" world was replaced more and more by the unfreedom of sinking into the narrow world of the grave and the swamp. "World," however, signifies not only world-formation and predesign of world, but—on the basis of the pre-design and model-image—also the *how* of being-*in*-the-world and the attitude *toward* world. Thus, the transformation of the ethereal into a grave-world could also be established in the change of the existence as expressed by an exultingly soaring bird to an existence in the form of a slowly crawling, blind earthworm.

All this takes us only to the outermost gate of Heidegger's fundamental ontology or *"Daseins* Analytics" and just to the gates of anthropological or existential analysis which has been inspired by and founded on the former. But I hasten to outline the method of existential analysis and the area of its scientific function. At this point, I have to mention that my positive criticism of Heidegger's theory has led me to its extension: being-in-the-world as being of the existence for the sake of *myself* (designated by Heidegger as "care") has been juxtaposed with "being-beyond-the-world" as being of the existence for the sake of *ourselves* (designated by me as "love"). This transformation of Heidegger's system has to be considered especially in the analysis of psychotic forms of existence where we frequently observe modifications of transcendence in the sense of the "over-swing" of love, rather than in the sense of the "overclimb" of care. Let us

only remember the enormously complex shrinkage of the existential structure which we so summarily call "autism."

* * * * *

As compared with biological research, which exhausts or interprets the
life-content of the phenomena, existential-analytical research has a double
advantage. Firstly, it does not have to deal with so vague a "concept" as
that of life, but with the widely and completely uncovered *structure of
existence* as "being-in-the-world" and "beyond-the-world." Secondly, it
can let existence actually speak up about itself—let it have its say. In
other words, the phenomena to be interpreted are largely language phenomena. We know that the content of existence can nowhere be more
clearly seen or more securely interpreted than through language; because it is in language that our world-designs actually ensconce and articulate themselves and where, therefore, they can be ascertained and
communicated.

As to the first advantage, knowledge of the structure or basic constitution of existence provides us with a systematic clue for the practical
existential-analytical investigation at hand. We know, now, what to focus
on in the exploration of a psychosis, and how to proceed. We know that
we have to ascertain the kind of spatialization and temporalization, of light-
ing and coloring; the texture, or materiality and motility, of the world-
design toward which the given form of existence or its individual configuration casts itself. Such a methodical clue can be furnished only by the
structure of being-in-the-world because that structure places a norm at
our disposal and so enables us to determine deviations from this norm in
the manner of the exact sciences. Much to our surprise it has turned out
that, in the psychoses which were so far investigated, such deviations could
not be understood merely negatively as abnormalities, but that they, in
turn, represent a new norm, a new *form* of being-in-the-world. If, for example, we can speak of a manic form of life or, rather, of existence, it
means that we could establish a norm which embraces and governs all
modes of expression and behavior designated as "manic" by us. It is this
norm which we call the "world" of the manic. The same holds true for the
far more complicated, hitherto incalculably manifold world-designs of the
schizophrenic. To explore and ascertain the world of these patients means,
here as everywhere, to explore and ascertain in what way everything that
is—men as well as things—is accessible to these forms of existence. For we
know well enough that that-which-is as such never becomes accessible to
man, except in and through a certain world-design.

As to the second advantage, the possibility of exploring language phenomena, it is the essence of speech and speaking that they express and
communicate a *certain content of meaning*. This content of meaning is, as
we know, an infinitely manifold one. Everything, therefore, depends upon
the precise criteria by which we explore the language manifestations of

our patients. We do not—as the psychoanalyst systematically does—focus merely upon the historical content, upon references to an experienced or conjectured pattern of the inner life-history. And we do not at all watch the content for all possible references to facts pertaining to life function, as does the psychopathologist in focusing on disturbances of speech or thinking functions. What attracts our attention in existential-analysis is rather the content of language expressions and manifestations insofar as they point to the world-design or designs in which the speaker lives or has lived or, in one word, their world-content. By world-content, then, we mean the content of facts pertaining to worlds; that is, of references to the way in which the given form or configuration of existence discovers world designs and opens up world—and is, or exists, in the respective world. There are, furthermore, indications of the way in which the existence is *beyond-the-world*; that is, how it *is*, or *is not*, at home in the eternity *(Ewigkeit)* and haven *(Heimat)* of love.

THREE MODES OF BEING-IN-THE-WORLD: UMWELT, MITWELT, AND EIGENWELT[4]

The existential analysts distinguish three modes of world, that is, three simultaneous aspects of world which characterize the existence of each one of us as being-in-the-world. First, there is *Umwelt*, literally meaning "world around"; this is the biological world, generally called the environment. There is, second, the *Mitwelt*, literally the "with-world," the world of beings of one's own kind, the world of one's fellow men. The third is *Eigenwelt*, the "own-world," the mode of relationship to one's self.

The first, *Umwelt*, is of course what is taken in general parlance as world, namely, the world of objects about us, the natural world. All organisms have an *Umwelt*. For animals and human beings the *Umwelt* includes biological needs, drives, instincts—the world one would still exist in if, let us hypothesize, one had no self-awareness. It is the world of natural law and natural cycles, of sleep and awakeness, of being born and dying, desire and relief, the world of finiteness and biological determinism, the "thrown world" to which each of us must in some way adjust. The existential analysts do not at all neglect the reality of the natural world; "natural law is as valid as ever," as Kierkegaard put it. They have no truck with the idealists who would reduce the material world to an epiphenomenon or with the intuitionists who would make it purely subjective or with anyone who would underestimate the importance of the world of biological determinism. Indeed, their insistence on taking the objective world of nature seriously is one of their distinctive characteris-

[4]Rollo May, "Contributions of Existential Psychotherapy," in Rollo May, Ernest Angel, and Henri F. Ellenberger, eds., *Existence: A New Dimension in Psychiatry and Psychology* (New York: Basic Books, 1958), from pp. 61-63.

tics. In reading them I often have the impression that they are able to grasp the *Umwelt*, the material world, with greater reality than those who seg- ment it into "drives" and "substances," precisely because they are not limited to *Umwelt* alone, but see it also in the context of human self- awareness.[e]. . . They insist strongly that it is an oversimplification and radical error to deal with human beings as though *Umwelt* were the only mode of existence or to carry over the categories which fit *Umwelt* to make a procrustean bed upon which to force all human experience. In this connection, the existential analysts are *more empirical,* that is, more re- spectful of actual human phenomena, than the mechanists or positivists.

The *Mitwelt* is the world of interrelationships with human beings. But it is not to be confused with "the influence of the group upon the indi- vidual," or "the collective mind," or the various forms of "social de- terminism." The distinctive quality of *Mitwelt* can be seen when we note the difference between a herd of animals and a community of people. Howard Liddell has pointed out that for his sheep the "herd instinct con- sists of keeping the environment constant." Except in mating and suckling periods, a flock of collie dogs and children will do as well for the sheep pro- viding such an environment is kept constant. In a group of human beings, however, a vastly more complex interaction goes on, with the meaning of the others in the group partly determined by one's own relationship to them. Strictly speaking, we should say animals have an *environment,* human beings have a *world.* For world includes the structure of meaning which is designed by the interrelationship of the persons in it. Thus the meaning of the group for me depends in part upon how I put myself into it. And thus, also, love can never be understood on a purely biological level but depends upon such factors as personal decision and commitment to the other person.[f]

The categories of "adjustment" and "adaptation" are entirely accurate in *Umwelt.* I adapt to the cold weather and I adjust to the periodic needs of my body for sleep; the critical point is that the weather is not changed by my adjusting to it nor is it affected at all. Adjustment occurs between two objects, or a person and an object. But in *Mitwelt,* the categories of adjustment and adaptation are not accurate; the term "relationship" offers the right category. If I insist that another person adjust to me, I am not taking him as a person, as *Dasein,* but as an instrumentality; and even if I adjust to myself, I am using myself as an object. One can never accurately speak of human beings as "sexual objects," as Kinsey for one example

[e]In this respect it is significant to note that Kierkegaard and Nietzsche, in contrast to the great bulk of nineteenth-century thinkers, were able to take the body seriously. The reason was that they saw it not as a collection of abstracted substances or drives, *but as one mode of the reality of the person.* Thus when Nietzsche says "We think with our bodies," he means something radically different from the behaviorists.

[f]Martin Buber has developed implications of *Mitwelt* in his *I and Thou* philosophy. See his lectures at the Washington School of Psychiatry, printed in *Psychiatry,* May 1957, Vol. 20, No. Two, and especially the lecture on "Distance and Relation."

does; once a person is a sexual object, you are not talking about a person any more. *The essence of relationship is that in the encounter both persons are changed.* Providing the human beings involved are not too severely ill and have some degree of consciousness, relationship always involves mutual awareness; and this already is the process of being mutually affected by the encounter.

The *Eigenwelt,* or "own world," is the mode which is least adequately dealt with or understood in modern psychology and depth-psychology; indeed, it is fair to say that it is almost ignored. *Eigenwelt* presupposes self-awareness, self-relatedness, and is uniquely present in human beings. But it is not merely a subjective, inner experience; it is rather the basis on which we see the real world in its true perspective, the basis on which we relate. It is a grasping of what something in the world—this bouquet of flowers, this other person—means to *me.* Suzuki has remarked that in Eastern languages, such as Japanese, adjectives always include the implication of "for-me-ness." That is to say, "this flower is beautiful" means *"for me* this flower is beautiful." Our Western dichotomy between subject and object has led us, in contrast, to assume that we have said most if we state that the flower is beautiful entirely divorced from ourselves, as though a statement were the more true in proportion to how little we ourselves have to do with it! This leaving of *Eigenwelt* out of the picture not only contributes to arid intellectualism and loss of vitality but obviously also has much to do with the fact that modern people tend to lose the sense of reality of their experiences.

It should be clear that these three modes of world are always interrelated and always condition each other. At every moment, for example, I exist in *Umwelt,* the biological world; but how I relate to my need for sleep or the weather or any instinct—how, that is, I see in my own self-awareness this or that aspect of *Umwelt*—is crucial for its meaning for me and conditions how I will react to it. The human being lives in *Umwelt, Mitwelt,* and *Eigenwelt* simultaneously. They are by no means three different worlds but three simultaneous modes of being-in-the-world.

Several implications follow from the above description of the three modes of world. One is that the reality of being-in-the-world is lost if *one of these modes is emphasized to the exclusion of the other two.*

CHAPTER 8

VIKTOR E. FRANKL

LOGOTHERAPY APPROACH TO PERSONALITY

Founder of the third school of Viennese psychiatry, Viktor E. Frankl was born on March 26, 1905, and educated at the University of Vienna where he received his M.D. and Ph.D. degrees, the former in 1930 and the latter in 1949. The World War II years found him in several concentration camps, out of which materialized his *From Death-Camp to Existentialism* in 1959, revised in 1962 as *Man's Search for Meaning: An Introduction to Logotherapy*. His speciality since 1936 has been neurology and psychiatry, and since the postwar years he has enjoyed a long tenure as Head of the Department of Neurology at the Poliklinik Hospital at Vienna and as Professor of Psychiatry and Neurology at the University of Vienna.

In recent years, Frankl has been writing extensively and lecturing at universities throughout the world, especially in the United States, where he spent the 1970-1973 school seasons at the Institute of Logotherapy at the United States International University and the summer of 1972 at Duquesne University. Prior to that time he offered courses at Harvard and Southern Methodist.

Although Frankl is quite fluent in English, having written a number of books and numerous papers in English, most of his books are in German and have not as yet been translated. His first article was published at the age of nineteen at Freud's invitation in the *International Journal of Psychoanalysis*. His first book to appear in English, *Arztliche Seelsorge*, appeared under the title *The Doctor and the Soul: From Psychotherapy to Logotherapy* (1955; revised, 1965). The book was more than an autobiography; it enunciated the principles of logotherapy. Though Frankl minimizes his concentration camp experiences of three years duration, those experiences serve for many as credentials of his logotherapeutic theory of personality. Speaking of them, Gordon W. Allport exclaimed: "How could he—every possession lost, every value destroyed, suffering from hunger, cold and brutality, hourly expecting extermination—how could he find life worth preserving? A psychiatrist who personally faced such extremities is a psychiatrist worth listening to." These words by Allport serve as part of the Preface to Frankl's *Man's Search for Meaning,* the best of the autobiographies by the founder of logotherapy. That work includes as well a précis of logotherapy. In 1967 his most widely quoted papers were gathered and published as *Psychotherapy and Existentialism,* and two years later an updated version of his views on personality appeared in integrated form under the title *The Will to Meaning* (1969). In 1975, he revised as well as translated his *The Unconscious God,* a work emphasizing his humanistic approach to personality.

One of the most articulate spokesmen for the humanistic theory of personality, Frankl has been in the forefront championing humanistic psychology. Though sympathetic to existentialism and one of the first psychologists to use that term in a psychological context, he is more than an existential psychologist because of his emphasis on optimism, rationality, and meaningfulness in opposition to pessimism, cynicism, irrationality, nihilism, and meaninglessness. The humanistic emphasis of Frankl exceeds even that of Maslow and is readily seen and appreciated in his concepts: unique meanings, meaning-universals or values, noëtic dimension of man, will to meaning, freedom of will, existential frustration, existential neurosis, in addition to *logotherapy,* which means therapy through meaning. His personality theory will challenge others with its adherence to "tension" and refreshingly new concepts such as existential vacuum, self-transcendence, the tragic triad, and the meaning of life. His repertoire of contributions would extend considerably if those related to psychotherapy were included, such as paradoxical intention, deflection, and logodrama. Ideas in his mind germinate viably.

THREE PREMISES OF LOGOTHERAPY: FREEDOM OF WILL, WILL TO MEANING, MEANING OF LIFE[1]

Insofar as logotherapy is concerned its concept of man is based on three pillars: (1) freedom of will; (2) will to meaning; and (3) meaning of

[1] "The Concept of Man in Logotherapy," *Journal of Existentialism,* VI (1965), from pp. 53-55.

life. They are opposed to those three principles which characterize the bulk of current approaches to man, namely, (1) pan-determinism, as I am used to calling it; (2) homeostasis theory; and (3) reductionism, an approach, that is, which—rather than taking a human phenomenon at its face value—traces it back to sub-human phenomena.

Pan-determinism accounts for the fact that the majority of psychologists are preferring either "the machine model," or "the rat model." As to the first, I deem it to be remarkable a fact that man, as long as he regarded himself as a creature, interpreted his existence in the image of God, his creator; but as soon as he started considering himself as a creator, henceforth interpreted his existence merely in the image of his own creation, the machine, that is to say, along the lines of LaMettrie's book *"L'homme Machine."* Now we may understand how justified Stanley J. Rowland, Jr. was in contending that "the major chasm" is not "between religion and psychiatry" but rather "between those who" take "a methodological and mechanistic approach and those who" take "an existential approach, with special emphasis on the question of life's meaning."

*   *   *   *   *

Because if one continues teaching young people that man is nothing but the battleground of the clashing claims of personality aspects such as id, ego and superego, or if one continues preaching that man is nothing but the victim of conditions and determinants, be they biological, psychological or sociological in nature and origin, we cannot expect our students to behave like free and responsible beings. They rather become what they are taught to be, i.e., a set of mechanisms. Thus a pan-deterministic indoctrination makes young people increasingly susceptible of manipulation.

Is this to imply that I deny that man is subject to conditions and determinants? How could this be possible? After all, I am a neurologist and psychiatrist and as such, of course, I am fully aware of the extent to which man is not at all free from conditions and determinants. But apart from being a worker in two fields (neurology and psychiatry) I am a survivor of four camps, that is, concentration camps, and as such I bear witness of the inestimable extent to which man, although he is never free from conditions and determinants, is always free to take a stand to whatever he might have to face. Although he may be conditioned and determined, he is never fully determined, he is not pan-determined.

Man's intrinsically human capacity to take a stand to whatever may confront him includes his capacity to choose his attitude toward himself, more specifically, to take a stand to his own somatic and psychic conditions and determinants. By so doing, however, he also rises above the level of somatic and psychic phenomena and thereby opens up a dimension of its own, the dimension of those phenomena which, in an at least heuristic contradistinction to the somatic and psychic ones, are termed noëtic phenomena, or, as I am used to calling this dimension, the noölogical dimension. Man passes this dimension whenever he is reflecting upon himself—or rejecting himself; whenever he is making himself an object—or making objections to himself; whenever he displays his being conscious of himself—or whenever he exhibits his being conscientious. Indeed, conscience presupposes the distinctly human capacity to rise above oneself in order to judge and evaluate one's own deeds in moral terms. And this is certainly something which is not accessible to a beast. A dog which has wet the carpet may well slink under the couch with its tail between the legs; but this is no manifestation of conscience but rather the expression of fearful expectation of punishment and, thus, might well be the result of conditioning processes.

By opening up the noölogical dimension man becomes capable of putting a distance between himself and his own biological and psychological make-up. In logotherapy, we speak of the specifically human capacity of self-detachment. This quality, however, not only enables a human being victoriously to overcome himself in a heroic way but also empowers him to deal with himself in an ironic way. In fact, humor also falls under the category of definitely human phenomena and qualities. After all, no beast is capable of laughing.

In logotherapy, both the capacity of self-detachment and a sound sense of humor are being utilized in the form of a specifically logotherapeutic technique which is called paradoxical intention. The patient is, then, encouraged to do, or wish to happen, the very things he fears.

*   *   *   *   *

Definition of Logotherapy

In context with logotherapy, logos means meaning as well as spirit. Spirit, however, is not conceived with a religious connotation but rather in the sense of noëtic phenomena or the noölogical dimension. By making therapeutic use of a noëtic phenomenon such as man's capacity of self-detachment, paradoxical intention is logotherapy at its best.

Once more the noölogical dimension was mentioned; but what was the reason that I spoke of a dimension rather than a stratum? Conceiving of man in terms of strata, for example, along the lines of the concepts propounded by Nicolai Hartmann and Max Scheler would disregard and neglect what I should like to call human coexistence of anthropological wholeness and unity on the one hand and ontological differences on the other hand; or, as Thomas Aquinas put it, the *"unitas multiplex"* quality of existence. By anthropological wholeness and unity I mean that man is not composed of somatic, psychic and noëtic components; while by ontological differences I wish to indicate that the somatic, psychic and noëtic modes of being are qualitatively rather than quantitatively different from each other. This coexistence of both unity and multiplicity in man is taken into account by an anthropological theory which I have developed in logotherapy and called dimensional ontology.

Two Laws of Dimensional Ontology

There are two laws of dimensional ontology. Its first law reads: One and the same thing projected into different dimensions lower than its own, yields contradictory pictures.

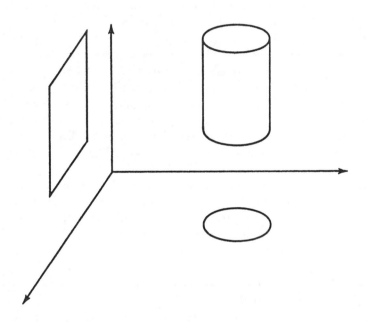

Imagine a cylinder, say, a cup. Projected out of its three-dimensional space down into the horizontal and vertical two-dimensional planes it yields in the first case a circle and in the second one a rectangle. These pictures contradict one another. What is even more important, the cup is an open vessel contrary to the circle which is a closed figure. Another contradiction.

Let us proceed to the second law of dimensional ontology which reads: Different things projected into one and the same dimension lower than their own, yield ambiguous pictures.

Imagine a cylinder, a cone and a sphere. The shadows they cast upon the horizontal plane depict them as three circles which are indiscriminate, interchangeable and ambiguous inasmuch as we cannot infer whether they *belong to a cylinder, a cone or a sphere.*

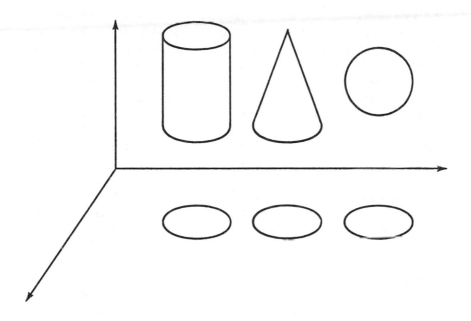

HUMAN MOTIVATION: UNIQUE MEANINGS AND MEANING-UNIVERSALS (VALUES)[2]

Meaning is relative inasmuch as it is related to a specific person who is entangled in a specific situation. One could say that meaning differs in two respects: first, from man to man, and second, from day to day—indeed, from hour to hour. It is true that if I read a speech, the situation unites me and my audience. But the meaning of the situation is still different. Our tasks are different. They have to listen. I have to talk.

To be sure, I, for one, would prefer to speak of uniqueness rather than relativity. Uniqueness, however, holds not only for a situation but also for life as a whole since life after all is a chain of unique situations. Thus, man is unique in terms of both existence and essence. He is unique in that, in the final analysis, he cannot be replaced. And his life is unique in that no one can repeat it.

There is, therefore, no such thing as a universal meaning of life, but only the unique meaning of individual situations. However, we must not forget that among these situations there are also situations which have something in common, and consequently there are also meanings which are shared by human beings throughout society and, even more, throughout history. Rather than being related to unique situations these meanings refer to the human condition. And these meanings are what is understood

[3]"What Is Meant by Meaning," *Journal of Existentialism,* VII (1966), from pp. 21-23.

by values. So that one may define values as those meaning-universals which crystallize in the typical situations a society—humanity—has to face.

By values or meaning-universals man's search for meaning is alleviated inasmuch as, at least in typical situations, he is spared making decisions. But, alas, he has also to pay for this relief and benefit. For, in contrast to the unique meanings pertaining to unique situations, it may well be that two values collide with one another. And, as is well known, value collisions are mirrored in the human psyche in the form of value conflicts, and as such play an important part in the formation of noögenic neurosis.

Let us imagine that the unique meanings referring to unique situations are points, while values or meaning-universals are circles. It is understandable that two values may well overlap with one another whereas this cannot happen to unique meanings. But we must ask ourselves whether two values can really collide with one another, in other words, whether their analogy with two-dimensional circles is appropriate. Would it not be more adequate to compare values with three-dimensional spheres? Two three-dimensional spheres projected out of the three-dimensional space down into the two-dimensional plane may well yield two two-dimensional circles overlapping one another, although the spheres themselves do not even touch on one another. Likewise, the impression that two values collide with one another is due to the fact that a whole dimension is disregarded and this dimension is the hierarchical order of values. According to Max Scheler, valuing implicitly means preferring one value to another. Thus, the rank of a value is experienced together with the value itself. The experience of one value includes the experience that it ranks higher than another. There is no place for value conflicts.

However, this is not to say that the experience of the hierarchical order of values dispenses man from decision-making. Man is pushed by drives. But he is pulled by values. He is free to accept or reject a value he is offered by a situation. It is up to him to take a stand as to whether or not he wishes to realize a value. This is true of the hierarchical order of values as it is transmitted and channeled by moral and ethical traditions and standards. They still have to stand a test, the test of man's conscience, unless he refuses to obey his conscience and suppresses its voice.

One may discern and distinguish three chief groups of values. I have classified them in terms of creative, experiential, and attitudinal values. This sequence reflects the three principal ways in which man can find meaning in life: first, by what he gives to the world in terms of his creation; second, by what he takes from the world in terms of encounters and experiences; and third, by the stand he takes when faced with a fate which he cannot change. This is why life never ceases to hold meaning, since even a person who is deprived of both creative and experiential values is still challenged by an opportunity for fulfillment, that is, by the meaning inherent in an upright way of suffering.

STRUCTURE OF THE PERSONALITY:
TRIDIMENSIONAL MAN (SOMATIC, PSYCHIC, NOËTIC)[3]

One characteristic of human existence is its transcendence. That is to say, man transcends his environment toward the world (and toward a higher world); but more than this, he also transcends his *being* toward an *ought*. Whenever man transcends himself in such a manner, he rises above the level of the somatic and the psychic, and enters the realm of the genuinely human. This realm is constituted by a new dimension, the noëtic; it is the dimension of spirit. Neither the somatic nor the psychic alone constitute the genuinely human; rather, they represent only two sides of the human being. Thus, there can be absolutely no talk of a parellelism in the sense of dualism, nor of an identity in the sense of monism. Nevertheless, in spite of all the ontological variations of the somatic, psychic, and noëtic, the anthropological unity and wholeness of a human being are preserved and saved as soon as we turn from an analysis of existence to what I call a dimensional ontology.

In an exclusively one-sided psychodynamic approach the genuinely human is necessarily portrayed in distortion. Indeed, certain human phenomena will entirely escape one, such as meaning and value. They must disappear from the field of vision as soon as instincts and dynamics are alone considered valid, for the simple reason that values do not drive me, they pull me. A great difference exists between driving and pulling, which we must recognize whenever we seek, in the sense of a phenomenological analysis, an access to the total, unabridged reality of human being.

Furthermore, it must appear questionable to speak of a "moral instinct" in the same sense as of a sexual instinct, or of a "religious instinct" as of an "aggression instinct." This would tend to make us see the essence of something like morality in the satisfying of a moral drive, or in the quieting of the superego, or in the appeasing of conscience. A good man, however, is not good for the sake of his conscience, but for a cause, for the good cause, or, a man is good because of, or for the sake of a person, or for the sake of God. Were a good man really good only in order to have a good conscience, then we would be truly confronted with a case of Pharisaism. To have a good conscience can never be the purpose of our ethical behavior; it is the result. Also, it is scarcely to be assumed that the saints would have become holy if that had been their main concern. Then, they would actually have become perfectionists, and perfectionism is one of the typical hindrances on the way toward perfection. Certainly a good conscience is, as the saying goes, the best pillow; we must, nevertheless, beware of making morality into a sleeping pill and ethics into a tranquilizer.

[3]"The Spiritual Dimension in Existential Analysis and Logotherapy," *Journal of Individual Psychology*, XV (1959), from pp. 159-64.

The underlying factor here is the conception, or better said the misconception, of the human psyche as dominated by an entropy, an equilibrium principle, in a word, the stipulation that the principle of homeostasis is regulative. This principle proceeds as if the psyche of man were a closed system and as if it were man's paramount concern to maintain or restore certain psychic conditions through the reconciliation and satisfaction of the claims of the id and superego. In this manner such an anthropology slides into a monadology. The true, the normal man is not concerned about some condition in his soul but about objects in the world; he is primarily ordered and directed toward them. Only the neurotic man is no longer objectively oriented; he is primarily interested in his own subjective condition. A psychotherapy which would acknowledge only the principle of homeostasis and would allow itself to be led by a monadological picture of man, would only reinforce neurotic escapism.

Critique of Self-Actualizationism

In this connection we cannot refrain from critical remarks concerning the current catchwords of self-fulfillment and self-actualization. Self-fulfillment and self-actualization cannot possibly be life's final purpose or man's last aim; on the contrary, the more man directs himself toward them, the more he will miss them. This is true for every subjective condition, e.g., pleasure; the more man strives for pleasure, the more it eludes him, and many sexual neuroses have their etiological basis precisely in this law. The hunt for happiness frightens the object away; the pursuit of happiness borders upon a self-contradiction.

Actually, man's concern is not to fulfill himself or to actualize himself, but to fulfill meaning and realize value. Only to the extent to which he fulfills concrete and personal meaning of his own existence will he also actualize himself. Self-actualization occurs by itself—not through intention, but as effect.

When is man so concerned with self-actualization? When does he, in this sense, reflect upon himself? Is not such reflection in each instance an expression of an intention toward meaning that has missed its goal and been frustrated? Does not the forced striving after self-actualization betray a frustrated striving for the fulfillment of meaning? Here the analogy of a boomerang comes to mind. Its purpose, as it is generally supposed, is to return to the hunter who has thrown it. But this is not so; only that boomerang returns to the hunter which has missed its target, the prey. Likewise, only that man comes back upon himself and is intent upon his own condition who has forgotten that outside in the world a concrete and personal meaning awaits him, that out there a task is waiting to be fulfilled by him and him alone. Man is close to himself only to the extent that he is close to the things in the world, to the extent that he stands in and for the world.

Will to Meaning

We maintain: only when the primary, objective orientation is lacking and has run aground, does that interest in one's condition arise which is so strikingly manifest in neurotic existence. Therefore the striving for self-actualization is in no way something primary; rather we see in it a deficient mode and a reduced level of human existence. Man's primary concern is not self-actualization, but fulfillment of meaning. In logotherapy we speak of a will-to-meaning; with this we designate man's striving to fulfill as much meaning in his existence as possible, and to realize as much value in his life as possible.

The will-to-meaning is something elementary, something genuine and authentic, and as such ought to be taken seriously by psychotherapy. But a psychology that designates itself as an unmasking one, is out to unmask this too; it presents man's claim to a maximally meaningful existence as a camouflage of unconscious instincts, and disposes of it as a mere rationalization. What is needed, I would say, is an unmasking of the unmasker! Although in some cases unmasking may be right, the tendency to unmask must be able to stop in front of that which is genuine in man; else, it reveals the unmasking psychologist's own tendency to devaluate.

Least of all can psychotherapy afford to ignore the will-to-meaning; instead, calling upon it involves a psychotherapeutic principle of the first rank. This can, under some circumstances, not only effect the preservation of psychic or somatic health but may be outright life-saving. Here not only clinical but other types of experiences, though no less empirical and practical, present themselves. In the tormenting "experiment" *(experimentum crucis)* of war prisons and concentration camps scarcely anything enabled one more to survive all these "extreme situations" (*Grenzsituationen,* in the sense of Karl Jaspers) than the knowledge of a life task. This "experiment" has confirmed Nietzsche's words: "He who has a *why* to live for, can bear almost any *how.*" The validity of these words depends, however, upon the fact that such a "why" pertains not just to any situation: it *must* pertain to the unique life task, the singularity of which corresponds to the fact that each man's life is singular in its existence and unique in its essence.

Existential Frustration

The will-to-meaning can become frustrated. In logotherapy we speak of an *existential frustration* since it appears justified to designate as existential that which applies to the meaning of existence, including the will-to-meaning. The feeling of meaninglessness is not pathological; it is something generally human, even the most human of all that there may be in man; it is not something all-too-human, something morbid. We must learn to distinguish between the human and the morbid, lest we confuse two essentially different things, viz., spiritual distress and psychic illness

[Frankl, *From Death-Camp to Existentialism*. (Boston: Beacon Press, 1959), p. 101]. In itself existential frustration is far from being morbid.

A patient of our acquaintance, a university professor of Vienna, had been assigned to us because he had tormented himself with the question of the meaning of his life. It turned out that he suffered from a recurrent endogenous depression; however, he brooded over and doubted the meaning of his life not during the phases of his psychic illness, but rather in the intervals, that is, during the time of healthiness.

Today existential frustration plays a more important role than ever. Man today suffers not only an increasing loss of instinct but also a loss of tradition, and herein may well be one of the causes of existential frustration. We see its effect in a phenomenon which we in logotherapy call *existential vacuum,* that is, inner emptiness, the feeling of having lost the meaning of existence and the content of life. This feeling then spreads and permeates the whole of life.

The existential vacuum may become manifest or remain concealed. It becomes manifest in the condition of boredom. The phenomenon of boredom, incidentally, invalidates the principle of homeostasis as applied to man's psychic life. If complete satisfaction of our needs were our primary aim, then such satisfaction would not result in existential fulfillment but rather in emptiness in the deepest sense of existential vacuum.

When Schopenhauer once said that humanity apparently is doomed to swing back and forth between the two extremes of need and boredom, he was not only quite correct; he seems to have foreseen that in our generation boredom gives us psychiatrists more work than does need, including the sexual need. Increasing automation gives man a greater amount of leisure time than he has previously had and than he knows how to use. Also the aging population is faced with the problem of how to fill its time and with its own existential vacuum. Finally, we can also see many ways in which the will-to-meaning is frustrated in youth and adolescence. Delinquency can only in part be traced to the acceleration of physical development; spiritual frustration, as is more and more being recognized, is also decisive.

Existential frustration can certainly also lead to neurosis. And so we speak in logotherapy of a *noögenic neurosis,* by which we understand a neurosis which has originally and genuinely been caused by a spiritual problem, a moral conflict, or an existential crisis; and we place the noögenic neurosis heuristically over against neurosis in the strict sense of the word, which is by definition a psychogenic illness.

Logotherapy

The specific therapy of noögenic neurosis can only be a psychotherapy which dares to follow man, his sickness and its etiology into the noëtic, spiritual dimension. Such a therapy is logotherapy. When we distinguish between logotherapy and psychotherapy, we use the latter term in the narrow sense, and, at that, intend the distinction only in a heuristic way. *Logos* now means not only *meaning,* but also the *spiritual.* The will-to-meaning is the subjective side of a spiritual reality in which the meaning is the objective side; at least it is objective insofar as the will is concerned with "finding" meaning and not at all with "giving" it.

Noëtic therapy is, however, not only applicable in cases of noögenic neuroses; rather, a psychogenic neurosis often represents a psychic development that has become rampant because of a spiritual vacuum, so that the psychotherapy will not be complete unless the existential vacuum is filled and the existential frustration is removed.

Logotherapy is more concerned with the attitude of the patient toward the symptom than with the symptom itself; for all too often it is the wrong attitude that is really pathogenic. Logotherapy, therefore, distinguishes different attitude formations [Frankl, *Theorie und Therapie der Neurosen; Einfuehrung in Logotherapie und Existenzanalyse* (Wien: Urban & Schwarzenberg, 1936), p. 128], and attempts to bring about within the patient a transformation of attitude; in other words, it is really a conversion therapy (not implying the religious connotation). To this end it provides specific methods and techniques such as *dereflection* and *paradoxical intention* which have been described elsewhere.

Logotherapy attempts to orient and direct the patient toward a concrete, personal meaning. But it is not its purpose to *give* a meaning to the patient's existence; its concern is only to enable the patient to *find* such a meaning, to broaden, so to speak, his field of vision, so that he will become aware of the full spectrum of possibilities for personal and concrete meanings and values.

If the patient is to become conscious of a possible meaning, then the doctor must know and remain conscious of all the possibilities for meaning, above all the meaning of suffering. Suffering from an incurable disease, for example, conceals in itself not only the last possibility for the fulfillment of meaning and the realization of value, but the possibility for deepest meaning and highest value. In this view, life up to the last moment never ceases to have a meaning. Logotherapy, then, will not only aim toward the recovery of the patient's capacity for work, enjoyment, and experience, but also toward the development of his capacity to suffer, viz., his capacity to fulfill the possible meaning of suffering.

DYNAMICS OF PERSONALITY[4]

Man as a finite being, which he basically is, will never be able to free himself completely from the ties which bind him in many respects incessantly to the various realms wherein he is confronted by unalterable conditions. Nevertheless, ultimately there is always a certain residue of freedom left to his decisions. For within the limits—however restricted

[4]"Dynamics, Existence and Values," *Journal of Existential Psychiatry*, II (1961), from pp. 5-7, 11-13.

they may be—he can move freely and only by this very stand which he takes again and again, toward whatsoever conditions he may face, does he prove to be a truly human being. This holds true with regard to biological and psychological as well as sociological facts and factors. Social environment, hereditary endowment, and instinctual drives can limit the scope of man's freedom, but in themselves they can never totally blur the human capacity to take a stand toward all those conditions, to choose an option.

Let me illustrate this by a concrete example. Some months ago I was sitting with a famous American psychoanalyst in a Viennese coffeehouse. As this was a Sunday morning and the weather was fine I invited him to join me on a trip to climb mountains. He refused passionately, however, by pointing out that his deep reluctance against mountain climbing was due to early childhood experiences. His father had taken him as a boy on walking trips of long duration, and he soon began to hate such things. Thus he wanted to explain to me by what infantile conditioning process he was incapacitated to share my hobby of scaling steep rocky walls. Now, however, it was my turn to confess; and I began reporting to him that I, too, was taken on week-end trips by my father and hated them because they were fatiguing and annoying. But in spite of all that, as for myself, I went on to become a climbing guide in an Alpine club.

Whether any circumstances, be they inner or outer ones, have an influence on a given individual or not, and in which direction this influence takes its way—all that depends on the individual's free choice. *The conditions do not determine me but I determine whether I yield to them or brave them.* There is nothing conceivable that would condition a man wholly, i.e., without leaving to him the slightest freedom. Man is never fully conditioned in the sense of being determined by any facts or forces. Rather *man is ultimately self-determining*—determining not only his fate but even his own self for man is not only forming and shaping the course of his life but also his very self. To this extent man is not only responsible[a] for what he does but also for what he is, inasmuch as *man does not only behave according to what he is but also becomes according to how he behaves.* In the last analysis, man has become what he had made out of himself. Instead of being fully conditioned by any conditions he is rather constructing himself. Facts and factors are nothing but the raw material for such self-constructing acts, of which a human life is an unbroken chain. They present the tools, the means, to an end set by man himself.

To be sure, such a view of man is just the reverse of that concept which claims that man is a product or effect of a chain of diverse causes. On the

[a]Of course, man's responsibility is as finite as his freedom; for, though man is a spiritual being, he remains a finite being. E.g., I am not responsible for the fact that I have grey hair; however, I am certainly responsible for the fact that I did not go to the hairdresser to have him tint my hair (which under the same "conditions" a number of ladies might have done). So even there a certain amount of freedom is left to everyone, even if only the choice of the color of his hair.

other hand, our assertion of *human existence as a self-creating act* corresponds to the basic assumption that a man does not simply "be," but always decides what he will be in the next moment. In every moment the human person is steadily molding and forging his own character. Thus, every human being has the chance of changing at any instant. There is the freedom to change, in principle, and no one should be denied the right to make use of it. Therefore, we never can predict a human being's future except within the large frame of a statistical survey referring to a whole group. On the contrary, an individual personality is essentially unpredictable. The basis for any predictions would be represented by biological, psychological or sociological influences. However, one of the main features of human existence is the capacity to emerge from and rise above all such conditions—to transcend them. By the same token, man is ultimately transcending himself. The human person then transcends himself insofar as he reshapes his own character.

Existential Vacuum and Tension

This has been noted by logotherapists long before. We have known the detrimental impact of what we call a man's "existential vacuum," i.e., the result of the frustration of the above mentioned "will to meaning." The feeling of a total and ultimate meaninglessness of one's life often results in a certain type of neurosis for which logotherapy has coined the term *noögenic* neurosis; that is to say a neurosis of which the origin is a spiritual problem, a moral conflict or the existential vacuum. But other types of neuroses are also invading this vacuum! So that no psychotherapy can be completed, no neurosis of whatsoever kind can be completely and definitely overcome, if this inner void and emptiness in which neurotic symptoms are flourishing has not been filled up by supplementary logotherapy, be it applied unconsciously or methodically.

By this I do not want to give the impression that the existential vacuum in itself represents a mental disease: the doubt whether one's life has a meaning is an existential despair, it is a spiritual distress rather than a mental disease. Thus logotherapy in such cases is more than the therapy of a disease; it is a challenge for all counseling professions. The search for a meaning to one's existence, even the doubt whether such a meaning can be found at all, is something human and nothing morbid.

From the above it can easily be seen how much mental health is based on the presence of an adequate state of tension, like that which arises from the unbridgeable gap between what a man has achieved and what he should accomplish. The cleavage between what I am and what I ought to become is inherent in my being human and, therefore, indispensable to my mental well being. Therefore, we should not be timid and hesitant in confronting man with the potential meaning to be actualized by him, nor evoking his will to meaning out of its latency. Logotherapy attempts to make both events conscious to man: (1) the meaning that, so to speak, waits to be fulfilled by him, as well as (2) his will to meaning that, so to speak, waits for a task, nay, a mission to be assigned to him. Inasmuch as logotherapy makes the patient aware of both facts it represents an essentially analytical procedure for it makes something conscious; however, not anything psychic but something noëtic, not only the subhuman but the human itself.

To make the patient again aware of a meaning in his life is the ultimate asset in all psychotherapy simply because it is the final requirement in every neurosis. To be charged with the task to fulfill the unique meaning assigned to each of us is nothing to be avoided and feared at all.

The homeostasis principle, however, that underlies the dynamic interpretation of man maintains that his behavior is basically directed toward the gratification and satisfaction of his drives and instincts, toward the reconciliation of the different aspects of his own such as id, ego and superego, and toward adaptation and adjustment to society, in one word, toward his own bio-psycho-sociological equilibrium. But human existence is essentially self-transcendence. By the same token, it cannot consist in self-actualization; man's primary concern does not lie in the actualization of his self but in the realization of values and in the fulfillment of meaning potentialities which are to be found in the world rather than within himself or within his own psyche as a closed system.

What man actually needs is not homeostasis but what I call *noödynamics,* i.e., that kind of appropriate tension that holds him steadily oriented toward concrete values to be actualized, toward the meaning of his personal existence to be fulfilled. This is also what guarantees and sustains his mental health whereas escaping from any stress situation would even precipitate his falling prey to the existential vacuum.

What man needs is not a tensionless state but the striving and struggling for something worth longing and groping for. What man needs is not so much the discharge of tensions as it is the challenge by the concrete meaning of his personal existence that must be fulfilled by him and cannot be fulfilled but by him alone. In neurotic individuals, this is not less but even more valid. Integration of the subject presupposes direction toward an object. The tension between subject and object does not weaken but strengthens health and wholeness. If architects want to strengthen a decrepit arch they *increase* the load that is laid upon it for thereby the parts are joined more firmly together. So if therapists wish to foster their patients' mental health they, too, should not be afraid to increase the burden of one's responsibility to fulfill the meaning of his existence.

SELF-TRANSCENDENCE AND FREEDOM[5]

On the biological level, in the plane of biology, we are confronted with

[5]"Determinism and Humanism," *Humanitas,* VII (1971), from pp. 24-27.

the somatic aspects of man, and on the psychological level, in the plane of psychology, with his psychological aspects. Thus, within the planes of both scientific approaches we are facing diversity but missing the unity in man, because this unity is available only in the human dimension and must necessarily disappear within the cross sections through the human reality as they are used by biology and psychology. Only in the human dimension lies the *"unitas multiplex"* as man has been defined by Thomas Aquinas. And this unity now turns out to be not really a "unity *in* diversity" but rather a unity *in spite of* diversity.

What is true of man's oneness, also holds for his openness. . . .

[Man] is sometimes portrayed as if he were merely a closed system within which cause-effect relations are operant such as conditioned or unconditioned reflexes, conditioning processes or responses to stimuli. On the other hand, being human is profoundly characterized as being open to the world, as Max Scheler, Arnold Gehlen and Adolf Portmann have shown. Or, as Martin Heidegger has said, being human is "being in the world." What I have called the self-transcendence of existence denotes the fundamental fact that being human means relating to something, or someone, other than oneself, be it a meaning to fulfill, or human beings to encounter. And existence falters and collapses unless this self-transcendent quality is lived out. Let me illustrate this by simile. The capacity of the eye to perceive the world outside itself, paradoxically enough, is tied up with its incapacity to perceive anything within itself. In fact, to the extent to which the eye sees itself, for example, its own cataract, its capacity to see the world is impaired. That is to say, in principle the seeing eye sees something other than itself. Seeing, too, is self-transcendent.

That the self-transcendent quality of existence, that the openness of being human is touched by one cross section and missed by another, is understandable. Closedness and openness have become compatible. And I think that the same holds true of freedom and determinism. There is determinism in the psychological dimension, and freedom in the noölogical dimension which is the human dimension, the dimension of human phenomena. As to the body-mind problem, we wound up with the phrase "unity in spite of diversity." As to the problem of free choice, we are winding up with the phrase "freedom in spite of determinism." It parallels the phrase once coined by Nicolai Hartmann, "autonomy in spite of dependency."

As a human phenomenon, however, freedom also is an all too human phenomenon. Human freedom is finite freedom. Man is not free from conditions. But he is free to take a stand to them. The conditions do not completely condition him. For within limits it is up to him whether or not he succumbs and surrenders to the conditions. He may as easily rise above them and by so doing open up and enter the human dimension. As I once put it: As a professor in two fields, neurology and psychiatry, I am fully aware of the extent to which man is subject to biological, psychological and sociological conditions. But in addition to being a professor in two fields I am a survivor of four camps—concentration camps, that is—and as such I also bear witness to the unexpected extent to which man is capable of defying and braving even the worst conditions conceivable. Sigmund Freud once said, "Let us attempt to expose a number of the most diverse people uniformly to hunger. With the increase of the imperative urge of hunger all individual differences will blur, and in their stead will appear the uniform expression of the one unstilled urge." Actually, however, the reverse was true. In the concentration camps people became more diverse. The beast was unmasked—and so was the saint. The hunger was the same but people were different. In truth, calories do not count.

Ultimately, man is not subject to the conditions that confront him; rather, these conditions are subject to his decision. Wittingly or unwittingly, he decides whether he will face up or give in, whether or not he will let himself be determined by the conditions. Of course, it could be objected that such decisions are themselves determined. But it is obvious that this results in a *regressus in infinitum*. A statement by Magda B. Arnold epitomizes this state of affairs and lends itself as an apt conclusion of the discussion: "All choices are caused but they are caused by the chooser" (*The Human Person*, New York, 1954, p. 40).

Interdisciplinary research covers more than one cross section. It prevents us from one-sidedness. As to the problem of free choice, it prevents us from denying, on the one hand, the deterministic and mechanistic aspects of the human reality and, on the other hand, the human freedom to transcend them. This freedom is not denied by determinism but rather by what I am used to calling pan-determinism. In other words, the alternative really reads pan-determinism versus determinism, rather than determinism versus indeterminism. And as to Freud, he only espoused pan-determinism in theory. In practice, he was anything but blind to the human freedom to change, to improve, for instance, when he once defined the goal of psychoanalysis as giving "the patient's ego the freedom to choose one way or the other" (*The Ego and the Id*, London, 1927, p. 72).

Last but not least, human freedom implies man's capacity to detach himself from himself. I am used to illustrating this capacity of self-detachment, as I call it, by the following story. During World War I a Jewish army doctor was sitting together with his gentile friend, an aristocratic colonel, in a foxhole when heavy shooting began. Teasingly, the colonel said: "You are afraid, aren't you? Just another proof that the Aryan race is superor to the Semitic one." "Sure, I am afraid," was the doctor's answer. "But who is superior? If you, my dear colonel, were as afraid as I am, you would have run away long ago." What counts and matters is not our fears and anxieties as such but rather the attitude we adopt toward them. This attitude, however, is freely chosen.

The freedom of choosing an attitude toward our psychological make-up even implies the pathological aspects of this make-up. Time and again, we psychiatrists meet patients whose attitude toward what is pathological in them is anything but pathological. I have met cases of paranoia who, out of their delusional ideas of persecution, have killed their alleged enemies. And I have met cases of paranoia who have forgiven their alleged adversaries. The latter have not acted out of mental illness but rather reacted to this illness out of their humanness. To speak of suicide rather than homicide, there are cases of depression who commit suicide, and there are cases who managed to overcome the suicidal impulse for the sake of a cause or a person. They are too committed to commit suicide, as it were.

THE TRAGIC TRIAD: SUFFERING, GUILT, TRANSITORINESS[6]

Whenever speaking of meaning, however, we should not disregard the fact that man does not fulfill the meaning of his existence merely by his creative endeavors and experiential encounters, or by working and loving. We must not overlook the fact that there are also tragic experiences inherent in human life, above all that "Tragic Triad"—if I may use this term —which is represented by the primordial facts of man's existence: suffering, guilt, and transitoriness.

Of course, we can close our eyes to these "existentials." Also the therapist can escape from them and retreat into mere somato- or psychotherapy. . . . This would be the case, for instance, when the therapist tries to tranquilize away the patient's fear of death, or to analyze away his feelings of guilt. With special regard to suffering, however, I would say that our patients never really despair because of any suffering in itself! Instead, their despair stems in each instance from a doubt as to whether suffering is meaningful. Man is ready and willing to shoulder any suffering as soon and as long as he can see a meaning in it.

* * * * *

I wish to say that it is never up to a therapist to convey to the patient a picture of the world as the therapist sees it, but rather to enable the patient to see the world as it is. Therefore, he resembles an ophthalmologist more than a painter. . . . Also, in reference to meanings and values, what matters is not the meaning of man's life in general. To look for the general meaning of man's life would be comparable to the question put to a chess player: "What is the best move?" There is no move at all, irrespective of

6"Logotherapy and the Challenge of Suffering," *Review of Existential Psychology and Psychiatry*, I (1961), from pp. 4-7.

the concrete situation of a special game. The same holds for human existence inasmuch as one can search only for the concrete meaning of personal existence, a meaning which changes from man to man, from day to day, from hour to hour. Also the awareness of this concrete meaning of one's existence is not at all an abstract one, but it is, rather, an implicit and immediate dedication and devotion which neither cares for verbalization nor even needs it in each instance. In psychotherapy it can be evoked by the posing of provocative questions in the frame of a maieutic dialogue in the Socratic sense. I should like to draw your attention to an experience of such a dialogue during the group psychotherapeutic and psychodramatic activities of my clinic as they are conducted by my assistant, Dr. Kurt Kocourek.

It happened that I stepped in the room of the clinic where he was at the moment performing group therapy; he had to deal with the case of a woman who had lost her son rather suddenly. She was left alone with another son, who was crippled and paralyzed, suffering from Little's disease. She rebelled against her fate, of course, but she did so ultimately because she could not see any meaning in it. When joining the group and sharing the discussion I improvised by inviting another woman to imagine that she was eighty years of age, lying on her deathbed and looking back to a life full of social success; then I asked her to express what she would feel in this situation. Now, let us hear the direct expression of the experience evoked in her—I quote from a tape: "I married a millionaire. I had an easy life full of wealth. I lived it up. I flirted with men. But now I am eighty. I have no children. Actually, my life has been a failure." And now I invited the mother of the handicapped son to do the same. Her response was the following—again I am quoting the tape: "I would look back peacefully, for I could say to myself, 'I wished to have children and my wish was granted. I have done my best, I have done the best for my son. Be he crippled, be he helpless, he is my boy. I know that my life was not a failure. I have reared my son and cared for him—otherwise he would have to go into an institution. I have made a fuller life possible for this my son.' " Thereupon I posed a question to the whole group: "Could an ape which is being used to gain serum for poliomyelitis ever grasp what his suffering should be for?" The group replied unanimously, "Of course it cannot." And now I proceeded to put another question: "And what about man? Man's world essentially transcends an ape's "Umwelt." That is why the ape cannot become cognizant of the meaning of its suffering. For its meaning cannot be found in the "Umwelt" of the animal, but only in the world of man. "Well," I asked them, "are you sure that this human world is something like a terminal in the development of the cosmos? Shouldn't we rather admit that there is possibly a world beyond, above man's world, a world, let me say, in which the question of the ultimate meaning of our sufferings could be answered, and man's quest for this super-meaning could be fulfilled?"

TRANSITORINESS AND RESPONSIBILITY[7]

What threatens man is his guilt in the past and his death in the future. Both are inescapable, both he must accept. Thus man is confronted with the human condition in terms of *fallibility and mortality*. Properly understood, it is, however, precisely the acceptance of this twofold human finiteness which adds to life's being worthwhile, since only in the face of guilt does it make sense to improve, and only in the face of death is it meaningful to act.

It is the very transitoriness of human existence which constitutes man's responsibleness—the *essence of existence*. If man were immortal, he would be justified in delaying everything; there would be no need to do anything right now. Only under the urge and pressure of life's transitoriness does it make sense to use the passing time. Actually, the only transitory aspects of life are the potentialities; as soon as we have succeeded in actualizing a potentiality, we have transmuted it into an actuality and, thus, salvaged and rescued it into the past. Once an actuality, it is one forever. Everything in the past is saved from being transitory. Therein it is irrevocably stored rather than irrecoverably lost. Having been is still a form of being perhaps even its most secure form.

What man has done, cannot be undone. I think that this implies both activism and optimism. Man is called upon to make the best use of any moment and the right choice at any time: be it that he knows what to do, or whom to love, or how to suffer. This means activism. As to optimism, let me remind you of the worlds of Laotse: "Having completed a task means having become eternal." I would say that this holds true not only for the completion of a task, but for our experiences and, last not least, for our brave sufferings as well.

Speaking figuratively we might say: The pessimist resembles a man who observes with fear and sadness how his wall calendar from which he daily tears a sheet, grows thinner and thinner with the passing days. However, a person who takes life in the sense suggested above, is like a man who removes each leaf, files it carefully after having jotted down a few diary notes on it. He can reflect with pride and joy on all the richness set down in these notes, on all the life he has already lived to the full.

Even in advanced years one should not envy a young person. Why should one? For the possibilities a young person has, or for his future? No, I should say; instead of possibilities in the future, the older person has realities in the past: work done, love loved and suffering suffered. The latter is something to be proudest of—although it will hardly raise envy. . . .

[7]"Existential Dynamics and Neurotic Escapism," *Journal of Existential Psychiatry,* IV (1963), from pp. 27-42.

CHAPTER 9

CARL R. ROGERS

PHENOMENOLOGICAL THEORY
OF PERSONALITY

Rogers' PHENOMENOLOGICAL THEORY OF PERSONALITY is strongly influenced by his approach to clinical psychology, "nondirective" counseling or client-centered therapy. This approach is predicated on the following premises: (1) The focus of attention and importance should be on the individual rather than the problem, for if the individual has enough intelligence to create a problem for himself, he ought to have enough to extricate himself with the aid of a counselor. (2) Not intellectual problems per se, but emotive and value problems lie at the root of a person's maladjustment; if these are permitted to surface, so that the individual can recognize and accept them as part of a well-integrated personality, wholesome adjustment ensues. (3) Each individual is faced with his own peculiar problems; consequently, in treatment, no single concept, such as the Oedipus complex, will prove to be the source of all maladjustments. Moreover, emphasis must be placed on the individual's immediate situation rather than the past. (4) The lack of an individualized system of values, which is acceptable to the individual as well as harmonious with the values of his society, is basic in all maladjustment. The therapeutic relationship, as is true of any learning experience, is fundamentally a growth experience.

Rogers refers to his theory of personality as "phenomenological," because the significant factor which affects the individual is not *reality* as such, but what the individual *experiences as reality*— what he thinks, understands, or feels reality to be. For example, a thirsty man walking along the desert sands will run as eagerly to a pool of water which is only a mirage as he will to a real pool. A phenomenological theory of personality "pictures the end-point of personality development as being congruence between the phenomenal field of experience and conceptual structure of the self—a situation which, if achieved, would represent freedom from potential strain; which would represent the maximum in realistically oriented adaptation; which would mean the establishment of an individualized value system having considerable identity with the value system of any other equally well-adjusted member of the human race."

Carl R. Rogers was born in Illinois in 1902; he was educated at the University of Wisconsin (B.A., 1924) and Columbia University (M.A., 1928; Ph.D., 1931). His professional career opened in 1928 in Rochester, New York, where he was a psychologist in the Child Study Department at the Society for the Prevention of Cruelty to Children. He was a Director of the Department from 1930 until 1938 and in 1939 was Director of the Rochester Guidance Center. In 1940 he was appointed Professor of Clinical Psychology at The Ohio State University, where he remained until 1945. During 1944-1945 he was Director of Counseling Services for the U.S.O., and from 1945 to 1957 he was Professor of Psychology and Executive Secretary of Counseling at the University of Chicago. From 1957 to 1963 he was Professor of Psychiatry and Psychology at the University of Wisconsin and is currently a resident fellow at the Western Behavioral Sciences Institute.

Carl Rogers' publications include *Measuring Personality Adjustment in Children* (1931), *A Test of Personality Adjustment* (1931), *Clinical Treatment of the Problem Child* (1939), *Counseling and Psychotherapy* (1942), *Counseling with Returned Service Men* (with J. Wallen, 1946), *Dealing with Social Tensions* (1948), *Client-Centered Therapy* (1951), *Psychotherapy and Personality Change* (with others, 1954), *On Becoming a Person* (1961), *Person to Person* (with Barry Stevers, 1967), *Freedom to Learn* (1969), and *Becoming Partners* (1972). He also edited *The Therapeutic Relationship and Its Impact* (1967).

A THEORY OF PERSONALITY AND BEHAVIOR[1]

The Propositions

I. *Every individual exists in a continually changing world of experience of which he is the center.*

[1]*Client-Centered Therapy* (Boston: Houghton Mifflin, 1951), from pp. 483-524.

This private world may be called the phenomenal field, the experiential field, or described in other terms. It includes all that is experienced by the organism, whether or not these experiences are consciously perceived. Thus the pressure of the chair seat against my buttocks is something I have been experiencing for an hour, but only as I think and write about it does the symbolization of that experience become present in consciousness. It seems likely that Angyal is correct in stating that consciousness consists of the symbolization of some of our experiences.

It should be recognized that in this private world of experience of the individual, only a portion of that experience, and probably a very small portion, is *consciously* experienced. Many of our sensory and visceral sensations are not symbolized. It is also true, however, that a large portion of this world of experience is *available* to consciousness, and may become conscious if the need of the individual causes certain sensations to come into focus because they are associated with the satisfaction of a need. In other words, most of the individual's experiences constitute the ground of the perceptual field, but they can easily become figure, while other experiences slip back into ground. We shall deal later with some aspects of experience which the individual *prevents* from coming into figure.

An important truth in regard to this private world of the individual is that it can only be known, in any genuine or complete sense, to the individual himself. No matter how adequately we attempt to measure the stimulus—whether it be a beam of light, a pinprick, a failure on an examination, or some complex situation—and no matter how much we attempt to measure the perceiving organism—whether by psychometric tests or physiological calibrations—it is still true that the individual is the only one who can know how the experience was perceived. I can never know with vividness or completeness how a pinprick or a failure on an examination is experienced by you. The world of experience is for each individual, in a very significant sense, a private world.

This complete first-hand acquaintance with the world of his total experience is, however, only potential; it does not hold true of the individual's general functioning. There are many of the impulses which I feel, or the sensations which I experience, which I can permit into consciousness only under certain conditions. Hence my actual awareness of and knowledge of my phenomenal field is limited. It is still true, however, that potentially I am the only one who can know it in its completeness. Another can never know it as fully as I.

II. *The organism reacts to the field as it is experienced and perceived. This perceptual field is, for the individual, "reality."*

This is a simple proposition, one of which we are all aware in our own experience, yet it is a point which is often overlooked. I do not react to some absolute reality, but to my perception of this reality. It is this perception which for me *is* reality. Snygg and Combs give the example of two men driving at night on a western road. An object looms up in the middle of the road ahead. One of the two men sees a large boulder, and reacts with fright. The other, a native of the country, sees a tumbleweed and reacts with nonchalance. Each reacts to the reality as perceived.

This proposition could be illustrated from the daily experience of everyone. Two individuals listen to a radio speech made by a political candidate about whom they have no previous knowledge. They are both subjected to the same auditory stimulation. Yet one perceives the candidate as a demagogue, a trickster, a false prophet, and reacts accordingly. The other perceives him as a leader of the people, a person of high aims and purposes. Each is reacting to the reality as he has perceived it. In the same way, two young parents perceive differently the behavior of their offspring. The son and daughter have differing perceptions of their parents. And the behavior in all these instances is appropriate to the reality-as-perceived. This same proposition is exemplified in so-called abnormal conditions as well. The psychotic who perceives that his food is poisoned, or that some malevolent group is out to "get" him, reacts to his reality-as-perceived in much the same fashion that you or I would respond if we (more "realistically") perceived our food as contaminated, or our enemies as plotting against us.

To understand this concept that reality is, for the individual, his perceptions, we may find it helpful to borrow a phrase from the semanticists. They have pointed out that words and symbols bear to the world of reality the same relationship as a map to the territory which is represents. This relationship also applies to perception and reality. We live by a perceptual "map" which is never reality itself. This is a useful concept to keep in mind; for it may help to convey the nature of the world in which the individual lives.

*　　*　　*　　*　　*

For psychological purposes; reality is basically the private world of individual perceptions, though for social purposes reality consists of those perceptions which have a high degree of commonality among various individuals. Thus this desk is "real" because most people in our culture would have a perception of it which is very similar to my own.

That the perceptual field is the reality to which the individual reacts is often strikingly illustrated in therapy, where it is frequently evident that when the perception changes, the reaction of the individual changes. As long as a parent is perceived as a domineering individual, that is the reality to which the individual reacts. When he is perceived as a rather pathetic individual trying to maintain his status, then the reaction to this new "reality" is quite different.

III. *The organism reacts as an organized whole to this phenomenal field.*

Although there are still some who are primarily concerned with the segmental or atomistic type of organic reaction, there is increasing acceptance of the fact that one of the most basic characteristics of organic life is its tendency toward total, organized, goal-directed responses. This is true of those responses which are primarily physiological, as well as those which we think of as psychological. Take such a matter as the maintenance of the water balance in the body. It has been shown that this is ordinarily maintained by the activity of the posterior lobe of the pituitary gland, which, when the body loses water, secretes more of an antidiuretic hormone, thus reducing the secretion of water by the kidney. This reaction would appear to be definitely of the atomistic type, reducible in the last analysis to purely chemical factors. But where the posterior lobe is experimentally removed, the animal drinks very large amounts of water, and thus maintains a satisfactory water balance in spite of the loss of the regulating mechanism. It is thus the total, organized, goal-directed response which appears to be basic, as evidenced by the fact that, when one avenue is blocked off, the animal organizes to utilize another avenue to the same goal. The same would be true of various compensatory physiological phenomena.

In the psychological realm, any simple S-R type of explanation of behavior seems almost impossible. A young woman talks for an hour about her antagonism to her mother. She finds, following this, that a persistent asthmatic condition, which she has not even mentioned to the counselor, is greatly improved. On the other hand, a man who feels that his security in his work is being seriously threatened, develops ulcers. It is extremely cumbersome to try to account for such phenomena on the basis of an atomistic chain of events. The outstanding fact which must be taken into theoretical account is that the organism is at all times a total organized system, in which alteration of any part may produce changes in any other part. Our study of such part phenomena must start from this central fact of consistent, goal-directed organization.

IV. *The organism has one basic tendency and striving—to actualize, maintain, and enhance the experiencing organism.*

Rather than many needs and motives, it seems entirely possible that all organic and psychological needs may be described as partial aspects of this one fundamental need. It is difficult to find satisfactory words for this proposition. The particular phrasing is from Snygg and Combs. The words used are an attempt to describe the observed directional force in organic life—a force which has been regarded as basic by many scientists, but which has not been too well described in testable or operational terms.

We are talking here about the tendency of the organism to maintain itself —to assimilate food; to behave defensively in the face of threat, to achieve the goal of self-maintenance even when the usual pathway to that goal is blocked. We are speaking of the tendency of the organism to move in the direction of maturation, as maturation is defined for each species. This involves self-actualization, though it should be understood that this too is a directional term. The organism does not develop to the full its capacity for suffering pain, nor does the human individual develop or actualize his capacity for terror or, on the physiological level, his capacity for vomiting.

The organism actualizes itself in the direction of greater differentiation of organs and of function. It moves in the direction of limited expansion through growth, expansion through extending itself by means of its tools, and expansion through reproduction. It moves in the direction of greater independence or self-responsibility. Its movement, as Angyal has pointed out, is in the direction of an increasing self-government, self-regulation, and autonomy, and away from heteronomous control, or control by external forces. This is true whether we are speaking of entirely unconscious organic processes, such as the regulation of body heat, or such uniquely human and intellectual functions as the choice of life goals. Finally, the self-actualization of the organism appears to be in the direction of socialization, broadly defined.

* * * * *

It is our experience in therapy which has brought us to the point of giving this proposition a central place. The therapist becomes very much aware that the forward-moving tendency of the human organism is the basis upon which he relies most deeply and fundamentally. It is evident not only in the general tendency of clients to move in the direction of growth when the factors in the situation are clear, but is most dramatically shown in very serious cases where the individual is on the brink of psychosis or suicide. Here the therapist is very keenly aware that the only force upon which he can basically rely is the organic tendency toward ongoing growth and enhancement.

* * * * *

It would be grossly inaccurate to suppose that the organism operates smoothly in the direction of self-enhancement and growth. It would be perhaps more correct to say that the organism moves through struggle and and pain toward enhancement and growth. The whole process may be symbolized and illustrated by the child's learning to walk. The first steps often involve struggle, and usually pain. Often it is true that the immediate reward involved in taking a few steps is in no way commensurate with the pain of falls and bumps. The child may, because of the pain, revert to crawling for a time. Yet, in the overwhelming majority of individuals, the forward direction of growth is more powerful than the satisfactions of remaining infantile. The child will actualize himself, in spite of the painful experiences in so doing. In the same way, he will become independent, responsible, self-governing, socialized, in spite of the pain which is often involved in these steps. Even where he does not, because of a variety of circumstances, exhibit growth of these more complex sorts, one may still rely on the fact that the tendency is present. Given the opportunity for clear-cut choice between forward-moving and regressive behavior, the tendency will operate.

* * * * *

V. *Behavior is basically the goal-directed attempt of the organism to satisfy its needs as experienced, in the field as perceived.*

This proposition becomes somewhat modified in the human organism, as we shall see, by the development of the self. . . . Behavior is postulated as a reaction to the field as perceived. This point, like some of the other propositions, is proved every day in our experience, but is often overlooked. The reaction is not to reality, but to the perception of reality. A horse, sensing danger, will try to reach the safety and security which he perceives in his stall, even though the barn may be in flames. A man in the desert will struggle just as hard to reach the "lake" which he perceives in a mirage, as to reach a real water hole. At a more complex level, a man may strive for money as the source of emotional security, even though in fact it may not satisfy his need. Often, of course, the perception has a high degree of correspondence with reality, but it is important to recognize that it is the perception, not the reality, which is crucial in determining behavior.

It should also be mentioned that in this concept of motivation all the effective elements exist in the present. Behavior is not "caused" by something which occurred in the past. Present tensions and present needs are the only ones which the organism endeavors to reduce or satisfy. While it is true that past experience has certainly served to modify the meaning which will be perceived in present experiences, yet there is no behavior except to meet a present need.

VI. *Emotion accompanies and in general facilitates such goal-directed behavior, the kind of emotion being related to the seeking versus the consummatory aspects of the behavior, and the intensity of the emotion being related to the perceived significance of the behavior for the maintenance and enhancement of the organism.*

The intensity of the emotional reaction appears to vary according to the perceived relationship of the behavior to the maintenance and enhancement of the organism. Thus if my leap to the curb to escape the oncoming automobile is perceived as making the difference between life and death, it will be accompanied by strong emotion. The reading of another chapter tonight in a new psychology book, a behavior which is seen as having a slight relationship to my development, will be accompanied by a very mild emotion indeed.

Both these propositions have been worded and discussed as though behavior always had to do with the maintenance and enhancement of the *organism*. As we shall see in later propositions, the development of the self may involve some modification of this, since behavior is then often best described as meeting the needs of the self, sometimes as against the needs of the organism, and emotional intensity becomes gauged more by the degree of involvement of the self than by the degree of involvement of the organism. As applied, however, to the infra-human organism, or to the human infant, Propositions V and VI appear to hold.

VII. *The best vantage point for understanding behavior is from the internal frame of reference of the individual himself.*

It was mentioned in Proposition I that the only person who could fully know his field of experience was the individual himself. Behavior is a reaction to the field as perceived. It would therefore appear that behavior might be best understood by gaining, in so far as possible, the internal frame of reference of the person himself, and seeing the world of experience as nearly as possible through his eyes.

* * * * *

If we could empathetically experience all the sensory and visceral sensations of the individual, could experience his whole phenomenal field including both the conscious elements and also those experiences not brought to the conscious level, we should have the perfect basis for understanding the meaningfulness of his behavior and for predicting his future behavior. This is an unattainable ideal. Because it is unattainable, one line of development in psychology has been to understand and evaluate and predict the person's behavior from an external frame of reference. This development has not been too satisfactory, largely because such a high degree of inference is involved. The interpretation of the meaning of a given bit of behavior comes to depend upon whether the inferences are being made, say, by a student of Clark Hull or a follower of Freud. For this and other reasons, the possibility of utilizing the phenomenal field of the individual as a significant basis for the science of psychology appears promising. There can be agreement on the specific way in which the world is experienced by the individual, and his behavior follows definitely and clearly upon his perception. Consequently, with agreement possible on the datum for a science, science can conceivably grow.

To point out the advantages of viewing behavior from the internal frame of reference is not to say that this is the royal road to learning. There are many drawbacks. For one thing, we are largely limited to gaining an acquaintance with the phenomenal field as it is experienced in consciousness. This means that the greater the area of experience not in consciousness, the more incomplete will be the picture. The more we try to infer what is present in the phenomenal field but not conscious (as in interpreting projective techniques), the more complex grow the inferences until the interpretation of the client's projections may become merely an illustration of the clinician's projections.

Furthermore our knowledge of the person's frame of reference depends primarily upon communication of one sort or another from the individual. Communication is at all times faulty and imperfect. Hence only in a clouded fashion can we see the world of experience as it appears to this individual.

* * * * *

VIII. *A portion of the total perceptual field gradually becomes differentiated as the self.*

The point is made that gradually, as the infant develops, a portion of the total private world becomes recognized as "me," "I," "myself." . . . Angyal points out that there is no possibility of a sharp limit between the experience of the self and of the outside world. Whether or not an object or an experience is regarded as a part of the self depends to a considerable extent upon whether or not it is perceived as within the control of the self. Those elements which we control are regarded as a part of self, but when even such an object as a part of our body is out of control, it is experienced as being less a part of the self. The way in which, when a foot "goes to sleep" from lack of circulation, it becomes an object to us rather than a part of self, may be a sufficient illustration. Perhaps it is this "gradient of autonomy" which first gives the infant the awareness of self, as he is for the first time aware of a feeling of control over some aspect of his world of experience.

It should be clear from the foregoing that though some authors use the term "self" as synonmous with "organism" it is here being used in a more restricted sense, namely, the awareness of being, of functioning.

IX. *As a result of interaction with the environment, and particularly as a result of evaluational interaction with others, the structure of self is formed—an organized, fluid, but consistent conceptual pattern of perceptions of characteristics and relationships of the "I" or the "me," together with values attached to these concepts.*

X. *The values attached to experiences, and the values which are a part of the self-structure, in some instances are values experienced directly by the organism, and in some instances are values introjected or taken over from others, but perceived in distorted fashion, as if they had been experienced directly.*

It will probably be best to discuss these two important propositions together. . . . One of the first and most important aspects of the self-experience of the ordinary child is that he is loved by his parents. He perceives himself as lovable, worthy of love, and his relationship to his parents as one of affection. He experiences all this with satisfaction. This is a significant and core element of the structure of self as it begins to form.

At this same time he is experiencing positive sensory values, is experiencing enhancement, in other ways. It is enjoyable to have a bowel movement at any time or place that the physiological tension is experienced. It is satisfying and enhancing to hit, or to try to do away with, baby brother. As these things are initially experienced, they are not necessarily inconsistent with the concept of self as a lovable person.

But then to our schematic child comes a serious threat to self. He experiences words and actions of his parents in regard to these satisfying behaviors, and the words and actions add up to the feeling "You are bad, the behavior is bad, and you are not loved or lovable when you behave in this way." This constitutes a deep threat to the nascent structure of self.

*   *   *   *   *

Certain results then follow in the development of the ordinary child. One result is a denial in awareness of the satisfactions that were experienced. The other is to distort the symbolization of the experience of the parents. The accurate symbolization would be: "I perceive my parents as experiencing this behavior as unsatisfying to them." The distorted symbolization, distorted to preserve the threatened concept of the self, is: "*I* perceive this behavior as unsatisfying."

It is in this way, it would seem, that parental attitudes are not only introjected, but what is much more important, are experienced not as the attitude of another, but in distorted fashion, *as if* based on the evidence of one's own sensory and visceral equipment. Thus, through distorted symbolization, expression of anger comes to be "experienced" as bad, even though the more accurate symbolization would be that the expression of anger is often experienced as satisfying or enhancing. . . . These values come to be accepted as being just as "real" as the values which are connected with direct experience. The "self" which is formed on this basis of distorting the sensory and visceral evidence to fit the already present structure acquires an organization and integration which the individual endeavors to preserve. Behavior is regarded as enhancing this self when no such value is apprehended through sensory or visceral reactions; behavior is regarded as opposed to the maintenance and enhancement of the self when there is no negative sensory or visceral reaction. It is here, it seems, that the individual begins on a pathway which he later describes as "I don't really know myself." The primary sensory and visceral reactions are ignored, or not permitted into consciousness, except in distorted form. The values which might be built upon them cannot be admitted to awareness. A concept of self based in part upon a distorted symbolization has taken their place.

Out of these dual sources—the direct experiencing by the individual, and the distorted symbolization of sensory reactions resulting in the introjection of values and concepts *as if* experienced—there grows the structure of the self. . . . The self-structure is an organized configuration of perceptions of the self which are admissible to awareness. It is composed of such elements as the perceptions of one's characteristics and abilities; the percepts and concepts of the self in relation to others and to the environment; the value qualities which are perceived as associated with experiences and objects; and the goals and ideals which are perceived as having positive or negative valence. It is, then, the organized picture, existing in awareness either as figure or ground, of the self and the self-in-relationship, together with the positive or negative values which are associated with those qualities and relationships, as they are perceived as existing in the past, present, or future.

It may be worthwhile to consider for a moment the way in which the self-structure might be formed without the element of distortion and denial of experience.

*　　*　　*　　*　　*

If we ask ourselves how an infant might develop a self-structure which did not have within it the seeds of later psychological difficulty, our experience in client-centered therapy offers some fruitful ideas. Let us consider, very briefly, and again in schematic form, the type of early experience which would lay a basis for a psychologically healthy development of the self. The beginning is the same as we have just described. The child experiences, and values his experiences positively or negatively. He begins to perceive himself as a psychological object, and one of the most basic elements is the perception of himself as a person who is loved. As in our first description he experiences satisfactions in such behaviors as hitting baby brother. But at this point there is a crucial difference. The parent who is able (1) genuinely to accept these feelings of satisfaction experienced by the child, and (2) fully to accept the child who experiences them, and (3) at the same time to accept his or her own feeling that such behavior is unacceptable in the family, creates a situation for the child very different from the usual one. The child in this relationship experiences no threat to his concept of himself as a loved person. He can experience fully and accept within himself and as a part of himself his aggressive feelings toward his baby brother. He can experience fully the perception that his hitting behavior is not liked by the person who loves him. What he then does depends upon his conscious balancing of the elements in the situation—the strength of his feeling of aggression, the satisfactions he would gain from hitting the baby, the satisfactions he would gain from pleasing his parent. The behavior which would result would probably be at times social and at other times aggressive. It would not necessarily conform entirely to the parent's wishes, nor would it always be socially "good." It would be adaptive behavior of a separate, unique self-governing individual. Its great advantage, as far as psychological health is concerned, is that it would be realistic, based upon an accurate symbolization of all the evidence given by the child's sensory and visceral equipment in this situation. It may seem to differ only very slightly from the description given earlier, but the difference is an extremely important one. Because the budding structure of the self is not threatened by loss of love, because feelings are accepted by his parent, the child in this instance does not need to deny to awareness the satisfactions which he is experiencing, nor does he need to distort his experience of the parental reaction and regard it as his own. He retains instead a secure self which can serve to guide his behavior by freely admitting to awareness, in accurately symbolized form, all the relevant evidence of his experience in terms of its organismic satisfactions, both immediate and longer range. He is thus developing a soundly structural self in which there is neither denial nor distortion of experience.

* * * * *

XI. *As experiences occur in the life of the individual, they are either (a) symbolized, perceived, and organized into some relationship to the self, (b) ignored because there is no perceived relationship to the self-structure, (c) denied symbolization or given a distorted symbolization because the experience is inconsistent with the structure of the self.*

Let us look first at those experiences which are ignored because they are irrelevant to the self-structure. There are various noises going on at this moment, in the distance. Until they serve my intellectual need of this moment for an example, I am relatively oblivious to them. They exist in the ground of my phenomenal field, but they do not reinforce or contradict my concept of self, they meet no need related to the self, they are ignored. Often there might be doubt as to whether they existed in the phenomenal field at all, were it not for the ability to focus on those experiences when they might serve a need. I walk down the street a dozen times, ignoring most of the sensations which I experience. Yet today I have need of a hardware store. I recall that I have seen a hardware store on the street, although I have never "noticed" it. Now that this experience meets a need of the self it can be drawn from ground into figure.

* * * * *

A more important group of experiences are those which are accepted into consciousness and organized into some relationship with the self-structure either because they meet a need of the self or because they are consistent with the self-structure and thus reinforce it. The client who has a concept of self that "I just don't feel that I can take my place in society like everybody else" perceives that she hasn't learned from her schoolwork, that she fails when she attempts things, that she does not react normally, and so on. She selects from her many sensory experiences those which fit in with her concept of herself.

* * * * *

It is the third group of sensory and visceral experiences, those which seem to be prevented from entering awareness, which demand our closest attention, for it is in this realm that there lie many phenomena of human behavior which psychologists have endeavored to explain. In some instances the denial of the perception is something rather conscious. The client cited above, whose self-concept was so negative, reports: "When people tell me they think I'm intelligent, I just don't believe it. I just—I guess I don't want to believe it. I don't know why I don't want to believe it—I just don't want to. It should give me confidence, but it doesn't. I think they just really don't know." Here she can perceive and accept readily anyone's depreciation of her, because this fits in with her self-concept.

*　*　*　*　*

There is, however, an even more significant type of denial which is the phenomenon the Freudians have tried to explain by the concept of repression. In this instance, it would appear that there is the organic experience, but there is no symbolization of this experience, or only a distorted symbolization, because an adequate conscious representation of it would be entirely inconsistent with the concept of self. Thus, a woman whose concept of self has been deeply influenced by a very strictly moralistic and religious upbringing, experiences strong organic cravings for sexual satisfaction. To symbolize these, to permit them to appear in consciousness, would provide a traumatic contradiction to her concept of self. The organic experience is something which occurs and is an organic fact. But the symbolization of these desires, so that they become part of conscious awareness, is something which the conscious self can and does prevent.

Thus the fluid but consistent organization which is the structure or concept of self, does not permit the intrusion of a perception at variance with it. . . . For the most part, it reacts as does a piece of protoplasm when a foreign body is intruded—it endeavors to prevent the entrance.

*　*　*　*　*

The individual may deny experiences to awareness without ever having been conscious of them. There is at least a process of "subception," a discriminating evaluative physiological organismic response to experience, which may precede the conscious perception of such experience. This supplies a possible basic description of the way in which accurate symbolization and awareness of experiences threatening to the self may be prevented.

Here too we may have a basis for describing the anxiety which accompanies so many psychological maladjustments. Anxiety may be the tension exhibited by the organized concept of the self when these "subceptions" indicate that the symbolization of certain experiences would be destructive of the organization. If this experimental work is confirmed by further research, it will supply a needed link in the description of the way in which repression, or denial of experience to awareness, occurs. Clinically it would appear that some such process as indicated by the term "subception" is necessary to account for the observed phenomena.

XII. *Most of the ways of behaving which are adopted by the organism are those which are consistent with the concept of self.*

As the organism strives to meet its needs in the world as it is experienced, the form which the striving takes must be a form consistent with the concept of self. The man who has certain values attached to honesty cannot strive for a sense of achievement through means which seem to him dishonest. The person who regards himself as having no aggressive feelings cannot satisfy a need for aggression in any direct fashion. The only channels by which needs may be satisfied are those which are consistent with the organized concept of self. . . . In the typical neurosis, the organism is satisfying a need which is not recognized in consciousness, by behavioral means which are consistent with the concept of self and hence can be consciously accepted.

*   *   *   *   *

XIII. *Behavior may, in some instances, be brought about by organic experiences and needs which have not been symbolized. Such behavior may be inconsistent with the structure of the self, but in such instances the behavior is not "owned" by the individual.*

In moments of great danger or other emergency stress, the individual may behave with efficiency and ingenuity to meet the needs for safety or whatever other needs exist, but without ever bringing such situations, or the behavior called forth, to conscious symbolization. In such instances the individual feels "I didn't know what I was doing." "I really wasn't responsible for what I was doing." The conscious self feels no degree of government over the actions which took place. The same statement might be made in regard to snoring or restless behavior during sleep. The self is not in control, and the behavior is not regarded as a part of self.

Another example of this sort of behavior occurs when many of the organically experienced needs are refused admittance to consciousness because inconsistent with the concept of self. The pressure of the organic need may become so great that the organism initiates its own seeking behavior and hence brings about the satisfaction of the need, without ever relating the seeking behavior to the concept of self. Thus, a boy whose upbringing created a self-concept of purity and freedom from "base" sexual impulses was arrested for lifting the skirts of two little girls and examining them. He insisted that he could not have performed this behavior, and when presented with witnesses, was positive that "I was not myself." The developing sexuality of an adolescent boy, and the accompanying curiosity, constituted a strong organic need for which there seemed no channel of satisfaction which was consistent with the concept of self. Eventually the organism behaved in such a way as to gain satisfaction, but this behavior was not felt to be, nor was it, a part of the self. It was behavior which was dissociated from the concept of self, and over which the boy exercised no conscious control. The organized character of the behavior grows out of the fact that the organism on a physiological basis can initiate and carry on complex behavior to meet its needs.

*   *   *   *   *

XIV. *Psychological maladjustment exists when the organism denies to awareness significant sensory and visceral experiences, which consequently are not symbolized and organized into the gestalt of the self-structure. When this situation exists, there is a basic or potential psychological tension.*

To illustrate briefly the nature of maladjustment, take the familiar picture of a mother whom the diagnostician would term rejecting. She has as part of her concept of self a whole constellation which may be summed up by saying, "I am a good and loving mother." . . . With this concept of self she can accept and assimilate those organic sensations of affection which she feels toward her child. But the organic experience of dislike, distaste, or hatred toward her child is something which is denied to her conscious self. The experience exists, but it is not permitted accurate symbolization. The organic need is for aggressive acts which would fulfill these attitudes and satisfy the tension which exists. The organism strives for the achievement of this satisfaction, but it can do so for the most part only through those channels which are consistent with the self-concept of a good mother. Since the good mother could be aggressive toward her child only if he merited punishment, she perceives much of his behavior as being bad, deserving punishment, and therefore the aggressive acts can be carried through, without being contrary to the values organized in her picture of self. If under great stress, she at some time should shout at her child, "I hate you," she would be quick to explain that "I was not myself," that this behavior occurred but was out of her control. "I don't know what made me say that, because of course I don't mean it." This is a good illustration of most maladjustment in which the organism is striving for certain satisfactions in the field as organically experienced, whereas the concept of self is more constricted and cannot permit in awareness many of the actual experiences.

*   *   *   *   *

In other instances, the individual feels, as he explores his maladjustment, that he has no self, that he is zero, that his only self consists of endeavoring to do what others believe he should do. The concept of self, in other words, is based almost entirely upon valuations of experience which are taken over from others and contains a minimum of accurate symbolization of experience, and a minimum of direct organismic valuing of experience. Since the values held by others have no necessary relationship to one's actual organic experiencings, the discrepancy between the self-structure and the experiential world gradually comes to be expressed as a feeling of tension and distress. One young woman, after slowly permitting her own experiences to come into awareness and form the basis of her concept of self, puts it very briefly and accurately thus: "I've always tried to be what the others thought I should be, but now I'm wondering whether I shouldn't just see that I am what I am."

XV. *Psychological adjustment exists when the concept of the self is such that all the sensory and visceral experiences of the organism are, or may be, assimilated on a symbolic level into a consistent relationship with the concept of self.*

This proposition may be put in several different ways. We may say that freedom from inner tension, or psychological adjustment, exists when the concept of self is at least roughly congruent with all the experiences of the organism. To use some of the illustrations previously given, the woman who perceives and accepts her own sexual cravings, and also perceives and accepts as a part of her reality the cultural values placed upon suppression of these cravings, will be accepting and assimilating all the sensory evidence experienced by the organism in this connection. This is possible only if her concept of self in this area is broad enough to include both her sex desires and her desire to live in some harmony with her culture. The mother who "rejects" her child can lose the inner tensions connected with her relationship to her child if she has a concept of self which permits her to accept her feelings of dislike for the child, as well as her feelings of affection and liking.

＊　＊　＊　＊　＊

The best definition of what constitutes integration appears to be this statement that all the sensory and visceral experiences are admissible to awareness through accurate symbolization, and organizable into one system which is internally consistent and which is, or is related to, the structure of self. Once this type of integration occurs, then the tendency toward growth can become fully operative, and the individual moves in the directions normal to all organic life. When the self-structure is able to accept and take account in consciousness of the organic experiences, when the organizational system is expansive enough to contain them, then clear integration and a sense of direction are achieved, and the individual feels that his strength can be and is directed toward the clear purpose of actualization and enhancement of a unified organism.

One aspect of this proposition for which we have some research evidence, but which could be tested even more clearly, is that conscious acceptance of impulses and perceptions greatly increases the possibility of conscious control. It is for this reason that the person who has come to accept his own experiences also acquires the feeling of being in control of himself. . . . The term "conscious awareness" should be used almost interchangeably with "conscious control." . . . The sense of autonomy, of self-government, is synonymous with having all experiences available to consciousness.

The term "available to consciousness" in the last sentence is deliberately chosen. It is the fact that all experiences, impulses, sensations are *available* that is important, and not necessarily the fact that they are present in consciousness. It is the organization of the concept of self *against* the symbolization of certain experiences contradictory to itself, which is the significant negative fact. Actually, when all experiences are assimilated in relationship to the self and made part of the structure of self, there tends to be *less* of what is called "self-consciousness" on the part of the individual. Behavior becomes more spontaneous, expression of attitudes is less guarded, because the self can accept such attitudes and such behavior as a part of itself.

* * * * *

XVI. *Any experience which is inconsistent with the organization or structure of self may be perceived as a threat, and the more of these perceptions there are, the more rigidly the self-structure is organized to maintain itself.*

This proposition is an attempt to formulate a description of certain clinical facts. If the rejecting mother previously mentioned is told that several observers have come to the conclusion that she does reject her child, the inevitable result is that she will, for the moment, exclude any assimilation of this experience. She may attack the conditions of observation, the training or authority of the observers, the degree of understanding they possess, and so forth and so on. She will organize the defences of her own concept of herself as a loving and good mother, and will be able to substantiate this concept with a mass of evidence. She will obviously perceive the judgment of the observers as a threat, and will organize in defence of her own governing concept.

* * * * *

XVII. *Under certain conditions, involving primarily complete absence of any threat to the self-structure, experiences which are inconsistent with it may be perceived, and examined, and the structure of self revised to assimilate and include such experiences.*

It is clear that self-concepts change, both in the ordinary development of the individual, and in therapy. The previous proposition formulates facts about the defences of the self, while this one endeavors to state the way in which change may come about.

* * * * *

In therapy of a client-centered form, by means of the relationship and the counselor's handling of it, the client is gradually assured that he is accepted as he is, and that each new facet of himself which is revealed is also accepted. It is then that experiences which have been denied can be symbolized, often very gradually, and hence brought clearly into conscious form. Once they are conscious, the concept of self is expanded so that they may be included as a part of a consistent total.

* * * * *

A question sometimes raised is that if absence of threat to the self-concept were all that was required, it might seem that the individual could, at any time that he was alone, face these inconsistent experiences. We know that this does happen in many minor circumstances. A man may be criticized for a persistent failing. At the time he refuses to admit this experience at face value, because it is too threatening to his self-organization. He denies the fault, rationalizes the criticism. But later, alone, he rethinks the matter, accepts the criticism as just, and revises his concept of self, and consequently his behavior, as a result. For experiences which are deeply denied, however, because they are deeply inconsistent with the concept of self, this does not avail. It appears possible for the person to face such inconsistency only while in a relationship with another in which he is sure that he will be accepted.

*   *   *   *   *

It should also be obvious that what is being described here is a learning process, perhaps the most important learning of which the person is capable, namely the learning of self. It is to be hoped that those who have specialized in theory of learning may begin to utilize the knowledge from that field in helping to describe the way in which the individual learns a new configuration of self.

XVIII. *When the individual perceives and accepts into one consistent and integrated system all his sensory and visceral experiences, then he is necessarily more understanding of others and is more accepting of others as separate individuals.*

We find, clinically, that the person who completes therapy is more relaxed in being himself, more sure of himself, more realistic in his relations with others, and develops notably better interpersonal relationships. One client, discussing results which therapy has had for her, states something of this fact in these words: "I am myself, and I am different from others. I am getting more happiness in being myself, and I find myself more and more letting other people assume the responsibility for being selves."

If we try to understand the theoretical basis upon which this takes place, it appears to be as follows:

The person who denies some experiences must continually defend himself against the symbolization of those experiences.

As a consequence, all experiences are viewed defensively as potential threats, rather than for what they really are.

Thus in interpersonal relationships, words or behaviors are experienced and perceived as threatening, which were not so intended.

Also, words and behaviors in others are attacked because they represent or resemble the feared experiences.

There is then no real understanding of the other as a separate person, since he is perceived mostly in terms of threat or nonthreat to the self.

But when all experiences are available to consciousness and are integrated, then defensiveness is minimized. When there is no need to defend, there is no need to attack.

When there is no need to attack, the other person is perceived for what he really is, a separate individual, operating in terms of his own meanings, based on his own perceptual field. . . .

XIX. *As the individual perceives and accepts into his self-structure more of his organic experiences, he finds that he is replacing his present value system—based so largely upon introjections which have been distortedly symbolized—with a continuing organismic valuing* process.

Values are always accepted because they are perceived as principles making for the maintenance, actualization, and enhancement of the organism. It is on this basis that social values are introjected from the culture. In therapy it would seem that the reorganization which takes place is on the basis that those values are retained which are *experienced* as maintaining or enhancing the organism as distinguished from those which are said by others to be for the good of the organism. For example, an individual accepts from the culture the value, "One should neither have nor express feelings of jealous aggressiveness toward siblings." The value is accepted because it is presumed to make for the enhancement of the individual—a better, more satisfied person. But in therapy this person, as a client, examines this value in terms of a more basic criterion—namely, his own sensory and visceral experiences: "Have I felt the denial of aggressive attitudes as something enhancing myself?" The value is tested in the light of personal organic evidence.

It is in the outcome of this valuing of values that we strike the possibility of very basic similarities in all human experience. For as the individual tests such values, and arrives at his own personal values, he appears to come to conclusions which can be formulated in a generalized way: that the greatest values for the enhancement of the organism accrue when all experiences and all attitudes are permitted conscious symbolization, and when behavior becomes the meaningful and balanced satisfaction of *all* needs, these needs being available to consciousness. The behavior which thus ensues will satisfy the need for social approval, the need to express positive affectional feelings, the need for sexual expression, the need to avoid guilt and regret as well as the need to express aggression. Thus, while the establishment of values by each individual may seem to suggest a complete anarchy of values, experience indicates that quite the opposite is true. Since all individuals have basically the same needs, including the need for acceptance by others, it appears that when each individual formulates his own values, in terms of his own direct experience, it is not an anarchy which results, but a high degree of commonality and a genuinely socialized system of values. One of the ultimate ends, then, of an hypothesis of confidence in the individual, and in his capacity to resolve his own conflicts, is the emergence of value systems which are unique and personal for each individual, and which are changed by the changing evidence of organic experience, yet which are at the same time deeply socialized, possessing a high degree of similarity in their essentials.

Conclusion

This theory is basically phenomenological in character, and relies heavily upon the concept of the self as an explanatory construct. It pictures the end-point of personality development as being congruence between the phenomenal field of experience and the conceptual structure of the self—a situation which, if achieved, would represent freedom from internal strain and anxiety, and freedom from potential strain; which would represent the maximum in realistically oriented adaptation; which would mean the establishment of an individualized value system having considerable identity with the value system of any other equally well-adjusted member of the human race.

SELF-THEORY OF PERSONALITY[2]

In endeavoring to order our perceptions of the individual as he appears in therapy, a theory of the development of personality, and of the dynamics of behavior, has been constructed. It may be well to repeat the warning previously given, and to note that the initial propositions of this theory are those which are furthest from the matrix of our experience and hence are most suspect. As one reads on, the propositions become steadily closer to the experience of therapy. . . .

A. Postulated Characteristics of the Human Infant

It is postulated that the individual, during the period of infancy, has at least these attributes.

1. He perceives his *experience* as reality. His *experience* is his reality.
    a. As a consequence he has greater potential *awareness* of what reality is for him than does anyone else, since no one else can completely assume his *internal frame of reference.*
2. He has an inherent tendency toward *actualizing* his organism.
3. He interacts with his reality in terms of his basic *actualizing* tendency.

[2]Carl R. Rogers, "A Theory of Therapy, Personality, and Interpersonal Relationships as Developed in the Client-Centered Framework," from *Psychology: A Study of a Science*, Vol. III, from pp. 221-35, edited by Sigmund Koch. Copyright 1959 by McGraw-Hill. Used with permission of McGraw-Hill Book Company. Internal references have been deleted.

Thus his behavior is the goal-directed attempt of the organism to satisfy the experienced needs for *actualization* in the reality as *perceived*.
4. In this interaction he behaves as an organized whole, as a gestalt.
5. He engages in an *organismic valuing process,* valuing *experience* with reference to the *actualizing tendency* as a criterion. *Experiences* which are *perceived* as maintaining or enhancing the organism are valued positively. Those which are *perceived* as negating such maintenance or enhancement are valued negatively.
6. He behaves with adience toward positively valued *experiences* and with avoidance toward those negatively valued.

Comment. In this view as formally stated, the human infant is seen as having an inherent motivational system (which he shares in common with all living things) and a regulatory system (the valuing process) which by its "feedback" keeps the organism "on the beam" of satisfying his motivational needs. He lives in an environment which for theoretical purposes may be said to exist only in him, or to be of his own creation.

This last point seems difficult for some people to comprehend. It is the perception of the environment which constitutes the environment, regardless as to how this relates to some "real" reality which we may philosophically postulate. The infant may be picked up by a friendly, affectionate person. If his perception of the situation is that this is a strange and frightening experience, it is this perception, not the "reality" or the "stimulus" which will regulate his behavior. To be sure, the relationship with the environment is a transactional one, and if his continuing experience contradicts his initial perception, then in time his perception will change. But the effective reality which influences behavior is at all times the perceived reality. We can operate theoretically from this base without having to resolve the difficult question of what "really" constitutes reality.

Another comment which may be in order is that no attempt has been made to supply a complete catalogue of the equipment with which the infant faces the world. Whether he possesses instincts, or an innate reflex, or an innate need for affection, are interesting questions to pursue, but the answers seem peripheral rather than essential to a theory of personality.

B. The Development of the Self
1. In line with the tendency toward differentiation which is a part of the *actualizing tendency,* a portion of the individual's *experience* becomes differentiated and *symbolized* in an *awareness* of being, *awareness* of functioning. Such awareness may be described as *self-experience.*
2. This representation in *awareness* of being and functioning, becomes elaborated, through interaction with the environment, particularly the environment composed of significant others, into a *concept of self,* a perceptual object in his *experiential field.*

Comment. These are the logical first steps in the development of the self. It is by no means the way the construct developed in our own thinking. . . .

C. The Need for Positive Regard

1. As the awareness of self emerges, the individual develops a *need for positive regard.* This need is universal in human beings, and in the individual, is pervasive and persistent. Whether it is an inherent or learned need is irrelevant to the theory. Standal . . . who formulated the concept, regards it as the latter.
   a. The satisfaction of this need is necessarily based upon inferences regarding the experiential field of another.
      (1) Consequently it is often ambiguous.
   b. It is associated with a very wide range of the individual's *experiences.*
   c. It is reciprocal, in that when an individual discriminates himself as satisfying another's need for *positive regard,* he necessarily experiences satisfaction of his own need for *positive regard.*
      (1) Hence it is rewarding both to satisfy this need in another, and to experience the satisfaction of one's own need by another.
   d. It is potent, in that the *positive regard* of any social other is communicated to the total *regard complex* which the individual associates with that social other.
      (1) Consequently the expression of positive regard by a significant social other can become more compelling than the *organismic valuing process,* and the individual becomes more adient to the *positive regard* of such others than toward *experiences* which are of positive value in *actualizing* the organism.

D. The Development of the Need for Self-Regard

1. The positive regard satisfactions or frustrations associated with any particular *self-experience* or group of *self-experiences* come to be *experienced* by the individual independently of *positive regard* transactions with social others. *Positive regard experienced* in this fashion is termed *self-regard.*
2. A *need for self-regard* develops as a learned need developing out of the association of *self-experiences* with the satisfaction or frustration of the *need for positive regard.*
3. The individual thus comes to *experience positive regard* or loss of *positive regard* independently of transactions with any social other. He becomes in a sense his own significant social other.
4. Like *positive regard, self-regard* which is *experienced* in relation to

any particular *self-experience* or group of *self-experiences*, is communicated to the total *self-regard complex*.

E. The Development of Conditions of Worth

1. When *self-experiences* of the individual are discriminated by significant others as being more or less worthy of *positive regard*, then *self-regard* becomes similarly selective.

2. When a *self-experience* is avoided (or sought) solely because it is less (or more) worthy of *self-regard*, the individual is said to have acquired a *condition of worth*.

3. If an individual should *experience* only *unconditional positive regard*, then no *conditions of worth* would develop, *self-regard* would be unconditional, the needs for *positive regard* and *self-regard* would never be at variance with *organismic evaluation*, and the individual would continue to be *psychologically adjusted*, and would be fully functioning. This chain of events is hypothetically possible, and hence important theoretically, though it does not appear to occur in actuality.

Comment. This is an important sequence in personality development, stated more fully by Standal. . . . It may help to restate the sequence in informal, illustrative, and much less exact terms.

The infant learns to need love. Love is very satisfying, but to know whether he is receiving it or not he must observe his mother's face, gestures, and other ambiguous signs. He develops a total gestalt as to the way he is regarded by his mother and each new experience of love or rejection tends to alter the whole gestalt. Consequently each behavior on his mother's part such as a specific disapproval of a specific behavior tends to be experienced as disapproval in general. So important is this to the infant that he comes to be guided in his behavior not by the degree to which an experience maintains or enhances the organism, but by the likelihood of receiving maternal love.

Soon he learns to view himself in much the same way, liking or disliking himself as a total configuration. He tends, quite independently of his mother or others, to view himself and his behavior in the same way they have. This means that some behaviors are regarded positively which are not actually experienced organismically as satisfying. Other behaviors are regarded negatively which are not actually experienced as unsatisfying. It is when he behaves in accordance with these introjected values that he may be said to have acquired conditions of worth. He cannot regard himself positively, as having worth, unless he lives in terms of these conditions. He now reacts with adience or avoidance toward certain behaviors solely because of these introjected conditions of self-regard, quite without reference to the organismic consequences of these behaviors. This is what is meant by living in terms of introjected values (the phrase formerly used) or conditions of worth.

It is not theoretically necessary that such a sequence develop. If the infant always felt prized, if his own feelings were always accepted even though some behaviors were inhibited, then no conditions of worth would develop. This could at least theoretically be achieved if the parental attitude was genuinely of this sort: "I can understand how satisfying it feels to you to hit your baby brother (or to defecate when and where you please, or to destroy things) and I love you and am quite willing for you to have those feelings. But I am quite willing for me to have my feelings, too, and I feel very distressed when your brother is hurt (or annoyed or sad at other behaviors) and so I do not let you hit him. Both your feelings and my feelings are important, and each of us can freely have his own." If the child were thus able to retain his own organismic evaluation of each experience, then his life would become a balancing of these satisfactions. Schematically he might feel, "I enjoy hitting baby brother. It feels good. I do not enjoy mother's distress. That feels dissatisfying to me. I enjoy pleasing her." Thus his behavior would sometimes involve the satisfaction of hitting his brother, sometimes the satisfaction of pleasing mother. But he would never have to disown the feelings of satisfaction or dissatisfaction which he experienced in this differential way.

F. The Development of Incongruence Between Self and Experience

1. Because of the need for *self-regard*, the individual *perceives* his experience selectively, in terms of the *conditions of worth* which have come to exist in him.
   a. Experiences which are in accord with his *conditions of worth* are *perceived* and *symbolized* accurately in *awareness*.
   b. Experiences which run contrary to the *conditions of worth* are *perceived* selectively and distortedly as if in accord with the *conditions of worth*, or are in part or whole, *denied to awareness*.
2. Consequently some experiences now occur in the organism which are not recognized as *self-experiences*, are not accurately *symbolized*, and are not organized into the *self-structure* in *accurately symbolized* form.
3. Thus from the time of the first selective *perception* in terms of *conditions of worth*, the states of *incongruence between self and experience*, of *psychological maladjustment* and of *vulnerability*, exist to some degree.

Comment. It is thus because of the distorted perceptions arising from the conditions of worth that the individual departs from the integration which characterizes his infant state. From this point on his concept of self includes distorted perceptions which do not accurately represent his experience, and his experience includes elements which are not included in the picture he has of himself. Thus he can no longer live as a unified whole person, but various part functions now become characteristic. Certain experiences tend to threaten the self. To maintain the self-structure defensive reactions are necessary. Behavior is regulated at times by the self and at times those aspects of the organism's experience which are not included in the self. The personality is henceforth divided, with the tensions and inadequate functioning which accompany such lack of unity.

This, as we see it, is the basic estrangement in man. He has not been true to himself, to his own natural organismic valuing of experience, but for the sake of preserving the positive regard of others has now come to falsify some of the values he experiences and to perceive them only in terms based upon their value to others. Yet this has not been a conscious choice, but a natural—and tragic—development in infancy. The path of development toward psychological maturity, the path of therapy, is the undoing of this estrangement in man's functioning, the dissolving of conditions of worth, the achievement of a self which is congruent with experience, and the restoration of a unified organismic valuing process as the regulator of behavior.

G. The Development of Discrepancies in Behavior

1. As a consequence of the incongruence between self and experience described in *F*, a similar incongruence arises in the behavior of the individual.
    a. Some behaviors are consistent with the *self-concept* and maintain and actualize and enhance it.
       (1) Such behaviors are *accurately symbolized* in *awareness*.
    b. Some behaviors maintain, enhance, and actualize those aspects of the experience of the organism which are not assimilated into the *self-structure*.
       (1) These behaviors are either unrecognized as *self-experiences* or *perceived* in distorted or selective fashion in such a way as to be *congruent* with the *self*.

H. The Experience of Threat and the Process of Defense

1. As the organism continues to *experience*, an *experience* which is ingruent with the self-structure (and its incorporated *conditions of worth*) is *subceived as threatening*.
2. The essential nature of the *threat* is that if the *experience* were accurately symbolized in *awareness*, the *self-concept* would no longer be a consistent gestalt, the *conditions of worth* would be violated, and the *need for self-regard* would be frustrated. A state of *anxiety* would exist.
3. The process of *defense* is the reaction which prevents these events from occurring.
    a. This process consists of the selective *perception* or *distortion* of the *experience* and/or the *denial to awareness* of the *experience* or

some portion thereof, thus keeping the total *perception* of the *experience* consistent with the individual's *self-structure,* and consistent with his *conditions of worth.*

4. The general consequences of the process of *defense,* aside from its preservation of the above consistencies, are a rigidity of *perception,* due to the necessity of distorting *perceptions,* an inaccurate *perception* of reality, due to distortion and omission of data, and *intensionality.*

Comment. Section *G* describes the psychological basis for what are usually thought of as neurotic behaviors, and Section *H* describes the mechanisms of these behaviors. From our point of view it appears more fundamental to think of defensive behaviors (described in these two sections) and disorganized behaviors (described below). Thus the defensive behaviors include not only the behaviors customarily regarded as neurotic —rationalization, compensation, fantasy, projection, compulsions, phobias, and the like—but also some of the behaviors customarily regarded as psychotic, notably paranoid behaviors and perhaps catatonic states. The disorganized category includes many of the "irrational" and "acute" psychotic behaviors, as will be explained below. This seems to be a more fundamental classification than those usually employed, and perhaps more fruitful in considering treatment. It also avoids any concept of neurosis and psychosis as entities in themselves, which we believe has been an unfortunate and misleading conception.

Let us consider for a moment the general range of the defensive behaviors from the simplest variety, common to all of us, to the more extreme and crippling varieties. Take, first of all, rationalization. ("I didn't really make that mistake. It was this way....") Such excuses involve a perception of behavior distorted in such a way as to make it congruent with our concept of self (as a person who doesn't make mistakes). Fantasy is another example. ("I am a beautiful princess, and all the men adore me.") Because the actual experience is threatening to the concept of self (as an adequate person, in this example), this experience is denied, and a new symbolic world is created which enhances the self, but completely avoids any recognition of the actual experience. Where the incongruent experience is a strong need, the organism actualizes itself by finding a way of expressing this need, but it is perceived in a way which is consistent with the self. Thus an individual whose self-concept involves no "bad" sexual thoughts may feel or express the thought "I am pure, but you are trying to make me think filthy thoughts." This would be thought of as projection or as a paranoid idea. It involves the expression of the organism's need for sexual satisfactions, but it is expressed in such a fashion that this need may be denied to awareness and the behavior perceived as consistent with the self. Such examples could be continued, but perhaps the point is clear that the incongruence between self and experience is handled by the distorted perception of experience or behavior, or by the denial of experience in awareness (behavior is rarely denied, though this is possible), or by some combination of distortion and denial.

I. The Process of Breakdown and Disorganization

Up to this point the theory of personality which has been formulated applies to every individual in a lesser or greater degree. In this and the following section certain processes are described which occur only when certain specified conditions are present.

1. If the individual has a large or significant degree of *incongruence between self and experience* and if a significant experience demonstrating *incongruence* occurs suddenly, or with a high degree of obviousness, then the organism's process of *defense* is unable to operate successfully.

2. As a result *anxiety* is *experienced* as the *incongruence* is subceived. The degree of *anxiety* is dependent upon the extent of the *self-structure* which is *threatened*.

3. The process of *defense* being unsuccessful, the *experience* is *accurately symbolized* in *awareness*, and the gestalt of the *self-structure* is broken this *experience* of the *incongruence* in *awareness*. A state of disorganization results.

4. In such a state of disorganization the organism behaves at times in ways which are openly consistent with experiences which have hitherto been distorted or denied to awareness. At other times the self may temporarily regain regnancy, and the organism may behave in ways consistent with it. Thus in such a state of disorganization, the tension between the concept of self (with its included distorted perceptions) and the experiences which are not accurately symbolized or included in the concept of self, is expressed in a confused regnancy, first one and then the other supplying the "feedback" by which the organism regulates behavior.

Comment. This section, as will be evident from its less exact formulation, is new, tentative, and needs much more consideration. Its meaning can be illuminated by various examples.

Statements 1 and 2 above may be illustrated by anxiety-producing experiences in therapy, or by acute psychotic breakdowns. In the freedom of therapy, as the individual expresses more and more of himself, he finds himself on the verge of voicing a feeling which is obviously and undeniably true, but which is flatly contradictory to the conception of himself which he has held. Anxiety results, and if the situation is appropriate (as described under J) this anxiety is moderate, and the result is constructive. But if, through overzealous and ineffective interpretation by the therapist, or through some other means, the individual is brought face to face with more of his denied experiences than he can handle, disorganization ensues and a psychotic break occurs, as described in statement 3. We have known this to happen when an individual has sought "therapy" from several different sources simultaneously. It has also been illustrated by some of the early experience with sodium pentathol therapy. Under the drug the individual revealed many of the experiences which hitherto he had denied to himself, and which accounted for the incomprehensible elements in his behavior. Unwisely faced with the material in his normal state, he could not deny its authenticity, his defensive processes could not deny or distort the experience, and hence the self-structure was broken, and a psychotic break occurred. . . .

J. The Process of Reintegration

. . . A process of reintegration is possible, a process which moves in the direction of increasing the *congruence* between *self* and *experience*. This may be described as follows:

1. In order for the process of *defense* to be reversed—for a customarily *threatening experience* to be *accurately symbolized* in *awareness* and assimilated into the *self-structure*, certain conditions must exist.
   a. There must be a decrease in the *conditions of worth*.
   b. There must be an increase in *unconditional self-regard*.
2. The communicated *unconditional positive regard* of a significant other is one way of achieving these conditions.
   a. In order for the *unconditional positive regard* to be communicated, it must exist in a context of *empathic* understanding.
   b. When the individual *perceives* such *unconditional positive regard*, existing *conditions of worth* are weakened or dissolved.
   c. Another consequence is the increase in his own *unconditional positive self-regard*.
   d. Conditions 2a and 2b above thus being met, *threat* is reduced, the process of *defense is reversed*, and *experiences* customarily *threatening* are *accurately symbolized* and integrated into the *self-concept*.
3. The consequences of 1 and 2 above are that the individual is less likely to encounter *threatening experiences*; the process of *defense* is less frequent and its consequences reduced; *self* and *experience* are more *congruent*; *self-regard* is increased; *positive regard* for others is increased; *psychological adjustment* is increased; the *organismic valuing process* becomes increasingly the basis of regulating behavior; the individual becomes nearly fully functioning.

Comment. This section is simply the theory of therapy which we presented earlier, now stated in a slightly more general form. It is intended to emphasize the fact that the reintegration or restoration of personality occurs always and only (at least so we are hypothesizing) in the presence of certain definable conditions. These are essentially the same whether we are speaking of formal psychotherapy continued over a considerable period, in which rather drastic personality changes may occur, or whether we are speaking of the minor constructive changes which may be brought about by contact with an understanding friend or family member.

One other brief comment may be made about item 2a, above. Empathic understanding is always necessary if unconditional positive regard is to be fully communicated. If I know little or nothing of you, and experience an unconditional positive regard for you, this means little because further knowledge of you may reveal aspects which I cannot so regard. But if I know you thoroughly, knowing and empathically understanding a wide variety of your feelings and behaviors, and still experience an unconditional positive regard, this is very meaningful. It comes close to being fully known and fully accepted.

SPECIFICATION OF FUNCTIONAL RELATIONSHIPS IN THE THEORY OF PERSONALITY

In a fully developed theory it would be possible to specify, with mathematical accuracy, the functional relationships between the several variables. It is a measure of the immaturity of personality theory that only the most general description can be given of these functional relationships. We are not yet in a position to write any equations. Some of the relationships implied in [the previous section] may be specified as follows:

The more actualizing the experience, the more adient the behavior $(A5, 6)$.

The more numerous or extensive the conditions of worth, the greater the proportion of experience which is potentially threatening $(F1, 2)$.

The more numerous or extensive the conditions of worth, the greater the degree of vulnerability and psychological maladjustment $(F3)$.

The greater the proportion of experience which is potentially threatening, the greater the probability of behaviors which maintain and enhance the organism without being recognized as self-experiences $(G1a, b)$.

The more congruence between self and experience, the more accurate will be the symbolizations in awareness $(G1a, and H1, 2, 3)$.

The more numerous or extensive the conditions of worth, the more marked will be the rigidity and inaccuracies of perception, and the greater the degree of intensionality $(H4)$.

The greater the degree of incongruence experienced in awareness, the greater the likelihood and degree of disorganization $(I3)$.

The greater the degree of experienced unconditional positive regard from another, based upon empathic understanding, the more marked will be the dissolution of conditions of worth, and the greater proportion of incongruence which will be eliminated $(J2, 3)$.

In other respects the relationships in section J have already been specified in the theory of therapy.

Evidence. The first sections of this theory are largely made up of logical constructs, and propositions which are only partly open to empirical proof or disproof.

Section *F* receives some confirmation from Cartwright,[a] and Diller,[b] Section *H* from Chodorkoff[c] and Cartwright, whereas Goldiamond[d] introduces evidence which might modify the definition of subception. . . .

Because it is a closely reasoned and significant experimental testing of certain of the hypotheses and functional relationships specified in this portion of the theory, Chodorkoff's study [cited above] will be described briefly. His definitions were taken directly from the theory. Defensiveness, for example, is defined as the process by which accurate symbolizations of threatening experiences are prevented from reaching awareness.

He concentrated on three hypotheses which may be stated in theoretical terms as follows:

1. The greater the congruence between self and experience, the less will be the degree of perceptual defensiveness exhibited.

2. The greater the congruence between self and experience, the more adequate will be the personality adjustment of the individual, as this phrase is commonly understood.

3. The more adequate the personality adjustment of the individual (as commonly understood), the less will be the degree of perceptual defensiveness exhibited.

Thus it will be seen that he was testing one of the definitions of the theory (Congruence equals psychological adjustment) against clinical and common-sense reality. He was also testing one of the relationships specified by the theory (Degree of congruence is inversely related to degree of defensiveness). For good measure he also completes the triangle by testing the proposition that adjustment as commonly understood is inversely related to degree of defensiveness.

He gave the following operational meanings to the essential terms:

1. Self is defined as a *Q* sort of self-referent items sorted by the individual to represent himself as of now.

2. Experience. An exact matching of the theoretical meaning with given operations is of course difficult. Chodorkoff avoids the term "experience," but operationally defines it by an "objective description" which is a *Q* sort by a clinician of the same self-referent items, this sorting being based on a thorough clinical knowledge of the individual, gained through several

---

[a]D. Cartwright, "Self-Consistency as a Factor in Affecting Immediate Recall." Unpublished manuscript (mimeo.). (Chicago: University of Chicago Counseling Center, 1955).

[b]L. Diller, "Conscious and Unconscious Self-Attitudes after Success and Failure," *Journal of Personality*, 23 (1954), from pp. 1-12.

[c]B. Chodorkoff, "Self-Perception, Perceptual Defense, and Adjustment," *Journal of Abnormal and Social Psychology*, 49 (1954), from pp. 508-12.

[d]I. Goldiamond, "On the Asynchrony Between Responses in a Perceptual Experiment." Unpublished doctoral dissertation, University of Chicago, 1954.

projective tests. Thus the total experiencing of the individual, as distinct from the self-concept he possesses in awareness, is given a crude operational definition by this means.

3. Perceptual defensiveness is defined as the difference in recognition time between a group of neutral words tachistoscopically presented to the individual, and a group of personally threatening words similarly presented. (The selection of the words and the technique of presentation were very carefully worked out, but details would be too lengthy here.)

4. Personal adjustment as commonly understood was defined as a combined rating of the individual by four competent judges, the rating being based on biographical material, projective tests, and other information.

These definitions provide an operational basis for four measures entirely independent of one another.

Chodorkoff translates his hypotheses into operational predictions as follows:

1. The higher the correlation between the individual's self-sort and the clinician's sorting for his total personality, the less will be the difference in his recognition threshold between neutral and threatening words.

2. The higher the correlation between the self-sort and the clinician's sorting for the total personality the higher will be the rating of personal adjustment by the four judges.

3. The higher the adjustment rating by the four judges, the lower will be the difference in recognition threshold between neutral and threatening words.

All three of these predictions were empirically upheld at levels of statistical significance, thus confirming certain portions of the theory.

This study illustrates the way in which several of the theoretical constructs have been given a partial operational definition. It also shows how propositions taken or deduced from the theory may be empirically tested. It suggests, too, the complex and remote behavioral predictions which may be made from the theory.

A Theory of the Fully Functioning Person

Certain directional tendencies in the individual . . . and certain needs . . . have been explicitly postulated in the theory thus far presented. Since these tendencies operate more fully under certain defined conditions, there is already implicit in what has been given a concept of the ultimate in the actualization of the human organism. This ultimate hypothetical person would be synonymous with "the goal of social evolution," "the end point of optimal psychotherapy," etc. We have chosen to term this individual the fully functioning person.

Although it contains nothing not already stated earlier . . . it seems worthwhile to spell out this theoretical concept in its own right.

A. The individual has an inherent tendency toward *actualizing* his organism.
B. The individual has the capacity and tendency to *symbolize experiences* accurately in *awareness.*
    1. A corollary statement is that he has the capacity and tendency to keep his *self-concept* congruent with his *experience.*
C. The individual has a *need for positive regard.*
D. The individual has a *need for positive self-regard.*
E. Tendencies A and B are most fully realized when needs C and D are met. More specifically, tendencies A and B tend to be most fully realized when
    1. The individual *experiences unconditional positive regard* from significant others.
    2. The pervasiveness of this *unconditional positive regard* is made evident through relationships marked by a complete and communicated *empathic* understanding of the individual's *frame of reference.*
F. If the conditions under E are met to a maximum degree, the individual who experiences these conditions will be a fully functioning person. The fully functioning person will have at least these characteristics:
    1. He will be *open to his experience.*
        a. The corollary statement is that he will experience no *defensiveness.*
    2. Hence all *experiences* will be *available to awareness.*
    3. All *symbolizations* will be as accurate as the experiential data will permit.
    4. His *self-structure* will be congruent with his *experience.*
    5. His *self-structure* will be a fluid gestalt, changing flexibly in the process of assimilation of new *experience.*
    6. He will *experience* himself as the *locus of evaluation.*
        a. The *valuing process* will be a continuing *organismic* one.
    7. He will have no *conditions of worth.*
        a. The corollary statement is that he will *experience unconditional self-regard.*
    8. He will meet each situation with behavior which is a unique and creative adaptation to the newness of that moment.
    9. He will find his *organismic valuing* a trustworthy guide to the most satisfying behaviors, because
        a. All available experiential data will be available to *awareness* and used.
        b. No datum of *experience* will be *distorted in,* or *denied to, awareness.*
        c. The outcomes of behavior in *experience* will be *available to awareness.*

      d. Hence any failure to achieve the maximum possible satisfaction, because of lack of data, will be corrected by this effective reality testing.

    10. He will live with others in the maximum possible harmony because of the rewarding character of reciprocal *positive regard* *(C1c)*.

Comment. It should be evident that the term "the fully functioning person" is synonymous with optimal psychological adjustment, optimal psychological maturity, complete congruence, complete openness to experience, complete extensionality, as these terms have been defined.

Since some of these terms sound somewhat static, as though such a person "had arrived," it should be pointed out that all the characteristics of such a person are *process* characteristics. The fully functioning person would be a person-in-process, a person continually changing. Thus his specific behaviors cannot in any way be described in advance. The only statement which can be made is that the behaviors would be adequately adaptive to each new situation, and that the person would be continually in a process of further self-actualization. For a more complete exposition of this whole line of thought the reader may wish to see my paper on the fully functioning person.[e]

Specification of Functions. Our present state of thinking can be given in one sentence. The more complete or more extensive the conditions $E1$, $E2$, the more closely will the individual approach the asymptotic characteristics $F1$ through $F10$.

Evidence. The evidence regarding outcomes of therapy is in a general way confirmatory of the direction taken in this theory, though by its very nature it can never be completely tested, since it attempts to define as asymptote.

    [e]C. R. Rogers, "A Concept of the Fully Functioning Person." Unpublished manuscript (mimeo.). (Chicago: University of Chicago Counseling Center, 1953.)

PART THREE

Field, Holistic, and Organismic Approaches to Personality

CHAPTER 10

GEORGE A. KELLY

PERSONAL CONSTRUCT THEORY

Building a personality theory on his psychology of personal constructs, George A. Kelly developed his system from a phenomonological or cognitive approach. In Kelly's system, phenomonology means that a person's inner experiences and world view are paramount; the focus on the subjective life of an individual is of major importance. Kelly's cognitive approach is evident in his personal construct theory: that a person looks at his world through self-made "transparent patterns" which he tries to fit over the world's realities. Such a position closely juxtaposes Kelly's psychology of personal constructs with existentialism, as well as with phenomological psychology and cognitivism.

Compared to other professional scientists, Kelly regards each person as "man-the-scientist"; hypothesizing, exploring and viewing life as a psychological maze. To cope effectively with life, Kelly states that an individual must postulate constructs and (according to Kelly's constructive alternativism doctrine) experiment and exchange the constructs for more effective and usable ones. According to the personal construct theory, a balanced personality is one whose philosophy of life (or personal constructs) is integrated with and fits the objective circumstances.

Conversely, Kelly asserts that an imbalanced personality is one whose personal constructs are not compatible with perceived circumstances. When personal constructs fail, that is, prove ineffective, anxiety is the result. Threat is experienced when upheaval confronts the core structure of an individual's world view. While aggression is viewed as the pursuit of constructive experience, hostility is a desperate attempt to validate discredited personal constructs. Role playing is adapting another's personal constructs for one's own. Guilt erupts as a result of being dislodged from one's role. Dismissing motivation as redundant because being alive is itself evidence of motivation, Kelly introduced his fundamental postulate: "A person's processes are psychologically channelized by the ways in which he anticipates events,"[1] that is, in the light of his personal constructs.

Born in Perth, Kansas in 1905, George Alexander Kelly attended Friends University in Wichita before transferring to Park College in Missouri. After receiving his baccalaureate in 1926, Kelly attended the University of Kansas, where he received a master's degree in educational sociology in 1928. The following academic year was spent at the University of Edinburgh. Returning with a bachelor's degree in education, Kelly continued his graduate education at the University of Iowa, where he obtained a Ph.D. in 1931.

Kelly's post-doctoral career began in 1931 with an appointment at Fort Hays Kansas State College, and continued until World War II, when he served as an aviation psychologist with the U.S. Navy. In 1945 he accepted a faculty position with the University of Maryland, but left the following year as Professor and Director of Clinical Psychology at Ohio State University. It was during the Ohio tenure that Kelly's personal construct theory of personality matured. In 1965 Kelly left Ohio to assume the Riklis Chair of Behavioral Science at Brandeis University in Waltham, Massachusetts. At the height of his career and in the midst of preparing another book for publication, Kelly died on March 6, 1967. He was survived by but a few intellectual heirs, among them the Britishers, D. Bannister and J.M.M. Mair, who in 1968 published a volume on *The Evaluation of Personal Constructs,* and dedicated it "to the late George Alexander Kelly to whose work it is a footnote." While Brenden Maher was Kelly's successor at Brandeis University, he edited a book on Kelly's papers, many of which up to that time were unpublished. The volume, *Clinical Psychology and Personality* appeared in 1969. Kelly published only one book during his lifetime, a two volume tome on *The Psychology of Personal Constructs* in 1955.

---

[1]*The Psychology of Personal Constructs* (New York: Norton, 1955), from p. 46.

PERSONAL CONSTRUCTS[2]

The theory is based upon the philosophical position of constructive alter-nativism, the notion that there are many workable alternative ways for one to construe his world. The theory itself starts with the basic assumption, or postulate, that a person's processes are psychologically channelized by the ways in which he anticipates events. This is to say that human behavior may be viewed as basically anticipatory rather than reactive, and that new ave-nues of behavior open themselves to a person when he reconstrues the course of events surrounding him. Thus a thoughtful man is neither the prisoner of his environment nor the victim of his biography.

The patterns of man's construction are called *constructs*; and, since each person sets up his own network of pathways leading into the future, the con-cern of the psychologist is the study of personal constructs. Each personal construct is based upon the simultaneous perception of likeness and differ-ence among the objects of its context. There is no such thing as a difference without a likeness being implied, and vice versa. Each construct is, therefore, dichotomous or bipolar in nature; and, in dealing with a client, the psychol-ogist must frequently go off searching for the submerged poles in the client's thinking.

When a person finds his personal construction failing him, he suffers *anxiety*. When he faces an impending upheaval in his *core structure*, he ex-periences *threat*. A person who construes the construction system of another person sets the stage for playing a *role* in relation to that person. When he finds himself dislodged from his role, he experiences *guilt*. This has much to do with social organization. *Aggression* is merely the active pursuit of *con-structive* experience, but it may be *threatening* to one's associates. *Hostility*, while not necessarily violent, is the continued attempt to extort *validational evidence* in support of a personal construction which has already discredited itself.

* * * * *

Man looks at his world through transparent patterns or templets which he creates and then attempts to fit over the realities of which the world is composed. The fit is not always very good. Yet without such patterns the world appears to be such an undifferentiated homogeneity that man is unable to make any sense out of it. Even a poor fit is more helpful to him than nothing at all.

Let us give the name *constructs* to these patterns that are tentatively tried on for size. They are ways of construing the world. They are what enables man, and lower animals too, to chart a course of behavior, explicitly formu-lated or implicitly acted out, verbally expressed or utterly inarticulate, con-

[2]*Ibid.*, from pp. 8-9, 135-136, 550-565.

sistent with other courses of behavior or inconsistent with them, intellectually reasoned or vegetatively sensed.

In general man seeks to improve his constructs by increasing his repertory, by altering them to provide betters fits, and by subsuming them with super-ordinate constructs or systems. In seeking improvement he is repeatedly halted by the damage to the system that apparently will result from the alter-ation of a subordinate construct. Frequently his personal investment in the larger system, or his personal dependence upon it, is so great that he will forego the adoption of a more precise construct in the substructure. It may take a major act of psychotherapy or experience to get him to adjust his construction system to the point where the new and more precise construct can be incorporated.

Those construction systems which can be communicated can be widely shared.

*   *   *   *   *

We have long since committed ourselves to a point of view from which we see the world as being real and man's psychological processes as being based upon personal versions of that reality. The personal versions are personal constructs. Now we may ask ourselves the question whether, from this point of view, constructs are real. The answer is a qualified yes. Constructs are not to be confounded with the factual material of which they are personalized versions; they are interpretations of those facts. But constructs may be used as viewpoints for seeing other constructs, as in the hierarchical relationships of constructs within a system. In that sense the superordinate constructs are versions of those constructs which are subordinate to them. This makes the subordinate constructs a form of reality which is construed through the use of the superordinate constructs. The summary answer to our question of whether or not constructs are real is that a construct is indeed real, but its reality is not identical with the factual elements in its context. With respect to the factual elements it is representative, not identical. Its reality is not their reality. The construct has its own reality. The problem should not cause us trouble if we keep in mind that a construct and its elements are both real, but distinguished from each other.

Can a construct be communicated from one person to another without losing its reality? In a sense the answer is yes.

*   *   *   *   *

Fundamental Postulate and Corollaries

The theory of personality we have called the psychology of personal con-structs starts with a basic assumption upon which all else hinges. It is called the Fundamental Postulate. This postulate is then elaborated by means of eleven corollaries. These, also, are assumptive in nature, and they lay the groundwork for most of what follows. While it may be difficult to see the implications of this series of assumptions from a bare recitation of them, it seems appropriate to give the reader an opportunity to see what the statements are....

a. *Fundamental Postulate:* A person's processes are psychologically channelized by the ways in which he anticipates events.

b. *Construction Corollary:* A person anticipates events by construing their replications.

c. *Individuality Corollary:* Persons differ from each other in their constructions of events.

d. *Organization Corollary:* Each person characteristically evolves for his convenience in anticipating events, a construction system embracing ordinal relationships between constructs.

e. *Dichotomy Corollary:* A person's construction system is composed of a finite number of dichotomous constructs.

f. *Choice Corollary:* A person chooses for himself that alternative in a dichotomized construct through which he anticipates the greater possibility for extension and definition of his system.

g. *Range Corollary:* A construct is convenient for the anticipation of a finite range of events only.

h. *Experience Corollary:* A person's construction system varies as he successfully construes the replications of events.

i. *Modulation Corollary:* The variation in a person's construction system is limited by the permeability of the constructs within whose ranges of convenience the variants lie.

j. *Fragmentation Corollary:* A person may successively employ a variety of construction subsystems which are inferentially incompatible with each other.

k. *Commonality Corollary:* To the extent that one person employs a construction of experience which is similar to that employed by another, his psychological processes are similar to those of the other person.

l. *Sociality Corollary:* To the extent that one person construes the construction processes of another he may play a role in a social process involving the other person.

Formal Aspects of Constructs

Range of Convenience. A construct's range of convenience comprises all those things to which the user would find its application useful.

Focus of Convenience. A construct's focus of convenience comprises those particular things to which the user would find its application maximally useful. These are the elements upon which the construct is likely to have been formed originally.

Elements. The things or events which are abstracted by a person's use of a construct are called elements. In some systems these are called objects.

Context. The context of a construct comprises those elements among which the user ordinarily discriminates by means of the construct. It is somewhat more restricted than the range of convenience, since it refers to the circumstances in which the construct emerges for practical use, and not necessarily to all the circumstances in which a person might eventually use the construct. It is somewhat more extensive than the focus of convenience, since the construct may often appear in circumstances where its application is not optimal.

Pole. Each construct discriminates between two poles, one at each end of its dichotomy. The elements abstracted are like each other at each pole with respect to the construct and are unlike the elements at the other pole.

Contrast. The relationship between the two poles of a construct is one of contrast.

Likeness End. When referring specifically to elements at one pole of a construct, one may use the term "likeness end" to designate that pole.

Contrast End. When referring specifically to elements at one pole of a construct, one may use the term "contrast end" to designate the opposite pole.

Emergence. The emergent pole of a construct is that one which embraces most of the immediately perceived context.

Implicitness. The implicit pole of a construct is that one which embraces contrasting context. It contrasts with the emergent pole. Frequently the person has no available symbol or name for it; it is symbolized only implicitly by the emergent term.

Symbol. An element in the context of a construct which represents not only itself but also the construct by which it is abstracted by the user is called the construct's symbol.

Permeability. A construct is permeable if it admits newly perceived elements to its context. It is impermeable if it rejects elements on the basis of their newness.

Constructs Classified According to the Nature of Their Control Over Their Elements

Preemptive Construct. A construct which preempts its elements for membership in its own realm exclusively is called a preemptive construct. This is the "nothing but" type of construction—"If this is a ball it is nothing but a ball."

Constellatory Construct. A construct which fixes the other realm memberships of its elements is called a constellatory construct. This is stereotyped or typological thinking.

Propositional Construct. A construct which carries no implications regarding the other realm memberships of its elements is a propositional construct. This is uncontaminated construction.

General Diagnostic Constructs

Preverbal Constructs. A preverbal construct is one which continues to be used, even though it has no consistent word symbol. It may or may not have been devised before the client had command of speech symbolism.

Submergence. The submerged pole of a construct is the one which is less available for application to events.

Suspension. A suspended element is one which is omitted from the context of a construct as a result of revision of the client's construct system.

Level of Cognitive Awareness. The level of cognitive awareness ranges from high to low. A high-level construct is one which is readily expressed in socially effective symbols; whose alternatives are both readily accessible; which falls well within the range of convenience of the client's major constructions; and which is not suspended by its superordinating constructs.

Dilation. Dilation occurs when a person broadens his perceptual field in order to reorganize it on a more comprehensive level. It does not, in itself, include the comprehensive reconstruction of those elements.

Constriction. Constriction occurs when a person narrows his perceptual field in order to minimize apparent incompatibilities.

Comprehensive Constructs. A comprehensive construct is one which subsumes a wide variety of events.

Incidental Constructs. An incidental construct is one which subsumes a narrow variety of events.

Superordinate Constructs. A superordinate construct is one which includes another as one of the elements in its context.

Subordinate Constructs. A subordinate construct is one which is included as an element in the context of another.

Regnant Constructs. A regnant construct is a kind of superordinate construct which assigns each of its elements to a category on an all-or-none basis, as in classical logic. It tends to be nonabstractive.

Core Constructs. A core construct is one which governs the client's maintenance processes.

Peripheral Constructs. A peripheral construct is one which can be altered without serious modification of the core structure.

Tight Constructs. A tight construct is one which leads to unvarying predictions.

Loose Constructs. A loose construct is one leading to varying predictions, but which retains its identity.

Constructs Relating to Transition

Threat. Threat is the awareness of an imminent comprehensive change in one's core structures.

Fear. Fear is the awareness of an imminent incidental change in one's core structures.

Anxiety. Anxiety is the awareness that the events with which one is confronted lie mostly outside the range of convenience of his construct system.

Guilt. Guilt is the awareness of dislodgment of the self from one's core role structure.

Aggressiveness. Aggressiveness is the active elaboration of one's perceptual field.

Hostility. Hostility is the continued effort to extort validational evidence in favor of a type of social prediction which has already been recognized as a failure.

C-P-C Cycle. The C-P-C cycle is a sequence of construction involving, in succession, circumspection, preemption, and control, and leading to a choice precipitating the person into a particular situation.

Impulsivity. Impulsivity is a characteristic foreshortening of the C-P-C Cycle.

Creativity Cycle. The Creativity Cycle is one which starts with loosened construction and terminates with tightened and validated construction.

CONSTRUCTIVE ALTERNATIVISM[3]

We assume that all of our present interpretations of the universe are subject to revision or replacement. This is a basic statement which has a bearing upon almost everything that we shall have to say later. We take the stand that there are always some alternative constructions available to choose among in dealing with the world. No one needs to paint himself into a corner; no one needs to be completely hemmed in by circumstances; no one needs to be the victim of his biography. We call this philosophical position *constructive alternativism.*

* * * * *

For we must keep trying our alternative interpretations on nature for size, since she never offers to give us her measurements in advance. Only by comparisons of what we contrive to try on do we successively approximate the one ultimate hypothesis that is truer than any other. It should be clear, then, that what any scientist can hope to discover is not an absolute categorical truth, nor even a relative fraction of truth, but a categorical truth applied in a context of relationships. The relativity refers not to the truth—that is categorical—but to the hypotheses in the context of which truth is the abstraction.

[3]*Ibid.,* from pp. 15, 189.

MAN-THE-SCIENTIST[4]

Mankind, whose progress in search of prediction and control of surrounding events stands out so clearly in the light of the centuries, comprises the men we see around us every day. The aspirations of the scientist are essentially the aspirations of all men.

The universe is real; it is happening all the time; it is integral; and it is open to piecemeal interpretation. Different men construe it in different ways. Since it owes no prior allegiance to any one man's construction system, it is always open to reconstruction. Some of the alternative ways of construing are better adapted to man's purposes than are others. Thus, man comes to understand his world through an infinite series of successive approximations. Since man is always faced with constructive alternatives, which he may explore if he wishes, he need not continue indefinitely to be the absolute victim either of his past history or of his present circumstances.

Life is characterized, not merely by its abstractability along a time line, but, more particularly, by the capacity of the living thing to represent its environment. Especially is this true of man, who builds construction systems through which to view the real world. The construction systems are also real, though they may be biased in their representation. Thus, both nature and human nature are phenomenologically existent.

The constructs which are hierarchically organized into systems are variously subject to test in terms of their usefulness in helping the person anticipate the course of events which make up the universe. The results of the testing of constructs determine the desirability of their temporary retention, their revision, or their immediate replacement. We assume that any system may, in proper time, have to be replaced. Within the structure of a system determinism and free will are directional aspects of the same system; that is, a construct is determined by that with which one judges it must always be consistent, and it is free of that which one judges must always be subordinated to it.

ROLES AND ROLE-PLAYING[5]

In terms of the theory of personal constructs, a *role* is a psychological process based upon the role player's construction of aspects of the construction systems of those with whom he attempts to join in a social enterprise. In less precise but more familiar language, a role is an ongoing pattern of

[4]*Ibid.*, from pp. 43-44.
[5]*Ibid.*, from pp. 97-99.

behavior that follows from a person's understanding of how the others who are associated with him in his task think. In idiomatic language, a role is a position that one can play on a certain team without even waiting for the signals.

This definition of *role* lays emphasis upon several important points. First, like other patterns of behavior, it is assumed to be tied to one's personal construct system. This implies that it is anchored in the outlook of the role player and does not necessarily follow from his congregate relationship to other members of a group. It is a pattern of behavior emerging from the person's own construction system rather than primarily out of his social circumstances. He plays out his part in the light of his understanding of the attitudes of his associates, even though his understanding may be minimal, fragmentary, or misguided. This notion of role is, therefore, neither a typical stimulus-response notion nor a typical sociological notion. We believe it is essentially consistent with our Fundamental Postulate and with the various corollaries which have already been stated.

The second point to be emphasized is that this definition of role is not equivalent to the "self-concept" as used in some psychological systems. Seeing oneself as playing a role is not equivalent to identifying oneself as a static entity; but rather, as throughout the theory of personal constructs, the role refers to a process—an ongoing activity. It is that activity carried out in relation to, and with a measure of understanding of, other people that constitutes the role one plays.

The third point to be emphasized is that this definition ties up the role with a social process. While the concept of role is appropriate to a psychological system which is concerned with individual persons, it is defined herein so that it is dependent upon cognate developments within a group of two or more people. It is not enough that the role player organize his behavior with an eye on what other people are thinking; he must be a participant, either in concert or in opposition, within a group movement. This further restriction of the definition of a role places emphasis upon team membership on the part of the role player.

The fourth point to be emphasized is that, while one person may play a role in a social process involving the other person, through subsuming a version of that other person's way of seeing things, the understanding need not be reciprocated. Thus the one person is playing a role in a social process, but the other is not playing a role in that social process. This is the way we have chosen to define *role*. It does not mean that the other person is not a factor to be taken into account in explaining the social process.

The fifth and final point to be emphasized is that this definition of role does not insist upon commonality in the construct systems of the people involved in the social process or in the persons specifically involved in playing roles. Commonality between construction systems may make it more likely that one construction system can subsume a part of another, but that fact is incidental rather than essential in those cases where roles are played between people who think alike and understand each other. Moreover, commonality can exist between two people who are in contact with each other without either of them being able to understand the other well enough to engage in a social process with him. The commonality may exist without those perceptions of each other which enable the people to understand each other or to subsume each other's mental processes.

CHAPTER 11

KURT LEWIN

COGNITIVE OR FIELD THEORY
OF PERSONALITY

Kurt Lewin's COGNITIVE OR FIELD THEORY OF PERSONALITY was inspired by Einstein's concept of "fields of force." As a result, Lewin believes that objects do not exist or function in a vacuum, but rather in a field of interrelated wholes (*Gestalten*). His second major contribution consists in his application of *spatial* concepts to personality theory which up to this time had employed only the concept of *time*. Lewin's interest in mathematical principles has led him to apply the mathematical discipline of *topology* to psychology in order to give it the prestige and status of a science. For Lewin, the constructs of personality and its environment are as responsive to mathematical logic as are spatial relations. He favors the *Gestalt* approach to psychological problems inasmuch as his beliefs are predicated on the premise that each "part depends upon every other part."

Conceptualizing is the psychologist's primary task as a scientist; thus, it is his task to translate phenomenological experiences into mental concepts by taking into account both the quantitative and qualitative aspects of phenomena, together with their causal relations, and by seeking out operational definitions which issue in useful generalizations—those which encompass universals as well as concrete particular cases. Lewin describes the function of constructs, then, as a method whereby one is obliged "to consider qualitatively different geometrical entities (such as a circle, square, parabola) as the product of a certain combination of certain 'elements of construction' (such as points and movements). . . . It is sometimes called the method of 'genetic definition.' It is able, at the same time, to link and to separate; it does not minimize qualitative differences and still lays open their relation to general variables."[1] This method is applicable to the "empirical sciences where the 'elements of construction' are mathematically described empirical entities (such as forces, ions, atoms)."[2]

Kurt Lewin was born in 1890 in Prussia and died in 1947, at the height of his career, while serving as Director of the Research Center for Group Dynamics at the Massachusetts Institute of Technology. Prior to going to M.I.T., he served as Professor of Psychology in the Child Welfare Station at the University of Iowa. He also taught at Stanford University and, for two years, at Cornell University. Before coming to America, he was on the faculty of the University of Berlin and concurrently was affiliated with the Psychological Institute of Berlin in a research capacity.

Among his publications in English are "Environmental Forces" in *Handbook of Child Psychology* (ed. by C. C. Murchison, 1934), *A Dynamic Theory of Personality* (1935), *Principles of Topological Psychology* (1936), "The Conceptual Representation and Measurement of Psychological Forces" in *University of Iowa Contributions to Psychological Theory* (1938), *Resolving Social Conflicts; Selected Papers on Group Dynamics* (1948), and *Field Theory in Social Science; Selected Theoretical Papers* (1951).

PSYCHOLOGICAL ECOLOGY[3]

I do not expect ever to live down the misunderstandings created by my attack on some ways in which statistics have been used in psychology. I have always been aware that quantitative measurement demands statistics. That statement holds also for "pure cases"; i.e., situations where it is possible to link theory and observable facts in a definite way. Since psychology is increasingly abandoning the inadequate objectives of statistics, further discussion might have little pragmatic value.

However, Brunswik has brought into the open new and important aspects, and I feel that their clarification may be helpful for psychological methodology in general.

[1]*Field Theory in Social Science* (New York: Harper, 1951), from p. 45.
[2]"Constructs in Psychology and Psychological Ecology," *University of Iowa Studies in Child Welfare*, XX (1944), from pp. 1-29.
[3]"Defining the 'Field at a Given Time,'" *Psychological Review*, L (1943), 306-9. This material may also be found in *Field Theory in Social Science, op. cit.*, ch. 3.

Within the realm of facts existing at a given time one can distinguish three areas in which changes are or might be of interest to psychology:

1. The "life space"; i.e., the person and the psychological environment as it exists for him. We usually have this field in mind if we refer to needs, motivation, mood, goals, anxiety, ideals.
2. A multitude of processes in the physical or social world, which do not affect the life space of the individual at that time.
3. A "boundary zone" of the life space: certain parts of the physical or social world do affect the state of the life space at that time. The process of perception, for instance, is intimately linked with this boundary zone because what is perceived is partly determined by the physical "stimuli"; i.e., that part of the physical world which affects the sensory organs at that time. Another process located in the boundary zone is the "execution" of an action.

Brunswik states correctly: "The 'field' within which Lewin is able to predict, in the strict sense of the word, is the person in his life space." Then he proceeds, "But the life space is not to be confused with geographic environment of physical stimuli, nor with actually achieved results in the environment. It is post-perceptual, and pre-behavioral." This statement is partly incorrect, namely, in so far as perception and behavior, to my mind, are legitimate problems of psychology. This view is a necessary consequence of the field-theoretical approach according to which the boundary conditions of a field are essential characteristics of that field. For instance, processes of perception which should be related to the boundary zone depend partly on the state of the inner part of the psychological field; i.e., upon the character of the person, his motivation, his cognitive structure, his way of perceiving, etc., and partly on the "stimulus distribution" on the retina or other receptors as enforced by physical processes outside the organism. For the same reasons, the problems of physical or social action are legitimate parts of psychology proper.

Brunswik, however, is correct in assuming that I do not consider as a part of the psychological field at a given time those sections of the physical or social world which do not affect the life space of the person at that time. The food that lies behind doors at the end of a maze so that neither smell nor sight can reach it is not a part of the life space of the animal. If the individual knows that food lies there this *knowledge*, of course, has to be represented in his life space, because this knowledge affects behavior. It is also necessary to take into account the subjective probability with which the individual views the present or future state of affairs because the degree of certainty of expectation also influences his behavior.

The principle of representing within the life space all that affects behavior at that time, but nothing else, prevents the inclusion of physical food which is not perceived. This food cannot possibly influence his behavior at that time under the conditions mentioned. Indeed, the individual will start his journey if he thinks the food is there even if it is actually not there, and he will not move toward the food which actually is at the end of the maze if he does not know it is there.

According to Brunswik, it is possible to think in terms of laws rather than mere statistical rules if one limits the psychological field in the way described. However, he claims that for this gain one has to pay "the price of an encapsulation" into the realm of problems which actually leaves out the most dynamic aspects of psychology. He wishes to include in the psychological field those parts of the physical and sociological world which, to my mind, have to be excluded. These parts, he states, have to be studied in a statistical way, and the probability of the occurrence of events calculated.

To my mind, the main issue is what the term "probability" refers to. Does Brunswik want to study the ideas of the driver of a car about the probability of being killed or does he want to study the accident statistics which tell the "objective probability" of such an event. If an individual sits in a room trusting that the ceiling will not come down, should only his "subjective probability" be taken into account for predicting behavior or should we also consider the "objective probability" of the ceiling's coming down as determined by the engineers. To my mind, only the first has to be taken into account.

I can see why psychology should be interested even in those areas of the physical and social world which are not part of the life space or which do not affect its boundary zone at present. If one wishes to safeguard a child's education during the next years, if one wishes to predict in what situation an individual will find himself as a result of a certain action, one will have to calculate his future. Obviously, such forecast has to be based partly on statistical considerations about nonpsychological data.

Theoretically, we can characterize this task as discovering what part of the physical or social world will determine during a given period the "boundary zone" of the life space. This task is worth the interest of the psychologists. I would suggest calling it "psychological ecology."

Some problems of the "life history" of an individual have their places here. The boundary conditions of the life space during long as well as short time-periods depend partly on the action of the individual himself. To this degree they should be linked to the psychological dynamics of the life space. The rest of the calculation has to be done, however, with other than psychological means.

The essence of explaining or predicting any change in a certain area is the linkage of that change with the conditions of the field at that time. This basic principle makes the subjective probability of an event a part of the life space of that individual. But it excludes the objective probability of alien factors that cannot be derived from the life space.

The relation[4] between psychological and nonpsychological factors is a

4The remainder of this section is from "Forces behind Food Habits and Methods of Change," *Bulletin of the National Research Council,* CVIII (1943), from pp. 35-36.

basic conceptual and methodological problem in all branches of psychology, from the psychology of perception to the psychology of groups. A proper understanding of this relationship must be achieved before we can answer the many questions raised in efforts to produce an integration of the social sciences. A field-theoretical approach to these problems of "psychological ecology" suggests some of the ways in which these questions may be answered. . . .

Any type of group life occurs in a setting of certain limitations to what is and what is not possible, what might or might not happen. The nonpsychological factors of climate, of communication, of the law of the country or the organization are a frequent part of these "outside limitations." The first analysis of the field is done from the point of view of "psychological ecology": the psychologist studies "nonpsychological" data to find out what these data mean for determining the boundary conditions of the life of the individual or group. Only after these data are known can the psychological study itself be begun to investigate the factors which determine the actions of the group or individual in those situations which have been shown to be significant. . . .

The Field Approach: Culture and Group Life as Quasi-Stationary Processes

This question of planned change or of any "social engineering" is identical with the question: What "conditions" have to be changed to bring about a given result and how can one change these conditions with the means at hand?

One should view the present situation—the *status quo*—as being maintained by certain conditions or forces. A culture—for instance, the food habits of a given group at a given time—is not a static affair but a live process like a river which moves but still keeps a recognizable form. In other words, we have to deal, in group life as in individual life, with what is known in physics as "quasi-stationary" processes.

Food habits do not occur in empty space. They are part and parcel of the daily rhythm of being awake and asleep; of being alone and in a group; of earning a living and playing; of being a member of a town, a family, a social class, a religious group, a nation; of living in a hot or a cool climate; in a rural area or a city, in a district with good groceries and restaurants or in an area of poor and irregular food supply. Somehow all of these factors affect food habits at any given time. They determine the food habits of a group every day anew just as the amount of water supply and the nature of the riverbed determine from day to day the flow of the river, its constancy, or its change.

Food habits of a group, as well as such phenomena as the speed of production in a factory are the result of a multitude of forces. Some forces support each other, some oppose each other. Some are driving forces, others restraining forces. Like the velocity of a river, the actual conduct of a group depends upon the level (for instance, the speed of production) at which these conflicting forces reach a state of equilibrium. To speak of a certain culture pattern—for instance, the food habits of a group—implies that the constellation of these forces remains the same for a period or at least that they find their state of equilibrium at a constant level during that period.

Neither group "habits" nor individual "habits" can be understood sufficiently by a theory which limits its consideration to the processes themselves and conceives of the "habit" as a kind of frozen linkage, as "association" between these processes. Instead, habits will have to be conceived of as a result of forces in the organism *and* its life space, in the group *and* its setting. The structure of the organism, of the group, of the setting, or whatever name the field might have in the given case, has to be represented and the forces in the various parts of the field have to be analyzed if the processes (which might be either constant "habits" or changes) are to be understood scientifically. The process is but the epiphenomenon; the real object of study is the constellation of forces.

Therefore, to predict which changes in conditions will have what result we have to conceive of the life of the group as the result of specific constellations of forces within a larger setting. In other words, scientific predictions or advice for methods of change should be based on an analysis of the "field as a whole," including both its psychological and nonpsychological aspects.

* * * * *

THE LIFE SPACE
(PERSON AND ENVIRONMENT)[5]

As far as the *content* is concerned, the transition from Aristotelian to Galilean concepts demands that we no longer seek the "cause" of events in the nature of a single isolated object, but in the relationship between an object and its surroundings. It is not thought then that the environment of the individual serves merely to facilitate or inhibit tendencies which are established once for all in the nature of the person. One can hope to understand the forces that govern behavior only if one includes in the representation the whole psychological situation.

In psychology one can begin to describe the whole situation by roughly distinguishing the person (P) and his environment (E). Every psychological event depends upon the state of the person and at the same time on the environment, although their relative importance is different in different cases. Thus we can state our formula $B = f(S)$ for every psychological event as $B = f(PE)$. The experimental work of recent years shows more

[5]*Principles of Topological Psychology* (New York: McGraw-Hill, 1936), from pp. 11-12.

and more this twofold relationship in all fields of psychology. Every scientific psychology must take into account whole situations, *i.e.*, the state of both person and environment. This implies that it is necessary to find methods of representing person and environment in common terms as parts of one situation. We have no expression in psychology that includes both. For the word situation is commonly used to mean environment. In the following we shall use the term psychological life space to indicate the totality of facts which determine the behavior of an individual at a certain moment.

TOPOLOGICAL SPACE[6]

The mathematical concept of space can be developed from different fundamental relationships. From the point of view of psychology it is especially interesting that one can use the part-whole relationship as the basic one. This basic theorem states that for any two objects, U and V, of a system for which certain conditions hold, the following relationship shall or shall not be valid: U is a part of V (that is equivalent to "V includes U"). By means of certain monotonous series of inclusion one can characterize the concept of a "point" and further the concept of "surrounding."

Space thus defined is called topological space. By this term is meant that we are dealing with mathematical relationships which can be characterized without measurement. No distances are defined in topological space. A drop of water and the earth are, from a topological point of view, fully equivalent. A cube and a sphere also are not distinguishable. Nevertheless these nonmetrical spaces exhibit characteristics which are fundamental also for metrical space. There is a highly developed branch of mathematics which has grown up around the concept of connectedness. It deals with separated and connected spaces, with the different kinds of connectedness, with the relationship of part sets in different regions, with boundaries, with cuts, etc. Problems of dimension can also be treated on the basis of topological concepts without recourse to metrical properties.

It is now generally recognized that the whole-part relationship, and the relationships of the parts to each other play a fundamental role in psychology. This is true for all branches of psychology. The concept of connectedness, for instance the distinction between separate and connected regions, the distinction between different groupings of regions, is . . . of prime importance for characterizing both the person and the psychological environment. Changes of connection, especially the uniting and separating of regions, are just as important for the psychology of perception as for the psychology of intention, satisfaction, or friendship. The basic idea of a person in an environment is in its conceptual content a statement of a certain topological relationship between two regions.

[6]*Ibid.*, from pp. 53-55.

Certain binary relationships, *i.e.*, relationships between two points of topological space, play an essential role in topology. In this place we must call attention to the topological concept of "path" that connects two points. How parts of a space are connected can be determined to a large extent by the possibility of such paths and the fact that the path does or does not intersect certain boundaries. We will see that the concept of path plays a fundamental role in the constitution of psychological spaces. One can coordinate certain psychological facts which have the function of a psychological connection between two psychological "points" to a "path" which mathematically connects two points. For instance, any kind of locomotion of the person in the quasi-physical, the quasi-social, or the quasi-conceptual field can be designated as a connecting process which corresponds to a topological path.

In addition to the locomotion of the person or other parts of the psychological space we must call attention to that type of real connection which one can call "dynamic communication." The fact that certain regions in the psychological environment and within the person influence other regions, both of the environment and of the person, may be taken as a criterion for connectedness in the topological sense.

*   *   *   *   *

I hope it is now clear that from the point of view of mathematics there is no reason why these concepts should not be applied to psychological problems and that psychology has already used, and cannot avoid using, concepts which are of a topological nature.

The Psychological Region[7]

Definition: To each part of the life space a region is to be coordinated.

Thus we have to represent as a region (1) everything in which an object of the life space, for instance a person, has its place; in which it moves; through which it carries out locomotions; (2) everything in which one can distinguish several positions or parts at the same time, or which is part of a more inclusive whole.

This definition implies that the person itself has to be represented as a region in the life space, further that the life space as a whole is a region.

The reverse of the definition of a psychological region also holds: everything that is shown as a region in representing a situation must be a part of the life space.

In determining whether we are dealing with one or with several psychological regions one can build on either of two facts: (1) one can characterize a region by its qualitative properties and can find out its relations of position by determining which regions are contained in others, which regions have common boundaries. (2) One can build on psychological

---

[7]*Ibid.*, from pp. 93-95.

processes which connect different points (part regions) in the life space, for instance on locomotions. The locomotions cross or do not cross certain boundaries or other regions. This characteristic makes it possible, on the basis of the coordination of locomotion and path, to make topological statements about the regions to which the points (part regions) belong. . . .

The determination of a region, for instance by certain qualitative characteristics, does not in itself imply whether or not this region is a connected one. For instance, the region which corresponds to the property of a person or the region which corresponds to a certain social group has to be represented sometimes as a connected, sometimes as a non-connected region according to the actual distribution of the property or the members of the group. Also in this point therefore the psychological concept of region agrees with that of mathematics.

Psychological Locomotion[8]

Definition: A path is to be coordinated mathematically to each psychological locomotion.

One understands by path a part of a Jordan curve, *i.e.*, a curve which does not intersect itself. On the other hand psychological lomotion can, at least in a certain sense, pass the same place twice. In these cases locomotion would have to be represented by a curve which intersects itself. . . . It should be emphasized once more that in the following discussion we mean by locomotion not only quasi-physical but also quasi-social or quasi-conceptual locomotion.

The question arises whether this coordinating definition can be reversed. Such a reversal would take the following form: To each path in the life space corresponds a locomotion. However, there are cases in which one can connect mathematical points in two different regions of the life space, but when the corresponding locomotion can actually not be carried out. For instance, the prisoner cannot carry out bodily locomotion from the region within the prison to the region outside. Nevertheless, in this case other objects in the life space of the prisoner can carry out such a locomotion and he himself can move in his thoughts from one region to the other. But it is at least conceivable that there can be regions in the life space into which even a conceptual locomotion cannot be carried out. . . . For our purposes we can state the definition in its reverse form as follows: To each path in the psychological life space corresponds a locomotion which can or cannot be carried out.

* * * * *

On the basis of these coordinating definitions of the psychological region and the psychological locomotion one can represent mathematically the topological relationships of an unlimited number of different situations.

[8]*Ibid.*, from pp. 95-96.

The Principle of "Concreteness"[9]

Only what is concrete can have effects. This proposition may seem obvious. But one often ignores it in explaining an event by development, by adaptation, by the *Prinzip der wirkenden Seele*, by an abstract drive, and in treating these principles as concrete causes. . . . These fallacies arise in part from a confusion between the law that governs the effects of certain concrete events and these events themselves. Effects can be produced only by what is "concrete," *i.e.*, by something that has the position of an individual fact which exists at a certain moment; a fact which can be given a definite place in the representation of the psychological situation. All this is not true of "principles."

The Principle of "Contemporaneity"[10]

The question of the temporal relationship of the event and the dynamic conditions which produce it are very important and have a direct bearing on almost all psychological problems. By referring to our formula $B = f(PE)$ we can state these questions more precisely: What is the temporal relationship of behavior (B) to the two factors which make up the situation, person (P) and environment (E)? Furthermore, what is the temporal relationship between the different parts of the life space?

These questions have usually been discussed in such a way that one asked whether only past or whether future events also could cause change. Wundt, for instance, believed that the characteristic of the *causa finalis* (teleology) lies in the assumption that future events influence present events. In the case of the ordinary cause (*causa efficiens*) one generally takes for granted that something past is the cause of present events. This point of view occurs frequently in philosophical discussions that are based on physics.

This emphasis on past or future causes plays an important part, not only in philosophical discussions of psychology, but also—and that is more significant for us—in the actual construction of theories regarding concrete problems. The reference to future events occurs in more or less explicit form, for instance in the application of the concepts of drive or instinct, in the theories of play, etc.

Though we are justified in setting up "historical" questions and looking for causal sequences, yet we must be careful to avoid historical and half-historical answers to "systematic" questions of causation. . . . We shall here strongly defend the thesis that neither past nor future psychological facts but only the present situation can influence present events. This thesis is a direct consequence of the principle that only what exists concretely can have effects. Since neither the past nor the future exists at the present moment it cannot have effects at the present. In representing the life space therefore we take into account only what is contemporary. . . . From the point of view

[9]*Ibid.*, from pp. 32-33.
[10]*Ibid.*, from pp. 33-35.

of systematic causation, past events cannot influence present events. Past events can only have a position in the historical causal chains whose inter-weavings create the present situation. This fact has often not been given enough consideration in psychology.

THE PSYCHOLOGICAL WORLDS[11]

Physics treats its space as a closed system of causes and effects in the following sense: All physical changes are the result of conditions or changes within the same physical space. According to physics there are no influences on this space from outside.

In psychology also there is a more or less close dynamic connection between all the facts which belong to the same psychological space. The psychological events are determined by the life space according to the formula $B = f(S)$. So far therefore, as in physics, a change is the result of conditions or events within the same space.

Nevertheless, the matter is not so simple in psychology. That becomes clear if one asks, in connection with the question of "historical causality," how the situation S came into being. . . . We cannot avoid recognizing that there are such influences from outside on the psychological life space. That means that there are changes which cannot be derived from the dynamics of the psychological life space even if one assumes strict determinism in psychology and if one has a complete knowledge of the previous situation and of all psychological laws. These changes can only be thought of as influences on the psychological life space which are "alien to psychology."

> I do not use the expression "alien to psychology" to indicate physiological or other bodily influences which, as we have seen, have to be included in the system of psychobiological laws. Instead I use it to designate such influences on a situation as cannot be derived from the psychobiological properties of the preceding situation.

Such alien influences occur frequently. The field of perception and action can be changed for instance by the fact that an object is suddenly set in motion by physical causes, that another person encroaches, that the telephone rings, etc. These influences from outside can have a definitely social character. The announcement of new regulations for peddlers, about employment relief, about taxes, can entirely change the field of action of a peddler, of an employed person, or of the taxpayer. As mentioned above such influences can occur by way of perception or as gross somatic influences. In all these cases we find essential dynamic changes of the life space of an individual which do not depend on the psychological dynamics of the life space itself. The single psychobiological worlds do not therefore represent dynamically closed regions in the sense indicated above.

If one follows up this problem one sees that almost all processes which

[11]*Ibid.*, from pp. 68-75.

are based primarily on psychobiological dynamics depend to a certain degree on alien factors. If someone saws a board his behavior is determined not only by his goal but also by the nature of the wood and the properties of his saw. The same is true when a year-old child puts one block on another and finds that they do not stick together however hard he presses them; or when someone tries to influence a political group, or to solve a mathematical problem, and finds that things do not go as he had expected. If someone throws a ball at a mark, if he tries to influence another person through praise or blame, if he goes along a street, or looks around, in all these cases, the actual effects of the psychological event depend also on facts which are alien to psychology.

We have, further, to call attention to the connection between cognition and these alien factors. Cognition has always been treated as a specific characteristic of mental life although it has not at all such outstanding importance for inner-psychological dynamics. This may be one consequence of the fact that the psychological worlds are not closed. Perception and cognition often affect the life space in such a way that the structure of its parts corresponds in a high degree to the objective structure of what is perceived. How far and at what points the two structures correspond in concrete cases is very important for the success of an action, and is decisive for the value of a plan. The comprehension of the intrinsic nature of the alien factors, whether of physical relationships, of mathematical problems, or of social groups, is therefore of the greatest importance for every achievement.

> It is not always easy to decide, in particular cases, what is to be taken as alien and what as real psychological influences. A child may want to get a cloth to clean up water that the "naughty" doll has spilled. If he asks an adult where to find the cloth, then the adult's answer represents an alien factor, *i.e.*, it cannot be derived from the preceding situation in the life space of the child. But if the child already knows where the cloth is, one is inclined to speak of a simple psychological relationship. . . .

The concept of a world which is dynamically not "closed" but within which there exists nevertheless a strict determinism offers some difficulty at first, and one might ask whether it is at all possible to give a conceptually clear definition of such a space. Closer examination, however, shows that a mathematical representation of such a world is quite possible.

We have to consider two possibilities: The influence "from outside" can affect the psychological life space at every point or only in certain regions.

The mathematical representation of the second case is simple. It means that one has to distinguish within the life space "inner points" and "boundary points." The life space therefore would be a "limited" and "closed" region, *i.e.*, a region which includes its own boundary. The boundary points would correspond to those zones of the life space that can be influenced from the outside. This representation would be correct if for instance all influences on the life space from the outside were mediated by the surface of the body of the person. The boundary of the life space would be a simply connected region which, represented two-dimensionally, would correspond to Fig. 1. Only psychological laws would then govern the inner part of the life space. Alien influences would affect only these boundary points.

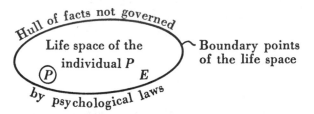

Fig. 1.
The life space as a "dynamically not closed" world. *P*, person; *E*, environment.

The other possibility, *viz.*, that each point of the life space can be affected by alien influences, can also be represented mathematically. It would mean that all points of the life space are boundary points. This postulate is fulfilled if one imbeds the space of psychological facts in a space which has one dimension more. Then, regardless of the number of dimensions of the psychological life space, every point becomes a boundary point in relation to the space of more dimensions. Let us assume that the life space could be represented by a two-dimensional manifold, for instance by a plane. Then the events that occurred could be derived according to psychological laws from the structure and the dynamic properties of the facts represented in this plane. Nevertheless, each point of the plane would be a boundary point in regard to a three-dimensional space. This three-dimensional "hull" would make it possible to represent those physical, social, or other facts which are alien to psychology and which do not influence the life space at the present moment but which can affect it in the future. Within this hull would hold not psychological, but other laws. In this case the life space could again be "limited" (as in Fig. 1). But it could also correspond to the unlimited plane. An analogous possibility of a transition to a hull of more dimensions exists mathematically also in the case in which the life space itself represents a manifold of three, four, or more dimensions.

In answering the question how the boundary points in the life space are distributed, one will have to take into account that not only is the life space influenced from the outside, but that effects can also work in the opposite direction; that is, behavior can affect those regions which are not subject to psychological laws.

One must not conclude from the unclosedness of the psychological worlds that there is no use in speaking of a psychological causal relationship. The task of dynamic psychology is to derive unequivocally the behavior of a given individual from the totality of the psychological facts that exist in the life space at a given moment ($B = f(S)$). To this also belong all those facts at the boundary points which influence the person at the present moment but which themselves owe their existence partly to alien events. Insofar, therefore, the task of deriving the behavior B from the totality of S remains unchanged and has not lost anything of its psychological character. Insofar there is no formal difference between psychology and physics. The difference consists in the fact that there are no boundary points in the physical world which depend on nonphysical factors.

It is obvious that psychology must take into account also physical and social facts which obey non-psychological laws and which control the events in the "foreign" hull of the life space. For these facts determine the boundary points of the life space and are therefore of great importance for all events in it. Every act of influencing another person, whether in laboratory experiment or in everyday life, consists in creating such a hull, one which affects the boundary points of the life space and thereby the life itself in a certain way.

To summarize: psychology has to assign a separate space to each single individual and his own environment. Each such space corresponds to the totality of a psychobiological world. (From the point of view of theory of science it is equivalent to the whole physical world.) These worlds are "dynamically not closed"; they have boundaries or each of their points exhibits boundary properties in relation to certain influences which are alien to psychology. [Lewin defines *dynamic* as "facts or concepts which refer to conditions of change, especially to forces. Dynamic facts can be determined indirectly only." A *construct* is "a dynamic fact which is determined indirectly as an 'intervening concept' by way of 'operational definition.' A construct expresses a dynamic interrelation and permits, in connection with laws, the making of statements about what is possible and what is not possible."—ED.]

The Person as a Differentiated Region in the Life Space[12]

Behavior depends on the state of the environment and that of the person: $B = f(PE)$. In this equation P and E are not independent variables. The structure of the environment and the constellation of forces in it vary with the desires and needs, or in general with the state of the person. It is possible to determine in detail the dependency of certain facts in the environment (*e.g.*, the extent to which they are satisfied). Thereby it becomes evident that a change of a certain need, for instance its satiation, does not change all needs in the same direction and to the same extent. This makes it necessary to distinguish within the person a multitude of different regions whose changes of state are to a certain extent independent of each other.

These considerations meet an objection which is sometimes raised against

[12]*Ibid.*, from pp. 166-67.

our representations. It is said that it suffices for the derivation of behavior to represent either environment or person. In reality however it is impossible to derive the psychological processes in the life space without including changes both of person and of environment in the representation. (All so-called physiological theories which do not contain a representation of the environment are for this reason inadequate.)

One will ask for criteria on the basis of which one can determine what is to be represented as a region of the environment and what as a region of the person. In answering this question it could be pointed out that the "self" is experienced as a region within the whole field. This criterion, however, is not sufficient. . . . The goals and concepts which popular psychology has often attributed to the inner person as a rule have to be represented as part of the environment. From a dynamic point of view the following facts may be considered: one can treat everything as environment in which, toward which, or away from which the person as a whole can perform locomotion.

One will have to treat the question whether a psychological region belongs to person or to environment with the same topological methods by means of which one determines other positions in the life space. The determinations depend on the concrete facts of the individual case. Therefore, for different life spaces there may be considerable differences in the structure and boundaries of the person.

*   *   *   *   *

STRUCTURE OF THE PERSON (AND HIS TOPOLOGY) [13]

Inner-Personal Regions and the Motor-Perceptual Region

If, on the basis of these considerations, we try to determine the structure of the person as a whole, we come to the following interpretation. The person is to be represented as a connected region which is separated from the environment by a Jordan curve. Within this region there are part regions. One can begin by distinguishing as such parts the "inner-personal" regions (I) from the motor and perceptual region (M). The motor and perceptual region has the position of a boundary zone between the inner-personal regions and the environment (E; Fig. 2). Two groups of facts stand in favor of such a representation.

1. Needs or other states of the inner-personal regions can influence the environment only by way of a bodily expression of a bodily action, that is, by way of a region which one can call the motor region. Koffka uses the term "the executive" for this region. . . . We have to represent the motor

---

[13]*Ibid.*, from pp. 177-88.

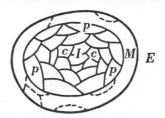

Fig. 2.
Topology of the person. M, motor-perceptual region; I, inner-personal region; p, peripheral parts of I; c, central parts of I; E, environment.

region as a boundary zone between the inner-personal regions and the environment. One of the most important processes in this motor region is speech. It plays a great role in the communication between the person and his social environment. The use of gestures, "smiling at" and "looking at," belongs here. The position of the motor region as an intermediate between the environment and the inner-personal regions holds for purposeful actions as well as for undirected affective discharges of tension, *i.e.*, for all changes of the environment E resulting from the state of the inner-personal region.

2. We find an intermediate region again when we consider the influence in the opposite direction, namely psychological changes of the inner-personal region resulting from changes of the environment. This intermediate region corresponds to the perceptual system in the broadest sense of the word, that is, to hearing, seeing, etc. It is identical in part with the motor region. The eye, for instance, can both express and perceive. Other parts, like the ear, serve with man to transmit events only in one direction, from outside in. In any case the boundary zone between the inner regions and the environment includes both motor and perceptual systems.

It is to a certain degree arbitrary where one draws the boundary between the motor-perceptual system and the inner regions, whether for instance one considers the understanding of speech as an event within the boundary zone or within the inner-personal systems. The essential task is to determine the relative position of the regions in question, and the degree of communication between them and their neighboring regions. The same is true of the boundaries between the motor region and the environment. Both determinations depend upon the nature of the person and also upon the momentary state of the life space. During a medical examination the boundaries of the body are at the same time the boundaries between the person and the environment. But usually the clothing has to be counted as part of the person. The outer boundary of a child may be different when he is in contact with his mother and when he is with a stranger. In cases of embarrassment, for instance when one is suddenly exposed to critical glances of a stranger, the clothing and the whole appearance are often strongly emphasized and stand out as a special zone within the boundary region of the person. Under certain circumstances regions which are usually hidden can lie open or can be easily discerned through the surface layers.

With the motor-perceptual region, as with every boundary zone, one must consider its dynamic properties. There are great individual differences which depend upon age and personality.

The difference between motor and inner regions is certainly not only a difference of position but is also a difference of function within the whole system. In a certain sense the motor systems have the position of "tools" of inner systems.

*   *   *   *   *

Within the motor-perceptual region one can distinguish again between more "peripheral" and more "central" regions. Such distinctions play an important role in the theory of perception. Insofar as action is concerned the motor region seems to possess a relatively high unity: it is difficult to carry out four or five unrelated activities at the same time. It seems that the motor system can be connected dynamically with only one inner region or one relatively unified group of such regions at a given moment. If the motor system were to be guided by all the needs of a person at the same time, his behaviour would become chaotic. The muscular tonus in one part of the motor region is closely connected with that in the others.

*   *   *   *   *

Central and Peripheral Inner-Personal Strata

Within the inner regions of the person one can distinguish between more central (c) and more peripheral strata (p, Fig. 2). . . . It is of great general importance whether a psychological process belongs to more central or to more peripheral strata. Dembo's experimental investigations on anger have shown the significance of this factor for emotions. If only the peripheral strata of the person are touched, manifestations of anger occur more easily. The outbreaks of anger are then more superficial. If more central strata are involved an open outbreak of affect is more rare. Indeed the boundary zone between the central strata (c, Fig. 2) and the environment (E) is stronger than the boundary zone between the peripheral strata (p) and the environment. Besides, the central regions may be surrounded by a specific functional wall (B_c, Fig. 3a). The peripheral strata come more easily into connection with the motor region to which they lie closer. Therefore expression usually occurs more readily when events of more peripheral strata are concerned. One speaks about personal matters only under special circumstances.

This is not only because the more central strata have on the whole less direct access to the motor region. Events in the opposite direction also, that is, from the environment to the inner regions of the person, usually reach the more central regions less easily. In conversation the way to the peripheral regions of the person is almost always open. But it is difficult to touch the real core of the person.

The relationship between the peripheral or the central position of an inner-personal region on the one hand and the degree of its accessibility and its ease of expression on the other hand, is not an entirely fixed one. It depends upon the momentary state of the person and upon the characteristics of the situation. With some persons it seems to be easy to touch certain central places and to injure them like an "open wound." Some of these central regions seem to be always ready to communicate with the motor systems. Not less important than the topological position of the systems therefore are their dynamic properties and the dynamic properties of their boundaries. These are usually quite different for the different regions within one stratum and may change for the whole stratum. An example of a relatively simple change of dynamic relations between the different strata is the transition from a state of superficial anger to a state of profound anger. When the person is in a quiet mood the boundary (B_p) between the peripheral strata and the motor region is dynamically relatively weak, but the boundary (B_c) between the peripheral and central regions of the person dynamically strong (Fig. 3a). If the situation of higher affective tension arises, the person usually replies with greater "self-control." To such self-control corresponds a greater separation of the peripheral strata from the motor region. At the same time the inner regions become relatively more unified (Fig. 3b). Dembo has shown that if the affective tension is increased the resulting unification can reduce the person to a more primitive level (Fig. 3c). If the tension in the inner regions is still further increased it can break through to the motor region.

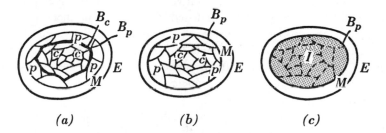

(a)   (b)   (c)

Fig. 3.
Relations between various strata of the person under different circumstances. (a) The person in an easy situation: the peripheral parts p of the inner-personal region I are easily accessible from outside E; the more central parts c are less accessible; the inner-personal region I influences the motor region M relatively freely. (b) The person under stress, in state of self-control: the peripheral parts p of the inner-personal region I are less accessible than in (a); peripheral and central parts (c and p) are more closely connected; communication between I and M is less free. (c) The person under very high tension: unification (primitivation, "regression") of the inner-personal region I. M, motor-perceptual region; I, inner-personal region; p, peripheral parts of I; c, central parts of I; E, environment; B_c, dynamic wall between c and p; B_p, dynamic wall between I and M.

The separation of the inner regions from each other and their connection with the motor region can undergo changes of very different kinds. In the state of joy the inner-personal regions seem to be relatively unified and especially little separated from the motor zone. Joy expresses itself easily. Here again we find important individual differences.

Dynamically a more central position and greater tension of the inner systems are in many respects equivalent.

Individual Differences in the Structure of the Person

A. Degree of Differentiation of the Person.   One of the most dynamic differences between child and adult is that the person of the child is less differentiated into part regions. The growth of the psychological environment and of the person of the child does not mean simply quantitative increase in size, but it is at the same time essentially a process of differentiation and, to some extent, of integration. . . .

One could say that the statement "the person A is more differentiated than B" is inadmissible for the following reason: it is a thesis about the number of part regions of a whole region, namely, the person, and it seems doubtful whether there is any value in comparing the number of part regions of two persons.

We distinguished between two possibilities of determining regions: the characterization by certain qualitative properties on the one hand and by locomotions or communications on the other. If one uses the qualitative characterization, one can speak of different regions whenever one can make qualitative distinctions between regions. It is clear that this is an entirely relative standard, for what seems to be a homogeneous region at a superficial examination may show qualitative differentiations when one looks more closely. The number of distinguishable regions would thereby be made dependent on the degree of accuracy of the examination. This seems to make an objective comparison of the number of part regions impossible. For instance in both child and adult the first analysis shows the same number of regions, namely, a central and a peripheral inner-personal stratum and the motor stratum.

If one determines regions by means of the concept of dynamic communication, their unity is determined by their dynamic wholeness. But in this way also we achieve only a relative determination of the units of regions since we find different degrees of wholeness. It is for instance possible to consider child and adult each as one single dynamic region.

Another way of approaching this problem is suggested by our discussion of finitely and infinitely structured spaces. It might be possible to designate as "smallest regions" those regions within the person which at a given moment can no longer be broken up into psychologically meaningful part regions. As a matter of fact the assumption that such objectively not-further-structured dynamic unities are the structural elements of the person seems to be justified. Unfortunately at the present time a comparison between the degree of differentiation of different persons is not possible in this way.

Nevertheless, the dynamic connection can be used in determining the degree of differentiation of the person. Even if we can designate child and adult each as one single dynamic region, still the degree of wholeness of this system is greater with the child than with the adult: a change of one part of the system in the child usually influences all other parts to a much greater extent than in the adult.

*   *   *   *   *

It would be a difficult and important task of a "general gestalt theory" to investigate how the degree of unity of a whole depends on its structure. The following proposition seems to contain a fundamental principle: the dynamic unity of a whole depends not only on the relation of the parts of the whole to each other but no less on the relation of the whole to its environment. As a rule a greater separation from the environment increases the inner unity of the whole.

In determining the degree of dynamic unity of the whole person one must therefore always take into account (1) the degree of differentiation, (2) the degree of dynamic separation of neighboring part regions, (3) the special structure. If we assume that the structure is roughly the same in different persons, we have still to consider factors 1 and 2. It is however possible to separate these two factors if one succeeds in comparing the dynamic strength of the walls between the single part systems of the person concerned.

Such a comparison can sometimes be made. Investigations of satiation and substitution have shown that the psychological systems of certain feeble-minded persons are separated from each other by relatively strong and rigid walls. On the other hand it is characteristic of the sensitive problem child that there is only a small degree of separation of the part regions from each other. One can express this also in the following way: the person of the problem child corresponds to a more fluid, the person of the feeble-minded child to a more rigid material. The normal child is intermediate in this respect. The lesser dynamic separation of the system in the problem child involves a closer connection between his central and peripheral strata. Therefore the condition of the central regions more readily expresses itself, for instance in a stormy affective outbreak. At the same time these expressions show a superficial character. The central strata of these children lie, from the point of view of dynamics, less deep; even if the degree of differentiation were the same as that of normal children, the boundary zone which lies between the central strata and the environment would sheath the central strata less than with the normal. Actually the degree of differentiation of the feeble-minded as well as of the problem child is less than of a normal child of the same age. This shows itself in their infantilism and in the primitiveness of their behavior.

*   *   *   *   *

B. The Kind of Structure of the Part Regions. Individuals differ not only in the degree of differentiation of the whole person but also in the way in which the different part regions are arranged, in the strength of the connections between the different individual part regions, and the function which they have in the life of the person. We shall call these characteristics the "kind of structure of the person."

Within the same person the different part regions are not differentiated to the same degree. This is obvious for the different regions which are connected with knowledge and skills. Individuals also differ markedly as to which part regions are highly and which are poorly differentiated. We find similar differences in kind and degree of differentiation in non-intellectual regions, for instance in those inner-personal regions which are connected with family, friendships, or occupation. With the feeble-minded certain "irreal" regions which are important for phantasy seem to be relatively little differentiated. Or again if one speaks of a "harmonious character" it is meant that the different part regions of the person are relatively well balanced.

The functional significance of such regions can be very different. The region related to occupation for instance can play either a fundamental or a more secondary role in the structure of the person. It can have its source in very different needs. The significance which a certain activity has for a person and the satisfaction which it offers him depend on the functional significance of this region in the life of the person.

The degree of dynamical connectedness of the different parts of the person can be nearly equal within the whole region of the person, or certain regions can separate themselves to an especially high degree from the others and develop relatively independently. This can be observed in the normal person and it seems to be important for certain mental diseases.

In those cases in which Freud speaks of "complex" and McDougall of "dissociation" there is probably also a considerable degree of isolation.

A person's structure is often relatively constant over a long period of time. Nevertheless a great change in the environment, falling in love, being "converted," or some other decisive event can bring about a far-reaching change of structure which may be either temporary or lasting.

The question of structure of the person has special bearing on developmental psychology. For the structure of an individual at any given time is a product of his development. The differentiation of the whole person, connectedness, relative differentiation, and function of the single part regions seem to undergo typical changes during individual development. The investigation of these processes about which we know very little will be possible only along with the investigation of the general laws and only if one carefully considers the different conceptual problems which we have discussed.

INTEGRATION AND DEDIFFERENTIATION[14]

Besides the process of differentiation there seems to occur a process of "integration" during development.

[14]*Ibid.*, from pp. 192-192a.

This process counteracts the process of differentiation insofar as it creates a greater degree of interdependence of the different systems of the person and in this way makes for a higher degree of unity of the person as a whole. Mathematically this integration could be viewed as a reversal of the differentiation so that there would be no difference between the dedifferentiation occurring under the specific (more or less "abnormal") conditions discussed above the normal process of developmental integration.

Dynamically speaking, however, these processes seem to be definitely different in character. The integration of the person during development seems not to be a strict reversal of the differentiation and also not a simple restructuring of the inner personal system. It is rather a process by which a certain system (or group of systems) becomes "dominant" insofar as it is able to impose certain patterns of action and to build up certain quasi needs. I am inclined to venture the theory that we have to deal here with the relation of an inducing field to an induced field. In other words, the position of the dominant system is dynamically equivalent to that of the center of a social power field. The same type of dynamic interdependence is probably characteristic for the relation between the inner psychological region and the motor region or between a person and a tool.

* * * * *

These problems can be considered in detail only in vector psychology. However, it might be well to limit the term "integration" in psychology to those cases where the unification of differentiated regions is due to the establishing of the hierarchic relation between an inducing field and an induced field. A unification due to destruction (or weakening) of the dynamic walls that separate systems might be called "dedifferentiation" as opposed to "integration."

Lewin's Glossary of Terms[15]

BEHAVIOR: By behavior we mean any change in the life space which is subject to psychological laws. Behavior (B) at a given time is a function of the life space (L) at that time. $B = f(L)$.

BOUNDARY, OF A PSYCHOLOGICAL REGION: Those points of a region for which there is no surrounding that lies entirely within the region. The presence of a boundary within the environment or person can be determined by means of locomotions or communications. A boundary of a psychological region is not necessarily an obstacle to locomotion or communication.

BOUNDARY POINT: Any surrounding of a boundary point of a region contains points which do not belong to that region.

BOUNDARY, SHARP: Psychologically one can distinguish sharp and unsharp

[15]*Ibid.*, from pp. 213-18.

boundaries. In the case of a sharp boundary it can be determined for every point of the life space whether or not it belongs to the region in question.

CONCRETE: That which has the position of an individual fact which exists at a certain moment. In psychology the concrete can be represented as a part of the life space or as a property of such a part.

CONSTRUCT: A dynamic fact which is determined indirectly as an "intervening concept" by way of "operational definition." A construct expresses a dynamic interrelation and permits, in connection with laws, the making of statements about what is possible and what is not possible.

CUT: A path which connects two boundary points of a region and which, aside from these boundary points, lies wholly within the region.

DIMENSION: The boundary of an n-dimensional space is $(n-1)$-dimensional. Points of spaces of different numbers of dimensions can be co-ordinated to each other in one-to-one correspondence only when their topological relations are destroyed.

DYNAMIC: Facts or concepts which refer to conditions of change, especially to forces, are called dynamic. Dynamic facts can be determined indirectly only (*see* CONSTRUCT).

ENVIRONMENT: Everything in which, toward which, or away from which the person can perform locomotions is part of the environment.

EXISTENCE: That which has effects. The existence and the time index of a psychological fact are independent of the existence and the time indices of the facts to which its content refers.

FIELD: Space, conceived as having a certain characteristic at every point.

GESTALT: A system whose parts are dynamically connected in such a way that a change of one part results in a change of all other parts. This unity may differ for different kinds of changes.

INFLUENCES "FROM OUTSIDE": influences on a life space which cannot be derived by psychobiological laws from the psychobiological properties of the preceding situation.

JORDAN CURVE: A topological image of a circle.

LAW, EMPIRICAL: A law defines the functional relationship between various facts. These facts are conceived as types, *i.e.*, historical time indices do not enter a law. A psychological law can be expressed by an equation, *e.g.*, of the form $B = f(L)$. The laws serve as principles according to which the actual events may be derived from the dynamic factors of the situation.

LIFE SPACE: Totality of facts which determine the behavior (B) of an individual at a certain moment. The life space (L) represents the totality of possible events. The life space includes the person (P) and the environment (E). $B = f(L) = f(P, E)$. It can be represented by a finitely structured space.

LIFE SPACE, FOREIGN HULL OF: Facts which are not subject to psychological laws but which influence the state of the life space.

LOCOMOTION: Change of position. Locomotion can be regarded as a change of structure: the moving region becomes a part of another region. Locomotion can be represented by a path which can or cannot be carried out. This path characterizes a change of position within a field which otherwise remains sufficiently constant. One can distinguish quasi-physical, quasi-social, and quasi-conceptual locomotions.

MEDIUM: A region through or in which locomotions can be carried out.

NEED: A need corresponds to a tension system of the inner-personal region.

PERSON: The person is represented as a differentiated region of the life space; however in the first approximation he can be represented as an undifferentiated region or a point.

PERSON, PARTS OF: (1) Motor-perceptual stratum (region); (2) inner-personal stratum (region): (*a*) peripheral regions, (*b*) central regions. The motor-perceptual stratum has the position of a boundary zone between the inner-personal regions and the environment.

PHENOMENAL FACT: Fact which can be observed directly.

PLASTICITY: The plasticity of a region corresponds to the ease of producing a relatively lasting and stable change in its structure.

POWER FIELD: The sphere of influence of a person. It can be represented as a field of inducing forces.

REALITY: The epistemological concept of reality (*see* EXISTENCE) is to be distinguished from the psychological concept of "degree of reality," which refers to certain strata of the life space.

REALITY, DEGREE OF: A property of psychological facts. Differences of degree of reality can be coordinated to a special dimension of life space. The more irreal levels show a greater fluidity. The structure of a more real level depends upon the will of the person. The degree to which the life space is structured in the dimension reality-irreality depends upon the specific character, *e.g.*, age, of the person and the momentary situation.

REGION, PSYCHOLOGICAL: Part of the life space. Everything that is represented as a region in characterizing a psychological situation must be a part of the life space. A region is not necessarily a connected one.

REGRESSION: Corresponds to a decrease in the differentiation of a person.

RIGIDITY: Boundaries (barriers, walls) are the more rigid the greater the forces necessary to overcome them. Rigidity of a region can differ for different types of processes.

RESTRUCTURING: Change of the relative position of part regions without change of their number.

SITUATION: Life space or part of it conceived in terms of its content (meaning). The life space may consist of one situation or of two or more overlapping situations. The term situation refers either to the general life situation or the momentary situation.

SITUATION, OVERLAPPING: Two or more situations which exist simultaneously and which have a common part. The person is generally located within this common part.

SPACE OF FREE MOVEMENT: Regions accessible to the person from his present position. The space of free movement is usually a multiple connected region. Its limits are determined mainly by (1) what is forbidden to a person, (2) what is beyond his abilities.

SPACE, PHYSICAL: The whole physical world.

SPACE, TOPOLOGICAL: Nonmetrical space, for which certain axioms hold. Part-whole relation and connectedness are among its basic concepts.

STRUCTURE, COGNITIVE: Structure of the life space corresponding to the knowledge of the person.

STRUCTURE OF A REGION: Refers to (1) degree of differentiation of the region, (2) arrangement of its part regions, (3) degree of connection between its part regions.

SYSTEM: A region considered in regard to its state, especially to its state of tension.

THING: A region in or through which locomotions can be carried out.

VALENCE: A valence corresponds to a field of forces whose structure is that of a central field. One can distinguish positive and negative valences.

WALL: Boundary (boundary zone) considered as to its influence on communication. A stronger wall corresponds to a smaller degree of communication.

WORLD, PHYSICAL: Totality of more or less interdependent physical facts. All physical changes are the result of conditions or changes within one connected physical space. According to physics there are no influences upon physical objects "from outside" this space.

WORLD, PSYCHOLOGICAL: Totality of more or less interdependent psychological facts. There exists a plurality of psychological worlds, corresponding to a plurality of not connected psychological spaces (life spaces). These worlds are influenced "from outside."

PART FOUR

Holistic and Organismic
Approaches to Personality

CHAPTER 12

KURT GOLDSTEIN

ORGANISMIC PSYCHOLOGY:
HOLISTIC THEORY OF PERSONALITY

The theory of Kurt Goldstein, who entered the science of psychology through the field of neuropsychiatry, has been called ORGANISMIC PSYCHOLOGY. Like other adherents of the holistic or organismic school of psychology, Goldstein asserts that (1) the atomistic approach, *i.e.*, the analytical method of diagnosing personality, is inadequate; (2) personality must be studied as an organism in a given environment; and (3) personality must be viewed as a whole, *i.e.*, a *Gestalt* in which the whole is greater than the sum of the individual parts.

There are other concepts which are essential to Goldstein's theory: (1) *Coming to terms with one's environment*. This concept signifies more than mere adjustment; rather, it is a natural adaptation by which the individual experiences a wholesome human development in an environment conducive to a healthful mental life. Under such conditions, anxiety is reduced to a minimum and the human organism is capable of enduring greater amounts of anxiety-producing tension emanating from catastrophic situations. (2) *Self-actualization*. This is the proper course or direction for a personality to pursue in the interests of a wholesome and normal development. All organisms, human or subhuman, instinctively and/or consciously, seek self-actualization (that state in which one is free from anxiety and enjoys living), which is best effected through a societal relationship. (3) *Figure and ground (back-*

ground). These factors, which are the area of concentration and its surroundings, constitute the primary organization of organismic functioning.

Kurt Goldstein was born on November 6, 1878, in Upper Silesia, which was at that time a part of Germany; in 1903 he received his doctorate in medicine from the University of Breslau. Several years later he accepted an assignment in the area of teaching and research at the Psychiatric Hospital in Koenigsberg, where he stayed for eight years. Here his reputation grew and spread, partly through the many papers which he published, and he gained the position of Professor of Neurology and Psychiatry and Director of the Neurological Institute at the University of Frankfurt. During World War I he directed the Military Hospital for Brain-Injured Soldiers. In 1930 he was appointed Professor of Neurology and Psychiatry at the University of Berlin and was affiliated in a similar capacity at Moabit Hospital. When he came to the United States, in 1935, he practiced first at the New York Psychiatric Institute for a period of about a year, and then at Montefiore Hospital in New York. Later he accepted an appointment as Clinical Professor of Neurology at Columbia University. During World War II he held the same position at Tufts Medical School in Boston. In 1945 he returned to New York and resumed private practice. Goldstein died on September 18, 1965.

Among his publications are *The Organism* (1939), *Human Nature in the Light of Psychopathology* (1940), *After-Effects of Brain Injuries in War* (1942), and *Language and Language Disturbances* (1948). Other writings include: "Organismic Approach to the Problem of Motivation" in *Transactions of the New York Academy of Science* (1947), "Frontal Lobotomy and Impairment of Abstraction" in *Journal of Nervous and Mental Diseases* (1949), "On Emotions" in *Journal of Psychology* (1951), and "New Ideas on Mental Health" in *Personal Problems and Psychological Frontiers* (ed. by J. Fairchild, 1957).

THE HOLISTIC APPROACH[1]

In the approach towards healing today we are no longer preoccupied with the innumerable single phenomena in disease; we know that these phenomena are not the essentials of the disease. More and more we approach

[1]*Human Nature in the Light of Psychopathology* (Cambridge, Mass.: Harvard University Press, 1940), from pp. 5-25.

the conviction that the essential element of disease is the shock to the existence of the individual caused by the disturbance of the well-regulated functioning of the organism by disease. If restoration is out of the question, the only goal of the physician is to provide the patient with the possibility of existing in spite of his defect. To do this one has to consider each single symptom in terms of its functional significance for the total personality of the patient. Thus it is obviously necessary for the physician to know the *organism as a whole,* the total personality of his patient, and the change which this organism as a whole has suffered through disease. The whole organism, the individual human being, becomes the center of interest.

Naturally one cannot fail to observe that a true insight into the condition of the individual is to be gained only if the individual is considered as part of the whole of nature, particularly of the human society to which it belongs. Many manifestations of disease can be understood only in the light of their social origin and can be eliminated only by considering this origin. Such a view leads to the study of the interrelationships between the individual and society, the differences between nations and peoples, and the variations in individuals themselves.

*   *   *   *   *

It was natural that, in the development of this approach to man in his entirety, interest in the single phenomenon, which till then science had stressed in all its various fields, should have diminished. This meant a turning away from the atomistic and mechanistic approach, from a mere theoretical attitude, toward empiricism and concreteness. This tendency was to be observed in the procedure in the individual departments of science as well as in the increasing concern with synthesizing the results of the diverse sciences which are concerned with the nature of man.

*   *   *   *   *

With our holistic approach to human nature, we are faced with a very difficult epistemological problem. For us there is no doubt that the atomistic method is the only legitimate scientific procedure for gaining facts. Knowledge of human nature has to be based on phenomena disclosed in this way. But is it possible to proceed from material gained by the use of this method to a science of the organism as a whole, to a science of the nature of man?

If the organism were a sum of parts which we could study separately, there would be no difficulty in combining our knowledge about the parts to form a science of the whole. But all attempts to understand the organism as a whole directly from these phenomena have met with very little success. They have not been successful, we may conclude, because the organism is not such a sum of parts. The analytic experiment may not be suitable in principle for finding out the real constituent attributes of an organism and leading to a recognition of the organism as a whole.

If the organism is a whole and each section of it functions normally within that whole, then in the analytic experiment, which isolates the sections as it studies them, the properties and functions of any part must be modified by their isolation from the whole of the organism. Thus they cannot reveal the function of these parts in normal life. There are innumerable facts which demonstrate how the functioning of a field is changed by its isolation. If we want to use the results of such experiments for understanding the activity of the organism in normal life (that is, as a whole), we must know in what way the condition of isolation modifies the functioning, and we must take these modifications into account. We have every reason to occupy ourselves very carefully with this condition of isolation; as we shall see later, many a phenomenon of human life is understandable only in terms of the effects of isolation.

*   *   *   *   *

The organism, we assume, is a unit. We shall consider the functioning of this unit by means of the facts gained through studies of the nervous system, because the functioning of this system lends itself especially well to explanation. The nervous system is an apparatus which always functions as a whole. It is always in a state of excitation, never at rest. All performances are expressions of changes in this condition of perpetual activity, which are caused by the stimuli that impinge upon the organism. These changes always concern the entire system, but not in the same manner throughout, the special effect of any stimulus becoming apparent in one particular place. Stimulation of the eyes by light is usually followed by movements of the pupils or of other eye muscles, and by vision. If we assume that stimulation spreads over the whole system, this localized effect can be explained in the following way. Stimulation may change the excitation in the whole system, but it changes it in an effective way particularly in the part of the body near the entrance of the stimulus. We call this the local or *spacial near effect.* The particular effect of a stimulus, however, results not only from the special excitation of those parts of the body which are in the neighborhood of the point of entrance of the stimulus, but also from the specific receptiveness of definite parts of the nervous system to specific stimuli. The eyes, for example, are specifically adapted to be affected by light, the nose by odor, and so on. We call this the *functional near effect,* in distinction to the spacial near effect. The performance caused by a stimulus is the expression of the excitation of both the spacial and the functional near effect. The processes set off by the stimulus are not restricted to a part of the nervous system the excitation of which corresponds to the performance—for example, the perception of an object; the rest of the nervous system is also more or less involved, and there is a characteristic relationship between the excitation in the near part and excitation arising in the distant parts. We speak in this connection of the near effect as the *figure* process and of the excitation in the rest of the nervous system as the *ground* process. In the same way we speak of *figure* and *background* in a performance. Any excitation in the nervous system has the character of a figure-ground process. Any performance invariably shows this figure-ground character.

When you look at a picture you see and understand at once what is figure and what background. The terms "figure" and "ground" have, indeed, been borrowed from our visual experience. However, they fit not only visual configurations but all other configurations as well. For example, if you raise your arm vertically, the exact execution of this movement requires, as you can feel in yourself and observe in others, a quite definite position of the rest of the body. The raised arm is a figure; the rest of the body is the background. Figure and background can be discriminated as readily in speaking, thinking, feeling, etc. A word, for instance, is understandable only within a definite context, within a definite sentence, within a certain cultural sphere.

Habitually we ignore the background of a performance and pay attention only to the figure. From the standpoint of systematic observation and methodology this is false, for figure and background are intimately interconnected. Neither can be properly evaluated without the other.

As an example of the influence of the background on the figure let me recall first how the impression of simple color changes if it is presented on different backgrounds. Just so, the execution of any precise movement of a limb demands a definite attitude of the rest of the body. The most superficial glance at the way we walk will show that the correct movements of our legs in walking depend upon definite movements of our arms and head. When for any reason freedom of arms and head is impeded, the gait changes immediately; in short, when the background changes, the figure (the performance) also changes.

In the normal organism a definite stimulus produces under the same conditions approximately the same figure and ground configuration, and with it approximately the same reaction. For example, a person always has about the same visual acuity; that is, the same visual stimulus—a point of definite extension and color on a definite background—produces the same visual experience. The reaction is based on what is called the threshold of vision. If the threshold did not remain approximately equal under normal conditions, it would not be possible for a given object or part of the physical world to arouse the same experience again and again nor should we be able to react to the same situation in a consistent way. Only through such uniformity is an ordered life possible. Otherwise our world would change constantly, and we ourselves would change, too. But this is not the case. Our world remains relatively constant despite all the changes in it, and we, too, remain about the same.

On the other hand, there is no doubt that each stimulus produces a change in the substratum which changes its excitability, with the result that a new stimulus—equal to the former one—gives rise to an effect different from the previous one. Now how is it possible that in spite of this change of excitability through stimulation the threshold remains approximately the same, that the organism remains about the same, and that it reacts in about the same way to a late stimulus? This constancy is achieved only by virtue of the fact that in normal life excitation which has been changed by a stimulus returns, after a period of time, to its former state; that is, if no new stimulation occurs, it returns to a state of equilibrium. The presupposition of constancy is that the change in excitability caused by the stimulus is only temporary.

This equalization process fixes the threshold and, with this, creates constancy, ordered behavior, and secures the very existence of the organism. Normal equalization demands the working of the whole organism; that is, in fact, an equalization between the excitation in near and distant parts. Normal life is ordered because the equalization process takes place in relation to the tasks of the whole organism. This is not the case under experimental and pathological conditions. In an experiment we deliberately isolate the parts we wish to study.

*　　*　　*　　*　　*

Now how does isolation change the functioning of the nervous system and modify its reactions? We shall mention here only such facts as are important for the explanation to follow.

1. The reactions to stimuli in an isolated part are *abnormally strong*. For example, knee jerks in an animal with a lesion of the upper part of the spinal cord are exaggerated. The explanation is that the excitation produced by the stimulus, which normally spreads over the whole nervous system, is now restricted to a smaller part of the organ and therefore has a greater effect.

2. The reactions are of *abnormal duration*, because the normal equalization process is disturbed.

3. The reactions are bound to the stimulus in an abnormal way. We call this phenomenon *abnormal stimulus bondage*, or *forced responsiveness to stimuli*. . . . Now if the stimulated part is more or less detached from the rest of the organism, those processes cannot be utilized in the reaction as they normally would. In consequence, the outside stimuli gain an abnormal predominance and compel the organism to react in a more than normal way. This effect of isolation is to be seen particularly clearly in sick people. They are in general much more under the influence of external stimuli, less capable of freeing themselves from a stimulus which has touched them, than well people.

*　　*　　*　　*　　*

Thus *isolated processes within the organism may determine the reactions of the sick individual in an abnormal, compulsive way*. In the mental field this finds its expression in the abnormal predominance of particular thoughts, ideas, or compulsive activities. To the individual himself these phenomena seem strange and not part of him.

4. A further change of the form of the reaction in an isolated part is the

appearance of abnormal rigidity on the one hand and alternating reactions to a single stimulus on the other. This is the consequence of a disturbance of the normal figure-ground process. If the stimulus which touches an isolated part is adequate for the activity of this part, the reaction, the "figure," becomes abnormally fixed because of the lack of the equalization process. If the stimulus is adequate only to a section of this part, then a reaction may appear which corresponds to that section. But this excitation, the "figure," has no constancy, because the rest of the isolated part does not represent an adequate background. Excitation of this part may gain preponderance after a certain time, and a phenomenon appears that corresponds to the stimulation of the rest of the part. After a time this reaction, which is also not a "good" figure and therefore has no stability, disappears, and a reaction corresponding to the excitation of the first stimulated section returns, and so on, in alternation. This we call "lability." Such alternating reactions are frequently observed in patients with mental diseases.

5. The detachment of a part of the organism from the rest more or less deprives the activities of that part of content. Therefore actions in isolation are simpler or, as we say, more "primitive."

Isolation phenomena are characteristic of pathological conditions. They may also occur in normal life if stimulation gains an abnormal strength or an abnormal duration which hinders the normal equalization process.

We can isolate processes in our own bodies by special experimental procedure. We can expose our visual apparatus to abnormal stimulation, as in after-image experiments, where we allow a color to act intensively on our eyes. In that case we obtain both an abnormal after-effect and repeated alternations of opposite (complementary) color sensations. Or take a similar phenomenon in the motor field. If, with the arm hanging loosely, one presses the hand against a wall so that the deltoid muscle is strongly innervated, the arm rises by itself. The less attention the subject pays to the arm, thereby isolating it, the more striking the phenomenon is. If one succeeds in this isolation, one experiences an alternating movement, the arm rising and falling several times.

*　　*　　*　　*　　*

The more complete the approach of the whole organism to an object in the outer world, the more constant the object. Because in everyday life we usually make the complete approach, the objects of the outer world are definitely figures, and there is never under normal conditions a change of figure and ground or even an uncertainty about what is figure and what is ground.

*　　*　　*　　*　　*

We do not try to construct the architecture of the organism by a mere addition of brick to brick; rather we try to discover the actual *Gestalt* of the intrinsic structure of this building, a *Gestalt* through which some phenomena may become intelligible as belonging to a unitary, ordered, relatively constant formation of a specific structure, and other phenomena may become intelligible as not belonging to it. The picture of the organism must be of such a kind that it allows us to differentiate among the observed phenomena between the members which really belong to it and phenomena corresponding to less relevant arbitrary connections between contingent parts.

*   *   *   *   *

In essence the biological knowledge we are seeking is akin to this phenomenon in which the capacity of the organism becomes adequate to environmental conditions. This is the fundamental biological process by virtue of which the actualization of the organism, and with that its existence, is made possible. Whenever we speak of the nature of the organism, of the idea, the picture, or the concept of the organism, we have in mind the essentials for the occurrence of an adequate relationship between the organism and its environment. From these, in principle, that picture arises which we have to grasp in determining the nature of man.

*   *   *   *   *

Only[2] knowledge of the whole organism leads us to understand the various reactions we observe in isolated parts. The response to a special stimulus depends upon the significance of that stimulus for the performance required of the whole organism at the moment of stimulation and is intelligible only from this point of view.

I should like to demonstrate this by example. The tendon reflex is usually considered as the contraction of a muscle as the result of the stimulation of its tendon. Very careful investigations by a physiologist, Hoffman, have shown that the tendon reflexes are not elicited by the stimulation of the tendon but by the striking of the tendon. Hoffman therefore called these reflexes "proprioceptive" reflexes (*eigenreflexe*), reactions to stimuli arising through the processes in the functioning of the stimulated apparatus itself.[a] The reflex action takes place in the following way. The muscle is stretched abnormally by the stroke. This tension is followed by a reflexively produced innervation by which the muscle is brought back to the average state of tension of the muscle. This is the activity of the tendon reflex. . . . To the change produced by a stimulus belongs the process of equalization by which the state of excitation is brought back to the "average" condition which makes possible the best performance. Here it makes possible the exact innervation of the muscle. The correct innervation corresponds to a definite average tone of the muscle.

The average state of tension of the single muscle is not determined by the condition of the muscle alone but by the situation of the whole organism. This might be demonstrated in the following way. If you jump down a

[2]*Ibid.*, from pp. 123-33.
[a]Paul Hoffman and Ernst Kretschmer, *Untersuchungen Über Eigenreflexe* (Berlin, 1922).

steep incline in such a way that you always touch the ground first with your heel, then the muscles located on the anterior part of the lower segment of the leg and the quadriceps are first passively stretched and then contracted reflexively. This very sensible reaction seems to take place without any voluntary innervation and to be the consequence of a reflex process. It seems to happen without any relation to the organism as a whole. But, correct and plausible as such an explanation seems to be, it is not really so. This is to be seen by the fact that, under other conditions of the whole organism, we observe a totally different phenomenon during the same kind of abnormal tension of these muscles. If, as one walks, let us say, through the forest, one's foot sticks fast behind an object, say a stone, the muscles we mentioned before are stretched. They do not contract, however, in response to that tension. On the contrary, they extend, and the opposite muscles—those of the back of the leg—contract, for only so can the foot be released and a fall be avoided. This reaction, too, takes place without our knowledge, without our will—which means reflexively; yet it is certainly not an innervation caused by the abnormal tension alone, but one determined rather by the condition of the organism as a whole.

Now if we assume that the change of peripheral innervation in *this* case is determined by the whole organism, we have no reason not to assume the same in the other case. Thus we obtain the following result: The reflexive reaction to a change in the periphery is determined by the condition of the whole organism. This means that the so-called reflexive reactions are reactions corresponding to the condition of the whole organism.

We might also react in a voluntary way to the peripheral change, i.e., to the overtension. But this voluntary reaction would come too late, and the organism would be in danger of injury. In such situations reflex actions take place, but, as we have seen, they are determined by the condition of the entire organism. They represent a special type of reaction of the organism as a whole. We may say then that so-called reflexive reactions appear during certain states of the organism as a whole, i.e., in situations of danger in which the organism cannot react quickly enough voluntarily. But what is most important is that they are reactions corresponding to the situation involving the organism as a whole.

* * * * *

Thus, after having reviewed all the facts in this field, one reaches the following conclusion: We are dealing with a system in which the single phenomena mutually influence one another through a circular process, which has no beginning and no end. If, starting with the observation of reflexes, we try in unbiased fashion to understand the behavior of an organism, the facts everywhere force such a point of view upon us. In this disappointing situation the adherents of the reflex theory are forced to build up supporting hypotheses by introducing factors which integrate the mechanisms of single processes and thus account for the total behavior of an organism, which is always an ordered behavior. But these regulative and integrative factors in themselves—for example, the assumed regulative higher nerve centers or a metaphysical entelechy (in Aristotle's sense) or a vitalistic principle, as Driesch[b] would call it—are all of an order totally different from the reflexes. Thus we face a situation in which one has to assume *two* essentially different determining factors in the organism: reflexes and higher regulating principles. With such a twofold assumption the essential significance of the reflex theory—its claim to explain behavior entirely on the plane of reflexes—is abandoned. But it is not merely that these adventitiously introduced factors differ in principle from the reflexes; implicitly they are usually thought of as an expression of the function of the whole organism. Consequently, the whole organism again comes into the discussion, and the very situation arises which the simple reflex theory tried to avoid.

* * * * *

Certainly any reaction is understandable only if we consider the individual phenomenon in reference to the condition of the whole organism. In animal psychology, too, such a conception has of late gained more ground. I should like to mention especially the work of K. S. Lashley and Kantor. A follower of Kantor, I. W. Carter, after a very careful analysis of all the different types of conceptions advanced for understanding the facts, holds that only an organismic or interactional conception, as he calls it, can do justice to the facts.[c] Thus he comes to the same conclusion as I did from my investigations in man: that the stimulus has to be considered from the point of view of "its stimulating function or value" for the individual, and that the response is an expression of the adjustment of the organism *as a whole* to the given situation. The special action by which this adjustment is reached is understandable. I would add, only in relation to the task which the organism faces at the moment, and in terms of the law that it is the organism's tendency to fulfill a task in such a way that its capacities are realized as fully as possible. This tendency represents the drive by which the organism is set going, a topic we shall have to discuss very soon.

We come to the conclusion therefore that what we usually call reflexes are performances of the organism which are understandable only from a knowledge of the organism.

* * * * *

COMING TO TERMS[3]

We shall try to gain an understanding of the way in which men come to terms with the outside world. In discussing this important problem we shall

[b]Hans Driesch, *Philosophie des Organischen* (Leipsig, 1928).

[c]"An Experimental Study of Psychological Stimulus Response," *Psychological Record*, vol. II, 1938.

[3]*Human Nature in the Light of Psychopathology, op. cit.,* from pp. 85-119.

draw upon observations of our patients' ways of adapting themselves to the difficulties caused by their defects.

Let us begin with the observation of the behavior of one of our patients in a task which seems very simple.[d] We give him a problem in simple arithmetic which before his sickness he would without any doubt have been able to solve. Now he is unable to solve it. But merely noticing and recording the fact that he is unable to perform a simple multiplication would be an exceedingly inadequate account of the patient's reaction. By simply looking at him we discover a great deal more than his arithmetical failure. He looks dazed, changes color, becomes agitated and anxious, starts to fumble. A moment before, he was amiable; now he is sullen and evasive or exhibits temper. He presents a picture of a very much distressed, frightened person, a person in a state of anxiety. It takes some time to restore him to a state which will permit the examination to continue. In the presence of a task which he can perform, the same patient behaves in exactly the opposite manner. He looks animated and calm, and appears to be in a good mood; he is well-poised and collected, interested, coöperative; he is "all there." We may call the state of the patient in the situation of success, *ordered behavior;* his state in the situation of failure, *disordered* or *catastrophic behavior.*[e]

In the catastrophic condition the patient not only is incapable of performing the required task, which exceeds his impaired capacity, but he also fails, for a longer or shorter period, in performances which he is able to carry out in the ordered state. The whole organism is in great disorder for some time. Observation of the patient over a longer period of time reveals that his behavior fluctuates between these two opposing states and that the catastrophic type of behavior appears very often in examinations. After a while the patient becomes calmer, and catastrophic situations more or less disappear, even if the disturbance of functions remains unaltered. In normal life as well, in his attempt to come to terms with the outer world, the individual has to go through such states of disorder or catastrophe. Thus, in our attempt to understand human nature we cannot fail to be much interested in scrutinizing the structure of the catastrophic condition in our patients and in learning how the abnormal person overcomes it.

*   *   *   *   *

What do we mean by the phrase "adequate stimuli"? We know the organism does not react to all stimuli in the same way. There are many events to which a particular organism is not sensitive. I need not mention the fact that every organism, including the human organism, is insensitive to stimuli

---

[d]See Kurt Goldstein, "The Significance of the Frontal Lobes for Mental Performances," *Journal of Neurology and Psychopathology,* vol. XVII, 1936.
[e]See Kurt Goldstein, *The Organism,* pp. 35ff.

to which other organisms react. Each has its special organization as to sensory equipment, etc., and usually is responsive only to stimuli relevant to this, its "nature." As we shall see later, it is the basic tendency of the organism to actualize itself in accordance with its nature. All performances that can be observed are expressions of the activity of the organism in this direction. This actualization means existence, life. Normally the organism responds only to those stimuli which are "adequate"—that is, relevant—to its nature. Normal equalization is possible, and the organism is in a state of ordered behavior, only so long as it is not affected by inadequate stimuli; and only in this ordered state is it able to carry on the performances that correspond to its nature. Therefore, to live in a milieu, which allows for normal equalization, is requisite for the organism's living at all. The proper milieu of the organism is not the entire environment but only that part with which it can come to terms in such a way that normal equalization is possible. Each organism has its own characteristic milieu. Only that, a certain segment of all that surrounds it, constitutes its world. We call this milieu the adequate milieu, that is, the milieu that is appropriate to the nature of the organism. Contact with it does not alter the organism in such a way that it becomes unable to realize its own nature. The stimuli arising from it we call adequate stimuli.

The very existence of the organism is tied up with the possibility of finding an adequate milieu within its environment. Normally, the adaptation of the organism to its environment—that is, congruency between the two—is developed to such a degree that existence is guaranteed.

The organism ordinarily does not react at all to stimuli which are inadequate to it. Such stimuli can become effective only if they are very strong and force themselves upon the organism; then it is driven into the catastrophic situation, not only because it is so shocked and disturbed in its functioning that, for a longer or shorter period, it is unable to react at all. This brings it into the danger of not being able to carry on even those performances which are essential for its existence, and in this sense we may consider catastrophic behavior as a threat to the existence of the organism.

For several reasons this situation takes place more often in abnormal persons than in normal ones. . . . Furthermore, [catastrophic situations] endanger the existence of the abnormal person more than that of a normal one because his performances are so limited by his illness that he is more likely to be unable to realize essential capacities.

It may be difficult to understand how failure in such unimportant tasks as, for example, simple arithmetic, can bring an individual into a state that actually endangers his existence. In order to understand it, one must bear in mind that any failure or lack of ability, which to a normal person would be merely somewhat disagreeable, may produce in the abnormal one a sense of such inadequacy that it blocks his ability to perform at all. The danger to his existence does not depend upon a special task but on the fact that the task places him in the situation of not being able to react in accordance with his essential capacities. With that, realization of the essential capacities is endangered—that is, life, existence itself.

As we have said before, the phenomenon of anxiety belongs to the catastrophic condition. That is, anxiety corresponds on the subjective side to a condition in which the organism's existence is in danger. Anxiety is *the subjective experience of that danger to existence.* The catastrophic condition and the phenomenon of anxiety, in short, have a special significance for life. We feel that we are correct in assuming that both of them are to be found in all living creatures, in animals as well as in man—that they belong to life itself.

* * * * *

Anxiety, as we have said, belongs to the life of all organisms; fear, however, seems to be confined to the "higher" organisms, perhaps only to man, because, as we shall see, it presupposes the abstract attitude. Let us call attention to some phenomenological differences between anxiety and fear. In the state of fear we have an object before us that we can meet, that we can attempt to remove, or from which we can flee. We are conscious of ourselves as well as of the object; we can deliberate as to how we shall behave toward it, and we can look at the cause of the fear, which actually lies before us. Anxiety, on the other hand, gets at us from the back, so to speak. The only thing we can do is to attempt to flee from it, but without knowing what direction to take, because we experience it as coming from no particular place.

* * * * *

Now how does the abnormal person get rid of his catastrophic reaction and, with it, anxiety?

We have stressed the fact that catastrophic situations are especially dangerous for the sick man. The tendency to avoid them therefore is a dominant feature of his whole behavior. Avoiding catastrophic situations is possible only if he is able to come to terms with the world in spite of his defects—that is, only if he finds a new milieu which is appropriate to his defective condition, a milieu from which no stimuli arise which put him into a catastrophic condition. As I have said before, sooner or later after the injury to the brain, catastrophic reactions become rarer, and the patient grows quiet, happier, and more friendly.

* * * * *

One way to escape catastrophe consists in voluntarily withdrawing, to a greater or less degree, from the world. In extreme cases the only way out is through loss of consciousness, a factor which plays an important role in the disturbance of consciousness appearing in epileptics. One of my patients, living in an adequate milieu, as in the hospital, was usually quiet and well behaved. This state lasted as long as he had to do only those tasks to which he was equal. When faced with a task to which he was not equal, he began to tremble violently, showed signs of catastrophic behavior, and often fell into unconsciousness for a short time. In his case a catastrophic reaction of the severest type, leading to unconsciousness, could be produced experimentally. If, after the patient had returned to his normal condition, he was asked what had been the matter wth him and what had been demanded of him, he could give no information whatever.

Resorting to unconsciousness is, of course, hardly a suitable means of avoiding catastrophic situations, since it totally abolishes contact between the patient and his environment. The organism, therefore, commonly seeks protection in another way—namely, by avoiding particularly dangerous situations and by seeking other situations which promise a minimum of irritating stimuli. In discussing this avoidance of situations, we must bear in mind that the mentally sick cannot achieve such a thing by conscious effort; our patients, as we have seen, were unable to recognize whether or not a situation was dangerous for them, because they were impaired in the capacity which makes this judgment possible. Avoidance takes place in a rather passive way. If the patient has had some experience of being disturbed in a catastrophic way in certain situations, and if he is able to recognize these situations by certain particulars, then, warned by such criteria, he may withdraw from the dangerous approach. In such cases he does not recognize the real cause of the danger but is influenced by some warning signal. We often observe that patients persistently resist certain tasks which, to us, seem entirely harmless. We can understand the behavior of the patient in these cases only when we see the situation from the point of view of the danger it presents to that patient.

Another method of escaping danger is found in not reacting at all to the required task. If the examiner urges the patient, he often gives an answer which is not correct but by which he can escape the situation—for example, "I don't know"; "That does not interest me"; "I don't like it." Usually the patient gives these answers very quickly, with a much quicker reaction than in other situations. One gets the impression that he has a great desire to hurry out of a dangerous situation.

*　　*　　*　　*　　*

He avoids a catastrophic situation indirectly *by busying himself with those things which he is able to do*. No stimulus is so dangerous for him as an unexpected one, because the quick readjustment which the reaction demands is very difficult for him, and may even be impossible. We observe again and again that patients start violently when suddenly addressed. It is not necessary that what is said be irritating in itself. What acts as the irritant is the mere fact that the stimulus comes from a situation not belonging to the patient's immediate milieu and therefore demands a particular adjustment which he cannot make. Very often he does not react at all to such stimuli, and this has been explained as inattention. If spoken to with great vehemence, however, he will respond. By keeping busy he is aided in his desire to avoid these sudden irritations. The activities which engross him need not be of great value in themselves; their usefulness consists in their protective character. We call them "substitute reactions." Just what performances appear as substitute reactions depends on the individuality of the patient and upon the particular conditions of the environment. Wherever we find such performances we have to remember that the patient is in a condition in which he is afraid of catastrophic situations. The value of these substitute reactions is not primary but secondary.

These phenomena have received much attention in neurotics. . . . In the neurotic it is due to the fact that he is incapable of mastering the battle in his own soul.

*   *   *   *   *

Another protection from catastrophic situations is excessive and fanatical orderliness. Suppose, in sitting and talking with a patient, you put several objects at random on a table. If he becomes aware of them, he will at once arrange them in some order. . . . Apparently such a state of disorder is unbearable to him. . . . Patients fulfill required tasks meticulously, and become unhappy, even excited, if they are interrupted by anyone in their work before it is finished. They are punctual in their daily activities, in bathing, in going to bed, etc., doing everything at the prescribed time.

*   *   *   *   *

I once had a patient who had been shot through the optic nerve *(Chiasma opticum)* and was at first totally blind. As long as this lasted he was not conscious of being totally blind. He used to talk to visual things like any seeing person; he was quiet, his behavior was orderly, and one could see that he managed to get along with the help of his other senses and that he adjusted without difficulty in the hospital environment. Later his injury improved and to a certain degree he regained his sight. Then he became upset; he sought to orient himself by means of sight but, owing to its imperfection, succeeded badly. He was thus less well adapted to his world than when he had been blind. Now, for the first time, he spoke of something's not being right in his vision, and this previously quite reasonably contented man dropped into a state of depression. "What's to become of me if I can't see?" he would cry.

*   *   *   *   *

Using what we have learned by studying patients with brain defects, we are ready to discuss the role which anxiety and fear play in normal human life. In normal life, unquestionably, incongruities often arise between the capacities of the organism and the tasks imposed by constellations of stimuli in the environment; for example, an organism may have to cope continually with new tasks—i.e., with tasks which contain factors not in keeping with the condition of the organism. The conquest of the world inevitably forces the organism over and over into such situations. Consequently we assume that the "coming to terms" with the world must proceed by way of constantly recurring catastrophic situations, with concomitant emotions of the character of anxiety. This is actually the case. To be sure, anxiety in its full strength does not always appear when one is incapable of solving the problems. It occurs only when the situation is of a particular kind. In patients with brain injuries it is induced by the fact that the impossibility of solving any given problem acts very easily as a menace to the existence of the individual. In normal persons such a situation—i.e., not being able to solve a given problem—usually does not really put the individual into such danger. The normal person has many possibilities for managing the situation without threat to his existence.

* * * * *

Like the person with a brain injury, though to a much smaller degree, the normal person has the urge to diminish his anxiety. As an expression of it, we find the tendency toward order, norms, continuity, and homogeneity similar in principle to the tendency exhibited by our patients. But, on the other hand, the normal person is also driven by his inherent desire for new experiences, for the conquest of the world, and for an expansion of the sphere of his activity in a practical and spiritual sense. His behavior oscillates between these two tendencies, and is influenced now by one, now by the other. The outcome of the interaction of the two is the development of culture and the products of culture. But one can in no way maintain that the ordered world which culture represents is the product of anxiety, the result of the desire to avoid anxiety. Freud, for example, conceives of culture as a sublimation of repressed drives. This is a complete misapprehension of the creative trend of human nature, and at the same time leaves one question completely unanswered: why the cultural world should have taken shape in certain patterns, and why just these forms should be suited to win security for man. The matter becomes intelligible only if one regards the forms of his tendency to effect a realization of his nature. Only when the world is adequate to man's nature do we find what we call security.

* * * * *

Whenever anxiety, as the mainspring of the activity of an organism, comes into the foreground, we find that something is awry in the nature of that organism. To put it conversely, an organism is normal and healthy when its tendency toward self-actualization issues from within, and when it overcomes the disturbance arising from its clash with the world not by virtue of anxiety but through the joy of coming to terms with the world. How often this perfect form of actualization occurs, we leave open to question. In any event, even life in its most nearly perfect manifestation must go through the disturbances which emerge from the adjustment to the environment. The creative person, who ventures into many situations which expose him to shock, gets into these anxiety situations more often and more readily than the average person. The more original the human being is, the deeper his anxiety is, said Søren Kiekegaard. According to this philosopher, the cause of not being able to come to terms with the world, the cause of anxiety, is the inability to come to terms with the phenomenon of sin. The more original a human being is, the more he experiences this inability—and with it, anxiety.

Individuals differ as to how much anxiety they can bear. For a patient with a brain injury, the amount is very low; for a child it is greater; and for the creative individual it is still greater. The capacity for bearing anxiety is the manifestation of genuine courage, in which ultimately one is concerned not with the things of the world but with a threat to existence. *In the final analysis courage is nothing but an affirmative answer to the shocks of existence, to the shocks which it is necessary to bear for the sake of realizing one's own nature.* This form of overcoming anxiety requires the ability to view a single experience within a larger context, i.e., to assume the "attitude toward the possible," to maintain freedom of decision regarding different possibilities. This attitude is peculiar to man, and it is because persons with brain injuries have lost it, and have suffered a consequent impairment of freedom, that they are so completely helpless when facing an anxiety situation. They surrender entirely to the anxiety situation, unless they are safeguarded against it through limitation of their world, which reduces their existence to the simplest forms.

*   *   *   *   *

When normal people are beset to an abnormal degree by anxiety, they are unable to actualize themselves, and the result is catastrophic situations, with their consequences. Abnormal states of anxiety grow out of various causes, but fundamentally they result from the fact that the individual is in a state of uncertainty about his existence, taking this term in its broadest meaning. This uncertainty may be based upon external or internal difficulties; it may rest upon events in the personal life of the individual or upon the condition of a group, a class, a people, a nation, and so on.

Uncertainty and anxiety force the individual into abnormal activities (i.e., substitute phenomena) or into neurosis or suicide. Substitute phenomena reveal their abnormal character, their origin in the abnormal isolation produced by anxiety, by their abnormal stress on *partial* aspects of human action or nature, and by their compulsiveness, their lack of freedom and relationship to reality, to life. Their true nature is sometimes misunderstood because they have a high value in themselves, as, for example, when they consist in religious beliefs, in valuable scientific ideas, in sacrificing oneself for political reasons. However, as long as these activities are not spontaneous, are not outlets for the free personality, but are merely the sequelae of anxiety, they have only a pseudo value for the personality. They always mean a shrinkage of the freedom of one's world. This can be well illustrated by the difference between the sincere faith of the really religious man, which is based upon willing devotion to the infinite, and superstitious beliefs.

* * * * *

If the shrinkage of personal life reaches too high a degree and nature does not help the individual by blinding him to the danger to existence which this state involves, then courage reaches its limit. The person involved may then fall into insanity, as very often happened in the horrible situations of the first World War. Or he may become conscious of the conflict within him and turn to suicide as the only means of protecting himself from the perpetual fear of catastrophic situations and the terrible experience of not being able to carry out tasks which appear to him as the essence of life. A deliberate decision to commit suicide presupposes that the individual gives an account of the situation to himself and willingly chooses death as the ultimate solution. Suicide, therefore, is a phenomenon we observe only in man. No animal commits suicide. Neither do patients with brain injuries, except in states of transition in which they are aware of their situation. With them, suicide—at least, the kind of suicide we have in mind—is a very rare phenomenon, and the same is the case with animals. An animal which is in great anxiety or a patient who is in the same situation or who is suffering to an extreme degree may react to this situation in such a way that he hurts himself and dies, as a man running amok runs into death. Here, however, we are not dealing with an action of the will but with a sequence of disorder and confusion belonging to the catastrophic situation, in which the actions of the individual inadvertently cause death. Death then is a mere accident; it is not desired by the individual and should not be called suicide. Suicide is a voluntary act, and, with that, a phenomenon belonging to abstract behavior and thus characteristic of human nature alone.

* * * * *

From what we have said, it is plain that we can understand the behavior of an organism, and so also of a human being, only if we take into account the mechanisms used to avoid catastrophic situations. In pathological cases the tendency to avoid catastrophies is very prominent; yet even here the individual is not governed by this tendency alone, for he tries to make use of his capacities. This is even more strongly the case in normal people. An understanding of normal behavior, consequently, asks especially for knowledge of the capacities that are characteristic of a particular individual.

SELF-ACTUALIZATION[4]

I doubt whether in the natural life of an animal there can be such complicated conditions in the environmental situation as to build up conditioned reflexes, and, further, I doubt whether, if these conditions exist, they are constant enough to enable the conditioned responses to be maintained and thus become important for the life of the animal. Here is a problem which we have not enough experience to discuss. We can say somewhat more about the significance of conditioned responses in human children. Here, too, the experimenter, the educator, has to bring the infant into a situation which is suited for building up conditioned reflexes, and he has to maintain this condition for as long as the response is to be maintained. In immature children this is achieved by reward and punishment, but later the acquired actions can be preserved without these measures and by other factors, which are given in the *characteristic organization* of the human being. Two factors have to be considered. The first is the possibility of transition from a conditioned response to a natural, normal, adequate performance. For example, the baby must learn to control urination. He is not able to understand why, or how to manage it. Now a conditioned response may be built up by using reward and punishment, but later the habit is no longer based on these factors. His behavior comes to be determined by will, insight, and the purposeful use of his organic capacities—i.e., a special habit becomes part of the behavior as a whole that is characteristic of a grown child. Here the conditioned response shows its significance as a reaction built up in a state of immaturity as preparation for real performances in mature life. If this mature status is not achieved—because, for example, of retardation in the child's general, especially his mental, development— then the proper habit will never be perfectly attained. Conditioned responses are characteristic drill actions. Normal learned performances are not the result of *drill* but of *training*.

Both these proceedings aim at performances that are as good as possible. *Training* attempts to achieve them by exercising the natural capacities of the individual organism and by bringing them to the level of greatest efficiency. The performances in question are related to the nature of the organism, and the intended effect is the highest possible adequate relationship between the individual organism and the environment. In *drill* the performance aimed at is not related to the nature of the organism. It is achieved by building up a connection between a particular stimulus and a reaction by an *isolated* part of the organism. This connection, created by the method of conditioning, is intended to become so well set that whenever the stimulus is present the reaction appears automatically. The building up of such drill-reactions is possible only if the rest of the organism is in a definite situation which is held constant by certain means. In animals

[4]*Human Nature in the Light of Psychopathology, op. cit.*, from pp. 134-47.

this is controlled by the trainer. Later the animal may be in a condition in which the isolation of parts required for conditioned responses occurs passively, without pain, but supported by reward and punishment. The best results are achieved, however, if the trainer uses performances which are natural to the animal. Then the performance will be executed most accurately and may also give the animal some pleasure. The best drills one sees in circuses are of this kind. An expert in drilling animals must be an expert in knowledge of their nature. In any case, the maintenance of the action demands the presence of the human being; it can never occur through the efforts of the animal itself.

In human beings, as well, the best learning is that which is based on the natural capacities of the individual. Nevertheless, the human adult is also forced to subject himself in some measure to learning by drill. Because of the complex structure of civilization, his environment is not consistently natural. As a result, men are compelled to build up external connections between certain stimuli and definite reactions which make it possible for them to respond to the sometimes very unnatural demands of civilization.

There is a special capacity of human nature which enables human beings to build up such unnatural connections and to maintain them; it is the capacity for abstraction. A human being is able to separate functionally parts of his own organism from the rest, subject them to specific isolated stimuli, and let the reactions run off by themselves. In this way he can drill himself. The only thing he has to do is to avoid hindering these reactions. It is insight into the necessity for such reactions which leads the human being to build them up and to maintain them. From this point of view it is obvious why conditioned responses can be built up more easily and maintained better in human beings than in animals.

Thus we come to the conclusion that conditioned responses cannot be considered as basic for understanding human behavior. They represent only secondary phenomena; abstract behavior is necessary for building them up and maintaining them. In animals they depend upon the experimenter's or trainer's capacity for abstraction; in infants on that of the educator; and in adult men on their own. This interpretation of conditioned reflexes in no way conflicts with our own conclusions about unconditioned reflexes. True, conditioning is an essential factor in human behavior which must not be neglected. It can be used successfully, however, only if we consider it within the framework of the organism as a whole.

Our discussion of the stimulus-response theory has revealed that it is impossible to understand the behavior of organisms in terms of constant reactions of isolated apparatuses to external stimuli. We have always been brought back to the organization of the individual organism as a whole. We come to the same result if we try to understand human behavior on the basis of the so-called *instincts*.

*   *   *   *   *

A careful analysis leads to the conclusion that these phenomena are of various kinds. Some—the reactions of infancy, as, for example, the toe-turning reactions or first grasping and sucking movements—are reactions caused through the immaturity of the organism; they represent the equalization processes of immature living matter. For their understanding the assumption of special instincts is not necessary. A second group—sitting, walking, speaking, etc.—represents performances of the same order as any other performance. They are also grounded in inborn potentialities and developed through experience. They have to be distinguished from other performances only by the fact that inborn and non-conscious factors play a much greater role than in other performances—than, for example, in the highest form of performance, voluntary actions. Although the latter, too, are based upon inborn potentialities, they are determined to a much higher degree by experience and learning. In a voluntary action the "drive" works through the medium of intention, thinking, decision, and motivation on the part of the individual; in an instinctive action the performance is set going directly by the "drive." Both types of performance are dependent, however, upon the activity of the organism as a whole. The third and last group of instinctive actions is made up of habits and customs, actions which are distinguished from other performances by the fact that they occur in relative isolation from the organism and thus seem to represent a special type. They are actions acquired by the activity of the whole organ which later gain a great independence of it.

In common with the voluntary actions, all these so-called "instinctive" actions represent the organism's means for coming to terms with the outer world in an adequate way; they make possible the organism's actualization of its capacities. They differ from voluntary actions, however, in the variety of capacities which are actualized under various conditions.

The tendency to actualize itself is the motive which sets the organism going; it is the *drive* by which the organism is moved. This idea about drives is in contradiction to most theories of drives, which assume (1) that the goal of the drive is to release the tension which corresponds to it, and (2) that a number of different drives exists. In my opinion both assumptions are wrong. What can we learn from the observation of patients with brain injuries in connection with a theory of drives? First, that the tendency to release tension is a characteristic phenomenon of pathological life. In pathology abnormal tensions occur relatively often in single fields, because reactions tend to take place in isolated parts and because the process of equalization is disturbed. Through abnormal tissues with which the organism cannot cope, catastrophic situations are favored. The sick person has the tendency to avoid catastrophic reactions, and therefore has a special tendency to remove abnormal tensions. This gives the impression that he is governed by a drive to do this. For example, the sick who suffer from a tension in the sex sphere seem to be forced to release this tension. From this observation the idea has arisen that it is the real goal of all drives to lift and discharge tension, and to bring the organism into a state of non-tension—i.e., that it is the goal of the drive to release itself.

The tendency to discharge any tension whatsoever is a characteristic expression of a defective organism, of disease. It is the only means the sick organism has to actualize itself, even if in an imperfect way. But the entire existence of a sick organism depends upon other organisms. Clearly, life under such conditions is not normal, and the mere discharge of tensions cannot therefore be characteristic of normal life. Innumerable instances teach us that it is the basic tendency of the sick organism to utilize what capacities it has in the best possible way (considered, of course, in relation to the normal nature of the organism concerned). The behavior of patients with brain injuries, for example, is to be understood only from such a point of view. A comparison of the behavior of our patients with that of normal persons leaves us no doubt that the life of the normal organism is also governed by this rule. We may say, then, that an organism is governed by the tendency to actualize its individual capacities as fully as possible. This tendency is frequently regarded as a tendency to maintain the existent state, to preserve oneself. We learn from pathology, however, that the tendency to self-preservation is characteristic of sick people and is a sign of anomalous life, of decay of life. For the sick person the only form of actualization of his capacities which remains is the maintenance of the existent state. This is not the tendency of the normal person. Sometimes, it is true, the normal organism also tends primarily to avoid catastrophies and to maintain a state which makes this possible, but this occurs only when conditions are unfavorable and is not at all the usual behavior. Under adequate conditions the tendency of normal life is toward activity and progress.

Since the tendency to actualize itself as fully as possible is the basic drive, the only drive by which the sick organism is moved, and since the life of the normal organism is determined in the same way, it is clear that the goal of the drive is not a discharge of tension, and that we have to assume only one drive, the drive of self-actualization. Under various conditions various actions come into the foreground; and since they seem thereby to be directed toward different goals, they give the impression of existing independently of each other. In reality, however, these various actions occur in accordance with the various capacities which belong to the nature of the organism, and in accordance with those instrumental processes which are the necessary prerequisites of the self-actualization of the organism.

The concept of different separate drives is based on observations of the sick, of young children, and of animals under experimental conditions—that is, on observations made under circumstances in which some activities of the organism are isolated from the whole. This is the case in pathology; it is the case in children because the organism of the child lacks a center; and it is the case in experimental conditions. One of the basic errors of the Freudian theory is that the tendencies observable in sick people are considered as the basic drives of the normal human being.

The impression that there are separate drives arises easily because the organism is governed at one time by one tendency, at another time by another, because one or the other tendency in a given condition becomes more important for self-actualization. This is especially the case when the organism is living under inadequate conditions. If a human being is forced to live in a state of hunger for a long time, or if there are conditions in his body which produce a strong feeling of hunger, so that he is urged to relieve this feeling, it disturbs the actualization of his whole personality. Then it appears as if he were under a hunger drive. The same may be true with sex. A normal organism, however, is able to repress the hunger feeling or sex urge if it has something very important to do, the neglect of which would bring the whole organism into danger.

The behavior of a normal individual is to be understood only if considered from the point of view that those performances are always fulfilled which are most important for the organism. This presupposes a normal, adequate environment. Because these conditions are not always fulfilled, even in normal life, the organism may often appear to be governed transitorily by a special tendency. In this case we have to deal with an emergency situation, not with a normal one, and as a result one gets the impression of a special, isolated drive. This is to be found particularly if the organism is not allowed to actualize one potentiality or another for an abnormally long time, as, for example, if the reception of food is hindered for a long time. Then the harmonious relationship between the organism and the outer world is thrown out of gear, and the individual is driven to fulfill that particular potentiality because only in this way can its existence be guaranteed. We are confronted here with a behavior corresponding to that in which only the activities prevail that are important for mere existence in situations of danger. But these are not the activities by which normal behavior can be understood.

On the basis of our discussion I believe that we are in no way forced to assume the existence of special drives. I believe that the facts which are taken as foundations for the assumption of different drives are more or less abstractions from the natural behavior of the organism. They are special reactions in special situations, and represent the various forms by which the organism as a whole expresses itself.

The traditional view assumes various drives which come into the foreground under certain conditions. We assume only one drive, the drive of self-actualization, but are compelled to concede that under certain conditions the tendency to actualize one potentiality is so strong that the organism is governed by it. Superficially, therefore, our theory may not appear to be much in conflict with the others, but I think there is an essential difference. From our standpoint we can understand the latter phenomenon as an abnormal deviation from normal behavior under definite conditions, but the theory of separate drives can never comprehend normal behavior without positing another agency which makes the decision in the struggle between the single drives. This means that any theory of drives has to introduce another, a "higher" agency. Here the same situation confronts us as in the discussion of reflexes, and we must again reject the auxiliary hypothesis as unsuitable in solving the problem. In the tendency of the organism to actualize itself we are faced with only one question. We do not need to assume drives.

We reject the theory of drives from yet another point of view. If one of these potentialities,[f] or one which we can abstract from the whole of the organism, is taken as a distinct faculty, we fall into the errors of faculty psychology. It is isolated, and isolation changes the capacity, exaggerates it, just as it changes every behavioral aspect taken apart from the rest of the organism. If we start from the phenomena to be observed in such situations of isolation, we can never understand behavior. False concepts arise, as of the determining importance of single drives, sex or power, etc. A judgment about such phenomena as sex and power is to be made only if one considers them outside of their appearance in the natural life of the organism, where they present themselves as embedded in the activities of the *organism as a whole*.

* * * * *

What are usually called drives are tendencies corresponding to the capacities and the nature of the organism, and to the environment in which the organism is living at the time. It is better to speak of "needs." The organism has definite potentialities, and because it has them it has the need to actualize or realize them. The fulfillment of these needs represents the self-actualization of the organism. Driven by such needs, we experience ourselves as active personalities and are not passively impelled by drives that are felt to conflict with the personality.

A special form of such self-actualization is the need to complete incomplete actions, a tendency which explains many of the activities of the child. In the innumerable repetitions of children we are not dealing with the manifestation of a senseless drive for repetition but with the tendency toward completion and perfection. The driving force is given in the experience of imperfection, be it thirst, hunger, or the inability to fulfill any performance which seems to be within our capacities; the goal is the fulfillment of the task. The nearer we are to perfection, the stronger is the need to perform. This is valid for children as well as for adults.

The urge to perfection brings about the building up of more or less perfect instruments in any field. These in themselves become a further impulse for the use of the instrumental mechanisms, because this makes possible perfection in other fields. As long as the child's walking is imperfect, he tends to walk and walk, often with no other goal than walking. After he has perfected the walking, he uses it in order to reach a special point which attracts his attention—that is, to complete another performance, and so on.

[f]Henceforth the terms "potentiality" and "capacity" will be used interchangeably.

THE STRUCTURE OF THE PERSONALITY[5]

Our analysis has disclosed some characteristic trends in the structure of the organism. We have seen the specific significance of the abstract attitude for human behavior, the relation between abstract and concrete behavior, and the role both play in human life. . . . We have become acquainted with some of the general rules that determine the human being's coming to terms with the outer world. We have learned that man is a being who does not merely strive for self-preservation but is impelled to manifest spontaneity and creativeness, that man has the capacity of separating himself from the world and of experiencing the world as a separate entity in time and space. All these features we have inferred from the changes which patients with brain injuries show as a result of the loss of various capacities.

* * * * *

We arrived at the conclusion that the drive which sets the organism going is nothing but the forces which arise from its tendency to actualize itself as fully as possible in terms of its potentialities. But what are the potentialities of a given individual?

In making definite general statements about human potentialities we must be mindful of the fact that any such general statements are abstractions from what has been observed in individuals, and that we have learned nothing about how to investigate these potentialities. Unquestionably, we have to go back to concrete findings as offered by the isolating methods. But how, among the innumerable observable phenomena, shall we discriminate between those which really correspond to the nature of the individual and those which are only more or less accidental reactions produced by the method that has been used? To decide this method we are in need of a criterion. We are faced here with a problem which lies at the center of modern psychology, the problem of how to characterize personality.

* * * * *

We can assume that those factors belong essentially to an organism which guarantees its existence. There is no question that, in spite of its changing in time and under varying conditions, an organism remains to a certain degree the same. Notwithstanding all the fluctuations of the behavior of a human being in varying situations, and the unfolding and decline that occur in the course of life, the individual organism maintains a relative constancy. If this were not the case, the individual would not experience himself as himself, nor would the observer be able to identify a given organism as such. It would not even be possible to talk about a definite organism.

* * * * *

[5]*Ibid.*, from pp. 171-200.

Consistency appears in pathology in a special form, in the abnormally ordered behavior of the patient. It is true that we have to deal here with a pathologically exaggerated phenomenon, but, as we have explained above, the tendency to ordered behavior belongs to the normal organism as well. Consequently, in their content observable activities during ordered behavior can be considered as reflecting essential capacities belonging to the individual concerned.

If we consider an organism first in the usual atomistic way, as composed of parts, members, and organs, and then in its natural behavior, we find that in the latter case many kinds of behavior which on the grounds of the first consideration can be conceived of as possible are not actually realized. Instead, a definite selective range of kinds of behavior exists. These we shall classify as "preferred" behavior.

*   *   *   *   *

For example, one can point forward while the body remains fixed. But this is not the natural way. In the pointing movement, then, the organism seems to have the tendency to prefer a definite relation between the positions of arm and trunk, and does not conform to the varying environmental demands, although this could very well be done by changing the relation between the arm and trunk positions. To take another example, if one asks a person who is standing to describe a circle, one type of individual usually describes a circle of medium size in a frontal plane parallel to the line of the body, using the index finger of the right hand, the arm being half flexed at the elbow. Larger circles and circles in other positions, possibly executed with the extended arm, seem unnatural and uncomfortable to such persons, who naïvely proceed in the manner we have described. When the trunk is bent forward, however, it is natural for this type to describe the circle in a horizontal plane. One might think the horizontal circle simply the result of the movement of the arm in the same relationship to the upper part of the body as before, and due only to the change in bodily position. If this were true, we should have a circle in an oblique plane; actually, however, it is in the horizontal plane. In this position, apparently, the circle in the horizontal plane corresponds to the preferred behavior. Accurate analysis shows that the manner of describing the circle is unequivocally determined by the *total* situation of the subject. In "total situation" the factor of the subject's attitude toward the task is included; consequently, the circle is not made by all subjects the same way. In a specific situation, however, each one makes it in a specific way which he prefers, quite naïvely, to all other possible ways.

Through this simple experiment one can detect some characteristic properties of individuals belonging to different types of personality. In the one type the objectifying attitude prevails. This type prefers to describe a small circle in an almost frontal parallel plane. Another type is more subjective and has a prevailing motor attitude. This type describes a large circle with the extended arm, with excessive movement in the shoulder joint; actually the subject does not describe a true circle, but moves his arm around in a circular fashion, for which an excessive excursion is most natural. These variations in the execution of the circle reveal differences between men and women, between persons of different character, vocations, and so on. But each person has his own preferred way of performing, and it is this that is essential for the point under discussion.

If one who is accustomed to hold his head somewhat obliquely is forced to hold it straight, it requires a special effort, and, in addition, after a certain time the head will return into the usual, "normal" position, unless the subject prevents this by continuously paying attention to the position of his head. If, in going to sleep, one assumes a variety of positions, one will very soon take a certain position which leads naturally to sleep. Much wakefulness is due simply to the fact that one is prevented by some circumstance from assuming this natural position. If we trace the causes for the assumption of such positions, we find a great variety of bodily and psychological factors, but they are almost always fixed for a given individual. In abnormal persons such phenomena can be observed even better than in normal persons. We have stressed the fact that in our patients we are dealing with states of disintegration or decreased differentiation of personality. The reduced and narrowed personality of the patient is cut off from many events in the outer world which the normal person experiences; it is confined to a more limited order, as is shown by the tendency to abnormal orderliness as a means of avoiding catastrophes. In an organism thus reduced to a simpler form of organization and to a shrunken range of activities, preferred behavior comes strikingly to the foreground and it ought therefore to be easier to discover its qualitative characteristics.

There are two further circumstances which bring preferred behavior to the foreground in abnormal persons. A normal person, because of his capacity for abstraction and voluntary action, is able to execute tasks in a not-so-preferred condition and to maintain a not-preferred behavior. In addition, he is not restricted to the type of preferred behavior we have been discussing; he is capable also of preferred performances on a higher level, which correspond to his higher level of performance in general. The abnormal person is either wholly incapable of this, or less capable of it, because of his lack of the capacity for abstraction. As a consequence, he is subject in a higher degree to preferred behavior. This is manifest in the fact that a patient who is asked to execute a movement in an uncomfortable position invariably shifts into a more comfortable one unless his attention is concentrated entirely on the task demanded of him. To prevent such concentration it usually suffices to have him carry out the movement with closed eyes. We find then that, even against his will, and usually without his knowledge, he assumes the preferred position. The second circumstance is as follows. In normal persons preferred performances have a certain range of variability within which a performance is still adequate. In abnormal persons this realm is narrowed and the preferred performances are restricted to more rigid positions and to more fixed relations between positions. Thus, for example, in a patient with a disturbance of the left frontal lobe, the preferred position of the head is a slight tilting to the right. This is his natural position. If the examiner brings the head into a straight position or tilts it to the left or even further to the right, the head returns without the subject's knowledge into the natural position, where it ultimately will remain. The same thing happens if the patient himself intentionally holds his head in an abnormal position and then pays no further attention to it. A normal person can hold his head in a position that is to a certain degree oblique without discomfort and without having an irresistible tendency to bring the head to its normal position. The patient is forced to bring his head back.

What we have said about these simple motor actions is valid for all other performances. Every individual reveals preferences not only in the motor sphere, in walking, standing, sitting, eating, and so on, but in the sensory and intellectual processes, in the realm of feeling and voluntary activities.

* * * * *

Performances under preferred conditions show two characteristics. (1) They represent the most exact execution of the required task under the circumstances given; for example, pointing in the preferred realm is much more exact than elsewhere. (2) They are executed with a feeling of comfort and ease, of fitness and adequacy. Natural performances under not-preferred conditions are experienced as disagreeable, unsatisfactory, unnatural.

As I have explained elsewhere, observation shows that preferred performances are determined not only by the processes in the area where we observe them but also by the condition of the rest of the organism. On the basis of many facts reported elsewhere I reached the conclusion that preferred behavior in one field always means preferred behavior on the part of the whole organism; the tendency toward preferred behavior is an expression of the fact that the organism constantly seeks a situation in which it can perform at its best and with optimal comfort. Preferred performances are the performances which correspond best to the capacities of the organism. Thus observation of such performances may serve as a means of finding out the capacities—the constants—of the organization and functioning of the individual.

* * * * *

For every task there is an objective optimal manner of adequate execution, and for every individual there is a certain range of possible variations within the realm of his preferences. Consequently, we may call the preferred way of execution a constant of the individual. Ultimately these constants are basic traits of the constitutional and character make-up of the individual. Wherever the individual does his best, notwithstanding the fact that another solution may be more adequate in the light of the objective optimal execution, we are dealing with a constant.

In all these investigations, of course, we have to be mindful of certain positive and negative criteria.

1. No matter what the behavioral field in which we may test an individual, we are justified in speaking of a constant only when and if other pertinent tests show that, concomitantly with the execution in that field, the rest of the organism is in *ordered* condition; for example, definite behavior in a sensory field can be called constant only when we ascertain that, among other things, blood pressure, respiration, pulse rate, threshold of reflexes, etc., correspond to the norm of the individual, which is to be determined for each field in the way just described.

2. If a required task falls outside the realm of the preferred ways that are peculiar to an individual, the corresponding capacity is wanting in a greater or less degree. In such a case we have to vary the methods of examination until the subject is able to cope with the task in some way that he finds natural.

*   *   *   *   *

3. The preferred and ordered behavioral forms (constants) are not identical in all the performances of an individual. On the contrary, the individual responds to every type of task in a special way. This is determined by the organism's tendency to come to terms with the requirements of the outer world in the best possible condition of the whole.

*   *   *   *   *

The constant in the temporal course of processes must be regarded as particularly characteristic of individuality. The important role of the specific temporal sequence of processes for the ordered activity of the normal organism can be seen in the fact that many pathological phenomena may be regarded as being predominantly the expression of changes in the normal temporal course. This is shown not only by the analysis of symptoms but also by investigations with time-measuring methods (e.g., chronaxie and electroencephalography). Every human being has his own rhythm. This rhythm manifests itself in various temporal measures in various performances, but in any given performance it is always in the same measure. A performance is normal only when an individual can accomplish it in the rhythm that is natural to him for this performance. This holds true for psychological events like emotion or thought processes, like the beating of the heart and respiration, and in physicochemical processes. All these time constants indicate particular characteristics of the personality.

From my experience to date I believe that we are justified in selecting a number of factors as guiding for the determination of constants. We have pointed out that each person prefers a definite medium for the performance of certain tasks—for instance, a definite sense modality, or the motor apparatus, or speech; all this is indicative of certain constants. The preference for a concrete or abstract approach falls under the same aspect.

* * * * *

In connection with the question of the functional relation between those factors of personality which we call preferred, I should like to suggest that factor analysis might offer an appropriate method of approach. Factor analysis tries to discover the factors on the basis of which personality can be understood. If it were possible to determine with this instrument the performances that are preferred (in the sense in which we have defined the term), then we might hope to discover by objective mathematical methods some consistent traits of personality. But this cannot be attained through a comparative investigation of a great number of subjects by means of standardized tests. How can we tell whether we grasp the essential factors with these tests? Methodologically this would be possible only if we could study the tested group under conditions which represent an ordered state for each individual within the group. This presupposes, however, that we are acquainted with the nature of each person in that group; and so we are brought back to the individual as our point of departure. Factor analysis may have value as a technique if it is applied fruitfully to the individual proper, here the major determinants of preferred performances and their structural interrelation within the whole personality may become susceptible of mathematical representation.

The methods which till now we have considered instrumental for determining the basic constants of an individual are more or less confined to a cross-sectional aspect of his *present* behavioral state, but there can be no doubt that we ought to include the temporal aspect of his total behavior—that is, the course of life and the biographical span of the personality explored. In other words, the biographical method or "anamnesis," as we call it in medicine, is an indispensable supplementary source of information. It can furnish a distinction between the factors which make for ordered or disordered behavior, between genuine constants and the more casual phenotypic reaction patterns, habits, and so on. Only on the basis of information regarding the course of the individual's life can we really identify unequivocally the constants in question, by recognizing their consistency and persistence in the pattern of that person's development.

I am, of course, well aware of a question which probably has beset the mind of the reader since I began to outline the importance of preferred behavior. In what way are the individual's constants influenced and modified by *experience,* and in what way do they in turn shape and mold the experiences of the individual? In attempting to answer this question, we must first of all recognize the ultimate consequence which follows from the conception of preferred behavior. If there are any constants at all, then they must operate as selective and accentuating factors upon the experiences of the individual and the stimuli by which he is affected.

In order to appreciate this rule we must recall the result of our discussion of the problem of drives. It will be remembered that we came to the conclusion that the only drive or basic tendency of the organism is to actualize itself according to its potentialities in the highest possible degree. This is possible only if the organism is faced with situations it can cope with. From what we have learned about the behavior of our patients we know that, if the patient is faced with environmental conditions with which his changed personality cannot come to terms, then he is either not touched at all or he responds with a catastrophic reaction. He can exist—that is, actualize his capacities—only if he finds a new milieu that is appropriate to his capacities. Only then can he act in an orderly way, and only then can his powers of recognition, attention, memory, and learning be at their best.

These facts offer us the key to our question regarding the relation between preferred performances and experience in the normal person. The experiences a person has, or is able to assimilate or acquire, hinge upon his capacities, and these we can infer from his preferred ways of behavior. Only if given the opportunity to realize himself in these ways will he be in an ordered state, which is the basis of good performance; in other words, the more the demands made upon him correspond to his preferred ways of behaving, the more nearly perfect will his achievements be. Of course, these preferred ways of behaving have a determinable range of variation and should not be treated as fixed and rigid patterns. The experienceable environmental segments may vary within certain limits according to this range of variability. And it is this scale of variability which has to be carefully studied and weighed by the investigator of the mutual interdependence of preferred behavior and environmental demands. In order to determine and secure the best possible performances of an individual, and in order to develop his manifold potentialities to their full capacity, we have to know the extent of this interdependence. In pathology this fact is quite obvious. We have acquainted ourselves with the rule that patients have catastrophic reactions, and that their intact performance fields are also reduced, if the demands of the outer world exceed the scope of their impaired capacities. Such a diminution of capacity for performance also takes place if the demands are too low, and the capacities which remain are not called upon and utilized to their full extent. Then a shrinkage of the patient's milieu and personality sets in which is greater than the actual impairment would entail.

From this it follows that, if we wish to prompt the development of an organism in the way best suited to its potentialities, our demands must be neither too low nor too high. The measure of the commensurate degree is to be found in the organism's range of preferred ways of behaving.

* * * * *

⸴he drive to actualize one's potentialities also operates as a motivating force in one's emotional valuation in accordance with one's preferred ways of acting.

THE SOCIAL MILIEU[6]

We have elaborated the contention that there is only one motive by which human activity is set going: the tendency to actualize oneself.

*　　*　　*　　*　　*

Our observation of our patients shows that they cannot actualize themselves without respect to their surroundings in some degree, especially to other persons. The sick man is exposed to catastrophic reactions to a higher degree than the normal man; he can perform only if he finds a milieu which allows him to avoid catastrophic reactions. This implies that his behavior has to presume definite environmental conditions, in particular the existence of other men. The patient must develop an adjustment to others and limit himself according to the social actuality of others.

*　　*　　*　　*　　*

One can hardly find a better example of the fact that the attitude of self-restriction belongs to natural human behavior than that given by the behavior of normal persons toward the sick, which is characterized by active self-restriction in the interest of the sick. This fact gains greater significance in view of the contrasting behavior of our patients, who lack the capacity for voluntary self-restriction. It is because they seem so self-centered and that they are unable to build up by themselves a real community or social world.

*　　*　　*　　*　　*

There is still another behavioral interrelation between individuals which is inherent in man. The self-actualization of the individual in his social environment can take place only by his encroaching upon another's freedom, by claiming something from another, by imposing upon another to a certain degree. The primary fact that the individual does not exist alone, but with other creatures, necessarily implies the incomplete realization of every individual's nature; it entails impact, antagonism, conflict and competition with others.

Self-actualization on the part of one individual can be attained only by some renunciation on the part of another, and each must ask from others that renunciation. . . . Being individual, being free, implies the necessity of encroaching upon the freedom of others. The two things are the same. Therefore, we may say that the activity of encroaching also belongs to the nature of man.

These two kinds of behavior, self-restriction and encroachment, have been spoken of (by McDougall, for example), under the names of "submission" and "aggression," as two basic drives of human nature. In terms

6*Ibid.*, from pp. 201-36.

of our general criticism of the theory of drives and instincts we have no reason to assume such inherent drives. These two types of behavior are not separate and antagonistic tendencies operating in the human being. Man is neither aggressive nor submissive by nature. He is driven to actualize himself and to come to terms with his environment. In doing so, he has at times to be submissive and at times aggressive, depending on the situation.

Whenever either form of behavior achieves dominance in such a way that all the activities of the individual seem to be under its control, then something has gone wrong in the relationship between the individual and the surrounding world. Either the individual lacks adequate centering or the demands arising from the world are so difficult that he is not able to cope with them. Under such conditions one or the other of these two types of behavior comes abnormally to the foreground, and, according to the law of isolation, behavior takes on an abnormal character. Then we encounter either self-sacrifice or aggressiveness. Abnormal aggressiveness or submissiveness we observe especially in patients who lack the capacity for abstraction and in those in whom there is a pathological isolation of certain personality sectors. In the latter case the individual may be driven by an irresistible urge to fulfill the needs—say abnormal hunger or sexual desire— that result from this isolation. Then he is inconsiderate, reckless, and highly aggressive in seeking the release of this urge. This can be observed in patients with organic as well as functional diseases. Thus we find aggression as a characteristic symptom of neurosis. Abnormal aggression is always combined with abnormal submission, however, and what we observe in our patients is an abnormal exaggeration of normal behavior. Normally behavior fluctuates in adequate proportions between self-restriction and an encroachment upon the freedom of others. The exaggeration in pathology is the sequel of a lack of proper centering, which, as we have explained, always produces opposed reactions that alternate abnormally. As in normal persons, the situation determines which type of behavior becomes the figure, comes to the foreground; the only difference is that the intensity is abnormally exaggerated. That behavior always appears by which in a given condition the organism can best come to terms with the outer world; and this rule holds for a changed personality as well as a normal one.

*　　*　　*　　*　　*

Normal, ordered life asks for a balanced relation between compliant and encroaching behavior. Only then can the individual realize himself, and assist others in their self-realization. Furthermore, the highest forms of human relationship, such as love and friendship, are dependent on the individual's ability and opportunity to realize both these aspects of human behavior. This is evident so far as self-restriction is concerned. It acquires then the character of self-restriction without resentment. But encroachment also belongs to every relationship between individuals. Love is not merely a mutual gratification and compliance; it is a higher form of self-actualization, a challenge to develop both oneself and another in this respect.

* * * * *

If this conception of the relationship between one individual and another fits the facts, if all relations between individuals are determined by the tendency of each to realize himself, then we may draw the general conclusion that the individual is primary in all social organization. Very often the "we"—that is, the relationship between the individual and others—is considered the primary factor, and the individual's behavior is supposed to be understandable only in terms of that "we." Indeed, there is no question that in a concrete situation it is often the case that the individual is determined to a high degree by the community in which he lives. But the question is: Is this a normal situation—that is, does it correspond to the nature of man, or is it merely an accidental phenomenon? In other words, is the "we" empirically given? Can it serve to make understandable in terms of human nature the self-realization of the individual? . . . From this point of view, not all "we" phenomena are real, but only those which guarantee the realization of the individual. All other concepts of the relationship between the individual and other individuals represent accidental connections related to a variety of factors, such as the concept of reflexes or of "higher centers," all of which are more or less inadequate. . . . It is not simply a sum made up of individuals. Real group life, social life, is not an accidental living-together, nor is it based on a voluntary "social contract.". . . He cannot exist without the "we"; he can realize his nature only within the group. The individual and the "we" depend upon each other. Even though the individual is primary to society, without question he is influenced to a very high degree by society.

* * * * *

A habit is a means of adaptation on the part of the individual to the conditions of the non-human environment; habits help particularly to guarantee one's physical existence. A custom is a means of adaptation to the general conditions of life in a *group*. An institution is an adaptive measure that has to do with the socio-economic conditions of a group. Common to all these adaptive forms is the fact that, once built up, they can function without continual voluntary acts on the part of the individual. They achieve a certain independence of the individual. The formation of habits calls for very little volitional participation on the part of the individual; that of institutions calls for much. For this reason institutions vary greatly, and it is easy to misuse them. From all these adaptive processes there emerges a strong impulse toward action. They become valuable aids in the accomplishments of individuals and make the self-actualization of the organism easier; there is therefore a strong urge to preserve them.

* * * * *

Normal society means a type of organization through which the fullest possible actualization on the part of all individuals is assured. This presupposes the possibility that both aspects of human nature, self-restriction and encroachment, can be effective in a balanced fashion. The attempt to build up a social life based on the notion of a drive to submission or to aggression, or of an antagonistic struggle between the two, is futile. If we acknowledge and utilize social organization as an instrument by means of which all individuals may actualize themselves to an optimal degree, then a genuine social life becomes possible. Only under these conditions is a social organization capable of doing justice to every individual; only this makes it a real social organization and secures its duration. . . . The basic reason for failure in this respect, it seems to me, lies in the misinterpretation of human nature. Ultimately all failures in social organization are caused by an underestimation of the significance of the abstract attitude and by a misjudgment of the detrimental influence which can emanate from human traits if one changes them through artificial isolation. With the help of the abstract attitude the fallacy which is basic to all false social organization can be disclosed.

*   *   *   *   *

Some sacrifices are rightly to be considered an expression of an unusually high development of human nature. But self-sacrifice *in itself* is not of value. It is of value only if it is important for the actualization of the individual; it is of value only if the rescue of others is of such importance to the individual that his own self-realization demands this sacrifice. This is the border situation similar to one we have already discussed, in which voluntary suicide is sometimes the last way out in the attempt to preserve the personality. One has to be very careful in the evaluation of self-sacrifice, because it is often nothing more than an escape from the difficulties of normal self-actualization. If society has to ask for general self-sacrifice on the part of its members, then there is something wrong with the organization of that society.

*   *   *   *   *

We recognize further that a more nearly perfect realization can take place only through a process of mutual adaptation between peoples, which will permit a fuller actualization of all the different factors that, harmoniously combined, represent human nature.

CHAPTER 13

ABRAHAM H. MASLOW

SELF-ACTUALIZATIONISM: META MOTIVATIONAL THEORY OF PERSONALITY

Maslow's SELF-ACTUALIZATIONISM or META MOTIVATIONAL THE-ORY OF PERSONALITY shows marked signs of the influence of Goldstein and Adler—indebtedness to Goldstein for the concept of self-actualizationism, and to Adler for the concepts of need gratification and structure. Meta motivationalism in this optimistic personality theory assumes that there is innate goodness in man, and that normality is the ideal state which man seeks to achieve through successful need-gratification, hierarchically ordered; hence, Maslow's theory implies ascending degrees of psychological health which are to be attained through proper growth motivation. Maslow's is a synthetic theory, as the *holistic-dynamic* concept intimates.

Maslow was born in 1908 in New York. He received his academic training (B.A., 1930; M.A., 1931; Ph.D., 1934) from the University of Wisconsin. However, the decisive educational influences in his life came in the late thirties through his association with various theorists in the New York area: Max Wertheimer and Kurt Koffka and *Gestalt* psychology at The New School for Social Research; Kurt Goldstein and organismic psychology; psychoanalysis under Erich Fromm, Karen Horney, and David Levy; Alfred Adler and individual psychology; Ruth Benedict and Margaret Mead and their anthropological contributions; and E. L. Thorndike, under whom Maslow worked as a research assistant. Maslow died in 1970.

Maslow's books include *Principles of Abnormal Psychology* (with B. Mittelmann, 1941), *Motivation and Personality* (1954, rev. ed., 1970), *Toward a Psychology of Being* (1962, rev. ed., 1968), *Religions, Values, and Peak-Experiences* (1964), and *The Farther Reaches of Human Nature* (1971).

THE HOLISTIC-DYNAMIC POINT OF VIEW[1]

The general point of view that is being propounded here is holistic rather than atomistic, functional rather than taxonomic, dynamic rather than static, dynamic rather than causal, purposive rather than simple-mechanical. In spite of the fact that these opposing factors are ordinarily looked upon as a series of separable dichotomies, they are not so considered by the writer. For him they tend strongly to coalesce into two unitary but contrasting world views. This seems to be true for other writers as well, for those who think dynamically find it easier and more natural to think also holistically rather than atomistically, purposively rather than mechanically, and so on. This point of view we shall call the holistic-dynamic point of view. It could also be called organismic in Goldstein's sense.

Opposed to this interpretation is found an organized and unitary viewpoint that is simultaneously atomistic, taxonomic, static, causal, and simple mechanical. The atomistic thinker finds it much more natural to think also statically rather than dynamically, mechanically rather than purposively, etc. This general point of view I shall call arbitrarily general-atomistic. I have no doubt that it is possible to demonstrate not only that these partial views tend to go together but that they *must* logically go together.

A few special remarks on the causality concept are necessary at this point since it is an aspect of the general-atomistic theory that seems to me to be centrally important and that psychological writers have slurred or neglected altogether. This concept lies at the very heart of the general-atomistic point of view and is a natural, even necessary, consequence of it. If one sees the world as a collection of intrinsically independent entities, there remains to be solved the very obvious phenomenal fact that these entities nevertheless have to do with each other. The first attempt to solve this problem gives rise to the notion of the simple billiard-ball kind of causality in which one separate thing does something to another separate thing, but in which the entities involved continue to retain their essential identity. Such a view is easy enough to maintain, and actually seemed absolute so long as the old physics gave us our world theory. But the advance in physics and chemistry made modification necessary. For instance, the usually more sophisticated phrasing today is in terms of multiple causation. It is recognized that the interre-

[1]"Dynamics of Personality Organization," *Psychological Review*, L (1943), from pp. 519-24, reprinted in *Motivation and Personality* (New York: Harper, 1954, 1970), from pp. 27-31.

lationships holding within the world are too complex, too intricate to describe in the same way as we do the clicking of billiard balls on a table. But the answer is most often simply a complexifying of the original notion rather than a basic restructuring of it. Instead of one cause, there are many, but they are conceived to act in the same way—separately and independent of each other. The billiard ball is now hit not by one other ball, but by ten simultaneously, and we simply have to use a somewhat more complicated arithmetic to understand what happens. The essential procedures are still addition of separate entities into an "and-sum" to use Wertheimer's phrase. No change is felt to be necessary in the fundamental envisagement of the complex happenings. No matter how complex the phenomenon may be, no essentially new thing is happening. In this way the notion of cause is stretched more and more to fit new needs until sometimes it seems to have no relation but a historical one to the old concept. Actually, however, different though they may seem, they remain in essence the same, since they continue to reflect the same world view.

It is particularly with personality data that the causality theory falls down most completely. It is easy to demonstrate that within any personality syndrome, relationship other than causal exists. That is to say, if we had to use causal vocabulary we should have to say that every part of the syndrome is both a cause and an effect of every other part as well as of any grouping of these other parts, and that furthermore we should have to say that each part is both a cause and effect of the whole of which it is a part. Such an absurd conclusion is the only one that is possible if we use only the causality concept. Even if we attempt to meet the situation by introducing the newer concept of circular or reversible causality we could not completely describe the relations within the syndrome nor the relations of the part to the whole.

Nor is this the only shortcoming of causality vocabulary with which we must deal. There is also the difficult problem of the description of the interaction or interrelation between a syndrome as a whole and all the forces bearing upon it from the "outside." The syndrome of self-esteem, for instance, has been shown to tend to change as a whole. If we try to change Johnny's stammering and address ourselves specifically to this and only this, the chances are very great that we shall find either (1) that we have changed nothing at all, or else (2) that we have changed not Johnny's stammering alone but rather Johnny's self-esteem in general, or even Johnny as a whole individual. External influences usually tend to change the whole human being, not just a bit or a part of him.

There are yet other peculiarities in this situation that defy description by the ordinary causal vocabulary. There is one phenomenon in particular that is very difficult to describe. The nearest I can come to expressing it is to say that it is as if the organism (or any other syndrome) "swallows the cause and emits the effect." When an effective stimulus, a traumatic experience let us say, impinges upon the personality, there are certain consequences of this experience. But these consequences practically never bear a one-to-one or a straight-line relationship to the original causal experience. What actually happens is that the experience, if it is effective, changes the whole personality. This personality, now different from what it was before, expresses itself differently and behaves differently from before. Let us suppose that this effect would be that his facial twitch gets a little worse. Has this 10 percent increase of the tic been caused by the traumatic situation? If we say it has, it can be shown that we must, if we wish to be consistent, say that every single effective stimulus that has ever impinged on the organism has also caused this 10 percent increase in the facial tic. For every experience is taken into the organism, in the same sense that food is digested and by intussusception becomes the organism itself. Is the sandwish I ate an hour ago the cause of the words I now set down, or was it the coffee I drank, or what I ate yesterday, or was it the lesson in writing I got years ago, or the book I read a week ago?

It would certainly seem obvious that any important expression, such as writing a paper in which one is deeply interested, is not caused by anything in particular, but is an expression of, or a creation of the whole personality, which in turn is an effect of almost everything that has ever happened to it. It should seem just as natural for the psychologist to think of the stimulus or cause as being taken in by the personality by means of a readjustment, as to think of it as hitting the organism and pushing it. The net result here would be, not a cause and effect remaining separate, but simply a new personality (new by however little).

Still another way of demonstrating the inadequacy for psychology of conventional cause-effect notions is to show that the organism is not a passive agent to which causes or stimuli *do* something, but that it is an active agent entering into a complex mutual relationship with the cause, doing something to it as well. For readers of the psychoanalytic literature this is a commonplace, and it is necessary only to remind the reader of the facts that we can be blind to stimuli, we can distort them, reconstruct, or reshape them if they are distorted. We can seek them out or avoid them. We can sift them out and select from among them. Or finally, we can even create them if need be.

The causality concept rests on the assumption of an atomistic world with entities that remain discrete, even though they interact. The personality, however, is not separate from its expressions, effects, or the stimuli impinging upon it (causes) and so at least for psychological data it must be replaced by another conception.[a] This conception—holistic-dynamics—cannot

[a]More sophisticated scientists and philosophers have now replaced the causality notion with an interpretation in terms of "functional" relationships, i.e., A is a function of B, *or* If A, then B. By so doing, it seems to me that they have given up the nuclear aspects of the concept of cause, that is to say, of necessity, and of acting upon. Simple linear coefficients of correlations are examples of functional statements, which are, however, often used as *contrasting* with cause-effect relationships. It serves no purpose to retain the word "cause" if it means the very opposite of what it used to mean. In any case, we are then left with the problems of necessary or intrinsic relationship, and of the ways in which change comes about. These problems must be solved, not abandoned nor denied.

be stated simply, since it involves fundamental reorganization of viewpoint, but must be expounded step by step.

BASIC NEEDS AS INSTINCTOID[2]

[Several] considerations encourage us to the hypothesis that basic needs are in some sense, and to some appreciable degree, constitutional or hereditary in their determination. Such a hypothesis cannot be directly proved today, since the direct genetic or neurological techniques that are needed do not yet exist. Other forms of analysis, e.g., behavioral, familial, social, ethnological, are generally of more service in disproving, rather than in proving the hereditary hypothesis, except in unequivocal cases, and our hypothesis is by no means unequivocal.

In the following pages are presented such available data and theoretical considerationns as can be marshaled in support of the instinctoid hypothesis.

1. The chief argument in favor of offering new hypotheses is the failure of the old explanation. The instinct theory was drummed out by a complex of environmentalistic and behavioristic theories that rested almost entirely on associative learning as a basic, almost an all-sufficient tool of explanation.

On the whole it may fairly be said that this approach to psychology has failed to solve the problems of dynamics, e.g., of motives, their gratification and frustration, and the consequences thereof, e.g., health, psychopathology, psychotherapy.

It is not necessary to go into a detailed argument to substantiate this conclusion. It is sufficient to note that clinical psychologists, psychiatrists, psychoanalysts, social workers, and all other clinicians use behavioristic theory almost not at all. They proceed stubbornly in an *ad hoc* way to build an extensive practical structure on inadequate theoretical foundations. They tend to be practical men rather than theorists. Be it noted that to the extent that theory *is* used by the clinicians it is a crude and unorganized dynamic theory in which instincts play a fundamental role, i.e., modified Freudian theory.

In general nonclinical psychologists agree in admitting as instinctoid only such psychological impulses as hunger, thirst, etc. On this basis, and with the aid of the conditioning process alone, it is assumed that all higher needs are derived or learned.

That is to say, we learn to love our parents because they feed us and in other ways reward us. Love, for this theory, is the by-product of a satisfactory business or barter arrangement, or, as the advertising people might say, it is synonymous with customer satisfaction.

No single experiment known to the writer has ever been performed that shows this to be true for the needs for love, safety, belongingness, respect, understanding, etc. It has always been simply assumed without further ado.

[2]"The Instinctoid Nature of Basic Needs," *Journal of Personality*, XXII (1954), from pp. 326-47, and reprinted in *Motivation and Personality, op. cit.*, from pp. 136-45.

This assumption may have survived only for that reason—that it has in fact never been closely examined.

Certainly the data of conditioning do not support such a hypothesis: on the contrary, such needs behave far more like the unconditioned responses on which conditioning is originally based than like secondary conditioned responses.

As a matter of fact, the theory runs into many difficulties even at the common-observation level. Why is the mother so eager to give out rewards? What are *her* rewards? How rewarding are the nuisances of pregnancy and the pains of parturition? If indeed the relationship is at bottom a *quid pro quo* arrangement, why should she enter into such a poor business deal? Furthermore, why do clinicians unanimously affirm that a baby needs not only food, warmth, good handling, and other such rewards, but also love, as if this were something over and above the rewards? Can this be no more than redundancy? Is the efficient and unloving mother more loved than the inefficient (or poverty-stricken) and loving mother?

Many other disquieting questions suggest themselves. What exactly is a reward—even a physiological reward? We must assume that it is a physiological pleasure, since the theory in question purports to prove that all other pleasures are derived from physiological ones. But are safety gratifications physiological, e.g., being held gently, not roughly handled, not dropped sharply, not frightened, etc.? Why do cooing to the infant, smiling at it, holding it in one's arms, paying attention to the young child, kissing him, embracing him, etc. *seem* to please him? In what sense are *giving*, rewarding, feeding the child, sacrificing for it, rewarding to the giver?

Evidence is accumulating that indicates the *manner* of rewarding to be as effective (or as rewarding) as the reward itself. What does this mean for the concept of reward? Do regularity and dependability of feeding reward the hunger need? Or some other? Which need is rewarded by permissiveness? By respect for the child's needs? By weaning or toilet training the child when *he* wishes? Why do institutionalized children develop psychopathologically so often, no matter how well cared for they may be, i.e., physiologically rewarded? If love hunger is ultimately a request for food, why can it not be stilled by food?

Murphy's concept of canalization is highly useful at this point. He points out that arbitrary associations may be made between an unconditioned stimulus and any other stimulus because this latter arbitrary stimulus is only a signal and not itself a satisfier. When one deals with physiological needs, like hunger, *signals will not do—only satisfiers will do. Only* food will allay hunger. In a fairly stable world, such signal learning will take place and be useful, e.g., the dinner bell. But a far more important kind of learning that is *not* merely associative in nature is canalization, i.e., learning which objects are proper satisfiers and which not, and which of the satisfiers are *most* satisfying or most to be preferred for other reasons.

The relevance to our argument lies in the writer's observation that healthy gratification of love needs, respect needs, understanding needs, and the like is by canalization, i.e., by some intrinsically proper gratification and not by arbitrary associations. Where the latter do occur, we speak of neurosis and of neurotic needs, e.g., fetishism.

2. The ordinary biological criteria of instinct do not help us much, partly because we lack data, but also because we must now permit ourselves considerable doubt about these criteria themselves. (See, however, Howells' challenging papers, which indicate a new possibility of by-passing the difficulty.)

As we have seen above, a serious mistake of the early instinct theorists was to overstress man's continuity with the animal world, without at the same time stressing the profound differences between the human species and all others. We can now see clearly in their writings the unquestioned tendency to define and list instincts in a universal animal way, i.e., so as to cover any instinct in any animal. Because of this, any impulse found in men and *not* in other animals was often thought, *ipso facto*, to be noninstinctive. Of course it is true that any impulse or need found in man *and* all other animals is thereby proved to be instinctive beyond the need for any further evidence. This does not, however, disprove the possibility that some instinctoid impulses may be found only in the human species, or as appears to be the case with the love impulse, in common with chimpanzees alone of all the animal world. Homing pigeons, salmon, cats, etc., each have instincts peculiar to the species. Why could not the human species also have characteristics peculiar to it?

The commonly accepted theory has been that instincts steadily drop out as we go higher in the phyletic scale, to be replaced by an adaptability based on a vastly improved ability to learn, to think, and to communicate. If we define an instinct, in lower animal style, as a complex of innately predetermined urge, readiness to perceive, instrumental behavior and skill, and goal object (and possibly even affective accompaniment if we could ever find a way of observing it), then this theory seems to be true. Among the white rats, we find by this definition a sexual instinct, a maternal instinct, a feeding instinct (among others). In monkeys, the maternal instinct remains, the feeding instinct is modified and modifiable, and the sexual instinct is gone, leaving behind only an instinctlike urge. The monkey has to learn to choose his sexual mate and has to learn to perform the sexual act efficiently. The human being has *none* of these (or any other) instincts left. The sexual and feeding urges remain, and perhaps even the maternal urge although very faintly, but instrumental behavior, skills, selective perception, and goal objects must be learned (mostly in the sense of canalization). He has no instincts, only instinct remnants and instinct anlagen.

Side by side with this evolutionary development, there may be found another, namely, for the gradual appearance as we ascend the phyletic scale, of new (and higher) urges, instinctoid in nature, i.e., predetermined in greater or lesser degree by the structure and functioning of the organism. We say *may* because, although we present our hypotheses confidently for human beings, practically nothing is known about higher urges in subhuman animals. It remains a task for the future to decide to what degree, and in what sense, rats, dogs, cats, and monkeys show urges to safety, belongingness, love, respect, autonomy, self-confidence, curiosity, understanding, or beauty. (Be it noted again that we speak here of instinctoid *impulses* or *urges* and *not* of predetermined instrumental behaviors, abilities, or modes of gratification, i.e., *not* of instincts.)

One group of experiments shows that this is a testable hypothesis. It has been shown by Crawford, Yerkes, Maslow that the young chimpanzee is an altruistic, undominating, friendly, and fostering animal. This, too, is the impression of all who have worked with them. Wolfle, repeating Crawford's experiments with rhesus macaques, found this *not* to be true for them. We may for the moment say then that humans share with chimpanzees *alone* of all the species in the animal kingdom behavior that is altruistic, friendly, loving, etc., in a nonreflex sense (perhaps dogs should be included on the basis of common observation). Other needs of this same sort, i.e., *stronger* in the human being than in other animals, are those for information, for understanding, and for beauty (or symmetry, order, perfection, etc.). Certainly no one will deny that these urges come to climax rather than to obsolescence in the human being. Men are the most scientific, the most philosophical, the most theological, and the most artistic of all animals. Furthermore, there can be little doubt that, at least for some people, these are needs in the same sense that safety, love, etc., are needs, but that they are instinct anlagen rather than instinct remnants.

Unfortunately, we have practically no experimental or even clinical information about these needs, important though they obviously are.

It may be supposed on a priori grounds that extrinsic, acquired determinants of these urges, though undoubtedly present, are just as undoubtedly minimal. Most theorists hold or assume that the love need is created or constructed by conditioning upon physiological need satisfaction, e.g., that we *learn* to love because in the past the loved one has been a food-warmth-protection giver. This doctrine of derived needs would have to maintain then that the needs for knowledge, understanding, and beauty were acquired through conditioning upon physiological satisfaction, i.e., that they were and are signals for food, etc. Common experience supports such a contention almost not at all. It is, on the face of it, even less likely than the similar theory of acquisition of the love need.

3. The cultural criterion of instinct ("Is the reaction in question independent of culture?") is a crucial one, but unfortunately the data are as yet equivocal. It is the opinion of this writer that as far as they go, they either support or are compatible with the theory under consideration. However, it must be admitted that others, examining the same data, could conceivably come to an opposite conclusion.

Since the writer's field experience has been confined to a short stay with but one Indian group, and since the issue rests with the future findings of ethnologists rather than of psychologists, we shall not here consider the matter further.

4. One reason for considering basic needs to be instinctoid in nature has already been mentioned. Frustration of these needs is psychopathogenic, all clinicians agree. This is not true for neurotic needs, for habits, for addictions, for the preferences of familiarization, for instrumental needs, and it is true only in a special sense for the act-completion needs and for the talent-capacity-expression needs. At least this variety of needs *can* be differentiated on operational or on pragmatic grounds and *should* be differentiated for various theoretical and practical reasons.

If society creates and inculcates all values, why is it that only *some* and not others are psychopathogenic when thwarted? We learn to eat three times a day, say thank you, use forks and spoons, table and chair. We are forced to wear clothes and shoes, to sleep in a bed at night, and to speak English. We eat cows and sheep but not dogs and cats. We keep clean, compete for grades, and yearn for money. And yet any and all of these powerful habits can be frustrated without hurt and occasionally even with positive benefit. Under certain circumstances, as on a canoe or camping trip, we acknowledge their extrinsic nature by dropping them all with a sigh of relief. But this can *never* be said for love, for safety, or for respect.

Clearly, therefore, the basic needs stand in a special psychological and biological status. There is something different about them. The burden of proof that they are not appreciably instinctoid rests upon anyone who denies this.

5. The gratification of basic needs leads to consequences that may be called variously desirable, good, healthy, self-actualizing. The words desirable and good are used here in a biological rather than in an a priori sense and are susceptible to operational definition. These consequences are those that the healthy organism itself tends to choose, and strives toward under permissive conditions.

These psychological and somatic consequences have already been sketched out in the chapter on basic need gratification and need not be examined further here except to point out that there is nothing esoteric or nonscientific about this criterion. It can easily be put on an experimental basis, or even on an engineering basis, if we remember only that the problem is not very different from choosing the right oil for a car. One oil is better than another if, with it, the car works better. It is the general clinical finding that the organism, when fed safety, love, and respect, works better, i.e., perceives more efficiently, uses intelligence more fully, thinks to correct conclusions more often, digests food more efficiently, is less subject to various diseases, and so forth.

6. The requiredness of basic need gratifiers differentiates them from all other need gratifiers. The organism itself, out of its own nature, points to an intrinsic range of satisfiers for which no substitute is possible as is the

case, for instance, with habitual needs, or even with many neurotic needs. This requiredness is also responsible for the fact that the need is finally tied to its satisfiers by canalization rather than by arbitrary associations.

7. The effects of psychotherapy are of considerable interest for our purpose. It seems to the writer to be true for all major types of psychotherapy that, to the degree that they consider themselves successful, they foster, encourage, and strengthen what we have called basic, instinctoid needs, while they weaken, or expunge altogether the so-called neurotic needs.

Especially for those therapies that explicitly claim only to leave the person what he essentially and deep-down *is*, e.g., the therapies of Rogers, Fromm, Horney, etc., is this an important fact, for it implies that the personality has some intrinsic nature of its own, and is not created *de novo* by the therapist, but is only released by him to grow and develop in its own style. If insight and the dissolution of repression make a reaction disappear, this reaction may reasonably thereafter be considered to have been foreign and not intrinsic. If insight makes it stronger, we may thereafter consider it to be intrinsic. Also, as Horney has reasoned, if the release of anxiety causes the patient to become more affectionate and less hostile, does this not indicate that affection is basic to human nature, while hostility is not?

There is here, in principle, a gold mine of data for the theory of motivation, of self-actualization, of values, of learning, of cognition in general, of interpersonal relations, of acculturation and de-acculturation, etc. Unfortuately these data on the implications of therapeutic change have not yet been accumulated.

8. The clinical and theoretical study of the self-actualizing man, as far as it has gone, indicates unequivocally the special status of our basic needs. On the satisfaction of these needs, and no other, is the healthy life conditioned. Furthermore, these individuals are readily seen to be impulse-accepting as the instinctoid hypothesis would demand rather than impulse-controlling. On the whole, however, we must say for this kind of research that like the research on therapeutic effects, it is yet to be done.

9. Within anthropology, the first rumbles of dissatisfaction with cultural relativism came from field workers who felt that it implied more profound and irreconcilable differences between peoples than actually existed. The first and most important lesson that the writer learned from a field trip was that Indians are first of all people, individuals, human beings, and only secondarily Blackfoot Indians. By comparison with similarities, the differences, though undoubtedly there, seemed superficial. Not only they but all other peoples reported in the literature seemed to have pride, to prefer to be liked, to seek respect and status, to avoid anxiety. Furthermore, the constitutional differences observable in our own culture are observable all over the world, e.g., differences in intelligence, in forcefulness, in activity or lethargy, in calmness or emotionality, etc.

Even where differences have been seen they may confirm the feeling of universality since they are very often immediately understandable as reactions of the sort that *any* human being would be prone to in similar circumstances, e.g., reactions to frustration, to anxiety, to bereavement, to triumph, to approaching death.

It is granted that such feelings are vague, unquantifiable, and hardly scientific. Yet, taken together with other hypotheses presented above, as well as further on, e.g., the weak voice of instinctoid basic needs, the unexpected detachment and autonomy of self-actualizing people and their resistance to acculturation, the separability of the concepts of health and adjustment, it seems fruitful to reconsider the culture-personality relationship so as to give a greater importance to determination by intraorganismic forces, at any rate in the healthier person.

If he is shaped without regard to this structuring, it is true that no bones are broken and no obvious or immediate pathology results. It is, however, completely accepted that the pathology *will come,* if not obviously, then subtly, and if not sooner, then later. It is not too inaccurate to cite the ordinary adult neurosis as an example of such early violence to the intrinsic (though weak) demands of the organism.

The resistance of the person to enculturation in the interests of his own integrity and of his own intrinsic nature is then, or should be, a respectable area of study in the psychological and social sciences. The person who gives in eagerly to the distorting forces in his culture, i.e., the well-adjusted man, may be less healthy than the delinquent, the criminal, the neurotic, who may be demonstrating by his reactions that he has spunk enough left to resist the breaking of his psychological bones.

From this same consideration, furthermore, arises what seems at first to be a topsy-turvy, hind-end-to paradox. Education, civilization, rationality, religion, law, government, have all been interpreted by most as being primarily instinct-restraining and suppressing forces. But if our contention is correct that instincts have more to fear from civilization than civilization from instincts, perhaps it ought to be the other way about (if we still wish to produce better men and better societies): perhaps it should be at least one function of education, law, religion, etc. to safeguard, foster, and encourage the expression and gratification of the instinctoid needs.

Man's Inner Nature[3]

Let us sum up then. What has been affirmed is that man's inherent design or inner nature seems to be not only his anatomy but also his most basic needs, desires, and psychological capacities. And second, this inner nature is usually not obvious and easily seen, but is rather hidden and unfilled, weak rather than strong.

And how do we know that these needs and constitutional potentialities *are* inherent design? Of the twelve separate lines of evidence and tech-

[3]*Motivation and Personality, op. cit.,* from pp. 345-52.

niques of discovery . . . , I shall mention now only the four most important. First, frustration of these needs and capacities is psychopathogenic, i.e., it makes people sick. Second, their gratification is healthy-character-fostering (eupsychogenic), as neurotic need gratifications are not. That is, it makes people healthy and better. Third, they spontaneously show themselves as preferences under free conditions. Fourth, they can be directly studied in relatively healthy people.

If we wish to differentiate basic from nonbasic, we cannot look alone to introspection of conscious needs or even to description of unconscious needs because, phenomenologically, neurotic needs and inherent needs all feel alike. They press equally for gratification, for the monopolizing of consciousness, and their introspected qualities are not different enough from each other to enable the introspector to differentiate them except perhaps at the end of his life and in retrospect (as did Tolstoy's Ivan Ilyitch), or in moments of special insight.

No, we must have some other external variable to correlate with, to covary with. In effect this other variable has been the neurosis-health continuum. We are now pretty well convinced that nasty aggressiveness is reactive rather than basic, effect rather than cause, because as a nasty person gets healthier in psychotherapy, he gets less vicious; and as a healthier person gets more sick, he changes in the direction of *more* hostility, *more* venom, and *more* viciousness.

Furthermore, we know that giving gratification to neurotic needs does *not* breed health as does gratification of basic inherent needs. Giving a neurotic power seeker all the power he wants does not make him less neurotic, nor is it possible to satiate his neurotic need for power. However much he is fed he still remains hungry. . . . It makes little difference for ultimate health whether a neurotic need be gratified or frustrated.

It is very different with basic needs like safety or love. Their gratification *does* breed health, their satiation *is* possible, their frustration *does* breed sickness.

The same seems to be true for individual potentialities like intelligence, or strong tendency to activity. (The only data we have here are clinical.) Such a tendency acts like a drive that demands fulfillment. Gratify it and the person develops nicely; frustrate it and block it, and various subtle troubles, not yet very well known, develop at once.

The most obvious technique of all, however, is the direct study of people who are *actually* healthy. We certainly know enough now to be able to select *relatively* healthy people. Granted that we cannot find perfect specimens, still it may be expected that we can learn more about the nature, for example, of radium when it is relatively concentrated than when it is relatively dilute.

[Earlier] research . . . has demonstrated the possibility that a *scientist* could study and describe normality in the sense of excellence, perfection, ideal health, the fulfillment of human possibilities. If we know what good people are like or can be like, it becomes possible for the human species (who mostly want to be good) to model themselves on these paragons and improve thereby.

The most fully studied example of inherent design is the love need. With this we can illustrate all four of the techniques so far mentioned for differentiating the inherent and universal in human nature from the accidental and local.

1. It is agreed by practically all therapists that when we trace a neurosis back to its beginnings we shall find with great frequency a deprivation of love in the early years. Several semiexperimental studies have confirmed this in infants and babies to such a point that radical deprivation of love is considered dangerous even to the life of the infant. That is to say, the deprivation of love leads to illness.

2. These illnesses, if they have not gone so far as to be irreversible, are now known to be curable, especially in young children, by giving affection and loving kindness. Even in adult psychotherapy and analysis of more serious cases, there is now good reason to believe that one thing that the therapy does is to make it possible for the patient to receive and utilize the love that heals. Also there is a mounting mass of evidence to prove a correlation between affectionate childhood and a healthy adulthood. Such data add up to the generalization that love is a basic need for healthy development of the human being.

3. The child in the situation where he is permitted free choice, and granted that he is not yet warped and twisted, prefers affection to nonaffection. We have no true experiments yet to prove this, but we have a huge amount of clinical data and *some* ethnological data to support this conclusion. The common observation that children prefer an affectionate teacher or parent or friend to the hostile or cold teacher or parent or friend illustrates what I mean. The crying of infants tells us that they prefer affection to nonaffection, for instance in the Balinese situation. The adult Balinese does not need love as the adult American does. Balinese children are taught by bitter experiences not to ask for it and not to expect it. But they do not *like* this training; the children weep bitterly while being trained not to ask for love.

4. Finally, what do we find descriptively in healthy adults? That practically all (though not quite all) have led loving lives, have loved and been loved. Furthermore, they are *now* loving people. And finally and paradoxically they *need* love *less* than the average man does, apparently because they already have enough.

A perfect parallel that makes these points more plausible and more commonsense is supplied by *any* other of the deficiency diseases. Supposing an animal lacks salt. First this produces pathology. Second, extra salt taken into the body cures or helps these sicknesses. Third, a white rat or a human that lacks salt when given a choice will prefer salt-laden foods, that is, will eat salt in unusually large quantities and in the case of the human, will report subjective cravings for salt and will report that it tastes especially good. Fourth, we find that healthy organisms, already having enough salt, do *not* specially crave it or need it.

We may therefore say that just as an organism needs salt in order to attain health and avoid illness, so also does it need love for the same reasons. In other words, we can say that the organism is so designed that it needs salt and love, in the same way that automobiles are so designed that they need gas and oil.

We have spoken much of good conditions, of permissiveness, etc. These refer to the special conditions of observation that are so often necessary in scientific work and are the equivalent of saying, "This is true under such and such circumstances."

DEFINITION OF GOOD CONDITIONS[4]

Let us turn to this problem of what constitutes good conditions for the revelation of original nature to see what contemporary dynamic psychology has to offer on the subject.

If the upshot of what we have already said is that the organism has a vaguely delineated, intrinsic nature of its own, it is quite clear that this inner nature is a very delicate and subtle something rather than being strong and overpowering as it is in lower animals, who are never in any doubt about what they are, what they want, and what they do not want. The human needs for love, or for knowledge or for a philosophy, are weak and feeble rather than unequivocal and unmistakable; they whisper rather than shout.

In order to discover what a human being needs and what he *is*, it is necessary to set up special conditions that foster expression of these needs and capacities that encourage and make them possible. In general these conditions may all be summed up under the one head of permissiveness to gratify and to express. How do we know what is best for pregnant white rats to eat? We give them free choice from among a wide range of possibilities, and we let them eat whatever they want, whenever they want it, and in any quantities or patterns they choose. We know it is best for a human infant to be weaned in an individual fashion, i.e., whenever it is best for *him*. How do we determine this? Certainly we cannot ask the infant, and we have learned not to ask the old-school pediatrician. We give the baby a choice; we let him decide. We offer him both the liquid and the solid food. If the solid food appeals to him, he will spontaneously wean himself from the breast. In the same way we have learned to let the child tell us when he needs love, or protection or respect or control, by setting up a permissive, accepting, gratifying atmosphere. We have learned that this is the best atmosphere for psychotherapy, indeed, the *only* possible one, in the long run. Free choice from among a wide range of possibilities has been found useful in such diverse

[4]*Ibid.*, from pp. 348-49.

social situations as choosing roommates in institutions for delinquent girls, choosing teachers and courses in college, choosing bombadier crews, etc. (I leave aside the knotty but important question of *desirable* frustration, of discipline, of setting limits to gratification. I wish to point out only that while permissiveness may be best for our experimental purpose, it need not also be sufficient in itself for teaching consideration of others and awareness of their needs.)

From the point of view, then, of fostering self-actualization or health, a good environment (in theory) is one that offers all necessary raw materials and then gets out of the way and stands aside to let the organism itself utter its wishes and demands and make its choices (always remembering that it often chooses delay, renunciation in favor of others, etc., and that *other* people also have demands and wishes).

Eupsychia (A Psychological Utopia)[5]

It has been my pleasure recently to work up a speculative description of a psychological Utopia in which all men are psychologically healthy, Eupsychia, I call it. From what we know of healthy people, could we predict the kind of culture that they would evolve if 1000 healthy families migrated to some deserted land where they could work out their own destiny as they pleased? What kind of education would they choose? Economic system? Sexuality? Religion?

I am very uncertain of some things—economics in particular. But of other things I am *very* sure. And one of them is that this would almost surely be a highly anarchistic group, a laissez-faire but loving culture, in which people (young people too) would have much more free choice than we are used to, and in which wishes would be respected much more than they are in our society. People would not bother each other so much as we do, would be much less prone to press opinions or religions or philosophies or tastes in clothes or food or art or women on their neighbors. In a word, the inhabitants of Eupsychia would tend to be permissive, wish-respecting and gratifying (whenever possible), would frustrate only under certain conditions that I have not attempted to describe, and would permit people to make free choices wherever possible. Under such conditions, the deepest layers of human nature could show themselves with great ease.

I must point out that adult human beings constitute a special case. The free-choice situation does not necessarily work for people in general—only for intact ones. Sick, neurotic people make the wrong choices; they do not know what they want, and even when they do, have not courage enough to choose correctly. When we speak of free *choice* in human beings, we refer to sound adults or children who have not yet been twisted and distorted. Most of the good experimental work with free choice has been done with

5*Ibid.*, from p. 350.

animals. We have also learned a great deal about it at the clinical level from the analysis of psychotherapeutic processes.

ENVIRONMENT AND PERSONALITY[6]

There is another important problem that confronts us as we struggle to understand this newer conception of normality and its relationship to environment. One theoretical consequence would seem to be that perfect health needs a perfect world to live in and to make it possible. In actual research, it does not seem to work out that way exactly.

It *is* possible to find extremely healthy individuals in our society, which is very far from perfection. Certainly these individuals are not perfect but they certainly are as fine people as we can now conceive. Perhaps at this time and in this culture we just do not know enough about how perfect people can get.

In any case, research has established an important point in discovering that individuals can be healthier, even *much* healthier, than the culture in which they grow and live. This is possible primarily because of the ability of the healthy man to be detached from his surroundings, which is the same as saying that he lives by his inner laws rather than by outer pressures.

Our culture is democratic enough to give a very wide latitude to individuals to have the characters that they please, so long as their external behavior is not too unusual. Healthy individuals are not externally visible; they are not marked off by unusual clothes, or manners, or behavior. It is an *inner* freedom that they have. So long as they are independent of the approval and disapproval of other people, and seek rather *self*-approval, so long may they be considered to be psychologically autonomous, i.e., relatively independent of the culture. External freedom seems to be less important than inner freedom, and it will probably turn out that influences like Senator McCarthy are more dangerous to psychological health than Al Capone. Tolerance and freedom of taste and opinion seem the key necessities.

To sum up, what research we have points to the conclusion that while a good environment fosters good personalities, this relationship is far from perfect, and furthermore, the definition of good environment has to change markedly to stress spiritual and psychological rather than material and economic forces.

NORMALITY AS AN IDEAL[7]

Now coming back to the question with which we started, the nature of normality, we have come close to identifying it with the highest excellence

[6]*Ibid.*, from p. 351.
[7]*Ibid.*, from p. 352.

of which we are capable. But this ideal is not an unattainable goal set out far ahead of us; rather it is actually within us, existent but hidden, as potentiality rather than as actuality.

Furthermore, it is a conception of normality that I claim is discovered rather than invented, based on empirical findings rather than on hopes or wishes. It implies a strictly naturalistic system of values that can be enlarged by further empirical research with human nature. Such research should be able to give us answers to the age-old question "How can I be a good man?" "How can I live a good life?" "How can I be fruitful?" "Happy?" "At peace with myself?" If the organism tells us what it needs—and therefore what it values—by sickening and withering when deprived of these values, this is the same as telling us what is good for it.

One last point. The key concepts in the newer dynamic psychology are spontaneity, release, naturalness, self-acceptance, impulse-awareness, gratification. They *used* to be control, inhibition, discipline, training, shaping, on the principle that the depths of human nature were dangerous, evil, predatory, and ravenous. Education, family training, bringing up children, acculturation in general were all seen as a process of bringing the darker forces within us under control.

See how different are the conceptions of society, law, education, and family that are generated by these two different conceptions of human nature. In the one case they are restraining and controlling forces; in the other they are gratifying and fulfilling. . . .

If this conception that identifies normality with ideal health holds up, we shall have to change not only our conceptions of individual psychology but also our theories of society.

TRANSCENDENT OR PEAK-EXPERIENCES[8]

The very beginning, the intrinsic core, the essence, the universal nucleus of every known high religion (unless Confucianism is also called a religion) has been the private, lonely, personal illumination, revelation, or ecstasy of some acutely sensitive prophet or seer. The high religions call themselves revealed religions and each of them tends to rest its validity, its function, and its right to exist on the codification and the communication of this original mystic experience or revelation from the lonely prophet to the mass of human beings in general.

But it has recently begun to appear that these "revelations" or mystical illuminations can be subsumed under the head of the "peak-experiences" or "ecstasies" or "transcendent" experiences which are now being eagerly investigated by many psychologists. That is to say, it is very likely, indeed almost certain, that these older reports, phrased in terms of supernatural

[8]*Religions, Values, and Peak-Experiences* (Columbus: The Ohio State University Press, 1964), from pp. 19-23.

revelation, were, in fact, perfectly natural, human peak-experiences of the kind that can easily be examined today, which, however, were phrased in terms of whatever conceptual, cultural, and linguistic framework the particular seer had available in his time (Laski).

In a word, we can study today what happened in the past and was then explainable in supernatural terms only. By so doing, we are enabled to examine religion in all its facets and in all its meanings in a way that makes it a part of science rather than something outside and exclusive of it.

Also this kind of study leads us to another very plausible hypothesis: to the extent that all mystical or peak-experiences are the same in their essence and have always been the same, all religions are the same in their essence and always have been the same. They should, therefore, come to agree in principle on teaching that which is common to all of them, i.e., whatever it is that peak-experiences teach in common (whatever is *different* about these illuminations can fairly be taken to be localisms both in time and space, and are, therefore, peripheral, expendable, not essential). This something common, this something which is left over after we peel away all the localisms, all the accidents of particular languages or particular philosophies, all the ethnocentric phrasings, all those elements which are *not* common, we may call the "core-religious experience" or the "transcendent experience."

To understand this better, we must differentiate the prophets in general from the organizers or legalists in general as (abstracted) types. (I admit that the use of pure, extreme types which do not really exist can come close to the edge of caricature; nevertheless, I think it will help all of us in thinking through the problem we are here concerned with.) The characteristic prophet is a lonely man who has discovered his truth about the world, the cosmos, ethics, God, and his own identity from within, from his own personal experiences, from what he would consider to be a revelation. Usually, perhaps always, the prophets of the high religions have had these experiences when they were alone.

Characteristically the abstraction-type of the legalist-ecclesiastic is the conserving organization man, an officer and arm of the organization which has been built up on the basis of the prophet's original revelation in order to make the revelation available to the masses. From everything we know about organizations, we may very well expect that people will become loyal to them, as well as to the original prophet and to his vision; or at least they will become loyal to the organization's version of the prophet's vision. I may go so far as to say that characteristically (and I mean not only the religious organizations but also parallel organizations like the Communist Party or like revolutionary groups) these organizations can be seen as a kind of punch card or IBM version of an original revelation or mystical experience or peak-experience to make it suitable for group use and for administrative convenience.

It will be helpful here to talk about a pilot investigation, still in its beginnings, of the people I have called non-peakers. In my first investigations, in collaboration with Gene Nameche, I used this word because I thought some people had peak-experiences and others did not. But as I gathered information, and as I became more skillful in asking questions, I found that a higher and higher percentage of my subjects began to report peak-experiences. . . . I finally fell into the habit of expecting everyone to have peak-experiences and of being rather surprised if I ran across somebody who could report none at all. Because of this experience, I finally began to use the word "non-peaker" to describe, not the person who is unable to have peak-experiences, but rather the person who is afraid of them, who suppresses them, who denies them, who turns away from them, or who "forgets" them. My preliminary investigations of the reasons for these negative reactions to peak-experiences have led me to some (unconfirmed) impressions about why certain kinds of people renounce their peak-experiences.

Any person whose character structure (or Weltanschauung, or way of life) forces him to try to be extremely or completely rational or "materialistic" or mechanistic tends to become a non-peaker. That is, such a view of life tends to make the person regard his peak- and transcendent experiences as a kind of insanity, a complete loss of control, a sense of being overwhelmed by irrational emotions, etc. The person who is afraid of going insane and who is, therefore, desperately hanging on to stability, control, reality, etc., seems to be frightened by peak-experiences and tends to fight them off. For the compulsive-obsessive person, who organizes his life around the denying and the controlling of emotion, the fear of being overwhelmed by an emotion (which is interpreted as a loss of control) is enough for him to mobilize all his stamping-out and defensive activities against the peak-experience. I have one instance of a very convinced Marxian who denied—that is, who turned away from—a legitimate peak-experience, finally classifying it as some kind of peculiar but unimportant thing that had happened but that had best be forgotten because this experience conflicted with her whole materialistic mechanistic philosophy of life. I have found a few non-peakers who were ultra-scientific, that is, who espoused the nineteenth-century conception of science as an unemotional or anti-emotional activity which was ruled entirely by logic and rationality and who thought anything which was not logical and rational had no respectable place in life. (I suspect also that extremely "practical," i.e., exclusively means-oriented, people will turn out to be non-peakers, since such experiences earn no money, bake no bread, and chop no wood. So also for extremely other-directed people, who scarcely know what is going on inside themselves. Perhaps also people who are reduced to the concrete à la Goldstein, etc., etc.) Finally, I should add that, in some cases, I could not come to any explanation for non-peaking.

CHAPTER 14

HENRY A. MURRAY

PERSONOLOGY

Henry A. Murray's PERSONOLOGY is the "science of men, taken as gross units"; as a term it stands for "methods of inquiry or doctrines rather than realms of knowledge." It is a science which lacks theories which are "securely proved," much less certainty. Personology conceives of personality as a "temporal integrate of mutually dependent processes (variables) developing in time"; an explanation of a single one of these variables involves the recognition of a large number of others and their reciprocal relations. Murray's "divisions of personality" draw upon psychoanalytic theory for the structure of the personality, but the psychoanalytic source is appreciably modified, apparently by Murray's research and training in biochemistry with Lawrence J. Henderson at Harvard University and Sir Gowland Hopkins at Cambridge. Divergence from psychoanalytic psychology is especially true of Murray's treatment of needs.

Murray's studies in personality have issued in some unusual, but nevertheless fruitful, results. "One result, for instance, was this: after trying to complete a number of tasks, the majority remembered their successes better than their failures. Another was this: that the majority remembered best the tasks on which they had cheated. Yet another was this: that the majority persisted longer in an attempt after they had been humiliated in the initial attempt than they did after they had been commended."[1]

Murray was born in New York City in 1893 and was educated

[1] *Explorations in Personality*, ed. Henry A. Murray (New York: Oxford, 1938), from p. viii.

at Groton, Harvard, Columbia (M.D., 1919), and Cambridge (Ph.D., 1927). His training in psychotherapy was under Carl Jung in Zurich and Morton Prince at Harvard. Murray served on the teaching faculty at Harvard and in research as Director of the Harvard Psychological Clinic for thirty-six years. He retired from his teaching duties at Harvard in 1962, when he was appointed Professor of Clinical Psychology Emeritus, but he resumed psychological research at that institution. His research includes studies in religion, fear, humor, fantasies, dreams, sentiments, creativity, and myth-making. He is best known for his Thematic Apperception Test, which is widely used in the assessment of personality to uncover degree of emotional stability, personality traits, and other factors.

Murray's best known work is *Explorations in Personality* (1938); among his other publications are "Basic Concepts for a Psychology of Personality" in *Journal of General Psychology* (1936), "What Should Psychologists Do About Psychoanalysis?" in *Journal of Abnormal and Social Psychology* (1940), *Manual of Thematic Apperception Test* (1943), "A Clinical Study of Sentiments" in *Psychological Monographs* (with C. D. Morgan, 1945), "Problems in Clinical Research" in *American Journal of Orthopsychiatry* (1947), *Assessment of Men* (1948), "Some Basic Psychological Assumptions and Conceptions" in *Dialectica* (1951), "Toward a Classification of Interaction" in *Toward a General Theory of Action* (ed. by T. Parsons and E. A. Shils, 1951), "Outline of a Conception of Personality, and Personality Formation: The Determinants" in *Personality in Nature, Society, and Culture* (ed. by C. Kluckhohn, H. A. Murray, and D. M. Schneider, 1953), "American Icarus" in *Clinical Studies in Personality* (ed. by A. Burton and R. E. Harris, 1955), "Preparations for the Scaffold of a Comprehensive System" in *Psychology: A Study of a Science*, vol. 3 (ed. by S. Koch, 1959), "Studies in Stressful Interpersonal Disputations" in *American Psychologist* (1963), "Components of an Evolving Personological System" in the *International Encyclopedia of the Social Sciences* (1968), and *Encounter with Psychology* (1969).

PERSONOLOGY DEFINED[2]

Man is to-day's great problem. . . . The point of view adopted in [*Explorations in Personality*] is that personalities constitute the subject matter of

[2]*Ibid.*, from pp. 3-10.

psychology, the life history of a single man being a unit with which this discipline has to deal. It is not possible to study all human beings or all experiences of one human being. The best that can be done is to select representative or specially significant events for analysis and interpretation. Some psychologists may prefer to limit themselves to the study of one kind of episode. For instance, they may study the responses of a great number of individuals to a specific situation. They may attempt to discover what changes in the situation bring about important changes in response. But, since every response is partially determined by the after-effects of previous experiences, the psychologist will never fully understand an episode if he abstracts it from ontogeny, the developmental history of the individual. Even phylogeny, or racial history, may have to be considered. The prevailing custom in psychology is to study one function or one aspect of an episode at a time—perception, emotion, intellection or behaviour—and this is as it must be. The circumscription of attention is dictated by the need for detailed information. But the psychologist who does this should recognize that he is observing merely a part of an operating totality, and that this totality, in turn, is but a small temporal segment of a personality. Psychology must construct a scheme of concepts for portraying the entire course of individual development, and thus provide a framework into which any single episode—natural or experimental—may be fitted.

The branch of psychology which principally concerns itself with the study of human lives and the factors that influence their course, which investigates individual differences and types of personality, may be termed "personology" instead of the "psychology of personality," a clumsy and tautological expression.

Personology, then, is the science of men, taken as gross units, and by definition it encompasses "psycho-analysis" (Freud), "analytical psychology" (Jung), "individual psychology" (Adler) and other terms which stand for methods of inquiry or doctrines rather than realms of knowledge.

In its intentions our endeavour was excessively ambitious. For we purposed nothing less than (1) to construct methodically a *theory* of personality; (2) to devise *techniques* for getting at some of the more important attributes of personality; and (3) by a study of the lives of many individuals to discover basic *facts* of personality. Our guiding thought was that personality is a temporal whole and to understand a part of it one must have a sense, though vague, of the totality. It was for this that we attempted comprehensiveness, despite the danger that in trying to grasp everything we might be left with nothing worth having.

We judged the time had come when systematic, full length studies of individuals could be made to bring results. And more than this, indeed, it seemed a necessary thing to do. For if the constituent processes of personality are mutually dependent, then one must know a lot to comprehend a little, and to know a lot that may be used for understanding, good methods must be systematically employed. In our attempt to envisage and portray the general course of a person's life, we selected for analysis certain happenings along the way and, using these as points, made free drawings of the connected paths. We judged that the spaces without definition would attract attention and it would become more evident than it has been in what quarters detailed research might yield important facts. For without some notion of the whole there can be no assurance that the processes selected for intensive study are significant constituents.

Actually, the scheme of concepts we employed was not exhaustive, one reason being the inability of the mind to hold so many novel generalities in readiness. The amount of space and time and the number of examiners available put a limit to the number of experimental subjects and the number of techniques that could be used. Thus, in the end, our practices and theories were not as comprehensive as we thought they could and should be.

Since in the execution of our plan we went from theory down to fact, then back to theory and down to fact again, the book may be regarded either as a scheme of elementary formulations conceived of to explain the ways of different individuals, or as an assemblage of biographic data organized according to a certain frame of reference.

The Present State of Personology

In psychology there are few generally valued tests, no traits that are always measured, no common guiding concepts. Some psychologists make precise records of their subjects' overt movements, others inquire into sentiments and theories. Some use physiological techniques, others present batteries of questionnaires. Some record dreams and listen for hours to free associations, others note attitudes in social situations. These different methods yield data which, if not incommensurate, are, at least, difficult to organize into one construction. There is no agreement as to what traits or variables are significant. A psychologist who embarks upon a study of normal personality feels free to look for anything he pleases.

*   *   *   *   *

A little order is brought out of this confusion—though somewhat arbitrarily—by dividing psychologists into two large classes holding opposite conceptual positions. One group may be called *peripheralists*, the other *centralists*. The peripheralists have an objective inclination, that is, they are attracted to clearly observable things and qualities—simple deliverances of sense organs—and they usually wish to confine the data of personology to these. . . . Agreement, it is pointed out, is common among trained observers when interpretations are excluded, and since without agreement there is no science, they believe that if they stick to measurable facts they are more likely to make unquestionable contributions. . . . In this respect they are *positivists*. Now, since we are reasonably certain that all phenomena within the domain of personology are determined by excitations in the brain, the things which are objectively discernible—the outer environment, bodily changes, muscular movements and so forth—are peripheral to the personality proper and hence those who traffic only with the former may be called *peripheralists*. ... [The peripheralist] is an *elementarist* because he regards personality as the sum total or product of interacting elements rather than a unity which may, for convenience, be analysed into parts. Furthermore, the implicit supposition of this class of scientists is that an external stimulus, or the perception of it, is the origination of everything psychological. For them, the organism is at the start an inert, passive, though receptive, aggregate, which only acts in response to outer stimulation. From the point of view of consciousness, as Locke would have it, mind is at first a sensorium innocent of imprints which, as time goes on, receives sensations from external objects and combines them variously, according to objective contiguities and similarities, to form ideas and ideologies. Those who hold this view are called *sensationists*.

In contrast to these varieties of scientists are a heterogeneous group, the *centralists*. The latter are especially attracted to subjective facts of emotional or purposive significance: feelings, desires, intentions. They are centralists because they are primarily concerned with the governing processes in the brain. And to these they think they are led directly by listening to the form and content of other people's speech. Their terminology is subjectively derived. For instance, to portray a personality they do not hesitate to use such terms as wishes, emotions and ideas. Though most of them make efforts to observe behaviour accurately, interpretation usually merges with perception, and overt actions are immediately referred to psychic impulses. Since the latter are intangible, personologists must imagine them. Hence, men of this complexion are *conceptualists* rather than positivists; and further, in so far as they believe that personality is a complex unity, of which each function is merely a partially distinguished integral, they are *totalists*, naturally inclined to doctrines of immanence and emergence. Craving to know the inner nature of other persons as they know their own, they have often felt their wish was realized, not by making conscious inferences from items of observation but by an unanalysable act of empathic intuition. For this, perceptions, naturally, are necessary, but the observer is only dimly aware of the specific sensa which were configurated to suggest the underlying feeling or intention of the subject's momentary self. So hold the *intuitionists*. Finally, as opposed to the *sensationists* are the *dynamicists*, who ascribe action to inner forces—drives, urges, needs, or instincts—some of which, inherited or suddenly emerging, may be held accountable for the occurrence of motility without external stimulation. These inner energies of which the personality may be wholly unaware seem to influence perception, apperception and intellection. The more or less mechanical laws of the sensationists are only true, it is believed, when a passive, disinterested attitude is adopted by the subject. But under most conditions, attention and conceptualization are directed by wants and feelings.

These two general classes of psychologists are heterogeneous. It is only certain underlying similarities which prompt us to put in one class peripheralists, objectivists, positivists, mechanists, elementarists, and sensationists; and to put in another centralists, subjectivists, conceptualists, totalists, and dynamicists. It is clear that a psychologist may belong in certain respects to one class and in others to another. For instance, some psychologists are eclectic, others vaguely hold to a middle ground, still others attempt with more or less success to encompass both positions. Then there are those whose natural temper is emotionally subjective but who come to adopt, for their own equilibration, the extreme behaviouristic point of view. These are holy zealots, the modern puritans of science. Mixtures and contrasts of this sort are not uncommon, but in the main the two classes are distinguishable.

*   *   *   *   *

In summary, it may be said that the peripheralists are apt to emphasize the physical patterns of overt behaviour, the combination of simple reflexes to form complex configurations, the influence of the tangible environment, sensations and their compounds, intellections, social attitudes, traits, and vocational pursuits. The centralists, on the other hand, stress the directions or ends of behaviour, underlying instinctual forces, inherited dispositions, maturation and inner transformations, distortions of perception by wish and fantasy, emotion, irrational or semi-conscious mental processes, repressed sentiments and the objects of erotic interest.

Primary Propositions[3]

1. The objects of study are individual organisms, not aggregates of organisms.
2. The organism is from the beginning a whole, from which the parts are derived by self-differentiation. . . .
3. The organism is characterized from the beginning by rhythms of activity and rest, which are largely determined by internal factors. The organism is not an inert body that merely responds to external stimulation. . . .
4. The organism consists of an infinitely complex series of temporally related activities extending from birth to death. Because of the meaningful connection of sequences the life cycle of a single individual should be taken as a unit, the *long unit* for psychology. . . .
5. Since, at every moment, an organism is within an environment which largely determines its behaviour, and since the environment changes—sometimes with radical abruptness—the conduct of an individual cannot be formulated without a characterization of each confronting situation, physical and social. . . . The organism and its milieu must be considered together, a single creature-environment interaction being a convenient short unit for psychol-

[3]*Ibid.*, from pp. 38-49.

ogy. A *long unit*—an individual life—can be most clearly formulated as a succession of related short units, or *episodes*.

6. The stimulus situation (S.S.) is that part of the total environment to which the creature attends and reacts. It can rarely be described significantly as an aggregate of discrete sense impressions. The organism usually responds to patterned meaningful wholes, as the gestalt school of psychology has emphasized. . . .

7. The reactions of the organism to its environment usually exhibit a *unitary trend*. This is the necessary concomitant of behavioural coordination, since co-ordination implies organization of activity in a *certain direction*, that is, towards the achievement of an effect, one or more. . . .

8. A specimen of adaptive behaviour can be analysed into the bodily movements as such and the effect achieved by these movements. We have found it convenient to use a special term, *actone*, to describe a pattern of bodily movements *per se*, abstracted from its effect . . . .

9. A behavioural trend may be attributed to a hypothetical force (a drive, need or propensity) within the organism. . . . It is a force which (if uninhibited) promotes activity which (if competent) brings about a situation that is opposite (as regards its relevant properties) to the one that aroused it. Frequently, an innumerable number of sub-needs (producing sub-effects) are temporally organized so as to promote the course of a major need.

10. The organism frequently seeks for a certain press—in which case the press is, for a time, expectantly imaged—more frequently the press meets the organism and incites a drive. Thus, the simplest formula for a period of complex behaviour is a particular press-need combination. Such a combination may be called a *thema. A thema* may be defined as the dynamical structure of a simple *episode*, a single creature-environment interaction. In other words, the endurance of a certain kind of *press* in conjunction with a certain kind of *need* defines the duration of a single *episode*, the latter being a convenient molar unit for psychology to handle. Simple episodes (each with a simple thema) may relatedly succeed each other to constitute a *complex episode* (with its *complex thema*). The biography of a man may be portrayed abstractly as an historic route of themas (*cf.* a musical score). Since there are a limited number of important drives and a limited number of important presses, there are a greater (but still limited) number of important themas. Just as chemists now find it scientifically profitable to describe a hundred thousand or more organic compounds, psychologists some day may be inclined to observe and formulate the more important behavioural compounds.

11. Each drive reaction to a press has a fortune that may be measured in degrees of realization ("gratification"). Whether an episode terminates in gratification or frustration (success or failure) is often decisive in determining the direction of an organism's development. Success and failure are also of major importance in establishing the "status" of an organism in its community.

12. In the organism the passage of time is marked by rhythms of assimi-

lation, differentiation and integration. The environment changes. Success and failure produce their effects. There is learning and there is maturation. . . . There is the "eternal return" ("spiritual evolution"). These phenomena make biography imperative.

13. Though the psychologist is unable to find identities among the episodes of an organism's life, he can perceive uniformities.

14. Repetitions and consistencies are due in part to the fact that impressions of situations leave enduring "traces" (a concept for a hypothetical process) in the organism, which may be reactivated by the appearance of situations that resemble them; and because of the connections of these evoked traces with particular reaction systems, the organism is apt to respond to new situations as it did to former ones (redintegration). Some of the past is always alive in the present. . . . ("The child is the father of the man.")

15. The progressive differentiations and integrations that occur with age and experience are, for the most part, refinements in stimulus discrimination and press discrimination and improvements in actonal effectiveness. Specific signs become connected with specific modes of thought, and certain aptitudes (abilities) are developed. . . .

16. Since in the higher forms of life the impressions from the external world and from the body that are responsible for conditioning and memory are received, integrated and conserved in the brain, and since all complex adaptive behaviour is evidently co-ordinated by excitations in the brain, the unity of the organism's development and behaviour can be explained only by referring to organizations occurring in this region. It is brain processes, rather than those in the rest of the body, which are of special interest to the psychologist. . . . A need or drive is just one of these hypothetical processes. . . .

17. It may prove convenient to refer to the mutually dependent processes that constitute dominant configurations in the brain as *regnant* processes; and, further, to designate the totality of such processes occurring during a single moment (a unitary temporal segment of brain processes) as a *regnancy*. According to this conception regnancies correspond to the processes of highest metabolic rate in the gradient which Child has described in lower organisms. It may be considered that regnancies are functionally at the summit of a hierarchy of subregnancies in the body. Thus, to a certain extent the regnant need dominates the organism. Occurrences in the external world or in the body that have no effect upon regnancies do not fall within the proper domain of psychology.

18. Regnant processes are, without doubt, mutually dependent. A change in one function changes all the others and these, in turn, modify the first. Hence, events must be interpreted in terms of the many interacting forces and their relations, not ascribed to single causes. . . .

19. According to one theory of the double aspect theory—seemingly the most fruitful working hypothesis for a psychologist—the constituents of regnancies in man are capable of achieving consciousness (self-consciousness)

though not all of them at once. The amount of introspective self-consciousness is a function of age, emotional state, attitude, type of personality, and so forth. . . .

20. During a single moment only some of the regnant processes have the attribute of consciousness. Hence, to explain fully a conscious event as well as a behavioural event the psychologist must take account of more variables than were present in consciousness at the time. Consequently, *looking at the matter from the viewpoint of introspective awareness,* it is necessary to postulate unconscious regnant processes. An unconscious process is something that must be conceptualized as regnant even though the S (subject) is unable to report its occurrence.

21. It seems that it is more convenient at present in formulating regnant processes to use a terminology derived from subjective experience . . . (perception, apperception, imagination, emotion, affection, conation).

22. One may suppose that regnancies vary in respect to the number, relevance and organization of the processes involved, and that, as Janet supposes, a certain amount of integrative energy or force is required to unify the different parts. Regnancies become disjunctive in fatigue, reverie and sleep, as well as during conflicts, violent emotion and insanity. The chief indices of differentiated conjunctive regnancies are these: alertness, nicety of perceptual and apperceptual discrimination, long endurance of a trend of complex action, increasingly effective changes of actone, rapidity of learning, coherence, relevance and concentration of thought, absence of conflict, introspective awareness and self-criticism.

23. Because of the position of regnancies at the summit of the hierarchy of controlling centres in the body, and because of certain institutions established in the brain which influence the regnancies, the latter (constituting as they do the personality) must be distinguished from the rest of the body. The rest of the body is as much outside the personality as the environment is outside personality. Thus we may study the effects of illness, drugs, endocrine activity and other somatic changes upon the personality in the same fashion as we study the changes produced by hot climate, strict discipline or warfare. In this sense, regnant processes stand between an inner and an outer world.

24. There is a continuous interaction between regnancies and other processes in the body. . . .

25. *Time-binding.* Man is a "time-binding" organism, which is a way of saying that, by conserving some of the past and anticipating some of the future, a human being can, to a significant degree, make his behaviour accord with events that have happened as well as those that are to come. Man is not a mere creature of the moment, at the beck and call of a stimulus or drive. What he does is related not only to the settled past but also to shadowy preconceptions of what lies ahead. Years in advance he makes preparations to observe an eclipse of the sun from a distant island in the South Pacific and, lo, when the moment comes he is there to record the event. With the same confidence another man prepares to meet his god. Man lives in an inner

world of expected press (pessimistic or optimistic), and the psychologist must take cognizance of them if he wishes to understand his conduct or his moods, his buoyancies, disappointments, resignations. Time-binding makes for continuity of purpose.

THE CONCEPT OF NEED OR DRIVE[4]

A need is a hypothetical process the occurrence of which is imagined in order to account for certain objective and subjective facts. . . . Though the introduction of new terms is sometimes confusing and should be avoided if possible, I require, at this point, a single term which will refer only to bodily movements as such (the mechanisms, means, ways, modes) and not at all to the effects of such movements. The word "action" cannot be used because it is commonly employed to describe both the movements and the effect of the movements. Hoping, then, for the reader's tolerance, I shall introduce the term *actone* to stand for any action pattern *qua* action pattern. And, since action patterns are mostly of two sorts, I shall divide *actones* into: motones (muscular-motor action patterns) and verbones (verbal action patterns).

A motone is a temporal series of more or less organized muscular contractions and a verbone is a temporal series of more or less organized words or written symbols. The verbone is constituted by the actual words used. The intended or actual effect of a verbone is something quite different.

Now, since the first systematic step in the construction of any science is that of classification, we, as students of behaviour, must find proper criteria for distinguishing one form of conduct from another. The problem arises, shall we classify in terms of actones or in terms of effects? We may, of course, and shall, eventually, classify according to both criteria, but the question is, which method is more profitable for scientific purposes? We can predict that the two classifications will not correspond. According to one method we shall find in each category a number of similar actones, and according to the other method we shall find in each category a number of similar effects. Since it is obvious that similar actones—putting food in the mouth and putting poison in the mouth—may have different effects, and different actones—putting poison in the mouth and pulling the trigger of a revolver—may have similar effects, *the aspects of conduct that are described when we classify in terms of actones are different from those described when we classify in terms of effects.*

Practical experience has led me to believe that of the two the classification in terms of effects organizes for our understanding something that is more fundamental than what is organized by the classification in terms of actones:

1. Physical survival depends upon the attainment of certain effects; not upon what actones are employed.

[4]*Ibid.*, from pp. 54-61.

2. Certain effects are universally attained by living organisms, but the actones that attain them vary greatly from one species to another.

3. During the life history of a single individual certain effects are regularly attained, but actones change.

4. According to the Law of Effect, which is widely accepted in one or another of its modifications, the actones which become habitual are for the most part those which, in the past, have led most directly to "satisfying" end situations. Hence, effects determine what actones become established.

5. When confronted by a novel situation, an organism commonly persists in its "efforts" to bring about a certain result, but with each frustration it is apt to change its mode of attack. . . .

6. There are some effects which can only be attained by entirely novel actones.

7. That actones are of secondary importance is shown by the fact that many biologically necessary effects may be brought about by the activity of another person. . . .

At this point a new concept should be introduced, for there are many acts which, because of some accident or because of the organism's lack of innate or acquired ability, never reach an end situation, that is, the total effect is never realized. In such cases, the direction of the movements is usually evident enough, or their preliminary result sufficient, to allow an experienced observer to predict with a reasonable degree of accuracy what total effect is being promoted. Such a succession of minor, subsidiary effects (sub-effects) may be called a *trend*. Thus, a *trend* describes the direction of movements *away from* the B.S. [initial existing conditions]—movements which, if unembarrassed, would reach a certain kind of E.S. [conditions that exist at the cessation of activity]. By the use of this concept we may include for classification actions which, though incomplete, manifest a tendency to achieve a certain end.

"Trend" should be a satisfactory term for psychologists who admit the directional character of behaviour but do not wish to employ a concept that points to something "behind" the tangible facts. . . .

On the basis of this characterization we have constructed a hypothetical entity which has been termed a *need* (or *drive*). Each need has (a) a typical directional or qualitative aspect (B = E) [effect produced], form, which differentiates it from other needs, as well as (b) an energetic or quantitative aspect, which may be estimated in a variety of ways. Thus, the first and best criterion for distinguishing a certain need is the production by the subject of a certain effect, or, if not this, the occurrence of a certain trend.

> Between what we can directly observe—the stimulus and the resulting action—a need is an invisible link, which may be imagined to have the properties that an understanding of the observed phenomena demand. "Need" is, therefore, a hypothetical concept.

Strictly speaking, a need is the immediate outcome of certain internal and external occurrences. It comes into being, endures for a moment and perishes. It is not a static entity. It is a resultant of forces. One need succeeds another. Though each is unique, observation teaches that there are similarities among them, and on the basis of this, needs may be grouped together into classes, each class being, as it were, a single major need. Thus, we may speak of similar needs as being different exhibitions of *one need,* just as when we recognize a friend we do not hesitate to call him by name though he is different from the person with whom we conversed yesterday. Between the different appearances of a certain kind of need there may be nothing to suggest it, but everyday experience and experiment show that if the proper conditions are provided, the need (i.e., another manifestation of the same kind of need) will be activated. Thus, we may loosely use the term "need" to refer to an organic potentiality or readiness to respond in a certain way under given conditions. In this sense a need is a latent attribute of an organism. More strictly, it is a noun which stands for the fact that a certain trend is apt to recur. We have not found that any confusion arises when we use "need" at one time to refer to a temporary happening and at another to refer to a more or less consistent trait of personality.

Needs, Viscerogenic and Psychogenic[5]

Needs may be conveniently divided into: 1, primary (viscerogenic) needs, and 2, secondary (psychogenic) needs. The former are engendered and stilled by characteristic periodic bodily events, whereas the latter have no subjectively localizable bodily origins; hence the term "psychogenic." They are occasioned by regnant tensions, with or without emotion, that are closely dependent upon certain external conditions or upon images depicting these conditions. Thus, speaking loosely, we may say that from a subjective standpoint the viscerogenic needs have to do with physical satisfactions and the psychogenic needs with mental or emotional satisfactions.

The viscerogenic needs are: 1, n Air, 2, n Water, 3, n Food, 4, n Sex, 5, n Lactation, 6, n Urination, 7, n Defecation, 8, n Harmavoidance, 9, n Noxavoidance, 10, n Heatavoidance, 11, n Coldavoidance, and 12, n Sentience. We also recognize a need for Passivity, which includes relaxation, rest and sleep, but this may be neglected for the present. . . .

The secondary or psychogenic needs, which are presumably dependent upon and derived from the primary needs, may be briefly listed. They stand for common reaction systems and wishes. It is not supposed that they are fundamental, biological drives, though some may be innate. The first five pertain chiefly to actions associated with inanimate objects.

n *Acquisition* (Acquisitive attitude). To gain possessions and property. To grasp, snatch or steal things. To bargain or gamble. To work for money or goods.
n *Conservance* (Conserving attitude). To collect, repair, clean and preserve things. To protect against damage.

[5]*Ibid.,* from pp. 76-124.

n Order (Orderly attitude). To arrange, organize, put away objects. To be tidy and clean. To be scrupulously precise.

n Retention (Retentive attitude). To retain possession of things. To refuse to give or lend. To hoard. To be frugal, economical and miserly.

n Construction (Constructive attitude). To organize and build.

Actions which express what is commonly called ambition, will-to-power, desire for accomplishment and prestige have been classified as follows:

n Superiority (Ambitious attitude). This has 'been broken up into two needs: the n Achievement (will to power over things, people and ideas) and the n Recognition (efforts to gain approval and high social status).

n Achievement (Achievant attitude). To overcome obstacles, to exercise power, to strive to do something difficult.

n Recognition (Self-forwarding attitude). To excite praise and commendation. To demand respect. To boast and exhibit one's accomplishments. To seek distinction, social prestige, honours and high office.

n Exhibition (Exhibitionistic attitude). To attract attention to one's person. To excite, amuse, stir, shock, thrill others. Self-dramatization.

Complementary to Achievement and Recognition are the desires and actions which involve the defence of status or the avoidance of humiliation.

n Inviolacy (Inviolate attitude). This includes desires and attempts to prevent a depreciation of self-respect, to preserve one's "good name," to be immune from criticism, to maintain psychological "distance." It is based on pride and personal sensitiveness. . . .

n Infavoidance (Infavoidant attitude). To avoid failure, shame, humiliation, ridicule. To refrain from attempting to do something that is beyond one's powers. To conceal a disfigurement.

n Defendance (Defensive attitude). To defend oneself against blame or belittlement. To justify one's actions. To offer extenuations, explanations and excuses. To resist "probing."

n Counteraction (Counteractive attitude). Proudly to overcome defeat by restriving and retaliating. To select the hardest tasks. To defend one's honour in action.

The next five needs have to do with human power exerted, resisted or yielded to. . . .

n Dominance (Dominative attitude). To influence or control others. To persuade, prohibit, dictate. To lead and direct. To restrain. To organize the behaviour of a group.

n Deference (Deferent attitude). To admire and willingly follow a superior allied O (object). To co-operate with a leader. To serve gladly.

n Similance (Suggestible attitude). To emphasize. To imitate or emulate. To identify oneself with others. To agree and believe.

n Autonomy (Autonomous attitude). To resist influence or coercion. To defy an authority or seek freedom in a new place. To strive for independence.

n Contrarience (Contrarient attitude). To act differently from others. To be unique. To take the opposite side. To hold unconventional views.

The next two needs constitute the familiar sado-masochistic dichotomy. . . .

n Aggression (Aggressive attitude). To assault or injure an O. To mur-

der. To belittle, harm, blame, accuse or maliciously ridicule a person. To punish severely. Sadism.
n *Abasement* (Abasive attitude). To surrender. To comply and accept punishment. To apologize, confess, atone. Self-depreciation. Masochism.

The next need has been given a separate status because it involves a subjectively distinguishable form of behaviour, namely *inhibition*. Objectively, it is characterized by the absence of socially unacceptable conduct. . . .

n *Blamavoidance* (Blamavoidance attitude). To avoid blame, ostracism or punishment by inhibiting asocial or unconventional impulses. To be well-behaved and obey the law.

The next four needs have to do with affection between people; seeking it, exchanging it, giving it, or withholding it.

n *Affiliation* (Affiliative attitude). To form friendships and associations. To greet, join, and live with others. To co-operate and converse sociably with others. To love. To join groups.
n *Rejection* (Rejective attitude). To snub, ignore or exclude an O. To remain aloof and indifferent. To be discriminating.
n *Nurturance* (Nurturant attitude). To nourish, aid or protect a helpless O. To express sympathy. To "mother" a child.
n *Succorance* (Succorant attitude). To seek aid, protection or sympathy. To cry for help. To plead for mercy. To adhere to an affectionate, nurturant parent. To be dependent.

To these may be added with some hesitation:

n *Play* (Playful attitude). To relax, amuse oneself, seek diversion and entertainment. To "have fun," to play games. To laugh, joke and be merry. To avoid serious tension.

Finally, there are two complementary needs which occur with great frequency in social life, the need to ask and the need to tell.

n *Cognizance* (Inquiring attitude). To explore (moving and touching). To ask questions. To satisfy curiosity. To look, listen, inspect. To read and seek knowledge.
n *Exposition* (Expositive attitude). To point and demonstrate. To relate facts. To give information, explain, interpret, lecture.

*   *   *   *   *

Under sex has been subsumed:

1. The sex instinct proper, as biologists have described it, that is, the force which leads to the development of sexual characteristics and to intercourse between the sexes (n Sex).

2. All tendencies which seek and promote sensuous gratification (n Sentience), particularly the enjoyment of tactile sensations originating in certain sensitive regions of the body (the erogenous zones). Thus, analysts speak of oral, anal, urethral and genital eroticism.

Periodicity of Needs

Many of the viscerogenic needs are characterized by rather regular rhythms of activity and rest, rhythms which seem to be determined by an

orderly succession of physiological events: inspiration and expiration, inges-
tion and excretion, waking and sleeping. . . .

For convenience, a single need cycle may be divided into: 1, a *refractory*
period, during which no incentive will arouse it; 2, an *inducible* or *ready*
period, during which the need is inactive but susceptible to excitation by appropriate stimuli; and 3, an *active* period, during which the need is determining the behaviour of the total organism.

A need which is aroused in a subject and not completely objectified may
perseverate for some time afterwards. During this period the subject will
meet situations that present themselves with a *need set*. That is to say, the
need in question will be in a state of high *inducibility* or high *readiness*, with
a low *threshold of stimulation*. For example, if it is anger (n Aggression)
that has been aroused, the subject will be apt to vent his emotion upon the
first object that crosses his path, the object, in such a case, being called the
substitute object (Freud). . . .

Fusion of Needs

When a single action pattern satisfies two or more needs at the same time
we may speak of a fusion (F) of needs. Confluences of this kind are extremely common.

Subsidiation of Needs

When one or more needs are activated in the service of another need, we
may speak of the former as being *subsidiary* (S) and the latter as being
determinant. The determinant need regulates the action from the beginning,
but may not itself become overt until the terminal phase of the total event. . . .

Conflicts

Needs may come into conflict (C) with each other within the personality,
giving rise when prolonged to harassing spiritual dilemmas. Much of the
misery and most of the neurotic illness in the world may be attributed to
such inner conflicts.

Needs, Emotions and Affections

Without pretending to settle anything we may state that for us "emotion
is a *hypothetical concept* that stands for an excitatory process in the brain
—most probably in the interbrain (thalamic region)—that may manifest itself subjectively and objectively or both. Thus an emotion may occur without
the subject's being aware of it (unconscious emotion). Usually it is felt, the
subjective manifestation being that quality of an experience which is generally designated by the word "emotional" ("excited"). The objective manifestation is a compound of autonomic disturbances ("autonome"), affective actones, and the intensification or disorganization of effective behaviour
(motor and verbal). Sometimes the faintest moistening of an eye or the
quiver of the voice is enough for a diagnosis. At other times the experi-

menter requires more evidence: the occurrence of a sufficient press, signs of vegetative upset, characteristic tremors, gestures and exclamations, confusion of thought, disorganization of actones and a subjective report of having been "much upset." . . .

We are using the word "affection" to refer to hedonic feelings: pleasure, happiness, "eupathy," contentment and elation (positive affection), and unpleasure, unhappiness, "dyspathy," discontent and dejection (negative affection). . . .

Affection is considered to be a hypothetical concept which stands for some process in the brain—probably in the interbrain—that manifests itself subjectively as feelings of pleasure or unpleasure (which vary in intensity), and objectively (with much less clearness) as a compound of affective actones (a certain bearing, demeanour, intonation of speech, tempo of movement, etc.). Our most direct information about feelings must come from introspection, but it should not be supposed that an affection (as defined above) is always or even usually conscious.

Needs, Actones, Vectors

The word "actone" has been used to stand for a simple bodily movement, such as pouting, lowering the eyes, smiling, coughing, extending the hand (simple motone); a compound of movements, such as rising from a recumbent position, walking, manipulating, kneeling and bowing (complex motone); a single word or phrase, such as "Yes," "Hurry up," "I like you," "Go to Hell" (simple verbone); and a compound of words, such as occurs in a long conversation or speech (complex verbone). Now, these are all objective occurrences and they may be recorded and measured in terms of frequency, speed (tempo), strength (emphasis), duration, conjunctivity (organization) and a host of other defining dimensions. Many of these actones are commonly considered to be outward signs of a particular emotional state, whereas others are regarded as manifestations of temperament or temper. The term "expressive movements," which indicates that these events reveal something that is "inside" and are not to be taken merely as patterns, is currently used to include all such phenomena. . . .

There is, in addition to the actonal viewpoint, another conception which remains to be considered. It is one which affirms that all people have the same needs in the same measure and, consequently, they cannot be differentiated on this basis; what distinguishes them are the modes (other than actones) which they employ to satisfy their needs. . . . But besides these and others, there are modes which are distinguishable according to the type or general direction of spatial movement. For example, adience and abience describe movements towards and away from external objects. Following Lewin, these may be termed *vectors* (v). The Adience vector furthers the positive needs (Food, Sex, Sentience, Achievement, Recognition, Affiliation, Deference, Nurturance, Dominance, Exhibition, Succorance), whereas the Abience vector favours the negative needs (Harmavoidance, Noxavoidance, Blamavoidance, Infavoidance). . . . This gives us a dichotomy that roughly corresponds to extraversion-introversion.

* * * * *

Cathected Objects, Interests

An object (O) that evokes a need is said to "have cathexis" (c) or to "be cathected" (by the subject or by the need). This is one of Freud's valuable concepts. If the object evokes a positive adient need (indicating that the S (subject) likes the O) it is said to have a positive cathexis (value); if it evokes a positive contrient or a negative abient need (indicating that the S dislikes the O) it is said to have a negative cathexis. Such cathexes may be temporary or enduring. . . .

A personality is largely revealed in the objects that it cathects (values or rejects), especially if the intensity, endurance and rigidity of each cathection is noted, and if observation is extended to the cathected groups with which the individual is *affiliated* (has "belongingness"). In this fashion a reasonably adequate portrait of the social personality may be composed. Institutions and cultures can also be profitably analysed from the standpoint of their cathected objects, what they value and what they depreciate.

* * * * *

Need Integrates

Everyday observation instructs that with development each need tends to attach itself (to be commonly evoked by) certain objects or certain classes of objects, other objects or classes being disregarded. And, likewise, each cathected object attaches to *itself* an aggregate or fusion of needs. Also, certain characteristic modes (actones, sub-trends, agency objects and pathways) become quite regularly utilized in connection with these needs and objects. Such consistencies of connection lead to the conception of relatively stable organizations in the brain, a notion which is substantiated by introspection. One might say that traces (images) of cathected objects in familiar settings become integrated in the mind with the needs and emotions which they customarily excite, as well as with images of preferred modes. A hypothetical compound of this sort may be called a *need integrate,* or *complex.* The integrate may enter consciousness as a fantasy or plan of action, or, under appropriate circumstances, it may be objectified, in which case it can be operationally defined as a reaction pattern that is evoked by certain conditions.

* * * * *

Manifest and Latent Needs

Need integrates commonly become objectified and exhibit themselves in overt action, when they are aroused. One can observe repeatedly in some people the same directional tendency carried along by the same mode towards the same object. Integrates of this sort tend to become loosely organized into a characteristic temporal sequence: a daily schedule which gives shape to a person's life. Some need integrates, however, do not become objectified in real action when evoked. They take one of a number of other forms, all of which we have termed latent. "Covert" or "imaginal" would have been a happier word, since in these cases the complexes are not strictly speaking latent. They are active fantasies which are merely not manifested objectively, or, if so manifested, follow an "irreal" (Lewin's term) course.

*　　*　　*　　*　　*

Conscious and Unconscious Needs

It is important to distinguish the needs which are relatively *conscious* from those which are relatively *unconscious* (un). By consciousness we mean introspective or, more accurately, immediately-retrospective awareness. Whatever a subject can report upon is considered conscious; everything else which, by inference, was operating in the regnancy is considered unconscious. According to this convenient pragmatic criterion, consciousness depends upon verbalization. Thus, conscious facts (for the experimenter) are limited to those which the subject is able to recall. Consequently, in all organisms below man every regnant variable, being unverbalizable, is treated as if it were unconscious.

Definition of Need

Marshalling the facts and reflections reviewed in this section it is possible to enlarge upon our initial definition of a need.

A need is a construct (a convenient fiction or hypothetical concept) which stands for a force (the physico-chemical nature of which is unknown) in the brain region, a force which organizes perception, apperception, intellection, conation and action in such a way as to transform in a certain direction an existing unsatisfying situation. A need is sometimes provoked directly by internal processes of a certain kind (viscerogenic, endocrinogenic, thalamicogenic) arising in the course of vital sequences, but, more frequently (when in a state of readiness) by the occurrence of one of a few commonly effective press (or by anticipatory images of such press). Thus, it manifests itself by leading the organism to search for or avoid encountering or, when encountered, to attend and respond to certain kinds of press. It may even engender illusory perceptions and delusory apperceptions (projections of its imagined press into unsuitable objects). Each need is characteristically accompanied by a particular feeling or emotion and tends to use certain modes (sub-needs and actones) to further its trend. It may be weak or intense, momentary or enduring. But usually it persists and gives rise to a certain course of overt behaviour (or fantasy), which (if the organism is competent and external opposition not insurmountable) changes the initiating circumstance in such a way as to being about an end situation which stills (appeases or satisfies) the organism.

From this definition it appears that the indices by which an overt or manifest need can be distinguished are these:

1. A typical behavioural trend or effect (transformation of external conditions).

2. A typical mode (actones or sub-effects).

3. The search for, avoidance or selection of, attention and response to one of a few types of press (cathected objects of a certain class).

4. The exhibition of a characteristic emotion or feeling.

5. The manifestation of satisfaction with the achievement of a certain effect (or with a gratuity), or the manifestation of dissatisfaction when there is failure to achieve a certain effect.

* * * * *

CONCEPTS OF PRESS AND THEMA

Press

It may be readily seen that when the objects of the environment are human or animal, they can be symbolized as the subject is symbolized in terms of this or that drive. The natural environment, as we shall see, may be treated in much the same fashion. Thus, the external world appears in the guise of a dynamical process and the complete behavioural event as an interaction of forces.

We have selected the term *press* (plural *press*) to designate a directional tendency in an object or situation. Like a need, each press has a qualitative aspect—the kind of effect which it has or might have upon the subject (if the S comes in contact with it and does not react against it)—as well as a quantitative aspect, since its power for harming or benefiting varies widely. Everything that can supposedly harm or benefit the well-being of an organism may be considered *pressive*, everything else *inert*. The process in the subject which recognizes what is being done to him at the moment (that says "this is good" or "this is bad") may be conveniently termed *pressive perception*. The process is definitely egocentric, and gives rise almost invariably to some sort of adaptive behaviour.

Most stimulus situations are not in themselves directly effective. As such, they are not harms or benefits to the organism. But they are potent evokers of behaviour because they appear as signs of something that is to come. Some people, for example, are more disturbed by omens of disaster than they are by actual misfortune; and others are more thrilled by thoughts of future events than by these events when they occur. Similarly, there is such a thing as fore-pleasure and fore-unpleasure. Indeed, the power of a stimulus situation does not usually depend upon *pressive per-*

ception—"the object is doing this or that to me"—but rather upon *pressive apperception*—"the object may do this to me (if I remain passive) or I may use the object in this or that way (if I become active)."

*   *   *   *   *

What we have been describing is the external world in the guise of a psychological environment: objects in changing settings characterizable as foods, poisons, sensuous patterns, supports, harbingers of danger, friends, guides, enemies, suppliants that are prospective of certain consequences if approached, manipulated, embraced, commanded, flattered, obeyed or otherwise responded to. The *press* of an object is what it can *do to the subject* or *for the subject*—the power that it has to affect the well-being of the subject in one way or another. The cathexis of an object, on the other hand, is what it can *make the subject do*.

In our work we concentrated upon press that were manifested by human objects (mobile, autonomous press) and we enlarged the notion to include lacks and losses of positive press (ex.: a barren monotonous environment, lack of food objects, poverty, no friends, etc.). A few illustrations will suffice:

p Affiliation, a friendly, sociable companion
p Nurturance, a protective, sympathetic ally
p Aggression, a combative O, or one who censures, belittles or fleers
p Rival (Recognition), a competitor for honours
p Lack (Economic), the condition of poverty
p Dominance, Restraint, an imprisoning or prohibiting object.

The diagnosis of press is fraught with the same difficulty as the diagnosis of need. It is always an interpretation, but an important one. Every individual must make such guesses many times a day: "Will this object please and benefit me, or will it displease and harm me?" The knowledge of what is good and what is bad for man is a large part of wisdom. In identifying press we have found it convenient to distinguish between 1, the *alpha* press, which is the press that actually exists, as far as scientific inquiry can determine it; and 2, the *beta* press, which is the subject's own interpretation of the phenomena that he perceives. An object may, in truth, be very well disposed towards the subject—press of Affiliation (*alpha* press)—but the subject may misinterpret the object's conduct and believe that the object is trying to depreciate him—press of Aggression: Belittlement (*beta* press). When there is wide divergence between the *alpha* and *beta* press we speak of delusion.

*   *   *   *   *

Concept of Thema

A thema is the dynamical structure of an event on a molar level. A simple thema is the combination of a particular press or pre-action or outcome (o) and a particular need. It deals with the general nature of the environment and the general nature of the subject's reaction. For example:

p Rejection → *n Rejection:* The S is rejected (snubbed by the O) and responds in kind.

o Failure → *n Achievement:* The S makes renewed, counteractive attempts to succeed after failure.

Thus, a thema exhibits the press of the stimulus to which a subject is exposed when he reacts the way he does. Since fantasies as well as actual events have themas, every need integrate is also a thematic tendency, the theory being that in such cases there is an inhibited need for a particular form of behaviour to be aroused by a press which the individual secretly (perhaps unconsciously) hopes to find embodied in some actual person. In our experience, the unconscious (*alter ego*) of a person may be formulated best as an assemblage or federation of thematic tendencies.

THEMATIC APPERCEPTION TEST[6]

Purpose

The purpose of this procedure is to stimulate literary creativity and thereby evoke fantasies that reveal covert and unconscious complexes.

The test is based upon the well-recognized fact that when a person interprets an ambiguous social situation he is apt to expose his own personality as much as the phenomenon to which he is attending. Absorbed in his attempt to explain the objective occurrence, he becomes naïvely unconscious of himself and of the scrutiny of others and, therefore, defensively less vigilant. To one with double hearing, however, he is disclosing certain inner tendencies and cathexes: wishes, fears, and traces of past experiences. Another fact which was relied upon in devising the present method is this: that a great deal of written fiction is the conscious or unconscious expression of the author's experiences of fantasies.

The original plan was to present subjects with a series of pictures each of which depicted a dramatic event of some sort with instructions to interpret the action in each picture and make a plausible guess as to the preceding events and the final outcome. It was anticipated that in the performance of this task a subject would necessarily be forced to project some of his own fantasies into the material and thus reveal his more prevailing thematic tendencies. As the subjects who took this test were asked to interpret each picture—that is, to apperceive the plot or dramatic structure exhibited by each picture—we named it the "Thematic Apperception Test." Only by experience did we discover that much more of the personality is revealed if the S is asked to create a dramatic fiction rather than to guess the probable facts.

[6]*Ibid.*, from pp. 530-34. Much of this material is taken from C. D. Morgan and H. A. Murray, "A Method for Investigating Fantasies," *Arch. Neur. and Psychiat.*, XXXIV (1935), from pp. 289-306.

Since, for purposes of comparison, it is desirable to devise a procedure which is as uniform as possible, the attempt was made to arrive at a set of pictures which could be considered standard. Each picture should suggest some critical situation, and be effective in evoking a fantasy relating to it. The set must be comprehensive. Ideally, there should be a picture which could act as a trellis to support the unfolding of every primal fantasy. It was considered, and the idea was later confirmed by experience, that in most pictures there should be at least one person *(evocative object)* with whom the subject could easily empathize and identify himself. Thus, there should be a separate set of pictures for males and females, and also for children, young adults and elders. Since in the present experiments the subjects were all young men between the ages of twenty and thirty, most of the pictures in our set included at least one figure of that sex and age. After a preliminary selection from several hundred pictures and an elimination of those which on repeated trials proved unproductive, we arrived at a set of twenty which gave good results.

Procedure

The subject was seated in a comfortable chair with his back to the experimenter and the following directions were read to him:

This is a test of your creative imagination. I shall show you a picture and I want you to make up a plot or story for which it might be used as an illustration. What is the relation of the individuals in the picture? What has happened to them? What are their present thoughts and feelings? What will be the outcome? Do your best. Since I am asking you to indulge your literary imagination you may make your story as long and as detailed as you wish.

The subject was then handed picture No. 1 and the experimenter wrote down everything he said. If, in giving his story, the subject omitted the antecedent circumstances or the outcome, he was prompted by such remarks as, "What led up to this situation?" "How will it end?" and so forth. When the subject finished his story he was handed picture No. 2 and asked to proceed as before. There were twenty pictures in the series, but as the test was stopped after an hour, most of the subjects did not have time to make up stories for more than two-thirds of them.

After a few days had elapsed each subject was interviewed. This time the experimenter explained that he was studying the factors which operate in the imaginative construction of literary plots, and that he wished to know whether what eminent writers had written about their creative experiences was true for everyone. The subject was asked whether he would co-operate by saying what came to his mind when certain words or topics were mentioned. The S was then reminded one by one of the more important items or situations which he had recounted. The S was also asked whether his story had come from something which he had seen or read or whether it had come out of his personal experience.

Results

Examination of the stories concocted by our subjects in conjunction with material obtained from introspections, autobiographies, hours of free association, interviews and so forth, shows that there were four chief sources from which the plots and the items of the plots were drawn: 1, books and moving pictures; 2, actual events in which a friend or member of the family participated; 3, experiences (subjective or objective) in the subject's own life; and 4, the subject's conscious and unconscious fantasies.

Although the material from the first two of these four sources may seem at first blush to be of little importance, it was discovered that even here much of significance was revealed. It would appear that the external events which excite sympathetic vibrations (empathy) within the psyche are generally those which make the deepest impression and are most enduringly remembered, and so when we hear the recounting of such events we may tentatively suppose that the theme of the objective occurrence is a clue to the subject's personality.

That every subject almost immediately projects his own circumstances, experiences or preoccupations into the evocative object was only too obvious. For instance, in one of the early experiments six of the eleven college men who took the test said that the youth in one picture was a student; whereas none of the twelve non-college men who acted as subjects described him as such. To take another case, one of our subjects, whose father had been a ship's carpenter, wanted to go to sea himself, to travel and see the world. This was his dominant fantasy. In his stories three of the scenes were laid on board ship, two in the Orient. About a picture which illustrates a middle-aged man talking to a younger man, the subject said: "The older man is educated and has traveled a lot. He convinces the other to travel; to take a job that will take him to different places." In a picture which illustrates a young man sitting in a chair brooding rather disconsolately, this subject said: "This is a business man who runs quite a business in town. He is weighing the possibility of a European trip. He has been arguing with his wife on the subject. She got angry because he would not go, and finally took up her hat and left. He is thinking it over. He changes his opinion, goes out and buys tickets." In another picture illustrating two labourers engaged in conversation, the same subject said: "These two fellows are a pair of adventurers. They always manage to meet in out-of-the-way places. They are now in India. They have heard of a new revolution in South America, and they are planning how they can get there. . . . In the end they work their way on a freighter."

Many other examples of this sort of thing could be cited. No subject failed to exemplify it. Some of them, in fact, gave stories which were frank and unabashed autobiographies.

If the procedure had merely exposed conscious fantasies and remembered events it would have been useful enough, but it did more than this. It gave the experimenter excellent clues for the divination of unconscious thematic formation. The following mode of analysis and summary was used: each of the subject's stories was read and diagnosed separately and then the attempt was made to find a unifying thema. If such was evident, each story, if necessary, was re-interpreted and with some elimination and curtailment the series was re-arranged in such a way as to emphasize the important trends, and demonstrate their interrelations.

MISCELLANEOUS CONCEPTS[7]

Energy

Among the facts of subjective experience is the feeling or the quality of feeling to which the term "energy" is very commonly applied. Not only can an individual introspect at any moment and give an estimate of the degree to which he feels "energetic"; but his judgment will often be found to correspond with what an observer would say on the basis of external signs. Evidently we are dealing here with a continuum between two extreme states, subjectively and objectively discernible: *zest* and *apathy*. The various aspects of zest may be designated by such words as alertness, reactivity, vigilance, ardour, freshness, vitality, strength, "fire," "pep," verve, eagerness, ardour, intensity, enthusiasm, interest; whereas under apathy may be subsumed lassitude, lethargy, loginess, "brain fag," indolence, ennui, boredom, fatigue, exhaustion. The former state yields prompter, faster, stronger, more frequent and persistent reactions—reactions that are apt to be more correct, relevant, novel, adaptive, intelligent, imaginative or creative than those produced during the latter state. Zest is highly correlated with pleasure and activity (physical and mental), apathy with displeasure and inactivity.

To the topic of energy (vital energy, psychic energy) much thought and many words have been devoted, but, as yet, no theory acceptable to the majority of psychologists has been proposed. . . .

Divisions of the Personality:

        (1) The Id
        (2) The Superego System
        (3) The Ego System
        (4) Interests
        (5) The Habit System

The Id. This is the generic term under which all innate drives are subsumed, among which the viscerogenic needs should be especially emphasized. We are apt to use the term when we observe the excitation of emotional impulses associated with primitive actones (savage assault, panicky

[7]*Explorations in Personality, op. cit.,* from pp. 129-41.

fear, flagrant exhibitionistic sexuality). At such times conscious control is in abeyance and the individual merely reacts. He feels that he is overcome by irresistible forces outside himself. Strong temptations and compulsions are also assigned to this category.

The Id, however, is not composed entirely of active passions. The need for Passivity (which may manifest itself as indolence and slovenliness) belongs to it. Hence it is often necessary to stir up the Id instead of checking it.

Furthermore, all impulses of the Id are not asocial or antisocial as most analysts affirm. There are, for example, certain gregarious and conforming tendencies (empathy, imitation, identification) which operate instinctively and unconsciously. Also, the highest as well as the lowest forms of love come from the Id.

Viewing the Id from the point of view of perception and intelligence, we find that its operations are carried on by associations of imagery, mostly unconscious, that do not conform closely to the course of natural events. To the Id we ascribe hallucinations, delusions, irrational beliefs, as well as fantasies, intuitions, faith and creative conceptions. Thus almost everything, good and bad, has its primitive source in the Id.

The Superego System. The tpmo (time-place-mode-object) pattern, as a loose organization of "Do's" and "Don't's," preached and perhaps practised by the parents, asserted to be the only "Right," sanctioned by religion and strengthened by the image of an avenging deity, becomes, to a greater or less degree, internalized as a complex institution, known commonly as conscience. This may be termed the Superego system. A strong Superego is usually more exacting than current laws and conventions. It may be elevated far above worldly considerations by fusion with the Ego Ideal. It endures, with certain modifications, throughout life. It is, as it were, always there to influence the composition of regnancies. Its first function is to inhibit asocial tendencies, its second is to present cultural or religious aims as the "highest good." Its operations are largely unconscious.

The Ego System. Everyone has experienced "resolving to do something" or "selecting a purpose." Such an experience must modify the brain (i.e., must leave a latently perseverating disposition), because at some future date it will be found that behaviour is not the same as it would have been if the "resolving" experience had not occurred. Decisions and intentions of this sort—"accepting a goal," "planning a course of action," "choosing a vocation," as well as promises, compacts and "taking on responsibility" (all of them related to time-binding and the establishment of expectations and levels of aspiration)—seem to be attended by a relatively high degree of consciousness, and, what is more, by a feeling that the "self" is making the decision, freely *willing* the direction of its future conduct. We should say that such conscious fixations of aim were organized to form the "Ego system."

*   *   *   *   *

The concept of Ego emphasizes the determining significance of 1, conscious, freely-willed acts: making a resolution (with oneself) or a compact (with others) or dedicating oneself to a life-long vocation, all of which "bind" the personality over long periods of time; 2, the establishment of a cathected Ego Ideal (image of a figure one wants to become); and 3, the inhibition of drives that conflict with the above mentioned intentions, decisions and planned schedules of behaviour. One index of the degree of structuration (strength) of the Ego is the ability of an individual to "live by" his resolutions and compacts.

The Ego system stands, as it were, between the Id and the Superego. It may gradually absorb all the forces of the Id, employing them for its own purpose. Likewise, it may assimilate the Superego until the will of the individual is in strict accord with the best principles of his society. Under such circumstances what the individual feels that he wants to do coincides with what he has to do (as prescribed by his culture). The Ego, however, may side with the Id against the Superego. It may, for example, inhibit or repress the Superego and "decide" in favour of a criminal career. A strong Ego acts as mediator between Superego and Id; but a weak Ego is no more than a "battleground."

Interests. If we observe a series of objective episodes (external and overt trends) occurring in the life of an individual, we never fail to notice certain resemblances. The personality exhibits sameness. We say that the man possesses certain consistent traits. However, we can usually observe more than this. Viewing successive episodes over a sufficient span of time we can note developments. We can perceive that some episodes are the logical outgrowths of others and that together they form temporal systems bound together by the persistence (constant repetition) of one or more needs integrated with certain modes and directed towards certain cathected objects (things, people, institutions, ideologies). Every such system may be called an *interest* (complex need integrate).

The Habit System. Behaviour that has become automatic, that proceeds without much conscious intervention, that recurs repeatedly in the same form, may be conveniently ascribed to a *habit system*. This is formed by the structuralization (mechanization) of what has frequently recurred, whether determined by the Superego, the Ego or the Id. The habit system accounts for most rigidities, particularly those which the individual himself cannot abandon.

Thus, as we see it, regnancies are the resultants of external press, of freshly aroused needs (Id), of conscious intentions (Ego), of accepted cultural standards (Superego) and of customary modes of behaviour (habit system) in varying proportions. The relative strength of these influences determines what tendencies will be objectified.

This brings us to the end of this long, yet all-too-brief, summary of the theory and concepts that guided our researches.

CHAPTER **15**

GARDNER MURPHY

THE BIOSOCIAL THEORY
OF PERSONALITY

Murphy's BIOSOCIAL APPROACH TO PERSONALITY lays particular stress on the social factors influencing the cultivation and molding of personality. Because of his conviction that personality is capable of change, growth, and proper adjustment at any period in one's life, Murphy's outlook is pleasantly optimistic: man has the capacity for change and self-fulfillment through self-discovery or self-understanding.

The psychology of personality, Murphy believes, has made indolent advances: "Not much, I believe, is known about man; and what is known relates mostly to Homo sapiens as a species, not to persons as known to others and to themselves."[1] Murphy aspires to ameliorate the situation by writing "about personality in such a way as to help in clarifying the little that we know and to show its possible relations to the vast and confused domain that we do not yet understand—this is my aim."[2] Thus far, the data collected in this field are not of great value because "the psychology of personality is spreading in all directions, and no one can make it stand still to be assessed."[3]

Man, as a result of the process of discovering more and more

[1]*Personality: A Biosocial Approach to Origins and Structure* (New York: Harper, 1947), from p. ix.
[2]*Ibid.*
[3]*Ibid.*

357

about his nature, is undergoing a change himself: "The potentialities of this process are radically new kinds of human nature."[4] And, in *Human Potentialities*, Murphy writes: "I have believed for a long time that human nature is a reciprocity of what is inside the skin and what is outside; that is, definitely not 'rolled up inside us' but our way of being one with our fellows and our world. I call this field theory."[5]

Gardner Murphy was born on July 8, 1895, in Chillicothe, Ohio. His formal education in psychology began at Yale University, from which he received his A.B. in 1916; the following year he received the A.M. from Harvard University, and in 1923 the Ph.D. from Columbia University. After completing three years as Hodgson Fellow in Psychology at Harvard, he went to the Department of Psychology at Columbia University in 1925 and stayed there until 1940, when City College of New York appointed him Professor and Chairman of the Department of Psychology. At the invitation of the Indian government he spent 1950 in New Delhi, India, as a consultant on behalf of the United Nations Educational, Scientific, and Cultural Organization. The fruits of his efforts there were summed up and evaluated in his book, *In the Minds of Men* (1953). From 1952 to 1967, Murphy was in Topeka, Kansas, as Director of Research at the Menninger Foundation. The results of that research are found in his *Development of the Perceptual World* (with Charles M. Solley, 1960). Currently he is visiting professor at George Washington University.

Murphy's other major publications are *Experimental Social Psychology* (with Lois B. Murphy, 1931), *Approaches to Personality* (with F. Jensen, 1932), *Personality: A Biosocial Approach to Origins and Structure* (1947), "The Nature of Man" in *Stephanos: Studies in Psychology Presented to Cyril Burt* (ed. by C. Banks and P. L. Broadhurst, 1965), and "Psychological Views of Personality and Contributions to Its Study" in *The Study of Personality* (ed. by E. Norbeck et al., 1968).

THE BIOSOCIAL APPROACH TO THE STUDY OF PERSONALITY[6]

There are two current uses of the term "personality," which involve basic differences in point of view and method. In the commoner usage the term

---

[4]"A Cosmic Christmas Carol," *Saturday Review*, December 13, 1958, from p. 47.
[5]*Human Potentialities* (New York: Basic Books, 1958), from p. viii.
[6]*Personality: A Biosocial Approach*, op. cit., from pp. 1-26.

embraces the sphere of *individual differences,* or such of these differences as are relatively persistent, or such of them as are effective and volitional as distinct from intellectual. Thus a psychology of personality deals with all the individual aspects of a given human organism except for certain expressly excluded ones. It is a catalogue of certain human variabilities. The second usage embraces the thing which all personalities, *as such,* possess—the thing that marks off a personality from all other objects, such as a tree or a triangle. From this vantage point one tries to discover the nature of personality in general, as he might try to discover the nature of trees in general. This double usage of the term is natural and inevitable, because we are interested both in man in general and in the individual man for his own sake. But an author must say what he means; and if he writes a book about two subjects at once, bracketed under a common term, he must "show cause."

Both of these conceptions of personality have to be used, but in every discussion of personality it makes a considerable difference where interest lies. In the present volume the emphasis is upon the general rather than upon the particular; we are more interested in formulating a working conception of personality than in endeavoring to define in detail the infinite variability of personalities. It is hard to see what serious purpose could be served by attempting a catalogue of all the individual differences in all the traits known to psychology—a manual of human diversities. Inventories of definable traits and full descriptions of the ways of studying and measuring them have already given place, as the literature has piled up, to more specifically defined trait areas; there are compact summaries of childhood social traits, of vocationally significant traits in the adolescent, of methods of identifying and measuring adult socio-economic attitudes.

But there is another reason for preferring the general to the particular. The man who tells you about the peculiarities of a radio must think and talk in terms proceeding from the general properties of radios; it is out of the general consideration of radio construction that the meaning of a particular emerges. Personality traits, in inventories or elsewhere, presuppose a working conception as to what traits are and, a fortiori, a working conception as to what a personality is. For the present writer at least, it is compellingly necessary to keep the focus on the central problem of defining the nature of personality, drawing upon data which clarify a working conception and allowing the particulars, the individual forms of response, in traits or in their mode of interrelation, to gather about the focus, just as an individual who is studying internal combustion engines or architectural form finds the specific engine and the specific cathedral more interesting and more meaningful when the general philosophy of the total construction precedes the analysis of particulars. Methods, which, like the case study or the biography or psychoanalysis, seek to understand the organized totality of a person are presumably richer in their perception of their problem when they are fortified by a broad and clear conception of the laws governing such totalities.

But if one is thinking of personality in general, is he not simply thinking of man in general? If one wishes to talk about man as man, man in the abstract, are there not already enough disciplines concerned with him? And is not general psychology itself, with its principles relating to perception, motivation, learning, thinking, sufficient to the theme? The answer will be in the affirmative if this general psychology includes and emphasizes the interactions, the organic wholeness of all these functions, and, in particular, the awareness of self and of individuality which is one of the central facts about being human. The use of the principles of general psychology in such a view of the whole individual would constitute, I believe, *general psychology of personality*, which deals with the universal fact of organization, and awareness of such organization and individuality, the sense of personal identity, continuity, distinctiveness, responsibility. This sense of personal identity will of course vary from man to man, but we are at the moment concerned solely with the legitimacy of a general inquiry into a general phenomenon.

Beneath all the limitless complexity of personal acts there is the general organic substratum, the system of organic potentialities—in short, the organism. This is approachable from many vantage points, by many techniques. When one combines several, and tries to see the whole organism at once, he may, if he wishes, say that he is studying personality. The organism the biologist studies and the personality the psychologist studies would be the same thing, except that the psychologist would tend to emphasize more complex functions, and more expressly indicate his desire to see all interrelations within the organism at once, as well as the hierarchy of laws governing those interrelations. Psychology of personality would then be that particular kind of general psychology that emphasizes totality and the organic systematic relations which obtain within it.

THREE LEVELS OF COMPLEXITY

At least three levels of complexity must be considered when confronting personality problems. Personality may be conceived, first, as an object or an event in a larger context—a dot on a chart, a billiard ball on a table. It is identifiable, strictly localized in time-space, and homogeneous. Its internal structure need not be considered. This view is useful in many sociological and some psychological problems, especially those of a statistical character. For example, just as we may compare large dots with small dots, or red balls with white, we may compare adults with children, men with women, Chinese with Japanese.

At a second level of complexity, personality may be likened to a chrysalis. It is again identifiable and strictly bounded, but it has internal structure. It is no longer homogeneous; it is organized. One chrysalis differs from another not only in size, weight, and color, as in the first-level analysis, but in the character of its constituent parts and their interrelations. This second level requires patient and penetrating consideration of the nature of the internal structure from one such chrysalis to another, and of problems of types, or classes of organization. This approach is currently being used more and more with great improvement in prediction and control.

At the third level of analysis, however, the chrysalis is an unsatisfactory model. It is encapsulated and it stays put. When you find one in the woods you may wonder whether there is still life in it. Something may have snuffed out its capacity to yield a butterfly. This something indicates that encapsulated though it was, it was not really self-contained. It could live only as long as a delicate relation obtained between its own structure and the outer structure of its habitat. The inner structure was supported and partly guided in its development by a field of external relations.

If this is true even of a chrysalis, it is much more compellingly true of the butterfly or the mouse or the man. Here there is even less encapsulation. The world of atmosphere, food, light, gravitation flows into the defenceless organism. The organism exists because outer changes and inner adjustments are nicely attuned, because in the broad sense of the evolutionist the organism evolved only so far as it maintained itself in intimate unity with the environment at each stage of its development—literally as a node in a physical field, defined, limited, governed by the field relations. The organism has a *practical boundary* for some purposes—for example, the skin and mucous membranes. The air we breathe is "within us" not when it passes valve-like barriers, but by degrees as it passes through nostrils, bronchi, the red blood cells and, with chemical reshuffling, back through veins and breath to the windowpane or to the people around us. To find a sharp barrier between self and non-self is a nice metaphysical task. If this is true of the simplest facts of biological existence, it is hard to see how people can be considered solely from the point of view of internal structure, of the personality that lies within the skin. If biology is right in considering the organism not as an encapsulated unit but as a node, an organizing point in a field, there is a level of analysis at which the man-world relation, the organism-environment field, may be studied.

Such a view may, if we wish, be called a *field* view, if we note that fields studied by biology are in a state of perpetual *redefinition.* Inner and outer structures are unstable; indeed, in the chemistry of nutrition and respiration there are structures which are neither outer nor inner, but lie in a zone where the two flow together or apart, moment by moment. The perpetually resulting changes mean that the time dimension is as essential to biology as it is to physics. The word "field" may remind us of the surveyor, and the maps used to portray a field are, after all, just maps; but world and self flow into one another. The boundary is often vague or non-existent, but the flow is always *directed* to some extent by the relations between the outer and inner structures.

No single word is likely to serve perfectly for this conception. The word "field" will perhaps serve if we expressly state that it is used as it is in physics; an electromagnetic field, for example, permits no strict demarcation of a boundary and may change continually as a result of varying currents.

All three conceptions of personality just indicated will need to be used. In discussing the simplest relations of age to behavior, the first will often suffice. In discussing the interaction of conflicting motives, the second will often be adequate; at least, it will suffice when we are gathering data about events within the organism (strictly, within the skin). When the thing we recognize as personality in our daily doings confronts us, we shall find ourselves pushing forward to the third level of analysis, knowing that in doing so we are abandoning simplicity, courting trouble, and raising far more questions than we can solve.

It has become accepted doctrine that we must attempt to study the whole man. Actually we cannot study even a whole tree or a whole guinea pig. But it is a whole tree and a whole guinea pig that have survived and evolved, and we must make the attempt. When it comes to studying the whole man, we are confronted by three ways in which he refuses to cooperate. First, his traits do not seem intelligible in their own right; they express something complicated going on inside. This is what has driven us from the first level to the second, namely, the study of inner structure. Second, some of the phases of this inner structure are hidden, pocketed off, oriented with respect to some long past situation which man had to confront; the students of conditioning and of psychoanalysis tell us we need to reconstruct the man historically after the manner of the archeologist. Often there is only a fragment, and the reconstruction fails or is incomplete. Third, the man is reacting to something in the present that we do not understand. We have, if you like, the response but not the stimulating situation, and we are driven into an arduous and often futile search for what the environmental structure means to him, so that the field relations will be clear.

But let us suppose that we succeed at all three levels. We discover events relating to the whole man as he is and as he changes. Since whole personalities in their interrelations make a society, we have, if our logic is sound, made a first approach to a theory of interpersonal relations, a theory of society. Man is a creature that responds to other men in as full a sense as he responds to oxygen or gravity; he is as fully anthropotropic as geotropic. Man as man is in some degree social; the inner-outer structure which is the product of a particular organism-culture interaction gives at the same time the first law of cultural reaction, the key to cultural nexus itself. If all the man and all of the culture—its geographic, economic, institutional patterns —are held in view at once, personality study becomes a biosocial, not only a biological pattern that embraces interorganism events.

But man is not only one with his immediate physical environment in the sense that he is enmeshed within it, and in the same sense enmeshed with his social environment. He is part of a still larger context, as an aspect not only of a community but of a cosmos. This is the cosmos which has, as one of its limitless propensities, the propensity of producing man. Man is the kind of creature that can love his Mother Earth, and the sun and stars beyond. Because, as man has wondered at the beauty of the world and striven with tubes and numbers to fathom it all, personality is actualized not only through his being drawn to other men but through his being drawn, as artist, to patterns of color and tone or, as scientist, to schemata in time and space. Such patterns are sought, seized, appropriated, lived for. Personality is social, but it is more. It is a drop of the cosmos, and its surface tensions bespeak only a fragile and indefinite barrier that marks a region of relative structuring, relative independence. This structuring and independence can exist only because they are relative, that is, because of the confluence of the self and the non-self. As the musician melts into and identifies with his beloved instrument, the Hopi Indian on the rim melts into his Grand Canyon.

Man is, then, a nodal region, an organized field with a larger field, a region of perpetual interaction, a reciprocity of outgoing and incoming energies. We shall need, from time to time, sharp definition of our terms, and visual schemata with which to show their relations to other terms. The three conceptions of personality may now be put into definitions and portrayed in such visual schemata.

1. A personality is a distinguishable individual, definable in terms of a qualitative and quantitative differentiation from other such individuals.

A, B, C, and *D* are individuals; their interrelations, their manifest external likenesses and differences, may be studied without reference to their internal organization, which need not even be portrayed.

2. A personality is a structured whole, definable in terms of its own distinctive structural attributes.

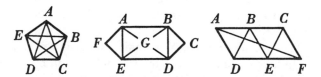

The letters constitute parts or attributes, such as the different organs of the body, which stand in specific interrelations.

3. A personality is a structured organism-environment field, each aspect of which stands in dynamic relation to each other aspect. There is organization within the organism and organization within the environment, but it is the cross organization of the two that is investigated in personality research.

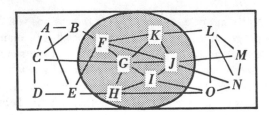

All the functional relations within the shaded area, and between the shaded and unshaded areas, constitute personality. The shaded area is the organism.

These three schemata are presented as if the organism were static, "frozen," at a moment of time. Considered developmentally and dynamically in the time dimension, the first would imply gradual qualitative or quantitative change (e.g., change in size or shape); the second would involve a reshuffling of inner relations (e.g., change in relative activity of parts, or inner equilibrium); the third would mean a reordering of inner-outer relations conjointly with a reordering of inner structure (e.g., the biosocial process by which personality adjustments at puberty involve simultaneous alterations of social demands upon the individual and of inner endocrine balance, so that the "changed personality" both reflects a biological change and is determined by a large field).

To illustrate the three standpoints: We may say from the first standpoint that each two-year-old has his own patterns of language; from the second, that these language patterns, though "acquired" from his environment, express his own inner pattern of needs and bodily dispositions; from the third, that both his own unique inner organization and his own unique personal environment are in intimate, fluid reciprocity; that just as his language reflects his whole organic system, it reflects the response of the system that envelops and engulfs it, and the outflowing response by which this system pervades and engulfs many aspects of the enveloping environment.

All three points of view have their regions of adequacy. All three, for example, take account of the reality of individual differences, and of both temporary and permanent forms of uniqueness. But in relation to developmental problems such as those just mentioned, the second has an advantage over the first, because the dynamics of change become clearer when attention is directed to the reordering of parts. The third view, moreover, has a considerable advantage over the second, because the uniqueness of the individual is seen to lie in his peculiar capacity for interaction with his environment, the peculiar field properties which, during growth, express his potential relation to his specific environmental situation, a situation which would draw out and express different reaction tendencies in any other organism. It is the interaction of the two that is available for study, and nothing psychological can be observed except in such interaction field.

Consequently, though the first two points of view will at times be sufficient, our preference for the third must be clearly indicated at the outset. We shall, in this way, attempt for personality study a point of view that has long been commonplace in the biological sciences, a view which emphasizes the full reciprocity of inner and outer events. This outer-inner reciprocity means that the *life process* is itself a matter of world as much as organism. The organism is structurally definable for some purposes in terms of an adaptation polarity which gives the environment pole the same relation of absolute necessity to the process, the field, as that held by the organism pole.

THE BIAS OF OUR CULTURE REGARDING PERSONALITY

Though this last principle is so central in biology, and though general psychology based upon biological conceptions has necessarily adopted it, it seems to have been given only scant attention in our studies of individual persons. These are conceived as self-contained objects of contemplation; pressed flowers, or gems, interesting or beautiful or instructive in themselves.

The reasons for this disparity of approach are clear and intelligible. First, there is and always has been, at least from Plato's time, a profound esthetic satisfaction in the contemplation of an ordered and self-contained unity. Persons are even more interesting and beautiful than gems. . . . The encysted person must be idealized because he is so obviously ideal—that is, in Plato's sense, the *real* person. For the Platonist, the fluctuations, the fuzzy boundaries characterize only the *apparent* person.

The other reason is the moralistic. People can be relied on if their boundaries are definite and fixed; you know where to put them; you know they will stay put. Above all, they can be held responsible. A society made up of persons of this sort can manage itself.

*   *   *   *   *

Psychological conceptions are regularly guided in some measure by esthetic, moralistic, and other normative attitudes. Personalities differ in value, but personality in general is "good." There are clear cultural-historical reasons for these attitudes. . . . Here and elsewhere I hope only to describe, not to sit in judgment. All these tendencies are natural and intelligible. So also are the counter-tendencies which arise in such eras of confusion and disillusionment: the picture of robots, "hairy apes." The counter-tendencies are themselves only facets of the truth, and any appreciation of or protest against these tendencies is merely another tendency to be put into its own perspective. But there is no danger that anyone will succeed in this century in getting the perspective completely right or, indeed, in defining what personality is.

If personality is half as complex as this suggests, it may be viewed in all sorts of ways and from all sorts of vantage points. There are perennial counter-views as to what it is: a primordial stuff; a pattern of accidentally imposed conditionings; an achieved inner structure; a cultural mold. Here, then, is much quarreling. But I have no stomach for these controversies. These views have all arisen in genuine efforts to seize the thing and to articulate what is seen. . . . Personality is a biological conception and a cultural-science conception, a sum and a fusion, a laboratory datum and a next-door neighbor. You will see in it what you are trained to see, and in some measure all the things that are seen are really seen, not hallucinated. The views differ in value and in range of utility, but in general there are not too many but too few. Considering how little is known, it is said that there are only eight or nine coherent living views of personality that are widely shared by psychologists; and of these, two or three (Janet, Ward, McDougall) are almost moribund. Not that they have been outlived; they have been lost in the whirl-wind of excitement about other more complicated and in some ways more exciting doctrines, the teachings of behaviorism, Gestalt, Freud, Jung, and Adler. There might well be more boldness in ordering the data of laboratory and clinic to freshly conceived schemata of structure.

SCIENCE, ART, AND ENGINEERING

Personality study is an art and an engineering enterprise as well as a science, and at the present stage in its development the three often flow together and refuse to be separated. The data to be used in such an enterprise are of every conceivable sort: experimental, biographical, clinical; gleanings from anthropological and sociological field studies; oddments from general biology and general sociology, as well as general psychology; educational experience; artistic perception of meanings; impressions of an individual observer of an individual subject; tables of statistical findings from large groups.

METHODS

The value of data depends, of course, a good deal upon the *methods* by which they have been derived. We have as major research tools (1) the genetic methods (the cross-sectional comparison of groups at different developmental levels, and the longitudinal-biographical study of individuals); (2) the comparative methods (the phylogenetic and the anthropological-sociological); and (3) the experimental method. We might add the statistical method, but with the development of statistical procedures for the study of small groups, it now seems reasonable to regard statistical methods as tools to accompany all the other methods whenever the data assume quantitative form and suggest the possibility of functional dependencies.

THE STAIRCASE OF PERSONALITY STUDY

In view of the difficulty of the task confronting us, it will be necessary to order our conceptions on a scale from the simplest to the most complex.

*   *   *   *   *

First, we will consider personality as a biological system, an organic matrix, from which, through outer and inner pressures, evolves the socially known individual. . . . When the conception of the organic system seems developed with reasonable clarity, we shall turn to the study of responses arising through the interaction of the individual constitution and a specific environment—the problem of learning. . . . Along with the behavior modifications of the organic system, we encounter the development of a world of perception and thought. . . . But major steps remain to be taken. The organism perceives, thinks about, and responds to itself. The study of the resulting functions of self or ego presupposes an understanding of the earlier steps. . . . The search for the dynamics of selfhood reflects the special genius of Freud. The Freudian conception of the self proceeds from, and is a much needed extension of, the cognitive-affective psychology just mentioned. The notion of a self struggling against tendencies of which it is unaware, or only partially aware, leads into the theory of unconscious dynamics and into a system of principles defining the relation of self and non-self; it helps therefore to extend and enrich the theory of integration and of conflict. . . . Unconscious dynamics, the enhancement and defense of the self, necessarily call our attention to conflict, disunity. But personality also achieves a kind of genuine unity or wholeness.

*   *   *   *   *

Wholeness, however, does not stop with the skin. We have already seen that the individual-environment relation involves larger fields, the organism being an aspect of such a field. Each individual is a member of a community; is guided, inhibited, moulded, structured by the life of the community; each personality is a reflection of a developmental history in a specific cultural whole. This is often called a social science view. Wholeness of culture and wholeness of organic response are conjointly stressed.

From this social science view two others develop. The first of these is that personality at a given time is a reflection and an epitome of specific cultural requirements. This we shall call *situationism*. The other, which is as much concerned with the capacity of the organism to select from the dispositions of the organism, might well be called simply the personality-and-culture view. But since this type of mutual selection between organism and environment involves the necessity of regarding the barrier between individual and environment as indefinite and unstable, and requires the consideration of an organism-environment field whose properties are studied as field properties, the approach will be called *field theory*. Personality is considered here as a flowing continuum of organism-environment events. The general nature of these events, and the problem of individuality in their history, are considered jointly.

CANALIZATION[7]

Needs tend to become more specific in consequence of being satisfied in specific ways. Children all over the world are hungry; their hunger may be satisfied by bread, by ice cream, by peanuts, by raw eggs, by rice, or by whale blubber. Eventually they develop, when hungry, not a demand for food in general, but a demand for what they are used to; in one part of the world peanuts are good food, whale blubber disgusting, and vice versa. So, too, over the face of the earth, children enjoy rhythms; the need is satisfied by different kinds of rhythms, different games, different types of music. Soon they find the ones which they are "used to" natural and satisfying; others seem awkward, difficult, unsatisfying.

* * * * *

This process by which general motives (which are at first rather non-specifically related to a class of stimuli) tend, upon repeated experience, to become more easily satisfied through the action of the specific satisfier than of others of the same general class, has been known so long that it would be impossible to name its discoverer. But good names are a great convenience, and Janet's term *canalization* is a good name for this process. The energies awaiting an outlet break through the barrier at a given spot, are channeled or canalized in the process, and, as the barrier weakens, tend more and more to focus their pressure upon it.

The strength of such canalizations appears to depend first upon the initial selectivity, the preference of the organism; and second, upon frequency of opportunities for specific response. The tone-hungry child may, despite years of deprivation, find his way to music through the force of the original need, but even the run of the people in a German village may come uniformly to love their folk songs and their Schumann through sheer iteration of musical experience.

* * * * *

Rather closely related to this problem are the experiments which indicate the tendency of familiar objects to become better and better liked. Under the term "familiarization" Maslow studied the tendency to prefer stimuli with which one had had earlier experience. On one occasion a series of thirty Russian names for women was divided into two groups of fifteen each. One of the lists was read aloud to a group of student clerical workers every

[7]*Ibid.*, from pp. 161-72.

evening for six evenings, the students being asked to write them down, spelling them as well as they could. At the end of the experiment all thirty names were read aloud, and the students were asked to indicate their preference for the names in each pair, one name in each pair being familiar, the other unfamiliar, and also to indicate which was superior in euphony. The familiar terms are better liked and more "euphonious," the critical ratios being, respectively, 1.9 and 5.0.

* * * * *

Canalizations can be broken, but apparently, as Holt points out, only by more powerful responses which in their essence block the energies originally established. From this point of view, the canalization could be destroyed only if another more potent behavior tendency could be set up to compete with it so powerfully, so dominantly, as to prevent its physiological expression. Sometimes this does occur. But canalizations are in general free of interference from one another. The love of Bach does not destroy the love of Shakespeare, nor does the love of raspberry sherbet destroy the love of baseball. There seems to be room for a practically infinite variety of tastes. One may develop many acquired wants within one modality; he may learn to like many kinds of food, many kinds of music. Canalization at one point leaves many other points relatively unaffected. One may like Raphael or Rembrandt, and later, Hokusai, or Sung Dynasty paintings, or Picasso; there is room for them all. When tastes are incompatible, as when a man says his love of Bach tends to prevent his enjoyment of jazz, the clue appears to lie in secondary habits such as a "fear of being low-brow," just as another man may find his tastes competing because of a "fear of being inconsistent" or a "desire to be at home in all sorts of worlds."

* * * * *

Not everyone may become catholic in his tastes. When one does, he has, through a broad development of affective response or through the cultivation of insight into the meaning of many different aspects of experience, transcended the narrow channels of his first developmental needs. Many people, moreover, typically give objective value to personal preferences, whether they be for thirteenth-century primitives or for Grant Wood. One derives a sense of status from feeling: "I am one of the rare ones who realize that. . .is the only real art, or music, or literature."

Canalizations, then, are not, so far as we know, subject to extinctions, whether by disuse or by displacement by other canalizations. Let one compare, for example, the length of time between extinction to a dinner bell which now means "mail man" rather than "dinner," with the extinction that can be acquired in losing one's interest in corn on the cob or peaches and cream which one in a strange clime has not eaten for many years. It is quite possible that the reason for this lies in the simple fact that the stimulus is by definition satisfying. Every time that the canalized food is eaten, it satisfies.

Extinction which is due to the satisfier's failure to satisfy is a contradiction in terms.

*   *   *   *   *

Whatever its ultimate explanation, the fact is of the utmost importance for any theory of personality wants or any doctrine of human values. It is not the bare wants or any interrelation of wants that makes the adult personality; it is not the adventitious pattern of connections between these inner wants and the conditioning stimuli of daily life. It is to a large degree the system of wants as organized in a directed form toward familiar satisfiers; it is a system of anticipations and preparations for a round of experiences which have compelling value because they are the specific ways in which the diffuse and generalized wants have in the past been converted from tension to satisfaction. The process appears irreversible, as the life process moves forward, consolidating itself into more and more differentiated, firmly constructed patterns. Two of the major clues to personality seem therefore to be the study of the specific ways in which canalized patterns are implanted in children by any society, and the study of the individual differences in content and form which such canalizations may assume in any society.

*   *   *   *   *

If the term canalization marked off no specific kind of event but were purely an alternative for such terms as conditioning, positive adaptation, or reintegration, there would be no justification in using it; we have enough terms already. In summary, however, there appears to be (1) a general tendency for motives to move toward greater specificity; (2) evidence that the consummatory responses, not the preparatory alone, are involved; (3) a hint that such responses are not merely connected with new signals but are intrinsically modified; and (4) a strong indication that they are not subject to extinction—the trend is unidirectional.

SOCIALIZATION[8]

Each individual serves to create in some measure the world in which others may live. Certain generic human traits—the capacity to be aroused, the capacity to learn, the capacity to be stimulated by others—predispose toward cultural living when once the attitude of adults to children is such that they readily transmit to them the skills they have learned. And children are deeply predisposed through affection, interests, dependence, to learn what parents have to teach. Furthermore, much is learned avidly without formal teaching. It is therefore not true that social participation is imposed upon or used as a mold for human personality. For the nature of human existence has slanted man's response in the social direction; man is deeply ready for society. The

[8]*Ibid.*, from pp. 765-67.

little child is called into activity by the sheer presence of others; and the activity, when aroused, tends to take a social direction by virtue of the ordinary mechanisms of social facilitation, by virtue of a selective awareness of this or that activity prominently carried out by the parents, and later, when self-evaluation has become clearcut, by virtue of competition for status within the group and between groups. Moreover, he shows affective spread of response, coming to love more widely and to hate more widely than his first family patterns require; he is canalized and familiarized, and he develops in the group that elementary social response, that primitive sympathy. . . .

Most important, perhaps, in the early formulation of his sense of his own membership character, is the figure-ground relation which develops between in-group and out-group, the consequent affective anchorage on the activities of parents, and on the parents as values. This cannot, however, be separated from the process of self-realization; for as Cooley and G. H. Mead have well taught us, it is only by constant reciprocity between perception of others and perception of self that individuality can come clearly into existence. Self-realization is not in opposition to, it is a positive phase of socialization.

In the same way membershp in any or all social groups, small or large, involves some balance between defensive and competitive tendencies on the one hand, and tendencies toward participation or even self-immolation on the other. The positive impulse to crowd membership is merely a dramatic manifestation of this impulse to sociality. The group suggestibility so much lamented by writers about mobs involves a positive need of one's fellows. And though it is a full realization of a deep social dependence, it is always mixed in some degree with the countervailing need of the leader, and likewise of the follower, to maintain their individuality. The normal figure in the figure-ground perception of the social group in which one participates is oneself; it is *one's own* group, not just "*a group of people.*" If the mob is pathological, it may be because the self has ceased to be the figure.

Indeed, a cardinal concept for the approach to personality through culture is the notion that the individual perceives himself as figure in the figure-ground pattern that is each social group, and that personality develops organically with this perception of the entire figure-ground system. It is for this reason that family membership, specifically in terms of age and sex roles, constitutes the first factor to be emphasized in the shaping of individuality. It likewise follows from this that the structuring of the earliest attitudes—attitudes towards parents, brothers, sisters, and so on—comes to the child in field-structured terms. The complex linkage or interlocking of attitudes which Newcomb has described in young adults is no mere late expression of a learning process that appears during adolescence. It is rather a late and complex form of a field-structuring process which has been occurring from the time of birth. The transfer of canalized and conditioned responses and the slow development of verbal symbols to integrate and mediate between them have brought into more articulate form a structuring or even a fusion of dispositions which are there as soon as is the capacity for responding to objects not physically present.

In the same way, social discovery and the capacity for group thinking develop within the contexts of the face-to-face group, usually the family, as big sister tries to thread a needle, or father to hang a picture. The suggestions, the sharing of experience in relation to a new problem, make *individuality* more definite at the same time that one becomes aware of non-membership, as we see in Benedict's studies of the deviant; but even the deviant has his own world, his own deviant group, in which membership is experienced. Most individuals have a wide variety of membership roles.

The Gestalt psychologists have taught us that every aspect of experience reflects the context in which it appears; every color, feeling, or act expresses its place in a system, its "membership character." Just as each aspect of an individual life reflects its context, so each person's role in society reflects the system of group relations. It is, therefore, more than just a play on words when we refer to the membership character in the social group. For certain purposes the biologist may treat the cell as if it were a self-contained unit; and for certain purposes a personality may be treated as if it were a self-contained unit. But for the most vital purposes a cell must be understood as an aspect of the life of a man. In the same way personality must be understood as an aspect of a social process; it cannot, in most cases, be considered as a self-contained unit. Individually we balk at this fact, for it is very deflating; nevertheless, we are reflections of a broad social process. We should have neither our biological nor our social individuality but for specific cultural processes that have mingled our ancestral strains and our social norms in highly specific ways. Exactly as the Gestalt psychologist shows in the study of perception that the value of a color or a tone depends upon its context, so the individual personality can be understood only if the membership character which it sustains in society at large is made clear. Personalities are not independent building stones of society; they are interdependent. Their interaction makes the social world, and the social world acting on the young makes new personalities.

ROLES[9]

The Manus tribe consists of about two thousand people. They live as merchants; the life of the group is centered in the processes of trade. They deal in futures; a man calculates that six months hence he will have received payments with which he will meet an obligation due at that time. Not only must he be competent in handling boats and overseeing production, he must also be shrewd and remorseless, must allow no one to get the better of him. The physical wear and tear of fulfilling his business responsibilities resemble that experienced by an active member of the New York Stock Exchange.

[9]*Ibid.*, from pp. 785-88.

The Manus are as aggressive and as hard in their competitive life as any business leader in our own society.

This tribe is deliberately chosen as an extreme example of what can be "predicted" from knowledge of the self-maintenance mores, from the kind of knowledge just cited. We may predict that marriage will be a matter of cold calculation, that love will mean little; that children will be reared without affection; that because affection is lacking in sexual matters and maternal relationships, the people will be extreme prudes. We may predict that their arts will be practical, not aimed at esthetic experience; that their politics will be unadulterated power politics, and their religion a straightforward barter with the unseen. These "predictions" are right on every count.

* * * * *

Thus far, this has seemed to be a very simple, clear example of the way in which self-maintenance mores influence other mores and serve to structure the personalities of those who grow up in a world constituted by these patterns of social relations. Our interest in all this lies not in the Manus' behavior as such, but in the light thrown upon *social roles,* defined by the cultural organization of the group and implemented by the family in such a way as to prepare the individual for enacting the role. Our primary hypothesis has been that the self-maintenance mores serve in large measure to determine the pattern of the mores as a whole; this hypothesis seems to be validated, as far as this analysis has gone, and our second hypothesis is apparently confirmed, in that such roles genuinely serve to mold personality. This is the writer's view; he does not seek, here or elsewhere, to attribute this interpretation to the ethnologists whom he cites.

But the self-maintenance mores act in different ways on different individuals, according to the role they must play. Among the Manus, almost all adult males share in the commercial system, and almost all adult females participate in a supporting way. Age and sex are therefore the two clear bases for the behavior roles to be assumed by the individual. Personality is congruent with the specific parts which persons of each age and sex must enact. Each role is specified by the number, variety, and quality of the interrelated tasks that the society defines, and each role depends to a large degree upon the self-maintenance roles. The point applies in detail; e.g., the subroles enacted by merchants at varying levels of power and success reflect their economic success. Thinking more broadly about human society as a whole, we may suspect that only those who are functionally capable of carrying out a role will be admitted to it, and that among those who are capable, only those will be admitted who are acceptable to those who control the society. Moreover, most economic tasks are sex-defined, for both men and women, partly in terms of what each can do, partly in terms of what the men will let the women do. And the day-by-day situation plunges the individual into the role more and more fully; the personality cannot help expressing it more and more profoundly.

As with the Manus, so with other primitive men, and ourselves. The assignment of roles is to a considerable extent incorporated in the child's early education, each family willingly or unwillingly preparing the children for roles analogous to those of the parents. But the roles defined by a person's relation to the whole system of mores are not determined solely by the family; they reflect the total culture. If a child grows up as a member of an Irish policeman's family or Swiss jeweler's family, there is considerable cultural pressure upon him to play the same role in society as his father, much as his role in other respects depends upon growing up in an ethnic or a religious group, e.g., as a French Canadian or a Russian Jew. Much of the resemblance between children and their parents is due to this carrying forward of specific roles in society.

Sociologists have gone far toward providing a characterology based squarely on these factors of role playing. They have shown that if a boy is a Portuguese cranberry picker—so that we know his age, sex, subculture, and economic position—we can go a long way rather safely in describing his personality. The compelling force of the socially assigned roles is so tremendous that we can sketch a series of personality interpretations which may be very useful without benefit of any further concepts. The Portuguese cranberry picker, the Maine lobsterman, the Georgia cracker, the fruit vendor from little Italy—all these and countless others can be defined in a rough general way, not at all because of blood but because of the coercive power of the roles in which their lives are cast.

SITUATIONISM[10]

By following the logic of this psychology of roles a systematic and revolutionary approach has been engendered under the name of *situationism.* . . . The fundamentals are simple, almost of the nature of axioms; and like other axioms they lead, when rationally pursued, to many paradoxical and revolutionary results.

We begin with the fact that any normal person must discover, in consequence of experience, the requirements necessary to fulfill each role which society expects him to enact. He learns what is standard and acceptable behavior in terms of the age, sex, race, economic status, and other standards that are socially assigned to him. His adaptation to such roles may not be as prompt and unequivocal as is that of the chameleon to a new color, but we may predict just as clearly that those who are required to discover and make use of the attributes of each role will be so deeply colored—stained, we might say—by the requirements of the situation that all who have similar roles will be fundamentally alike. Differences between persons will be fundamentally the differences in the roles which different individuals must enact. These differences may, of course, be quantitative in the sense that re-

[10]*Ibid.,* from pp. 867-91.

sponse to a situation, e.g., race discrimination, will naturally vary with the stimulus intensity of the situation, or that response according to sex may differ with the sharpness of the male-female differentiation emphasized by various cultures. Situationism maintains simply that human beings respond as situations require them to respond; and that whatever their biological diversities, they will, if capable of learning, take on the attributes which the situations call for. Although some adaptations to situations may be practically instantaneous, the requirements of the situationist theory are met if, after a reasonable opportunity for learning, all human individuals are found to have learned both what is required and how to carry out the required assignment.

Given a changed situation, there is a changed role and consequently a changed personality. For this reason situationism is unlike the current behavioristic systems which emphasize the slow accumulation of habits. Though the situational doctrine may appear at first sight to be rather similar to behavioristic views of social learning, the fact is that situationism is in sharp antithesis to all types of environmentalism which emphasize the fixation of character early in childhood. For the situationist it is not the slow and arduous process of fundamental character formation that is involved; it is not the slow shaping into the pattern required by parents; it is rather the fulfillment, in the adult as in the child, of the *day-to-day requirements*. In fact, in most instances the situationist has no need for the more elaborate emphasis upon childhood experience that characterizes behaviorism on the one hand and psychoanalysis on the other. Indeed, a child may throw to the winds his entire previous experience and react almost like a chameleon to his new environment. As a matter of fact, most of the literature on individual differences in childhood, in which such differences are related to farm vs. city, or to good vs. poor neighborhood, or to Catholic vs. Protestant vs. Jewish upbringing, or to differences of family pressures, tends to overwork the past and the concept of habit, and to forget that all these pressures dominate the *present moment*. The case history is frequently merely a "history" that makes too much of bygones; it may obscure the fact that we must be concerned with the present experience of the child. The present situation may be far more important than any past experience.

* * * * *

In the light of . . . strong emphasis upon individuality, we may ask whether the older formulations cannot be made to serve, whether field theory is necessary. Yes, indeed; the old *can* be "made to serve"; we can stretch Gestalt psychology in the situational direction and stretch situationism in the Gestalt direction, and hold the two, thus stretched, in contact. But what is gained by clinging to the old it is difficult to see. Unless we are forever alert to the oversights made by Gestalt without situationism, or by situationism without Gestalt, we cannot make these two work without constant and crude errors. The stretching process has to be continuous, for an unstretched

Gestalt will try to define organization within the organism first, and then look for organization in the situation, whereas in point of fact the organization *within* the organism depends partly on the organization of the situation. Similarly, situationism will try to define the organization of the situation first, before turning to the organism, forgetting that it is partly by virtue of the structure of the organism that the situation achieves structure. *We cannot define the situation operationally except in reference to the specific organism which is involved; we cannot define the organism operationally, in such a way as to obtain predictive power for behavior, except in reference to the situation. Each serves to define the other; they are definable operationally while in the organism-situation field.*

Autism[11]

As Nietzsche remarked, "My memory says that I did it, my pride says that I could not have done it, and in the end, my memory yields." This chapter is our attempt to show why and how, memory—and all the intellectual kin of memory—*yield.*

* * * * *

Nothing is more fatuous than the assumption that by making a voluntary effort, by "leaning over backwards," one can nicely separate thought from impulse and "correct" for one's biases. These mechanisms by which personal needs guide each individual's outlook go right to the bottom of personal existence; the more profoundly his needs are involved, the greater the danger of the complete captivation of the cognitive apparatus within their vise-like grip. Doctors, lawyers, ministers know this as they deal with men and women faced with grave and ultimate matters, with problems of life and death. Congressmen and statesmen know it as they read history or view men of other lands. But how often they see only a microscopically small distance into the process by which the inward aspects of their own determining motives guide their stormy convictions—perhaps about as much as psychiatrists and psychologists, who also frequently peer into other people's sorry tricks of self-deception with a microscope but remain well "defended" against too close a view of their own.

How does all this come about? Do we not, after all, have an elaborate machinery for making contact with *reality,* do we not have sense organs, brains, and action systems which lead us to adapt not to our whims but to our *environment?* Yes, perception depends upon the structure and function of receptors, and mediates the environment to us. In the long run, organic needs are satisfied through the adaptive behavior which results from the effective functioning of the reporting and communicating system. *But there is another way in which needs relate to perception.* Since all behavior is

11*Ibid.,* from pp. 364-65.

drive-motivated, the process of interpretation may fail to lead to behavior upon which adjustment depends, yet may, through past experience, pattern the perceptual world so that it conforms *directly* to the need. The molding of perception or thought or memory in the drive-satisfying direction follows from the satisfying or frustrating quality of past perception; one learns to perceive, think or remember in this way or that because such a habit is satisfying, just as one learns to *behave* this way or that because such behavior is satisfying. All cognitive processes are apparently continually shaped in greater or lesser degree by the pressure of wants.

This movement of the cognitive processes in the direction of need satisfaction is called autism. The term comes from Bleuler, who was especially concerned with autism in adult psychotics, yet saw clearly the almost universal role of the process in human life.

PART FIVE

Constitutional Approach
to Personality

CHAPTER 16

WILLIAM H. SHELDON

CONSTITUTIONAL PSYCHOLOGY

CONSTITUTIONAL PSYCHOLOGY, as William H. Sheldon chooses to designate his system of psychology, is a method whereby one derives a basic taxonomy of human beings on the basis of each person's physical and psychological constitution. There exist three types of physical constitution, each with its corresponding temperament: (1) the *endomorphic* constitution with its *viscerotonic* temperament; (2) the *mesomorphic* constitution with its *somatotonic* temperament; and (3) the *ectomorph* in whom is found the *cerebrotonic* temperament. Endomorphy is characterized by massive viscera which are highly developed; such individuals are exceptionally fat. Mesomorphs are muscular in build, high in specific gravity, hard, relatively strong, and tough; ectomorphs, by contrast, are fragile and linear, lanky, long-limbed, slender and delicate. In temperament, the viscerotonic person is relaxed, gluttonous, readily sociable, dependent and complacent; the somatotonic is aggressive, assertive, energetic, dominating, ruthless, loud, manic, active, and fond of risks; the cerebrotonic is tense, restrained, sensitive, secretive, and inhibited; he recoils from social situations, particularly those in which he must make new acquaintances, and is, hence, considered to be introverted.

Each person possesses some characteristics of all three types, but he is identified by the type which predominates. For each type, the units of measurement ascend in a numerical scale from 1 to 7, and are calculable in terms of the strength of the dominant traits in each area. The scores in endomorphy-viscerotonia, mesomorphy-somatotonia, and ectomorphy-cerebrotonia, listed in that order respectively, will indicate which type predominates. Consequently, the score for a person who is predominantly endomorphic and shows minimal traces of mesomorphy and ectomorphy, would be 7-1-1; such extreme types as this are rare.

Sheldon, born in 1899 in Warwick, Rhode Island, was reared on a farm where he acquired much practical knowledge under the tutelage of his father, a naturalist. After spending his undergraduate days at Brown University, he left for the University of Colorado where he received the A.M. degree; in 1926 he received the Ph.D. in psychology from the University of Chicago, and in 1933 the M.D. In 1924 he taught in the Department of Psychology at the University of Chicago, and in 1927 he accepted an appointment as an Assistant Professor at the University of Wisconsin. Following the award of his medical degree, he secured a grant which enabled him to spend two years in Europe where he came into contact with Freud, Jung, and Kretschmer. The theories of Jung and Kretschmer, particularly Jung's theory of psychological types and Kretschmer's constitutional types, influenced Sheldon greatly and left an imprint on his entire psychology.

In 1936 he was appointed Professor of Psychology at the University of Chicago; in 1938 he left for Harvard University where he met S. S. Stevens. They collaborated in the work which eventually led to the publication of *The Varieties of Temperament*. Since 1947 Sheldon has been directing the Constitutional Laboratory at Columbia University's College of Physicians and Surgeons.

His works include *The Varieties of Human Physique* (1940), *The Varieties of Temperament* (1942), *Varieties of Delinquent Youth* (1949), *Atlas of Men* (1954), and (with N. D. C. Lewis and A. M. Tenney) "Psychotic Patterns and Physical Constitution" in *Schizophrenia: Current Concepts and Research* (ed. by D. V. Siva Sankar, 1969).

THE VARIETIES OF TEMPERAMENT[1]

The Primary Components of Morphology

Having failed in several efforts to arrive at a useful morphological taxonomy through anthropometric techniques alone, we very early came to the conclusion that in order to set up the framework of such a taxonomy *ab initio*

[1]*The Varieties of Temperament* (New York: Harper, 1942), from pp. 5-11.

it would be desirable to scrutinize a large number of physiques all at one time. Photography would make this possible, but also would permit us to see each physique from as many directions at once as might be desirable. Accordingly, a procedure was adopted in which the individual is photographed in a standardized posture from the frontal, lateral, and dorsal positions on a single film.

When four thousand photographs were assembled in one place, so that they could be arranged experimentally in series, it was found that a certain orderliness of nature could be made out by the unaided eye. Certainly there were no "types," but there were obvious dimensions of variation.

The first problem, then, was to determine how many dimensions or components of structural variation could be recognized. The criteria we employed in seeking "Primary structural components" were two: (1) Could the entire collection of photographs be arranged in an ascending (or a descending) progression of strength in the characteristic under consideration, with agreement between experimenters working independently? (2) In the case of a suspected new component of structural variation, is it, upon examinations of the photographs, found to be impossible to define this apparently new component in terms of mixtures, regular or dysplastic, of the other components already accepted? Application of these two criteria revealed the presence of three primary components of structural variation, and we were unable to find a fourth structural variant that was not obviously the result of a mixture of the three.

To arrange the entire series of four thousand along each of the three accepted axes of variation was relatively easy, not only for the body as a whole but also for different regions of the body separately (thus providing a method for the ultimate measurement of dysplasia). The distributions for the body as a whole were then scaled tentatively by the method of equal-appearing intervals, and we had at hand a rough approximation to the general patterning of a continuous tridimensional distribution that was true to life. This was not yet an objectively defined distribution, but the first step toward meaningful objectification had been taken. We now had a fairly good idea of what could most profitably be measured, and were ready to make use of anthropometry.

The second problem was to find such anthropometric measurements as would (1) most reliably reflect those obvious differences in physique that anthroposcopic inspection had already shown to be present, and (2) refine and objectify these differences so that precise allocations of physiques on the tridimensional distribution could be made. Such measurements were selected by trial and error. It was found that the measurements most valuable for the purpose were certain diameters expressed as ratios to stature, and that most of these diameters could be undertaken with needle-point dividers from the film more accurately (more reliably) than from the living subjects, provided the photographs were posed in a standardized manner.

The question of how many such diameters to use is simply the question of how precisely accurate an allocation is desired. In dealing with groups statistically, we scale the strength of each of the primary components on a 7-point scale. For this purpose a minimum of seventeen diameter measurements is adequate for determining what is called the *somatotype*. In the detailed analysis of an individual, more precise differentiation may be made by using a greater number of measurements.

In order more readily to determine the somatotype from a series of measurements, a machine was constructed into which the measurements may be entered. The manipulation of switches then discloses the correct somatotype.

*   *   *   *   *

The somatotype is a series of three numerals, each expressing the approximate strength of one of the primary components in a physique. The first numeral always refers to *endomorphy* (see below), the second to *mesomorphy*, and the third to *ectomorphy*. Thus, when a 7-point scale is used, a 7-1-1 is the most extreme endomorph, a 1-7-1 is the most extreme mesomorph, and a 1-1-7 the most extreme ectomorph. The 4-4-4 falls at the mid point (of the scale, not of the frequency distribution) with respect to all three components.

*   *   *   *   *

Now for a description of the static components:

When *endomorphy* predominates, the digestive viscera are massive and highly developed, while the somatic structures are relatively weak and underdeveloped. Endomorphs are of low specific gravity. They float high in the water. Nutrition may vary to some degree independently of the primary components. Endomorphs are usually fat but they are sometimes seen emaciated. In the latter event they do not change into mesomorphs or ectomorphs any more than a starved mastiff will change into a spaniel or a collie. They become simply emaciated endomorphs.

When *mesomorphy* predominates, the somatic structures (bone, muscle, and connective tissue) are in the ascendency. The mesomorphic physique is high in specific gravity and is hard, firm, upright, and relatively strong and tough. Blood vessels are large, especially the arteries. The skin is relatively thick, with large pores, and it is heavily reinforced with underlying connective tissue. The hallmark of mesomorphy is uprightness and sturdiness of structure, as the hallmark of endomorphy is softness and sphericity.

Ectomorphy means fragility, linearity, flatness of the chest, and delicacy throughout the body. There is relatively slight development of both the visceral and somatic structures. The ectomorph has long, slender, poorly muscled extremities with delicate, pipestem bones, and he has, relative to his mass, the greatest surface area and hence the greatest sensory exposure to the outside world. He is thus in one sense overly exposed and naked to his world. His nervous system and sensory tissue have relatively poor protection. It might be said that the ectomorph is biologically "extraverted," as the endomorph is biologically "introverted." Psychologically . . . these characteristics are usually reversed—the ectomorph is the introvert, the endomorph is *one type* of extravert.

The digestive viscera (dominant in endomorphy) are derived principally from the endodermal embryonic layer. The somatic tissues (dominant in mesomorphy) are derived from the mesodermal layer, while the skin and nervous system, which are relatively predominant in ectomorphy, come from the ectodermal embryonic layer.

The anthropometric measurements used to determine the somatotype are standardized for normal or average nutrition within a particular age range. Therefore those measurements which change with nutritional changes readily detect the under- or over-nourished individual. But apparently no nutritional change can cause the measurements of a person of one somatotype exactly to simulate those of another somatotype. Nutritional changes are recognized as such by the somatotyping process. When an individual's measurements are posted in the somatotyping machine, the machine indicates where the somatotype lies. If a severe nutritional disturbance is present, the machine does not indicate a false somatotype but indicates only an unusual aberration from a normal pattern. We have as yet seen no case in which metabolic or nutritional changes led us to the assignment of two different somatotypes for the same individual, although we have somatotyped people from photographs taken at different periods in their (adult) lives when a weight change of as much as one hundred pounds had taken place.

When the relative strength of the three primary components of morphology has been determined, the physical analysis may be said to be anchored. But identification of the somatotype is only a beginning. So many secondary variables still remain to be described that the horizon of individuality seems only to broaden and recede to greater distance as the techniques of physical description mature to usefulness.

Some of the more important secondary variables are dysplasia (different mixtures of the primary components in differing regions of the body), gynandromorphy (physical bisexuality), texture (fineness or coarseness of tissue, aesthetic harmony of structure), secondary local dysplasias or hereditary local patternings of the primary components often called racial characteristics, pigmentation, distribution of secondary sexual characteristics (gynandromorphic dysplasias and characteristic patterns), hirsutism and hair distribution, and so on. We have tried to standardize the scaling of most of these characteristics just mentioned, but many other important physical variables lie on beyond these. Furthermore the work on secondary factors is for the most part new and incomplete, since none of this work could be done in a meaningful frame of reference until the somatotyping techniques and the norms for the primary components were well established.

The Dynamic Components of Temperament

As in the studies of morphology, the first problem at this more complex level of personality was to discover and define criteria for a useful basic taxonomy. It was necessary at the beginning to determine what first-order components are present in temperament. The method which has finally yielded fruitful results is a variation on the technique of factor analysis applied to quantitative ratings on a group of traits.

We have been able to standardize the descriptions of sixty traits—twenty in each of three correlated clusters—which collectively make up a scale for measuring what appear to be three primary components of temperament. Within each of the clusters the traits are positively correlated, while all of the intercorrelations between traits not of the same cluster are negative.

* * * * *

Names have been given to the three correlated groups of traits. *Viscerotonia*, the first component, in its extreme manifestation is characterized by general relaxation, love of comfort, sociability, conviviality, gluttony for food, for people, and for affection. The viscerotonic extremes are people who "suck hard at the breast of mother earth" and love physical proximity with others. The motivational organization is dominated by the gut and by the function of anabolism. The personality seems to center around the viscera. The digestive tract is king, and its welfare appears to define the primary purpose of life.

Somatotonia, the second component, is roughly a predominance of muscular activity and of vigorous bodily assertiveness. The motivational organization seems dominated by the soma. These people have vigor and push. The executive department of their internal economy is strongly vested in their somatic muscular systems. Action and power define life's primary purpose.

Cerebrotonia, the third component, is roughly a predominance of the element of restraint, inhibition, and of the desire for concealment. Cerebrotonic people shrink away from sociality as from too strong a light. They "repress" somatic and visceral expression, are hyperattentional, and sedulously avoid attracting attention to themselves. Their behavior seems dominated by the inhibitory and attentional functions of the cerebrum, and their motivational hierarchy appears to define an antithesis to both of the other extremes.

Physique and Temperament

In a study extending through a period of five years we have been able to analyze 200 young men both morphologically and temperamentally, measuring in addition to the primary components a number of apparently secondary temperamental characteristics. Correlations of the order of about $+.80$ between the two levels of personality (morphological and temperamental) indicate that temperament may be much more closely related to the physical constitution than has usually been supposed.

However, the correlation between the two levels is by no means perfect, and from the point of view of individual analysis it seems to be the disagreements or inconsistencies between the physical and temperamental pattern that throw the most light on behavior. We find, roughly, at least four general factors at work in the development of personality: (1) the total strength of endowment in each of the three primary components, (2) the quality of such endowments, (3) the mixture of components, or their order of relative strength, and (4) the incompatibilities between morphology and manifest temperament. Of the latter, several subvarieties can be made out and are often encountered in the analysis of personalities having a history of severe internal conflict.

THE SCALE FOR TEMPERAMENT[2]

I VISCEROTONIA	II SOMATOTONIA	III CEREBROTONIA
*1. Relaxation in posture and movement	*1. Assertiveness in posture and movement	*1. Restraint in posture and movement, tightness
*2. Love of physical comfort	*2. Love of physical adventure	2. Physiological overresponse
*3. Slow reaction	*3. The energetic characteristic	*3. Overly fast reactions
4. Love of eating	*4. Need and enjoyment of exercise	*4. Love of privacy
5. Socialization of eating	5. Love of dominating, lust for power	*5. Mental overintensity, hyperattentionality, apprehensiveness
6. Pleasure in digestion	*6. Love of risk and chance	*6. Secretiveness of feeling, emotional restraint
*7. Love of polite ceremony	*7. Bold directness of manner	*7. Self-conscious motility of the eyes and face
*8. Sociophilia	*8. Physical courage for combat	*8. Sociophobia
9. Indiscriminate amiability	*9. Competitive aggressiveness	*9. Inhibited social address
10. Greed for affection and approval	10. Psychological callousness	10. Resistance to habit and poor routinization
11. Orientation to people	11. Claustrophobia	11. Agoraphobia
*12. Evenness of emotional flow	12. Ruthlessness, freedom from squeamishness	12. Unpredictability of attitude

[2]*Ibid.*, from p. 26. The thirty traits with asterisks constitute collectively the short form of the scale.

I VISCEROTONIA	II SOMATOTONIA	III CEREBROTONIA
*13. Tolerance	*13. The unrestrained voice	*13. Vocal restraint, and general restraint of noise
*14. Complacency	14. Spartan indifference to pain	14. Hypersensitivity to pain
15. Deep sleep	15. General noisiness	15. Poor sleep habits, chronic fatigue
*16. The untempered characteristic	*16. Overmaturity of appearance	*16. Youthful intentness of manner and appearance
*17. Smooth, easy communication of feeling, extraversion of viscerotonia	17. Horizontal mental cleavage, extraversion of somatotonia	17. Vertical mental cleavage, introversion
18. Relaxation and sociophilia under alcohol	18. Assertiveness and aggression under alcohol	18. Resistance to alcohol, and other depressant drugs
19. Need of people when troubled	19. Need of action when troubled	19. Need of solitude when troubled
20. Orientation toward childhood and family relationships	20. Orientation toward goals and activities of youth	20. Orientation toward later periods of life

THE PRIMARY COMPONENTS OF TEMPERAMENT[3]

1. Viscerotonia

Given a measure of poetic license, we might describe the first dynamic component as a manifest desire to embrace the environment and to make its substance one with the substance of the individual's own person. At the most unsublimated level this is the drive to ingest and to assimilate food, which is then transmuted into the flesh of the self. The predominantly viscerotonic personality generally remains close to the earth. Viscerotonia means earthiness. Such a person seems to express a dominant mood not far from the mood of the nourishing soil: he is unhurried, deliberate, and predictable. At high levels of culture he radiates warmth, stability, and (if cerebrotonia is low) indiscriminate amiability. At low levels he is gross, gluttonous, and possessive. In any event he knows what he wants, and his wants are tangible.

In contrast to viscerotonic motivation, the somatotonic desire is centered upon action and somatic expression, and in cerebrotonia the whole visceral and somatic organism seems to be held in a state of subjugation to the inhibitory, attentional function.

The viscerotonic's craving is for food, for comfort, and for the mental

3*Ibid.*, from pp. 248-79.

and somatic relaxation which accompanies the digestive process at its full best, when the main blood supply is withdrawn from the brain and from the peripheral somatic structures, and is vested in the digestive viscera. For cultured viscerotonics, the food-taking time is the high spot of the day, and the principal focus of feeling-awareness is in the assimilative business. The soul has its seat in the splendid gut.

Such a personality rarely can understand the cerebrotonic, who wants to eat quickly and have it over with, who prefers to eat in private, and cares little for service and ceremony or for fancy dishes. The viscerotonic is likely to devote a tremendous interest to *cuisine*, and he achieves ecstasy in the imagination and anticipation of fine food. Furthermore, he is prone to carry into adult life his natural early childhood interest in faeces and in the eliminative functions, for viscerotonia loves all digestive activity, including the peristalsis of defecation.

At lower cultural levels the viscerotonic becomes simply the glutton, growing heavier and more hoglike in his obesity if the food supply holds out, and less so when kept on a limited diet or on a rigid schedule of work and exercise. Peasant stock from all lands appears to carry a heavy viscerotonic component. The great majority of the overly fat, full-gutted personalities so conspicuous in American urban and political life have presumably sprung from stock which for many generations had lived on a limited diet under sterner conditions. Rioting now in the rich spoils of a newly exploited continent, some of these men and women of strong first component fail to maintain the balance, and they go to gut and fat.

The viscerotonic may of course express his temperamental predominance in a wide variety of ways. He may be culturally polished and urbane, or crude and uneducated. He may be bishop or bumpkin, scholar or butcher, aggressive or meek, energetic or lazy, courageous or cowardly, ruthless or squeamish, loud or quiet—in short he may live out *any* role in life which permits the expression of a predominant viscerotonia. The predominant component is but one of the variables determining the personality. How that component is to be expressed must depend upon the relative endowment in the other two primary components and upon many other factors, including the cultural influences to which the man has been exposed. We see that to know the strength of one of the primary components *and that alone* is to take but one short step toward describing or predicting a personality.

Viscerotonic people tend to be hypoattentional and to remain overrelaxed. The viscerotonic gives the impression of being slow. Yet although his conscious response may seem sluggish to the faster reacting cerebrotonic, the basic conscious orientation of the viscerotonic is surer and in some respects more accurate. Viscerotonics can always be trusted to maintain a close grip upon immediate, practical reality. They are certain to know where they are at all times, in relation to their jobs, to their marriage, to their social status, to their basic likes and dislikes. Attitudes toward these things do not change readily or suddenly in the viscerotonic personality, and for some reason, both viscerotonic and somatotonic people possess a better sense of spatial orientation than do cerebrotonics.

The cerebrotonic is also concerned with the problem of orientation, but this worry usually concerns orientation in time. He lies awake nights thinking of distant plans, of the general course and objectives of his life as a whole, of the state of his religion, of the ethics of some projected undertaking, or of the future of his progeny, of mankind, and of the universe. In both kinds of minds the problem of *orientation* is vital and urgently important, but the reference of the orientation in the two cases is different. For the somatotonic and viscerotonic components, orientation is essentially a spatial, earthly, immediate need. For cerebrotonia the orientational need seems to take the form primarily of a craving for a sense of direction in time, and for some hierarchy of values transcending the apparent value hierarchy of present experience. This is a relative difference. There seems to be no necessity for calling one kind of orientation religious, and the other nonreligious.

The viscerotonic digests his food with the highest efficiency. All of it is utilized, and made the most of. Food is eagerly absorbed into the organism. The organism consequently tends to expand, and in a realistic sense to glue itself more closely to the earth. If given full sway, the viscerotonic component seems to lead the organism back to the earth and insidiously to bring about a reunion with the basic earth stuff. The cerebrotonic is always in danger of flying too far from the earth and suffering an Icarian fall. The viscerotonic runs the danger of growing back and becoming attached to this earth like a Siamese twin, losing his conscious individuation and remerging prematurely with the maternal stuff from which he was molded. He must watch his diet with great care, or he grows heavy of body. If then he fails to master the desire to absorb, he degenerates, spreads out in a clod of flesh, and the mental and somatic functions are drowned in a rising tide of biological surfeit.

In well-developed viscerotonia the actual food requirement is less per unit of bodily weight than that in cerebrotonia. Furthermore, the digestive apparatus in viscerotonia is equipped to accommodate larger quantities of food at more infrequent intervals. Two meals a day are therefore probably ample for any predominantly viscerotonic person, and we have seen viscerotonic symptoms clear up in persons of this pattern through the simple expedient of changing temporarily to a program of *one* meal a day. Similarly, a pronounced viscerotonic probably requires less sleep than a cerebrotonic, but here, as in the matter of food, the viscerotonic is prone to take more than is good for him, or perhaps we should say, more than is conducive to his best mental development. The viscerotonic *loves to sleep*, in marked contrast with the somatotonic, who loves to wake up and be active, and in contrast with the cerebrotonic, who hates to *go to sleep*, but who, when once asleep, also hates to wake up and be severed from his dreams.

Viscerotonics are remarkably susceptible to habit formation. Food taking and sleeping in overdoses become habitual, and if drugs once are taken, especially sedative drugs, there is danger of the development of a drug habit. The habit of constant dependence upon tobacco is very common among viscerotonic people, who often tend to use this drug to hold down their weight, thus substituting a habit for internal (cerebrotonic) discipline.

The mechanism of viscerotonic susceptibility to habit is a matter of speculation. The same phenomenon is seen in somatotonia, at times even more conspicuously. It is possible that this phenomenon is related directly to the relative degree of cerebral dominance in the personality. Where cerebral dominance is pronounced, there is marked resistance to habit formation. Where the cerebrotonic component is low, the organism appears readily and willingly to fall into all sorts of habits which obviate the recurrent necessity of making choices and decisions. Habit is a psychological antithesis to hyperattentionality, which is perhaps associated with an innately determined taste for mental conflict, and is certainly a cerebrotonic trait. It may be that the common habit addictions of mankind are simply manifestations of relative failure of the cerebrotonic component.

Viscerotonic people like alcohol. They are frequently connoisseurs of alcoholic beverages. But they are rarely drunkards. The overuse of alcohol is almost certainly a response to conflict, not to a temperamental predominance. The common picture of the alcoholic personality is one in which is seen an intense struggle for dominance between the cerebrotonic and the somatotonic components, usually with the third component slightly the weaker. The chronic excessive use of any depressant drug seems psychologically to constitute an attempt to achieve internal peace by putting down the cerebrotonic component. Alcohol attacks this component selectively, depressing the higher centers of the forebrain first, then the intermediate brain centers, and if in sufficient concentration, finally paralyzing the lower nerve centers.

In moderate quantities alcohol appears to be good food for the viscerotonic and seems to agree with him, as tobacco seems to agree with him. These two relatively mild depressants appear to balance the internal economy of the biologically overefficient viscerotonic organism in an ordinarily pleasant and innocuous manner. At any rate there is no convincing evidence that either of them in moderate quantity is injurious to one who possesses a good viscerotonic component, and for such a person alcohol and tobacco seem to add materially to the comfort and enjoyment of life.

Sir Arthur Conan Doyle pictured his immortal Sherlock Holmes as an indefatigable smoker, capable of smoking half a pound of strong tobacco in a single night. Yet the Holmes of Doyle's fertile imagination was also a cerebrotonic ectomorph who in most respects conspicuously lacked the viscerotonic component. Holmes, as Doyle *generally* pictured him, could no more have smoked a strong pipe in such a manner than the late Calvin Coolidge could have put away a case of 6 per cent beer at a sitting. But Doyle himself had a flourishing viscerotonic component, and he loved his tobacco. The Holmes he created, like many legendary heroes, was a composite ideal, but not quite psychologically probable. Holmes was partly

Doyle, and partly what Doyle dreamed of being. Viscerotonics and somato-tonics dream of being *also* cerebrotonic. We all dream of being *also* what we are not.

Viscerotonia means realism. Viscerotonic ecstasy lies in the achievement of a "real" surrounding made up of nice things that taste good, smell good, look good, sound good, feel good. The viscerotonic wants to dig in, to establish himself in a good place on his earth, and to feel the warming and nourishing earth juices flowing in his veins. In the face of trouble and dis-may, this personality does not go off into solitude and think it through alone, but seeks social support at once, and finds respite in outward lamentation. Sorrow and grief are inhibiting things. They are foreign to the inner organic economy of the viscerotonic personality. Sorrow is not to be cherished and reflected upon, but must be expressed and thrown off and got rid of. After a little time of dismay and lamentation, the viscerotonic component asserts itself like the returning tide, again takes over the management of affairs, and demands the satiation of appetites. Then there may be feasting, drinking, and spending. The viscerotonic bruises easily but recovers rapidly. A cere-brotonic, however, may carry his deep emotional hurts close to the con-scious focus for a lifetime.

The viscerotonic youth does not get "buck fever" in the face of crises and opportunities. He does not lose his nerve and go to pieces at the time when it is most vital that he should be normal and relaxed. His mind is not so vulnerable to distraction as is that of the cerebrotonic, whose attention can be reached in an instant by almost any distracting stimulus. The viscero-tonic controls are deeper, harder to reach, and slower to respond. This individual is thus insulated against the danger of hasty, confused, rattle-brained action. He is not likely to flinch or to lose his head in an emergency. He has good kidney, good intestinal fortitude, a strong stomach. He has guts, bowels. Indeed, it is remarkable that so much of our common language descriptive of stability in the face of emergency should point so consistently to the digestive tract. The somatotonic has courage (a strong heart). He is the one who goes out to meet danger. The cerebrotonic sees too much, too many alternatives and consequences, and he is frightened.

Neurodermatitis, nervous disorders, functional bowel distress and the like are not often found in predominant viscerotonia, nor do we often encounter sexual hypereroticism (quick, intense sexual excitability). This is a cere-brotonic characteristic.

With the viscerotonic component high, there is excellent thermal adapt-ability. Such people typically enjoy both cold weather and hot weather, although hot weather may be uncomfortable in cases where the physique has been permitted to degenerate to obesity. The heavy layer of subcutane-ous fat prevents the normal irradiation of heat in hot weather, but this same fat layer acts as an insulation against cold. Viscerotonia loves the water, loves to swim.

Viscerotonic emotional expression is direct and sincere, in the sense that the outward response tends to reveal what the individual feels within. Since the restraining cerebral controls are relatively inactive and weak, outward expression of feeling in viscerotonia is a more accurate barometer of the true state of inner feeling than is the case in cerebrotonia. Viscerotonics are relatively predictable, and therefore in a superficial sense more trustworthy, and more trusted. They are open. There is relatively little about them that is mysterious. To live with them is to know them, to understand them, and therefore to sympathize with them.

It is far different with the cerebrotonic, whose sharp, watchful countenance and overly responsive eyes advertise that something is going on among the inner workings which is not revealed to the light of day. There is no predicting what such men are thinking. They work, as it were, behind an intervening screen, and the screen may cover the darkest morass or the brightest garden of thought. It is possible to live for years with a cerebrotonic and be totally mistaken as to what manner of man he really is. People like that make life interesting, but they also make life complicated. In viscerotonia there is surety, although perhaps also boredom.

Persons with a good viscerotonic component can *cry*. They can pour out their souls. It is *real* crying, sobbed up wholebelliedly from the depths of the abdomen. The entire abdominal musculature joins in with a will and a rhythm. The cerebrotonic cries through clenched teeth, usually in silence. His crying is not so convincing to the uninstructed listener. This viscerotonic ability to cry convincingly is at times a remarkably potent weapon. Many a resistant heart has been melted by it, and many a marital fortress taken, which could never otherwise have been scaled. When a viscerotonic male sets his heart upon a woman whose quality lies a little beyond his reach, he is apt sooner or later to resort to this weapon, and in such a beginning many unfortunate marriages take shape. Men as a rule may be fairly well disciplined in resisting feminine tears, but against good viscerotonic masculine tears the female is at a serious disadvantage, for her own weapons are turned against her.

The cerebrotonic who has not been embittered and beaten back by a relatively unsympathetic outer world tends frequently toward anthropomorphism. He becomes affectionately attached to *things*, reads human qualities and feelings into them, and often focuses deep affection upon things that are not human. In predominant viscerotonia this anthropomorphism is not found. The viscerotonic has in the beginning better natural rapport with other human beings, and the main targets of his affection usually remain through life essentially direct human objects.

* * * * *

In summary, viscerotonia refers to a motivational organization dominated by the gut and hence by the function of anabolism. The primary desire seems to be to assimilate the earth and to merge with it. Viscerotonia means warmth, earthiness, and in general, *indiscriminate* good will.

Predominance of this component generally means a slowness of reaction, but it means also a tenacious grip on reality, especially upon social reality, and a sure orientation in the spatial and personal sense. Viscerotonia means practicality. It provides the central *thema* for a group of religions older than Christianity, and in terms of total number of sincere adherents, probably more influential.

2. Somatotonia

The second component is the "motional" element in life. Somatotonia is the craving for vigorous action and (when fully admitted to consciousness) the resolution to subdue the environment to one's own will. Successful somatotonics are conquerors. They conqueror mountains, oceans, forests, wild beasts, Chinese, and other less somatotonic or less strongly united peoples. Somatotonic ecstasy is that of vigorously overcoming obstacles, and somatotonic hell is inaction.

A constant characteristic of predominant somatotonia is physical endurance, accompanied by a low sleep requirement and a relatively infrequent food requirement. When the second component is predominant, without the complication of a strong first or third, we find typically a person who requires from a fifth to a third less sleep than the average individual of his age. These are the voluntary early risers of youth and middle age, and sometimes in the later decades of life they give the impression of being almost independent of the need for sleep. It is not uncommon to find a somatotonic 6 with the established habit of sleeping only five or six hours nightly, while retaining seemingly boundless energy and evidencing no signs of fatigue.

Extremes in the second component have solid, compact bodies, ruddy complexions, large blood vessels, and usually they have high blood pressure. They are rarely very long lived, but are prone to go out suddenly with a "coronary or cerebral accident," not infrequently in the sixth decade of life. The somatotonic mesomorph is certainly closer to the *habitus apoplecticus* of Hippocrates than is the viscerotonic endomorph. In our own studies we have found that it is principally mesomorphs and not endomorphs who tend to develop manic-depressive psychoses. (We suspect that many of Kretschmer's manic-depressive "pyknics" were really fat mesomorphs.)

Somatotonics do not require frequent feeding, but often they are voracious, eat too much, and grow fat. For the full-fledged somatotonic, two meals a day probably constitute a better feeding schedule than three. These people like to "wolf" a large quantity of food at a sitting, and if permitted, are inclined to gorge themselves. In middle life, somatotonics almost invariably eat too much. In several instances when confronted with the picture of a somatotonic complaining in middle life of boredom, loss of interest, and of disturbing somatic symptoms, we have recommended a change of two meals a day instead of three. This recommendation has in certain cases been followed by remarkable improvement.

Both viscerotonic and somatotonic people can often be benefited by a stern dietary regimen. . . . Somatotonics love a vigorous life and are at their best when meeting physical hardship. Under such conditions they reach their peak of energy output and when in the best of training are capable of enduring great exertion for long periods without food, eating enormously when the opportunity is presented.

Somatotonics feel good in the morning. They love to jump out of bed, take a shower, make a lot of noise, and greet the sun. Normally they become sleepy or tired rather suddenly at about their usual bedtime, and typically drop off to deep sleep at once upon retiring. A person in whom either the first or second component predominates strongly over the third is not likely to have chronic difficulty in going to sleep.

Somatotonic sleep is deep and seems to be relatively dreamless. Such sleep is refreshing and it may be that an explanation of the lower sleep requirement of people high in the second component lies partly in the fact that they sleep *better*, or more thoroughly, than do cerebrotonics. Whoever has attempted to use a dream analysis technique in the therapeutic or diagnostic study of somatotonic people is aware of the peculiar early difficulty which they present. Most somatotonics will state that they rarely dream and never remember their dreams upon awakening (see trait S-17). Cerebrotonics nearly always, and viscerotonics usually, are more or less aware of the trend of their own dreaming, and can without practice recite their recurrent dreams in some detail. But for individuals of predominant somatotonia an introduction to their own dream world often amounts to revelation, and the event not infrequently constitutes a religious (conversional) experience. These people then tend to become converts in quite a religious sense to the analytic procedure which has introduced them to their "other side," and if wealthy they make very satisfactory patients or communicants. The somatotonic mind offers an admirable target for exploitation by conversion because by its nature such a mind is cut off from its own subconscious levels. But that people who are successfully analyzed or suddenly converted to a religion are generally somatotonic reflects no discredit on the devices through which the conversion experience has historically been exploited. If there is to be criticism, it should be directed at commercial exploitation, not at the priestly function itself.

Somatotonic people tend to lack introspective insight. They are loaded guns and they want to be pointed somewhere and set off. Their function is action. Hence it is that the clever medicine men of all time have made a good living by pointing and exploiting the action-loving somatotonic component in their contemporaries.

In general, somatotonia lives for the present, cerebrotonia for the future. The cerebrotonic often feels as if the present were a sort of valley or depression between a better yesterday and a potentially brighter tomorrow. The somatotonic tends to feel that the present is like a high and sunny ridge between the dead valley of the past and the misty nothingness of the future.

Somatotonics typically like high or mountainous country and sunny weather. Cerebrotonics show a predilection for low country, and for rainy weather. However, this trait is so obscured by the individual history that it is hard to get at, and its diagnostic value is questionable. Ectomorphs are usually more comfortable in wet weather, possibly due in part to their peculiar susceptibility to dehydration (relatively greater surface exposure). They tend to be uncomfortable in strong sunlight, probably because of visual and general cutaneous oversensitivity. Cerebrotonics love the twilight, and if the preliminary evidence of general observation is to be trusted, they often see better at night than do either somatotonics or viscerotonics.

Somatotonic people are generally tolerant of noise and are frequently noise-makers. The cerebrotonic hates noise. His hyperattentional responsive mechanism is especially sensitive to noise and renders him at the mercy of his environment. He is physiologically unable to prevent responding to what is going on, especially to what is making a noise. He is like a delicate instrument which records a slight disturbance in its environment, but can be ruined or destroyed by heavier, more violent disturbances. Noise therefore exhausts and frustrates cerebrotonic people.

Cerebrotonics seem to have suffered a misfortune in the invention of the radio, for this is a weapon against which, in full-fledged cerebrotonics, no dissociative effort can prevail. Somatotonics, however, *like* the noise bombardment. To them the radio is mild stimulation, comparable perhaps to what the distant voice of wildfowl is to a nature lover. Their threshold of attention is high, and relatively little really breaks through. Rhythmic noise lulls and only gently stimulates the somatotonic mind when the same noise may distract and disrupt a cerebrotonic mind. Automobile horns often constitute a pleasant sound to somatotonia. Such sounds mean fellowship, action and high health. The cerebrotonic, with his more labile attentional focus, has to attend to every noise as though it were a meaningful stimulus. But for the somatotonic, the noise may constitute merely an encouraging and reassuring background item in the total complex of stimulation, like the distant voices of children. These two kinds of people are different inside.

To highly cerebrotonic people the experience of attempting to converse with the deaf is a traumatic one. The cerebrotonic is not able to raise his voice well, and the effort to do so in order to make himself heard sometimes constitutes a sereve strain. Some time ago the writer was asked to consult a young woman who had been suffering from a number of cerebrotic manifestations, among them neurodermatitis, insomnia, return of a childhood habit of fingernail biting, and a peculiar sense of impending disaster. She was morphologically 2-2-6, very shy and quiet, and her motivational components seemed to be also about 2-2-6. She had unusual beauty, of her delicate type, and was engaged to marry a young man of excellent standing. This girl had been to a psychiatrist and had been encouraged to proceed with her marriage. The young man to whom she was engaged turned out to be a hearty, athletic 3-5-2 in his early thirties. He had been successful in a business job, was aggressive and popular, fond of somatotonic activities, and as innocent of cerebrotonia as a Chicago congressman. But he was partially deaf. To one who had noted the pain of the cerebrotonic who is forced to raise the voice, it may not be surprising to learn that today the girl is institutionalized. Diagnosis, "schizophrenia, type undetermined."

Could this girl have been saved from a fatal breakdown? That we do not know, but at least her departure could have been made more pleasant. A cerebrotonic 2-2-6 should not have been forced to make her final struggle against such odds as the combination of somatotonia and deafness. (Incidentally, is there a genuine correlation between somatotonia and deafness—do vulnerable ears go with the second component—or is it merely that somatotonic deaf people are the most conspicuous?)

It is excessively rare to find a cerebrotonic who snores, even in deep sleep. Snoring is probably due to relatively complete relaxation, especially of the structures in the upper respiratory path. The cerebrotonic goes to sleep very slowly, and his body relaxes incompletely. This is probably why he does not snore. Somatotonics seem to snore only when a fairly good viscerotonic component is also present. They then are inclined to snore noisily. The heavy, rafter-shaking snoring that is sometimes heard in army barracks or Pullman cars will usually be found upon investigation to emanate from a viscerotonic-somatotonic throat. But the more frequent, regular, musical snoring which is nearly always heard in such places comes from the softer, shallower-breathing viscerotonics.

Psychologically the most important thing about snoring is doubtless its devastating effect upon cerebrotonic morale. Cerebrotonics typically cannot sleep within range of the sound of snoring, particularly somatotonic snoring. But snoring is a habit almost impossible to break because it takes place when the organism is so completely relaxed that the cerebral inhibitory (habit-breaking) functions are entirely cut off. When a snorer and a cerebrotonic are married there is often little to do except sleep in different parts of the house, or better, in different parts of the city.

* * * * *

In older children somatotonia gives rise to rough and dynamic play, to self-assertiveness, and to pugnacity and dominational qualities. As the child grows on toward maturity these somatotonic manifestations either yield to sufficient sublimation and "socialization" to render the emerging personality socially acceptable, and to lend it the quality of leadership, or they settle it at relatively unsublimated levels and the individual takes on the nature of incorrigibility.

Most people in our present crowded world become gradually discouraged in the twenties and early thirties, and after the discouragement has well set in they typically fall back upon some simple and usually innocuous routine expression of the inherently dominant motive. Somatotonics tend to enter upon the most tragic of all human quests, the quest of lost youth. One of the cardinal indicators of somatotonia is a horror of growing old. Somatotonics want their bodies to stay young, and they want to continue to do the things of youth. Athletic games, gadgets of locomotion, competitions, money, status, power, success—these are the things are preoccupy somatotonia growing older against its will. Somatotonics love to keep up with tennis, the football, the hunting, the races. Professional athletics and gambling are so highly commercialized and so vulgarized that their following is a variegated one. You see more than vicarious somatotonia at the horse races, ball parks and gambling places. You see also the backwash of human life. But when you see a man in the fifth or sixth decade of life faithfully practicing his tennis or religiously following the hunts, you are looking upon gentlemanly somatotonia. So gentlemanly that sportsmanship means more than victory, and so somatotonic that the mind has long since surrendered to the muscles.

Alcohol depresses the cerebrotonic component selectively, and therefore acts as a relative stimulant, especially to the somatotonic component. This drug seems to release hidden springs of action in people whose motivation reveals the stress of conflict between the second and third components. Such people seem to be natural candidates for chronic alcoholism (possibly because of the peculiar incompatibility between these two components). They are frequently and, so far as anyone knows, are rightly fond of alcohol. If cerebrotonia predominates, it presumably protects them from being entirely mastered by the habit. If somatotonia predominates in a close struggle with cerebrotonia, alcohol may offer an easy way out of a difficult struggle.

Somatotonic people who are free from cerebrotonic interference are singularly open, guileless people. (The open face is the somatotonic passport, the amiable face is the viscerotonic passport, and the cerebrotonic face has no passport, but wears a lean danger sign which arouses universal suspicion.)

Somatotonia means susceptibility to habit. The even regulation of habitual overt behavior in somatotonics is striking, but is perhaps relatively unimportant in comparison with the same habitual ordering of mental activities. Somatotonic people who have more viscerotonia than cerebrotonia think in orderly, habitual patterns, and they rarely change their minds or their internal attitudes. They are prone to wear the same mental clothes through life, and whatever cerebrotonia may be present is readily bent to the role of rationalization or self-justification.

In adult cerebrotonics, on the contrary, an astounding capacity for changing the mind is encountered. To live with a cerebrotonic is to walk in a forest thickly planted with surprises. Yet the other side of the story may also be a painful one. The deep habit formation and mental inflexibility of somatotonia often spell ineducability, and many a bright cerebrotonic-somatotonic marriage, after dawning with a brave reeducation program, has sobered into the gray drizzle of sullen conflict.

Predominant somatotonia carries relative immunity to the common nervous or functional disorders, but somatotonics frequently have high blood pressure and are susceptible to cardiac, vascular and renal ailments associated with hypertension. Somatotonic people are also peculiarly susceptible to staphylococcic infections, particularly to acne and boils. But the most characteristic of all somatotonic afflictions is acute, fulminating appendicitis. There is ground for believing that this condition is rare where somatotonia is low.

Bodily coordination is one of the most conspicuous of somatotonic characteristics. Where somatotonia is predominant the body appears to function as a unit. Legs, arms, head, and trunk are never in each other's way. Somatotonics move with grace, swim, skate and climb easily, and adapt readily to athletic games. They seem to think with the body as a whole, so perfectly does the physical self hang together.

* * * * *

Somatotonia is generally the most difficult of the components to gauge. Since it is a dynamic concept, referring to somatic expression, there is conspicuously present in it a gradient which extends from a latent to a manifest extreme. Depending on the predominant environmental pressures, somatotonia may be largely latent and potential, or largely a manifest, surface expression. To gauge this component accurately, it is necessary to know how the individual behaves under *all* circumstances, including those which fully challenge or fully test somatotonia (crucial athletic competition, physical attack, apparent discrimination against the individual, insulting offense, the challenge to competition, etc.). Also it is necessary to study in detail the breathing habits, the cough, laugh, manner of movement and the like. In short it is necessary to look beneath the veneer of civilization.

One of the major skills to be developed by the student of constitution is the ability accurately to detect latent somatotonia. Were it not for this factor, the diagnosis of temperament might be almost child's play. When not immediately needed, somatotonia exhibits a tendency to disappear from sight, like a cat's claws. This is especially the case with the more intelligent and more successfully adapted somatotonics. In a superficial sense they simulate viscerotonia when not excited (as do the cats). Yet when subjected to appropriate stimulation the somatotonia makes itself clearly enough manifest. People showing this characteristic are frequently quiet-spoken, although the cough, the laugh, and especially the vigorous breathing are fairly certain to reveal signs of the latent second component. (Trait S-13, *Unrestrained Voice*, is thus not always a loud voice. It may be loud only in the cough or laugh, and under conditions which bring the somatotonia to the front.)

For a long time we were confused and puzzled by this phenomenon of latent somatotonia.

* * * * *

In summary, somatotonia means dynamic expression of the soma. This component is closely associated with physical drive and endurance, with a relatively low sleep requirement, with infrequent food requirement, with high blood pressure and the danger of apoplexy, and with a youthfully athletic body which tends to become solid and heavy as life advances. Somatotonia needs exercise and loves a vigorous life. Dreaming is very remote from waking consciousness and dream analysis is often suddenly revealing to somatotonic people. Somatotonics love noise and the strong voice and the strong walk. They snore irregularly but loudly.

There is about the same proportion of somatotonia in young children as in adults, if noisiness is a good criterion. Somatotonics are likely to enter upon the pathetic quest of the springs of youth. Alcoholism seems typically to be associated with a motivational conflict in which somatotonia and cerebrotonia are at war within a personality, with the former barely holding the upper hand. Somatotonia implies habit susceptibility. The functional or nervous disorders are rare when this component is predominant, but acute appendicitis is common (and dangerous) with somatotonia. People high in the second component love rhythm, the dance, and martial music.

* * * * *

3. Cerebrotonia

The third component is the element of restraint, inhibition and attentionality. The forebrain holds in check both visceral and somatic functions, apparently to maintain a closer and more sensitive attentional focus. The cardinal symptom of cerebrotonia is tense hyperattentionality. The physical foundation for it seems to lie in relative predominance of exposed surface over mass.

The cerebrotonic is tense, incapable of peripheral relaxation, and chronically aware of his internal tension, although not necessarily disturbed by it. Cardia distress or heart consciousness, and temporary digestive distress of all sorts are normal manifestations of cerebrotonia, a fact which if generally known might save the public millions of clinical dollars, and the medical profession many headaches. Cerebrotonics are often called nervous or neurotic when they are quite normal, just as viscerotonics are sometimes accused of gluttony and lethargy when they are behaving normally.

The cerebrotonic uses up a great amount of "nervous energy" and flirts with the danger of "nervous exhaustion." He needs more sleep than a person high in one of the other dynamic components. His basal metabolic rate is usually high and he tends to become chronically fatigued in the normal routines of life. The history of fatigability, poor sleep habits, inability to get up in the morning, abnormal caloric requirement, and a chronic sense of internal tension are good clinical indicators of cerebrotonia. These people sleep lightly. The forebrain seems never to let go its dominance completely even in sleep. Dreaming is constant. The dreaming is relatively close to the threshold of clear consciousness, and the process of going to sleep is invariably a slow one. All relaxation is slow. The sphincters "let go" slowly and incompletely. In cerebrotonia the urinary stream is small, and the length of time required for urination is relatively great.

Cerebrotonia is accompanied by resistance to depressant drugs, and nothing is gained by attempting to use the violence of drug depression against the stubbornly resistant forebrain, except possibly in acute pathological conditions. Many cerebrotonics learn in middle life to go to sleep by a routine of "relaxational" exercises. But along with the remarkable resistance to drug depression there is usually a similar resistance to habit. The cerebrotonic avoids enslavement by habit, but often fails to form the routine habits which play so important a part in a normal and comfortable life.

Cerebrotonia gives rise to many manifestations of chronic fatigue in an overstimulated and hurried world. Among these the commonest are the various skin conditions called neurodermatitis, and the symptoms collectively called functional bowel distress.

* * * * *

For a person high in the third component, the process of getting up in the morning is often an exceedingly painful business. It is only after several hours in bed that this individual descends to really refreshing and recuperative sleep. His deepest sleep is his latest sleep. . . . Cerebrotonics often become most alert and do their best work in the evening of the day. They are usually most wide awake at about bedtime, and they are often worthless in the early part of the morning.

These people perhaps need to eat four times a day instead of three. They need more food than they have usually been taught to believe. They particularly need protein and the easily digested carbohydrates. Their digestive tracts are under predominantly thoracico-lumbar control, which is really forebrain control. Normally this means tension. Under emotional circumstances it means virtual intestinal paralysis. Absorption is relatively poor, hunger is quick in onset, poorly sustained, and promptly relieved. In cerebrotonia the stomach is ordinarily small, of low capacity, and best adapted to taking frequent small amounts of food rather than infrequent large amounts. The cerebrotonic should never go without breakfast, for to do so is to draw heavily upon his slender store of reserve energy, and this means flirting with the danger of chronic fatigue.

* * * * *

Cerebrotonic hunger is quick in onset and sharp in quality. But it is poorly sustained. Cerebrotonics do not for long *suffer* from hunger. In them hunger tends soon to give way to a (sometimes rather pleasant) sense of exhaustion and dissociation from physical reality. For viscerotonics, prolonged hunger is extremely painful and death by starvation presents a terrifying prospect. Hunger and solitary confinement are potent weapons of punishment against viscerotonics but not against cerebrotonics. Viscerotonics do not enter upon hunger strikes.

Alcohol is a selective depressant, acting first on the higher cerebral centers, and theoretically releasing the rest of the organism from the inhibition which the cerebrum exerts. This produces a transient exhilaration or feeling of well-being in somatotonic and viscerotonic personalities. There is nothing imaginary about the exhilaration. In persons whose basic motivation is for some reason caught in a state of poorly tolerated conflict, alcoholic removal of cerebral control sometimes comes to be the main ecstasy of life. These people may become as incurably alcoholic as a dementia praecox patient is incurably schizoid.

*   *   *   *   *

Cerebrotonics can often resist the depressant effect of alcohol with remarkable fortitude, and sometimes they acquire the social custom of drinking, perhaps following the path of least resistance, but they pay well for it. Instead of yielding graciously to the effect of the drug, the cerebrotonic constitution resists violently, using up its reserve energies in its resistance, and a cerebrotonic bout with alcohol tends to be followed by fatigue and low energy for days afterwards. For the individual of cerebrotonic motivation, alcohol is a poison. For viscerotonics and for some somatotonics the drug is without doubt beneficent. For all temperaments, alcohol possesses diagnostic value.

It is to be observed that stress or emotional crisis of any sort appears to exert nearly the same effect as alcohol, so far as revealing the relative strength of the primary temperamental components is concerned. Upon this general principle the logic of the "third degree" is perhaps grounded. If a suspected person is badgered long enough, or deprived of sleep for a sufficient length of time, he falls back at last upon his true character and tends to reveal his true nature.

The concept of intelligence, or of intellectuality, must not be confused with cerebrotonia.

*   *   *   *   *

The cerebrotonic may be literate or illiterate, may be trained or untrained in the conventional intellectual exercises of his *milieu*, may be an avid reader or may never have read a book, may be a scholastic genius or may have failed in every sort of schooling. He may be a dreamer, a poet, philosopher, recluse, or a builder of utopias and of abstract psychologies. He may be a schizoid personality, a religious fanatic, an ascetic, a patient martyr, or a contentious crusader. All these depend upon the intermixture of other components, upon other variables in the symphony, and also upon the environmental pressures to which the personality has been exposed. The essential characteristic of the cerebrotonic is his acuteness of attention. The other two major functions, the direct visceral and the direct somatic functions, are subjugated, held in check, and rendered secondary. The cerebrotonic eats and exercises to attend, the viscerotonic attends and exercises to eat, the somatotonic eats and attends in order to exercise. Loss of one of the major exteroceptive media—eyesight, for example—would be more tragic for the cerebrotonic than for one in whom the first or second component predominates.

The cerebrotonic component finds its primary ecstasy and its freedom not in eating or drinking, not in fellowship or for long in sexual relationship, not in physical adventure or in the power of social domination, but in a certain intensification of consciousness which appears to arise from *inhibition* of all of these (somatotonic and viscerotonic) "freedoms." Freedom is perhaps only a general name for the ultimate objective of all striving, and our historical difficulty in defining it possibly takes origin from the polydimensionality of the first order of components of motivation. For cerebrotonia, freedom seems to be activity of attention relatively unhampered by objective "reality." Even in schizophrenia, which whatever else it may be, is one condition closely associated with cerebrotonia, the dissociated mind achieves a freedom to suppress the objective reality and to range in its own delusional system, or within its own chaos. For somatotonia, freedom is freedom of direct action, and for viscerotonia it is freedom to be comfortable, to have a full belly, and to feel possessive toward the world. Cerebrotonic freedom appears to arise as a direct function of inhibition—inhibition of viscerotonic and somatotonic freedom.

The major cerebrotonic danger is dissociation from reality. The freedom of the forebrain is likely to be purchased at the price of a biological losing of the way, and hence at an apparent end-cost of suicide. . . . The cerebrotonic can become suicidally schizoid and can thereby escape all these dangers at once. He throws the baby overboard to keep it from falling out of the boat.

The nature of the basic motivation in a personality can easily be determined if an observer can discover what has been the typical behavior in the face of trouble and stress. The cerebrotonic in trouble may lose appetite and all desire for action, exercise, travel or companionship. He may resent intrusion and may resist any attempt on the part of others either to cheer him up or to distract him. Intense contemplation of the thing may leave him sleepless for many days and nights, may finally exhaust him altogether, but if the cerebrotonic temperament is predominant, this is his way out.

Much harm is done to cerebrotonics by persons who do not comprehend the nature of this process. Cerebrotonia means that the function of thought is the naturally dominant one, and that in the face of crisis it is this function which must take over the responsibility to find the way out. This may be why cerebrotonics can rarely act effectively in crises. The cerebrotonic finds both his delights and his defenses in the system and detail of his own consciousness. He is internally self-sufficient. He may be kind and affectionate, according to the strength and quality of his first component, and he may be fond of action, according to the strength of the second component, but he is not in the final analysis dependent upon affection or action. In the face of trouble the cerebrotonic must always fall back upon the system and organization which is in his own head, even though the resulting delay may be fatal.

Cerebrotonia is probably the major characteristic of what Jung originally called *introversion*. The principal difficulty with this term is that it some-times implies pathology and in its common use indicates something unde-sirable or unhealthy. In the popular conception introversion is a thing which, like ectomorphic posture, ought to be "corrected."

Cerebrotonic skin is typically dry and finely lined, with notable sensi-tivity to insect bites and to itching. The outer layer of the skin is rapidly shed and replaced. In this sense cerebrotonic skin is highly active. Such people produce large crops of dandruff, but they hold their hair. The bald-headed cerebrotonic is relatively rare.

In cerebrotonia the basal metabolic rate (thyroid function) is typically high. Appendicitis, furunculosis (boils), gall bladder infections, nephritis, and indeed nearly all of the common overwhelming infections except those of the upper respiratory tract are distinctly rarer among people with predom-inant third component than among the general population. Cancer also appears to be rare among cerebrotonics. The swallowing and gagging reflexes are overly sensitive, and rapid edematous swelling of the laryngeal region presents a peculiar danger in cerebrotonia. Many cerebrotonics appear to have been killed by acute streptococcal infections of the throat, accompanied by edema and strangulation.

Cerebrotonics show remarkable resistance to general anaesthetics. Recov-ery from a general anaesthetic is slow, however, for the cerebrotonic appears to use up his energy resources in fighting the depressant effect. There is often marked sensitivity to tobacco, and the cerebrotonic constitution cannot as a rule stand up to regular pipe smoking. Tobacco produces a rapid heart, dizziness, and if persisted in, loss of weight.

Cerebrotonics, for some reason, can rarely sing. The difficulty is probably associated with their inability to relax, and with what is called self-con-sciousness. There is so much internal restraint that it is very difficult for a cerebrotonic to "throw out" his voice.

*   *   *   *   *

In summary, cerebrotonia is related to what has been called introversion but it has more specific meaning than that term has carried, and it has no normal-abnormal connotation. It carries its own norms, as do the other basic dynamic components.

There are a number of distinctive, although not necessarily diagnostic, clinical correlates of cerebrotonia. The more conspicuous of these are (1) tenseness, unrelaxability and apprehensiveness, associated with a low, labile blood pressure, (2) neurodermatitis, dry skin, sensitivity to insect bites, and a history of itching, (3) functional digestive disturbances, (4) high sexual eroticism with intense crisis in both sexes, (5) poor voice control and "the paralysis of overawareness" in crucial or emotional situations, (6) thermal instability and poor toleration of both heat and cold—especially of cold water, (7) resistance to contagious diseases except colds, (8) oversensitive upper respiratory tract, with consequent laryngeal irritation and overly active gagging reflexes, (9) resistance to alcohol and to all general depressants, (10) sensitivity to tobacco, (11) suppression (paralysis) of visceral activity in the face of emotion, (12) increased food requirement with inability to gain weight, (13) increased sleep requirement, light sleeping, and resistance to hypnotic drugs, (14) easy or chronic fatigability but with quick recovery, (15) overawareness of or overresponse to pain and to normal organic processes, and (16) a moderately elevated basal metabolic rate which is permanently sustained and therefore not due to intercurrent thyroid pathology.

PART SIX

Trait and Factor Theoretical Approaches to Personality

CHAPTER 17

GORDON W. ALLPORT

PERSONALISTIC PSYCHOLOGY:
A TRAIT APPROACH TO PERSONALITY

Allport's PERSONALISTIC PSYCHOLOGY suggests that the personality of the individual is a self-contained system which merits consideration in its own right, independent of such factors as interpersonal relations, culture, or roles, however much they may contribute indirectly to the psychologist's knowledge of personality. Since the person is an individual, it is the individual's motives, traits, and personal style which are of major import in the study of personality. *Uniqueness* is the keynote, both in form and in pattern, of the whole of human nature. "Molecular biology shows increasingly that life-substances are identical across species. The building blocks of life —vegetable and animal—turn out to be strikingly uniform in terms of nucleic acids, protein molecules, and enzymatic reactions. Yet a sparrow differs from a pine tree, a man from a sparrow, and one man is very unlike another. The challenge of morphogenesis (accounting for pattern) waxes more and more acute as we discover the commonalities of life."[1]

Allport would place the emphasis in personality theory upon the normal and integrated person rather than upon the abnormal and the degenerate, who are so often the sources of much of the material which psychiatrists use in their personality theories. Allport also puts major emphasis upon the concept of "functional

[1]*Pattern and Growth in Personality* (New York: Holt, Rinehart and Winston, 1937, 1961), from p. x.

autonomy," a belief that motivation is not solely attributable to in-stincts or other propensities stemming from birth, but is, rather, a "contemporary system," possessing an autonomy in its own right and responsible for the governance of the personality.

Allport was born in 1897. Until his death in 1967 he was Pro-fessor of Psychology at Harvard, where he received his A.B. in 1919, A.M. in 1921, and Ph.D. in 1922. Allport studied also at the University of Berlin, the University of Hamburg, and Cam-bridge. He was editor of the *Journal of Abnormal and Social Psy-chology* from 1937 to 1949. His honors included presidency of the American Psychological Association and honorary memberships in the German, British, French, and Austrian psychological societies.

Among his publications are *A—S Reaction Study* (with his brother, Floyd H., 1928), *A Study of Values* (with P. E. Vernon, 1931), *Studies in Expressive Movement* (with P. E. Vernon, 1933), "Judging Personality from Voice" in *Journal of Social Psychology* (with H. Cantril, 1934), "Attitudes" in *A Handbook of Social Psychology* (ed. by C. C. Murchison, 1935), *The Psychology of Radio* (with H. Cantril, 1935), "Trait-Names: A Psycho-Lexical Study" in *Psychological Monographs* (with H. S. Odbert, 1936), "The Functional Autonomy of Motives" in *American Journal of Psychology* (1937), *Personality: A Psychological Interpretation* (1937), "Motivation in Personality: Reply to Mr. Bertocci" in *Psychological Review* (1940), "The Psychologist's Frame of Ref-erence" in *Psychological Bulletin* (1940), *The Psychology of Rumor* (with L. Postman, 1947), "Scientific Models and Human Morals" in *Psychological Review* (1947), *The Individual and His Religion* (1950), *The Nature of Personality: Selected Papers* (1950), "The Trend in Motivational Theory" in *American Journal of Orthopsychiatry* (1953), *The Nature of Prejudice* (1954), *Be-coming: Basic Considerations for a Psychology of Personality* (1955), *Personality and Social Encounter* (1960), *Pattern and Growth in Personality* (1961), and *The Person in Psychology: Se-lected Essays* (1968). In 1970 Allport's personality system was in-formally presented to R. I. Evans in *The Man and His Ideas*.

A DEFINITION OF PERSONALITY[2]

Since there is no such thing as a wrong definition of any term, if it is sup-

[2]*Personality: A Psychological Interpretation* (New York: Holt, Rinehart and Win-ston, 1937), from pp. 47-50.

ported by usage, it is evident that no one, neither the theologian, the philosopher, the jurist, the sociologist, the man in the street, nor the psychologist, can monopolize "personality." For the psychologist, to be sure, some definitions seem to be more serviceable than others. Completely unsuitable are biosocial formulations in terms of social reputation or superficial charm. The distinction between reputation (social effectiveness) and the true personality is one that will be observed rigidly throughout this book. Omnibus definitions must likewise be rejected. More helpful are those conceptions that ascribe to personality a *solid organization* of dispositions and sentiments. Valuable likewise are definitions that refer to the *style of life*, to *modes of adaptation* to one's surroundings, to *progressive growth* and development and to *distinctiveness*.

Might we not merely say that, psychologically considered, personality is what man really is?

This terse expression states the essential biophysical position, and is acceptable enough in principle. Yet it is too brief and vague as it stands. The following amplification seems to serve the purpose better:

PERSONALITY IS THE DYNAMIC ORGANIZATION WITHIN THE INDIVIDUAL OF THOSE PSYCHOPHYSICAL SYSTEMS THAT DETERMINE HIS UNIQUE ADJUSTMENTS TO HIS ENVIRONMENT.

This formulation contains the seeds of the hierarchical, integrative, adjustive, and distinctive classes of definitions described above. In a sense, therefore, *it represents a synthesis of contemporary psychological usage.* But each portion of the definition is to be accurately understood.

Dynamic Organization. To escape from the sterile enumerations of the omnibus definitions it is necessary to stress active organization. The crucial problem of psychology has always been mental organization (association). . . . Hence "organization" must appear in the definition. Yet this organization must be regarded as constantly evolving and changing, as motivational and as self-regulating; hence the qualification "dynamic." Organization must also imply at times the correlative process of *disorganization*, especially in those personalities that we are wont to regard as "abnormal."

Psychophysical Systems. Habits, specific and general attitudes, sentiments, and dispositions of other orders are all psychophysical systems. In later chapters these dispositions will be ordered within a theory of *traits.* The term "system" refers to traits or groups of traits in a latent or active condition. The term "psychophysical" reminds us that personality is neither exclusively mental nor exclusively neural. The organization entails the operation of both body and mind, inextricably fused into a personal unity.

Determine. This term is a natural consequence of the biophysical view. Personality *is* something and *does* something. It is not synonymous with behavior or activity; least of all is it merely the impression that this activity makes on others. It is what lies *behind* specific acts and *within* the individual. The systems that constitute personality are in every sense *determining tendencies,* and when aroused by suitable stimuli provoke those adjustive and expressive acts by which the personality comes to be known.

Unique. Strictly speaking every adjustment of every person is unique, in time and place, and in quality. In a sense, therefore, this criterion seems redundant. It becomes important, however, in our later discussions of the problem of *quantitative* variation among individuals in respect to the so-called "common" traits and is therefore emphasized in the definition.

Adjustments to His Environment. This phase has a functional and evolutionary significance. Personality is a mode of survival. "Adjustments," however, must be interpreted broadly enough to include maladjustments, and "environment" to include the behavioral environment (meaningful to the individual) as well as the surrounding geographical environment.

Above all, adjustments must not be considered as merely reactive adaptation such as plants and animals are capable of. The adjustments of men contain a great amount of spontaneous, creative behavior toward the environment. Adjustment to the physical world as well as to the imagined or ideal world—both being factors in the "behavioral environment"—involves *mastery* as well as passive adaptation.

STAGES OF PERSONALITY DEVELOPMENT[3]

Early Infancy

We do not know what an infant's conscious experience may be like. . . . One thing is quite certain: the young infant is not aware of himself as a *self*. He does not separate the "me" from the rest of the world. And it is precisely this separation that is the pivot of later life. Consciousness and self-consciousness are not the same, neither for the infant nor for the adult. The infant, though presumably conscious, lacks self-consciousness completely; the adult has both, but they are not identical.

The Early Self

Three aspects of self-awareness gradually evolve during the first three years of life:

Aspect 1: Sense of bodily self
Aspect 2: Sense of continuing self-identity
Aspect 3: Self-esteem, pride

Contributing to the development are many influences: maturation (anatomical and physiological), recurrent bodily sensations, memory aided by verbal concepts, one's proper name as an anchorage point, frustrations dur-

[3]*Pattern and Growth in Personality, op. cit.,* from pp. 111-27.

ing the process of exploring and manipulating the environment, a period of negativism where the child practices his emerging sense of self. At this stage the child begins to feel himself autonomous and separate from others. But even now he can easily "depersonalize" in play, and feel himself to be an object, an animal, or another person.

It is, of course, *people* who stimulate the child most of all. He learns that their acts and his response, as well as his acts and their response, always go together. The ego and the alter play a constant game of interaction—like adults at tennis. There is a continuous "conversation of gestures" between them.

*   *   *   *   *

The self, says Mead, in all its aspects, is predominantly a social product. In general we agree with Mead, though he inclines to overstate his case.

Four to Six

During this period we may date the appearance of two aspects of selfhood in addition to the three we have previously discussed.

Aspect 4: The extension of self
Aspect 5: The self-image

The sense of competition starts only after the age of three. With it comes the sense of possession. This ball is *mine. I* own the tricycle. My daddy, my brother, my dog, my house are felt to be warm parts of one's self. The child cannot yet, of course, extend himself to embrace his country, his church, or his career. But the foundations are laid for this important extension of selfhood. At the adult level we sometimes say, "A man is what he loves." By this statement we mean that we know personality best by knowing what the extended-self embraces. But the young child has only the rudiments of such self-extension.

Rudimentary, too, is the *self-image*. The child begins to know that his parents want him to be a "good" boy, and also that at times he is "naughty." By the interaction process he comes to know what his parents expect of him, and to compare this expectation with his own behavior. Of course, as yet, he has no clearly developed conscience, nor any image of himself as he would like to be in adulthood. . . . In childhood the capacity to think of oneself as one is, as one wants to be, and as one ought to be is merely germinal.

Six to Twelve

The child's sense of identity, his self-image, and his capacity for self-extension are greatly enhanced by his entrance into school. . . . All the while the child's intellectual life is developing. Early in the school years he becomes addicted to riddles and puns, and a little later to codes, cryptograms, and foreign words. Objective knowledge fascinates him, and the question

"Why?" is always on his lips. He begins to sense a new power, a new aspect of his selfhood:

Aspect 6: The self as rational coper

It is true that from early months the child has been able to solve simple problems, but only now does he fully realize that he has a rational capacity to bring to bear upon them. Previously he *thought*, but now he *thinks* about thinking. The self as a "coper" coincides fairly well with Freud's definition of the ego.

Adolescence

The core of the identity problem for the adolescent is the selecting of an occupation or other life-goal. The future, he knows, must follow a *plan*, and in this respect his sense of selfhood takes on a dimension entirely lacking in childhood. Often youth aims too high. Idealism is a frequent, and loveable, quality. Many adolescent ideals are so high that a bad tumble is in store. Perhaps during the late twenties the youth will discover that he has less talent than he thought, that he will make less of a mark on the world, and that his marriage is less perfect than he had hoped. Paring down the self-image and aspirations to life-size is a task for his adult years.

But the important point is that in adolescence long-range purposes and distant goals add a new dimension to the sense of selfhood. We shall speak therefore of

Aspect 7: Propriate striving

Various writers maintain that the cement holding life together is its "directedness" or "intentionality." In order to be normal an adolescent, and especially an adult, needs a defining objective, a line of promise. It is not necessary that the goals be rigidly focused, but only that a central theme of striving be present.

THE PROPRIUM[4]

Is there no way to unite these seven aspects of selfhood? They are all states of self-relevance that we *feel*. Each in its way is an intimate region of personality involved in matters of importance to the organized emotional life of the individual. Together they compose the me as felt and known.

So it seems reasonable to unite these aspects (even though they are phenomenologically different, *i.e.*, differently experienced) under a single name. Let us choose the term *proprium*. Why not simply the term *self?* There are two reasons: (1) Most writers, as we have seen, use *self* or *ego* for only one or two of the limited aspects we have treated. We prefer a fresher and

[4]*Ibid.*, from pp. 127-28.

broader label. (2) There is one remaining philosophical problem pertaining to the self to which we now turn, the question of "the knower." Since this aspect of selfhood is also properly termed *self*, we suggest using *proprium* to cover the self "as object" of knowledge and feeling. We are directly aware of the proprium in a sense that we are never directly aware of the "knower."

Before proceeding with this issue let us explain why it is necessary in personality theory to give a place to the proprium in its various aspects. One reason, of course, is that the subjective (felt) side of personality is what everyone knows about; it would be foolish to overlook it as some psychologists prefer to do. Another reason, very important, is that people's *behavior* varies greatly according to whether they feel self-involved or merely task-involved in what they are doing.

       *   *   *   *   *

The concept of the proprium, therefore, we find to be not only justified, but entirely indispensable in psychological theory.

It is important to point out that the proprium is not at all moments conscious. True, we *derive* the concept from experiences of self of which we are fully aware. But the traces of these experiences are effective even when we are not observing them. In propriate striving, for example, we characteristically "lose ourselves," because we are deeply absorbed in what we are doing. But it is nonetheless true that ego-involved interest is still playing a persistent role.

CHARACTER[5]

Character is a term frequently used as a synonym of personality. It has a history as long and nearly as intricate. As employed by Theophrastus it possessed much of the same adverbial significance that Woodworth ascribed to personality. It was the "engraving" of the individual, his style of life as determined by his dominant trait. There is no historical reason why the term should not be used interchangeably with personality, as indeed it frequently is. But in modern psychology there are two divergent lines of meaning, both of which give an independent significance to the term, thereby lessening the practice of equating the terms.

Many writers identify character with some special phase of personality, making it a subdivision of the whole. For example, it is said that personality may be viewed as intelligence plus character, or as intelligence, temperament, and character. Since personality is never an additive phenomenon such statements serve to characterize neither personality nor character.

Whenever character is considered to be a subdivision of personality, it is nearly always identified with volition in some way. . . . This is the meaning endorsed not only by many psychologists but by the church, by educators,

[5]*Personality: A Psychological Interpretation, op. cit.*, from pp. 50-52.

and by common speech as well. . . . When a man shows "character" by resisting temptation, or when it is said that the aim of education should be the "development of character," what is really meant is that the man has behaved, or the child should be trained to behave, in ways that are approved by prevailing social and ethical standards. The exercise of "will" in each case is a phenomenon of personality. *Character enters the situation only when this personal effort is judged from the standpoint of some code.* . . . Social standards as well as psychology are brought in when we label such conduct "character." . . .

Therefore, instead of defining character as the volitional aspect of personality, it is sounder to admit frankly that it is an ethical concept. Sir John Adams writes, "Character is the moral estimate of the individual, an evaluation." Defined in this way, the psychologist does not need the term at all; personality alone will serve. *Character is personality evaluated, and personality is character devaluated.*

*   *   *   *   *

TEMPERAMENT[6]

The classical doctrine that ascribed peculiarities of temperament to the humors of the body has persisted throughout the ages so that the meaning of the term has varied but little. The term found its way into English in the Middle Ages along with the doctrine of the humors. It meant then and still means a "constitution or habit of mind, especially depending upon or connected with physical constitution." Today in America psychological writers stress particularly the constitutional basis; for them temperament is the "internal weather" in which personality develops; it is the subjective climate provided by native physiological and kinetic endowment. The usage of the term in Great Britain is somewhat different, tending to equate temperament with personality, as in the phase "temperament tests" (rather than "tests of personality").

Temperament, like intelligence and physique, might be said to designate a certain class of raw material from which personality is fashioned. Strictly speaking, there is no temperament apart from personality, nor any personality devoid of temperament. It is merely convenient to employ the term in speaking of dispositions that are almost unchanged from infancy throughout life (dispositions saturated with a constant emotional quality, with a peculiar pattern of mood, alertness, intensity, or tonus). The more anchored a disposition is in native constitutional soil the more likely it is to be spoken of as temperament.

*   *   *   *   *

Work dealing primarily with glands, physical build, or blood composition (to name only a few popular fields of contemporary study) frequently claims

[6]*Ibid.*, from pp. 53-54.

416

to be seeking the biological foundations of *personality*. And so it is—indirectly; but first of all it is seeking the physical correlates of *temperament*. There is a danger of exaggeration in labels such as "Glands Regulating Personality," "Biological Foundations of Personality," "Physique and Character." The implication in these titles is that no factors other than the constitutional need be considered. It would clarify the problem if biologists and endocrinologists would drop the term personality altogether, and speak exclusively of temperament.

*   *   *   *   *

The following definition of temperament fits standard psychological usage and meets the requirements of this book. *Temperament refers to the characteristic phenomena of an individual's emotional nature, including his susceptibility to emotional stimulation, his customary strength and speed of response, the quality of his prevailing mood, and all peculiarities of fluctuation and intensity in mood; these phenomena being regarded as dependent upon constitutional make-up, and therefore largely hereditary in origin.*

FUNCTIONAL AUTONOMY[7]

To understand the dynamics of the normal mature personality a new and somewhat radical principle of growth must be introduced to supplement the more traditional genetic concepts thus far considered. For convenience of discussion this new principle may be christened the *functional autonomy of motives*.

*   *   *   *   *

Before describing the principle of functional autonomy, its theoretical significance should stand out clearly. The stress in this volume is constantly on the ultimate and irreducible uniqueness of personality. "But how," cry all the traditional scientists, including the older dynamic psychologists, "how are we ever to have a *science* of unique events? Science must generalize." Perhaps it must, but what the objectors forget is that *a general law may be a law that tells how uniqueness comes about*. It is manifest error to assume that a general principle of motivation must involve the postulation of abstract or general motives. The principle of functional autonomy, here described, is general enough to meet the needs of science, but particularized enough in its operation to account for the uniqueness of personal conduct.

The dynamic psychology proposed here regards adult motives as infinitely varied, and as self-sustaining, contemporary systems, growing out of antecedent systems, but functionally independent of them. Just as a child gradually repudiates his dependence on his parents, develops a will of his own, becomes self-active and self-determining, and outlives his parents, so

[7]*Ibid.*, from pp. 191, 193-95.

GORDON W. ALLPORT

it is with motives. Each motive has a definite point of origin which may lie in the hypothetical instincts, or, more likely, in the organic tensions and diffuse irritability. Theoretically all adult purposes can be traced back to these seed-forms in infancy. But as the individual matures the bond is broken. The tie is historical, not functional.

Such a theory is obviously opposed to psychoanalysis and to all other genetic accounts that assume inflexibility in the root purposes and drives of life. (Freud says that the structure of the Id *never* changes.) The theory declines to believe that the energies of adult personality are infantile or archaic in nature. Motivation is *always* contemporary. The life of modern Athens is *continuous* with the life of the ancient city, but it in no sense *depends* upon it for its present "go." The life of a tree is continuous with that of its seed, but the seed no longer sustains and nourishes the full-grown tree. Earlier purposes lead into later purposes, but are abandoned in their favor.

William James taught a curious doctrine that has been a matter for incredulous amusement ever since, the doctrine of the *transitoriness of instincts*. According to this theory—not so quaint as sometimes thought—an instinct appears but once in a lifetime, whereupon it promptly disappears through its transformation into habits. If there *are* instincts this is no doubt their fate, for no instinct can retain its motivational force unimpaired after it has been absorbed and recast under the transforming influence of learning. Such is the reasoning of James, and such is the logic of functional autonomy. The psychology of personality must be a psychology of post-instinctive behavior. If, as in this volume, instincts are dispensed with from the beginning, the effect is much the same, for whatever the original drives or "irritabilities" of the infant are, they become completely transformed in the course of growth into contemporaneous systems of motives.

THE DOCTRINE OF TRAITS[8]

In everyday life, no one, not even a psychologist, doubts that underlying the conduct of a mature person there are characteristic dispositions or traits. His enthusiasms, interests, and styles of expression are far too self-consistent and plainly patterned to be accounted for in terms of specific habits or identical elements. Nor can the stability and consistency of behavior be explained away by invoking nominalistic theories; stability and consistency are not due to the bio-social arrangement of unrelated activities into categories with verbal tags. Traits are not creations in the mind of the observer, nor are they verbal fictions; they are here accepted as biophysical facts, actual psychophysical dispositions related—though no one yet knows how—to persistent neural systems of stress and determination.

[8]*Ibid.*, from pp. 339-42.

Traits are not, like the faculties of old, abstractions derived from a theory of mind-in-general. There is no essential resemblance between impersonal faculties, as Memory, Will, and Sagacity on the one hand, and the focalized sub-structures of a particular mind (interests, sentiments, general attitudes) on the other. Faculties are universal, traits personal; faculties are independent, traits inter-dependent; faculties are a priori, traits must be ascertained empirically in the individual case.

The doctrine of traits differs also from the theory of factors or any other system of common dimensions into which every individual is fitted categorically. Conceptualized nomothetic units (factors, instincts, needs, and the like) stress what is universal in men, not what is organized into integral, personal systems. The doctrine of traits emphasizes concrete individuality.

Traits are not directly observable; they are inferred (as any kind of determining tendency is inferred). Without such an inference the stability and consistency of personal behavior could not possibly be explained. Any specific action is a product of innumerable determinants, not only of traits but of momentary pressures and specialized influences. But it is the repeated occurrence of actions having the *same significance* (equivalence of response), following upon a definable range of stimuli having the same personal significance (equivalence of stimuli), that makes necessary the postulation of traits as states of Being. Traits are not at all times active, but they are persistent even when latent, and are distinguished by low thresholds of arousal.

It is one thing to admit traits as the most acceptable unit for investigation in the psychology of personality, but another to determine authoritatively the precise character of these traits in a given life. In order to avoid projection of his own nature and many other sources of error, the psychological investigator must use all the empirical tools of his science to make his inferences valid. Traits cannot be conjured into existence; they must be discovered.

In naming the traits that are discovered, there are many pitfalls, the chief one being the confusion of personality with character through the use of eulogistic and dyslogistic terms. Whenever this occurs the existential pattern of personality becomes hopelessly entangled with social judgments of merit and demerit. It is possible, though difficult, to achieve a psychological vocabulary of noncensorial trait-names. Most of these terms antedate psychology by centuries; they were invented because they were needed. Simply because it is difficult to employ them circumspectly, the investigator is not on that account justified in dispensing with them altogether and attempting to put mathematical or artificial symbols in their place. Regrettable though it may seem, the attributes of human personality can be depicted only with the aid of common speech, for it alone possesses the requisite flexibility, subtlety, and established intelligibility.

For the purposes of comparison and measurement certain segments of behavior (by virtue of the similarity of human equipment and the common exigencies of the cultural and physical environments) may be considered as distributed in a general population. These *common* traits as conceptualized by the investigator may, in a rough and approximate way, be scaled on a linear continuum. The "normality" of distribution obtained for such traits is a complex product of chance-biological variation, cultural conformity, and artifact. However carefully conceived and scaled, a common trait is at best an abstraction, for in its concrete form, in each particular life, it operates always in a unique fashion. *Individual* traits cannot be scaled at all in a general population, and for that reason they have been hitherto neglected by all except clinical investigators.

Some traits are clearly motivational, especially those subclasses ordinarily known as interests, ambitions, complexes, and sentiments. Other traits are less dynamic in their operation, having an ability to steer (to stylize) behavior rather than to initiate it. But often the traits that are first directive acquire driving power, and those that are at one time driving become merely directive.

Traits are not wholly independent of one another; nor are any other neuro-psychic systems. They frequently exist in clusters, the arousal of one portion tending to spread to all regions in readiness for communication. Throughout this elaborate interplay, different foci of organization can be detected, a fact that justifies the conception of a *manifold* of traits even where they clearly overlap.

As this segregation among traits is only relative, so too is their self-consistency. In fact, the usefulness of any trait to its possessor depends to a great extent upon its flexibility. Even while it stabilizes conduct and economizes effort, the trait must not be rigid in its operation; for effective judgment and mastery require variation. The range of situations that arouses traits must be expected to change according to circumstances. Also in any personality one must expect to find some contradiction and conflict among traits, as novelists and clinicians never tire of telling.

Variable though they are, still in every mature personality certain *central* traits can normally be identified. So too can *secondary* traits, though these are less distinctive, less prominent, and more circumscribed in their operation. Whenever a disposition is so little generalized that it is aroused by only a narrow range of stimulus situations, it is more properly called an *attitude* than a trait. Somewhat rarely a personality is dominated by one outstanding *cardinal* trait, to which other dispositions serve as merely subsidiary congruent foci.

As is the case with all other forms of mental organization, the structure of true (individual) traits is a question of degree. But however much they may vary in respect to their consistency, scope, and independence, they have—according to the theory developed in these chapters—certain essential characteristics. They are always biophysical in nature, concrete and personal in their organization, contemporaneous in their effect, capable of functional autonomy, but not structurally independent of one another; they are generalized (to the extent that the effective stimuli are equivalent, and to the extent that the resultant responses are equivalent). They are *modi vivendi*, ultimately deriving their significance from the role they play in advancing adaptation within, and mastery of, the personal environment.

*   *   *   *   *

We[9] are left with a concept of trait as *a generalized and focalized neuro-psychic system (peculiar to the individual), with the capacity to render many stimuli functionally equivalent, and to initiate and guide consistent (equivalent) forms of adaptive and expressive behavior.*

Psychological Concepts Equivalent to, Subordinate to, or Partially Overlapping the Concept of Traits

Charakterzug	mode of adjustment
complex	motor-perceptual region (Lewin)
directional tendency	need integrate (Murray)
ego-system (Koffka)	*Neigung* (Lazurski)
Eigenschaft (Baumgarten, Stern)	phobia
foci of development	*Richtungsdisposition* (Stern)
general attitude	*Rüstungsdisposition* (Stern)
generalized habit (Dewey)	sentiment (McDougall)
ideal	style of life (Adler)
inner-personal region (Lewin)	subjective value (Spranger)
interest	taste
linéament (Boven)	*Triebfeder* (Klages)
mode of adaptation	trend

Attitude and Trait[10]

→ Both *attitude* and *trait* are indispensable concepts. Between them they virtually cover every type of disposition with which the psychology of personality concerns itself. Ordinarily *attitude* should be employed when the disposition is bound to an object or value, that is to say, when it is aroused by a well-defined class of stimuli, and when the individual feels towards these stimuli a definite attraction or repulsion. In some cases either of the terms (trait or attitude) is correct, as in the case of extroversion or patriotism . . . or conservatism or radicalism. If in the last two cases the object or value against which the person is rebelling, or which he is intent on conserving, can be specified, the term attitude is preferable. If, on the other hand, the radicalism or the conservatism is chronic and "temperamental," expressed in almost any sphere of the person's behavior, then the

[9]*Ibid.*, from p. 295.
[10]*Ibid.*, from p. 294.

term *trait* fits the situation better. Narrow or specific attitudes are never traits. A man is fond of his dog: he has a kindly attitude toward it. But if in general he is thoughtful of, and sympathetic toward men and beasts, he has a trait of kindliness. The more generalized an attitude (the more difficult it is to specify its object or its polarity of affect), the more does it resemble a trait.

Trait and Type[11]

We refer to the sharp contrast between the theory of traits and the doctrine (any doctrine) of types. Unlike traits, types always have biosocial reference. A man can be said to *have* a trait; but he cannot be said to *have* a type. Rather he *fits* a type. This bit of usage betrays the important fact that types exist not in people or in nature, but rather in the eye of the observer. Type includes more than is in the individual. Traits, on the contrary, are considered wholly within the compass of the individual. The crux of the distinction is that in type the reference point is always some attribute, or cluster of correlating attributes abstracted from various personalities, a biosocial reference defined by the interest of the particular investigator.

Individual versus Common Traits[12]

Strictly speaking, no two persons have precisely the same trait. Though each of two men may be *aggressive* (or *esthetic*), the style and range of the aggression (or estheticism) in each case is noticeably different. What else could be experienced in view of the unique hereditary endowment, the different developmental history, and the never-repeated external influences that determine each personality? The end product of unique determination can never be anything but unique.

This evident fact is one that most psychologists have great difficulty in accepting. If individuals cannot be compared with one another in respect to the same traits, what is to become of the psychology of personality as a "scientific" (*i.e.*, nomothetic) discipline? Outraged at the prospect, one psychologist exclaimed, "I think it is nonsense to say that no two men ever have the same trait. I mean, of course it is true, but it is one of those truths that can't be accepted." The die-hard nomothetist feels that in sheer loyalty to science, he *must* search for nothing but common and basic variables, however great the resulting distortion of the individual structure.

* * * * *

For all their ultimate differences, normal persons within a given culture-area tend to develop a limited number of *roughly comparable* modes of adjustment. The original endowment of most human beings, their stages of growth, and the demands of their particular society, are sufficiently standard and comparable to lead to some basic modes of adjustment that from in-

[11]*Ibid.*, from pp. 295-96.
[12]*Ibid.*, from pp. 297-99.

dividual to individual are *approximately* the same. . . . The psychologist does well to recognize all these possible gradations and to postulate a common variable which, though rough and approximate, permits quantitative scaling. He does not measure directly the full-bodied individual trait that alone exists as a neuropsychic disposition and as the one irreducible unit of personality. What he does is to measure a common *aspect* of this trait, such a portion thereof as takes common cultural forms of expression and signifies essentially the same manner of adjusting within the social group.

*   *   *   *   *

In the strict sense of the definition of traits only the individual trait is a true trait: (a) because traits are always in individuals and not in the community at large, and (b) because they develop and generalize into dynamic dispositions in unique ways according to the experiences of each individual. The common (continuum) trait is not a true trait at all, but is merely a measureable aspect of complex individual traits.

Cardinal, Central, and Secondary Traits[13]

In every personality there are traits of major significance and traits of minor significance. Occasionally some trait is so pervasive and so outstanding in a life that it deserves to be called the *cardinal trait*. It is so dominant that there are few activities that cannot be traced directly or indirectly to its influence. . . . No such trait can for long remain hidden; an individual is known by it, and may even become famous for it. Such a master quality has sometimes been called *the eminent trait, the ruling passion, the master-sentiment,* or *the radix* of a life.

It has been objected that the conception of a cardinal trait is essentially tautological, for, one asks, is not the cardinal trait identical with the personality itself? This objection cannot be admitted; however well integrated a life may be around the cardinal trait there remain specific habits, incidental and non-organized tendencies, and minor traits of some degree that cannot be subsumed functionally under the cardinal trait. Though pervasive and pivotal, a cardinal trait still remains within the personality; it never coincides with it.

It is an unusual personality that possesses one and only one eminent trait. Ordinarily it seems that the foci of personality (though not wholly separate from one another) lie in a handful of distinguishable *central traits*. Central traits are those usually mentioned in careful letters of recommendation, in rating scales where the rater stars the outstanding characteristics of the individual, or in brief verbal descriptions of a person.

One may speak, on a still less important level, of *secondary traits*, less conspicuous, less generalized, less consistent, and less often called into play than central traits. They are aroused by a narrower range of equivalent

[13]*Ibid.*, from pp. 337-38.

stimuli and they issue into a narrower range of equivalent responses. Being so circumscribed they may escape the notice of all but close acquaintances.

Trait and Habit[14]

Ordinarily the term *habit* connotes an invariable and inflexible type of response following the recurrence of a definite stimulus situation with which it is, by experience and practice, tied. . . . A trait arises, in part at least, through the integration of numerous specific habits having in common not identical elements, but the same adaptive significance to the person. . . . But however acquired, a trait is always a fusion of habits and endowment rather than a colligation or chain of habits alone.

By tracing the hypothetical history of another generalized habit, sociability, we can see the process more clearly. A young child, finding that his mother is nearly always present to satisfy his wants, develops for her an early affective attachment (conditioning). But later other social contacts likewise prove to be conducive to this child's happy and successful adjustment: playmates, for example, or family gatherings, or crowds at the circus. Unless markedly timorous in temperament, or fearful and shy because of experiences of punishment or public ridicule, the child gradually comes to seek people, rather than avoid them. A trait (not an instinct) of gregariousness develops. The child grows eager for social intercourse; he enjoys being with people. When isolated from them for some time, he misses them and becomes restless. The older he grows the more ways he finds of expressing his gregarious interest. He seeks to ally himself with groups of people at a lodge, at the theatre, at church; he makes friends and keeps in touch with them, often entertains them, and corresponds with them. These separate activities are not habits. They are varied (but equivalent) aspects of a trait of sociability. On occasion this trait may become dynamic almost to the point of compulsiveness, leading to such excess of sociability that the person is morbid or unhappy unless with people.

Under the guidance of this trait new and effective expressions may be found to satisfy the craving for social intercourse. Habits no longer dominate the trait; rather it is the trait that forces the formation of new habits, congenial and serviceable to the trait. The transformation of motives from the simple conditioned responses of infancy is complete. The trait has transcended its specific foci of origin. Neither conditioned response, nor specific habit, nor identical elements, nor instinct represents the condition that prevails. Sociability has become a deep and characteristic quality of this individual's personality. Its expression is variable; a wide range of equivalent stimuli arouse it. Furthermore, its structure has changed with time; for not only has it become a pervading style of behavior, but also a motivational system basic in the structure of this personality. The trait has become autonomous.

14*Ibid.*, from pp. 292-93.

CHAPTER 18

RAYMOND B. CATTELL

FACTOR THEORY PSYCHOLOGY: A STATISTICAL APPROACH TO PERSONALITY

Cattell's theory of personality may well be termed "a trait theory of personality," for in many points it strongly resembles Gordon Allport's trait psychology; however, unlike Allport, Cattell depends heavily upon results derived from statistical factor analysis, particularly in reference to variables. An important aspect of Cattell's FACTOR THEORY PSYCHOLOGY is the formulation of laws of personality which will enable the psychologist to predict behavior.

Raymond B. Cattell, born in Staffordshire, England, in 1905, was trained at Kings College, University of London, from which he received the B.S. in 1924, the Ph.D. in 1929, and an honorary D.Sc. in 1937. From 1928 to 1931 he was a lecturer at University College, Exeter, England; and from 1932 to 1937 he directed the City Psychological Clinic in Leicester, England. From 1937 to 1938 he was a research associate at Teachers' College, Columbia University, from 1938 to 1941 Professor of Psychology at Clark University, and from 1941 to 1944 Lecturer in Psychology at Harvard University. From 1944 to the present he has been Research Professor in Psychology at the University of Illinois.

Among his major publications are *A Guide to Mental Testing for Psychological Clinics, Schools and Industrial Psychologists* (1936; rev. ed., 1948), *The Factors of the Mind* (1941), *General Psychology* (1941), *The Culture-Free Test of Intelligence* (1944),

Description and Measurement of Personality (1946), *An Introduction to Personality Study* (1950), *Personality: A Systematic Theoretical and Factual Study* (1950), *Factor Analysis: An Introduction and Manual for the Psychologist and Social Scientist* (1952), *Personality and Motivation Structure and Measurement* (1957), *The I.P.A.T. Anxiety Scale* (1958), "Personality Theory Growing from Multivariate Quantitative Research" in *Psychology: A Study of a Science,* vol. 3 (ed. by S. Koch, 1959), *Personality and Social Psychology* (1964), *The Scientific Analysis of Personality* (1965), and the edited work *Handbook of Multivariate Experimental Psychology* (1966).

METHODOLOGY[1]

Inductive-Hypothetico-Deductive Spiral

Since a name can perpetually mislead, and the difference here is important, let us henceforth speak of the inductive-hypothetico-deductive method— or IHD method for short. Even with this correction to IHD method, let us never forget that the scientific process is a spiral, as shown in [Fig. 1]. The penny-in-the-slot concept of scientific method as testing the deduced consequences of a single, miraculously-produced-from-nowhere hypothesis by a single, final, experimental verdict must give way to the more realistic concept of the IHD spiral.

In this IHD spiral, nevertheless, there is a steady change of emphasis from inductive activity, which emphasizes the personality qualities of an explorer and a detective, in the first stages, to deduction, which emphasizes the qualities of the lawyer, in the later stages. The mistake of much research description is to bring the case into court and dwell on the skills of the lawyer too soon. In a good detective story, the advent of the police court, as when Sherlock Holmes hands over the case to Inspectors Gregory and Lestrade, signals the end of the really exciting part of the story. There is admittedly much good intellectual exercise still to be had in the courtroom, but the skills of the explorer and detective are more essential and characteristic of scientific research than the skills of the lawyer. These are most involved in the formative stage of hypotheses. And, as psychologists, we must by no means overlook the substantial role of unconscious processes in the generation of hypotheses, especially at the stage of the intuition and the hunch. To demand that all shall be as explicit as courtroom procedure is to sterilize the spirit of science, which is born in mystery.

*   *   *   *   *

[1]"The Principles of Design and Analysis and Theory Building," in Raymond B. Cattell, ed., *Handbook of Multivariate Experimental Psychology* (Chicago: Rand McNally, 1966), from pp. 15-16, 18, 64-66.

DIAGRAM 1-1. The Inductive-Hypothetico-Deductive Spiral

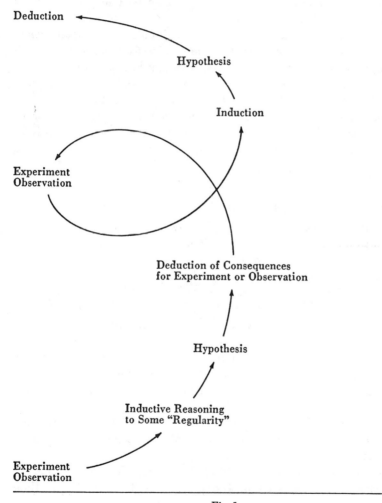

Fig. 1.

Galton-Spearman Tradition vs. the Wundt-Pavlov Methodology

(1) The Wundt-Pavlov methodology is a direct imitation of the physical sciences, undertaken partly in reaction against the diffuse, non-operational, and frequently irresponsible theory-building of the persisting literary-philosophical and clinical phases. It is bivariate and manipulative ("controlled"), but, except in perception, the special senses, and a learning theory that avoids human personality learning, it has not equalled in psychology its effectiveness in the physical sciences.

(2) The Galton-Spearman experimental tradition has been multivariate and non-manipulative, and has developed more directly as a response to the inherent needs of the behavioral sciences, whence it has spread to other life sciences. It enables wholistic real-life action to be analyzed without manipulative control. For too long, it was regarded and used as a method for psychometrics and the study of abilities, but it actually admits of manipulative experimental control and has been the main contributor more recently to personality and dynamics, and, potentially, to learning.

* * * * *

Mathematico-Statistical Method

(3) In their current form, however, these two traditions actually present only a limited perception of the full possible range of experimental designs. Their historical rivalry is as obsolete as the idea that together, in their present form, they cover the ground.

(4) An experiment is defined as *a controlled gathering of data aimed to discover significant relations.* As such, it is one phase in the inductive-hypothetico-deductive (IHD) spiral of scientific investigation. Whether it occurs within the walls of a laboratory or not is irrelevant to the definition.

(5) The laws that are first established are about either *structures* or *processes.* Theories rest on empirically checked laws, but the actual order of establishment of laws, hypotheses, and theories in the scientific process varies.

(6) Experimental designs can be more usefully classified and evaluated by parameters (dimensions) than by types. Most varieties are covered by six parameters:

1. Dimension N (Number of variables) Bivariate to Multivariate (b to m)
2. Dimension M (Manipulation degree) Interfered with to Freely Happening (i to f)
3. Dimension T (Time relation dimension) Dated to Simultaneous (d to s)
4. Dimension C (Control of non-focal variables) Constant to Uncontrolled (c to u)
5. Dimension R (Representativeness of "relative" variables) Abstractive to Representative (a to r)

6. Dimension D (Distribution of "referees," i.e., population sample)
Known Bias to Normal Representative (k to n)

Except for a few impossible, non-viable combinations, the parameters can be combined in all ways, yielding at least thirty varieties of experiment, of which the historical Wundt-Pavlov "classical" (A.P.A. Division 3) and the Galton-Spearman "multivariate" (A.P.A. Divisions 4, 5, 6, 8, etc.) cover only a minority.

(7) Mathematico-statistical methods of analyzing data are to a degree independent of design and offer a distinct taxonomy. They can likewise, but perhaps more arbitrarily, be classified according to four parameters:

1. Dimension E (e to v) (Power of significance test)
2. Dimension B (j to h) (Degree of mathematical complexity of the model)
3. Dimension S (o to g) (Number of relations simultaneously evaluated)
4. Dimension I (p to l) (Degree of utilization of information)

With some obvious exceptions, each of the 2^4 possible combinations ("types" of method) can be combined with the thirty or so experimental design possibilities, though there will be certain naturally greater congenialities. A combination of an experimental *design* with a statistical *method* will be called an *operational procedure,* since it defines what is actually done in the research.

(8) Theories are both ends and instruments in scientific investigation.— Definitions are given for law, postulate, working hypothesis, model, and theory. The difference between theoretical concept and empirical (working) construct is defined in terms of the imported or surplus meaning in the former, which can be classified by the distance from which the analogy is brought, or, alternatively, by the ideality of its origin. A dimension of imported meaning exists in which an *immediate construct* (formerly "intervening variable") is lowest, a hypothetical construct middling, and a theoretical concept highest. Theory in the behavioral sciences is affected more than theory in other areas by the limits to timeless generalization imposed by the incompleteness of the irreversible emergent process in Nature in any given era.

Tentatively, dimensions for a taxonomy of theory can be stated as (a) Degree of strictness of expression in a model, (b) Extent of role of imported or postulate-derived concepts, (c) Breadth of base, defined as the number of areas of observation inductively and deductively tied to the theory, and (d) Degree of complexity of internal relationships.

(9) The complete description of an investigation requires definition of (a) hypothesis *structure,* (b) relational *system,* (c) experimental *design,* and (d) mathematico-statistical analysis *method.* In conducting research it is useful also to consider these in various couplings, such as *procedure,* covering design and analysis method, *technique,* covering relational system and statistical analysis, etc. Each of these combinations normally involves

emphasis on the work of a different kind of specialist in an investigatory team.

(10) Understanding the structure of theory, and the best sequences for theory construction, assists, but does not insure, healthy development. Outside the logical structure are the personality of the researcher and the values and prejudices arising from socio-historical accidents. Since theories exist only in the minds of men, their historical development has suffered from partisan excesses and educational prejudices, from being exploited as status symbols, from being less easily separable, in psychology, from popular verbalizations, from the greater ease of stating a theory than finding a law, from the proliferation of oversimplified models out of touch with observation, and from fixation on conflict within pairs of alternative theories, encouraged by legalistic debate and emotional overvaluation of theories.

(11) In the light of the intrinsic structure of theory, and in catering to the perversions to which its development has proved historically susceptible, different scientific *procedures* (i.e., *designs* plus *methods*) have characteristic advantages and disadvantages. The multivariate procedures have the greatest potential for generating concepts, and suffer only from the inconvenience of the large demands they make on experimental time and the restriction that relations have to be first examined in a simple linear form. In generating theoretical concepts, their advantages are great but in theory-examination, as distinct from theory-construction, the gain is smaller. However, checking a whole pattern still usually offers a more significant conclusion than checking a correlation or difference of means using only two variables. Moreover, the simultaneous multivariate procedure offers opportunities to analyze higher-order interactions and relations commonly missed in bivariate and atomistic experimental steps.

DESCRIPTION AND DEFINITION OF PERSONALITY

A Preliminary Definition of Personality[2]

The initial definition of personality put forward by the writer, in addition to the delimitation of the data areas, will be a *denotative* one, as follows: *The personality of an individual is that which enables us to predict what he will do in a given situation.* Mathematically expressed it is "*P*" in the following equation,

$$R = f(P.S.)$$

where S is a definition of the situation (or stimulus) and R is a description of the behaviour (or reaction). What P connotes, in terms of all its elements, is the object of our investigation of personality.

However, common experience and the accumulated good sense of centuries

[2]*An Introduction to Personality Study* (London: Hutchinson House, 1950), from pp. 21-23.

permits us even at the outset to be a little more specific about the description of these elements and aspects of personality. Thus experience has, for example, led to agreement on those divisions into which personality traits may be sorted: (1) dynamic traits, which have to do with motivation, action and purpose, (2) temperament traits, which deal with pervasive, unchanging *qualities* and tempos in our actions, and (3) ability or "cognitive" traits which concern *how well* a person can do anything. These demand fuller illustration.

Dynamic or "driving" traits include acquired interests, such as attitudes, sentiments and complexes, as well as the presumably innate drives which used to be called "instincts" or propensities and which we shall call ergs. Under these subdivisions or dynamic traits, the student may like to classify, as an exercise, such trait forms as are described by the terms desire, need, habit, inhibition, prejudice, will, disposition. A person's disposition, for example, is determined by which innate drives predominate, so that where the sex drive predominates we speak of an "amorous" disposition, where the fear erg is always active, a "timid" disposition, and so on.

The term "character" has long been specialized (in English, but not so clearly in German) to mean that group of dynamic traits (sentiments and attitudes) united in a structure which controls unorganized impulses in the interest of ethical standards and other more remote goals of the self. The will is character in action. The relation of character to personality is thus not quite that of the division of dynamic traits to the total personality, but it is at least that of the most important structure among dynamic traits.

Abilities include such powers as general intelligence, verbal ability, spatial ability, musical aptitude, various powers of memory, and many acquired skills and capacities. We can classify them into perceptual and effector abilities and also, as a cross classification, into ability to acquire and ability to retain, in each of the above fields.

The definition of temperament traits has caused most difficulty to psychologists. Some wish to define them as those traits which are constitutional, while McDougall would have defined them as the aspects of behaviour determined by physiological conditions. But both must be rejected, for many abilities, notably general intelligence, are largely innate and many dynamic traits, e.g., the hunger drive and the sex drive, can be shown to be partly determined by the physiological state of the organism. It is better to define dynamic traits as those in which the person's performance is quickly affected by change in an incentive; abilities as those in which it changes with change in difficulties, and temperament traits as those in which the performance is independent of stimulus conditions. For example, a temperamentally excitable person will show this excitability equally in response to a fear, a sex or a pugnacity stimulus. Among temperament traits we shall then include such items as high-strungness; sensitivity to fatigue, drugs, etc.; tolerance of monotony; speed, acceleration and decline of performance; level of energy and so on.

The real point of difficulty, at which scientific method has to come to the rescue of common sense, is reached when we want to measure one of these traits, in order to say whether Jones is more or less temperamentally high-strung than Smith, or whether the intelligence of Johnny Brown has improved since he had his adenoids removed. *Then* we find it necessary to discover first if there are two or three different kinds of high-strungness and whether intelligence is a unitary trait and if so with what boundaries. Where gross, salient, abnormal traits are concerned this can be answered by simple clinical observation and psychiatrists have thus established certain "syndromes," e.g., mania, anxiety hysteria and so on, in which a collection of behaviour manifestations are known to "go together as a unity."

*　*　*　*　*

A Conclusive Definition of Personality[3]

Philosophically, one may ask whether there is anything in definitions beyond what is given in description and prediction. In Allport's scholarly survey of the origin and history of the term personality, we encounter, among his fifty definitions, such representatives of different approaches as Locke's revised "individuality which has become objective to itself"; Goethe's view of personality as the "supreme value" in life; the juristic definition of "any individual enjoying legal status"; a sociologist's (Burgess's) definition as "social effectiveness" and the related definition by the psychologist, May, as "social stimulus value" or personality defined as "the response made by others to the individual as a stimulus" and Morton Prince's "the sum total of all the biologically innate dispositions, impulses, tendencies, and the dispositions acquired by experience."

Many of these stress particular qualities of personality—its tendency to have a façade or layers, its uniqueness, its dynamic nature, its tendency to be integrated—but the whole escapes them, and perhaps in our present state of knowledge it is impossible to say what is essential about personality in a few words, for the foundation of precise but complex concepts which would need to be covered in these few words does not exist. That is true of connotative definition, i.e., definition which attempts to include all the far-flung connotations of that which is defined, or to describe in a nut-shell. It is not true of the denotative definition given below, which like many precise scientific definitions, avoids description and says simply that so-and-so is "that which" does some precisely definable operation.

Definition as concentrated description must therefore either deal with description from restricted viewpoints, confessed as such, or else ramify into a whole book—and still be incomplete, for to define a thing completely, thus, is to know *all* its relationships. So we come to the awesome fact that all entities or wholes we talk about are in fact only parts of the one whole that is the universe and never perfectly definable till we know the universe. Glimpsed

[3]*Ibid.*, from pp. 220-24.

in special aspects, however, personality can be defined, first, factorially, as *the dimensions of behavioural space for human beings,* secondly, biologically, as *the patterns of reaction to the environment required to maintain internal chemical states* (homeostasis), thirdly, clinically, as *a more or less integrated set of originally discrete dynamic trends,* fourthly, sociologically, as *a transmitting and creating element in the culture pattern,* and so on.

A single denotative definition is possible, as indicated by the writer elsewhere, to the effect that "Personality is that which determines *behaviour in a defined situation.*" It is the unknown "*x*" in an equation predicting behaviour from a given stimulus. More precisely an individual's behaviour can be predicted (in general, theoretically, and in actual performances, especially in the field of abilities, to an actual, practical extent) by the following type of equation....

$$P_{ij} = s_{1j}T_{1i} + s_{2j}T_{2i} + s_{3j}T_{3i} + \text{etc.}$$
$$\phantom{P_{ij} = }{}_{1 \cdot 1} \phantom{T_{1i} + } {}_{1 \cdot 2} \phantom{T_{2i} + } {}_{1 \cdot 3}$$

where P_{ij} is the performance of the individual in the situation j, T_{1i}, T_{2i}, T_{3i}, etc. are the individual's endowments in abilities, temperament and dynamic source traits and s_{1j}, s_{2j}, etc. are the stimulus situation constants for the situation s_1 with respect to the source traits T_1, T_2, etc. For example, the prediction required might be with respect to performance in a game of chess, and T_1 might be general intelligence, T_2 persistence and T_3 general emotionality. Then s_1 would be very large and positive, because chess demands a lot of intelligence, s_2 would be appreciable, and s_3 would be negative since emotionality interferes with good chess play. All other source traits would be involved, in this as in every piece of behaviour, but presumably with negligible situational indices.

Now the structure which is implied by this "specification equation" in factor terms is essentially the same as what the clinical and general psychologist means when he speaks of structure, the ego, attitudes, etc. The two lines of definition converge. The only difference is that the specification equation abstracts, in a number of primary dynamic traits, only the most important aspects of the dynamic lattice structure. Actually this comparative reduction of emphasis on the dynamic in relation to the complete absorption in it by the clinician presents a truer picture of the problem of integration of the total personality. Dynamic, ability and temperament traits are always acting as an approximately integrated whole, in which the dynamic traits assume whatever equilibrium positions are possible in an adjustment between the given abilities and temperament traits and the demands of the environment.

However, the total personality is not to be represented only as an integrated set of factors—integrated by their common action in the specification equation. Personalities differ not only in their factor strengths but also (in respect to dynamic traits) in the particular, unique attachments of these traits to things in the environment. The common trait specification equation does not show this; for the situational indices are common and only the trait endowments are unique. But the equation derived from *P*-technique *does* show this, the loading in particular situations being peculiar to that person. The idiosyncratic history of the individual shows itself in these unique attachments shown by unique situational indices.

One must not forget that there are *two* general problems of prediction in personality: (1) Predicting what a given person will *do* in a given stimulus situation; (2) Predicting what a person of given endowments will *become* in a given environment. The laws governing the first are implicit in the above equation. Those governing the second are the general laws of psychology applied quantitatively to the particular endowments of the individual and the situation. It is the aim of all personality study to explain personality change in terms of a few basic laws of learning, of disposition rigidity, of conflict, of energy expenditure and of the nature of intelligence, etc., so that the calculation of developmental change can be encompassed by some such simple formulation as that given above for prediction of a reaction in a given situation.

Some general laws, of a relatively unconfirmed nature, can be formulated in this area. We can, for example, organize many of the facts about adjustment by a law of constant mental energy, according to which the investment of interest in one field tends to impoverish others. We can get approximate laws regarding mental conflict, such as the tendency of the more powerful drive to establish itself, the tendency for dissociation and repression with increasing intensity of conflict, and the tendency for ambivalence with increasing freedom of drives from conscious association and connection. Learning theory, though it has been too preoccupied with cognitive memory to the neglect of dynamic traits, is on the brink of crystallizing laws governing the effect of repetition and ergic strength upon habit formation and maintenance. And before long we may be able to calculate the effect—now dimly indicated—of various degrees of disposition rigidity upon the development and stability of new adjustments.

* * * * *

The study of individual differences thus has as its ultimate goal the understanding of entirely general laws. Psychology is only now beginning to realize that personality study has been the most effective path to that goal. Indeed the experimentalist, with the traditional philosophical attempt at naïve, direct approaches to mind in the abstract and to laws about basic processes, has been perhaps not only relatively ineffective but positively in error. Perhaps the true psychological laws—as distinct from physiological ones—can only be established when we study the reactions of *the organism as a whole*. Our formula above suggests that no item of performance by the individual is unaffected by all aspects of the individual make-up, and the same is probably true of personality development, i.e., of prediction in the second realm of observation. Thus personality is the integration of the partial reactions of the organism, but it promises also to be the integration of psychology.

434

Structure and Dynamics of the Personality[4]

Surface Traits and Source Traits

The means by which psychology seeks larger unitary traits . . . consists in correlating trait elements until one discovers those which correlate positively in every possible internal combination. Such a collection is called a syndrome in abnormal psychology and in normal psychology a surface trait. If the surface trait is very broad we may prefer to call the extremes of it "types." A surface trait is in any case simply a collection of trait-elements, of greater or lesser width of representation, which obviously "go together" in many different individuals and circumstances.

Statistical Meaning of Source Traits and Surface Traits

At this point the student needs to cross a rather difficult methodological bridge involving statistics. For, statistically, this "going togetherness" can have two meanings. These correspond to (*a*) the notion of "surface trait" as already defined, and (*b*) the notion of "source trait," whose understanding and definition require a *general* idea of the aims and methods of *factor analysis.*

Actually the essential meaning, at least, of *source trait* can be made clear to common sense without statistical technicalities. It is only in grasping the methods of discovering and delimiting source traits that factor analysis is necessary. Consider, for example, one of the surface traits or types already mentioned—that revealed by the three positive correlations that exist among the three measures: (*a*) size of vocabulary, (*b*) arithmetical ability, (*c*) tactfulness in social situation. If we ask how this surface trait might have come into existence, attention turns first to the influence of innate mental capacity. Other things being equal the individual of greater general mental capacity will achieve a greater size of vocabulary, will handle arithmetical problems more capably, and will also be more clever and tactful in social situations. Some of the observed positive correlations among the three variables in the surface trait will therefore have their *source* in the fact that the performances all spring in part from a single root, namely, general mental capacity. But it also happens that these three performances are about equally the objects of educational attention, so that the individual who has longer or better schooling will tend to do better at all three of them. Consequently another part (perhaps the remaining part) of the positive intercorrelation seen in the surface trait goes back to this second source— length of education. *General mental capacity* and *amount of education experienced* may therefore be considered two *source traits* accounting for the observed *surface trait.*

* * * * *

[4]*Personality: A Systematic Theoretical and Factual Study* (New York: McGraw-Hill, 1950), from pp. 21-22. The bibliography and references have been omitted.

RAYMOND B. CATTELL

Unique and Common Traits[5]

... The pattern discovered in a surface trait is merely an average trend. Individual differences of heredity and upbringing will cause the pattern to be slightly different in different people. For this reason Allport has contrasted *common traits* with *unique traits*. The common trait is a trait which all people possess in some degree, insofar as human beings have more or less of the same fund of heredity possibilities and are subjected to more or less of much the same pattern of social pressures, *e.g.*, the pressures of family, school, and so on. On the other hand a unique trait is peculiar to the individual, in that no one else has just that pattern. Common traits may be illustrated by cyclothymia-schizothymia, general mental capacity, or degree of character integration. Unique traits, on the other hand, are probably more obvious in the field of interests and attitudes, where a man might have a powerful interest in Korean butterflies or a strong attitude in favor of reducing the tax on tricycles, which extremely few people would share to any scorable degree.

Intrinsically Unique Traits

However, one might distinguish between an *intrinsically unique trait* which, like a six-fingered hand, introduces an entirely new *dimension* to be measured and a *relatively unique trait* in which, as in any individual hand, there is only the usual slight deviation from the *pattern* of the average or common-trait pattern. Intrinsic or relative unique-trait patterns can be found by *P*-technique studies of the given individual; whereas common-trait forms are found by *R* and *Q* techniques. The evidence now available suggests that unique-trait patterns do not depart much from the common-trait form, at least in the major dimensions of personality.

General and Specific Source Traits

... A factor or source trait is a source of variation that covers a great number of trait-elements. In extracting these "general" factors—"general" because they spread over most trait-elements—it usually happens, however, that some part of the variability of a specific trait-element remains unaccounted for when all the general factor variances are taken out. This part has to be considered due to error or to a "specific factor." That is to say, the variations in this particular piece of behavior cannot be accounted for entirely by the action of general characteristics such as run through the whole personality, but must be partly due to something absolutely specific to the act or organ. Ability to sort colors or fear of nails might be forms of behavior in which more general factors (intelligence and timidity, respectively) are less important than traits due to specific experience.

A specific factor is some narrow ability or highly particularized source

[5]*Ibid.*, from pp. 32-35.

436

of personality reaction which operates in that situation and that only, and of which all people have a certain amount, *i.e.*, it is a common trait.

* * * * *

Constitution and Environmental-Mold Traits

Surface traits, as we have seen, are often the consequence of two or more source traits overlapping in their effects, producing steeper correlation between trait-elements than either influence would produce alone. If source traits found by factorizing are pure, independent influences, as present evidence suggests, a source trait could not be due both to heredity and environment but must spring from one or the other.

* * * * *

. . . It is easy to see that internal conditions like alcohol, hyperthyroid states, or fatigue yield a set of covarying manifestations which factor analysis would reveal as a source trait. For example, in the case of alcohol, we should discover a pattern of increasing carelessness, talkativeness, lack of control of impulse, and so on. . . . Patterns thus springing from *internal* conditions or influences we may call *constitutional source traits*. The term "innate" is avoided, because all we know is that the source is physiological and *within the organism*, which will mean inborn only in a certain fraction of cases.

On the other hand, a pattern might be imprinted on the personality by something external to it. Thus it is said that one can always recognize by a pattern of disciplined habits and values the products of a certain famous school, as some detectives claim also to be able to recognize a man who has been in prison, and as we are mostly able to recognize, say, a strongly religious person from one who has not been interested in any church. The pattern of a powerful social institution, formed by the consistent rewarding of some habits and suppression of others, should thus be revealed by correlation, because the total constellation has impinged, on a whole, with different strength on different people. Thus a person who has one of the constituent trait-element habits poorly developed will tend to have others poorly developed, and another person strongly marked in one habit of the pattern will also be strongly possessed of the others. Such source traits, appearing as factors, we may call *environmental-mold* traits, because they spring from the molding effect of social institutions and physical realities which constitute the cultural pattern.

* * * * *

Ability, Temperament, and Dynamic Traits

Psychologists have long found it convenient to divide traits into three modalities, though the formal basis of this division has never been clearly set out. In *dynamic traits or interests* are included basic drives or ergs, on the one hand, and acquired interests, such as attitudes, sentiments, complexes, superego and ego formations, on the other. Dynamic traits are characterized by behavior arising from a stimulus situation or incentive and directed to some goal, at which the action ceases. *Abilities,* by contrast, are shown by *how well* the person makes his way to the accepted goals. Dynamic traits are thus traits in which performance varies as the *incentive* varies; whereas abilities can be recognized as those in which performance varies in response to changes in complexity. *Temperament traits* are definable by exclusion as those traits which are unaffected by incentive or complexity. These are traits like high-strungness, speed, energy, and emotional reactivity, which common observation suggests are largely constitutional.

* * * * *

Dynamic Subsidiation[6]

In whatever other ways dynamic traits may be interconnected, the briefest observation suffices to show that they are at least connected in some sort of "purposive" sequence. The intractable environment continually compels a man to do one thing in order to be able to do another. In order that he may enjoy eating habits he must acquire working habits. We then say that the interests in work are subsidiated to the hunger drive. Constant repetition of such situations sets up a series of response habits in which one member of the chain serves the next, and so on to some ultimate goal. Each habit of reacting—each dynamic trait—is directed to a certain interim satisfaction, but complete discharge of psychic tension comes only at the end of such a series.

* * * * *

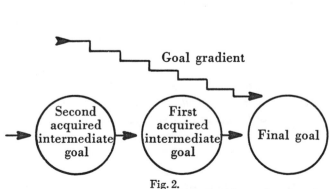

Fig. 2.
Subsidiation (means-end activities) and the hypothesis of goal gradient.

[6]*Ibid.*, from pp. 155-56. The diagrams in this and subsequent selections have been renumbered.

By rudely reiterating "Why?" to each answer, we can, therefore, in the simplest case, expose a series of *subsidiary* goals to a final goal. The person does *A* in order to do *B*, having gained the vantage point of *B* he is still unsatisfied and wants to attain *C*—and so on to the final satisfying goal at which activity ceases. This we shall call a dynamic *subsidiation* sequence . . . the lesser satisfactions between may be called intermediate or subsidiary goals, or means-end activities.

* * * * *

SENTIMENTS[7]

It behooves us now to look more closely at these relatively permanent and more stable channels of discharge which have been called *sentiments*, and which so far have been only roughly defined by "depth" or subsidiation position on a series of attitudes.

* * * * *

It is rare for one sentiment to absorb the whole energy of a drive, or vice versa. For the lines of dynamic subsidiation both converge and diverge with respect to sentiments, as we have seen that they do for all dynamic traits except final drives. However, in the psychoanalytic sense, a sentiment can be described as the cathexis of an object, but not a cathexis of libido alone. A sentiment will generally, but not always, be acquired earlier in life than the attitudes with which it is found associated. Frequently the attitudes will have developed simply to satisfy the sentiment.

* * * * *

For the present it suffices to define sentiments as major acquired dynamic trait structures which cause their possessors to pay attention to certain objects or classes of objects, and to feel and react in a certain way with regard to them.

ERG AND METANERG

Definition of an Erg[8]

These considerations lead to the following final definition of an erg: *An innate psycho-physical disposition which permits its possessor to acquire reactivity (attention, recognition) to certain classes of objects more readily than others, to experience a specific emotion in regard to them, and to start on a course of action which ceases more completely at a certain specific*

---

[7]*Ibid.*, from pp. 160-61.
[8]*Ibid.*, from p. 199.

goal activity than at any other. The pattern includes also preferred behavior subsidiation paths to the preferred goal.

The pattern clearly has four parts: (*a*) a preferential attention to certain situations, *i.e.*, an innate *cognitive*, perceptual organization; (*b*) a specific emotional pattern, revealing itself consciously and physiologically, *i.e.*, an innate *affective* side; (*c*) a specific goal satisfaction; (*d*) an innate

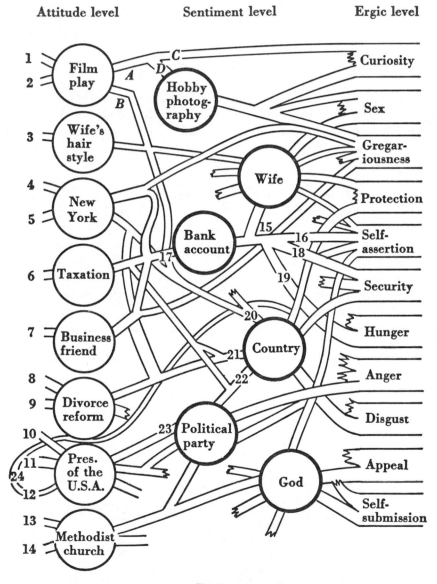

Fig. 3.
Fragment of a dynamic lattice, showing attitude subsidiation, sentiment structure, and ergic goals.

preference for certain ways of behaving (in reaching the goal). Parts (c) and (d) *may* be considered together as the innate, *cognitive* organization, reducing the aspects to three.

* * * * *

Ergic and Metanergic Patterns[9]

On the one hand we have glanced at the typical structure of sentiments and attitudes developed in the civilized adult. On the other we have attempted to uncover the raw material of innate dynamic source traits or "ergs" which man shares with the higher mammals. This contrast between what we have called "ergic" and "metanergic" structure (from Greek *meta,* meaning "beyond") provokes us to understand systematically what laws govern the transformation from one to the other during the individual's lifetime. These are, in the broadest sense, the laws of learning.

Let us agree on some definite terminology here. It is obvious that all actual dynamic traits owe their structure to two influences, (a) the inner constraint exercised by the hereditary maturation patterns, which develop the ergs. These are revealed by correlation as constitutional source traits in the realm of dynamic manifestations; (b) the environmental-mold source traits resulting from cultural constraints, corresponding to institutions in the culture pattern. To such environmental-mold traits, falling in the dynamic realm, we have given the name of *metanergs,* to indicate that they constitute the patterning of dynamic traits *beyond* that due to ergs. Any given dynamic surface trait is thus neither an erg nor a metanerg: it is an actual dynamic trait structure resulting from the interaction of ergic and metanergic patterns. The latter are abstractions analyzed out of concrete behavior habits, and the observed surface traits can therefore properly be regarded as a synthesis of ergic and metanergic influences.

* * * * *

THE SELF[10]

The self is something very obvious to the man in the street but very illusive to psychologists. Introspectionists have tried to turn around so quickly as to introspect on what the introspecting self is; but all they return with is conflicting observations that the self is a conscious awareness of doing, or a set of muscle tensions and visceral sensations, or an act of willing. . . . Unfortunately, dynamic psychology, which deals with behavior, has not succeeded much better in its attempts to define, operationally and scientifically, what the self-structure is in terms of behavior.

The psychoanalytic concept of the ego is lacking in precision and has not

9*Ibid.,* from p. 207.
10*Ibid.,* from pp. 240-41.

been brought into relation with experimental psychology and the study of learning. Let us now, therefore, seek a definition of a more exact nature, to enable operational tests to be applied. First it is clear that the self or ego is not that which is responsible for (*i.e.*, the source of) all actions of the organism. If a man sneezes in your face and says "Pardon me," he is politely assuming responsibility for something not willed (not emanating from "me"), and if a man charged in court with manslaughter pleads that he was "beside himself" with terror at the time, he may be exonerated on the grounds that the action sprang from the organism and not the ego. Reflexes and drives operating in unintegrated isolation are not the ego.

On the other hand, anything that is deliberately willed comes from the ego: indeed in the history of psychology the psychology of the will and the psychology of the ego are themes which constantly interweave, suggesting that they are aspects of the same thing. The essential features of the psychoanalytic ego are that (*a*) it is a structure formed from several drives, attempting by confluence to achieve the greatest satisfaction of the greatest number; (*b*) it is guided in this action by intelligent perception of the situation and by access to memories of past experiences of punishment and reward, by which the integration of the drives is maintained. These memories give stability to behavior in spite of big fluctuations in the appetitive state of the organism. When a man is hungry he does not behave as if gaining food were his only aim: he is influenced also by the need to retain his self-respect, or by considerations of loss of other satisfactions if he spends too much money on food, and so on. The self is thus the integrated "pilot" of the organism, seeking for it the greatest possible long-term satisfaction.

FACTOR ANALYSIS[11]

Spatial Representation of a Correlation

The algebraic presentation of the idea of factor analysis is somewhat forbidding to students lacking college mathematics; but the equivalent geometrical picture can be grasped readily by anyone fit for so complex a study as psychology. In the first place it is necessary to get used to the convention of representing correlation coefficients as angles, as in [Fig. 4].

By this geometrical representation, if two trait indicators *A* and *B* are highly correlated as at *(i)* in the diagram they will occur close together separated by only a small angular distance. If they are quite uncorrelated they are set at right angles *(ii)* like the independent coordinates of a graph. If they are negatively correlated they are set at an obtuse angle, as at *(iii)*. The convention is that the *cosine* of the angle is made exactly equal to the given correlation coefficient, as shown at *(iv)*. This convention, faithfully followed through, continues to give results consonant with all that we know about the arithmetical behavior of correlation coefficients.

[11]*Ibid.*, from pp. 23-32.

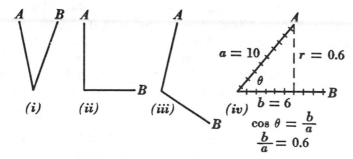

Fig. 4.
Spatial representation of correlations.

Factors as Coordinates

If now a group of trait elements have all possible correlations among them positive, as in the surface trait illustrated numerically in 3, they will appear in the geometrical representation as a bunched mass, like the ribs of a half-closed umbrella or a sheaf of arrows, as shown in [Fig. 4]. Now if it should happen that this surface trait, like that in the example above, is the result of only *two* general factors, these two factors can appear as the co-ordinates in [Fig. 5]. To each of the trait elements—*A, B, C,* and *D*—there can now be given a *factor loading* representing the extent to which the given factor determines (for the average person) the extent of possession

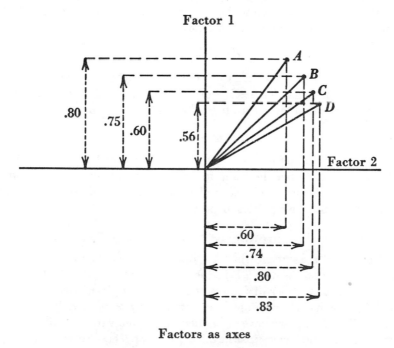

Factors as axes

Fig. 5.
Factors as coordinate axes.

of that particular trait-element. For example, the loadings of the four trait-elements—A, B, C, and D—by Factor 1 are 0.80, 0.75, 0.60, and 0.56, as shown, while the loadings in Factor 2 correspond similarly to the projections shown on the second, horizontal coordinate. In short, the factors obtained by the complex processes of factor analysis are nothing more than the coordinates—the axes—in the space created by representing the correlations between tests as angles between "test vectors."

Some idea of the meaning of the particular magnitudes of loading may be gained from the familiar case of the general intelligence factor. There it is found that ability in mathematics is loaded about 0.8 or 0.9 with the general factor, whereas ability in drawing is loaded only about 0.3 or 0.4. (The reader can imagine that A and D are, respectively, problem arithmetic [mathematics] and drawing in the above diagram, and that intelligence is Factor 1.) This means that a large part of the variability in mathematics is due to individual differences in the source trait "intelligence." Consequently, if a class of children were selected so that all had the same intelligence (mental age) the variability in mathematical performance would fall tremendously. On the other hand a group of people all of the same intelligence would still show almost as much variance in drawing ability as a group subtending the normal variability in intelligence.

The Meaning of Factor Loadings

From the facts behind [Fig. 5] it follows that the variability in any particular trait element can be broken down into variability in the two factors concerned, by an equation of the following form:

$$A = 0.8_1 + 0.6_2$$

and, as we shall see later, this can be used for any particular person, i, to predict or estimate his possession of A from what we know about his personal endowment in the source traits F_1 and F_2, thus:

$$A_i = 0.8F_{1i} + 0.6F_{2i}$$

This means that if his personal endowment in source trait F_1, namely F_{1i}, is high it will do more to help him in performance A than a high endowment in source trait F_2, for the loading of F_1 is greater in this situation, i.e., F_1 is more relevant to this particular performance.

Discovering the Number of Source Traits Involved

At this point the student will ask, "But how did you know that there were just *two* source traits at work in the surface trait of [Fig. 5]? And how do you find the *number* of factors at work in any given array of trait elements?" It is then clear that *we are given in the first place only the correlation coefficients* that we have calculated among the various trait indicators (variables subtests) measured in the experiment. These correlations, represented graphically, will arrange themselves in various experiments in different ways, giving some relatively isolated "test vectors" and also a number of clusters of vectors, called surface traits. The surface traits can be seen simply from inspection of the "rays" (vectors) drawn from the central origin. *But these same correlations (this same spatial "structure") will also tell us how many factors we need.* This fact can best be seen from an actual example. Consider the three correlations among trait elements X, Y, and Z as shown in [Fig. 6]. The angles are already drawn in the proper convention such that their cosines are equal to the correlations found. Now if one were to cut out these angles with scissors he would find that X, Y, and Z cannot be made to lie in a single plane, the plane of the diagram, as A, B, and C can in [Fig. 5]. Instead, they force one to make a pyramid, so that the points X, Y, and Z can only be represented in three-dimensional space, as shown to the right of [Fig. 6]. *Three coordinate axes are now required, to fix the positions of X, Y, and Z.* This means three factors. Consequently, there will

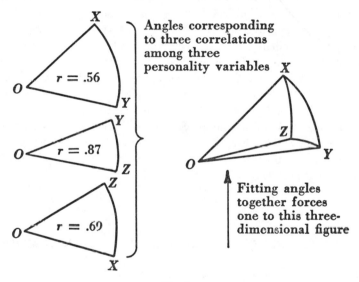

Fig. 6.
Correlations demanding axes in three dimensions.

be three coordinate values for each point, *i.e.*, there will be three factor loadings for each trait element and the *specification equation* for any one test performance, X, will be

$$X = aF_1 + bF_2 + cF_3$$

Actually it is the rule rather than the exception for the correlations to force the model out into three-dimensional space or more (when there are many vectors). If the student will experiment cutting out paper sectors to represent the correlations among any three or four variables known to him he may find some fitting in two dimensions, many fitting into three, but still others unrepresentable in three and requiring a model of four or more dimensions—a model in "hyperspace" which only a mathematician could conceive, for it cannot be visualized or constructed.

Since most models from personality and ability correlations would require more than two- or three-dimensional space, the discovery of the number of factors required and of the projections of the test points upon them is actually found from the correlations by algebraic methods. This process begins by finding the average correlation of each test with every other test, but its further steps need not be studied in this general text on personality and can be left for special technical reading.

Source Traits as Dimensions of Personality

The process of correlating trait elements and factorizing them may therefore be regarded as a search for the dimensions of personality, *i.e.*, for the number of truly independent *directions* in which personality needs to be measured in order completely to describe it. Similarly we need, in describing any physical object, to know the number of dimensions involved, *e.g.*, that a box requires numbers for each of three dimensions, but a lawn for only two. Incidentally, the student will find that the terms factor, vector (but not "test vector"), dimension, and source trait are used interchangeably by most writers as we do here. Obviously the first great advantage of factor analysis is that it leads to a method whereby we substitute measurements on a few (about a dozen so far) factors for measurements on hundreds or even thousands of trait-elements. The second advantage is that the source traits promise to be the real structural influences underlying personality, which it is necessary for us to deal with in developmental problems, psychosomatics, and problems of dynamic integration.

*   *   *   *   *

R, P, AND Q TECHNIQUES OF INVESTIGATION

Existing Syndromes Based on R Technique

Before we can examine the actual findings about personality, and before we can satisfy our curiosity about actual and particular unitary traits, it is necessary to clarify still one more point of method. So far we have dealt with the way in which correlation coefficients are analyzed in order to yield evidence of unitary traits, but have said very little about how the correlation coefficients are gathered.

As very student knows, all the important types and syndromes of the past are based on correlations of measures concerning individual differences. If we assert that extraversion is a unitary (surface) trait we mean that as we pass from individuals who are low in, say, gregariousness to individuals who are higher and higher in that trait-element we also find these individuals higher and higher in another element of the extraversions cluster, say, impulsiveness. The unitariness is revealed by *a common fate of these trait elements as we make person-to-person contrasts.* In correlation terms this means that we take any two trait-indicators or tests and measure them on *a series of persons*, obtaining a correlation coefficient between the two series thus formed. This traditional method of correlation, with the resulting extraction of clusters and factors, has been called R technique. The argument for general intelligence or g, as a single power, as well as Thurstone's discovery of seven primary abilities, such as verbal and spatial ability, rest on R technique.

*   *   *   *   *

The Meaning of Functional Unity

It may be argued, however, that the concept of "unitary trait" means more than that the parts "go together" in person-to-person variation. A functional unity means not only that the function behaves as a unity as we compare person with person but also that in the growth (learning or maturation) within one person the parts increase (or decline) together, and further, that when the trait is active (in one person) the parts have a simultaneous interaction. Thus, if general ability is a unitary trait by R technique—the correlation of individual differences—we should expect it also to show up as a factor when we correlate increments of growth.

*   *   *   *   *

The *P*-Technique Design

How can we investigate, however, the third criteria of a functional unity—that the parts function as a unity in a single individual? First, it is noticeable that most human behavior characteristics *fluctuate* slightly from day to day. Some of this variation, as shown in the repeated application of intelligence tests to the same person, is due to experimental error of measurement. But it can be shown that an appreciable part is also caused by "function fluctuation," *i.e.*, by a true fluctuation of that function from day to day. On some days one's intelligence is a little clearer than on others, or one's appetite is stronger, or one's memory is a little poorer, or one's pugnacity is greater, and so on. If several trait-elements are actually manifestations of the same unitary trait then they should fluctuate together from day to day, with changes of internal, appetitive condition and of external stimulus situation.

This common fluctuation can be discovered by correlation. Thus we take a single individual, measure him on a number of trait-indicators daily for a considerable number of days, plotting the trends of fluctuation as shown in [Fig. 7]. Inspection will show that some of these go together in some degree of functional unity, whereas others fluctuate in quite different patterns. Thus A, D, and E would correlate in [Fig. 7], while C and F would form a second cluster or a second factor by P technique.

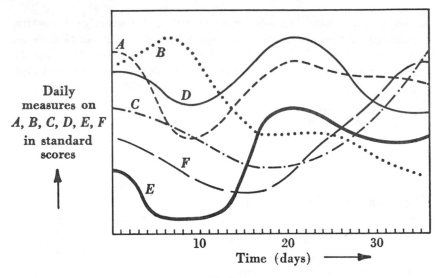

Fig. 7.
Traits in temporal covariation: the basis of *P* technique.

Typology and *Q* Technique

It has been pointed out by Burt and Stephenson that there exists yet another way in which correlation can be used, namely, the correlation of persons and, to complete the trio, this has been called *Q* technique. . . . Suppose we ask Jones to rank fifty jokes in order of funniness and then ask Robinson to do the same. These two orders (or "profiles" on a series of tests) can be correlated and might in this case yield a Jones-Robinson correlation of +0.6. Now we might test Smith and find his *r* with Jones to be +0.1 and with Robinson −0.1. We can conclude that Jones and Robinson have a decidedly similar sense of humor, but that Smith is unlike either of them. Later, however, we might find two other people forming a correlation cluster with Smith, independent of the Jones-Robinson cluster. *Q* technique has for this reason been called the ideal method for discovering types.

The purest representative of a type (as revealed by such a correlation cluster of people) is the individual who shows the highest average correlation with all others in the cluster. Whereas in *R* technique one would point to a particular trait-indicator test and say, "This is the best measure of the surface trait or factor in question," in *Q* technique one would point to Mr. Baker and say, "This man is the most perfect expression of the type" (or he "has a 0.8 loading in it"). Individuals highly correlating in *Q* technique and forming a type are similar with respect to their endowment in *all* factors.

* * * * *

The Covariation Chart

The search for functional unities by *R*, *Q*, and *P* techniques begins in each with correlation coefficients worked out on a *series* peculiar to each.

In *R* technique a correlation is between two tests (or symptoms) on a series of persons; in *P* technique it is between two tests on a series of days or occasions, and so on. While we are thinking of the general theory of manifestation and of the method of discovery of functional unities it is instructive to glance at the covariation chart shown in [Fig. 8].

Tests (personality variables)

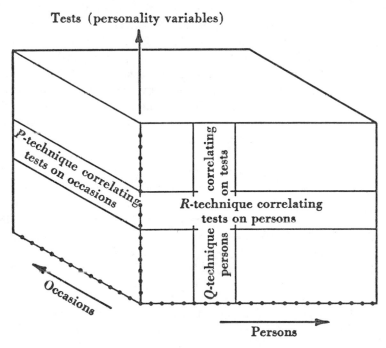

Fig. 8.
The covariation chart, showing exhaustively the possibilities of behavior correlation.

This is a device . . . reminding us that there are essentially *three* fundaments, or, rather, series of fundaments, among which the relations of correlation can be established in psychology. They are: people (or organisms); tests (or behavioral performances of any kind); and occasions (on which tests or people interact). The series in each constitute the three dimensions of the chart. Whenever two parallel lines are drawn on or through the parallelepiped there exist two correlatable series. Thus the band running horizontally to the right on [Fig. 8] starts with two tests (each represented by a dot in the vertical line of test series). The length of each line is represented by a series of persons—a projection upward of the series of persons along the bottom edge. The band lies in a single vertical plane, corresponding to a single-occasion lamina (the first one) from the series of occasions represented by dots along the left lower edge. In short, it is an R-technique band, representing the correlation between two tests administered on one occasion to a series of people.

* * * * *

The Specification Equation[12]

The above conception of traits culminates in the principle . . . that any given performance or reaction can be expressed by the specification equation:

$$P_{ij} = S_{1j}T_{1i} + S_{2j}T_{2i} + \cdots + S_{Nj}T_{Ni} + S_jT_{ji}$$

where P is the performance or reaction of the individual i in the situation j, S_{Nj} is the *situational index* for the source trait T_N in the situation j, T_{Ni} is the individual i's degree of possession (in standard score) of the source trait T_N, S_j, T_j are the index and the trait specific to this particular situation (whereas the other traits operate also in many other situations).

P_j can be anything measurable along an acceptable continuum, *e.g.*, the number of items scored on a test, the intensity of a neurotic symptom, the frequency of a social act in time sampling, the strength of a libidinal fixation or an attitude. The S's, as previously described, are situational indices which collectively define the "meaning" (or "valence" or "stimulus value") of the situation j for the typical person (in the case of R-technique values) or for the particular individual (in the case of P-technique variables). Any single S defines the emotional meaning (incentive value) or complexity (respectively for conditional dynamic and cognitive traits) of that situation for one particular source trait. The T's represent the source traits (of single or mixed modality, according to manner of extraction, and of common or unique character, according to their origin in R or P technique) which give the dimensions of the individual's personality.

STAGES OF PERSONALITY DEVELOPMENT[13]

Infancy

Infancy (0 to 6) is the great formative period of personality. There, in the relations to mother, in the reactions to the father, in the experiences of weaning and toilet training, and in the earliest reaction to siblings are built up the basic social attitudes, the degree of goodwill and the stability and strength of the moral super-ego, the sense of security or insecurity, the tendency to be with or against authority, and the strength of the various defence mechanisms which decide whether the individual shall be prone to neuroticism.

Childhood

Childhood (6 to 14) by comparison with the preceding critical developments of infancy and the succeeding upheavals of adolescence is a period of plain sailing and consolidation. The physical proportions are more constant and the incidence of disease is lower than before or after. Psychologically there are likewise no problems akin to those of infancy, while the

---

[12]*Ibid.*, from pp. 628-29.
[13]*An Introduction to Personality Study, op. cit.*, from pp. 212-19.

responsibilities of the adult world which fret adolescence with difficulties and anxieties are still far off. It has been called the period of the "hardy little savage." There is growth toward independence, out of the family into the gang or the general group of his peers, with a spreading of emotional contacts, affections and dependencies, in a "homosexual sublimation" or fond gregariousness with many objects. Moral feeling is not deep: to do what everyone else does and what is decreed by the group is the main regulation; but this is accepted as a rigid and unquestionable law. The chief virtues are those of personal prowess, of courage and of loyalty to the group. There is little intellectual questioning and little originality of thinking. That control of the body, which has occupied the child from infancy, has now reached practically a plateau of high skill, and preoccupation with physical skills as such declines hereafter, except where it is involved in the rivalry and assertion of adolescence.

Adventure stories are the chief reading diet. Successes and disappointments, and the general ego involvement of the self-regarding sentiment, centre most upon the school area, upon social acceptance in the gang and upon prowess in games. It is here that the child of limited intelligence shows his greatest frustration in school with resultant behaviour problems, while the physically defective or awkward shows the most typical Adlerian inferiorities and compensations. In general the mental life of make-believe is less than in infancy and less than the internal life and introspection of adolescence. Because the child longs for the status and privilege of adult life he may still have a vigorous day-dream life, mostly of adult adventure, but he is primarily a realist and even a materialist.

Adolescence

That adolescence (14 to 23) is outstandingly a period of storm and stress and readjustment has long been understood by psychologically gifted literary men, e.g., Goethe, but doubt has existed as to whether "endogenous" (biological) or "exogenous" (cultural) difficulties were chiefly responsible. The personality stress that goes on in the average person is more strikingly revealed by what happens to the more extreme personalities. Between 15 and 25 years of age the curves of incidence of first delinquencies, both for those who offend once only and for those who become recidivists, reach high peaks, falling away towards minima in earlier and later years. Similarly mental disorders and neurosis rise steeply; indeed, adolescence shows the greatest onset for the commonest of mental disorders—schizophrenia dementia praecox.

* * * * *

A considerable part of adolescent conflict arises from the increased strength of the drive to independence and self-assertion which is associated with increased sex drive and also with the new adult pattern expected by society. This development of self-assertion nevertheless begins with vacillating behaviour, e.g., bravado alternating with embarrassment. The vacillation springs partly from the youth's inner uncertainty, wanting to grow up yet wanting to return to family protection, partly from society's own uncertainty as to how far the individual should be regarded and treated as a grown-up and partly from the existence of such institutions as the school, which, however flexible they try to be, are apt to go on expecting the same pattern of conformity from the adolescent as from the child.

The greater part of the conflict, however, centres upon the developing sex drive and its derivatives by sublimation, etc. The individual's emotions experience innovation not only through the appearance of lust, the specific emotion of the mating erg, but also by powerful increments in the parental protective erg and in gregariousness. This introduces a sense of altruism and social belonging not felt before. The individual has to learn to control not only sex behaviour but also this increased capacity for sympathy, empathy and the need to give love where previously he received it, largely from the parents. It is from these sources that the adolescent draws that deeper quality and depth in intellectual activity and that nascent interest in social, political and religious problems, which observers have marked.

The sexual source motivates also the increased attention to smart appearance and manners, as well as the increased social and sexual awareness. Psycho-analytic studies show us that the sexual resurgence tends also to revive whatever "abnormal" sexual fixations the individual acquired in the infantile period. It is true in general that the adolescent adjustments tend to some extent to repeat the modes that have been found useful before, but it is still more certain that the adolescent sexual life—the degree of autoeroticism, the type of sex object chosen, the pattern of constancy or conflict—will repeat at least in brief recapitulation, the infantile experiences. For example, there is frequently seen in those in whom heterosexuality has to some extent been covered by a "blanket" repression of the Oedipus relation, a phase of more or less sublimated homosexual attachment. And there are "crushes" on individuals whose position or characteristics make them both parents and lovers. Some of the reappearance of nervous or neurotic traits lost during middle childhood must be ascribed to this same sexualization, but other instabilities arise rather from the disorganization already mentioned and now to be evidenced.

Evidence of some degree of personality disorganization is seen in the young adolescents, increased moodiness and irritability, in an unwonted instability, and in increased day dreaming, perhaps in the search for new ego ideals demanded by the changing self-regarding sentiment.

*   *   *   *   *

The disorganization is partly the result of having to adjust to new expectations, partly of having to absorb new ergic forces into an old metanergic system. Trial and error experimentation has to go on. The gaucherie in self-assertion as the individual struggles out of the family and towards acceptance in the larger community arises from the same causes as the physical clumsiness in handling the new bodily strength and proportions. Experimentation and increased inner conflict lead to increased need for privacy, and the break from the family sometimes requires secrecy, too. Poetry, religion, drama—the arts of emotionality and of love—come into their own. Indeed adolescence is the time when even the dullest clod knows that he possesses a soul; and it has been said of the genius that he lives in a perpetual adolescence.

Maturity

By "maturity" is meant here specifically the period from about 23 to 46, though in our complex civilization there are some respects in which men and women can go on maturing until the day they die. Indeed, as Shaw indicates in "Back to Methuselah," one of the chief causes of defect in civilization is that we do not live long enough to use mature interests and judgment.

At the beginning of this period the average person solves willy-nilly and rightly or wrongly the question of career; and perhaps also the problem of choosing a mate. The energies of adolescence become absorbed constructively in earning a living, building a home and rearing a family. In characterizing it as a busy and happy period, in which the chosen habits of adolescence become settled, we must not forget that we speak only of the majority. Adolescence has been a parting of the ways, and a minority has become shipwrecked in physical disease, in mental disorder, in a persistent inability to solve the questions of work and wife (the hoboes, the bachelors-about-town and the starving geniuses) and in fast hardening attitudes of delinquency or rebellion against established society.

Whatever course has been taken, there is ample evidence that the personality in general tends to become set. As we have seen, there is surprisingly little change of interest and attitude pattern between 25 and 50. This happens partly because psychological adjustment has been reached, partly because abilities and physical energy remain reasonably constant and partly because the external problems have decreased, harassing uncertainties have receded and the individual has generally become embedded as a substantial citizen in a stable community.

* * * * *

Middle Age

Middle age, characterized by a relatively sharp menopause, with obvious glandular changes, in women, and a slower, but equivalent change in men, is again a period of personality readjustment. In this case it is comparatively certain that most of the readjustment is occasioned by inner changes, by decline of sex and its sublimations, loss of energy and an increase in physical ills. But an increase in leisure, through the departure of the children, through voluntary partial or complete retirement or through incapacities reducing one's sphere of activity probably also contributes appreciably to the need for readjustment. At any rate, in the forties and fifties there is often a re-examination of life values and a search for a philosophy not unlike that which occurred at adolescence, except for its greater composure.

Senility

The meaning of senility is still uncertain. Research has not demonstrated which of the changes are normal and necessary and which are due to obscure disease. Some very old people retain their general intellectual capacity, for example, unimpaired till death, others show rather marked decline. Some, probably the majority, of very old people as now known, show restriction of interest, "crabbiness" of temper and worries about economic and social state and physical health, while others retain their geniality through the frostiness of December. As in adolescence, the ageing individual has to cope with a vacillating uncertain attitude towards him by society. Is he still capable of holding the reins wisely or has he already shown signs of dotage? He has to face also the readjustment to loss of company—relatives, work associates, etc.—so that loneliness and lack of status and security become problems. As Pressey has aptly said, he suffers "isolation from the swift traffic of life" and a feeling that it all goes on regardless of his views and needs. Some index of the problem may be seen in the suicide statistics, which rise towards old age—an index of declining satisfactions and increasing difficulties. A very different picture this seems from the poet's "Grow old along with me, the best is yet to be; the last of life, for which the first was made." Perhaps the values of our civilization are, in an unhealthy period, not such as to give due status and expression to the wisdom and interests of age. At any rate, because of our ageing population, psychologists are now beginning research on the psychology of old age which may answer questions that cannot now be answered here.

CHAPTER 19

H. J. EYSENCK

FACTOR THEORY PSYCHOLOGY:
A DIMENSIONAL APPROACH
TO PERSONALITY

Eysenck, whose FACTOR THEORY PSYCHOLOGY closely resembles
Cattell's, also uses factor analysis in order to derive scientifically
sound concepts of personality, but his theory is differentiated from
Cattell's by its dimensional rather than statistical approach. Factor
analysis provides Eysenck with dimensions of personality, as it did
Cattell, but he normally limits his factors to two or three, and works
toward establishing a *criterion analysis* or control group. He has
been influenced by Jung's two dimensions or types of personality—
introversion and extraversion—and also by the constitutional dimensions of Kretschmer. Utilizing statistical methods, Eysenck seeks
to study personality by the *hypothetico-deductive* method; that is, he
sets up a hypothesis concerning the structure of personality and then
tests the theories deductively.

Eysenck, born in Germany in 1916, left in 1934 for England,
receiving his Ph.D. from the University of London in 1940. During
World War II he served as a research psychologist at the Mill Hill
Emergency Hospital; in 1946 he was Reader in Psychology at
the University of London, where since 1955 he has been Professor
of Psychology.

His major works include *Dimensions of Personality* (1947), *The
Scientific Study of Personality* (1952), *The Structure of Human
Personality* (1953), *Uses and Abuses of Psychology* (1953), *Psy-*

chology and the Foundations of Psychiatry (1955), *The Psychology of Politics* (1955), *The Dynamics of Anxiety and Hysteria* (1957), *Perceptual Processes in Mental Illness* (1957), *Sense and Nonsense in Psychology* (1957), *The Causes and Cures of Neuroses* (with S. Rachman, 1965), *The Eysenck Personality Inventory* (with S. B. G. Eysenck), *The Biological Basis of Personality* (1967), *Personality Structure and Measurement* (with S. B. G. Eysenck, 1969), and *The Structure of the Human Personality* (3rd ed., 1970). He also edited the three-volume *Encyclopedia of Psychology* (1972).

FACTOR THEORY[1]

Ultimately, any view of personality must be based on experimental results treated by statistical methods. The mutually complementary nature of experiment and statistics has not always been recognized sufficiently, and may be stressed here in connection with our view of the nature of statistical factors. As will be seen, the statistical tool on which we have relied in the main is factorial analysis, and in view of the very strong opinions which have been held on the nature of factors, and on the proper method of analysis, a few words may be useful in indicating our own position.

Historically, factor analysis is merely an extension of the underlying logical postulate of all correlation procedures, viz. Mill's so-called "method of concomitant variation." The aim of factor analysis is to discover the smallest number of independent factors or variables which will adequately describe and classify mental abilities and temperamental traits; it attempts to give the most parsimonious account of the experimental findings insofar as these are interdependent. In doing so, it gives rise to four different types of factors: (1) General factors, which are common to all the tests or traits used in the investigation; (2) Group factors, common to certain of the tests or traits only, but absent in others; (3) Specific factors, which are peculiar to a single test or trait whenever it occurs; and (4) Error factors, which are present only on one occasion, and absent on all others. These four types of factors, as Burt has shown, correspond closely to the categories of the scholastic logicians: Genus, Species, Proprium, and Accidens.

The status of these factors once they have been isolated has given rise to much argument. Thurstone and Holzinger, for instance, regard factors as primary or fundamental abilities; similarly, Spearman regards them as fundamental functions of the mind. If factor analysis is to be applied to the study of personality as well as to the study of abilities, this definition has to be broadened somewhat, and it would become necessary to think of factors as elementary or unitary traits of personality, or as elementary or unitary

---

[1]*Dimensions of Personality* (London: Routledge & Kegan Paul, 1947), from pp. 16-18. The bibliography and references have been omitted.

traits of the mind. On the other hand, Anastasi, Allport and Thomson consider that factors are statistical artefacts, having no "reality" of any kind.

Our own position is very similar to that of Burt, who regards factors as principles of classification. "Rigorously speaking, factors cannot be regarded as substances or as parts of a substance, or even as causal attributes inhering in a substance. They are not separate 'organs' or isolated 'properties' of the mind; they are not 'primary abilities,' 'unitary traits,' 'mental powers or energies.' They are principles of classification described by selective operators. The operand on which these operators operate is not 'the mind,' but the sum total of the relations between minds and their environment."

There is, however, one way in which we would venture to modify and extend this view. If there are "unitary" or "primary" abilities, or fundamental dimensions of the mind, factor analysis alone is not sufficient to reveal them *and to prove them to be such.* If a factorial study of temperament showed the existence of one fundamental factor of introversion-extraversion, we would have to regard this demonstration merely as evidence that a classification along these lines would be expedient. If later on introversion could be shown to be due to demonstrable Mendelian factors, inherited in predictable ways, then our factor would surely deserve a higher status scientifically than a mere principle of classification; it could rightly be regarded as a fundamental dimension of the mind. It is on this interdependence of factor analysis and experiment, based on the results of such analysis, that we have laid particular stress in this book.

The nature of factors can perhaps best be understood by reference to the difference between *denotative* and *connotative* concepts. The characteristics of a denotative concept are given by abstraction, and its meaning can always be demonstrated by pointing to something, or by apprehending something, that is given or presented with immediacy. Thus we may consider the green of the grass and abstract from it the concept "green."

In contradistinction, a connotative concept is designated by the basic assumptions and postulates of the scientific theory in which it occurs. An electron, for instance, is not observed; it is defined by the postulates of electron theory. These unobserved concepts may be defined in any desired way as long as their properties are specified unambiguously in the terms of the general theory, and as long as logical deductions can be made from them, and verified or checked in terms of directly observable facts.

The relation of these two types of concepts to factor theory may be made explicit by a historical parallel. Newton, in the *Scholium* at the beginning of the Principia, points out that sensed time and sensed space are not to be confused with "true or mathematical" time or space; it is the former type of concept (denotative) which is experienced in everyday activity, while he is concerned with the latter type of concept (connotative) in his book. Anyone who confuses the two, he goes on to say, is guilty of vulgar ignorance.

Now clearly a statistical factor is a connotative concept, not a denotative one; yet much criticism of factorial work has been based on a misunderstanding of this position. The intelligence and suggestibility, the sense of humour and persistence which are observed and talked about by the man in the street are denotative concepts; stripped by experimental and factorial studies of popular misconceptions closely bound up with them, and of emotional elements inevitably mixed with them, they become *connotative* concepts. Certainly, Spearman's "g" bears some relation to the popular concept of "intelligence," just as Newton's or even Einstein's concept of space bears some relation to popular notions. But in spite of these similarities, the origin and meaning of the respective denotative and connotative concepts are sufficiently diverse to make it necessary to distinguish between them with great care.

When, therefore, we find factors in our work which bear certain resemblances to such denotative concepts as "neuroticism" or "introversion," it should be borne in mind that these terms are not used in their ordinary, denotative meaning, but that they are connotative concepts, designated by the basic assumptions and postulates of factorial theory.

* * * * *

STRUCTURE OF THE PERSONALITY[2]

Temperament

Temperament has frequently been used synonymously with personality, but in the interests of economy and clarity the term has partly shed its protean character and is used by many writers to cover "the general affective nature of an individual as determined by his inheritance and life history." Allport and Vernon has distinguished three main aspects under which temperament has been viewed in the past: the emotional, the physiological, and the kinetic. Many writers have considered temperament to be defined largely by the habitual emotional reactivity of an individual; others have emphasized physiological and biochemical factors; yet others have stressed the motor responses characteristic of the individual. These three aspects are happily combined in Allport's definition, which will constitute the basis of our own usage of the term: "Temperament refers to the characteristic phenomena of an individual's emotional nature, including his susceptibility to emotional stimulation, his customary strength and speed of response, the quality of his prevailing mood, and all peculiarities of fluctuation and intensity in mood." We have not been able to accept the final part of Allport's definition, ". . . these phenomena being regarded as dependent upon constitutional make-up, and therefore largely hereditary in origin" because

[2]*Ibid.*, from pp. 23-28.

of lack of evidence on this point; the theories of social learning associated with the Yale Institute of Human Relations may on *a priori* grounds be as capable of giving a satisfactory account of the presence of such observed differences between individuals as an hereditary view, and in the absence of very strong evidence in either direction we consider it premature to express in a definition an opinion as to their origin.

Character

The next term to be discussed, character, has been defined in two different and unrelated ways, one definition stressing the moral or ethical aspect of personality, the other stressing the conative aspect. The former type of definition, although more usual in non-technical writing, is of little use in psychology because of its evaluative nature, and the second type, introduced into psychology mainly through the writings of McDougall, seems more promising. In this sense, Warren's definition of character as a "system of directed conative tendencies" seems to cover the ground satisfactorily. In this way of looking at character, "the emphasis is upon the force of activity rather than upon its direction, upon the quality of behaviour in terms of strength, persistence, readiness, rapidity, etc., rather than upon its value as right or wrong, good or bad, wise or foolish, etc."

Character, as thus defined, is clearly closely related to the concept of "will," as studied by James, Ach, Michotte, Aveling, and others; it may be regarded as "an enduring psychophysical disposition to inhibit instinctive impulses in accordance with a regulative principle." As such, it will be seen to have many points in common with Freud's ego and superego, with Webb's "w" factor, with McDougall's self-regarding sentiment, with Luria's "functional barrier," and with the concepts of "conscience" and "will-power" of popular terminology. This identity is brought out very clearly in McDougall's view that character is that in man which "gives, or rather is, the ground of consistency, firmness, self-control, power of self-direction or autonomy."

Intelligence

Intelligence is another concept notoriously difficult to define; in the main, definitions can be subsumed under three headings, derived respectively from clinical studies, animal experimentation, and educational measurement. "The respective representative definition issuing from these fields are: (1) The capacity to think abstractly, (2) the ability to learn, and (3) the capacity to adapt means to ends." Perhaps Burt's definition of intelligence as "innate, all-round mental ability" comes closest to a generally acceptable usage. It is well-known that the existence of a general factor of this kind has for long been denied by some critics of Spearman's fundamental work, notably Thurstone; recent demonstrations, however, that in Thurstone's own correlational studies a general factor plays an important part, and the admission on Thurstone's part that the group factors to which his own analysis gives rise can themselves be analysed into what he calls a "second order general factor" have between them led to a close rapprochement [among] factorists of all views.

Personality

. . . Quite generally, however, definitions of personality may be grouped according to whether they stress superficial, observable, objective appearances (*persona* or mask definitions), or whether they stress rather underlying inner, subjective essentials (*anima* or substance definitions). Watson's famous definition of personality as "the end product of our habit systems" may stand as an example of the first type of definition, Allport's view that it is "the dynamic organization within the individual of those psychophysical systems that determine his unique adjustments to his environment" as an example of the latter type of definition.

Definitions which lay stress on the outward, observable appearance are usually associated with a behaviouristic, nomothetic approach, while definitions stressing the inner, subjective organization are usually associated with an analytical, idiographic approach. To some extent, these differences in approach are nationally conditioned; the nomothetic approach is predominantly American, the idiographic approach German.

While seemingly antagonistic, these two different methods of approaching the fundamental problem of psychology are in reality complementary. There is after all no scientific way of investigating the inner, subjective organization of a person's fundamental needs and drives except by studying "the sum of activities that can be discovered by actual observation over a long enough time to give reliable information." And there is no way of accounting for observed consistencies and characteristic tendencies except by assuming some kind of inner organization, embracing "every phase of human character: intellect, temperament, skill, morality, and every attitude that has been built up in the course of one's life."

A definition which includes both views and comes perhaps nearest to a general consensus of psychological thought at the present time is Warren's view of personality as "the integrated organization of all the cognitive, affective, conative, and physical characteristics of an individual as it manifests itself in focal distinctness to others." It is in this sense that the term has been used throughout this book.

*　　*　　*　　*　　*

Combining the definitions we have presented so far, we may say that personality is the sum-total of the actual or potential behaviour-patterns of the organism, as determined by heredity and environment; it originates and develops through the functional interaction of the four main sectors into which these behaviour-patterns are organized: the cognitive sector (intelligence), the conative sector (character), the affective sector (temperament) and the somatic sector (constitution).

Trait and Type

In the description of personality, two further terms are often invoked which may require brief definition. These are *type* and *trait*. Many authors consider that a theory invoking "traits" must inevitably be opposed to a theory invoking "types," on the grounds that trait theory presupposes a normal distribution of the characteristic measured, while type theory presupposes a bimodal distribution. "Type theory tends to classify people into sharply divided groups, while trait theory assumes a continuous gradation with most people near the average." Thus type theory would call all people either introvert or extravert, while trait theory would find that most people tended to be ambivert.

*　　*　　*　　*　　*

A view which attempts to reconcile type and trait theory has been presented by Murphy and Jensen. These writers maintain that true types of personality consist of *necessary interconnections* between traits, rather than of mere classifications on a trait scale. This view has been criticized by Stagner on the grounds that writers on type theory conceive of the connections between traits not as being *necessary*, but rather as being *habitual*. He quotes Jung, who says: "When the orientation to the object and to objective facts is so predominant that the most frequent and essential decisions and actions are determined, not by subjective values but by objective relations, one speaks of an extraverted attitude. *When this is habitual, one speaks of an extraverted type*" (... our italics). Stagner concludes, "it seems more correct to speak of introversion-extraversion as a trait continuum describing habitual forms of behaviour, rather than as definite types with necessary connections between responses."

Our own definitions of "type" and "trait" bear some resemblance to the view of Murphy and Jensen, except that instead of *necessary connections* we will speak rather of *observed connections*. We shall speak of "Types" as *observed constellations or syndromes of traits*, and of "Traits" as *observed constellations of individual action-tendencies*. Thus we make the distinction between types and traits not in terms of their distribution, but in terms of their *relative inclusiveness as determined experimentally*.

A FACTOR THEORY OF PERSONALITY[3]

This view is presented graphically in Figure 1. It will be seen that we are here dealing with four levels of behaviour-organization. At the lowest level, we have specific responses, $S.R._1$, $S.R._2$, $S.R._3$, ... $S.R._n$. These are acts, such as responses to an experimental test or to experiences of everyday life, which are observed once, and may or may not be characteristic of the individual.

[3]*Ibid.*, from pp. 28-32. The figure has been renumbered.

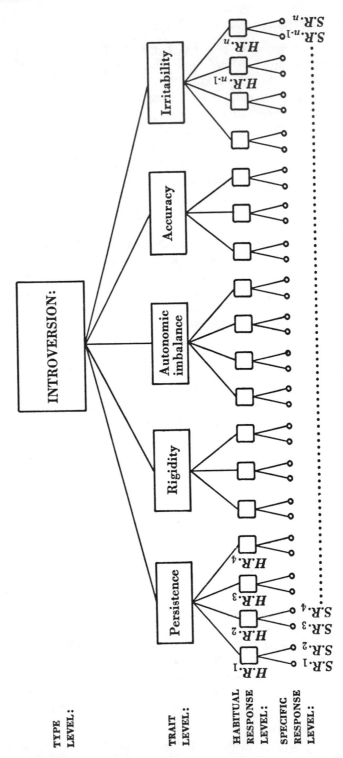

Fig. 1.
Diagrammatic representation of hierarchical organization of personality.

At the second level, we have what are called habitual responses, $H.R._1$, $H.R._2$, $H.R._3$, ... $H.R._n$. These are specific responses which tend to recur under similar circumstances; i.e., if the test is repeated, a similar response is given, or if the life-situation recurs, the individual reacts in a similar fashion. This is the lowest level of organization; roughly speaking, the amount of organization present here can be measured in terms of reliability coefficients, i.e., in terms of the probability that one repetition of a situation behaviour will be consistent.

At the third level, we have organizations of habitual acts into traits, T_1, T_2, T_3, ... T_n. These traits, accuracy, irritability, persistence, rigidity, etc., are theoretical constructs, based on observed intercorrelations of a number of different habitual responses; in the language of the factor analyst, they may be conceived of as group factors.

At the fourth level, we have organization of traits into a general type; in our example, the *introvert*. This organization also is based on observed correlations, this time on correlations between the various traits which between them make up the concept of the type under discussion. Thus in our example, persistence, rigidity, suggestibility, irritability and various other traits would form a constellation of traits intercorrelating among themselves, thus giving rise to a higher-order construct, the type. It will be noted that our four levels of personality organization correspond closely to the four types of factor distinguished in our discussion of factorial methods: error factors, specific factors, group factors, and general factors. An "habitual response" is merely a "specific response" divested of its error component, and made into a specific factor; a "trait" is a system of "specific responses" divested of its error and specific variance; a "type" is a system of "specific responses" which has lost its error, specific, and group factor variance.

Two consequences follow from this analysis. In the first place, as the field covered by each term grows, so the predictability of each "specific response" falls. It is much easier, and more rewarding, to predict a "specific response" from knowledge of a person's "habitual response" than from knowing his "trait" score, or from knowing his "type." If we wished to predict a person's score on the body-sway test of suggestibility, for instance, we should do well to give him the actual test, and make the result the basis of our prediction for future behaviour. As the test-retest correlation in this case is over .9, we can be fairly sure that our prediction will come true within a narrow margin of error.

If we cannot do that, then knowing his performance on other suggestibility tests, such as the Chevreul Pendulum, the Arm Levitation, or the Press-release test, would give us a predictive score with somewhat less certainty than if we knew his "habitual response." But as this trait is a comparatively well-defined one in terms of "habitual response" intercorrelations, our prediction would still be of some value. To take a practical example, we found that it was possible to predict hypnotizability with considerable accuracy from knowing a person's score on two other suggestibility tests.

If we were deprived even of this knowledge, and were told only a person's general type, then our prediction, while still better than chance, would be rather inaccurate, and would not inspire much confidence. Thus as we go up in the scale of generality, our ability to predict specific acts decreases; if our ability to predict is to be increased we must confine ourselves more and more closely to the actual "habitual response" in question.

The other consequence of the identification of our four levels of personality organization with the four types of factor is clearly implicit in Burt's discussion of the differences between these types of factor. He points out that "the differences throughout are principally differences of degree; the 'general factor' is simply the 'group factor' that has the most widespread occurrence; and the 'specific factors' are simply the 'group factors' that are most narrowly limited in their operation. . . . Thus the distinctions between general, group-, and specific factors are formal rather than material, relative rather than fixed. . . . By itself no factor can be styled general, group, or specific; such designations have reference solely to the particular set of tests and traits that have been correlated."

These admissions may appear to lower considerably the value of the type of analysis proposed. If predictability decreases as generality grows, then what is the value of discovering such general factors, the reader may ask; or he may enquire what is the purpose of analysing tables of correlations into factors which have no absolute but only relative value. The first type of criticism is made explicitly by Thomson, who doubts the usefulness of factor analysis because a better prediction of individual behaviour can usually be obtained by direct regression equations, the second is made implicitly by Thurstone, who seeks for "invariance."

In reply it may be pointed out that the investigation of the structure of the mind is in itself of scientific interest, regardless of the predictive powers, narrowly conceived, which such an analysis may bring. If a hierarchical structure such as we have outlined above succeeds in giving a more or less accurate picture of the kind of organization which obtains in the mind, then we are justified in using the methods outlined, and treating the problem of prediction as a secondary one, for whose solution other methods may be more appropriate. On the other hand, we do not claim that the factorial method can give us a definitive, final answer to all our questions. It is only as a first approach, as an approximation, that we regard our data and our theories; no more than heuristic value is claimed for them. As Burt has pointed out, "if factor analysis tells the truth and nothing but the truth, we need not condemn it for failing to tell the whole truth."

Summary

. . . A theory of personality organization was proposed which was based on Burt's views of factorial analysis and the nature of statistical factors, and on the hierarchical theories of sentiment-formation of McDougall. The view proposed, which attempts to reconcile the two main points of view in personality research (belief in specificity and belief in generality), stresses the actual amount of organization present, thus turning a qualitative difference of viewpoint into a quantitative problem of research.

THE DIMENSIONAL APPROACH[4]

This chapter will be devoted to a discussion of the relation between factor analysis and dimensional research, as well as to an investigation of certain criticisms often made of the factorial method. It will also contain an elementary introduction to the method of *criterion analysis* which has been introduced to overcome some of these criticisms, and to bring factor analysis into closer touch with the hypothetico-deductive method.

All through this book, then, we are concerned with problems of psychological dimensions. These problems are absolutely fundamental in science. If science depends on measurement, we must know what to measure. Thus we cannot make direct comparisons of magnitude between things which are qualitatively unlike, i.e., which do not lie along one dimension. We cannot form a dimensionally inhomogeneous equation, such as "23 hours + 14 horses = 20 sacks of potatoes + 17 miles" without violating common sense as well as physical propriety. Yet similarly dimensionally inhomogeneous equations are formed constantly by psychologists and psychiatrists because of our fundamental lack of knowledge regarding "dimensional homogeneity."

The reader may object that choice of dimensions in psychology, particularly if such choice is dependent on statistical procedures such as factor analysis, is arbitrary, thus setting psychology off from the remainder of science. This implies a profound misunderstanding of the procedures of physical science. In a very real sense, we may say that in physics "the choice of dimensions is arbitrary."

*　　*　　*　　*　　*

If, then, dimensions are in a sense arbitrary in physics, it seems unreasonable to expect factor analysis or any other statistical procedure to give us psychological dimensions which are not up to a point arbitrary. All possible systems of dimensions to describe a given set of facts must be convertible into each other, as they all must agree with the experimental facts; if two systems of dimensions disagree an empirical test becomes possible to decide which of the two leads to deductions verifiable by experiment. Whenever two factor analysts disagree in their analysis of a given table of intercorrelations, it is possible either (1) to convert one set of factors into the other through a set of intermediate equations, thus showing that these are merely alternative dimensional systems equally adequate to represent the facts, or else it is possible (2) to show that one solution is statistically unsound, or

[4]*The Scientific Study of Personality* (London: Routledge & Kegan Paul, 1952), from pp. 42-44.

leads to deductions which can be disproved. The argument between Spearman and Thurstone was of the latter kind, leading to a disproof of Spearman's original position; most arguments in the literature, however, are of the former kind.

To acknowledge that one's choice of dimensions is arbitrary does not mean, of course, that *any* set of dimensions may be chosen. In practice, the restriction imposed by the requirement that dimensions "may be anything consistent with a set of definitions which *agree with the experimental facts*" rules out all but a very few alternative sets of dimensions, and as facts accumulate choice becomes very restricted indeed. Even to find one single set of dimensions to embrace all the known facts of personality research may appear a tall order; to find several such sets would tax the imagination of most psychologists unduly. The undoubted existence of several sets of dimensions, proposed by the various schools, is accountable in the main by the very simple procedure of unmercifully rejecting all facts not fitting into a given scheme. If psychologists followed the example of physicists and rejected any model which was clearly in opposition to experimentally verified facts, the ground would be cleared of much rubbish the main effect of which is to hinder the advance of psychological knowledge.

THREE DIMENSIONS OF PERSONALITY: (1) EXTRAVERSION-INTROVERSION, (2) NEUROTICISM, (3) PSYCHOTICISM[5]

The great majority of psychologists who deal with the concept of personality either experimentally or clinically have adopted the organismic point of view; the present book, like its predecessor, takes an outspokenly atomistic, elementalistic point of view.

*　　*　　*　　*　　*

How, then, it may be asked, does the atomistic psychologist view the problem of personality organization? We may perhaps attempt to answer this question by reference to an urgent psychiatric problem, namely, that of diagnosis. Reference has already been made in an earlier chapter to the conflicting views, and the often self-contradictory pronouncements, of psychiatrists and clinical psychologists. In their terminology, they regard the patients under their care as falling into one of a number of different classes (hysteria, schizophrenia, neurasthenia, etc.), a view which is only permissible if these different disorders are regarded as qualitatively different; yet in much of their writing and even more so in their practice they regard these different classes as blending into one another, as being mutually overlapping, as being in fact differentiated along quantitative lines. Clearly the

[5]*Ibid.*, from pp. 276-86. The figure has been renumbered.

qualitative and the quantitative aspects must be reconciled in some way, but little guidance is to be found in the text-books.

The answer to this problem is implicit in the experiments described in the previous chapters of this book: we must determine the required number of dimensions, locate them accurately, and measure them with a given degree of reliability and validity. Figure 2 may serve as a very rudimentary model of the kind of structure we have in mind. Using our experimentally demonstrated three factors of neuroticism, psychoticism, and extraversion-introversion as three axes of a co-ordinate system, we can now locate a given patient in terms of his exact position within this system. Leaving out of account the extravert dimension for the moment, we can see that the average person would lie in the centre of the diagram, at *A;* a strongly psychotic person, undifferentiated with respect to neuroticism, would be located at *P,* while a strongly neurotic patient, undifferentiated with respect to psychoticism, would be located at *N.* A person suffering from both psychotic and neurotic disorders would be found at point *P* + *N.* In terms of this diagram, the question: "Is this person psychotic or neurotic?" becomes as unreasonable as the question: "Is this patient intelligent or tall?" "Two

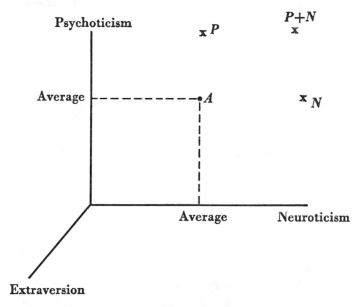

Fig. 2.
The organization of personality; three-dimensional representation.

orthogonal vectors, like neuroticism and psychoticism, generate a plane on which the position of an individual has to be indicated by reference to *both* vectors; we can only describe an individual by giving both his I.Q. and his height, or by giving both his degree of neuroticism and of psychoticism. All positions on the plane thus generated are possible locations for a given individual, and it will be seen that *mixed cases* are far more likely than *pure cases*—we are more likely to find individuals in the plane of the diagram than on the ordinate or on the abscissa. This preponderance of mixed cases of course agrees well with clinical experience. Diagnosis on this showing should consist in the accurate determinations of an individual's position on the plane, rather than, as is now usual, in a simple either-or judgment."

It is not hypothesized, of course, that the three dimensions dealt with in this book are the only ones into which personality can be analysed, and along which measurement should take place. To take but one example, there is the case of intelligence, operationally defined in terms of Thurstone's second-order factor, which is approximately orthogonal to all the dimensions so far discussed. In due course, other dimensions will no doubt be isolated and measured, and much prospecting has already been done by Cattell into possible lines of progress. But regardless of the actual number of independent dimensions which our picture of personality may require, it is clear that categorical diagnosis of the "either-or" kind are not warranted by the experimental findings; what is required is a separate assessment and measurement of each dimension in turn. It is not claimed that more than a beginning has been made in the complex, time-consuming, and difficult proceeding; it is believed, however, that results to date are fully in agreement with the general model of personality on which our procedures have been predicated.

Two Orthogonal Personality Factors:
Extraversion-Introversion,
Emotionality-Stability[6]

An attempt has been made to bring our picture of the structure of human personality up to date by introducing certain theoretical concepts and experimental techniques which originated in an endeavour to state causal postulates from which the observed behaviour patterns and descriptive factors could be deduced in a more or less rigorous fashion. The factorial literature in the last few years has grown to such an extent that the detailed historical review which we have followed in the preceding chapters [of *The Structure of Human Personality*] could not be maintained, without extending the book to twice its present length; such a detailed review has in fact been presented elsewhere [in Eysenck and Eysenck, *Personality Structure and Measurement* (London: Routledge & Kegan Paul, 1969)]. The main conclusion which can be drawn from the several hundred recent studies there reviewed, and the original work presented, serve largely to underline the conclusions derived from the earlier studies discussed in the present volume; results from the different universes of discourse presented by Cattell, Guilford, the MMPI, and many other apparently separate and

---

[6]*The Structure of Human Personality* (London: Methuen, 3rd ed., 1970), from p. 425.

independent sets of investigations all support very strongly the thesis that two orthogonal personality factors, extraversion-introversion and emotionality-stability, are omnipresent in empirical studies and analyses, and account for a large and important portion of the total variance, for children as much as for adults, and for mentally ill as well as for mentally normal people. Not all investigators are agreed on the nomenclature, of course, and many different terms are still used to designate these major personality variables, but it is now reasonable to say that there is almost complete agreement among experimental investigators that these two factors enjoy a predominant and assured position in the descriptive system of personality measurement.

CRITERION ANALYSIS:
A COMBINATION OF FACTOR ANALYSIS
AND THE HYPOTHETICO-DEDUCTIVE METHOD[7]

. . . This question is taken up directly by Cattell. He points out that the psychologist, as a scientist, will want to find the set of factors which corresponds to a set of psychologically real influences because he is interested in understanding the psychological meaning of his predictions and because he is curious to gain truth for its own sake. "In that case he may (1) devise possible ways of overdetermining the analysis of the given correlation matrix so that only the one set of true factors will emerge, or (2) start from the opposite shore and propound, on psychological grounds alone, a hypothesis about what source traits are operative in the variables. Then he will see if these factors correspond to any of the possible mathematical factors found in the matrix."[a] Cattell rejects the second, or hypothetico-deductive, type of method.

*   *   *   *   *

It is the purpose of this paper to suggest a method of rotation of factor axes which will give a unique, invariant solution along the lines of the hypothetico-deductive method; in other words, we believe that Cattell dismisses too easily the most powerful instrument of scientific methodology so far devised, and advocates instead methods which we shall try to show to be in no way adequate substitutes for it. First, we shall turn to an examination of these "methods of overdetermining the analysis of the given correlation matrix," and to a review of the results which may be expected from the use of these methods; then we shall describe the principles on which the method of criterion analysis was devised, in an attempt to get over the

[7]"Criterion Analysis—An Application of the Hypothetico-Deductive Method to Factor Analysis," *Psychological Review*, LVII (1950), from pp. 39-44.

[a]R. B. Cattell, *Description and Measurement of Personality* (London: George Harrap & Co., 1946), from p. 273.

difficulties pointed out by Cattell; the principles will be discussed by reference to a worked example to show the application of this new method to a concrete problem.

Principles of Factor Rotation

Cattell lists seven principles for determining the choice of factors: (1) Rotation to agree with clinical and general psychological findings; (2) Rotation to agree with factors from past factor analyses; (3) Rotation to put axes through the centre of clusters; (4) The principle of orthogonal additions; rotation to agree with successively established factors; (5) The principle of expected profiles; rotation to produce loading profiles congruent with general psychological expectation; (6) The principle of "simple structure" relative to the given correlation matrix; (7) The principle of proportional profiles or "simultaneous simple structure." These seven principles may in our discussion be reduced to two: rotation where there is an outside criterion, and rotation where reliance is placed exclusively on statistical properties of the correlation matrix.

When there is an outside criterion, there are many different ways of making use of the criterion; these all reduce ultimately to the most simple and direct—inclusion of the criterion in the correlation matrix, and subsequent rotation of factors in such a way that all the common-factor variance of the criterion score is taken up by one factor, which is then identified with the principle of classification underlying the criterion. As an example of this approach, we may quote the correlational analysis by Cox of Rorschach scores, taken on 60 normal and 60 neurotic children matched for age, sex, and I.Q. Each score was also correlated with the normal-neurotic dichotomy, which thus became the criterion score in the matrix of intercorrelations. After factorization, axes were rotated in such a way that all the common-factor variance of the criterion score was taken up by one factor, thus identified as "neuroticism," leaving only zero projections for this item on the remaining factors. While this method has certain advantages, it suffers from two great and fundamental drawbacks. In the first place, if the correlations between the individual scores and the criterion score are significant (if, in other words, several test scores discriminate significantly between the criterion groups), then it follows inevitably that a factor should be produced from the intercorrelations of the scores which, when rotated in conformity with the principle outlined, would have high loadings for the criterion score. In other words, it is doubtful if the factorial approach adds anything of fundamental scientific interest that would not be given equally well, and more quickly, by some form of multiple regression or discriminant function analysis.

The other objection is even more fundamental; the procedure outlined begs the questions which is really the ultimate justification for the factorial quest. We assume that the criterion groups are situated along what Cattell calls a "source trait"; this fundamental assumption cannot be proved by means of the procedure described here. The fundamental assumption that neuroticism is a source trait remains an assumption, and if, as the writer believes, it be true that the main *raison d'être* of factorial methods lies in their ability to prove or disprove fundamental taxonomic questions of this kind, then clearly the method of rotation through an outside criterion is not of great general importance.

*   *   *   *   *

Having rejected the method of external criteria, we must now turn to the method of internal criteria, *i.e.*, the methods of simple structure and of proportional profiles. There is such a large body of discussion dealing with these principles that we shall merely indicate with extreme briefness why we consider that they also fail to solve the problem which factor analysis sets out to attack. . . . Thurstone and Cattell make the assumption that if some "general guiding principles" could be arrived at from an analysis of the matrix of intercorrelations itself, then we would be ensured of finding "factors corresponding to realities." Thurstone phrases this point rather differently by saying that only when factors are rotated in conformity with his principles do they become "psychologically meaningful." It is this fundamental assumption underlying the work of both Thurstone and Cattell which appears doubtful to the present writer.

*   *   *   *   *

Criterion Analysis

Any statistical method of analysis is appropriate only to certain types of problems. The type of problem to which criterion analysis is appropriate may be described most easily by reference to an actual investigation. On the basis of a number of experimental and statistical investigations described elsewhere, the writer has advanced the heuristic hypothesis that there exists "a general factor of neuroticism, similar in mode of derivation and general interpretation on the orectic side to the general factor of intelligence on the cognitive side." This hypothesis assumes the existence of some strong, innate tendency predisposing individuals toward definite degrees of emotional adjustment or maladjustment, maturity or immaturity, neurotic or non-neurotic reactivity to environmental stress. It also assumes that the amount of environmental stress suffered by any given individual will affect the likelihood of his actual breakdown. We are not concerned here with the relative contribution of heredity and environment to neurotic maladjustment; what does concern us here is the hypothesis that his putative factor of "neuroticism" forms a quantitative continuum at one extreme of which are to be found hospitalized neurotics, while so-called normals are to be found all the way from the near-neurotic and neurotic to the conspicuously non-neurotic, mature, stable and integrated type of personality.

A second heuristic hypothesis was also advanced, again on the basis of various empirical investigations, to the effect that within the general field of temperament, a general factor of extraversion-introversion could be found which was orthogonal to the factors of intelligence and neuroticism, and which found its prototypes in the neurotic disorders known as hysteria and dysthymia (psychasthenia, neurasthenia, anxiety neurosis) respectively. While this scheme of organization was based on factorial studies, it was recognized that the researches reported did not contain any definite proof regarding the feasibility of the assumptions made. The possibility could not be ruled out that certain qualitative differences existed between normal and neurotic groups, for instance, which gave rise to differences in test scores between these groups; if this were so, the assumption of a quantitative continuum would clearly be untenable.

A similar problem arises in conjunction with a much more widely held theory, namely, that associated with the name of Kretschmer. This author believes that there exists a normality-abnormality continuum whose one extreme is not the neurotic, but the psychotic; he also posits that the main factor in the temperamental field finds its prototypes in the main functional psychoses (schizophrenia and manic-depressive insanity), rather than in the neuroses. Instead of a taxonomic system based on neuroticism and extraversion-introversion, Kretschmer therefore has an entirely different system based on psychoticism and cyclothymia-schizothymia. The present writer has outlined Kretschmer's position at length elsewhere, and is publishing experimental evidence regarding the adequacy of his theoretical position; here he only desires to draw attention to the fact that both theories (Kretschmer's and the writer's) cannot be right, although they may well both be wrong, and that consequently some form of proof becomes indispensable. Kretschmer has attempted such a proof, which has much methodological interest; the writer has examined it elsewhere, and does not wish to repeat his arguments here; the conclusion arrived at was that this alleged proof really leaves the issue indeterminate. Clearly what is wanted is a deduction from the hypotheses presented which can be tested by means of statistical procedures; a deduction, needless to say, which is sufficiently precise to avoid an equivocal answer.

Deduction 1. The type of deduction on which our method relies may be illustrated by reference to a hypothetical example in which we are dealing with the "neuroticism" factor, and two tests, T_1 and T_2, which discriminate significantly between a normal and a neurotic group. (We shall leave aside for the time being a consideration of the question of how these groups are chosen, or of problems of sampling which arise.) On the hypothesis that neuroticism is a continuous variable, a "normal" group would include persons differing in degree of "neuroticism." Now clearly the more highly "neurotic" subjects in the normal group should have higher "neurotic" scores on the two tests than the less highly "neurotic" subjects (we are assuming here that the tests have a threshold and a ceiling sufficiently far apart to allow differentiation at all levels of "neuroticism," an assumption which will be discussed below). It would follow from this argument that on the average T_1 and T_2 should be correlated in the normal population, a deduction which can easily be verified. (This correlation should of course be purified of the effects of irrelevant factors, such as intelligence, etc.)

This suggested proof could of course be extended to any number of tests; if a battery of n tests discriminates between normal and neurotic subjects, then on the basis of our hypothesis we should expect all the intercorrelations between these tests within the normal group to be positive on the average. We may, however, go further than this and add another specification which also follows directly from our hypothesis. This specification takes into account, not only the fact that our n tests discriminate between normals and neurotics, but also the additional fact that they do so with widely differing success.

Deduction 2. Let us correlate each of our n tests with the criterion, *i.e.*, the normal-neurotic dichotomy, by means of biserial or tetrachoric correlations; we thus obtain a criterion column (C_N) consisting of the correlations of tests $T_1, T_2, T_3, \ldots T_n$ with the criterion. Let us next take the table of intercorrelations between the n tests *for the normal population only*, and submit it to a process of factorization, using either Burt's summation method or Thurstone's centroid method. This will result in the reduction of the large original table of correlations to a small number of factors in terms of which the original correlations can be reconstructed.[b] The actual factors found are purely arbitrary, as their position in the factor space depends on the original selection of tests, conditions of univariate and multivariate selection of the population, and other considerations of a similar kind. Our suggestion for deriving a unique, invariant, and psychologically meaningful solution of the problem posed by this fortuitous structure of factor positions is to *rotate the first summation or centroid factor into a position of maximum correlation with the criterion column, C_N.*

The reasoning behind this suggestion follows directly from the two-test example given earlier. If the fact that two tests discriminate between the criterion groups results in a correlation between the two tests, then clearly the greater the discrimination effected by a test, the higher *(ceteris paribus)* the correlations that test will show with other discriminant tests. Similarly, the lower the discriminative ability of a test, the lower will be its correlations with other discriminant tests. Now a factor is the expression of a pattern of intercorrelations existing between a set of tests; if a pattern of intercorrelations such as the one posited here exists in the matrix which is being analyzed, then it should be possible to arrive at a corresponding factor by suitable rotation of the arbitrary factors which emerge from the original analysis. The factor which embodies, as it were, our hypothesis, is of such a kind that the test which best discriminates normals from neurotics would have the highest loadings, while the test which least discriminated between

[b]Only significant factors should be included in the analysis, of course, using one of the twenty or so available approximate criteria discussed by Vernon.

normals and neurotics would have the lowest loadings; the other tests would be intermediate between these two extremes, having factor loadings proportional to the criterion column values. Rotation according to the principle of maximizing the correlation between factor and criterion column would enable us to discover to what extent the hypothesis was borne out; in this sense the principle suggested enables us to use factorial methods as part of the general hypothetico-deductive procedure.

It should be noted that if the hypothesis which is being tested is not borne out by the data, no amount of rotation would succeed in giving us any but a chance correlation between the criterion column and the rotated factors. In other words, the appearance of a high correlation between factor and criterion column may be interpreted as definite support of the correctness of the hypothesis; failure of such correlation to appear is proof of the incorrectness of the hypothesis. These statements are subject to a number of qualifications.

*　　*　　*　　*　　*

Conclusion[8]

The essential points in "criterion analysis" will now have become clear. We start with a given criterion for some hypothetical continuum which we suspect, on purely psychological grounds, to be of general interest and importance. This criterion will in all probability be very impure, attenuated, and inaccurate. We create measuring instruments which can be shown to give some rough measure of correspondence with the criterion; we then study the interrelations of these measuring instruments by means of factor analysis, to obtain evidence of the existence of our hypothetical continuum, and to discover whether it is related in some rough way to our criterion. As has been shown early in this chapter, we may in this way actually transcend our criterion. . . . We may therefore now use our factor to improve our criterion, until we reach a position of exact equivalence. When this is done, we may assume that our original hypothesis was justified. This process may appear like arguing in a circle, but in reality this method of argument corresponds precisely to the method used by physical science to define even such elementary concepts as "length."

*　　*　　*　　*　　*

The close similarity between this mutual interplay of rough-and-ready, common-sense observation, measurement based upon such observation, and modification to give more precise interrelations of measurements, with the procedure of "criterion analysis" will be obvious. Criterion analysis attempts to do in a formal manner in psychology what has always been done in the physical sciences. Our original hypotheses about temperature are derived from "clinical" observation of our own feelings of hot and cold; this

[8]*The Scientific Study of Personality, op. cit.,* from pp. 78-83.

forms our original criterion. There is no doubt that this criterion is inaccurate, fallible, unreliable, and impure. One person's judgments of "hot" and "cold" are not necessarily identical with another's, and may deviate considerably; external factors such as humidity play an important part in our judgment, as do internal factors such as our state of nutrition, or the amount of exercise we have taken. But roughly these feelings of "hot" and "cold" can be shown to correspond with certain physical phenomena, such as the contraction and expansion of metals, the pressure of gases, or the emission of electrons from a heated surface. As these physical phenomena constitute an interconnected system of observations which in turn fits in well with other observations (rigidity of bodies, measurement of distances) the criterion is revised to obtain the best possible fit (the highest possible correlations) between all these sets of phenomena.

In the same way, "clinical" observations of certain types of behaviour give us our original hypothesis regarding the existence of a continuum of "neuroticism"; these observations, regularized and formalized in legal and psychiatric practice, form our original criterion. There is no doubt that this criterion is inaccurate, fallible, unreliable, and impure. One person's judgments of "neurotic" and "normal" are not necessarily identical with another's, and may deviate considerably; external facts such as intelligence, or beauty, play an important part in our judgment, as do internal factors such as the state of our liver, or our general attitudes. But roughly these assessments of "neurotic" and "normal" can be shown to correspond with certain objective tests, such as body-sway suggestibility, or persistence. As these objective tests constitute an interconnected system of observations which in turn fits in well with other observations (employability of mental defectives, effects of prefrontal leucotomy, selection of nurses and students, monozygotic and dyzygotic twin differences) the criterion is revised to obtain the best possible fit (the maximum correlation) between all these sets of phenomena.

*　　*　　*　　*　　*

The method of criterion analysis will become clearer as its various applications are studied. . . . In essence, it is nothing but the application to the special taxonomic problems of human behaviour in its non-cognitive aspects of the general principles of scientific method, more particularly of the hypothetico-deductive method. It requires a main hypothesis regarding the existence of a quantitative continuum underlying a given area of human behaviour; it also requires subsidiary hypotheses regarding the nature of this continuum, which will determine the tests to be used, and the linearity or otherwise of the relations anticipated. . . . Deductions made from such a set of hypotheses can be disproved . . . or they may be supported with varying degrees of evidence by the results of specially planned experiments.

PART SEVEN

S-R Approaches to Personality

CHAPTER 20

B. F. SKINNER

STIMULUS-RESPONSE PSYCHOLOGY: OPERANT REINFORCEMENT APPROACH TO PERSONALITY

Born in 1904 in Susquehanna, Pennsylvania, the experimental psychologist Burrhus Frederic Skinner was educated at Hamilton College, which granted him an A.B. in English. After what he felt was less than a successful attempt at writing, Skinner looked to psychology, though he "had only the vaguest idea of what that meant." Turning to Harvard University for graduate studies in psychology, where, under Professor Edwin G. Boring he submitted a thesis on reflex, he was granted his M.A. in 1930 and Ph.D. in 1931.

The earlier years of the 1930s were invested in experimentation at Harvard, initially as a National Research Council Fellow and subsequently as a Junior Fellow in the Harvard Society of Fellows. Then followed his maiden teaching experience at Minnesota, where he "began to learn College psychology" and where W. K. Estes, who was preparing for engineering, was prevailed upon to alter his program to one of psychology. By 1939 Skinner attained the rank of Associate Professor but relinquished his position in 1945 to become Professor and Head of the Department of Psychology at Indiana University. His move to Harvard's Department of Psychology in 1948 followed his William James Lectures delivered at that university a year earlier. It was the course in human behavior, introduced at Harvard, that clarified the need for a text and led to the publication of *Science and Human Behavior* in 1953.

As early as 1938, Skinner published the now classic *The Behavior of Organisms,* a book that enjoys a lasting place in the history of psychology and in which he introduced his operant conditioning. Chiefly owing to this book, annual conferences began in 1946 in Indiana on the Experimental Analysis of Behavior, which led approximately a decade later to the founding of its organ, the *Journal of the Experimental Analysis of Behavior,* and the establishment of the Division for the Experimental Analysis of Behavior of the American Psychological Association.

Seminal ideas in programmed instruction, emerging in the late 1930s, were formulated in an unpublished book *Something to Think About.* His prompting to design a series of teaching machines arose from his discovery that a number of his daughter's teachers were ignoring some substantiated facts of the learning process. The machine, demonstrated in 1954 at the University of Pittsburgh during the conference on Current Trends in Psychology, was followed by the publication of Skinner's views on teaching machines and programmed instruction, a summary of which appeared in 1958 in the article "Teaching Machines."

Although Skinner disparagingly spoke of his literary ability, he was probably motivated out of modesty, inasmuch as his *Walden Two* (1948), required an incubation period of only seven weeks. Although its initial intent was the feasible description of the good life in a community, a community so designed was too utopian ever to have existed.

It was as early as 1941 that Skinner, as a Guggenheim Fellow, undertook the final draft of his *Verbal Behavior,* but interruptions (including World War II) delayed its publication until 1957, twenty-three years from the time of its inception. One reason for the delay was research that fructified in the publication of *Schedules of Reinforcement* in 1957 with Charles Ferster. Having written a number of important papers, Skinner decided to have them published as his *Cumulative Record* in 1959, enlarging the book twice since that time, once in 1961 and again in 1972. A new section on creative behavior highlighted the third edition. The most systematic and integrated articulation of his position is found in *Science and Human Behavior;* notwithstanding its publication in 1953, it is still the finest presentation of his stand. Recently he summarized his position in a small volume which he titled *Contingencies of Reinforcement* (1968). In his contribution, the controversial *Beyond Freedom and Dignity* (1971) is more of a philosophical excursion than are his previous publications. A later work, *About Behaviorism* (1974), offers a synthesis of his psychological and philosophical stance. Before leaving the subject of his publications, mention should be made of the book produced from informal chats with Richard I. Evans, *B. F. Skinner: The Man and His Ideas* (1969), vol. IV of the series "Dialogues with Notable Contributors to Personality Theory."

Skinner's operant behavior, a non-theoretical or descriptive approach to the study of personality, views behavior as subject to the regulation of its environmental consequences. That consequence termed reinforcement serves to heighten the probability or frequency of occurrence of a given mode of behavior. If the reinforcing consequence entails the initiation or strengthening of a stimulus, then it is a positive reinforcement. But if the stimulus is aversive or negative, so that the reinforcing consequence is one of stimulus termination, it is called negative reinforcement.

There are three conditions of interaction existing between an organism and its environment: (1) the occasion for the response, (2) the response per se, and (3) the reinforcing consequences. It is among these interrelationships that contingencies of reinforcement exist. Unless a stimulus plays an important role in the prevailing contingencies its effect upon the organism is but slight or negligible. A reinforcer contingent upon a response or, more accurately, a class of responses, is termed operant. While operant behavior is emitted behavior, respondent behavior is elicited reflexly as a reaction to a stimulus, the former being associated with instrumental and the latter with classical conditioning. According to the primary law of operant conditioning (type R, the other being type S): *"If the occurrence of an operant is followed by presentation of a reinforcing stimulus, the strength is increased."* Extinction ensues, or at least strength is diminished, when the reinforcing stimulus fails to follow an operant already strengthened. Reinforcement may assume a variety of schedules such as intermittent reinforcement, wherein a predetermined time schedule governs reinforcement, or continuous reinforcement, where reinforcement occurs with each operant response. Other forms are fixed interval, in which reinforcement follows after a given period of time, fixed ratio, where reinforcement follows after a set number of responses, variable interval or ratio, in which reinforcement varies within a given range, multiple schedules, calling for the shifting of schedules depending upon the type of stimulus (e.g., a red key activates a variable interval and a green key a fixed interval), and differential reinforcement of rate of responding, wherein reinforcement occurs following the "preceding response after a specified interval of time . . . or before the end of a given interval."

Verbal behavior, as understood by Skinner, accords verbal contingencies the same status as that maintained by laboratory equipment, except that a second organism is involved. The prevailing contingencies in verbal societies that "generate sentences" account for verbal behavior, without the benefit of the speaker's environment.

The principles of operant behavior are ingeniously applied by Skinner to the entire spectrum of personality. Not that Skinner believes that personality is structured or operates dynamically with internal mechanisms operating, nor does he postulate "needs"; rather he is concerned with a functional analysis of contingencies of reinforcement. Neither does he believe in an "empty organism" or *tabula rasa* mind. An avowed determinist who identifies himself as a behaviorist, Skinner believes that all types of personality (normal and abnormal) can be shaped and conditioned by his operant reinforcement principles. His abhorrence of theory arises from his view that a theory is the explanation of behavior in terms of a mind or nervous system, i.e., in terms of another universe. Although he is determined, man can nevertheless control his behavior by altering the environment by which he is controlled. Operant behavior not only explains the individual personality but the social behavior of a person as well.

CONTINGENCIES OF REINFORCEMENT[1]

A few contingencies which have been studied experimentally may be roughly described as follows. An experimental space contains one or more operanda such as a lever projecting from a wall which may be pressed by a rat or a translucent disc on the well which may be pecked by a pigeon, various sources of stimuli, such as sounds and lights, and reinforcing devices, such as a food or water dispenser, or a source of aversive stimulation, such as a bright light or an electric grid to deliver shocks. Any stimulus arising from the space, the operandum, or special stimulating devices prior to a response is designated "S^D." A response, such as pressing the lever or pressing the disc, is "R." Food presented to a hungry organism is a positive

[1]*Contingencies of Reinforcement* (New York: Appleton-Century-Crofts, 1969), from pp. 22-25.

reinforcer ("S^{rein}"), a bright light or shock a negative reinforcer. The interrelations among S^D, R, and S^{rein} compose the contingencies of reinforcement. All three terms must be specified.

(1) *Operant reinforcement.* A hungry rat presses the lever and receives food. (Frequency of pressing increases.) A pigeon pecks the disc and receives food. (Frequency of pecking increases.)

(2) *Escape.* The experimental space is brightly lighted. A rat presses the lever and reduces the intensity of the light. (The lever is then pressed more quickly when the light appears, or more often in sustained light.)

(3) *Avoidance.* A rat is shocked every twenty seconds except that a response to the lever postpones the next shock for twenty seconds. (Frequency of response increases and many shocks are avoided.)

(4) *Stimulus discrimination.* A rat presses the lever and obtains food when a light is on, but no food follows the response when the light is off. (Frequency of responding is higher in the presence of the light than in its absence—"S$^\triangle$.")

(5) *Response differentiation.* Food appears only when the lever is depressed with a force above a given value. (Responses showing the required force appear more frequently.)

(6) *"Superstition."* The food dispenser operates every twenty seconds regardless of the behavior of the rat. (Any behavior occurring just before the appearance of the food is reinforced, and similar coincidences become more likely as the behavior is strengthened. The rat develops a "superstitious ritual.")

(7) *Chained operants.* Pecking a green disc changes the color to red, and pecking the red disc is followed by food. (The frequency of occurrence of the chain of responses increases.)

(8) *Observation.* A discrimination is set up under which a pigeon pecks a red disc but not a green. The color slowly fades, however, until a discrimination becomes impossible. Pecking another disc reverses the fading. (The pigeon pecks the other disc to produce enough color to make a discrimination.)

(9) *Matching to sample.* Three discs are arranged in a row. The middle disc is either red or green, the other two unlighted. A response to the middle disc lights the side discs, one red and one green. A response to the matching disc is reinforced with food. (Responses to the matching disc increase in frequency.)

(10) *Delayed matching.* As in (9) but the middle disc is darkened before the side keys are illuminated. (If the side keys are presented immediately, the pigeon is able to match. A short delay makes matching impossible. "The pigeon cannot remember the color of the middle key.")

(11) *Mediated delayed matching.* There are five discs—one in the center and the others within easy reach at the four points of the compass. Center is either red or green. A response darkens it and projects white light on North and South. If Center was red, a response to North illuminates East

and West, one red and one green. A response to the matching disc is rein-forced. If Center was green, a response to South illuminates East and West, and a matching response is reinforced. Two chains are thus set up: (i) The pigeon pecks Center red, North white, and red on either East or West; (ii) The pigeon pecks Center green, South white, and green on East or West. The pigeon matches successfully because it responds to the red on East or West when it has just responded to North and to the green on East or West when it has just responded to South. Responding on North and South can then be protracted—for example, by requiring a number of responses to il-luminate East and West. The number can be greatly increased. A long de-layed matching response to East or West is mediated by the stimuli gener-ated by responding to North or South.

(12) *Schedules of reinforcement.* Reinforcements may be scheduled in many ways. Each schedule, with given values of the parameters, generates a characteristic performance.

a. Fixed interval. A response is reinforced only when it occurs after the passage of a period of time (for example, five minutes). Another period be-gins immediately after reinforcement.

b. A fixed ratio. Every nth response is reinforced.

c. Variable interval or ratio. The interval or number in *a* and *b* need not be fixed but may vary over a given range around some average value.

d. Multiple schedules. One schedule is in force in the presence of one stimulus, a different schedule in the presence of another stimulus. For exam-ple, a fixed interval prevails when the key is red, and a variable issue when the key is green. (A characteristic performance is obtained under each stimulus.)

e. Differential reinforcement of rate of responding. A response is rein-forced only if it follows the preceding response after a specified interval of time (DRL) or before the end of a given interval (DRH). In DRL, the in-terval might be, for example, 3 minutes; in DRH, one-half second.

(13) *Multiple deprivation.* Pecking one disc is reinforced by food, peck-ing another disc is reinforced by water, pecking a third disc is reinforced with either food or water at random. Under different conditions of hunger and thirst the rate of responding on the third disc is the average of the rates on the first two.

Some contingencies in the field of verbal behavior are as follows:

(14) *"Mand."* In the presence of a listener (S^D), the response *water* is reinforced when the listener gives the speaker water.

(15) *Echoic behavior.* When someone says *water*, the speaker says *water*, and reinforcement is contingent on the similarity of the two sounds.

(16) *Textual behavior.* When looking at the printed word *water*, the speaker is reinforced if he says *water*.

(17) *Intraverbal behavior.* Upon hearing or reading the word *water*, the speaker is reinforced if he emits a thematically related response such as *ice* or *faucet*.

(18) *"Tact."* In the presence of a glass of water, a river, rain, and so on, the speaker is reinforced when he says *water.*

DETERMINISM AND BEHAVIOR AS LAWFUL[2]

We certainly accept the fact that we are not beginning with an empty organism or a *tabula rasa.* . . . As a determinist, I must assume that the organism is simply mediating the relationships between the forces acting upon it and its own output, and these are the kinds of relationships I'm anxious to formulate. . . .

If by "machine" you simply mean any system which behaves in an orderly way, then man and all the other animals are machines. But this has nothing to do with the interests of the humanists or of the interests of any man of compassion who deals with his fellowman. The behaviorists, like scientists in general, are attempting to reach certain goals. They use their own techniques to arrive at these goals, just as the humanist uses his own techniques to arrive at his goals. Though I call myself a behaviorist, I don't particularly like the term.

* * * * *

People at times have charged this kind of analysis with various ignominious shortcomings, saying that somehow it reduced the dignity and nobility of man. But no analysis changes man; he is what he is. I take an optimistic view. Man can control his future even though his behavior is wholly determined. It is controlled by the environment, but man is always changing his environment. He builds a world in which his behavior has certain characteristics. He does this because the characteristics are reinforcing to him. He builds a world in which he suffers fewer aversive stimuli and in which he behaves with maximum efficiency. He avoids extremes of temperature; he preserves food to avoid hunger. He builds a world in which he is more likely to get on with his fellowman, in which he is more likely to educate himself so that he will be more effective in the future, and so on. If you want to argue from history, you can say that over a period of, say, a hundred thousand years there has been an accumulation of behavioral techniques which have improved the effectiveness of human behavior. Man controls himself, but he does so by controlling his environment.

FUNCTIONAL ANALYSIS[3]

The external variables of which behavior is a function provide for what may be called a causal or functional analysis. We undertake to predict and

[2]Richard I. Evans, *B. F. Skinner: The Man and His Ideas* (New York: E. P. Dutton, 1969), from pp. 23-24, 106-7.
[3]*Science and Human Behavior* (New York: The Macmillan Company, 1953), from p. 35.

control the behavior of the individual organism. This is our "dependent variable"—the effect for which we are to find the cause. Our "independent variables"—the causes of behavior—are the external conditions of which behavior is a function. Relations between the two—the "cause-and-effect relationships" in behavior—are the laws of a science. A synthesis of these laws expressed in quantitative terms yields a comprehensive picture of the organism as a behaving system.

STRUCTURE OF PERSONALITY:
OPERANT AND RESPONDENT BEHAVIOR[4]

We select a relatively simple bit of behavior which may be freely and rapidly repeated, and which is easily observed and recorded. If our experimental subject is a pigeon, for example, the behavior of raising the head above a given height is convenient. This may be observed by sighting across the pigeon's head at a scale pinned on the far wall of the box. We first study the height at which the head is normally held and select some line on the scale which is reached only infrequently. Keeping our eye on the scale we then begin to open the food tray very quickly whenever the head rises above the line. If the experiment is conducted according to specifications, the result is invariable: we observe an immediate change in the frequency with which the head crosses the line. We also observe, and this is of some importance theoretically, that higher lines are now being crossed. We may advance almost immediately to a higher line in determining when food is to be presented. In a minute or two, the bird's posture has changed so that the top of the head seldom falls below the line which we first chose.

When we demonstrate the process of stamping in in this relatively simple way, we see that certain common interpretations of Thorndike's experiment are superfluous. The expression "trial-and-error learning," which is frequently associated with the law of effect, is clearly out of place here. We are reading something into our observations when we call any upward movement of the head a "trial," and there is no reason to call any movement which does not achieve a specified consequence an "error." Even the term "learning" is misleading. The statement that the bird "learns that it will get food by stretching its neck" is an inaccurate report of what has happened. To say that it has acquired the "habit" of stretching its neck is merely to resort to an explanatory fiction, since our only evidence of the habit is the acquired tendency to perform the act. The barest possible statement of the process is this: we make a given consequence contingent upon certain physical properties of behavior (the upward movement of the head), and the behavior is then observed to increase in frequency.

It is customary to refer to any movement of the organism as a "response." The word is borrowed from the field of reflex action and implies an act

4*Ibid.*, from pp. 63-66.

which, so to speak, answers a prior event—the stimulus. But we may make an event contingent upon behavior without identifying, or being able to identify, a prior stimulus. We did not alter the environment of the pigeon to *elicit* the upward movement of the head. It is probably impossible to show that any single stimulus invariably precedes this movement. Behavior of this sort may come under the control of stimuli, but the relation is not that of elicitation. The term "response" is therefore not wholly appropriate but is so well established that we shall use it in the following discussion.

A response which has already occurred cannot, of course, be predicted or controlled. We can only predict that *similar* responses will occur in the future. The unit of a predictive science is therefore not a response but a class of responses. The word "operant" will be used to describe this class. The term emphasizes the fact that the behavior *operates* upon the environment to generate consequences. The consequences define the properties with respect to which responses are called similar. The term will be used both as an adjective (operant behavior) and as a noun to designate the behavior defined by a given consequence.

A single instance in which a pigeon raises its head is a *response*. It is a bit of history which may be reported in any frame of reference we wish to use. The behavior called "raising the head," regardless of when specific instances occur, is an *operant*. It can be described, not as an accomplished act, but rather as a set of acts defined by the property of the height to which the head is raised. In this sense an operant is defined by an effect which may be specified in physical terms; the "cutoff" at a certain height is a property of behavior.

The term "learning" may profitably be saved in its traditional sense to describe the reassortment of responses in a complex situation. Terms for the process of stamping in may be borrowed from Pavlov's analysis of the conditioned reflex. Pavlov himself called all events which strengthened behavior "reinforcement" and all the resulting changes "conditioning." In the Pavlovian experiment, however, a reinforcer is paired with a *stimulus*; whereas in operant behavior, it is contingent upon a *response*. Operant reinforcement is therefore a separate process and requires a separate analysis. In both cases, the strengthening of behavior which results from reinforcement is appropriately called "conditioning." In operant conditioning we "strengthen" an operant in the sense of making a response more probable, or, in actual fact, more frequent. In Pavlovian or "respondent" conditioning, we simply increase the magnitude of the response elicited by the conditioned stimulus and shorten the time which elapses between stimulus and response. (We note, incidentally, that these two cases exhaust the possibilities: an organism is conditioned when a reinforcer (1) accompanies another stimulus or (2) follows upon the organism's own behavior. Any event which does neither has no effect in changing a probability of response.) In the pigeon experiment, then, food is the *reinforcer* and presenting food when a response is emitted is the *reinforcement*. The *operant* is defined by the property upon which reinforcement is contingent—the height to which the head must be raised. The change in frequency with which the head is lifted to this height is the process of *operant conditioning*.

While we are awake, we act upon the environment constantly, and many of the consequences of our actions are reinforcing. Through operant conditioning, the environment builds the basic repertoire with which we keep our balance, walk, play games, handle instruments and tools, talk, write, sail a boat, drive a car, or fly a plane. A change in the environment—a new car, a new friend, a new field of interest, a new job, a new location—may find us unprepared, but our behavior usually adjusts quickly as we acquire new responses and discard old.

Two Types of Conditioning and Extinction: Type S and Type R[5]

In the course of this book I shall attempt to show that a large body of material not usually considered in this light may be expressed with dynamic laws which differ from the classical examples only in the nature of the operations. The most important instances are conditioning and extinction (with their subsidiary processes of discrimination), drive, and emotion, which I propose to formulate in terms of changes in reflex strength. One type of conditioning and its corresponding extinction may be described here.

The Law of Conditioning of Type S.—*The approximately simultaneous presentation of two stimuli, one of which (the "reinforcing" stimulus) belongs to a reflex existing at the moment at some strength, may produce an increase in the strength of a third reflex composed of the response of the reinforcing reflex and the other stimulus.*

The Law of Extinction of Type S.—*If the reflex strengthened through conditioning of type S is elicited without presentation of the reinforcing stimulus, its strength decreases.*

These laws refer to the Pavlovian type of conditioned reflex. . . . I wish to point out here simply that the observed data are merely changes in the strength of a reflex. As such they have no dimensions which distinguish them from changes in strength taking place during fatigue, facilitation, inhibition, or, as I shall show later, changes in drive, emotion, and so on. The process of conditioning is distinguished by what is done to the organism to induce the change; in other words, it is defined by the operation of the simultaneous presentation of the reinforcing stimulus and another stimulus. The type is called type S to distinguish it from conditioning of type R . . . in which the reinforcing stimulus is contingent upon a response.

*   *   *   *   *

[5]*The Behavior of Organisms: An Experimental Analysis* (New York: Appleton-Century-Crofts, 1938; paper edition, 1966), from pp. 18-19, 21-22.

Three of the operations already described in relation to respondent behavior involve the elicitation of the reflex and hence are inapplicable to operants. They are the refractory phase, fatigue, and conditioning of type S. The refractory phase has a curious parallel in the rate itself, as I shall note later, and a phenomenon comparable with fatigue may also appear in an operant. The conditioning of an operant differs from that of a respondent by involving the correlation of a reinforcing stimulus with a *response*. For this reason the process may be referred to as of type R. Its two laws are as follows.

The Law of Conditioning of Type R.—*If the occurrence of an operant is followed by presentation of a reinforcing stimulus, the strength is increased.*

The Law of Extinction of Type R.—*If the occurrence of an operant already strengthened through conditioning is not followed by the reinforcing stimulus, the strength is decreased.*

The conditioning is here again a matter of a change in strength. The strength cannot begin at zero since at least one unconditioned response must occur to permit establishment of the relation with a reinforcing stimulus. Unlike conditioning of type S, the process has the effect of determining the form of the response, which is provided for in advance by the conditions of the correlation with a reinforcing stimulus or by the way in which the response must operate upon the environment to produce a reinforcement. . . .

PERSONALITY DYNAMICS: ENVIRONMENTAL VARIABLES[6]

The practice of looking inside the organism for an explanation of behavior has tended to obscure the variables which are immediately available for a scientific analysis. These variables lie outside the organism, in its immediate environment and in its environmental history. They have a physical status to which the usual techniques of science are adapted, and they make it possible to explain behavior as other subjects are explained in science. These independent variables are of many sorts and their relations to behavior are often subtle and complex, but we cannot hope to give an adequate account of behavior without analyzing them.

Consider the act of drinking a glass of water. This is not likely to be an important bit of behavior in anyone's life, but it supplies a convenient example. We may describe the topography of the behavior in such a way that a given instance may be identified quite accurately by any qualified observer. Suppose now we bring someone into a room and place a glass of water before him. Will he drink? There appear to be only two possibilities: either he will or he will not. But we speak of the *chances* that he will drink, and this notion may be refined for scientific use. What we want to evaluate is the *probability* that he will drink. This may range from virtual certainty that drinking will occur to virtual certainty that it will not. The very consid-

[6]*Science and Human Behavior, op. cit.,* from pp. 31-33, 144, 146-47.

erable problem of how to measure such a probability will be discussed later. For the moment, we are interested in how the probability may be increased or decreased.

Everyday experience suggests several possibilities, and laboratory and clinical observations have added others. It is decidedly not true that a horse may be led to water but cannot be made to drink. By arranging a history of severe deprivation we could be "absolutely sure" that drinking would occur. In the same way we may be sure that the glass of water in our experiment will be drunk. Although we are not likely to arrange them experimentally, deprivations of the necessary magnitude sometimes occur outside the laboratory. We may obtain an effect similar to that of deprivation by speeding up the excretion of water. For example, we may induce sweating by raising the temperature of the room or by forcing heavy exercise, or we may increase the excretion of urine by mixing salt or urea in food taken prior to the experiment. It is also well known that loss of blood, as on a battlefield, sharply increases the probability of drinking. On the other hand, we may set the probability at virtually zero by inducing or forcing our subject to drink a large quantity of water before the experiment.

If we are to predict whether or not our subject will drink, we must know as much as possible about these variables. If we are to induce him to drink, we must be able to manipulate them. In both cases, moreover, either for accurate prediction or control, we must investigate the effect of each variable quantitatively with the methods and techniques of a laboratory science.

Other variables may, of course, affect the result. Our subject may be "afraid" that something has been added to the water as a practical joke or for experimental purposes. He may even "suspect" that the water has been poisoned. He may have grown up in a culture in which water is drunk only when no one is watching. He may refuse to drink simply to prove that we cannot predict or control his behavior. These possibilities do not disprove the relations between drinking and the variables listed in the preceding paragraphs; they simply remind us that other variables may have to be taken into account. We must know the history of our subject with respect to the behavior of drinking water, and if we cannot eliminate social factors from the situation, then we must know the history of his personal relations to people resembling the experimenter. Adequate prediction in any science requires information about all relevant variables, and the control of a subject matter for practical purposes makes the same demands.

Drives: Deprivation and Satiation

A need or want could simply be redefined as a condition resulting from deprivation and characterized by a special probability of response. Since it is difficult to lay the ghosts which hover about these older terms, there is a certain advantage in using a term which has fewer connotations. "Drive" is sometimes used. A drive need not be thought of as mental or physiological. The term is simply a convenient way of referring to the effects of deprivation and satiation and of other operations which alter the probability of behavior in more or less the same way. It is convenient because it enables us to deal with many cases at once. There are many ways of changing the probability that an organism will eat; at the same time, a single kind of deprivation strengthens many kinds of behavior. The concept of hunger as a drive brings these various relations together in a single term.

The simplicity of the concept of drive is only apparent. This is true as well of need and want. No concept can eliminate an actual diversity of data. A drive is a verbal device with which we account for a state of strength, and it cannot answer experimental questions. We cannot control the behavior of an organism by directly changing its hunger, its thirst, or its sex drive. In order to change these states indirectly, we must deal with the relevant variables of deprivation and satiation and must face all the complexity of these operations.

*   *   *   *   *

Deprivation is put to practical use when a child is made more likely to drink milk by restriction of his water intake; when guests are induced to eat a modest meal with greater gusto by a delay in serving the meal; when the prisoner is made more likely to talk to interrogators by being put in "solitary" ("depriving him of talking" as in the case of the "need for exercise"); when a population is made more likely to cooperate with the authorities who control food supplies by reducing rations; and when a child is kept interested in his toys by being given only one at a time. Operations which have a similar effect are put to practical use when guests are induced to consume more cocktails at a party at which salty hors d'oeuvres are served, and when sexual behavior is intensified by the administration of certain hormones or aphrodisiacs. Extensive engineering control is obviously necessary to achieve some of these conditions for either theoretical or practical purposes. It is sometimes possible to use conditions which arise fortuitously. For example, waterfront brothels and other amusement enterprises take advantage of the deprivations suffered by sailors at sea. Wartime shortages generate large-scale deprivations, and these are frequently exploited for both theoretical and commercial purposes.

Satiation is put to practical use when a *table d'hôte* restaurant serves a large supply of good bread while a meal is being prepared in order to serve small portions of the rest of the meal without complaint (it is obviously a bad practice to serve bread if the customer has still to order *à la carte*); when an abundance of hors d'oeuvres is used to conceal the scantiness of the dinner which follows; when legalized prostitution is recommended on the ground that it reduces the probability of sexual behavior in members of the population who might, if unsatiated, otherwise attack innocent women; when bread lines are set up to reduce the violence which would otherwise result from meager rations; and when a clinic reduces aggressive or otherwise undesirable behavior by giving the individual attention, approval, or even affection. An effect comparable to satiation is obtained when a drug is administered to reduce the probability of sexual behavior.

All these examples could be described by reference to "drives." We could say that the eating of salty hors d'oeuvres makes a guest thirsty and that his thirst then drives him to drink. It is simpler, in both theory and practice, to restrict ourselves to the fact that consuming salty hors d'oeuvres leads to drinking.

The Role of Needs[7]

I don't see any reason to postulate a need anywhere along the line. People often complain that in our experimental work we use specific biological reinforcers—such as those related to hunger, thirst, or sex—and then they ask how we deal with nonbiological reinforcers which don't appear to reduce needs. But food is not reinforcing because it reduces a need. Eating changes a biological condition, but food is not reinforcing because it does so. As far as I'm concerned, if a baby is reinforced by the sound made by a rattle, the sound is just as useful as a reinforcer in accounting for behavior as food in the baby's mouth. That kind of distinction doesn't worry me. As to achievement, however, people generally tend to overlook the extraordinary importance of the conditions of reinforcement. The important thing is not that you are getting something; it is what you are doing at the moment you get it. I could make a pigeon a high achiever by reinforcing it on a proper schedule. I can't do it by ordering the needs. I don't know how to order needs. There is no way in which you can put a key in a slot and twist a need. What you can do is make an individual hungrier or you can use food skillfully as a reinforcer so that he will work at a very high rate when scarcely hungry at all. If you want people to be productive and active in various ways, *the important thing is to analyze the contingencies of reinforcement, not the needs to be satisfied.*

PERSONALITY DEVELOPMENT: MOTIVATION AND SHAPING[8]

Shaping Behavior

Operant conditioning shapes behavior as a sculptor shapes a lump of clay. Although at some point the sculptor seems to have produced an entirely novel object, we can always follow the process back to the original undifferentiated lump, and we can make the successive stages by which we return to this condition as small as we wish. At no point does anything emerge which is very different from what preceded it. The final product seems to have a special unity or integrity of design, but we cannot find a

---

[7] *B. F. Skinner: The Man and His Ideas, op. cit.,* from p. 10.
[8] *Science and Human Behavior, op. cit.,* from pp. 91-92, 99-103.

point at which this suddenly appears. In the same sense, an operant is not something which appears full grown in the behavior of the organism. It is the result of a continuous shaping process.

The pigeon experiment demonstrates this clearly. "Raising the head" is not a discrete unit of behavior. It does not come, so to speak, in a separate package. We reinforce only slightly exceptional values of the behavior observed while the pigeon is standing or moving about. We succeed in shifting the whole range of heights at which the head is held, but there is nothing which can be accurately described as a new "response." A response such as turning the latch in a problem box appears to be a more discrete unit, but only because the continuity with other behavior is more difficult to observe. In the pigeon, the response of pecking at a spot on the wall of the experimental box seems to differ from stretching the neck because no other behavior of the pigeon resembles it. If in reinforcing such a response we simply wait for it to occur—and we may have to wait many hours or days or weeks—the whole unit appears to emerge in its final form and to be strengthened as such. There may be no appreciable behavior which we could describe as "almost pecking the spot."

The continuous connection between such an operant and the general behavior of the bird can nevertheless easily be demonstrated. It is the basis of a practical procedure for setting up a complex response. To get the pigeon to peck the spot as quickly as possible we proceed as follows: We first give the bird food when it turns slightly in the direction of the spot from any part of the cage. This increases the frequency of such behavior. We then withhold reinforcement until a slight movement is made toward the spot. This again alters the general distribution of behavior without producing a new unit. We continue by reinforcing positions successively closer to the spot, then by reinforcing only when the head is moved slightly forward, and finally only when the beak actually makes contact with the spot. We may reach this final response in a remarkably short time. A hungry bird, well adapted to the situation and to the food tray, can usually be brought to respond in this way in two or three minutes.

Motivation Through the Contingencies of Reinforcement

Intermittent Reinforcement. A large part of behavior, however, is reinforced only intermittently. A given consequence may depend upon a series of events which are not easily predicted. We do not always win at cards or dice, because the contingencies are so remotely determined that we call them "chance." We do not always find good ice or snow when we go skating or skiing. Contingencies which require the participation of people are especially likely to be uncertain. We do not always get a good meal in a particular restaurant because cooks are not always predictable. We do not always get an answer when we telephone a friend because the friend is not always at home. We do not always get a pen by reaching into our pocket because we have not always put it there. The reinforcements characteristic of industry and education are almost always intermittent because it is not feasible to control behavior by reinforcing every response.

As might be expected, behavior which is reinforced only intermittently often shows an intermediate frequency of occurrence, but laboratory studies of various schedules have revealed some surprising complexities. Usually such behavior is remarkably stable and shows great resistance to extinction. An experiment has already been mentioned in which more than 10,000 responses appeared in the extinction curve of a pigeon which had been reinforced on a special schedule. Nothing of the sort is ever obtained after continuous reinforcement. Since this is a technique for "getting more responses out of an organism" in return for a given number of reinforcements, it is widely used. Wages are paid in special ways and betting and gambling devices are designed to "pay off" on special schedules because of the relatively large return on the reinforcement in such a case. Approval, affection, and other personal favors are frequently intermittent, not only because the person supplying the reinforcement may behave in different ways at different times, but precisely because he may have found that such a schedule yields a more stable, persistent, and profitable return.

*　　*　　*　　*　　*

Interval Reinforcement. If we reinforce behavior at regular intervals, an organism such as a rat or pigeon will adjust with a nearly constant rate of responding, determined by the frequency of reinforcement. If we reinforce it every minute, the animal responds rapidly; if every five minutes, much more slowly. A similar effect upon probability of response is characteristic of human behavior. How often we call a given number on the telephone will depend, other things being equal, upon how often we get an answer. If two agencies supply the same service, we are more likely to call the one which answers more often. We are less likely to see friends or acquaintances with whom we only occasionally have a good time, and we are less likely to write to a correspondent who seldom answers. The experimental results are precise enough to suggest that in general the organism gives back a certain number of responses for each response reinforced. We shall see, however, that the results of schedules of reinforcement are not always reducible to a simple equating of input with output.

Since behavior which appears under interval reinforcement is especially stable, it is useful in studying other variables and conditions. The size or amount of each reinforcement affects the rate—more responses appearing in return for a larger reinforcement. Different kinds of reinforcers also yield different rates, and these may be used to rank reinforces in the order of their effectiveness. The rate varies with the immediacy of the reinforcement: a slight delay between response and the receipt of the reinforcer means a lower over-all rate. Other variables which have been studied under interval reinforcement will be discussed in later chapters. They include the degree of deprivation and the presence or absence of certain emotional circumstances.

Optimal schedules of reinforcement are often of great practical importance. They are often discussed in connection with other variables which affect the rate. Reinforcing a man with fifty dollars at one time may not be so effective as reinforcing him with five dollars at ten different times during the same period. This is especially the case with primitive people where conditioned reinforcers have not been established to bridge the temporal span between a response and its ultimate consequence. There are also many subtle interactions between schedules of reinforcement and levels of motivation, immediacy of reinforcement, and so on.

If behavior continues to be reinforced at fixed intervals, another process intervenes. Since responses are never reinforced just after reinforcement, a change eventually takes place in which the rate of responding is low for a short time after each reinforcement. The rate rises again when an interval of time has elapsed which the organism presumably cannot distinguish from the interval at which it is reinforced. These changes in rate are not characteristic of the effect of wages in industry, which would otherwise appear to be an example of a fixed-interval schedule. The discrepancy is explained by the fact that other reinforcing systems are used to maintain a given level of work. Docking a man for time absent guarantees his presence each day by establishing a time-card entry as a conditioned reinforcer. The aversive reinforcement supplied by a supervisor or boss is, however, the principal supplement to a fixed-interval wage.

A low probability of response just after reinforcement is eliminated with what is called *variable-interval* reinforcement. Instead of reinforcing a response every five minutes, for example, we reinforce every five minutes *on the average*, where the intervening interval may be as short as a few seconds or as long as, say, ten minutes. Reinforcement occasionally occurs just after the organism has been reinforced, and the organism therefore continues to respond at that time. Its performance under such a schedule is remarkably stable and uniform. Pigeons reinforced with food with a variable interval averaging five minutes between reinforcements have been observed to respond for as long as fifteen hours at a rate of from two to three responses per second without pausing longer than fifteen or twenty seconds during the whole period. It is usually very difficult to extinguish a response after such a schedule. Many sorts of social or personal reinforcement are supplied on what is essentially a variable-interval basis, and extraordinarily persistent behavior is sometimes set up.

Ratio Reinforcement. An entirely different result is obtained when the schedule of reinforcement depends upon the behavior of the organism itself—when, for example, we reinforce every fiftieth response. This is reinforcement at a "fixed ratio"—the ratio of reinforced to unreinforced responses. It is a common schedule in education, where the student is reinforced for completing a project or a paper or some other specific amount of work. It is essentially the basis of professional pay and of selling on commission. In industry it is known as piecework pay. It is a system of reinforcement which naturally recommends itself to employers because the cost of the labor required to produce a given result can be calculated in advance.

Fixed-ratio reinforcement generates a very high rate of response provided the ratio is not too high. This should follow from the input-output relation alone. Any slight increase in rate increases the frequency or reinforcement with the result that the rate should rise still further. If no other factor intervened, the rate should reach the highest possible value. A limiting factor, which makes itself felt in industry, is simple fatigue. The high rate of responding and the long hours of work generated by this schedule can be dangerous to health. This is the main reason why piecework pay is usually strenuously opposed by organized labor.

Another objection to this type of schedule is based upon the possibility that as the rate rises, the reinforcing agency will move to a larger ratio. In the laboratory, after first reinforcing every tenth response and then every fiftieth, we may find it possible to reinforce only every hundredth, although we could not have used this ratio in the beginning. In industry, the employee whose productivity has increased as the result of a piecework schedule may receive so large a weekly wage that the employer feels justified in increasing the number of units of work required for a given unit of pay.

Punishment and Negative Reinforcement[9]

You can distinguish between punishment, which is making an aversive event contingent upon a response, and negative reinforcement, in which the elimination or removal of an aversive stimulus, conditioned or unconditioned, is reinforcing. Aversive control is a way of generating behavior. When you say you punish a child to make him work, you are misusing the word "punish." You are arranging conditions which he can escape from by working. When you punish a child to keep him from misbehaving, however, you are trying to suppress behavior. In my earlier experiments punishment did not suppress behavior as it had been supposed to do. Punishment may only be reducing a current tendency to respond. As soon as punishment is withdrawn, the behavior bounces back. This isn't always the case, because extremely severe punishment may knock behavior out for good, at least so far as we are able to determine. But what is surprising is that if you make common punishing events contingent on behavior, the behavior will recover after the punishment ceases, and the organism will continue to behave, even though it has been rather severely punished. I object to aversive control in general because of its by-products. All sorts of emotions are generated which have negative side effects. If you make a student study to escape punishment, then he will soon escape in other ways;

[9]B. F. Skinner: The Man and His Ideas, op. cit., from pp. 33-34.

he'll play hookey, be a truant, or become a dropout. Or he may counter-attack. Vandalism against school property is easily explained just by looking at the techniques schools use to control their students. Another common reaction of students is a kind of inactivity—an apathy or stubborn do-nothingness. These are the inevitable by-products of aversive stimuli. Positive reinforcement does not generate comparable by-products, and that's why it's better.

OPERANT REINFORCEMENT THEORY APPLIED TO PERSONALITY[10]

Consider a young man whose world has suddenly changed. He has graduated from college and is going to work, let us say, or has been inducted into the armed services. Most of the behavior he has acquired up to this point proves useless in his new environment. The behavior he actually exhibits can be described, and the description translated, as follows: he lacks assurance or feels insecure or is unsure of himself (*his behavior is weak and inappropriate*); he is dissatisfied or discouraged (*he is seldom reinforced, and as a result his behavior undergoes extinction*); he is frustrated (*extinction is accompanied by emotional responses*); he feels uneasy or anxious (*his behavior frequently has unavoidable aversive consequences which have emotional effects*); there is nothing he wants to do or enjoys doing well, he has no feeling of craftsmanship, no sense of leading a purposeful life, no sense of accomplishment (*he is rarely reinforced for doing anything*); he feels guilty or ashamed (*he has previously been punished for idleness or failure, which now evokes emotional responses*); he is disappointed in himself or disgusted with himself (*he is no longer reinforced by the admiration of others, and the extinction which follows has emotional effects*); he becomes hypochondriacal (*he concludes that he is ill*) or neurotic (*he engages in a variety of ineffective modes of escape*); and he experiences an identity crisis (*he does not recognize the person he once called "I"*).

[10]*Beyond Freedom and Dignity* (New York: Alfred A. Knopf, 1971), from pp. 146-47.

CHAPTER 21

JOHN DOLLARD
NEAL E. MILLER

STIMULUS-RESPONSE PSYCHOLOGY: DRIVE-RESPONSE-CUE-REWARD THEORY OF PERSONALITY

Dollard and Miller have presented a learning theory of personality, based on their STIMULUS-RESPONSE PSYCHOLOGY, in which the influence of both Hull and Freud is clearly detectable. Learning theory is the study of the circumstances uniting *response* and *cue*, and of the principles which maintain in those conditions under which cue and response are strengthened. Learning is effected when the factors *drive, cue, response,* and *reward* are present. A learning theory could almost be considered a *habit* theory of personality.

John Dollard, born in Menasha, Wisconsin in 1900, received his B.A. from the University of Wisconsin in 1922 and M.A. (1930) and Ph.D. (1931) from the University of Chicago. He also received training in psychoanalysis at the Berlin Institute. In 1932 he was appointed Assistant Professor of Anthropology at Yale; in 1933 he was appointed to the same position at Yale's Institute of Human Relations. In 1935 he became Research Associate at the Institute; since 1948 he has been Professor of Psychology there.

Neal E. Miller, born in Milwaukee, Wisconsin, in 1909, acquired his B.S. in 1931 from the University of Washington, his M.A. (1932) from Stanford, and his Ph.D. (1935) from Yale. In 1935-1936 he pursued postdoctoral studies at the Vienna Institute of Psychoanalysis. From 1936 to 1966, with the exception of the war years, he was with Yale and its Institute of Human Relations, since 1950 as Professor of Psychology. Since 1966, Miller has been Professor of Psychology at Rockefeller University.

Dollard and Miller, in collaboration, have published *Frustration and Aggression* (with others, 1939), *Social Learning and Imitation* (1941), with Personality and Psychotherapy (1950). Miller's papers were published in 1971 as *Selected Papers on Conflict Displacement, Learned Drives and Theory* (vol. 1) and *Selected Papers on Learning Motivation and Their Psychological Mechanisms* (vol. 2).

STIMULUS-RESPONSE THEORY OF PERSONALITY[1]

Three great traditions, heretofore followed separately, are brought together. One of these is psychoanalysis, initiated by the genius of Freud and carried on by his many able students in the art of psychotherapy. Another stems from the work of Pavlov, Thorndike, Hull, and a host of other experimentalists. They have applied the exactness of natural-science method to the study of the principles of learning. Finally, modern social science is crucial because it describes the social conditions under which human beings learn. The ultimate goal is to combine the vitality of psychoanalysis, the rigor of the natural-science laboratory, and the facts of culture. We believe that a psychology of this kind should occupy a fundamental position in the social sciences and humanities—making it unnecessary for each of them to invent its own special assumptions about human nature and personality.

*　　*　　*　　*　　*

Advantages of Scientific Theory

This book is an attempt at integration of the data on mental and emotional life via scientific principles. As is well known, a scientific theory has great advantages over an aggregation of empirical facts. A theory is more powerful the more generally applicable its principles are. As Einstein has emphasized, the goal is to account for the most facts with the fewest principles.

Integrating facts around principles makes them easier to remember. In this connection we are reminded of the superiority of logical over rote memory. Facts which are easier to remember are likewise easier to teach.

Similarly, scientific principles are easier to adapt to new situations (the superior *transfer* of logical over rote learning). A purely empirical generalization ("This happened frequently in the past; therefore it is likely to

[1]*Personality and Psychotherapy* (New York: McGraw-Hill, 1950), from pp. 3-11.

happen again.") can only be applied when a similar situation repeats itself; but one can use principles to make predictions about what will occur in new situations. If one understands the principles, one knows better whether a new application will be relevant or not. Understanding the principles should make it easier for the student to adapt his techniques to the infinitely variable and complex problems of therapy.

In the same connection, correct principles can be used as a basis for creating innovations. Every adult can call the roll of deadly diseases which have been made harmless during his lifetime. These advances in the therapy of physical disease have been made possible as a result of fundamental theoretical advances in bacteriology, physiology, chemistry, and relevant natural sciences. Innovations have been made that were not hit upon previously by hundreds of generations of purely empirical trial and error.

There is a further advantage to scientific principles—the fact that they allow one to make predictions about new situations gives a powerful method of testing them in a greater variety of situations. Thus, after principles of psychotherapy have been systematized in general terms, one can predict what should happen under rigidly controlled experimental conditions and use this prediction as a powerful method of testing and refining the principles. We hope that deductions of effect in therapeutic situations will suggest innovations in therapeutic technique. New ways of meeting the inevitable dilemmas of therapy are much needed. Likewise, deductions of effect in experimental situations which are easier to control and measure may provide a method of testing and refining the principles of psychotherapy.

Similarly, the clinic is constantly suggesting new problems for laboratory study, such as the list of learned social drives discussed later in this book. If a systematic theory of psychotherapy can be created, the clinic and laboratory should interact to a much greater degree and in a much more potent way than heretofore.

If neurotic behavior is learned, it should be unlearned by some combination of the same principles by which it was taught. We believe this to be the case. Psychotherapy establishes a set of conditions by which neurotic habits may be unlearned and nonneurotic habits learned. Therefore, we view the therapist as a kind of teacher and the patient as a learner. In the same way and by the same principles that bad tennis habits can be corrected by a good coach, so bad mental and emotional habits can be corrected by a psychotherapist. There is this difference, however. Whereas only a few people want to play tennis, all the world wants a clear, free, efficient mind.

We believe that giving the solid, systematic basis of learning theory to the data of psychotherapy is a matter of importance. Application of these laws and the investigation of the new conditions of learning which psychotherapy involves should provide us with a rational foundation for practice in psychotherapy analogous to that provided by the science of bacteriology to treatment of contagious diseases. As a learning theorist sees it, the existence of neuroses is an automatic criticism of our culture of child rearing. Misery-producing, neurotic habits which the therapist must painfully unteach have been as painfully taught in the confused situation of childhood. A system of child training built on the laws of learning might have the same powerful effect on the neurotic misery of our time as Pasteur's work had on infectious diseases.

The Problem of Teaching Scientific Theory

As larger areas of psychology move nearer to the status of a natural science, a new dilemma is presented to the teacher. He may have to make sure, as in the natural sciences, that the first units of the theory are heavily overlearned. He may have to resist the temptation to give the students large amounts of material, hoping that they will get something out of the mere quantity. Good theory is the best form of simplification, and good teaching consists of hammering home the basic elements of such theory.

Basic Assumption That Neurosis and Psychotherapy Obey Laws of Learning

If a neurosis is functional (*i.e.*, a product of experience rather than of organic damage or instinct), it must be learned. If it is learned, it must be learned according to already known, experimentally verified laws of learning or according to new, and as yet undiscovered, laws of learning. In the former case, such laws, meticulously studied by investigators such as Pavlov, Thorndike, Hull, and their students, should make a material contribution to the understanding of the phenomenon. If new laws are involved, the attempt to study neuroses from the learning standpoint should help to reveal the gaps in our present knowledge and to suggest new principles which could be fruitfully submitted to investigation in the laboratory. It seems likely that not only laws we know but also those we do not know are involved. However, the laws that we *do* know seem sufficient to carry us a long way toward a systematic analysis of psychotherapy.

Main Consequences of This Approach

We have attempted to give a systematic analysis of neurosis and psychotherapy in terms of the psychological principles and social conditions of learning. In order to give the reader a better perspective on this attempt, we shall swiftly list some of its main consequences.

1. The principle of reinforcement has been substituted for Freud's pleasure principle. The concept of "pleasure" has proved a difficult and slippery notion in the history of psychology. The same is true of the idea that the behavior that occurs is "adaptive," because it is awkward to have to explain maladaptive behavior on the basis of a principle of adaptiveness. The principle of reinforcement is more exact and rigorous than either the

pleasure principle or the adaptiveness principle. Since the effect of immediate reinforcement is greater than that of reinforcement after a delay, the investigator is forced to examine the exact temporal relationships between responses, stimuli, and reinforcement. He is thus provided with a better basis for predicting whether or not some account must be given of the means by which the temporal gap is bridged.

2. The relatively neglected and catchall concept of Ego strength has been elaborated in two directions: first is the beginning of a careful account of higher mental processes; second is the description of the culturally valuable, learned drives and skills. The importance of the foregoing factors in human behavior can hardly be overemphasized. The functioning of higher mental processes and learned drives is not limited to neuroses or psychotherapy. It is an essential part of the science of human personality.

3. A naturalistic account is given of the immensely important mechanism of repression. Repression is explained as the inhibition of the cue-producing responses which mediate thinking and reasoning. Just what is lost by repression and gained by therapy is much clearer in the light of this account.

4. Transference is seen as a special case of a wider concept, generalization. This explanation draws attention to the fact that many humdrum habits which facilitate therapy are transferred along with those that obstruct it. The analysis shows also why such intense emotional responses should be directed toward the therapist in the transference situation.

5. The dynamics of conflict behavior are systematically deduced from more basic principles. Thus, a fundamental fact of neurosis—that of conflict —is tied in with general learning theory. A clear understanding of the nature of conflict serves to provide a more rational framework for therapeutic practice.

6. We have been obliged to put great stress on the fact that the patient gets well in real life. Only part of the work essential to therapy is done in the therapeutic situation. Reinforcement theory supplies logical reasons why this should be expected.

7. The somewhat vague concept of "reality" is elaborated in terms of the physical and social conditions of learning, especially the conditions provided by the social structure of a society. In order to predict behavior we must know these conditions as well as the psychological principles involved. Psychology supplies the principles while sociology and social anthropology supply the systematic treatment of the crucial social conditions.

8. The concepts of repression and suppression are supplemented by the parallel ones of inhibition and restraint. The idea that it is important to suppress and restrain tendencies to unconventional thoughts and acts is not a novelty with us, but our type of analysis has forced us to reaffirm and expand it. In a study of this kind, it is necessary to discuss matters that are not ordinarily the subject of polite conversation. But those who have used a misinterpretation of psychoanalysis to justify their own undisciplined behavior will find scant comfort in this [theory].

FOUR FUNDAMENTALS OF LEARNING[2]

Human behavior is learned; precisely that behavior which is widely felt to characterize man as a rational being, or as a member of a particular nation or social class, is learned rather than innate. We also learn fears, guilt, and other socially acquired motivations, as well as symptoms and rationalizations—factors which are characteristic of normal personality but show up more clearly in extreme form as neurosis. Successful psychotherapy provides new conditions under which neurosis is unlearned and other more adaptive habits are learned.

Certain simple basic principles of learning are needed for a clear understanding of the kinds of behavior involved in normal personality, neurosis, and psychotherapy. . . . The field of human learning covers phenomena which range all the way from the simple, almost reflex, learning of a child to avoid a hot radiator, to the complex processes of insight by which a scientist constructs a theory. Throughout the whole range, however, the same fundamental factors seem to be exceedingly important. These factors are: *drive, response, cue,* and *reinforcement.* They are frequently referred to with other roughly equivalent words—drive as motivation, cue as stimulus, response as act or thought, and reinforcement as reward.

* * * * *

Drive

Strong stimuli which impel action are drives. Any stimulus can become a drive if it is made strong enough. The stronger the stimulus, the more drive function it possesses. The faint murmur of distant music has but little primary drive function; the infernal blare of the neighbor's radio has considerably more.

While any stimulus may become strong enough to act as a drive, certain special classes of stimuli seem to be the primary basis for the greater proportion of motivation. These might be called the *primary* or *innate* drives. One of these is pain. Pain can reach stabbing heights of greater strength than probably any other single drive. The parching sensation of thirst, the pangs of extreme hunger, and the sore weight of fatigue are other examples of powerful innate drives. The bitter sting of cold and the insistent goading of sex are further examples.

The strength of the primary drives varies with the conditions of deprivation. For example, if you hold your breath for more than 60 seconds, you experience a tremendous drive to breathe. But this drive is important to only a few people like asthmatics because it is rare for anyone to have his breathing interrupted.

To people living in a society protected by a technology as efficient as ours, it is difficult to realize the full height to which these primary drives can

[2]*Ibid.,* from pp. 25-41.

mount. One of the basic aims of any social organization is to protect its members from the unpleasant force of severe motivation by providing satiation for drives before they mount to agonizing heights. Thus it is only when the social organization breaks down under extreme conditions of war, famine, and revolution that the full strength of the primary drives is realized by the social scientist in his usually secure social circumstances.

The importance of the innate drives is further obscured by social inhibitions. In those cases in which our society allows a primary drive, for example, the sex drive before marriage, to rise to considerable heights, a certain amount of negative sanction or social opprobrium generally attaches to frank statements about the drive and to vivid descriptions of its intensity. In some cases, the effects of this taboo upon speech spread even to thoughts, so that consciousness of the drive tends to be weakened and, in extreme cases, obliterated.

The conditions of society tend, besides obscuring the role of certain primary or innate drives, to emphasize certain *secondary* or *learned* drives. These learned drives are acquired on the basis of the primary drives, represent elaborations of them, and serve as a facade behind which the functions of the underlying innate drives are hidden. These learned drives are exceedingly important in human behavior.

*   *   *   *   *

Any teacher who has tried to teach unmotivated students is aware of the relationship between drive and learning. Completely self-satisfied people are poor learners.

*   *   *   *   *

Cue

The drive impels a person to respond. Cues determine when he will respond, where he will respond, and which response he will make. Simple examples of stimuli which function primarily as cues are the five o'clock whistle determining when the tired worker will stop, the restaurant sign determining where the hungry man will go, and the traffic light determining whether the driver will step on the brake or on the accelerator.

*   *   *   *   *

Differences and Patterns as Cues. Usually a change in an external source of stimulation is a more distinctive cue than the absolute value of that source. Thus if one is reading in a room illuminated by a floor lamp with a six-way switch, it is much easier to report when someone turns the lamp to a higher level of illumination than to say offhand at which of the six levels the light has been constantly burning. Relatively few people are able to learn to name the exact note that they hear played on a piano, but almost anyone can learn to report whether two notes hit in rapid succession are the same or different, and to report the direction of the difference, whether the second note is a little higher or lower than the first. Changes, differences, the direction of differences, and the size of differences all can serve as cues.

∗   ∗   ∗   ∗   ∗

Response

Drive impels the individual to respond to certain cues. Before any given response to a specific cue can be rewarded and learned, this response must occur. A good part of the trick of animal training, clinical therapy, and schoolteaching is to arrange the situation so that the learner will somehow make the first correct response. A bashful boy at his first dance cannot begin to learn either that girls will not bite him or how to make the correct dance step until he begins responding by trying to dance.

The role of response in human learning is sometimes rather difficult to observe. Because of the fact that the individual already has a good deal of social learning behind him, verbal and other nonovert anticipatory responses may play an important part in controlling his behavior. But cases of verbal behavior are no exception to the rule. A person cannot learn a new way of speaking or thinking until he has first tried a new statement or thought. Much of the difficulty in teaching arises in finding a situation which will produce thoughts that can be rewarded.

Hierarchies of Responses.   The ease with which a response can be learned in a certain situation depends upon the probability that the cues present can be made to elicit that response. It is a case of "to everyone that hath shall be given." If the response occurs relatively frequently, it is easy to reward that response and still further increase its frequency of occurrence. If the response occurs only rarely, it is difficult to find an occasion when it occurs and can be rewarded. Thus, the initial tendency for a stimulus situation to evoke a response is an important factor in learning.

In order to describe this factor, one may arrange the responses in the order of their probability of occurrence and call this the *initial hierarchy* of responses. The most likely response to occur is called the dominant response in the initial hierarchy; the response least likely to occur is called the weakest response. The same situation may be described in another way. It may be said that there is a strong connection between the stimulus and the dominant response and a weak connection between the stimulus and the weakest response. The word "connection" is used to refer to a causal sequence, the details of which are practically unknown, rather than to specific neural strands.

Learning changes the order of the responses in the hierarchy. The rewarded response, though it may have been initially weak, now occupies the dominant position. The new hierarchy produced by learning may be called the *resultant hierarchy*.

∗   ∗   ∗   ∗   ∗

Usually the order of responses in an initial hierarchy is the result of previous learning in similar situations. In those cases in which the order of the response is primarily determined not by learning, but by hereditary factors, the initial hierarchy may be called an *innate hierarchy*. In the human infant, crying occupies a higher position in the innate hierarchy than does saying the word "No." Therefore it is much easier for an infant to learn to respond to the sight of a spoonful of medicine by crying than by saying "No."

Reinforcement

Repetition does not always strengthen the tendency for a response to occur. When the little girl picked up the wrong book on the top shelf and did not find candy, her tendency to repeat this response was weakened. Such weakening of a response is called experimental extinction.

* * * * *

When the little girl picked up the correct book and found the candy, her tendency to repeat this response was strengthened. Any specified event, such as finding candy when you want it, that strengthens the tendency for a response to be repeated is called reinforcement.

* * * * *

Reduction in Painfully Strong Stimulation. When the glare of the sun is bright enough to have a high drive value, any reduction in the strength of this drive stimulus will have the effect of reinforcing any immediately preceding response. Thus a person will tend to learn any response (such as squinting, pulling down a sunshade, or putting on dark glasses) that acts to reduce the painful glare. Similarly when stimulation from a painful headache is intense, any act that produces a prompt reduction in this stimulation —turning off the radio, lying down, rubbing the back of the neck, or taking aspirin—will be reinforced and learned. In animal experiments, escape from the stimulation of an electric shock is frequently used as a strong reinforcement. . . . Observation of the foregoing type may be generalized into the principle that the prompt reduction in the strength of a strong drive stimulus acts as a reinforcement.

* * * * *

Drive and Reinforcement. Where the drive is a strong stimulus from an external source that is easy to measure independently (like an intense light or an electric current), the following relationships between drive and reinforcement are clear: (1) a prompt reduction in the strength of the drive acts as a reinforcement; (2) reinforcement is impossible in the absence of drive because the strength of stimulation cannot be reduced when it is already at zero; and (3) the drive must inevitably be lower after the reinforcement so that unless something is done to increase it, it will eventually be reduced to zero, at which point further reinforcement is impossible. This fact makes the process self-limiting and so provides a mechanism for causing the individual to stop one type of behavior and turn to another.

*　　*　　*　　*　　*

SIGNIFICANT DETAILS
OF THE LEARNING PROCESS[3]

A Learning Dilemma

As long as an individual is being rewarded for what he is doing, he will learn these particular responses more thoroughly, but he may not learn anything new by trial and error. This is partly because the further strengthening of the dominant responses makes the occurrence of any new responses less likely, and partly because its rewards, if ample, will keep the drive at a low level. Thus, in order to get the individual to try a new response which it is desired that he learn, it is often necessary to place him in a situation where his old responses will not be rewarded. Such a situation may be called a *learning dilemma*. The importance of a problem, or dilemma, in producing learning and thinking has been emphasized by John Dewey.

*　　*　　*　　*　　*

Extinction

Reinforcement is essential to the learning of a habit; it is also essential to the maintenance of a habit. When a learned response is repeated without reinforcement, the strength of the tendency to perform that response undergoes a progressive decrease. This decrement is called *experimental extinction*, or, more simply, *extinction*. . . . A fisherman who has been rewarded by catching many fish in a certain creek may come back to that creek repeatedly, but if these visits are never again rewarded by securing fish (as a subgoal with learned reward value), his visits will gradually become less frequent and less enthusiastic.

*　　*　　*　　*　　*

Rate of Extinction. The process of extinction is usually not immediate but extends over a number of trials. The number of trials required for the complete extinction of a response varies with certain conditions.

Stronger habits are more resistant to extinction than weaker habits. Other things equal, any factor which will produce a stronger habit will increase its resistance to extinction.

*　　*　　*　　*　　*

The resistance to extinction is also influenced by the conditions of extinction. Fewer trials are required to cause the subject to abandon a given

[3]*Ibid.*, from pp. 45-60.

response when the drive during extinction is weaker, when there is more effort involved in the responses being extinguished, when the interval between extinction trials is shorter, and when the alternative responses competing with the extinguished response are stronger.

Finally, the rapidity with which a response is abandoned can be influenced by habits established during previous experiences with nonreward in similar situations. . . . Under different circumstances, a fisherman who happens to cast many times in the same pool and then is rewarded by catching a fish on a cast, which follows the cue of a previously unsuccessful cast, can learn to try many casts in the same pool.

Learned drives and rewards seem to be as subject to extinction as in any other form of habit. . . . In conclusion, mere repetition does not strengthen a habit. Instead, nonrewarded repetitions progressively weaken the strength of the tendency to perform a habit. Usually the tendency to perform a habit does not disappear immediately. The number of trials required for extinction depends on the strength of the habit, on the particular conditions of extinction, and on past experience with nonrewarded trials.

Spontaneous Recovery

The effects of extinction tend to disappear with the passage of time. After a series of unsuccessful expeditions, a fisherman may have abandoned the idea of making any further trips to a particular stream. As time goes on, his tendency to try that stream again gradually recovers from the effects of extinction, so that next month or next year he may take another chance. This tendency for an extinguished habit to reappear after an interval of time during which no nonrewarded trials occur is called *spontaneous recovery*.

The fact of recovery demonstrates that extinction does not destroy the old habit but merely inhibits it. With the passage of time, the strength of the inhibiting factors produced during extinction is weakened more rapidly than the strength of the original tendency to perform the habit. In this manner, a net gain is produced in the strength of the tendency to perform the habit.

* * * * *

The function of extinction is to force the subject to perform new responses. If any of these responses are rewarded, they will be strengthened to the point where their competition may permanently eliminate the old habit. If none of these new responses is rewarded, however, their extinction plus the recovery of the old response will induce the subject to perform the old response again. Recovery is adaptive in those situations in which the absence of reward is only temporary.

Gradient of Generalization

The effects of learning in one situation transfer to other situations; the less similar the situation, the less transfer occurs. Stated more exactly, reinforcement for making a specific response to a given pattern of cues strengthens not only the tendency for that pattern of cues to elicit that response but also the tendency for other similar patterns of cues to elicit the same response. The innate tendency for transfer to occur is called innate stimulus generalization. The less similar the cue or pattern of cues, the less the generalization. This variation in the transfer is referred to as a *gradient of generalization.*

* * * * *

Examples of generalization are common in everyday experience. A child bitten by one dog is afraid of other animals and more afraid of other dogs than of cats and horses.

* * * * *

The gradient of generalization refers to the qualitative differences or cue aspect of stimuli. The *distinctiveness* of a cue is measured by its dissimilarity from other cues in the same situation, so that little generalization occurs from one cue to other cues in the situation. Thus the distinctiveness of a cue varies with the other cues that are present. A red book in a row of black books is a more distinctive cue than is the same volume in a row of other red books, because less generalization occurs from red to black than from one shade of red to another.

* * * * *

Discrimination

If a generalized response is not rewarded, the tendency to perform that response is weakened. By the reward of the response to one pattern of cues and the nonreward or punishment of the response to a somewhat different pattern of cues, a discrimination tends to correct maladaptive generalizations. It increases the specificity of the cue-response connection.

By being rewarded for stopping at tourist cabins in the West and nonrewarded for stopping at tourist cabins in the East, a person may gradually learn to discriminate between the two situations on the basis of the geographical cue. But the process of learning to discriminate is complicated by the fact that the effects of extinction also generalize. Thus, after being nonrewarded for stopping at a series of tourist cabins in the East, our heroes of the highway may be reluctant to stop at tourist cabins in the West.

The less different the cues in the two situations, the more generalization will be expected to occur, and hence the more difficult it will be to learn discrimination. If the cues are too similar, so much of the effects of reward may generalize from the rewarded cue to the nonrewarded one, and so much of the effects of extinction may generalize from the nonrewarded cue to the rewarded one, that it will be impossible to learn a discrimination.

Gradient in the Effects of Reinforcement

Delayed reinforcements are less effective than immediate ones. In other words, if a number of different responses are made to a cue and the last of these responses is followed by reward, the connection to the last response will be strengthened the most and the connection to each of the preceding responses will be strengthened by a progressively smaller amount. Similarly, in a series of responses to a series of cues—as when a hungry boy takes off his hat in the hall, dashes through the dining room into the kitchen, opens the icebox, and takes a bite to eat—the connections more remote from the reward are strengthened less than those closer to the reward. In this series, the connection between the sight of the hall closet and the response of hanging up the hat will be strengthened less than the connection between the sight of the icebox door and the response of opening it.

* * * * *

The gradient of reinforcement accounts for an increase in tendency to respond, the nearer the goal is approached. Because cue-response connections near the reward are strengthened more than connections remote from the reward, a hungry man on his way to dinner has a tendency to quicken his pace in rounding the last corner on the way home.

* * * * *

Anticipatory Response

From the principle of the gradient of reinforcement and from that of generalization, an additional principle can be deducted: that responses near the point of reinforcement tend, wherever physically possible, to occur before their original time in the response series, that is, to become anticipatory.

* * * * *

This tendency for responses to occur before their original point in the reinforced series is an exceedingly important aspect of behavior. Under many circumstances, it is responsible for the crowding out of useless acts in the response sequence; under other circumstances, it produces anticipatory errors.

* * * * *

A person at a restaurant orders a delicious steak, sees it, and then eats it. The taste and eating of the steak elicits and reinforces salivation. On subsequent occasions, the sight of the steak or even its ordering may elicit salivation before the food has actually entered the mouth.

A person sees a green persimmon, picks it up, and bites into it. The astringent taste evokes the response of puckering the lips and spitting out the fruit. This response is reinforced by a decrease in the extreme bitterness of the taste. Upon subsequent occasions, puckering of the lips and incipient spitting responses are likely to have moved forward in the sequence so that they now occur to the cue of seeing a green persimmon instead of to the cue of tasting it.

Anticipatory Tendency Is Involuntary. In the foregoing examples, the anticipatory aspect of the learned responses was adaptive. The tendency for responses to move forward in a sequence, however, does not depend upon the subject's insight into the adaptive value of the mechanism. That the principle of anticipation functions in a more primitive way than this is indicated most clearly by examples in which it functions in a maladaptive manner.

*　　*　　*　　*　　*

Shortening Behavior Sequence. A small boy comes home at night hungry from play. He cleans his shoes on the doormat, comes in, passes the door of the dining room, where he can see food on the table, hangs his hat carefully on the hook, goes upstairs, straightens his tie, brushes his hair, washes his face and hands, comes downstairs to the dining room, sits down, waits for grace to be said, and then asks, "May I have some meat and potatoes, please?" Eating the food is the reinforcing goal response to this long series of activities. On subsequent occasions, there will be a strong tendency for responses in this sequence to become anticipatory. He will tend to open the door without stopping to clean off his shoes, and to turn directly into the dining room without stopping to hang up his hat or to go through the remainder of the sequence. These acts will be likely to crowd out other preceding responses in the series because the connections to these acts have been strengthened relatively more by being nearer to the point of reward. If he secures food, the anticipatory responses will be still more strongly rewarded and will be more likely to occur on subsequent occasions. The response sequence will be short-circuited. In this way, the principle of anticipation often leads to the adaptive elimination of useless acts from a response sequence.

Discrimination of Anticipatory Responses. If the response of turning directly into the dining room without stopping to remove the hat and clean up is not followed by food, however, it will tend to be extinguished as a response to cues at this inappropriate point in the series. A discrimination may eventually be established. Similarly, the acts of washing, brushing the hair, waiting quietly during grace, and saying "please" will tend to be abbreviated and crowded out by competition with anticipatory responses unless the latter are either punished or continuously extinguished. Those short cuts which are physically and socially possible will be strengthened by more immediate rewards; others will be punished or extinguished. Thus behavior tends gradually to approximate the shortest, most efficient possible sequence.

*　　*　　*　　*　　*

Anticipatory Responses in Communication. Anticipatory responses may play an important role in communication between people by providing significant stimuli to other persons. An infant not yet old enough to talk was accustomed to being lifted up into its mother's arms. Because often followed by innate rewards, being in the mother's arms had achieved learned reward value. As a part of the response of being picked up, the infant learned to stand up on his toes, spread his arms, arch his back in a characteristic way. Subsequently, when the child was motivated to be picked up, this response moved forward in a series; the infant performed in an anticipatory manner the part of the subgoal response that was physically possible under the circumstances. He stood on his toes, spread his arms, and threw his head and shoulders back. He could not, however, bend his knees, which would have been a part of the total response, because this would have conflicted with the activity of standing. Since his parents rewarded this gesture by picking him up, he used it more and more often.

* * * * *

Higher Mental Processes[4]

One of the important normal functions of the higher mental processes is the solution of emotional problems. Analyzing this function will help the nonspecialist to dissipate the aura of spookiness surrounding psychotherapy and to understand it in terms of his own experience. It will show what resources have been tried and have failed before the person is driven to get help from the therapist, what is lost when neurosis interferes, and what is regained through proper therapy. It will clarify some of the extremely important functions that psychoanalysts subsume under the category of Ego strength.

* * * * *

Two "Levels" of Learned Behavior

A great deal of human behavior is made up of simple automatic habits. We respond directly to the cues in our environment and to our internal drives without taking time to think first. For example, a driver sees a child run in front of a car and quickly and automatically presses the brake. Even a passenger is likely to perform the useless response of pressing the floorboards. This shows that the response is direct and automatic rather than the product of thought.

In a second type of behavior people do not respond immediately and automatically to cues and drives. The final overt response follows a series of internal responses, commonly called a train of thought. For example, a

[4]*Ibid.*, from pp. 97-105.

driver may see a steep hill, remember that his brakes are poor, and then decide to shift gears.

Many acts are a complex blend of both types of behavior. Man has a much greater capacity for the second, or thoughtful, type called the "higher mental processes."

* * * * *

Cue-Producing Responses

In order to talk about the higher mental processes we need to make the distinction between instrumental and cue-producing responses. An instrumental act is one whose main function is to produce an immediate change in the relationship to the external environment. Opening a door, lifting a box, jumping back on the curb are examples of instrumental acts. A cue-producing response is one whose main function is to produce a cue that is part of the stimulus pattern leading to another response. Counting is a cue-producing response. The chief function of counting the money one receives is to produce the cue that will lead to the proper instrumental response of putting it in one's pocket, giving some back, or asking for more.

* * * * *

Role of Cue-producing Responses in Higher Mental Processes

Having made the distinction between instrumental and cue-producing responses, we can improve our description of the distinction between the "lower" and "higher" types of adjustment. In the former, the instrumental response is made directly to the pattern of external cues and internal drives; in the latter, one or more cue-producing responses intervenes.

Our basic assumption is that language and other cue-producing responses play a central role in the higher mental processes. This should be contrasted with the approach of some philosophers who seem to believe that language is a mere means of communicating thoughts which somehow "exist" independently of speech rather than an essential part of most thinking and reasoning. According to our theory, teaching a student the specialized "language" of tensor analysis may enable him to solve problems that for centuries baffled the best minds of the ancients.

It should be noted, however, that by emphasizing the hypothesis that verbal and other cue-producing responses play an essential role in the higher mental processes, *we are not denying the fact that the organism must possess certain capacities, the exact nature of which is still unknown, before such responses can operate in this way.* A parrot can learn to imitate words but not to become a great thinker.

* * * * *

Influence of Labeling on Transfer and Discrimination

Attaching the same cue-producing response to two distinctive stimulus objects gives them a certain *learned equivalence* increasing the extent to which instrumental and emotional responses will generalize from one to the other.

*   *   *   *   *

By facilitating a discrimination, cue-producing responses can have an important effect on emotional responses. A girl whose older brother had died of a ruptured appendix suffered acute fear when she learned that her other brother had a ruptured appendix. In this case the drive of strong fear was her emotional problem; it motivated trial-and-error behavior. The girl tried unsuccessfully to concentrate on cleaning the house and then on reading. She also tried thinking. Eventually she thought: "My first brother died before they had sulfa drugs and penicillin; now that they have these new drugs it is different." This labeling of before and after the availability of the new drugs made the two situations more distinctive and cut down on the generalization of fear from the case of the one brother to the other. At the same time the thoughts about the drugs mediated the generalization of fear-reducing responses from other situations in which drugs and medical science had been effective. Both of these effects reduced the fear. The reduction in fear reinforced the thoughts about the drugs so that they recurred whenever the fear was revived. In this example, the labeling that facilitated the discrimination between the cases of the two brothers was the solution to an emotional problem.

*   *   *   *   *

Language Contains Culturally Important Generalizations and Discriminations

The verbal responses of labeling are especially important because language contains those discriminations and equivalences that have been found useful by generations of trial and error in a given society. Common examples are "boy" vs. "girl," "big boy" vs. "little boy," "friend" vs. "enemy," "married" vs. "single," and "my wife" vs. "other woman."

*   *   *   *   *

Scientific terminology is often chosen to bring out similarities between superficially dissimilar phenomena and facilitate discrimination among the superficially similar. This is one of the reasons why logical learning transfers to new situations so much more adaptively than rote learning. Logical learning is in terms of words and sentences and scientific principles, the general applicability of which has already been discovered and conserved as a part of the culture.

Three Levels of Generalization and Discrimination

By way of summary and refinement, three "levels" of generalization and discrimination may be distinguished:

1. Those Based Solely on Innate Similarities and Differences. After the subject learns a response to one cue, this response will tend to generalize to other similar cues, with more generalization occurring to cues that are more similar. This is called a *gradient of innate stimulus generalization.* For example, a child who is burned by one object will tend to fear other similar objects, showing more fear of objects that are more similar.

If the response to the original cue is repeatedly reinforced and that to the dissimilar cue is repeatedly nonreinforced, the response to the former will tend to be strengthened while that to the latter will be weakened until a *discrimination* is established. With further experience of being burned by one object but not by others, the child's fear will tend to become restricted to the hot object. Because of generalization, the difficulty in establishing a discrimination will be a function of the similarity of the cues, and if the cues are too similar, it will be impossible to establish a discrimination.

2. Those in Which Innate Similarities or Differences Are Enhanced by Appropriate Labels or Other Cue-Producing Responses. Attaching the same label to different cues increases the amount of generalization. Attaching different labels to similar cues decreases the amount of generalization and thus makes subsequent discriminations easier to learn. For example, if a child has already learned to apply the words "hot" and "cold" to the right objects but has had no experience with being burned, he will be more likely to generalize the fear caused by his first serious burn to other objects labeled "hot," and it will be somewhat easier for him to learn to discriminate these from one labeled "cold."

3. Those in Which Labels or Other Cue-Producing Responses Mediate the Transfer of Already Learned Responses. If the correct instrumental or emotional responses have already been learned to the appropriate labels, these responses can be immediately transferred to a new cue by learning to label it correctly. For example, if the child has already learned to respond appropriately to objects labeled "hot" and "cold" it is possible to transfer this discrimination to the new objects by teaching him to label one "hot" and the other "cold."

It can be seen that the first "level" differs from the other two in that no labeling or other cue-producing response is involved. In the second, the label is already learned but the appropriate response to the label still has to be learned. In the third, the appropriate response to the label has already been learned and is thus available for immediate transfer as soon as new objects are given the correct labels.

Actually the three "levels" blend into one another, as when a child tends to fear a new object because it has been labeled "hot" but is overcome by curiosity, touches it, and is burned, so that fear is reinforced as a response to the label and also as a direct response to the new object. Furthermore, if the label elicits strong enough response, it may serve as a learned reinforcement. Then the responses that it elicits may become conditioned to the new stimulus object, so that by repeated labeling (without any primary reinforcement such as a burn) the new object becomes able to elicit the responses directly without the need for the continued intervention of the label.

SOCIAL CONDITIONS FOR THE LEARNING OF UNCONSCIOUS CONFLICTS[5]

Conflict itself is no novelty. Emotional conflicts are the constant accompaniment of life at every age and social level. Conflicts differ also in strength, some producing strong and some weak stimuli. Where conflicts are strong and unconscious, the individuals afflicted keep on making the same old mistakes and getting punished in the same old way. To the degree that the conflict can be made conscious, the ingenuity and inventiveness of higher mental life can aid in finding new ways out of the conflict situation. This applies to all emotional dilemmas, to those which survive from early childhood and to those which are created in the course of later life.

High drives produced during the nursing period can have disturbing side-effects. The child first faces severe cultural pressure in the cleanliness-training situation. At this time intense anger-anxiety conflicts can arise. Similarly, in the discipline of the masturbation habit and of heterosexual approach tendencies, the sex-anxiety conflict is regularly created in all of us. In some it has traumatic intensity. When the elements of this conflict are unconscious, they can have an abiding effect on life adjustment in the marital sphere. The culture takes a harsh attitude toward the angry and hostile behavior of children and regularly attaches anxiety to it, usually by direct punishment. Anger can be aroused in any of the situations of childhood where frustrating conditions are created. Conflicts centering around social class and mobility are known, especially in families where the parents have different social aspirations for the child.

Not all conflict arises through the pitting of primary drives one against the other, as in the case of hunger vs. pain. It is possible to have severe conflict based on one primary and one strong learned drive. This is exemplified by the sex-anxiety conflict. It is further possible to have severe conflict when two strong learned drives are involved—as in the case of anger-anxiety. In later life many of the strong learned drives, some quite remote from their primitive sources of reinforcement, can produce painful conflicts. "Ambition" can be pitted against "loyalty." The wish to be truthful can be arrayed against "tact." Wishes for social advancement may be deterred by the fear of appearing vulgar and "pushy." Many of these complex learned drives have never been effectively described in terms of the reinforcing circum-

[5]*Ibid.*, from pp. 154-56.

stances. We do know, however, that when they compete they can plunge the individual into a painful state.

We must admit that we do not know the exact conditions under which the common conflict-producing circumstances of life generate severe conflicts in some and not-so-severe conflicts in others. We know that the conditions and factors described here *do* occur in those who later turn out to show neurotic behavior. It may be that the circumstances of life are not really "the same for normals and neurotics," that this sameness is an illusion based on poor discrimination of the actual circumstances. Therefore it may actually be that some individuals have much stronger conflicts than others. It may be that some are less well able to use higher mental processes than others and are therefore less well able to resolve traumatic tension. It may be that some are more "predisposed" than others in that they have stronger primary drives, or stronger tendencies to inhibition, or in other unknown respects. It is quite likely that the provocative circumstances of later life which precipitate neuroses are more severe in some cases than others; or that some are exposed to just those circumstances which for them excite neurotic behavior but that others are luckier and do not come into contact with just those adverse conditions which would set them off.

BASIC FACTORS INVOLVED IN NEUROSIS[6]

Let us begin with fear, guilt, and the other drives that motivate conflict and repression. Since fear seems to be the strongest and most basic of these, we shall simplify the discussion by referring only to it.

In the neurotic, strong fear motivates a conflict that prevents the occurrence of the goal responses that normally would reduce another drive, such as sex or aggression. This is called overt inhibition. It is produced in the following way. The cues produced by the goal responses (or even first tentative approaches to the goal) elicit strong fear. This motivates conflicting responses such as stopping and avoiding. The reduction in fear, when the neurotic stops and retreats, reinforces these conflicting responses.

Because the conflicting responses prevent the drive-reducing goal responses from occurring, the drives (such as sex and aggression) build up and remain high. This state of chronic high drive is described as misery. At the same time, the high drives tend to evoke the approaches (or other incipient acts) that elicit the fear. Thus the neurotic is likely to be stimulated by both the frustrated drives and the fear. Finally, the state of conflict itself may produce additional strong stimuli, such as those of muscular tension, which contribute to the misery.

Fear or guilt also motivate the repression of verbal and other cue-producing responses. The fact that certain thoughts arouse fear motivates stopping them, and the reduction in fear reinforces the stopping. Repression is similar

[6]*Ibid.*, from pp. 222-25.

to overt inhibition except that it is a conflict that interferes with thinking instead of one that interferes with acting.

Since the verbal and other cue-producing responses are the basis for the higher mental processes, the repression of these responses makes the neurotic stupid with respect to the specific function of the responses that are repressed. One of the functions of the cue-producing responses is to aid in discrimination. When they are removed by repression, it is harder for the patient to differentiate the situations in which he has been punished from similar ones in which he has not. Interference with such discriminations greatly retards the extinction of unrealistic fears and thus helps to perpetuate the vicious circle of fear, repression, stupidity, lack of discrimination, and persistence of unrealistic fear.

The stupidity in the areas that are affected by repression also tends to prevent the neurotic from finding adequate solutions to his problems and to cause him to do maladaptive things that contribute to his state of high drive or, in other words, misery. At the same time the misery tends to interfere with clear thinking and thus contributes to his stupidity. The high drives make it harder for him to stop and think. They overdetermine or, in other words, motivate certain thoughts so strongly that they occur in inappropriate situations. They produce preoccupation that distracts him from thinking clearly about other matters.

Both the fear and the drives that build up when their goal responses are inhibited by fear tend to produce symptoms. Some of these are unlearned physiological effects of the chronic state of high drive. Others are learned responses that are reinforced by the immediate drive reduction that they produce. These symptoms may be motivated by either of the drives in the conflict, but they are often compromise responses that are motivated by both drives. Similarly they may be reinforced by producing a partial or complete reduction in either one or both drives. Where more than one conflict is involved, the symptom may have still more sources of motivation and reinforcement. Other things equal, the response with the most sources will be most likely to occur as a symptom.

Though the immediate effect of the learned symptoms is a partial reduction in the strength of the drive, the long range effects, as in the case of alcoholism or a phobia that prevents a man from going to work, may be to create new dilemmas that contribute to the fear, guilt, and other high drives. The unlearned symptoms, such as stomach acidity, also may create new dilemmas that increase the height of the drives.

The fact that repression has impaired the patient's ability to think intelligently about his problems is also an important factor in the production of maladaptive symptomatic responses. Repression often prevents the patient from labeling the cause of his symptoms and makes them seem something utterly mysterious and uncontrollable. Because he has not labeled the impulses involved, he is less able to be on his guard. He is also frequently prevented from thinking clearly about the consequences of his symptoms. At the same time, some of the symptomatic responses (such as rationalization, projection, delusions, and hallucinations) may seriously interfere with the higher mental processes and contribute to his stupidity.

This is a general sketch of the most important factors in neurotic behavior.

MAIN FACTORS IN THERAPY[7]

The normal person uses his higher mental processes to solve emotional and environmental problems. When strong drives arise, he learns the responses that reduce these drives. The neurotic has failed to solve his problems in this way. Since he has not learned to solve his problems under the old conditions of his life, he must have new conditions before he can learn a better adjustment.

* * * * *

In addition to permitting free speech, the therapist commands the patient to say everything that comes to mind. By the free-association technique the therapist sets the patient free from the restraint of logic. The therapist avoids arousing additional anxiety by not cross-questioning. By encouraging the patient to talk and consistently failing to punish him, the therapist creates a social situation that is the exact opposite of the one originally responsible for attaching strong fears to talking and thinking. The patient talks about frightening topics. Since he is not punished, his fears are extinguished. This extinction generalizes and weakens the motivation to repress other related topics that were originally too frightening for the patient to discuss or even to contemplate. Where the patient cannot say things for himself, the therapist helps by attaching a verbal label to the emotions that are being felt and expressed mutely in the transference situation.

* * * * *

As the fears motivating repression are reduced by reassurance, extinction, and discrimination, and the patient is urged to think about his problems, mental life is greatly intensified. The removal of repressions restores the higher mental processes, which in turn help with further fear-reducing discriminations, reasoning, foresight, hope, and adaptive planning.

The patient begins to try better solutions in real life as fears are reduced and planning is restored. Some of the fear reduction generalizes from thinking and talking to acting. Becoming clearly aware of the problem and of the unrealistic basis of the fear serves as a challenge to try new modes of adjustment. As these new modes of adjustment are tried, the fears responsible for inhibitions are extinguished. When the new responses produce more satisfactory drive reduction, they are strongly reinforced. The reduction in drive and the extinction of fear reduce the conflict and misery. As the motivation behind the symptoms is reduced, they disappear.

[7]*Ibid.*, from pp. 229-31.

TRANSFERENCE AS GENERALIZED RESPONSE[8]

Strong emotions occur during the course of therapeutic work. They are directed at the therapist and are felt by the patient to be real. They occur because the permissive conditions of therapy weaken repression and inhibition and thus increase the net strength of inhibited tendencies. These tendencies generalize more strongly to the therapist than to others just because the avoidance responses to him are less strong. These responses are ones which, having been long inhibited, have frequently never been labeled. By labeling these emotions while they are occurring, the therapist makes it possible for them to be represented in the patient's reasoning and planning activity. Frequently these responses block therapeutic progress. By identifying them and showing that they are generalized, the therapist mobilizes the learned drives to be reasonable and healthy, thus helping the patient to return to his project of self-understanding. Generalization of emotional response is not only useful but inevitable; it is not purposive and should not be thought of as a duel.

THERAPEUTIC LEARNING[9]

Much of therapy consists of teaching the patient new discriminations. Some of these are achieved by directing the patient's attention toward relevant aspects of his environment or behavior. Some are achieved by contrasting the patient's present inhibitions with the lack of punishment in his present environment. Others are achieved by reviving memories of traumatic conditions of childhood, so that they can be contrasted with the different conditions of adult status. When the contrast is clear and immediate, the effect can be direct and automatic. Verbal responses play an important role in discriminations. They can help to revive memories of the past and to direct attention toward relevant details. They can function to make past neurotic habits seem similar to present ones but to make past conditions of reinforcement seem highly different from those of the present. They can also be the means of contrasting neurotic inhibitions of the present with real-life possibilities of gratification. Verbal cues can prevent generalization of anxiety from past to present. They can mediate responses inhibitory of anxiety. They can excite acquired drives which impel the patient to view the world realistically and to act intelligently. As anxiety is reduced by discrimination, reassurance, and extinction, new responses occur. When they reduce neurotic drives, these responses can be the basis of new habits which will permanently resolve the neurotic conflict.

[8]*Ibid.*, from p. 280.
[9]*Ibid.*, from p. 320.

PART EIGHT

Social Learning Approaches to Personality

CHAPTER 22

ALBERT BANDURA

MODELING THEORY OF PERSONALITY

Canadian-born Albert Bandura (1925-   ) received his baccalaureate from the University of British Columbia in 1949 and
his master's and doctorate from the University of Iowa in 1951
and 1952 respectively. Following a post-doctoral internship at
Wichita Guidance Center in 1953, he accepted a post on the faculty
of Stanford University, where he is currently Professor of Psychology. During 1969-1970 he was a Fellow of the Center for Advanced Study in the Behavioral Sciences. He has also served at
various times as consultant for the Veteran's Administration,
Varian Associates, the U.S. Naval Medical Research Institute, and
the Division of Research Grants of the National Institutes of
Health. He was elected the 82nd president of the American Psychological Association, assuming responsibilities of that office in
1973.

One of the most prolific writers of our time, with over fifty
papers and other publications to his name, Bandura has also served
on the editorial boards of six psychology journals. Two of his
earlier books, written with Richard H. Walters, are *Adolescent
Aggression* (1959) and *Social Learning and Personality Development* (1963). It was the latter that contributed greatly to his first
being acknowledged as a leading contender in personality theory.
As his views unfolded systematically, he offered an integrated presentation of them in his magnum opus, *Principles of Behavior Modification* (1969). But the book that best summarizes his social learn-

ing theory, and in abbreviated form, is *Social Learning Theory* (1971; revised and enlarged in 1975). The same year he edited *Psychological Modeling: Conflicting Theories* and contributed its opening chapter on modeling processes, which synopsizes his theory. Two other important works in this area include his "Social Learning through Imitation" in *Nebraska Symposium on Motivation*, ed. by M. R. Jones, 1962, and "Vicarious Processes: A Case of No-Trial Learning" (in *Advances in Experimental Social Psychology*, ed. by L. Berkowitz, 1965).

As may have been surmised, modeling theory is a form of social learning theory, the two terms being virtually interchangeable for Bandura. His theory emphasizes the important roles played by vicarious, symbolic, and self-regulatory processes in psychological functions. By vicariously observing the behavior of other people and appreciating its attendant consequences, a person can learn, alter, and shape his personality from such direct experiences. In "Modeling Therapy" (in *Psychopathology Today*, ed. by W. S. Sahakian, 1970), Bandura cited cases of vicarious extinction of phobic behavior in which young children overcame their fear of dogs by observing a fearless peer-model progressively display more fear-arousing interactions with the animal but without sensing or displaying any fear. Personality development undergoes intricate response patterns merely through the observation of the performances of appropriate models, so that emotional responses are acquired observationally by witnessing the affective reactions of others undergoing any type of emotional experience. On the other hand, personality traits or behavior are extinguishable vicariously by observing the modeled approach behavior of a performer's behavior toward the object feared without there being any adverse consequences attending his actions as occurred in the above case of phobia for dogs. Moreover, observing others suffering punishment induces inhibition, and the expression of a well-learned response is controlled to a considerable extent by the modeling stimulus. Thus Bandura's personality theory is principally one of personality change and development by example.

To some extent, a person is able to regulate his own behavior by visualizing self-generated consequences, with a number of personality modifications accompanying conditioning operations explicable in the light of self-control processes instead of stimulus-response linkages. Conditioning outcomes are understood as "reflecting the operation of mediating mechanisms rather than the direct coupling of stimuli with responses evoked by other events" (*Principles of*

Behavior Modification, p. 444). Consequently, Bandura's modeling theory is a social learning theory that is quite compatible with the approach of humanistic psychology inasmuch as it accommodates humanistic value theory and morality.

Unlike learning theories of personality that reduce changes in behavior to coupling and recoupling stimuli to responses (associational processes), Bandura's theory holds that behavioral change is for the major part *cognitively mediated,* despite such changes entailing instrumental or classical conditioning, extinction or punishment. Without being cognitively aware of the responses necessary for reinforcement, operant conditioning cannot be achieved without considerable difficulty. For example, it is not the reinforcements actually in force that are more powerful in regulating behavior, but in certain circumstances the more potent are those schedules of reinforcement that a person *believes* to be in effect. It is not necessary for emotional development to have a physically aversive event as the unconditioned stimulus, for emotional conditioning may simply be produced by the substitution of a symbolically generated arousal. In the majority of cases, intervening between an external stimulus and an overt response is a symbolic self-stimulation system.

STAGES OF PERSONALITY DEVELOPMENT[1]

Stage theories of personality development have been widely accepted as providing explanations of prosocial as well as of regressive and other deviant forms of behavior. Although there is relatively little consensus among these theories concerning the number and characteristics of crucial stages, they all assume that social behavior can be categorized in terms of a relatively prefixed sequence of stages which are more or less discontinuous. Stage theories place emphasis on intraindividual variability over time and on similarities among individuals at specifiable age periods; consequently, they tend to minimize obvious and often marked interindividual variability in behavior due to biological, socioeconomic, ethnic, and cultural differences and to variations in the child-training practices of socialization agents. Since children from diverse backgrounds experience different reinforcement contingencies and are exposed to widely differing social models, there are marked group differences at any age level. Moreover, even children who come from similar social or cultural backgrounds and have similar biological characteristics may, as a result of differing social-training experiences, display marked

[1]Albert Bandura and Richard H. Walters, *Social Learning and Personality Development* (New York: Holt, Rinehart and Winston, 1963), from pp. 24-25.

interindividual variability in social behavior patterns. On the other hand, since familial, subcultural, and biological factors that partly determine an individual's social-training experiences are likely to remain relatively constant throughout much of his earlier lifetime, one would expect a good deal of intraindividual continuity in behavior at successive age periods. Thus, social-learning approaches, in contrast to stage theories, lay stress on interindividual differences and on intraindividual continuities.

Stage theories have at best specified only vaguely the conditions that lead to changes in behavior from one level to another. In some of these theories it is assumed that age-specific behavior emerges spontaneously as the result of some usually unspecified biological or maturational process. In others it seems to be assumed that the maturational level of the organism forces from socializing agents patterns of child-training behavior that are relatively universal, thereby predetermining the sequence of developmental changes. In contrast, social-learning theories would predict marked changes in the behavior of an individual of a given age only as a result of abrupt alterations in social-training and other relevant biological or environmental variables, which rarely occur in the social-learning histories of most individuals during pre-adult years.

Learning by Direct Experience[2]

Within the framework of social learning theory, reinforcement primarily serves informative and incentive functions, although it also has response-strengthening capabilities.

Informative Function of Reinforcement

During the course of learning, people not only perform responses, but they also observe the differential consequences accompanying their various actions. On the basis of this informative feedback, they develop thoughts or hypotheses about the types of behavior most likely to succeed. These hypotheses then serve as guides for future actions. . . . Accurate hypotheses give rise to successful performances, whereas erroneous ones lead to ineffective courses of action. The cognitive events are thus selectively strengthened or disconfirmed by the differential consequences accompanying the more distally occurring overt behavior. In this analysis of learning by experience, reinforcing consequences partly serve as an unarticulated way of informing performers what they must do in order to gain beneficial outcomes or to avoid punishing ones.

Motivation

Because of man's anticipatory capacity, conditions of reinforcement also have strong incentive-motivational effects. Most human behavior is not

[2]*Social Learning Theory* (New York: General Learning Press, 1971), from pp. 3, 25-26.

controlled by immediate external reinforcement. As a result of prior experiences, people come to expect that certain actions will gain them outcomes they value, others will have no appreciable effects, and still others will produce undesired results. Actions are therefore regulated to a large extent by anticipated consequences. Homeowners, for instance, do not wait until they experience the misery of a burning house to buy fire insurance; people who venture outdoors do not ordinarily wait until discomforted by a torrential rain or a biting snowstorm to decide what to wear; nor do motorists usually wait until inconvenienced by a stalled automobile to replenish gasoline.

Through the capacity to represent actual outcomes symbolically, future consequences can be converted into current motivators that influence behavior in much the same way as actual consequences. Man's cognitive skills thus provide him with the capability for both insightful and foresightful behavior.

The relative power of vicarious and direct reinforcements is reversed with respect to their motivational effects, as reflected in the capacity to maintain effortful behavior over a long period. One would not recommend to employers, for example, that they maintain the productivity of their employees by having them witness a small group of workers receive pay checks at the end of each month. Seeing others rewarded may temporarily enhance responsiveness but it is unlikely by itself to have much sustaining power. Observation of other people's outcomes, however, can have a continuing influence on the effectiveness of direct reinforcement by providing a standard for judging whether the reinforcements one customarily receives are equitable, beneficent, or unfair. Since both direct and vicarious reinforcements inevitably occur together in everyday life, the interactive effects of these two sources of influence on human behavior are of much greater significance than their independent controlling power. This assumption is borne out by evidence that seeing how others are reinforced can significantly increase or reduce the effectiveness of direct rewards and punishments in changing observers' responsiveness.

Consistent with the preceding findings, explanations of social behavior emphasize relative rather than absolute reinforcement in determining the level of productivity and discontent within a society. Disadvantaged people may be rewarded more generously than in the past but still experience greater discouragement and resentment because the more affluent members of society make more rapid progress, so that the disparity between the groups widens.

MODELING[3]

While reinforcement is a powerful method for regulating behaviors that have already been learned, it is a relatively inefficient way of creating them.

[3]*Ibid.*, from p. 5.

Although behavior can be shaped into new patterns to some extent by rewarding and punishing consequences, learning would be exceedingly laborious and hazardous if it proceeded solely on this basis. Environments are loaded with potentially lethal consequences that befall those who are unfortunate enough to perform dangerous errors. For this reason it would be ill-advised to rely on differential reinforcement of trial-and-error performances in teaching children to swim, adolescents to drive automobiles, and adults to develop complex occupational and social competencies. Apart from questions of survival, it is difficult to imagine a socialization process in which the language, mores, vocational activities, familial customs, and the educational, religious, and political practices of a culture are taught to each new member by selective reinforcement of fortuitous behaviors, without benefit of models who exemplify the cultural patterns in their own behavior.

Most of the behaviors that people display are learned, either deliberately or inadvertently, through the influence of example. There are several reasons why modeling influences figure prominently in human learning in everyday life. When mistakes are costly or dangerous, new modes of response can be developed without needless errors by providing competent models who demonstrate how the required activities should be performed. Some complex behaviors, of course, can be produced only through the influence of models. If children had no opportunity to hear speech, for example, it would be virtually impossible to teach them the linguistic skills that constitute a language. It is doubtful that one could ever shape intricate individual words, let alone grammatical speech, by differential reinforcement of random vocalizations. Where novel forms of behavior can be conveyed only by social cues, modeling is an indispensable aspect of learning. Even in instances where it is possible to establish new response patterns through other means, the process of acquisition can be considerably shortened by providing appropriate models. Under most circumstances, a good example is therefore a much better teacher than the consequences of unguided actions.

Social Learning Analysis of Observational Learning[4]

Social learning theory assumes that modeling influences produce learning principally through their informative functions and that observers acquire mainly symbolic representations of modeled activities rather than specific stimulus-response associations.... In this formulation, modeling phenomena are governed by four interrelated subprocesses.

Attentional Processes. A person cannot learn much by observation if he does not attend to, or recognize, the essential features of the model's behavior. One of the component functions in learning by example is therefore concerned with attentional processes. Simply exposing persons to

[4]*Ibid.*, from pp. 6-8.

models does not in itself ensure that they will attend closely to them, that they will necessarily select from the model's numerous characteristics the most relevant ones, or that they will even perceive accurately the aspects they happen to notice.

Among the numerous factors that determine observational experiences, associational preferences are undoubtedly of major importance. The people with whom one regularly associates delimit the types of behavior that one will repeatedly observe and hence learn most thoroughly. Opportunities for learning aggressive behavior obviously differ markedly for members of delinquent gangs and of Quaker groups.

Within any social group some members are likely to command greater attention than others. The functional value of the behaviors displayed by different models is highly influential in determining which models will be closely observed and which will be ignored. Attention to models is also channeled by their interpersonal attraction. Models who possess interesting and winsome qualities are sought out, whereas those who lack pleasing characteristics tend to be ignored or rejected, even though they may excel in other ways.

Some forms of modeling are so intrinsically rewarding that they can hold the attention of people of all ages for extended periods. This is nowhere better illustrated than in televised modeling. Indeed, models presented in televised form are so effective in capturing attention that viewers learn the depicted behavior regardless of whether or not they are given extra incentives to do so.

Retention Processes. A person cannot be much influenced by observation of a model's behavior if he has no memory of it. A second major function involved in observational learning concerns long-term retention of activities that have been modeled at one time or another. If one is to reproduce a model's behavior when the latter is no longer present to serve as a guide, the response patterns must be represented in memory in symbolic form. By this means past influences can achieve some degree of permanence.

Observational learning involves two representational systems—an imaginal and a verbal one. During exposure, modeling stimuli produce, through a process of sensory conditioning, relatively enduring, retrievable images of modeled sequences of behavior. Indeed, under conditions where stimulus events are highly correlated, as when a name is consistently associated with a given person, it is virtually impossible to hear the name without experiencing imagery of the person's physical characteristics. Similarly, reference to activities (golfing, skiing), places (San Francisco, Paris), and things (one's automobile, Washington Monument) that one has previously observed immediately elicits vivid imaginal representations of the absent physical stimuli.

The second representational system, which probably accounts for the notable speed of observational learning and long-term retention of modeled contents by humans, involves verbal coding of observed events. Most of the cognitive processes that regulate behavior are primarily verbal rather than visual. The route traversed by a model can be acquired, retained, and later reproduced more accurately by verbal coding of the visual information into a sequence of right and left turns (for example, RLRRL) than by reliance upon visual imagery of the itinerary. Observational learning and retention are facilitated by such codes because they carry a great deal of information in an easily stored form.

After modeled activities have been transformed into images and readily utilizable verbal symbols, these memory codes serve as guides for subsequent reproduction of matching responses.

*   *   *   *   *

Motoric Reproduction Processes. The third component of modeling is concerned with processes whereby symbolic representations guide overt actions. To achieve behavioral reproduction, a learner must put together a given set of responses according to the modeled patterns. The amount of observational learning that a person can exhibit behaviorally depends on whether or not he has acquired the component skills. If he possesses the constituent elements, he can easily integrate them to produce new patterns of behavior, but if the response components are lacking, behavioral reproduction will be faulty. Given extensive deficits, the subskills required for complex performances must first be developed by modeling and practice.

Even though symbolic representations of modeled activities are acquired and retained, and the subskills exist, an individual may be unable to coordinate various actions in the required pattern and sequence because of physical limitations. A young child can learn observationally the behavior for driving an automobile and be adept at executing the component responses, but if he is too short to operate the controls he cannot maneuver the vehicle successfully.

There is a third impediment at the behavioral level to skillful reproduction of modeled activities that have been learned observationally. In most coordinated motor skills, such as golf and swimming, performers cannot see the responses that they are making; hence, they must rely on ill-defined proprioceptive cues or verbal reports of onlookers. It is exceedingly difficult to guide actions that are not easily observed or to identify the corrective adjustments needed to achieve a close match of symbolic model and overt performance. In most everyday learning, people usually achieve rough approximations of new patterns of behavior by modeling and refine them through self-corrective adjustments on the basis of informative feedback from performance.

Reinforcement and Motivational Processes. A person can acquire, retain, and possess the capabilities for skillful execution of modeled behavior, but the learning may rarely be activated into overt performance if it is negatively sanctioned or otherwise unfavorably received. When positive

Subprocesses in the Social Learning View of Observational Learning[5]

MODELED EVENTS →

ATTENTIONAL PROCESSES	RETENTION PROCESSES	MOTOR REPRODUCTION PROCESSES	MOTIVATIONAL PROCESSES
Modeling Stimuli Distinctiveness Affective valence Complexity Prevalence Functional value *Observer Characteristics* Sensory capacities Arousal level Motivation Perceptual set Past reinforcement	Symbolic coding Cognitive organization Symbolic rehearsal Motor rehearsal	Physical capabilities Availability of component responses Self-observation of reproductions Accuracy feedback	External reinforcement Vicarious reinforcement Self-reinforcement

→ MATCHING PERFORMANCES

[5] Albert Bandura, "Analysis of Modeling Processes." In A. Bandura, ed., *Psychological Modeling: Conflicting Theories* (Chicago: Aldine • Atherton, 1971), from p. 24.

incentives are provided, observational learning, which previously remained unexpressed, is promptly translated into action. Reinforcement influences not only regulate the overt expression of matching behavior, but they can affect the level of observational learning by controlling what people attend to and how actively they code and rehearse what they have seen.

For reasons given above, the provision of models, even prominent ones, will not automatically create similar patterns of behavior in others. If one is interested merely in producing imitative behavior, some of the sub-processes included in the social learning analysis of modeling can be disre-garded. A model who repeatedly demonstrates desired responses, instructs others to reproduce them, physically prompts the behavior when it fails to occur, and then administers powerful rewards will eventually elicit match-ing responses in most people. It may require 1, 10, or 100 demonstration trials, but if one persists, the desired behavior will eventually be evoked. If, on the other hand, one wishes to explain why modeling does or does not occur, a variety of determinants must be considered. In any given instance lack of matching behavior following exposure to modeling influences may result from either failure to observe the relevant activities, inadequate cod-ing of modeled events for memory representation, retention decrements, motoric deficiencies, or inadequate conditions of reinforcement.

REINFORCEMENT IN OBSERVATIONAL LEARNING[6]

Social learning theory . . . distinguishes between learning and perform-ance of matching behavior. Observational learning, in this view, can occur through observation of modeled behavior and accompanying cognitive ac-tivities without extrinsic reinforcement. This is not to say that mere ex-posure to modeled activities is, in itself, sufficient to produce observational learning. Not all stimulation that impinges on individuals is necessarily observed by them, and even if attended to, the influence of modeling stimuli alone does not ensure that they will be retained for any length of time.

Anticipation of reinforcement is one of several factors that can influence what is observed and what goes unnoticed. Knowing that a given model's behavior is effective in producing valued rewards or averting negative con-sequences can enhance observational learning by increasing observers' at-tentiveness to the model's actions. Moreover, anticipated reinforcement can strengthen retention of what has been learned observationally by motivating people to code and to rehearse modeled responses that have high value. Theories of modeling primarily differ in the manner in which reinforcement influences observational learning rather than in whether reinforcement may play a role in the acquisition process. As shown in the schematization be-low, the issue in dispute is whether reinforcement acts backward to strengthen preceding imitative responses and their association to stimuli or

[6]Bandura and Walters, *Social Learning Theory, op. cit.,* from pp. 9-10.

whether it facilitates learning through its effects on attentional, organizational, and rehearsal processes. It would follow from social learning theory that a higher level of observational learning would be achieved by informing observers in advance about the payoff value for adopting modeled patterns of behavior than by waiting until observers happen to imitate a model and then rewarding them for it.

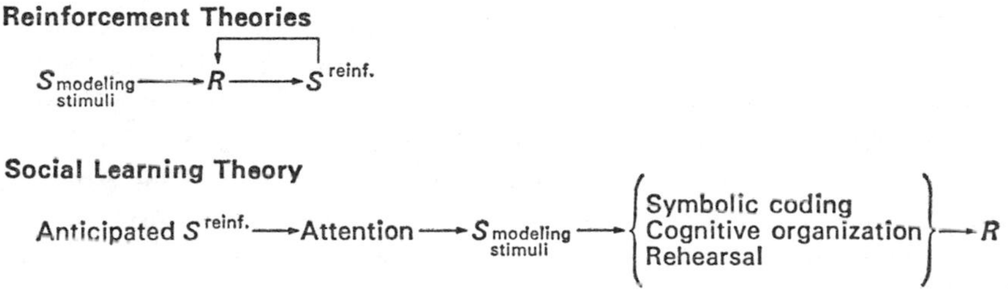

Reinforcement Theories

$$S_{\text{modeling stimuli}} \longrightarrow R \longrightarrow S^{\text{reinf.}}$$

Social Learning Theory

$$\text{Anticipated } S^{\text{reinf.}} \longrightarrow \text{Attention} \longrightarrow S_{\text{modeling stimuli}} \longrightarrow \left\{ \begin{array}{l} \text{Symbolic coding} \\ \text{Cognitive organization} \\ \text{Rehearsal} \end{array} \right\} \longrightarrow R$$

Fig. 1.

In social learning theory reinforcement is considered a facilitative rather than a necessary condition because there are factors other than response consequences that can influence what people will attend to. One does not have to be reinforced, for example, to hear compelling sounds or to look at prominent visual displays. Hence, when people's attention to modeled activities can be gained through physical means, the addition of positive incentives does not increase observational learning. . . . Children who intently watched modeled actions on a television screen in a room darkened to eliminate distractions later displayed the same amount of imitative learning regardless of whether they were informed in advance that correct imitations would be rewarded or given no prior incentives to learn the modeled performances. Anticipated reinforcement would be expected to exert greatest influence on observational learning under self-selection conditions where people can choose whom they will attend to and how intensely they observe their behavior.

Both operant conditioning and social learning theories assume that whether or not people choose to perform what they have learned observationally is strongly influenced by the consequences of such actions. In social learning theory, however, behavior is regulated, not only by directly experienced consequences from external sources, but by vicarious reinforcement and self-reinforcement.

Emotional Development[7]

Vicarious Conditioning

While many emotional responses are learned on the basis of direct experience, much human learning undoubtedly occurs through vicarious condi-

[7]*Ibid.*, from pp. 13-14.

tioning. The emotional responses of another person, as conveyed through vocal, facial, and postural manifestations, can arouse strong emotional reactions in observers. Affective social cues most likely acquire arousal value as a result of correlated experiences between people. That is, individuals who are in high spirits tend to treat others in amiable ways, which arouse in them similar pleasurable affects; conversely, when individuals are dejected, ailing, distressed, or angry, others are also likely to suffer in one way or another. This speculation receives some support in a study by Church[a], who found that expression of pain by an animal evoked strong emotional arousal in animals that had suffered pain together; it had much less emotional effect on animals that had undergone equally painful experiences but unassociated with suffering of another member of their species, and it left unmoved animals that were never subjected to any distress.

In vicarious conditioning, events take on evocative properties through association with emotions aroused in observers by affective experiences of others. In laboratory studies of this phenomenon, an observer hears a tone and shortly thereafter he sees another person exhibit pain reactions (actually feigned) as though he were severely shocked. Observers who repeatedly witness this sequence of events begin to show emotional responses to the tone alone even though no pain is ever inflicted on them. In everyday life, of course, pain may be witnessed from a variety of sources. Observation of failure experiences and the sight of terrified people threatened by menacing animals have, for instance, served as arousers for emotional learning.

Despite the importance of vicarious learning, there has been surprisingly little study of the factors determining how strongly people can be affectively conditioned through the experiences of others. The nature of the relationship between the observer and the sufferer is undoubtedly an influential factor. People are generally less affected emotionally by the adversities of strangers than by the suffering and joy of those close to them and on whom they depend. Observers' sensitivity to expressions of suffering, derived from their past social experiences, may be another contributor. Bandura and Rosenthal[b] for example, found that the degree to which observers were emotionally aroused affected their level of vicarious conditioning. Those who were under moderate emotional arousal displayed the highest rate and most enduring conditioned autonomic responses, whereas those who were either quite calm or highly aroused showed the weakest vicarious conditioning. Apparently, anguished reactions proved so upsetting to observers who themselves were beset by high arousal that they diverted their attention from the suffering person and sought refuge in distracting thoughts of a calming nature.

[a]Russell M. Church, "Emotional Reactions of Rats to the Pain of Others," *Journal of Comparative and Physiological Psychology*, 52 (1959), from pp. 132-34.

[b]Albert Bandura and Ted L. Rosenthal, "Vicarious Classical Conditioning as a Function of Arousal Level," *Journal of Personality and Social Psychology*, 3 (1966), from pp. 54-62.

It is evident from the preceding discussion that emotional learning is much more complex than is commonly assumed. Emotional responses can be brought under the control of intricate combinations of internal and external stimuli that may be either closely related to, or temporally remote from, physical experiences. The fact that stimulus events can be endowed with emotion-arousing potential on a vicarious basis further adds to the complexity of conditioning processes.

COGNITIVE CONTROL AND EMOTIONAL SELF-AROUSAL[8]

According to social learning theory, conditioned emotional responses are typically mediated through thought-produced arousal rather than being directly evoked by conditioned stimuli. The power to arouse emotional responses is by no means confined to external events. People can easily make themselves nauseated by imagining revolting experiences. They can become sexually aroused by generating erotic fantasies. They can frighten themselves by fear-provoking thoughts. And they can work themselves up into a state of anger by ruminating about mistreatment from offensive *provocateurs*. Indeed, Barber and Hahn[c] found that imagined painful stimulation produced subjective discomfort and physiological responses similar to those induced by the actual painful stimulation. The incomparable Satchel Paige, whose extended baseball career provided many opportunities for anxious self-arousal, colorfully described the power that thoughts can exert over visceral functioning when he advised, "If your stomach disputes you lie down and pacify it with cool thoughts."

VICARIOUS CONDITIONING OF EMOTIONAL RESPONSIVENESS[9]

It is generally assumed that persons develop emotional responses on the basis of direct painful or pleasurable stimulation experienced in association with certain places, people, or events. Although many emotional responses are undoubtedly acquired by means of direct classical conditioning, affective learning in humans frequently occurs through vicariously aroused emotions. Many phobic behaviors, for example, arise not from actual injurious experiences with the phobic objects, but rather from witnessing others either respond fearfully toward, or be hurt by, certain things. . . . Similarly, persons often acquire, on the basis of exposure to modeled stim-

---

[8]*Ibid.*, from p. 15.

[c]Theodore X. Barber and Karl W. Hahn, Jr., "Experimental Studies in 'Hypnotic' Behavior," *Journal of Nervous and Mental Disease,* 139 (1964), from pp. 416-25.

[9]*Principles of Behavior Modification* (New York: Holt, Rinehart and Winston, 1969), from p. 167.

ulus correlations, intense emotional attitudes toward members of unpopular minority groups or nationalities with whom they have had little or no personal contact.

As suggested above, vicarious emotional conditioning results from observing others experience positive or negative emotional effects in conjunction with particular stimulus events. Both direct and vicarious conditioning processes are governed by the same basic principle of associative learning, but they differ in the source of the emotional arousal. In the direct prototype, the learner himself is the recipient of pain- or pleasure-producing stimulation, whereas in vicarious forms somebody else experiences the reinforcing stimulation and his affective expressions, in turn, serve as the arousal stimuli for the observer. This socially mediated conditioning process thus requires both the vicarious activation of emotional responses and close temporal pairing of these affective states with environmental stimuli.

Vicarious Reinforcement[10]

Human functioning would be exceedingly inefficient, not to mention dangerous, if behavior were controlled only by directly experienced consequences. Fortunately, people can profit greatly from the experiences of others. In everyday situations reinforcement typically occurs within a social context. That is, people repeatedly observe the actions of others and the occasions on which they are rewarded, ignored, or punished. Despite the fact that observed rewards and punishments play an influential role in regulating behavior, vicarious reinforcement has, until recent years, been essentially ignored in traditional theories of learning.

There is a second reason why the study of vicarious reinforcement is critical to the understanding of reinforcement influences. Observed consequences provide reference standards that determine whether a particular reinforcer that is externally administered will serve as a reward or as punishment. Thus, for example, the same compliment is likely to be discouraging to persons who have seen similar performances by others more highly acclaimed, but rewarding when others have been less generously praised.

Research on the relational character of reinforcing events has shown that the same consequence can have rewarding or punishing effects on behavior depending upon the nature, frequency, or generosity with which one's performances were previously reinforced. However, incentive contrast effects, resulting from discrepancies between observed and directly experienced consequences, have received relatively little attention.

Vicarious Punishment

Vicarious reinforcement is defined as a change in the behavior of observers resulting from seeing the response consequences of others. Vicarious

---

[10]*Social Learning Theory, op. cit.,* from pp. 24-25.

punishment is indicated when observed negative consequences reduce people's tendency to behave in similar or related ways. This phenomenon has been studied most extensively with respect to aggressive behavior. In the typical experiment[d] children are shown a film depicting a model engaging in novel aggressive behaviors that are either rewarded, punished, or unaccompanied by any evident consequences. Witnessing aggression punished usually produces less imitative aggression than seeing it obtain social and material success or go unnoticed.

Because of the variety and complexity of social influences, people are not always consistent in how they respond to aggressive behavior. Rosekrans and Hartup[e] examined the effects of discrepant observed consequences on imitative aggression. Children who saw assaultive behavior consistently rewarded were most aggressive, those who saw it consistently punished displayed virtually no imitative behavior, while those who saw aggression sometimes rewarded and sometimes punished exhibited a moderate level of aggressiveness.

A second major set of experiments has been concerned with how vicarious punishment affects people's willingness to violate prohibitions. Walters and his associates have shown[f] that witnessing peer models punished for violating prohibitions increases observers' inhibition of transgressive behavior as compared with conditions in which modeled transgressions are either rewarded or simply ignored. Results of a comparative study by Benton[g] indicate that, under some conditions, observed and directly experienced punishment may be equally effective in reducing deviant behavior. Children who observed peers punished for engaging in prohibited activities later showed the same amount of response inhibition as the punished transgressors.

An interesting experiment by Crooks[h] reveals that lower species are also highly susceptible to observed punishments. After being tested for the extent to which they handled play objects, monkeys observed distress vocalizations sounded (through a tape recorder) whenever a model monkey touched a particular object; they also witnessed the model's contacts with a

[d]Albert Bandura, Dorothea Ross, and Sheila A. Ross, "A Comparative Test of the Status Envy, Social Power, and Secondary Reinforcement Theories of Identificatory Learning," *Journal of Abnormal and Social Psychology*, 67 (1963), from pp. 527-34.

[e]Mary A. Rosekrans and Willard W. Hartup, "Imitative Influences of Consistent and Inconsistent Response Consequences to a Model on Aggressive Behavior in Children," *Journal of Personality and Social Psychology*, 7 (1967), from pp. 429-34.

[f]Richard H. Walters, Marion Leat, and Louis Mezei, "Inhibition and Disinhibition of Responses Through Empathetic Learning," *Canadian Journal of Psychology*, 17 (1963), from pp. 235-43; Walters and Ross D. Parke, "Influence of Response Consequences to a Social Model on Resistance to Deviation," *Journal of Experimental Child Psychology*, 1 (1964), from pp. 269-80; Walters, Parke, and Valerie A. Cane, "Timing of Punishment and the Observation of Consequences to Others as Determinants of Response Inhibition," *Journal of Experimental Child Psychology*, 2 (1965), from pp. 10-30.

[g]Alan A. Benton, "Effects of the Timing of Negative Response Consequences on the Observational Learning of Resistance to Temptation in Children," *Dissertation Abstracts*, 27 (1967), from pp. 2153-154.

[h]Judith L. Crooks, "Observational Learning of Fear in Monkeys." Unpublished manuscript, University of Pennsylvania, 1967.

control object accompanied by the distress vocalizations played backwards, which did not sound like a pain reaction. In a subsequent test the observing animals played freely with the control item but actively avoided objects that supposedly produced painful experiences for another animal.

In all of the preceding studies the model was punished either verbally or physically by someone else. In many instances persons respond with self-punitive and self-devaluative reactions to their own behavior that may be considered permissible, or even commendable, by others. Numerous experiments, which are discussed later, demonstrate that witnessing punishments self-administered by a model has inhibitory effects on observers with respect to unmerited achievements. Observation of self-punishment by a model has been shown by Porro[1] to exert similar effects on transgressive behavior. For children who viewed a filmed model exhibit self-approving responses to her transgressions, 80 percent subsequently handled toys they were forbidden to touch, whereas the transgression rate was only 20 percent for children who had observed the same model respond self-critically toward her own transgressions.

Numerous experiments generally show that observed rewards produce a greater increase in similar responding than if the exemplified actions have no evident consequences. In the case of behavior that is ordinarily disapproved, however, seeing transgressions go unpunished seems to heighten analogous actions in observers to the same degree as witnessing models rewarded. To the extent that absence of anticipated punishment conveys permissiveness and allays fears, behavioral restraints are thereby reduced and transgressive actions are performed more readily.

[1]Catherine R. Porro, "Effects of the Observation of a Model's Affective Responses to Her Own Transgression on Resistance to Temptation in Children," *Dissertation Abstracts,* 28 (1968), from p. 3064.

JULIAN B. ROTTER

SOCIAL LEARNING THEORY
OF PERSONALITY

Julian B. Rotter has spent more than a quarter of a century developing his social learning theory (SLT) of personality. There are those critics, however, who would insist that Rotter's is a cognitive theory of personality, its cognitive character stemming from three basic constructs: behavior potential, a person's expectancy, and reinforcement value. Such comments are not repugnant to Rotter, who views social learning theory as a synthesis of two major trends in American psychology: (a) stimulus-response or reinforcement theories and (b) cognitive or field theories of psychology. The intellectual parents of this brand of social learning theory (since Bandura's is also a social learning theory as is that of Dollard and Miller) would include Lewin, Tolman, Adler, J. R. Kantor, Thorndike, and Hull.

The first extensive articulation of Rotter's social learning theory of personality appeared in his *Social Learning and Clinical Psychology* (1954) and ten years later in abbreviated form under the title *Clinical Psychology* (1964). The purpose of the former book was to offer a systematic personality theory that would prove viable for clinical practice. The latter, a small book, sought to provide the student with an understanding of clinical psychology realistically based but, nevertheless, oriented from a social learning theorist's position. A third and important contribution to social learning theory was published in 1972 by Rotter and two collaborators, June E.

Chance and E. Jerry Phares, who, in addition to editing the book, contributed a number of chapters to it. The book's title is self-explanatory: *Applications of a Social Learning Theory of Personality*. Rotter offered a later statement of his position in abbreviated form in a book entitled *Personality* (with D. J. Hochreich) in 1975. In addition, Rotter has contributed significant chapters to other books, including "Personality Theory" in *Theories and Data in Psychology* (ed. by H. Helson and W. Bevan, 1967), "Beliefs, Social Attitudes and Behavior: A Social Learning Analysis" in *Cognition, Personality, and Clinical Psychology* (ed. by R. Jessor and S. Feshback, 1967), and "Some Implications of a Social Learning Theory for the Practice of Psychotherapy" in *Learning Approaches to Therapeutic Behavior Change* (ed. by D. J. Levis, 1970).

Rotter grounds his social learning theory of personality on the four variables of (1) behavior potential, (2) expectancy, (3) reinforcement value, and (4) psychological situation. While utilizing the principles of expectancy and reinforcement, he adopts the empirical law of effect, though he does not accept drive reduction theory. According to Rotter, a person's behavior is directional or goal determined. An individual will learn to respond to that behavior which, under given circumstances, will issue in the maximum amount of satisfaction. The triune composition of a need includes *need potential* (the potential strength or likelihood that a set of behaviors will be employed in a particular circumstance), *expectancy* (the expectation that a given behavior will indeed fructify into the valued goal or satisfaction), and *need value* (the hierarchal preferences one ascribes to varying sets of satisfactions). In adding the *psychological situation* to these three components, one has the foundation of Rotter's social learning theory. The psychological situation is that environment or situation (internal and external) by which a person is stimulated, and by drawing upon past experiences, learns how to derive more satisfactions in any given set of circumstances. Six needs, decidedly humanistic, are adopted by Rotter: (1) recognition-status, (2) dominance, (3) independence, (4) protection-dependency, (5) love and affection, and (6) physical comfort. Other important Rotterian concepts are: freedom of movement, minimal goal level, generalized expectances, situational cues of positive and negative reinforcements, and a class of behavior called aggression.

A product of Brooklyn College with his terminal degree from Indiana University, Julian B. Rotter was born in Brooklyn, New York, on October 22, 1916. Having spent the World War II years as a psychologist and personnel consultant to the U. S. Army, after the war he accepted a position at Ohio State University, where eventually he became director of its Psychological Clinic. Since 1963 he has been with the University of Connecticut, directing its Clinical Psychology Training Program.

BASIC TENETS
OF ROTTER'S SOCIAL LEARNING THEORY (SLT)
OF PERSONALITY[1]

The unit of investigation for the study of personality is the interaction of the individual and his meaningful environment.

* * * * *

Personality constructs are not dependent for explanation upon constructs in any other field (including physiology, biology, or neurology). Scientific constructs for one mode of description should be consistent with constructs in any other field of science, but no hierarchy of dependency exists among them.

Behavior as described by personality constructs takes place in space and time. Although all such events may be described by psychological constructs, it is presumed that they may also be described by physical constructs, as they are in such fields as physics, chemistry, and neurology. Any conception that regards the events themselves, rather than the descriptions of the events, as different is rejected as dualistic.

* * * * *

Not all behavior of an organism may be usefully described with personality constructs. Behavior that may usefully be described by personality constructs appears in organisms of a particular level or stage of complexity and a particular level or stage of development.

A person's experiences (or his interactions with his meaningful environment) influence each other. Otherwise stated, personality has unity.

* * * * *

Behavior as described by personality constructs has a directional aspect. It may be said to be goal-directed. The directional aspect of behavior is inferred from the effect of reinforcing conditions.

* * * * *

The occurrence of a behavior of a person is determined not only by the nature or importance of goals or reinforcements but also by the person's

[1]Julian B. Rotter, June E. Chance, and E. Jerry Phares, *Applications of a Social Learning Theory of Personality* (New York: Holt, Rinehart and Winston, 1972), from pp. 4-11.

anticipation or expectancy that these goals will occur. Such expectations are determined by previous experience and can be quantified.

FOUR BASIC CONCEPTS:
(1) BEHAVIOR POTENTIAL, (2) EXPECTANCY,
(3) REINFORCEMENT VALUE,
(4) PSYCHOLOGICAL SITUATION[2]

Behavior Potential

Behavior potential may be defined as the potentiality of any behavior's occurring in any given situation or situations as calculated in relation to any single reinforcement or set of reinforcements.

Behavior potential is a relative concept. That is, one calculates the potentiality of any behavior's occurring in relation to the other alternatives open to the individual. Thus, it is possible to say only that in a specific situation the potentiality for occurrence of behavior *x* is greater than that for behavior *z*.

The SLT concept of behavior is quite broad. Indeed, behavior may be that which is directly observed but also that which is indirect or implicit. This notion includes a broad spectrum of possibilities—swearing, running, crying, fighting, smiling, choosing, and so on, are all included. These are all observable behaviors, but implicit behaviors that can only be measured indirectly, such as rationalizing, repressing, considering alternatives, planning, and reclassifying, would also be included. The objective study of cognitive activity is a difficult but important aspect of social learning theory. Principles governing the occurrence of such cognitive activities are not considered different from those that might apply to any observable behavior.

Expectancy

Expectancy may be defined as the probability held by the individual that a particular reinforcement will occur as a function of a specific behavior on his part in a specific situation or situations. Expectancy is systematically independent of the value or importance of the reinforcement.

While simple cognitions also may be regarded as having some of the characteristics of expectancies, throughout this book the term *expectancy* will be used to refer to the expectancy for behavior-reinforcement sequences (Rotter, 1960). Historically, expectancy has often been described as either an objective or subjective concept. Lewin (1951), for example, stressed the subjective nature of expectancy. Brunswik (1951), however, emphasized objective probability—a probability determined primarily by objectively describable past events.

---

[2]*Ibid.*, from pp. 12-15.

In SLT in concept of expectancy is defined as a subjective probability, but this definition does not imply inaccessibility to objective measurement. People's probability statements, and other behaviors relating to the probability of occurrence of an event, often differ systematically from their actuarial experience with the event in the past. A variety of other factors operate in specific instances to influence one's probability estimates. Such factors may include the nature or the categorization of a situation, patterning and sequential considerations, uniqueness of events, generalization, and the perception of causality.

Reinforcement Value

The reinforcement value of any one of a group of potential external reinforcements may be ideally defined as the degree of the person's preference for that reinforcement to occur if the possibilities of occurrence of all alternatives were equal.

Again, *reinforcement value* is a relative term. Measurement of reinforcement value occurs in a choice situation. That is, reinforcement value refers to a preference, and preference indicates that one favors something over something else. Such preferences show consistency and reliability within our culture and also, generally speaking, can be shown to be systematically independent of expectancy. These and other considerations will be discussed in greater detail later.

The Psychological Situation

Behavior does not occur in a vacuum. A person is continuously reacting to aspects of his external and internal environment. Since he reacts selectively to many kinds of stimulation, internal and external simultaneously, in a way consistent with his unique experience and because the different aspects of his environment mutually affect each other, we choose to speak of the psychological situation rather than the stimulus. Methods of determining generality or determining the dimensions of similarity among situations have been described by Rotter (1955).

Several writers have pointed out the difficulty of identifying situations independently of behavior. That is, how one can describe a situation, as one might a physical stimulus, independently of the particular S's response? However, the problem is not really so different from that of describing stimuli along dimensions of color, although it is perhaps vastly more complicated in social situations. In the case of color stimuli, ultimately the criterion is a response made by an observer, sometimes aided by an intermediate instrument. The response is one that is at the level of sensory discrimination and thus leads to high observer agreement. In the case of social situations, the level of discrimination is common sense based on an understanding of a culture rather than a reading from an instrument. As such, reliability of discrimination may be limited but still be sufficiently high to make practical predictions possible. Specific situations can be identified as school situations, employment situations, girl friend situations, and so on. For the purpose of generality, various kinds of psychological constructs can be devised to arrive at broader classes of situations having similar meaning to S. The utility of such classes would have to be empirically determined, depending on the S's response. The objective referents for these situations, which provide the basis for prediction, however, can be independent of the specific S. That is, they can be reliably identified by cultural, common sense terms.

Basic Formulas

The preceding variables and their relations may be conveniently stated in the formulas that follow. It should be remembered, however, that these formulas do not at this time imply any precise mathematical relations. Indeed, although the relation between expectancy and reinforcement value is probably a multiplicative one, there is little systematic data at this point that would allow one to evolve any precise mathematical statement.

The basic formula is stated thus:

$$BP_{x,s_1,R_a} = f(E_{x,R_a s,1} \,\&\, RV_{a,s_1}) \qquad (\cdot\,)$$

Formula (1) says, The potential for behavior x to occur, in situation 1 n relation to reinforcement a, is a function of the expectancy of the occur ence of reinforcement a, following behavior x in situation 1, and the value of reinforcement a in situation 1.

Formula (1) is obviously limited, inasmuch as it deals only with the potential for a given behavior to occur in relation to a single reinforcement. As noted earlier, description at the level of personality constructs usually demands a broader, more generalized concept of behavior, reflected in the following formula:

$$BP_{(x-n),s(1-n),R(a-n)} = f[E_{(x-n),s(1-n),R(a-n)} \,\&\, RV_{(a-n),s(1-n)}] \quad (2)$$

Formula (2) says, The potentiality of functionally related behaviors x to n to occur, in specified situations 1 to n in relation to potential reinforcements a to n, is a function of the expectancies of these behaviors leading to these reinforcements in these situations and the values of these reinforcements in these situations. To enhance communication by reducing verbal complexity, three terms—*need potential, freedom of movement,* and *need value*—have been introduced. A formula incorporating these latter terms is:

$$NP = f(FM \,\&\, NV) \qquad (3)$$

Thus, need potential is a function of freedom of movement and need value. In broader predictive or clinical situations, formula (3) would more likely be used, while formula (2) would be more appropriate in testing more specific, experimental hypotheses.

The fourth variable, *situation,* is left implicit in formula (3). SLT is highly committed to the importance of the psychological situation. It is emphasized that behavior varies as the situation does. But obviously, there is also transituational generality in behavior. If there were not, there would be no point in discussing *personality* as a construct or as a field of study. However, along with generality there is also situational specificity. While it may be true that person A is generally more aggressive than person B, nonetheless, there can arise many occasions on which person B behaves more aggressively than does person A. Predictions based solely on internal characteristics of the individual are not sufficient to account for the complexities of human behavior.

NEEDS, BEHAVIOR PATTERNS, AND FUNCTIONAL EXPECTANCIES[3]

Need Potential

The concept *need potential* is the broader analogue of behavior potential. The difference is that need potential refers to groups of functionally related behaviors rather than single behaviors. Functional relatedness of behaviors exists when several behaviors all lead to, or are directed toward, obtaining the same or similar reinforcements. The process of generalization occurring among functionally related behaviors allows for better than chance prediction from one specific referent of the category to another. (Similarity of re inforcement is not the only basis for functional relatedness of behaviors.) Need potential, then, describes the mean potentiality of a group of functionally related behaviors, directed at obtaining the same or a set of similar reinforcements, occurring in any segment of the individual's life.

The kinds of behaviors that can be grouped into functional categories may range from very molecular physical or objectively defined acts to implicit behaviors such as identifying with authority figures. Such categories may be progressively more inclusive depending upon one's predictive goal and the level of predictive accuracy required. For example, *need potential for recognition is more inclusive than need potential for recognition in psychology.*

In practice, estimates of need potential are made utilizing some sampling procedure. Perhaps, observations are made of how S behaves in selected or specified situations. Normally, the determination of the relation between behaviors and reinforcements is made on a cultural basis. That is, on a cultural basis we know that *studying* is related to a group of reinforcements called *academic recognition.* At this point a brief discussion of some need concepts used in social learning theory will be helpful in understanding the sections to follow.

It is crucial to the development of a theory of personality that a descriptive language be established which deals with the content of personality.

[3]*Ibid.*, from pp. 30-41.

One difficulty with many learning theories is their almost exclusive emphasis on the processes of acquisition of behavior and of performance and their almost total neglect of the content of personality. In contrast, many personality theories suffer from the reverse situation, emphasizing content (needs, traits, and so on) while neglecting process.

In developing content terms, SLT began by attempting to profit from the experience of clinicians, psychotherapists, and students of the culture generally. Development of a reliable, communicable, and valid language of description is an ever-evolving process. Furthermore, it is an empirical process, wherein the final test is predictive utility of the terms and not armchair rumination.

Based on the foregoing considerations, six need descriptions were developed at a fairly broad level of abstraction. From these relatively broad categories, more specific abstractions can be developed. Some of these can be included almost entirely within one of the broad categories, while some others might be related as well to one category as to another. The six broad categories arrived at and their definitions are the following:

Recognition-Status: Need to be considered competent or good in a professional, social, occupational, or play activity. Need to gain social or vocational position—that is, to be more skilled or better than others.

Protection-Dependency: Need to have another person or group of people prevent frustration or punishment, or to provide for the satisfaction of other needs.

Dominance: Need to direct or to control the actions of other people, including members of family and friends. To have any action taken be that which he suggests.

Independence: Need to make own decisions, to rely on oneself, together with the need to develop skills for obtaining satisfactions directly without the mediation of other people.

Love and Affection: Need for acceptance and indication of liking by other individuals. In contrast to recognition-status, *not* concerned with social or professional positions, but seeks persons' warm regard.

Physical Comfort: Learned need for physical satisfaction that has become associated with gaining security.

All of these categories were presumed to be at about the same general level of inclusiveness.

The general term *need* used in this context refers to the entire complex of *need potential, freedom of movement,* and *need value.* The term refers to a set of constructs describing directionality of behavior, *not* to a state of deprivation or arousal in the organism. Used in this way the concept *need* is neither the equivalent of *need value* (or preference for certain kinds of goals) only nor the equivalent of *need potential* only.

To return to the discussion of need potential, it should be apparent that relying exclusively on cultural definitions of terms can lead to problems in individual prediction. For example, even though many people may study in order to achieve academic reinforcements, it may be true that a few people study in order to attain affectional responses from their girl friends. Therefore, the latter kind of individual would not be demonstrating a high need potential for academic recognition, but rather, for love and affection from opposite sex peers.

Measurement of Need Potential. To measure need potential is to indicate the frequency of occurrence of certain behaviors. Perhaps one of the most striking examples of the confusion of concepts in attempts to assess personality is failure to differentiate among behaviors, preferences, and expectancies. This problem has been dealt with in considerable detail by Rotter (1960). For example, to say an individual places a high value on love and affection goals is *not* to say also that he behaves in such a way as to achieve need satisfaction in this area. Thus, although *need value* may be high, *expectancy* for the successful utilization of behaviors leading to such goals may be low, and therefore, *need potential* is low. Many psychological tests, for example, are composed of a confusing amalgam of items, some of which deal with frequency of behavior, others with preference for certain goals, and still others with expectancy. A total score summing these three classes of items can be very misleading. By the same token, how could one predict behavior from psychological tests were the test items to deal solely with need value? Behavior occurs not just on the basis of strength of preferences but also on the basis of expectancy that such behavior will lead to the goals in question. A study by Lesser (1957) clearly illustrates the utility of separating the concepts of *behavior, needs,* and *expectancies.* Lesser found little relation between aggressive needs and aggressive behavior among schoolchildren; evidently TAT responses did not predict overt behavior. However, when information regarding maternal control responses toward the child's aggression (responses SLT would regard as referents for the child's expectancy for punishment for overt aggression) was added to the need for aggression scores derived from the TAT, then significant predictions of overt behavior were possible.

A variety of measures of need potential are possible. These might include direct observation of S over a period of time, paper and pencil or verbal choice techniques, rankings, paired comparisons, forced-choice questionnaires, and so on. However, in utilizing paper and pencil techniques or verbal questionnaires, the emphasis must be on what the subject does and not on what he would like to do or expects to do.

Projective tests have, in the past, not been particularly useful in assessing need potential. Their best application would seem to be more in the direction of assessing *need values* and *freedom of movement.* Carefully applied sociometric techniques offer promise in measurement of *need potential.* Indeed, in some ways this method simply asks others to report on their observations of S and is thus very much akin to other observational techniques. Sociometric methods allow behavior to be assessed in natural settings and are carried out by people who know S well enough to make meaningful ratings. This technique was utilized by Fitzgerald (1958) to measure dependency behavior and by Phares (1959) to assess leaving-the-field behavior. Of course, crude predictions of need potential may be arrived at also by combining measures of freedom of movement and need value.

Need Value

Need value is defined as *mean preference value of a set of functionally related reinforcements.* Where *reinforcement value* indicates preference for *one* reinforcement over others, *need value* indicates preference for one *set* of functionally related reinforcements over another set (always assuming that expectancy for occurrence is held constant). Recall that functionality of reinforcements comes about either through stimulus generalization or through an extension of the principle of mediated stimulus generalization. Occurrence of functionality among reinforcements has been demonstrated empirically on a substitution basis, as in a study by Lotsof (1953), as well as in terms of generalization of expectancies among functionally related behaviors, as in the previously noted studies of Crandall, Jessor, and Chance. Demonstration of functionality by substitution involves a situation where behavior toward a goal is blocked, and it is then noted which behavior is adopted as a substitute.

Earlier, when need potential was discussed, it was emphasized that descriptions of need categories based on functionally related behaviors must ultimately be arrived at on an empirical basis. Likewise, given a workable culture-based definition, one is cautioned about generalizing beyond the confines of one's own culture. Similarly, one must be cognizant of individual devlopment of idiosyncratic need structures which may not follow those of the larger culture.

Measurement of Need Value. Interviews, objective tests, and projective tests have all been used to measure need value. It is also possible to use observations of behavior in situations where expectancies can be controlled.

One of the more systematic attempts to measure need value was made by Liverant (1958). Inasmuch as the SLT operational definition of need value implicitly suggests a choice or ranking technique for measurement, Liverant presented statements in a forced-choice arrangement and controlled *S*'s expectancies through instructions. An inventory, called the *Goal Preference Inventory*, resulted from this procedure and is designed to measure *S*'s relative need values for recognition *versus* love and affection. Item analysis, factor analysis, split-half and test-retest reliability, as well as correlations with the *Edwards Personal Preference Schedule* and use of criterion group methods, generally support the adequacy of the inventory as a valid and reliable indicator of relative need strength in the areas sampled.

Need value has been measured often by projective methods—most often with some version of the TAT. Rotter (1954) provides a general outline for construction of reliable judgmental procedures. Such procedures are illustrated in Fitzgerald's (1958) study. A somewhat different approach to measuring need value from interview data is presented by Tyler, Tyler, and Rafferty (1962).

Freedom of Movement

Freedom of movement is defined as *mean expectancy of obtaining positive satisfactions as a result of a set of related behaviors directed toward obtaining a group of functionally related reinforcements.* Thus, when an individual has a high expectancy of attaining reinforcements that define a given need area for him, he is said to have high freedom of movement in that need area. In short, he feels that his behavioral techniques will be successful for his goals. When freedom of movement is low, particularly in relation to a need area of high value, the individual may anticipate punishment or failure. Thus, the concept of *freedom of movement* bears a relation to the concept of *anxiety* as described by other theories. This correspondence will be discussed in more detail later.

Measurement of Freedom of Movement. Like its analogue *expectancy, freedom of movement* may be measured on either an absolute or on a relative basis. Furthermore, when it is possible to equate reinforcement values, freedom of movement can also be measured by assuming that the individual will choose the goal-directed behavior for which he has the highest set of expectancies. Direct methods of measurement include verbal statements of expectancy, behavioral techniques, such as betting on outcomes, and, possibly, decision times. Indirect methods of assessment often rely upon measures of avoidant behaviors or defensiveness. It seems reasonable to assume that to the extent an individual behaves defensively or in an irreal fashion in relation to certain goals, he possesses low freedom of movement in that need area. Low expectancy for success (or high expectancy for punishment) in a highly valued need area is correlated with defensiveness; thus, the latter can serve as a referent for the former. Naturally, the definition of what is *irreal, defensive,* or *avoidant* must derive from a study of the culture in which the individual operates. Such behaviors, although in some instances leading to immediate gratifications, do lead ultimately to negative reinforcements from society. It follows logically from this analysis that the person utilizing defensive behaviors is aware, at some level, of the potential for negative reinforcement involved. Put another way, if the person's defensive behaviors are characteristically followed by ultimate negative reinforcement, he uses the defensive behaviors because he expects greater punishment to result from his positive efforts than he does from negative or defensive efforts.

Possible origins of low freedom of movement are diverse. For example, the individual may simply not possess knowledge necessary to attain desired goals. An extreme illustration is the retardate, whose goals may be those of society's, but whose expectancy for goal attainment is low because he has neither the behavioral repertory nor the ability to acquire the appropriate behaviors. In other instances, the individual may have learned to value certain goals which others regard as undesirable. As a result, he comes to anticipate punishment in that area. In still other instances, the individual may develop low freedom of movement based on faulty interpretations of the past. For example, he may have, as a child, experienced severe criticism from his family. Generalizing erroneously from this experience to the present, he may anticipate failure or punishment from all others he encounters.

Rotter (1942, 1943, 1954) has described a variety of level-of-aspiration patterns derived from controlled observation of goal setting. These patterns frequently identify avoidant techniques, suggesting low freedom of movement.

A variety of other studies use projective techniques like the TAT and develop systematic scoring methods to assess avoidance. . . . When *freedom of movement is low while need value is high,* we have a situation of *conflict.* To escape punishment and failure in an area of great importance to him, the individual adopts various avoidant behaviors. He may also try to reach his goals in *irreal* or *symbolic* ways, such as fantasy, which do not run the risk of incurring failure or punishment. Most behavior regarded as psychopathological is avoidant or irreal behavior. . . .

In sumary, defensive behaviors provide an indirect measure of freedom of movement because such behaviors suggest the degree to which the individual expects negative reinforcement in a given need area. It is crucial in using this method that it first be established that the individual places a high value on the need in question. Otherwise, what seems avoidant may turn out to be an uncomplicated lack of interest.

Minimal Goal Level

Related to the concept of *low freedom of movement* is another SLT concept—*minimal goal level.* Specifically defined, *minimal goal level* refers to the *lowest goal in a continuum of potential reinforcements for some life situation which will be perceived by the person as satisfactory to him.* This definition suggests that reinforcements may be ordered from highly positive to highly negative. The point along this dimension at which reinforcements change from positive to negative in value for the person is his minimal goal level. Internalized minimal goals are responsible for the often observed instance where a person attains many goals that appear highly desirable to others and yet he, nonetheless, experiences a sense of failure or low freedom of movement. From his point of view, he is failing. When someone has extremely high minimal goals, whether in achievement, dominance, or love and affection, and is not obtaining reinforcements at or above this level, then by definition he has low freedom of movement.

The same analysis, in reverse, supplies the reason that a person may be contented, even though observers perceive his level of goal achievement to be exceedingly low. To the extent that problems in living often derive from a too high minimal goal level (or, more infrequently, from a very low minimal goal level), psychotherapy may concentrate on changing minimal goals by changing the value of reinforcements. As discussed in the preceding section on reinforcement values, value changes are accomplished by pairing the reinforcements in question with others of either a higher or lower value. For example, the individual is led to develop the expectancy that a previously negatively valued reinforcement—such as a grade of B—can lead to the positive reinforcements of praise and acceptance. . . .

While minimal goals are relatively stable, the values of all reinforcements are relative to others possible in a given situation. . . . For example, defensive and avoidant behaviors are acquired and maintained because they are positively reinforced by the avoidance of a strong negative reinforcement. At the same time, other behaviors leading to anticipated negative reinforcement may be negatively reinforced because anticipation itself can be negatively reinforcing. In situations of anticipation of strong negative reinforcement, minimal goals may shift markedly and avoidance (or partial avoidance) may be perceived as a positively reinforcing outcome. Similarly, in situations where strong positive reinforcements seem possible, a level of reinforcement that would be regarded as positive otherwise may be perceived as negative on that occasion.

The Situation

Implicit in all the preceding discussions has been the idea that the *psychological situation* is an extremely important determinant of behavior. This view is in sharp contrast to those positions that adopt a "core" approach to personality and assert that once the basic elements of personality are identified, reliable prediction follows. Core views are inherent in both psychoanalytic theories of dynamics and in trait and typological descriptive schemes. In short, many theories are so preoccupied with identifying highly stable aspects of personality that they fail to make systematic use of the psychological situation in the prediction of behavior. The SLT approach contends that such a posture severely limits prediction by permitting only global statements about future behavior which are limited to a very low level of accuracy in prediction.

From the SLT view, each situation is composed of cues serving to arouse in the individual certain expectancies for reinforcement of specific behaviors. For example, even though an individual may be described as possessing an extremely strong predisposition to aggressive behavior, he will not behave aggressively in a given situation if the latter contains cues suggesting to him that aggressive behavior is very likely to result in strong punishment. Meanings that cues acquire for the individual are based on prior learning history and can be determined in advance in order to help us predictively. Again, some of these meanings can be assumed on a cultural basis, but the possibilities raised by idiosyncratic life experiences must be recognized also.

Recognition that behavior is not determined solely by personal characteristics but also by situational considerations specifies the necessity for descriptive categories for different situations. Psychology can be accurately said to have made less progress in devising classifications for situations than in almost any other area. As a preliminary effort in this direction, Rotter (1955) described several methods for determining similarity among situations. As in the case of psychological needs, the number and kinds of situational categories developed would be a function of the purpose of classification and the level accuracy of prediction required. Fairly generalized predictions would require less subtle distinctions among situations than would more precise predictions.

At least four methods of categorizing situations are based on need concepts. The first method involves sampling expectancies. That is, within a given culture, Ss could estimate their expectations for potential occurrence of certain reinforcements in specific situations. Situations could then be classified as similar to the extent that they aroused similar expectancies for reinforcement. A second method requires that we sample, through observations, actual reinforcements that occur in specific situations. Thus, two situations in which it is observed that a high frequency of love and affection rewards occur would be classified as similar. The third technique utilizes behaviors. If we have already classified behaviors in terms of the goal toward which they are usually oriented, then situations which produce similar behaviors could be classified together. The fourth method utilizes generalization. For example, we might pretest some behavior (or expectancy or reinforcement) in several situations; then, increase or decrease this behavior potential in one situation and test in the other situations for a generalization of the increase or decrease. The greater the generalization between two situations, the greater their similarity.

* * * * *

Generalized Expectancies: Problem-Solving Skills

Man is a categorizing animal. He continuously forms concepts, changes concepts, and discovers new dimensions of similarity. While similarity of reinforcements is an extremely important basis for his conceptualizations, there are also other dimensions along which he perceives similarity. Within SLT any part of the environment to which the individual responds, or its totality, is referred to as a situational determinant. When an individual perceives that a number of people are alike because they are of the same sex, color, occupation, or age, he develops expectations about these people. Experience with one of them generalizes to others of the same class. When generalization takes place, we have the basis for believing that functional relations exist. That is, prediction of one referent from another referent of the same class can be made at a better than chance level. Generalized expectancies about people, and the behaviors and reinforcements connected with them, are part of the basis for what has been traditionally called *social attitudes* in psychology. In a later paper in this volume, Rotter (1967) describes in detail a social learning theory analysis of social attitudes and social action-taking behavior.

Situations, both social and nonsocial, may also be perceived as similar in that they present similar problems. For example, all of us are faced continuously with the problem of deciding whether what happens to us is contingent on our own behavior and can be controlled by our own actions, or whether it depends upon luck, the intervention of powerful others, or influences we cannot understand. We develop a generalized expectancy across situations which may differ in needs satisfied or reinforcements expected, but which are similar with respect to perception of control that we can exercise to change or maintain these situations. As with social attitudes, when generalization occurs from one situation to another, individual differences may develop in how the situations themselves are perceived or categorized. In such a case, generalized expectancies may deal with properties of situational stimuli. That is, the basis for similarity does not lie, in this instance, in the nature of reinforcements but in the nature of the situation. Behaviors relevant to these situational mediated expectancies are also functionally related because of similarity of the problems to be solved.

When a behavior directed toward a goal is blocked, or fails to achieve the goal, the failure itself may be regarded as a property of a new situation involving a problem to be solved. A generalized expectancy that problems can be solved by a technique of looking for alternatives may also be developed regardless of the specific need or reinforcement involved. The degree to which a generalized problem-solving expectancy is developed may be an important source of individual differences in behavior.

Another common human experience is that of being provided with information from other people—either promises of reinforcements to come or merely statements of presumed fact. Implicit in all these situations is the problem of whether to believe or not to believe the other person. A generalized expectancy of *trust* or *distrust* can be an important determinant of behavior.

The mature human can probably perceive an extremely large number of dimensions of similarities in problem characteristics in complex social situations. Some dimensions, however, are broader than others and some, undoubtedly, are far more relevant for particular kinds of psychological predictions than others. In recent years, many SLT investigations have concerned some of these dimensions. Two of these are the dimension of *internal versus external control of reinforcement* and the dimension of *interpersonal trust*. . . .

While inclusion of content dimensions makes the prediction of behavior more complex, it must be recognized that man is, in fact, a complex organism. A concept of generalized expectancies, as proposed here, requires some change in our previous formulation of expectancy. If we hypothesize that generalized expectancies derived from categorization of the problem will influence whether the individual anticipates that a particular behavior will lead to a particular reinforcement, then in addition to his generalized expectancy for the success of his behavior (GE) in obtaining that reinforcement, we have to make additional corrections to assess more accurately his expectancy about the particular character of the situation. For example, in a task where S believes that reinforcement (success) is controlled by the experimenter, a sequence of reinforcements such as $+ - - + - + + +$ might yield a low expectancy for success on the next trial. Where S believes reinforcement is determined by his own skill, the same pattern of reinforcements should yield a relatively high expectancy for success on the next trial.

Formula (8) schematizes this expansion. A subscript r is used to denote expectancies generalized from other similar attempts to obtain a given reinforcement, and the subscript ps denotes relevant generalized expectancies for classes of problem-solving situations cutting across specific need categories. As with other generalized expectancies for success in achieving a class of reinforcements, the more specific experience the individual has in that situation, the less influence generalized expectancies have; the more novel a situation, the greater is the influence wielded by generalized expectancies. As in preceding formulas, a hypothesis about the direction of influence of the variables is made, but no attempt to specify exact mathematical relations has been made. Predictions of increments and decrements in expectancy would have to be modified in many cases when particular generalized expectancies relevant to the situation being studied are present.

$$E_{s_1} = f(E' \& GE_r \& GE_{ps_1} \& GE_{ps_2} \cdots GE_{ps_n}) \qquad (8)$$
$$f(N_{s_1})$$

Positive and Negative Reinforcements as Situational Clues

Reinforcements, whether words, acts, or tangible objects, are also parts of the psychological situation, as are cues closely associated with occurrence of reinforcements. Content categories based on perceived similarities of reinforcement (needs), perceived similarities of social cues (social attitudes), and perceived similarities of the nature of the problems to be solved (generalized expectancies) have been discussed. There may also be similarities in situations based on the sign (whether positive or negative) or intensity of reinforcements, or combinations of these along with the circumstances in which they occur.

Occurrence of a negative reinforcement, or its anticipation, as already indicated, may lead to defensive or avoidant behaviors; and such behaviors can be understood as having a potential for a particular class of reinforcements. It may be characteristic of some people, however, that they respond with aggression, repression, withdrawal, projection, depression, and so on, somewhat independently of the kind (need category) of reinforcement. These responses may be a function of the sign or strength of the reinforcement rather than its particular form. In other words, we can talk not only about a behavior potential to repress competitive failures but a behavior potential to repress all strong negative reinforcements. How functional or general such potentials are across need areas is an empirical matter. Mild failure in an achievement-related task may increase the potential for some individuals to narrow their attention, increase concentration, and so on.

REFERENCES

Brunswik, E. The probability point of view. In M. H. Marx (Ed.), *Psychological theory.* New York: Macmillan, 1951.

Fitzgerald, B. J. Some relationships among projective test, interview, and sociometric measures of dependent behavior. *Journal of Abnormal and Social Psychology,* 1958, 56, 199-204.

Lesser, G. S. The relationship between overt and fantasy aggression as a function of maternal response to aggression. *Journal of Abnormal and Social Psychology,* 1957, 55, 218-222.

Lewin, K. The nature of field theory. In M. H. Marx (Ed.), *Psychological theory.* New York: Macmillan, 1951.

Liverant, S. The use of Rotter's social learning theory in developing a personality inventory. *Psychological Monographs,* 1958, 72 (Whole No. 455).

Lotsof, A. B. A study of the effect of need value on substitution. Unpublished doctoral dissertation, Ohio State University, 1953.

Phares, E. J. The relationship between TAT responses and leaving-the-field behavior. *Journal of Clinical Psychology,* 1959, 15, 328-330.

Rotter, J. B. Level of aspiration as a method of studying personality: II. Development and evaluation of a controlled method. *Journal of Experimental Psychology,* 1942, 31, 410-422.

Rotter, J. B. Level of aspiration as a method of studying personality. III. Group validity studies. *Character and Personality,* 1943, 11, 254-274.

Rotter, J. B. *Social learning and clinical psychology.* Englewood Cliffs, N.J.: Prentice-Hall, 1954.

Rotter, J. B. The role of the psychological situation in determining the direction of human behavior. In M. R. Jones (Ed.), *Nebraska symposium on motivation.* Lincoln: University of Nebraska Press, 1955. Pp. 245-269.

Rotter, J. B. Some implications of a social learning theory for the prediction of goal directed behavior from testing procedures. *Psychological Review,* 1960, 67, 301-316.

Rotter, J. B. Beliefs, attitudes and behavior: A social learning analysis. In R. Jessor and S. Feshbach (Eds.), *Cognition, personality and clinical psychology.* San Francisco, Calif.: Jossey-Bass, 1967.

Tyler, F. B., Tyler, B. B., and Rafferty, J. E. A threshold conception of need value. *Psychological Monographs,* 1962, 76 (Whole No. 530).

INDEX

PRINTED IN U.S.A.